PALATINE PUBLIC LIBRARY

S0-ARK-653

PRAISE FOR *THE GERALDO SHOW*

"Let me begin with an incontrovertible truth: It is simply impossible to know Geraldo personally and not love him as the true American original that he is. In my case, he is my adopted brother. The older brother I always wanted in life, and the older brother I am so proud of. His love of life is simply infectious. His fearlessness, and his courage are inspiring to everyone he comes into contact with. You have not lived a full and complete life unless and until you have the opportunity to listen to Geraldo tell the stories of each chapter in his life. To listen, to each and every detail, you marvel at the life Geraldo has lived. He has lived 500 full lives in one, and he loves every second of it, and he's building new chapters every single day. *The Geraldo Show* gives you insight into the man I know and love. The life lessons in this book will help all of us to grow and will inspire us to take more chances and 'go where the action is.' While some people recoil from danger, Geraldo dives in head first.

The passion and love he has for this country, our military, his work ethic, now almost 50 years on television, makes him The Godfather of tough hard-hitting, know-no-fear, go-anywhere reporting. *The Geraldo Show* takes us on a journey. A journey that few people in life will ever get to go on. A journey to some of the most remote places in the world. To me, Geraldo's greatest and most courageous journeys were those he took as a FNC war correspondent. I'll never forget the moment Geraldo pointed to the mountains of Tora Bora, emphatically telling the world 'Bin Laden is hidden right now in those mountains.' And Geraldo was correct.

This page-turning roller coaster ride Geraldo takes us on will truly inspire every reader to want to dive even deeper into themselves, to find that part of our souls that wish to be more courageous and bold in the lives we live. *The Geraldo Show* will also tell you the true story of how Geraldo and I first met, my initial skepticism when I first heard he was hired, and the evolution of one of the dearest friendships in my life."

—SEAN HANNITY, FOX News anchor, host of Hannity on Radio, bestselling author, motivational speaker, and producer

OFFICIALLY WITHDRAWN

Nov 2019

"With unrelenting pursuit, few were more dedicated to understanding the War on Terror than Geraldo Rivera. A must-read to understand the complexities of the battle overseas and the war over public opinion here at home."

—BILL HEMMER, FOX News anchor

"The Geraldo Show is a poignant account of combat as seen from the one person who has been there with our soldiers every step of the way. He captures war as it was fought; in all its ugliness, all its sacrifices, and all its heroism. As a war correspondent in Iraq and Afghanistan, there is no one who spent more time sharing in the hardships that our men and women endured than Geraldo; he also told their stories so that the true heroes . . . those selfless men and women that served our nation would not go uncelebrated. Geraldo's passion and love for GIs is unquestionable. I am proud to call Geraldo a true patriot and friend."

—JOHN F. CAMPBELL, General, US Army (Retired)

"Geraldo and I have been best buds since before I can remember smoking weed . . . which we never did together . . . even when no one was looking. I would go on an adventure with him anytime. The Geraldo Show is just the ticket."

—RICHARD "CHEECH" MARIN, author, comedian, and art collector

THE
GERALDO SHOW

*My Life as Roadkill in
the Age of Trump*

Geraldo Rivera

BenBella Books, Inc.
Dallas, TX

PALATINE PUBLIC LIBRARY DISTRICT
700 N. NORTH COURT
PALATINE, ILLINOIS 60067-8159

The events, locations, and conversations in this book, while true, are recreated from the author's memory. However, the essence of the story, and the feelings and emotions evoked, are intended to be accurate representations. In certain instances, names, persons, organizations, and places have been changed to protect an individual's privacy.

Copyright © 2018 by Geraldo Rivera
Interior photos © Craig Rivera

First trade paperback edition September 2019

All rights reserved. No part of this book may be used or reproduced in any manner whatsoever without written permission except in the case of brief quotations embodied in critical articles or reviews.

BenBella
10440 N. Central Expressway, Suite 800
Dallas, TX 75231
www.benbellabooks.com
Send feedback to feedback@benbellabooks.com

Printed in the United States of America
10 9 8 7 6 5 4 3 2 1

Library of Congress Cataloging-in-Publication Data is available upon request.
ISBN: 9781948836593
e-ISBN: 9781946885203

Editing by Glenn Yeffeth and Brian Nicol
Copyediting by Brian Buchanan
Proofreading by Michael Fedison and Cape Cod Compositors, Inc.
Text design and composition by Aaron Edmiston
Cover design by Sarah Avinger
Front cover photography by Benjamin West
Printed by Lake Book Manufacturing

Distributed to the trade by Two Rivers Distribution, an Ingram brand
www.tworiversdistribution.com

**Special discounts for bulk sales (minimum of 25 copies) are available.
Please contact bulkorders@benbellabooks.com.**

To wife Erica, and daughters Isabella, Simone, and Sol, the dauntless women in my life

CONTENTS

GERALDO CHRONOLOGY

Born, Manhattan, July 1943
Move to Long Island, 1951
Graduate from West Babylon High School, 1961
Maritime College, the Bronx, 1961–1963
Move to Los Angeles, 1963
University of Arizona, 1963–1965
Marry Linda Coblenz, Scottsdale, Arizona, August 1965
Reside Lower East Side, Manhattan, January 1966
Brooklyn Law School, 1966–1969
Intern, New York County District Attorney, summer 1967
Divorce Linda, 1968
Intern Harlem Assertion of Rights, summer 1968
Graduate from BLS, June 1969
Fellowship, Poverty Law, University of Pennsylvania, 1969–1970
Represent the Young Lords, 1969–1970
Fellowship, Fred Friendly, Columbia University Graduate School of
    Journalism, 1970
Hired, WABC *Eyewitness News*, September 1970
Marry Edith Vonnegut, Barnstable, Massachusetts, December 1971
Expose Willowbrook, January 1972
Win Peabody, 1973
Host ABC's *Goodnight America*, 1973–1977
Report Chile coup, September 1973
Report Yom Kippur War, October 1973

Divorce Edith, 1975

Debut, *Good Morning America*, November 1975

Meet Donald J. Trump, 1976

Establish Malibu residence, summer 1976

Marry Sheri Raymond, Malibu, December 1976

ABC Evening News, Barbara Walters, "Summer of Sam," Fidel Castro
    Debut, ABC's *20/20*, August 1977–1978

First child, Gabriel, born, Manhattan, July 1979

Divorce Sheri, 1981

Fired by ABC News, December 1985

Host *Al Capone's Vault*, Chicago, April 1986

Reporter, *Entertainment Tonight*, 1986–1987

Marry C.C. Dyer, Marion, Massachusetts, August 1987

Geraldo! syndicated talk show, 1987–1998

Brawl skinheads, 1987

Second child, Cruz, born, Dallas, Texas, November 1987

Interview Charles Manson, 1988

Third child, Isabella, born, Manhattan, November 1992

Fourth child, Simone, born, Manhattan, September 1994

CNBC's *Rivera Live*, April 1994–November 2001

O.J. Simpson murder trials, June 1994–1997

Clinton impeachment, 1997–1999

Begin sail around the world, July 1997

Kosovo War, 1999

Separate from C.C., 2000

Complete circumnavigation, 2000

Quit NBC, hired by Fox News, November 2001

Afghanistan, eleven assignments, December 2001–2012

Fox News, *Geraldo-at-Large*, 2002–2015

Tour of terror, January–April, 2002

Engaged to Erica Levy, August 2002

Iraq War, eleven assignments, 2003–2011

Marry Erica, Manhattan, August 2003

Mosul, Iraq, ambush, 2004

Hurricane Katrina, 2005

Fifth child, Sol Liliana, born, Manhattan, August 2005

Firefight, Libya, April 2011

Bin Laden killed, May 2011
Celebrity Apprentice, New York (Trump Tower), February 2015
Baltimore riots, 2015
Dancing with the Stars, Los Angeles, 2016
Roger Ailes fired, July 2016
Donald Trump elected, November 2016
Trump inaugurated, January 2017
Bill O'Reilly fired, April 2017
Move to Cleveland, Ohio, August 2017
Hurricane Maria with President Trump, Puerto Rico, October 2017
WTAM Cleveland Radio Show begins, September 2018
Trump cleared, no collusion, May 2019

PROLOGUE

In public life for half a century, my image and reputation have had more ups and downs than the Cyclone roller coaster at Coney Island. I have been called savior and sinner, fool and wise man, crusader and exploiter, hothead and dope. I am routinely scorned, admired, beloved, and belittled. Those passing judgment usually base it on when they tuned in. Were you around for my early days as a crusading local newsman? Did you waste an evening inside Al Capone's empty vault? Were you watching when the bombs dropped in Afghanistan or Iraq, or did you tune in to the raucous talk show when my nose got broken in the best television studio brawl ever caught on tape?

I am hard to nail down because of a shifting self-image. A moving target, even to myself, I have been intent variously on doing good or doing well, being taken seriously or just being successful. In the beginning it was easy. Money was a byproduct. The media was the message, and I used its power to fix what ails us. I made a historic start. In 1972, at age twenty-eight and with only two years in the news business, I changed the world for families touched by developmental disabilities. With a crusade targeting Willowbrook, a notorious institution that was America's largest and worst, I wrote and reported a searing exposé, "The Last Great Disgrace."

The blockbuster launched a movement that eventually closed all of the nation's major institutions for the population once described as mentally retarded. That was forty-five years ago, but in many ways it was my professional peak. I have never been more popular or highly regarded. The rest of my life since Willowbrook has been a postscript, a long and winding follow-up, never matching that period of renown and acceptance. Respected by peers and public, I had it all. I was famous. Coming from a mediocre background—a skinny, asthmatic, pimply-faced mutt—to have wealth and fame was enormously appealing. It drew me into the quandary that tormented much of my professional life. Am I a journalist or a celebrity? Juggling those sometimes-competing goals is a challenge I have not always won.

Since the attacks of September 11, 2001, and my employment by the conservative rabble-rousers of Fox News, and more recently with the coming of the Age of Trump, my professional life has been even more difficult to define. How could a sincerely progressive native-born Jew-Rican New Yorker like me ever work for an outfit better suited to the vibes of Orange County, Dixie, Appalachia, or the Mountain West? How could I not condemn and obstruct a wrecking ball like Donald Trump, who so many of my progressive friends abhor?

Don't get me wrong. I am not complaining about the choices I made. Sometimes seduced by the dark side of show business, I have been on a hell of a ride. Despite macho posturing and more serious lapses, I have also kicked some major journalistic butt. What makes me grind my teeth is that because of my tabloid history I am not taken as seriously as my work often deserves.

This narrative will reassure friends, infuriate enemies, and settle some grudges, especially surrounding my obsessive pursuit of Osama bin Laden, which is the real core of this book. It will also explain where my head and heart are late in a life lived in plain sight. Not as self-assured or certain as I once was, for better and worse, I have followed the traditional cliché that if you are not liberal as a young person, you have no heart, but if you are not more conservative deeper in life, you have no brain. I still support Roe v Wade, gun control, civil and immigrants' rights, and the need for universal health care, but detest liberals who shun responsibility and blame cops, rich white people, and corporations for everything that ails us. I call it pragmatic idealism.

Over five decades, I have met most of the era's good guys and bad, from Ronald Reagan to Charles Manson, Fidel Castro to Yasser Arafat, Muhammad Ali to Elvis, John Lennon, and Michael Jackson. Two from that larger-than-life crowd figure heavily in this book, both longtime friends. Donald J. Trump, who I met as an up-and-coming real estate

Erica and me with Roger and Beth Ailes. Chelsea Piers, New York, August 2003.

developer and playboy from Queens, New York, is our President. Despite the fact that I disagree with many of his policies, and despite the peer pressure from my old downtown crowd, our friendship endures.

The late Roger Ailes was a mentor and founding chief of Fox News. Once ruler of the media universe, and brilliant creator of the most important conservative news outlet ever, Roger was forced to resign in July 2016 after being accused of serial sexual harassment of young female staffers. The scandal that destroyed his career also ended his life. With his already deteriorating health, compromised by the stress and shame of his dismissal, he died less than a year after being outed by a ground-breaking lawsuit filed by former Fox News anchor Gretchen Carlson. His scandal was the fuse that helped ignite a firestorm of harassment allegations that burns to this day from New York newsrooms to Congress and the White House, to the casting couches of Hollywood, scorching scores of powerful old men including sixty-eight year-old Bill O'Reilly, another former colleague from my unfashionable era whose ratings long dominated cable news.

Ironically, many of those targeted in the purge had until recently been hailed as champions of progressive life. Celebrated actors Bill Cosby and Kevin Spacey and Democratic Party stalwart Harvey Weinstein apparently hid disgusting secrets behind masks of political correctness. Former

Saturday Night Live comedian Al Franken was forced to resign from the Senate when photos surfaced of him pretending to grope the breasts of a bulletproof vest-wearing female radio host as she slept. Civil rights icon, eighty-eight year old Congressman John Conyers left public life in tottering disgrace as did three more friends, CBS' Charlie Rose, PBS' Tavis Smiley and, stunningly, NBC *Today*'s long-reigning host Matt Lauer.

I tweeted in sympathy for the wreck of Lauer's career that "News is a flirty business & it seems like the current epidemic of #SexHarassmentAllegations may be criminalizing courtship & conflating it with predation." An explosion of anger and ridicule followed. In attempting to be compassionate to someone who always treated my family and me with respect, I was insensitive to his alleged victims. I survived the cacophony of outrage, but have much in common with those who did not. Our generation are dinosaurs, creatures of a bygone era struggling despite our success to remain relevant. Because our lives crisscrossed during this pivotal time in America's history and mine, some of my contemporaries are necessarily part of this narrative, especially Roger Ailes and President Trump. I am not here to tell their stories, only how they intersected and impacted my own.

Several months after I completed the first draft of this manuscript in 2016, all hell broke loose at Fox News. With Beth and Roger Ailes at Erica's fortieth birthday party at the Monkey Bar, New York, January 2015.

PREFACE

"The only thing in the middle of the road is roadkill," the inventor of partisan cable news, my friend and mentor Roger Ailes, once advised. In the supercharged, hyper-partisan second decade of the twenty-first century, to comment about politics on television meant you had picked an ideological lane. You were one side or the other, red or blue, conservative or liberal. I am both, or rather sometimes one and sometimes the other, depending on the issue. A pragmatic idealist. A compassionate capitalist.

A decade earlier, when I first came to Fox from NBC News, ideology really didn't matter as much. For several years following September 11, 2001, Americans shared a common goal: to punish the people who hurt us so grievously on that grim day. Our troops went to war to seek retribution and to insure a 9/11-scale violent attack never happened again.

When the George W. Bush–era financial crash came in 2007–2008, Americans lost interest in the ebb and flow of the wars overseas in Afghanistan and Iraq. Grizzled war correspondents like me came home. Our nation weathered the international banking crisis and the stock market bottom, and in November 2008 celebrated the historic election of Barack Obama, America's first black president. Tears flowed down my face when he won. For this old civil rights storefront attorney, Obama's election represented the triumph of the 1960s' ethos of inclusion and fair play. Racial equality would be attained. Historic wrongs were being righted, and all would soon be well with the world.

It didn't turn out that way. Instead, the nation soon re-fractured along racial and class lines. No doubt the increasing polarization was accelerated by reactionary white backlash against the elegant black man in the Oval Office. While generally scandal-free, President Obama's two terms were marred by racial violence. The deaths of Michael Brown in Missouri, Trayvon Martin in Florida, Eric Gardner on Staten Island, and Freddie Gray in Baltimore led to unrest, while on the political side, the growth of the right-wing Tea Party exemplified and accelerated our renewed and growing social and racial divisions.

I didn't talk about politics much on Fox News in the Obama years. When I wasn't overseas, I was covering my old beats—urban violence, drug abuse, and other gritty, crime-related topics—while seldom hanging with the DC crowd, although my wife Erica and I did attend several of the splashy annual White House Correspondents' Dinners and met President and Mrs. Obama. POTUS 44 (Obama) didn't exactly rub me wrong, but I never got the vibe that he wanted to hang out with me either. In my mind, he was like a lot of other Ivy League guys I had known over the years: super smart, slightly condescending, entitled, and affected—except when he was on camera.

I know I'm being harsh on this historic leader, and maybe I'm exaggerating, but you get the idea: for all my gushing respect and affection and support for his administration and policies, President Obama never gave me the time of day. Even though I worked for his archenemies at Fox News, I wanted to be friends, but I got nowhere. I joked that, because I worked at Fox, he would grant an interview to the Dog Food Channel before he would agree to sit down with me. His probable successor, secretary of state Hillary Clinton, was only marginally nicer, which likely had more to do with the fact that I saved her husband's ass during impeachment than any fondness she held for me.

Enter presidential contender Donald J. Trump, whose improbable election shocked the world, our country, and my family. Outside a cadre of Fox News colleagues and my grumpy old best friend, lawyer Leo Kayser III of Birmingham, Alabama, a rich, Yale-educated curmudgeon, no one close to me voted for the flamboyant billionaire businessman who had been background noise in my life for decades. As fate would have it, just three months before Trump declared his crazy longshot candidacy, I joined him as a cast member for his final season as host of *Celebrity Apprentice*. The elaborate production took about six weeks, during which he could not have been nicer or more supportive. Giving me every break, he acted like a true friend, or at least a fellow New Yorker of similar vintage with many shared experiences. He was so supportive that he put me in an embarrassing bind.

I wanted to vote for him. The problem was his hard-core, mostly right-wing politics. In 2011, he had joined forces with viciously anti-immigrant Arizona sheriff Joe Arpaio to embrace the bogus "birther" movement, which posited that Obama's presidency was illegitimate because Obama, allegedly born in Kenya, West Africa, was not a "natural-born Citizen," as required by Article Two, Section One of the Constitution. I recount in these pages how Erica and I, sitting at a nearby table, watched Trump ruthlessly made a mockery of by President Obama during the 2011 Correspondents' Dinner. ("What's next," joked Obama, "that we faked the moon landings?") I believe that, because he was so brutally mocked by Obama and host Seth Meyers, that was the night Trump decided to run for president. In his world, no insult can be left unanswered.

Four years later, like millions of other Americans, I watched my reality-show colleague's crazy, anti-immigrant announcement of his candidacy in June 2015. Coming down the long escalator at Trump Tower, my old friend made an emotional appeal to the nativist, conservative, mostly white crowd in the atrium and watching on television—the audience president Richard Nixon used to call the Silent Majority. "When Mexico sends its people, they're not sending their best," Trump said. "They're sending people that have lots of problems, and they're bringing those problems with us [sic]. They're bringing drugs. They're bringing crime. They're rapists. And some, I assume, are good people."

Yikes. The Trump I'd spent hours with over the years, on and off the air, was, I thought, a typical New York business guy who over-bragged and lived large, but was not ugly or bigoted. I was broadcasting live on my WABC New York radio show the morning of his announcement. I remember how my enthusiasm for his candidacy was dulled by those casually racist remarks about Mexican immigrants. Still, I would have voted for him anyway. After all, how often does a hangout buddy run for President of the Free World? Anyway, he'll pivot toward the center once elected and moderate his tone, I confidently assumed. He's a business guy, so he'll find a way to make the country work right and fairly.

When Election Day finally came around on November 8, 2016, my wife, Erica, and daughters Isabella, Simone, and Sol passionately intervened, imploring me not to vote for this man whose angry anti-immigrant politics were the opposite of my own.

It was literally an intervention. Knowing that I voted for Trump in the April 2016 New York Republican presidential primary when he ran against Ted Cruz of Texas (the most unpleasant person in the Senate), and that I was pondering the idea of voting for Trump again in the general election against Hillary Clinton, my wife Erica was incensed. She had been pleading with me for months not to take this big step to the dark side.

"How can you vote for a racist?" she asked, cutting to the quick.

"He's not a racist. Trump Tower is filled with racial and ethnic minorities in key jobs. I know him," I replied. "Anyway, Hillary is sure to win."

My marriage and family life was in turmoil as a result of my affection for this larger-than-life amateur politician who had bested seventeen other candidates in the knife fight for the Republican nomination. After interminable lobbying, I reluctantly agreed to vote for Hillary (to save the Supreme Court, etc.). As Sol, my then eleven-year old daughter, can attest, as she accompanied me into the voting booth as a lesson in civics, I did not vote for my friend. But a few hours later that Election Day, as the first results were coming in and after a spasm of shock and awe ("Oh my God!"), I immediately became President-elect Trump's first convert. "We only get one president at a time," I told anyone who questioned my instant enthusiasm for this longest of long shots, "and I have his back."

Continuing where he left off with *The Apprentice*, President Trump has remained gracious and loyal. On the day before he and First Lady-elect Melania were to move to Washington, DC, for their inauguration, he invited me to Trump Tower, the scene of our time together on the show. He has also hosted me at Mar-a-Lago, his legendary Florida home—which was, as he confided during a private tour of the complex, the "greatest private home in America, better than anything in Newport, Rhode Island, or LA"—and on the day I began my modest WTAM talk radio program in middle-market Cleveland, Ohio, he honored me with a forty-five-minute exclusive interview.

We follow each other on Twitter, and, while we sometimes disagree, especially on substantive issues like immigration and how to solve the crisis on the southern border, I have been broadly supportive of his presidency. I have also done my best to counter the vile and unfair coverage he receives from the establishment press corps vastly arrayed against him.

As I write this, special counsel Robert Mueller's long anticipated probe of allegations that Trump "colluded" with Russia to fix the 2016 elections has been newly released. The allegations' central thesis, for which there was never any real evidence, was that a criminal conspiracy existed between Trump and Russian president Vladimir Putin. The salacious fairy tale essentially alleged the two strongmen were in cahoots, with Putin doing everything in his power to tilt the election in Trump's favor, on the premise that Trump would then tilt American foreign policy in the Russian bully's direction.

Why would Trump do that, become a stooge for Russia? According to the so-called "Steele Dossier," a salacious compilation by an ex-British intelligence operator of opposition research paid for by the Hillary Clinton campaign and the Democratic National Committee, Putin had dirt on Trump. He was threatening to release it if Trump didn't commit treason and become a Russian spy. To cut to the grubby chase, the most sensational claim in the fictional dossier dated back to a visit Trump paid to Moscow in 2013 for his Miss Universe Pageant, when businessman Donald J. Trump was accused of either giving or receiving a "golden shower."

Bizarre and as unlikely as it now sounds, the fake dossier formed the unlikely backdrop for what became the second or third most significant presidential scandal in modern history after Nixon's Watergate and Clinton's Monica Lewinsky/Whitewater.

The fable gained currency late in Mr. Trump's audacious run for the White House and blossomed immediately following his shocking victory. At about the same time, in mid-to-late 2016, the Obama administration discovered a real, audaciously destructive, secret campaign by Russia to meddle in our election process. Russia, with the help of hacked emails released by Wikileaks, was indeed attempting to tilt the election toward Trump.

Critics of Trump were convinced Putin wanted Trump elected because Trump was compromised; I think Putin wanted Trump elected president because he's a fellow macho misogynist who thought Hillary Clinton a rigid, unpleasant foe. It doesn't matter. However bizarre their beginnings, so grave were the charges of criminal collusion between Trump and Putin that, for a time, there was talk that our president was "Putin's Bitch," a Russian spy, a traitor, a Manchurian candidate who, if elected, would bend US policy to suit his secret KGB bosses.

As the dark, tragicomic fantasy gained traction, it was used to explain everything from Trump's policies in Syria and Ukraine to his semisecret summit meeting with Putin in Helsinki, Finland, to his support of Brexit and his negative stance on NATO, our anti-Russia Atlantic alliance.

I never bought into the collusion hysteria. It all seemed far-fetched and stupid. Having known Trump for decades, I was convinced that the events depicted in Moscow never happened. For one thing, there was never any proof: no eyewitnesses, no photographs or social media, nothing. More broadly, Trump is not dumb. By 2013, when he visited Moscow for the pageant, he was already secretly deep in planning his run for the White House. Besides, even rookie travelers know that every room in Moscow occupied by an important guest is under surveillance.

Still, and despite its unlikely origins, the Trump/Russia collusion story dominated our politics for well over two years, especially after the appointment of Mueller to investigate the supposed conspiracy between Putin and Trump to subvert US interests and promote Russian ones.

During this period, early in Trump's presidency, turmoil and disorder in and around the Oval Office conspired with incompetence and backstabbing to create a sense of chaos and constant crisis. He became infuriated by his failure to stop the malignant investigation that ultimately cost at least $25 million, involved nineteen assistant U.S. attorneys and forty FBI agents, and featured interviews with five hundred witnesses. Exasperated, the president fired James Comey, the tall, creepy FBI director, among others, leading to further allegations that he was obstructing any probe of his conduct. His erratic behavior didn't help quell the controversy. His administration was further undermined by frequent firings, resignations, torrential leaks, West Wing treachery, and abrupt policy changes, and the chaos undermined confidence that the administration would even survive its four years. There was talk of impeachment, and all of it based on bullshit.

The story of what I came to call Collusion Illusion or Collusion Delusion exacerbated the political and ideological divide in this country, which was already riven by ethnic and racial strife.

Because I believed the allegation of criminal conspiracy to be empty nonsense, I vigorously defended the president in every possible forum, including a spirited on-air confrontation with Bill Maher in April 2018. It was clear to me that, disdainful of this president, critics and opponents both inside his administration and out were trying to oust him in a de facto coup, using the twenty-fifth amendment to have him declared unfit to continue in the Oval Office.

The eventual finding in April 2019 by the irreproachable Mr. Mueller that President Trump did not criminally conspire—i.e., collude—with Russia closed an improbable chapter in US history. The secondary issue of whether he improperly attempted to obstruct the investigation remains unresolved and maybe unresolvable.

What is relevant here is how tough it has been for me, the old-line New York progressive activist, to square my continued friendship with and support for this tempestuous, thin-skinned, and deeply controversial man. It was bad enough when I just had to explain to my family and longtime friends why I worked for conservative Fox News. In the words of Martin Garbus, a prominent civil rights attorney and activist I have known for decades, "Geraldo, look what you've become."

What have I become? Again quoting the late Roger Ailes, "I report, you decide."

Geraldo Rivera
April 2019

Chapter 1

ROGER & ME

"**N**ow is when you'll need all your courage," Roger Ailes said with his usual blend of bravado and brutal honesty. "You're getting near the end of the line and it's only going to get tougher."

"Getting near the end of the line?" Not me. Not Geraldo. It was a slap in the face for ageless Mr. Macho. In that twilight of Roger's glory days, two years before he was laid low by the toxic sexual harassment scandal that rocked my network and upended his world, my shrewd, blunt boss was still on top of the media world.

Before he became a pariah, scorned by friend and foe alike, he was the blustering genius who invented our mighty Fox News Channel. A kingmaker who made stars of O'Reilly, Hannity, and Kelly, he almost single-handedly invented the Tea Party, shaped the modern Republican Party, and enabled its eventual 2016 embrace of Donald Trump.

A short yet towering figure, Roger inspired respect and affection from hundreds of loyal staffers, including me. To be a F.O.R. at Fox News, a Friend of Roger, meant you were essentially untouchable, immune from management comings and goings. He was king and if you were a useful and, most important, loyal subject, then the old lion would make sure you were kept safe and secure. He demanded fealty, which he repaid with kindness, generosity, and, more practically, extended contracts.

1

Conversely, in his court, no crime was more infamous than disloyalty. If anyone chose publicly to challenge Roger on his decisions, he would savage them with an explosive, barely controlled temper that could rattle a stone sculpture. Even conservative idols who strayed from the boss in public felt his wrath.

Sean Hannity, my hangout buddy and the hardest of conservative hardliners, tells the story of how displeased he was personally when a liberal scoundrel like me came to Fox News from CNBC in 2001. The move was fraught with controversy within the Fox News family and Sean complained bitterly about my hire, both on his radio show and on his cable program, which was then called *Hannity and Colmes.*

Sean tells how he was summoned into Roger's office to be dressed down as if he were Benedict Arnold caught red-handed committing treason. At the time, before he was hobbled by age, infirmity, and scandal, Roger was a pear-shaped, pulsing human bomb, which could go nuclear if angered. His face could become a contorted mask that was terrible to behold.

"How dare you question my decision!" Sean quotes Roger at the time of my controversial hire. When Sean tried to explain to Roger that he did not have anything personal against me, that what he objected to were my liberal leanings, Roger went off on him again. Jabbing his pointed index finger, red-faced and spitting, he told Sean, "Don't you ever question me again!"

His occasional rages were not gender-specific. Most often wise, wise-cracking, insightful, and jocular, Roger sometimes exploded with no specific incident triggering his rage, at least none that we knew about. At a birthday dinner for my wife, Erica, I seated Roger across from Laurie Dhue, one of his star correspondents in the formative years of the Fox News Channel. A tall, blonde, self-described "Carolina Girl," Laurie was a terrific reporter/anchor with the charm and effervescence of a thirty-something cheerleader.

In a private dining room in a hip restaurant in SoHo, Roger out of the blue attacked her verbally. To the dismay of Roger's wife, Beth, and to the embarrassment of Erica and everyone at the long table, in his booming voice, he savaged Laurie's looks, specifically her big necklace that seemed made of brass marbles. "Didn't I tell you never to wear big necklaces?" he spat, unprovoked.

Laurie Dhue and Erica at our Edgewater, New Jersey, home. June 2015.

To break the ice, I made a lame joke about fashion. Laurie did her best to ride out the acute embarrassment with her usual grace, gently removing the offending jewelry. The moment passed, and the evening resumed course.

Still a family friend, Laurie for years afterward publicly attributed her downfall at Fox to her alcoholism, becoming a spokesperson for the anti-addiction cause. A decade later it was revealed that whatever else had been going on, she was one of at least five women who accused our star anchor Bill O'Reilly of sexual misconduct, and, according to the *New York Times*, "received payouts from either Mr. O'Reilly or the company in exchange for agreeing to not pursue litigation or speak about their accusations against him."

That initial report was followed six months later by the shocking news that O'Reilly paid another dear friend of ours, legal analyst Lis Wiehl, an extraordinary $32 million settlement for allegations including non-consensual sex. In accepting their settlements, both Lis and Laurie signed confidentiality agreements, and neither ever spoke of any misbehavior by anyone at Fox, either to Erica or me.

During Hurricane Roger's all-powerful reign, his wrath and rage were awesome in their ability to intimidate. With his friends scared quiet, the fear he instilled in his media enemies was even more daunting. To take on Roger Ailes was to risk humiliation and insult, much like those seeking to probe or criticize President Trump today. Roger buried any reporter digging for dirt in a ferocious campaign of opposition research. For years, his intimidating rage kept the world at bay, despite his closet filled with skeletons. In retrospect, maybe his roar was meant to scare away hunters of secrets.

At the time of our private meeting in his office on the second floor at Fox News in February 2014 he was still the Bully of Big Media, but not to me.

He had a heart of gold to those he let into his inner circle, a kindness and generosity that belies his sullied legacy. If he loved you, he was enormously supportive. At that meeting that February day, he delivered bad news about my career as a gentle older brother might. Eye-to-eye, he told me to buck up and get ready for my career's last dance. In fact, physically speaking we had both seen better days. He was heading to hip replacement surgery and just starting to walk with a cane. I was and am increasingly hobbled by the disastrous aftermath of back surgery that killed my right foot and gave me an increasingly pronounced limp.

Still, I was on a different page, personally and professionally, than he was that day, when he told me the end was in sight for my career in television news. I saw myself then as battle-scarred but still near the top of the news game. Old and busted up for sure, but not broken down.

A four-time-divorced, five-time-married, doting father of five more-or-less dependent children, including one then still in second grade, loving grandfather, and devoted husband of Erica, a stunning woman thirty-two years younger, I felt the last thing I needed to hear from the boss was essentially, "The end is near, so get over it."

For one thing, I need the dough. It's easy to spend money, not so easy to make or preserve it. Don't get me wrong, I am well enough off, just not compared to how things were during the fat days of my syndicated talk show, which I owned, produced, and starred in. Regardless of how flush a career you have had, as the legions of retiring Boomers are rapidly discovering, your nest egg cracks in a hurry once there is no salary to support it. That is especially true when the cost of maintaining multiple dwellings, alimonies, and the press of philanthropy is piled on top of prep-school and private-college tuitions, and the always-alarming price of an otherwise full life.

I am resigned now to never being rich. Gone is my benchmark dream of being flush enough to own a private jet one day like my pal Hannity, who started out nearly as humbly as I did. These days my financial goal is more down to earth. Mainly, I want enough to be comfortable and generous, helping the less fortunate, without outliving my stash or term life insurance policies, or worse, being forced to spend my wife's and kids' inheritance.

To prove my physical prowess and convince her friends that I was up to the role of Erica's husband, on the occasion of her twenty-sixth birthday in January 2001 we invited a bunch, and flew them all out to celebrate with us at our home in Malibu.

It was a great party with a guest list that included several of the supporting characters in the then-still-fresh O.J. Simpson saga, which had been one of my career preoccupations. Faye Resnick, a friend of O.J.'s murdered ex-wife, Nicole, and later a *Real Housewife* hanger-on, was there at the Malibu party with a posse of blonde, big-breasted, made-for-tabloid girlfriends, and so were Hollywood glitterati like Arianna Huffington, in those days before *The Huffington Post*.

What I remember most vividly about that day was playing touch football on the beach with Erica's girlfriends' boyfriends and husbands and outrunning them all. "Man, you've still got some wheels," I remember one of them exclaiming. Nowadays, they would use my carcass for second base.

When I went with Erica to Cleveland during that introductory period to spend some quality time with her parents, Howard and Nancy Levy, her dad and I went off alone to bond. We went to the Rock & Roll Hall of Fame, the city's gem. Howard offered to pay. I swaggered up to the booth alongside him only to be deflated when my future father-in-law asked the clerk, "Can I have two senior citizen tickets, please?"

Erica and me with baby Jace, my first grandchild, and his parents, Cruz and Lauren. November 2012.

SHE WAS TWENTY-EIGHT WHEN
WE MARRIED; I WAS SIXTY

Here is the rough domestic chronology of this phase of my life before the attacks of 9/11 unraveled everyone's plans for the future. After twenty years together, and several attempts at reconciliation, which lasted into the opening months of the new millennium, C.C. Dyer, my fourth wife and mother of our dear daughters, Isabella and Simone, and I separated forever. It was February 2000, and I wanted to be single.

The life lesson is to be careful what you wish for. After months of extraordinary indulgence I got sick of myself. At my age and position at the time, as many of my contemporaries today are discovering, there was no such thing as a casual date. It is fun playing the field, until you realize it is laden with land mines and opportunities for self-inflicted wounds.

This is one of the core reasons I was not as hard on President Trump during the 2015–2016 campaign as his noxious statements about people with disabilities, Muslims, Mexicans, and former Fox News and current NBC anchor Megyn Kelly probably required. I knew him when. Regardless of our ups and downs, and the obvious disparities in wealth, power, and notoriety, we were products of our time and circumstance. We grew to manhood in the chauvinistic promiscuity and nativist, clumsy closed-mindedness of the locker rooms of metro New York in the late 1950s and early 1960s, before JFK was killed and before civil rights, the Vietnam War, and the women's movement changed the rules, obviously for the better.

As a loyal and loving husband and father of five, including three daughters, I find it impossible not to be impressed by the progress women have made since Baby Boomers were teenagers. When Trump and I came of age, it was a much different time. Marilyn Monroe, Kim Novak, Jayne Mansfield, and Jane Russell were our cool cat's meow, and *Playboy* and *Esquire* magazines were the sexy style bibles. Women were to be admired, protected, and enjoyed. No one I knew spoke of gender equality in sports, academia, or professional life back in those dark ages before, say, the Summer of Love in 1967. As primitive and dumb as it seems today, our ethos was real-life *Mad Men* meets *Father Knows Best*. Cheerleaders and voluptuous centerfolds were the ideal, and trading in your partner when her warranty expired was routine. Divorce was not as common as infidelity, unless the protagonist was wealthy and irreligious, which for key decades the President and I both were. He and I navigated some hard social storms of our own making and figured out the grossness of that piggy approach at around the same phase in life.

Looking back at who I was back in the day, I feel uncomfortable with my old self, but I stopped being that person long before it became open season on horny old men. My bad was so last century, and even then, unlike the long and growing list of fallen contemporaries, I never took advantage of anyone. I joke that I married every woman I ever harassed. Why five marriages? It is because I am so old school, I believed my whole life that if you love and respect a woman, you (in the words of Beyoncé) "put a ring on it." Everybody was treated with generosity of spirit, and is doing well. They returned the favor with friendship and loyalty. None ever said anything negative about me, at least not out loud.

In Donald Trump's life, the tabloid lifestyle was also shed, and all's well that ends well, in his case very well, although by his own admission, the presidency is proving a bigger challenge than he ever imagined. Trump found Melania around 1998, and eighteen years later the two of them together forged an extraordinary path to the highest office in the land. Hate him if you must, but you cannot deny the guy has a great wife and family. I found Erica deep in life, along with humility and respect for family and fidelity.

Everything changed with Erica and our improbable match-up. We met and fell in love at first sight in December 2000. Both of us were working for CNBC in Fort Lee, New Jersey. We actually had met a bit earlier in the year at an office outing at ever-hip Tao restaurant on West Fifty-Eighth Street, but did not really notice each other until that winter day when she walked into my office wearing a black tube skirt and a white dress shirt, her arms filled with papers for me to review. I knew Erica was going to be my wife that first time I really looked at her.

With my bride celebrating her fortieth. January 2015.

Stunning inside and out, razor sharp, and straightforward, she happened also to be an excellent producer, with an adventurer's heart. Once our affair was exposed, she was urged by NBC News management and human resources to give up her staff job. Given appearances and my reputation, they were beyond freaked that I might be what I certainly seemed, an aging super predator and she, my helpless young victim.

The lawyers for the network made sure that even her parents were made aware of the situation; the resolution of the fraught issue required a signed contract between Erica and NBC. In return for giving up her staff job, she was simultaneously hired as my freelance field producer. As such, she was allowed to travel with me to the West Coast or wherever the story took us, and it took us most often to our lovely home on the sandy beach near Paradise Cove in Malibu, where our immediate neighbors included impresario Dick Clark, my former agent Jerry Weintraub, and queen diva Barbra Streisand and her husband, actor James Brolin. In addition to the perks, Erica was given a year to change her mind and return to her staff job if our relationship didn't work out. As with many of our friends and associates, the network was betting we would not last.

In our twentieth year together, she is my deeply connected partner for life and a wonderful mother to Sol, our daughter who celebrated her thirteenth birthday with an epic bat mitzvah at our home in Shaker Heights in October 2018. More than than mom and partner, Erica is the glue that keeps my wild bunch of older children together with us as a family. She handles with patience and intelligence the idiosyncrasies of our spreading herd, which ranges from Sol to Simone, aged twenty-four and an honors graduate of Northwestern University, on her way to Yale Law after being accepted to all the top law schools in the country, including Harvard and Stanford; Isabella, twenty-six, a graduate of NYU and an associate producer at CNN; Cruz, who graduated with a degree in engineering from Texas A&M after a rough skid through two other schools, who at thirty-two already has three kids of his own and, happily, a job as a union engineer installing elevators in New York City high-rises; and firstborn, but not least, Gabriel, forty, who just bought a home Topanga Canyon, ten miles from where he was raised in Santa Monica, where he lives with his wife, Deb, a brilliant scientist, and their four-year-old son, Desmond.

With four kids at the time, from three different mothers, and then getting married for the fifth time to a woman half my age, I realize what a long shot Erica and I were to succeed, how funky my personal life must seem to outsiders. Yet we have succeeded and thrived as a family. Despite the kids' religious, ethnic, and genetic potpourri, we are a functioning, caring unit. Like our daughter Sol, my older children love Erica and rely on her as a mom, although one much closer to their age than mine.

Spiritually, I feel forever young in Erica's presence, even though at the time we married she was twenty-eight and I was sixty. Our wedding at New York Central Synagogue in August 2003 was a party for the ageless. Before four hundred far-flung guests from the four corners of our lives, we lavishly celebrated our improbable pairing. I came down the aisle leading thirty groomsmen, including my two sons, two brothers, and best man: blood brother, stoner comic, art collector, *Celebrity Jeopardy!* champion, and all around Renaissance man, Cheech Marin. My wedding march was Tito Puente's "Oye Como Va," which I am reasonably certain had never been heard in Central Synagogue's ornate grand chamber.

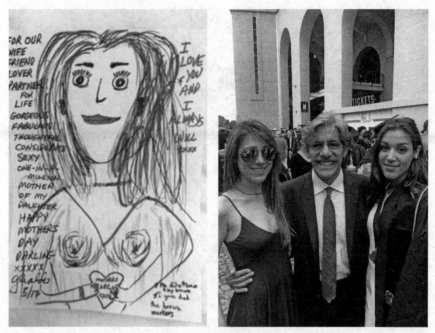

Left: "She is my deeply connected partner for life." Mother's Day, May 2017.
Right: Isabella and Dad at Simone's graduation from Northwestern University, June 2017.

At Erica's extravagant fortieth birthday party, January 2015.

Erica and I are wed at New York's Central Synagogue, August 2003.

Best man, blood brother, stoner comic, art collector, *Celebrity Jeopardy* champion, and all-around Renaissance man, Cheech Marin.

We capped it off with a blowout party at the now defunct Four Seasons Restaurant on Park Avenue and a honeymoon in the South of France, staying at the fabled Hotel du Cap-Eden-Roc in Cap Antibes, then to Monte Carlo, where we stayed in Winston Churchill's suite, St. Tropez, Nikki Beach. Exhausting, but Erica loved it all, saying at one point, "Can't we go to one more place? I have such a cute outfit on."

As I wrote during this wildly romantic interlude, "I am resolved that I will die married to this splendid, warm, loving, daring, beautiful, stylish, exhilarating, fun, Jewish temptress!!! And I will streamline my life for the big push ahead."

But back to Roger and me. My stunning, sobering 2014 meeting with him happened eleven years after Erica and I married. Until then, my career ambition had been relatively modest, given my notoriety and longevity. Mainly I was seeking to preserve a measure of success and swagger in the news business, while socially not looking ridiculous or mismatched out on the town with my stylish wife, who had blossomed into a sophisticated partner—glamorous, but not haughty, a lover of the arts, a fabulous mom, and a concerned citizen.

The only wrinkle to the honeymoon story is that, at the end, Erica had to fly home alone from Europe. I went the other direction, back to Iraq, where battles raged. Begun that past March, the fighting was already careening out of control. For the eleven years between 2001 and 2012, war was the setting and context for my life, preoccupying and defining all planning and perspective.

Our daughter, Sol Liliana, born in August 2005, is our unadulterated joy. Like her siblings, adorable and smart beyond her years, Sol is the antidote to the morbid melancholy that afflicts men my age when we realize our lives are best measured in days. That, by the way, is another of Roger's deep thoughts. "You realize that you've got about three thousand days left before someone's wheeling you around or throwing dirt on your dead body," he shared with me about a thousand days ago.

Like her big sisters, Sol is gifted with shocking wisdom. On the edge of a grown-up conversation and seemingly immersed in her book or video, she often pops her head up with a question or deep thought that is right on point. She wakes up happy and starts each day with an eager optimism that rubs off on her sometimes gloomy or melancholy dad. More than any other catalyst, she keeps me energized and positive about life.

"For the eleven years between 2001 and 2012, war was the
setting and context for my life." Afghanistan, 2003.

Through fifth grade, and until our move to the Midwest, Sol attended
Spence, the same private school on the Upper East Side of Manhattan as
older sisters Isabella and Simone graduated from a decade earlier. The
biggest difference from Sol's time in the school and theirs is that I was
that much older than most of the other fathers. The A-list superdads were
mostly around Erica's age, thirty or so years younger than I am. My only
comfort is that I had better hair than most of them, although since most
are either in big-time finance or the scions of big real estate families, they
already had more money.

During the several years I spent getting around to finally writing this
book, Erica, Sol, and I lived on the top floor of a Madison Avenue apartment opposite the Jackie Kennedy Reservoir in Central Park. From our
fortieth-floor windows we actually looked down on Sol's school about a
block away, which is why we lived there.

There is nothing pleasant about urban slipping and sliding when it
comes to getting your kid to school in a grueling New York City winter.
We sold the apartment in the summer of 2017. About the same time, we
also sold our most fanciful possession, a mile-square private island off
Playa Salinas on the southeast coast of Puerto Rico. Immodestly dubbed
Cayo Geraldo, our personal paradise island was the scene of raucous pig

roasts and countless clan reunions, but became expendable as we down-sized in anticipation of my running into the deep woods of old age, but it was a great fourteen years of rum-drenched fun while it lasted.

We still have a small but charming home alongside the Hudson River in Edgewater, New Jersey. Opposite Washington Heights in Manhattan, it is only eight miles from Fox News headquarters in Midtown. The "Edge" is our base when we are in the New York area, but unless or until I get drafted in a late-season career comeback, our principal residence is now a gracious old home in a perhaps surprisingly lovely neighborhood in suburban Cleveland, Ohio. I have a television and radio studio inside the modestly rambling manor with an indoor swimming pool, which would have cost far more than we paid for it were this a more favored location. Remember, after only Chicago, Boston, and Alaska, Cleveland has the worst winters in America.

Erica loves her hometown, which in recent years has shaken off its reputation as the "Mistake on the Lake." The lake would be Lake Erie, one of the Great Lakes, which together hold more freshwater than any other body in the world. The "mistake" was the awful industrial pollution that in the 1960s and 1970s mucked up the Cuyahoga River, which cuts through downtown, bearing the ships that bring the ore to the steel mills upriver. Randy Newman forever shamed the city with his epic satirical song "Burn On," which goes in part, "Cleveland, city of light, city of music . . . Even now I can remember. 'Cause the Cuyahoga River goes smokin' in my dreams. Burn on, big river, burn on . . ."

The idea of my moving to the Midwest, where I have never lived, may shock those who have followed my big-city public life, but aside from being about half as expensive as New York or Los Angeles, Cleveland has a lot going for it. A major article in the *Los Angeles Times* in July 2017 said the town was "on the cusp of cool." Aside from the Rock & Roll Hall of Fame, there is pretty good theater, a new casino, microbreweries, and trendy bars and restaurants. The town rolled out the red carpet for the flawless 2016 GOP Convention in which Trump was nominated, and it has some great sports teams, such as the 2016 NBA Champion Cleveland Cavaliers, the 2016 MLB American League Champion Cleveland Indians, and the reborn quarterback Baker Mayfield–led Cleveland Browns of the NFL. Nowadays, thanks to Mayfield, the legacy of LeBron James (who sadly went west to the L.A. Lakers) and slugger Francisco Lindor (pride of Puerto Rico, who we hope sticks around), folks call Cleveland "Believeland."

During the years spent writing this book, we lived behind
the Guggenheim Museum near Central Park.

Cayo Geraldo, the island off the south coast of Puerto Rico
we owned from 2004 to 2017. May 2016.

Anyway, Erica and I were ready for a change. After three-quarters of a century in the city at the center of the world, I think the slower pace of semisuburban life will either extend my life or kill me, leaving me buried under one of Cleveland's notorious lake-effect snowstorms.

OLD DADS

Like Mick Jagger, who had his eighth child at age seventy-three, having baby Sol at my age was even more controversial than my marriage to her mother. Sol was conceived just as all those reports were breaking about the dangers of birth defects or complications due to old sperm. Some of the people closest to me lobbied against it. "What's going to happen when she's in Little League and you're using a walker?" was a typical query. I told whoever doubted the decision that I had made up my mind, and that the main reason was that I could not marry a woman of childbearing age and not give her a child to bear.

Happily, Sol has ten fingers and toes, is healthy emotionally and physically, and loves math, swimming, piano, and theater. If any of my kids follow in my footsteps as an oversized media personality, it will probably be she. Sol is also her mom's hangout buddy. I joke that they should do a show like the *Gilmore Girls* where best-friend mom and daughter live, work, and play together in a quirky Connecticut town.

Less than 10 percent of men my age, seventy at the time of the 2014 Roger meeting, are still working. Even so, his mention at that meeting of my exit being imminent was stunning. My goal was and still is to stay in the game as long as I can compete with the endless flow of ambitious reporters and commentators, many of them less than a third my age, who continually swell the ranks of media.

In fire, flood, tornado, hurricane, eruption, earthquake, urban upheaval, dope-fiend confrontation, anarchy, and war, I managed to stay true to the No Guts, No Glory ethos in lands near and far. Even now, a beat-up old man, I am the reporter you do not want to compete against. Gimp or not, I will die before I let you beat me. Except for the bad foot and its accompanying, ever-growing limp, I am trim and relatively fit, with a solid exercise regimen and an undiminished competitive spirit. I might have trouble dodging bullets or blows these days, but I managed

to rouse myself to go to the aid of Puerto Rico in distress from historic
Hurricane Maria in September 2017, and I can still do hard interviews
as well as any reporter in the business, although it feels pathetic and
defensive to say so.

On our beloved Cayo in 2017 before Puerto Rico was ravaged by hurricanes Irma and Maria.

"DIDN'T YOU USED TO BE GERALDO RIVERA?" FEBRUARY 2014

In 2014 we thought our new millennium shooting wars were over or ending. At the time Roger told me to stiffen my upper lip and prepare for the
end of my active career, the world was a different place from what it was
when he hired me in the wake of the September 11, 2001, attacks. Our
combat forces were already out of Iraq, and the war in Afghanistan, the
longest in American history, was also ending, or at least downsizing. By
the end of 2014, no US ground forces were supposed to remain in that
hardscrabble country except trainers and security.

As we deflated our out-sized military presence everywhere, President
Barack Obama dismissed upstart ISIS as the "JV team." The extremists were just beginning to cut off heads and burn people alive. Syria was

screwed, but only a trickle of refugees had yet been set loose on Europe. Battlefield reports no longer interested our television audience, and demand for threescore-and-ten-year-old war correspondents was particularly low.

Roger called the meeting in his second-floor office at the Fox News World Headquarters on Avenue of the Americas, across from Radio City in Manhattan. It was a specific response to something I had said in an interview with commentator Will Cain. It was on *The Blaze*, that cable news and internet outfit owned and operated by Glenn Beck, a strange and powerful man, who is a whole other story.

Asked by Cain to comment on the recent death of a journalist in combat, I told him I envied the fallen reporter and wanted nothing less for myself. "I want to die with my boots on. That's half the reason why I go to these places—Libya, Afghanistan, Iraq, getting shot at—I'd rather die. I've been looking to get killed in action for years. That's one of the reasons I'm so bold, because I don't give a shit."

Cain asked, was I "addicted to fame"?

"I'm addicted to paying the bills," I quipped, but added straight from the heart, "I don't want people coming up to me and saying, 'Didn't you used to be Geraldo Rivera?'"

After I repeated the remarks on our own morning show *Fox and Friends*, Roger must have thought I was about to become a suicide bomber. His customarily gruff, direct, and strangely kind advice was to get a grip, take care of my family, and prepare for the ravages of old age. How could I not love the guy, and not recognize the monster he was later accused of becoming?

Chapter 2

WILLOWBROOK, O.J., AND THE SEMEN-STAINED DRESS

In rough strokes, I was a twenty-six-year-old, long-haired, radical street lawyer from a big, blue-collar New York Puerto Rican Catholic Jewish family when the media discovered me in 1970. Representing an East Harlem–based activist group called the Young Lords, I was thrust into the limelight as the group's spokesman when my clients refused to give interviews to the press. Their attitude toward the media was similar to President Trump's disdain for "fake news."

The first US-based Puerto Rican activist group not concerned primarily with the political status of the island, but rather with the social conditions of the Puerto Rican community in the States, the Lords had occupied a church complex in Spanish Harlem. They set up a free breakfast program for neighborhood children and were advocating testing for lead paint poisoning and addressing other health issues.

Even though the church congregation did not use the facility during the week, the Lords' occupation was illegal. The cops were surrounding the complex, and city officials under progressive Republican mayor John V. Lindsay were frantically trying to negotiate a peaceful end to the standoff.

For a week, it was a front-page story in the *New York Times* and even attracted national attention from the *Today* show and elsewhere. This was 1969–1970, during a period of urban rioting and widespread unrest. Harlem had burned before in 1964, followed by Watts in L.A., Newark, Baltimore, Detroit, and other battered cities. New York was a racial tinderbox that officials feared would be ignited by the church standoff.

After participating in the intense negotiations to resolve the crisis, I was singled out by pioneering news director Al Primo as a potential recruit for a new program at Columbia University's Graduate School of Journalism. I could not refuse the chance to attend that prestigious educational institution and learn how to be a television reporter, under Columbia's professor Fred Friendly.

The legendary producer for venerated CBS newsman Edward R. Murrow, Professor Friendly was running a program to train young black and brown professionals as reporters. It was designed to integrate the TV news business, which was overwhelmingly white and male. Mostly African Americans, with a sprinkling of Latinos, my class at Columbia was mostly lawyers, teachers, and law enforcement personnel. I turned twenty-seven on the Columbia campus and I was raring to go.

Funded by the Ford Foundation, the idea was to have a news team that reflected the racially diverse audience the particular channels were seeking to serve. It was a crash course during a tumultuous summer that saw the collision of the civil rights and anti-war movements and roughly spanned from the tragic Kent State massacre in May 1970 to the ruinous Asbury Park, New Jersey, race riots that July, which was my first assignment.

Each student was sponsored by a local TV station and had a promised job waiting upon graduation. None of the recruits had as high-octane a sponsor as mine. Al Primo had just come to the Big Apple bearing his potent invention, the *Eyewitness News* format, to WABC-TV, the huge ABC-owned and -operated station that was soon to begin a ratings dominance that has lasted almost a half-century in the nation's largest, most diverse market, the 23.7 million potential viewers in the New York metropolitan area.

Many years later, in December 2016, I was honored to introduce Al as he was inducted into the Golden Circle of the National Academy of Television Arts and Sciences, better known as the Emmys, for his more than fifty years in the business. Reaching that half-century milestone is a goal

I also covet. Only a handful of colleagues have managed to stick around that long. It's tough for lots of reasons, including the difficulty of staying relevant through five decades, a dozen wars, nine presidencies, countless fashion and style trends, and high-definition television. My fiftieth anniversary hits on Labor Day, 2020. Inshallah, which means "God willing," I will be around to celebrate.

Essentially I was hired in 1970 because of affirmative action, and I went on to my first fame as the Puerto Rican cog in the trailblazing news team's multiethnic wheel. During those action-packed early years, I covered gritty New York, a nightmarish city broke, broken, and reeling from racial tension, rampant crime, slashing graffiti, civic disengagement, filthy transit, and a heroin epidemic that was visible on virtually every stoop and alleyway. Those omnipresent junkie zombies could have been prototypes for *The Walking Dead*.

In 1971, I reported a special called "Drug Crisis in East Harlem," shot entirely on East 100th Street, which I said at the time was the worst street in America. It featured confrontational interviews with junkies shooting up, throwing up, and overdosing, and was the first time they were shown full-face on camera. It won my first major journalism acknowledgement, the Columbia DuPont Silver Baton. The city's response was to seize the entire street through eminent domain and bulldoze it. Now the block features attractive and hard-to-get public housing.

Reporting my Emmy-winning story, "Migrants, Dirt Cheap," 1974.

"THE LAST GREAT DISGRACE," JANUARY 1972

My life-altering crusade during that early period was a searing exposé targeting the nation's institutions for the developmentally disabled. There were several in the New York metropolitan area. On a bleak January morning, I broke into the Willowbrook State School on Staten Island. It was a chamber of horrors for more than five thousand so-called "residents," who were actually intellectually disabled inmates.

Two activist doctors, Mike Wilkins and Bill Bronston, whom I had met months before when they were volunteering at the Young Lords' health-care clinic in the occupied church in Spanish Harlem, were now working at Willowbrook. Both were planning to leave because of the abuse and neglect all around them. They told me they had a stolen key to the B Ward of Building 6, and that I could sneak in with my cameras rolling. It housed perhaps sixty severely and profoundly disabled children.

In exposing the wretched conditions at Willowbrook, I broadcast our searing footage (which you can still see on Geraldo.com) of naked children unattended and smeared with their own feces. They were making a pitiful sound, a kind of mournful wail that I will never forget.

As I reported in the plain, brutal language of the time:

> When Dr. Wilkins slid back the heavy metal door of B Ward, building No. 6, the horrible smell of the place staggered me. It was so wretched that my first thought was that the air was poisonous and would kill me. I looked down to steady myself and I saw a freak: a grotesque caricature of a person, lying under the sink on an incredibly filthy floor in an incredibly filthy bathroom. It was wearing trousers, but they were pulled down around its ankles. It was skinny. It was twisted. It was lying in its own feces. And it wasn't alone. Sitting next to this thing was another freak. In a parody of human emotion they were holding hands. They were making a noise. It was a wailing sound that I still hear and that I will never forget. I said out loud, but to nobody in particular, "My God, they're children." Wilkins looked at me and said, "Welcome to Willowbrook."

If I am remembered for anything, it will be these lines I wrote at the time: "This is what it looked like. This is what it sounded like. But how can I tell you about the way it smelled? It smelled of filth. It smelled of disease. It smelled of death."

Deeply shaken and enraged by what I had just seen, I hustled the fifteen miles' driving distance between Staten Island and the West Side studios of *Eyewitness News*. En route I interviewed Bernard Carabello, the Willowbrook resident whose story would come to represent those of many thousands of others forced to live in these horrible institutions. Bernard had just turned twenty-one and, under the sponsorship of the rebel doctors, had signed out of Willowbrook on his birthday to live on his own. His tragedy is that he was not retarded, and again I apologize for using that outdated "R" word. He was born with cerebral palsy. His intelligence is otherwise normal, but at age three his impoverished Puerto Rican immigrant mom had been persuaded by public health doctors to admit him to Willowbrook for his own good.

That is what parents did in those days, institutionalized their disabled youngsters. Even JFK and Robert F. Kennedy's sister Rosemary was institutionalized by her parents, Rose and Joseph Kennedy. So, for eighteen years, Bernard had been trapped in Willowbrook, physically handicapped but intellectually fully aware of the horrors all around him, which he charitably described as "a disgrace."

Leaving Bernard and calling ahead, I alerted management that my footage was earth-shaking: kids being treated worse than dogs at the worst kennel imaginable, and not in some distant land, but in a borough of New York City. The blockbuster reports did shake the world. I do not think there has ever been a bigger reaction to any investigative story, not even Edward R. Murrow's seminal "Harvest of Shame." The phones at the station rang off the hook. Politicians jumped all over themselves to deny responsibility and profess outrage and demand change. The station's ratings soared. In Bernard's honor, our half hour special was titled "The Last Great Disgrace."

A crusade to close Willowbrook and similar institutions began, including countless follow-ups, legislative lobbying, class action lawsuits, and, over the years, grand fund-raising events, including benefit boxing matches, golf outings, and concerts starring the likes of John Lennon and Yoko Ono, John Denver, the Allman Brothers, Stevie Wonder, and others, all of it helping change the way modern societies care for the developmentally disabled.

After Willowbrook, with friend-for-life Bernard Carabello. We joke that
the older we get, the more we look alike. September 1997.

With the funds raised and the high-profile promotions on programs
such as Donald Trump's last season of *Celebrity Apprentice*, of which I'll
have a lot more to say later, we have helped get the word out that this is
a population too long neglected and abused. More practically, we have
helped open scores of small, humane, community-based residences, and
have provided job training and educational facilities for a population once
condemned to short brutish lives, while also providing respite and support
for their often stressed-out parents.

When asked to speak about the Willowbrook experience, I am
unavoidably drawn to tears. There is hardly a day that I do not remember
those afflicted children in the B Ward of Building 6. In social situations
with relatives of intellectually and emotionally disabled folk, especially
kids, I am treated with the love and honor usually afforded a close friend
or family member. They know I get their special circumstance.

Advocating and fundraising for the disabled remains my principal charity, one especially necessary now that we are beset by the deeply troubling and mysterious epidemic of a developmental disability once known as mild retardation but now known as autism.

The crusade to humanize the care and treatment of the disabled is my best work and lasting legacy. The saga is the stuff of my pride and nightmares, and is still the main thing random strangers bring up, particularly in New York. They tell me how they remember the exposés, how the reports changed their lives and led them into social work or medicine, or how the stories saved the life of their brother or auntie or cousin, and how grateful they are that I am still involved in the cause.

In September 1987, Willowbrook was finally closed, along with virtually all similar large facilities for the disabled across the country and, eventually, around the civilized world. Community-based care—small, personal housing featuring remedial and vocational training—is now standard. At an emotional ceremony on the grounds, attended by families and activists, including Bernard, Governor Mario Cuomo presented me a commemorative award, the B Ward key I had used to gain entry. It is mounted on a small wooden plaque, with the inscription, "A Promise Fulfilled," and is my most treasured memento.

The lovely twenty-six acres of prime real estate on which the grim institution stood are now occupied by the College of Staten Island, which boasts a new Department of Sociology, with which Bernard and I remain involved.

Forty-seven years after that January 1972 day we met in the Staten Island diner, Bernard and I are still best friends, joking that the older we get the more we look alike, although my mustache is sexier. He went on to a full career as a client advocate and is still employed by the New York State Developmental Disabilities Services Office, although he keeps talking about his "imminent" retirement. We did a series of interviews together to commemorate the 30th anniversary of Willowbrook's closure, and he was honored at a gala dinner benefiting the College of Staten Island in December 2017 that brought together Willowbrook survivors, advocates, friends, and families who helped triumph over its bitter legacy, and who fight the never-ending battle to provide care and attention to the disabled.

YOM KIPPUR WAR, OCTOBER 1973

My first international assignment was the September 1973 coup in Chile, in which a military junta headed by armed forces chief Augusto Pinochet, and supported by our CIA, overthrew the democratically elected socialist government of Salvador Allende. Although I was still formally a WABC *Eyewitness* newsman, this was my first assignment for the big network, ABC News. Aside from tearing General Pinochet's throat out in a very aggressive interview, my most vivid memory from the trip was surviving the 8.3-magnitude earthquake that rocked our downtown Santiago high-rise hotel.

During my time in the Chilean capital, a full-blown war broke out halfway around the world in the Mideast. After a quick trip back to New York, during which I was the principal speaker at a fundraiser for Israeli charities, held at the home of Senator and Mrs. Jacob Javits, I flew in a chartered El Al flight to Tel Aviv. Everyone else onboard was a member of the Israeli Defense Forces.

I was reporting from the Golan Heights during the Yom Kippur War, when my team and I were bracketed by Syrian artillery, rounds exploding on both sides of our vehicle. At the time, this incident was the subject of intense scrutiny by critics alleging that it had been staged or misrepresented. Nothing is more damaging to a correspondent than to have his or her professional honor impugned.

The source of the false accusation was my *Eyewitness News* colleague, the late anchorman Roger Grimsby. In October 1973 he contacted a reporter from *Rolling Stone* to point out how miraculous it was for me to have survived a precisely targeted artillery strike just as the camera rolled.

When, given the gravity of the charge of staging, the magazine reporter ratted out Grimsby, telling me the details of his allegation, I was in a rage. I lured Grimsby to my office between his 6 PM and 11 PM newscasts. I told him we urgently had to talk about a matter of mutual importance. We were alone in the basement when I asked him face-to-face if he had indeed told the *Rolling Stone* reporter that I staged the barrage. He confessed. I started punching him, saying over and over that I was going to kill him, until he fell to the floor defenseless.

I stopped myself as my rage dissipated, leaving him seemingly unconscious on the newsroom basement floor. Worried that I had killed him, I went to my old friend producer Marty Berman's apartment on the Upper East Side of Manhattan. After I told Marty what had happened, we waited the hour or so until the 11 PM *Eyewitness News* came on. Needless to say, I was enormously relieved to see Roger give his signature line, "I'm Roger Grimsby, hear now the news." Or maybe it was "*here* now the news."

To his credit, the badly bruised Grimsby never told anyone what happened, as far as I know. The *Eyewitness* anchor unblinkingly went on the air and did the newscast flawlessly, even while sporting a badly made-over black eye.

My point is that war memories are cherished above all others. A glass top covers the wooden desk at which I write this; under the glass lies a field of service coins given me by hundreds of US combat units, mostly from Iraq and Afghanistan. Known as challenge coins, they are displayed with old press passes and a special service medal from an Iraqi general. All were personally handed to me by commanders of units large and small, here and abroad. Like the key to Willowbrook, the coins are cherished possessions, and each has a story attached.

Of course, we remember weddings and funerals, and especially children being born. But no memory is as vivid as a genuine war story, especially one caught on tape in a good cause. Those who have actually been in combat as warrior or reporter are ferocious defenders against "stolen valor" poseurs who claim peril they never experienced.

That is why NBC anchor Brian Williams got into such hot water in 2015 when caught embellishing his reporting during the Iraq War. He told a tallish tale of flying in a chopper in combat that got hit by an RPG, an enemy rocket. It turns out that although he did fly in a chopper at the time and place described, it was actually a different chopper in the unit that got hit by the rocket—a braggart's mistake that really was untrue, but at least the guy was there, unlike his critics. More about Brian's troubles later.

When Fox News and others began vigorously reporting Brian's scandal, liberal media wolves started hunting for similar misreporting by the right. That is when *Mother Jones*, the hard left-wing magazine, wrongfully attacked Bill O'Reilly. It was obviously a case of ideological tit-for-tat. A minor thirty-three-year-old discrepancy in O'Reilly's reporting over whether he was covering a "demonstration" or a "riot" in Buenos Aires, Argentina, during the 1982 Falklands War was being puffed to make it seem similar to Brian's fabrication, which it was not.

O'Reilly fought back with furious indignation. Fox News stuck by our star, which the network ultimately did not do when he was later forced out in the post–Roger Ailes frenzy over sexual harassment, but this time, his critics slunk away. By relentlessly revealing the left-wing agenda of the magazine and the paucity of facts in its reporting, O'Reilly defanged the critics of his war coverage. I should have done the same when my own scandal broke out in Afghanistan in 2001, but much more about that later.

HE'S NOT HEAVY, HE'S MY BROTHER, OCTOBER 1954–PRESENT

When Roger offered me the job at Fox in the fall of 2001, he promised substantial raises over time, if I lasted at the network, and agreed to hire my brother, Craig, as my field producer. Craig was middle-aged and desperate for a job after having a fight with his boss and quitting after thirteen years as a roving reporter at the syndicated show *Inside Edition*.

I remember the day Craig sheepishly told me he was taking that job at *Inside* for the chance to move from the role of sidekick field producer to on-air correspondent on his own. I was delighted for him, although miffed that he had kept the process secret from me. Until he made the jump, he had worked for me from the age of seventeen. He was tough and brave; in our time together before he went off on his own, Craig and I traveled near and far reporting for ABC News and later syndicated specials covering the KKK, devil worship, urban gangbangers, war, rebellion, the mob, militias, and mass murderers, including Charles Manson in an exclusive 1988 interview at San Quentin prison.

When Manson died in November 2017, I wrote, "It couldn't happen to a nicer guy." He was responsible for nine of the bloodiest murders ever committed, including that of the lovely actress Sharon Tate, who was eight-and-a-half months pregnant when Manson's devoted acolytes chopped her up and hung her upside down. The other victims were similarly savaged.

Devoid of remorse, his head filled with notions of grandeur, for decades, Manson enjoyed infamy among successive generations of young people seduced by the fact this murdering scum couched his crimes in environmental and antiracist babble. I hate the fact that, despite the brutality of his crimes, or perhaps because of them, his face adorned what were America's biggest-selling T-shirts. Thus, more popular than Che Guevara or Chairman Mao, Charlie was a charismatic snake charmer, an articulate, eco-friendly homicidal maniac who was part Jim Jones and part Adolf Hitler. His twisted soul shone through that hateful swastika tattoo carved on his forehead between those glaring, piercing, beady eyes.

He told me in our epic televised 1988 face-to-face confrontation inside San Quentin that he could save our overpopulated planet if he could just "kill 50 million" of us. I told him he was "a mass-murdering dog." He told me that if he didn't like the way our interview was presented he would have my head handed to my family in a basket. I told him that if anything happened to me his roomies in the joint would set him on fire again, as they did in 1984. As testament to his curious appeal, the hugely rated interview has been downloaded many millions of times.

Manson had been living on borrowed time anyway. He was originally sentenced to die in the gas chamber, but was spared in 1972 when the California Supreme Court ruled that the statute under which he was condemned was unconstitutional. His sentence commuted to life, he was denied parole twelve times. Most of his so-called family is either dead or still in prison. Only one of the largely well-educated, middle-class kids he convinced to kill for him has been granted parole. Just nineteen when she admittedly devolved into barbarism to please Charlie, now sixty-nine-year-old Leslie Van Houten remains behind bars as I write this, awaiting Governor Jerry Brown's decision to accept or reject the California parole board's recommendation that she be set free.

Manson was a lowlife whose enduringly perverse popularity was testimony to something dark in America's psyche. Don't rest in peace, Charlie. Go instead to be with your friend the devil. Go to hell.

Mass murders aside, in the decades before Fox News and the talk-show era, our real specialty was dope. Hands down, I am the Edward R. Murrow of dope reporters, which made Craig my *High Times* Fred Friendly. If there was a new stoner scourge, whether shooting, snorting, or smoking anything from heroin to crack to meth, we were on it. Often with brother Craig and/or Greg Hart, another fearless producer and cameraman by my side, I chronicled countless battles in the drug wars, from Bogota, Colombia, to Karachi, Pakistan, from Harlem to Hollywood. A wiry perpetual-motion machine, Greg came to work with me right out of Fordham University.

Together we patrolled the bloody hills of Guerrero State with the Mexican Army, the high seas with the United States Coast Guard, and across five continents with the Drug Enforcement Administration. We busted into countless homes and businesses with scores of SWAT teams, eager to put on a show, sometimes live, like *American Vice*, a revolution-ary program that in 1988 used multiple, simultaneous satellite remotes to show how deeply the nation had fallen into dope's embrace.

The danger with doing all those live remotes is that you never know exactly what you are going to get. In the case of the recklessly innova-tive *American Vice*, we snared a relatively innocent Texas woman, who happened to be at one of the locations when the cops busted in on live television, announcing that everybody there was under arrest. She was so transparently not a dope dealer that many audience members were out-raged that she was caught on camera. Actor Bruce Willis, a great guy who for years dated my third ex-wife, Gabriel's mother, Sheri, wrote me to say how unfair it was to expose her. When the cops cut her loose, she sued me for millions, but settled for about $200,000. She was subsequently busted on separate drug charges, a few months down the road.

CHASING DRAGONS, 1970–PRESENT

Chasing dope stories is a crazy, scary job. Peril is routine. Flying with bad pilots in overloaded airplanes or driving on heart-stopping roads, barely steering clear of the precipice, and dealing with scumbag drug killers and overly macho cops—it is a miracle we were not killed by bad guys or good intentions.

I have mixed feelings about narcotics enforcement. Pot should be universally legalized. Despite the best efforts of our retro Attorney Gen-eral Jeff Sessions, it already is, effectively, in about half the country. The harder stuff is a tougher call. As a believer in personal responsibility and as a libertarian, I think grown-ups should be allowed to get high as long as they are done working or studying and are not hurting others or infring-ing on their right to be sober and safe. Despite being open-minded and

Despite being open-minded and sometimes surrounded by forests of dewy pot plants, we almost never succumbed to the obvious temptations. March 2003.

sometimes surrounded by everything from wheelbarrows full of coke to forests of dewy pot plants, we never succumbed to the obvious temptations. Well, almost never. In Afghanistan and especially in South America, it is hard not to light up occasionally since it grows along the roads like crabgrass. But I have never been stoned or drunk on the air. We never bought any drugs for personal use on the job or brought anything home from the front. It just was not worth the career-destroying risk.

We were *Vice News* before cable. No story was too dangerous. I know that sounds like pretentious babble, but it is true. The criteria for doing a story were intrinsic worth and potential audience appeal, regardless of risk. Craig was experienced on both sides of the camera, correspondent and producer, and Roger's agreeing to hire both him and Greg Hart was a big reason I took the leap from NBC to Fox News after 9/11.

We knew the ground we were about to cover for Fox News in Afghanistan, because we had been there years before, on an assignment for ABC's *20/20*. In 1980, we traveled through the frontier town of Peshawar, the fabled Khyber Pass, and the lawless Tribal Territories, posing as opium buyers, shooting a gritty hour-long *20/20* special called "Chasing the Dragon," which is what junkies call smoking heroin.

Using a crude hidden camera in a gym bag, Craig managed to film me negotiating with representatives of local opium growers to buy a thousand kilos of opium paste neatly stuffed into a water-tank truck that was going to be delivered to our boat waiting in the dense, chaotic harbor of Karachi, Pakistan. Of course, we never consummated the deal, or took possession of the dope. Once we caught the sellers on hidden camera, we told them we would return soon with the cash . . . never to return. A correspondent for *Newsday* covering the area several years later reported that there was a price on my head, put there by the dope dealers whom our dramatic broadcast had acutely embarrassed.

That was 1980. Twenty-one years later, in 2001, as Craig and I started our careers at Fox News, the mastermind of the 9/11 attacks, Osama bin Laden, was thought to be in that same area along the Pakistan-Afghanistan border. He was said to be literally underground in a cave, certainly uncaught. I dreamed night and day of killing him with my own hands and was mocked for saying so publicly. I did not care. My main worry was that he would be caught or killed before I got there, and that there would be no war by the time we returned to the Khyber Pass, in November 2001.

ZAPRUDER, MARCH 1975

Eyewitness News propelled me to local celebrity, helping create a new one-name wonder to follow Elvis, Ringo, Dylan, Dion, and Lassie in those days before Oprah and Madonna. Because I was the most important New York media commentator of the period, TV critic John J. O'Connor of the *New York Times* predicted in 1973, "New York has a way of nationalizing its local celebrities." It is another way of phrasing Liza Minnelli's famous "New York, New York" lyrics, "If you can make it here, you can make it anywhere."

I went national soon after Willowbrook with a show called *Goodnight America*. It was a late-night, news-oriented variety show we called a "Second Generation TV Newsmagazine," a counterpoint to *60 Minutes*, which was so first generation. The bi-monthly show ran from 1973–1977. That show's theme song from Ringo Starr still applies. It features the lyrics, "You gotta pay your dues if you want to sing the blues. And you know, It Don't Come Easy."

GNA is best remembered for its pre–*Saturday Night Live*, late-night hipster sensibility and included interviews with all the Beatles and Rolling Stones, the Grateful Dead, and the Hell's Angels. I hung with Jerry Garcia before he was a flavor at Ben & Jerry's. The more notable *GNA* achievement was the first network airing of the Abraham Zapruder home movie of the 1963 Kennedy assassination.

In the grainy film, you see in the backseat of the open limousine driving through Dealey Plaza, the president's head jerk backward as he is shot. He instantly grabs his throat as his battered and bloodied head then snaps forward. The inevitable question became how could his head initially jerk backward if a lone assassin, Lee Harvey Oswald, shot from behind from his sniper's perch on the sixth floor of the Texas School Book Depository?

The enormous response to that airing on March 6, 1975, gave birth to generations of conspiracy theories claiming that dark forces within the US government or the Chicago mob or Cuba or extraterrestrials from a galaxy far, far away killed the young and gracious thirty-fifth president, who did not really live in Camelot and had lots of secrets in real life.

For the next several years, I investigated every facet of the disturbing mystery before concluding that the Warren Commission was probably right about Lee Harvey Oswald's being the lone assassin, and that JFK's apparently anomalous head movement was the result of a measurable involuntary reflex.

During those years, I was a hybrid reporter/celebrity, a role I describe as being the first "rock 'n' roll newsman." Until I decided life was too tempting to stay married, I was an accepted member of the jet set, or at least a tolerated presence. During that flashy period I was with Edith Vonnegut, the beautiful, skilled, spiritual artist and daughter of one of the twentieth century's literary lions, Kurt Vonnegut Jr., author of *Slaughterhouse Five* and other now-iconic novels. We married in the Vonnegut family home in Barnstable, Massachusetts, in December 1971.

THE HIGH LIFE, 1972–1991

It is no excuse, but in the early 1970s, in my late twenties and early thirties, I was a young man from nowhere, fresh to fame following the Willowbrook exposés and for the first time relatively flush with money. I ran in gauche and glittering circles and I am not blaming anyone but myself.

This was the time in New York before AIDS changed mores and Ronald and Nancy "Just Say No" Reagan became the social scene setters. It was the ten years from 1970 to 1980 when the drug- and sex-fueled arts crowd flourished in the midst of a horde of larger-than-life characters. Part of the scene centered on the mustachioed and flamboyantly erratic Salvador Dali, whom I met through billionaire Huntington Hartford, the A & P heir, who had the best bacchanals in his expansive crash pad inside his modern art museum, an entire building overlooking Columbus Circle.

The unparalleled Andy Warhol was out everywhere, his dead eyes and droll humor counterpoints to his vivacious talent. He was usually the quiet, unblinking center of attention, along with his Pop Art rivals Robert Rauschenberg and Jasper Johns, whose American flag paintings also became iconic. Warhol once complained how late one night I was the most famous person in Studio 54. When he published a book of his art, I asked him to autograph one for me. "I'll do more than that," he said with his perpetual smirk. Flourishing his magic marker, he started drawing random lines on a book's cover. "I'll make you priceless art." I have moved so many times since then and have no idea where that book is, although I am reasonably certain it will turn up when my estate does an inventory.

Thomas Hoving was often around. His family owned Tiffany, and he was the larger-than-life president of the Metropolitan Museum of Art. A connoisseur of art and existentialism, he later ran the NYC parks. Tom once told me how as parks commissioner he sometimes instructed his police officers on how to cut the skyrocketing crime wave sweeping the parks in the crime-riddled Manhattan of Mayors John Lindsay and later Abe Beame. "I told my cops to throw the bodies over the wall onto Central Park West, so the homicide would be recorded as having happened in the Nineteenth Precinct, not in Central Park," he told me, perhaps jokingly.

My first real home, a rehabilitated triplex apartment, over a cuchifritos (deep-fried Puerto Rican food) joint, on Avenue C in Manhattan's then predominantly poor and Puerto Rican Lower East Side, became party hearty central. If a street is ever named after me, it should be Avenue C, say between Third and Tenth Streets. Mayor Lindsay, Mick Jagger, ballet superstar Rudolph Nureyev, and many more luminaries frequented my soirees there. The wild night that Jagger and Nureyev put me in a grinding men sandwich convinced me that I could not be gay, because if I were, that would have been the night.

I especially enjoyed my late-night hangout royals, who unintentionally taught me the lesson never, ever to envy anyone, however high-born or hereditarily noble. Classically handsome Prince Egon Von Furstenberg made his wife, Diane, royalty. She went on to become one of the most successful designers in history. He basically drank himself to death. After not seeing him for several years, I ran into him by chance in 1983, drinking alone in a random bar in Rome. Having been undeniably blood royalty, he went from being baptized by the pope, to dying of hepatitis C in 2004 from an infection left over from years of self-indulgence and melancholia. He was fifty-seven.

I met my other royal hangout buddy taping a notable segment on the glitzy extravagant opening of a new resort called Las Hadas (the Fairies) near Manzanillo, Mexico. Three passenger jets were chartered for the gala, one coming in from Los Angeles, one from New York, and another from Europe. My main interview was with actor and perennially tanned playboy George Hamilton. What made the segment unusual is that it was done on the beach with each of us wearing a skin-tight Speedo. Much later, in an appearance on *Fox and Friends* in April 2016, George and I joked about the old "daze."

Baron Arnot des Rosnay, a French nobleman, arranged the event at Las Hadas. His wife's, Isabel Goldsmith's, enormously wealthy family owned the resort. When they divorced, Arnot became a daredevil who set long-distance surf-sailing records that to his rivals seemed too good to be true. In 1984, after other windsurfers had questioned his record surf sailing his thirteen-foot board the almost nine hundred miles from the Marquesas to Tahiti, he decided to sail solo on his tiny board through shark-infested waters from Mainland China to Taiwan, never to be heard from again. He was thirty-eight.

Through Kurt Vonnegut, I met and spent time with many of the macho, literary, and show business luminaries of the era, often at Elaine's extraordinary pub on Second Avenue. They included swaggering, confident, over-the-top role models such as novelist Norman (*The Naked and the Dead*) Mailer; filmmaker Sidney Lumet, who thought I should be an actor, which I took as high praise coming from the man who directed *12 Angry Men*, *Equus*, *Dog Day Afternoon*, and *Serpico*; elegant Gay Talese;

bitchy but brilliant Gore Vidal before his Italian sojourn; classy and cool, deep Harry Belafonte; Tom "White Suit" Wolfe; Joseph (*Catch 22*) Heller; Peter (*Valachi Papers*) Maas; tiny, chatty Truman (*In Cold Blood*) Capote; William F. Buckley, the inventor of modern smart conservatism, and his imperial wife, Patricia; unfailingly pleasant poet Allen Ginsberg; and occasionally, Chicago's blue-collar oracle Studs Terkel; among many others. There were also plenty of tough guy reporters around, including three I admired, Jimmy Breslin and Mike McAlary of the *New York Daily News* and Pete Hamill of the *New York Post*. The inventor of participatory journalism, George Plimpton, was also a regular. I learned from the *Paper Lion* author to be physically and emotionally involved with my stories, to live them and be them, not merely to report them. George and Kurt were both guests on the first edition of my show, along with the hero of the farmworkers' struggle, Cesar Chavez, who became a friend I idolized.

Vonnegut taught me another eye-opening lesson. He told me how witnessing the carnage and horror of World War II had convinced him that he was an atheist. He reasoned that if there was a God, then why did the heavens not open up and consume the Nazis, those ultimate doers of evil, or even our GIs, who in destroying cities and killing enemies were also taking lives?

I embraced that dark reflection. After sixty, seventy, or eighty years that fly by way too fast, you die. There is no moral cost for sins on this Earth. There might be a reckoning eventually, but unless you get caught, not here and now. When I succumbed to infidelity, I knew God was not going to punish me, at least not in this world. If God existed, he, she, or it did not care. Yet now that I'm an old man, my certainty that no judgment awaits has wavered, as it often does when showoffs face the end of their time onstage.

As the disco years faded, Edie and I divorced. Keeping to what became my sorry pattern of middle life, my philandering caused our breakup. For that, I am filled with regret and embarrassment, half a century later. I skipped around for a while, never staying put for too long. The party continued even as cadres of friends began dying of the mystery disease we thought was a "gay plague," including a dear friend, the incredible fashion designer and bon vivant Giorgio di Sant' Angelo. Still, I remained a glutton for the easy attention semi-stardom brings.

GOOD MORNING AMERICA, NOVEMBER 1975

My career moved forward in fits and starts. In November 1975, I was assigned to the inaugural cast of ABC's *Good Morning America*, roving the country for the team for the next several years until the network's *20/20* debuted in June 1978. In that year I investigated and exposed the drug-overdose death of Elvis Presley, setting a ratings record for the show that stood for twenty-one years, until Barbara Walters interviewed Monica Lewinsky in 1999.

Personal upheavals aside, those were fifteen great years with the ABC network, before I was ignominiously fired in 1985 by yet another legend, my boss Roone Arledge. The creator of modern sports and news programming, who coined the phrase "up close and personal," Roone fired me because I complained publicly when he killed a colleague's story about dark rumors concerning the Kennedy family.

Reported by Sylvia Chase, the story included allegations of an inappropriate relationship between Marilyn Monroe, the sex goddess of her time, and both President Kennedy and his brother, Attorney General Robert F. Kennedy. There were more whispers of Chicago mobster involvement—those criminals must have stayed busy nefariously plotting big stuff—and also malignant rumors that Monroe's accidental drug-overdose death was actually murder.

Roone claimed he canceled the story only because it was badly reported and poorly sourced, both of which were true. The salacious allegation of presidential infidelity at its core has since been widely published, but never proven. After decades pondering every major investigation on the subject, I have come to the conclusion that Marilyn, the aging and lonely sex symbol of my teens, just gave up on life. Like so many others, she took more of the drugs she was then taking than she should have and slipped into last, deepest sleep.

Anyway, I was furious that the story was spiked, and without proof foolishly alleged to *People* magazine and other media that Roone killed the report out of loyalty to his dear friend Ethel Kennedy, Bobby's widow.

Perhaps ironically, Ethel and Bobby Kennedy's second youngest of eleven children, Douglas Kennedy, is a friend and colleague of mine at Fox. He is a straight-arrow news correspondent, only assigned non-political stories, and he is never put professionally close to his legendary family's politics, which are antithetical to big Fox. He has no shortage of strong, smart political opinions, however, and if unleashed in private, he will set your clock right with intensity.

My career at *20/20* ended when two other friends, Hugh Downs and Barbara Walters, assured the staff that they were just as outraged as I was that the Kennedy story was being killed. They said they stood shoulder-to-shoulder with me, but in the end, I was the only one to speak out. Roone saw my accusatory rant as a personal betrayal. It was my stupidest career move because, at forty-two years old, I was soon the most famous unemployed person in the nation.

NATION'S MOST FAMOUS UNEMPLOYED PERSON, JANUARY 1986

Unable to move to another major network-news division because of that aggressive personal style so many news pros still consider too flamboyant, in desperation, and for $50,000 paid up front, I agreed in 1986 to solve *The Mystery of Al Capone's Vault* on live television. The vault was empty and I was a humiliated laughingstock—until the live telecast proved to be the highest-rated syndicated show in television history, which it still is. I like to say it was my greatest failure and most noteworthy commercial triumph; the only thing in the vault was ratings.

In April 2016, just about every news and entertainment outlet in the country made note of the thirtieth anniversary of the special. The *Chicago Tribune* commented how the show out-rated Super Bowl XX that year despite the fact that the big football game featured a 46-10 victory by the hometown Chicago Bears, *Da Bears*, over the New England Patriots. I was proud to have a thirtieth anniversary of anything to celebrate.

As a result of the Capone show's colossal commercial success, I was deluged with job offers from programs like *Entertainment Tonight*, where I worked long enough to interview the one Beatle I never spent any quality time with, the great "While My Guitar Gently Weeps" George Harrison. He had some of the same humility I saw in Elvis, too much for the occasion, but probably born of shyness. I stayed at *ET* only until I got my own syndicated show up and running the following year. Initially called *Geraldo!*, the shockingly successful program ran from 1987 to 1998, and along with some related business deals, earned my fortune, such as remains.

Opinion makers and critics soon forgot my hard work as an ABC News crusading reporter. During much of the talk-show period, I was best known for getting my nose broken in that genuinely violent on-air rumble with racist skinheads, for multiple interviews with the playboy of the era, Donald J. Trump, and for talk-show segments like "Men in Lace Panties and the Women Who Love Them."

TIES THAT BIND

My ghosts, and ultimate career redemption, help explain my mixed response to the alleged misdeeds of my late boss and friend Roger Ailes. Before he was exposed as an alleged misogynist, we had known each other for decades, introduced by another powerful media maestro, the late, great Jerry Weintraub.

One of Hollywood's most important producers, Jerry first met Roger when Roger was executive producer of *The Mike Douglas Show* in the late 1960s. Both men orbited the world of Kennebunkport's favorite son, George H.W. Bush, before, during, and after his presidency, the forty-first, from 1988 to 1992. Jerry was my first agent. He and I remained friends long after our professional relationship ended, until his death in July 2015. There is no mystery as to why so many big stars, from Elvis to Frank Sinatra, George Clooney to Matt Damon, adored the man.

He was a creative powerhouse, loving and loyal, and a terrific movie producer, with films such as *Karate Kid* and *Ocean's 11* to his credit. He played a big role in my life, helping to craft *Goodnight America*, my first network show. He negotiated my first, huge-for-those-days ABC News deal, which made me the first million-dollar street reporter. In the early 1970s especially, that was a ton of money, even for anchors like Barbara Walters.

Erica and I reminisced about the great man with Jerry's son Michael in March 2016 when we were staying out in L.A. during my improbable stint on *Dancing with the Stars*. At The Lobster, a Santa Monica restaurant overlooking the famous pier, we laughed remembering how I had brought two hookers to Michael's bar mitzvah at his family mansion on Doheny Road in Beverly Hills in 1975.

It was not as bad as it sounds. I was up in San Francisco with Jane Fonda doing a story about her speech on empowerment at an international hookers' convention. Jane wanted the world's oldest profession decriminalized and prostitutes given all the employment protections of any other profession.

A two-time Academy Award winner, Jane has been one of America's most underrated public personalities for the last couple of decades. The star of *Barbarella*, *Klute*, and *Coming Home* went from stunning ingénue to America's antiwar conscience. She did take her activism a step too far in making the pilgrimage to North Vietnam at the time that nation was killing American GIs. Showing obscene sympathy to our enemies, she became a pariah during the 1970s, cursed by everyone who ever wore the uniform of the United States. For that Jane was never forgiven. Indeed, host Megyn Kelly brought up the incident in 2018 when the two argued on the air about something totally unrelated, plastic surgery.

Typically, I saw Jane's notorious history differently. "Hanoi Jane's" visit to North Vietnam, even as hundreds of brave Americans were POWs in its prison camps, was a serious mistake, for which she apologized and deserved forgiveness. She is too smart, talented, and sincere to be written off for that lapse in judgment. Viewed by the prism of today, her actions seem treasonous, particularly to Vietnam vets. In the context of 1972, however, when tens of thousands were protesting the wildly unpopular war every day, what she did was not that egregious. Her biggest mistake was being photographed in a North Vietnamese antiaircraft gun emplacement wearing a commie helmet.

Vietnam was a long way from San Francisco, where, after interviewing two of Jane's ladies of the night at the hookers' convention, I invited them to Michael Weintraub's grand Beverly Hills bar mitzvah. Both were immediately eager to attend. Even more eager were the ABC television executives who were guests at the bar mitzvah, and the teenagers, all of them buzzing around my special guests. What can I say, other than it was a different era, the ethos of which seemed cool, but feels boorish in the retelling decades later?

Michael brought pictures of the girls to our dinner at The Lobster. Erica said how classy they looked: "They look like college girls, not at all trampy." Michael, who is now in his fifties, told me how thankful he was at the time. In a town where these Jewish rites of passage can be outrageously excessive, I helped make his celebration special. We also laughed about how his fabulous father managed to balance wife and mistress so well that the women lived together after Jerry passed. Isn't that the best evidence that Jerry was a remarkable negotiator and a terrific agent?

My second agent was Jon Peters, a dramatic-looking, long-haired, part-Native American, mostly-Italian former hairstylist to the stars. I call him Cochise of Beverly Hills. He was the real-life *Shampoo*; the Warren Beatty character in the movie was obviously modeled after Jon. Through pure chutzpah and charisma, he courted Hollywood's biggest prize, wooing and landing Barbra Streisand, the ultimate show-business icon. The power couple enjoyed a long-time passionate, tumultuous love and business relationship.

Our friendship started when Jon and Barbra watched some of my Willowbrook exposés. As with John Lennon and Yoko before them, that story was our introduction. Jon and I have been best buds for four decades, during which I watched his evolution from hairdresser to one of Hollywood's most powerful tycoons. His movies include the Oscar-winning *The Color Purple*, Barbra's hugely successful remake of *A Star Is Born*, *Footloose*, *Batman*, *Superman*, and about a hundred others.

A couple of years after we met, in 1976, Sheri, my third wife and mother of my firstborn child, Gabriel, and I moved next door to Jon and Barbra in Malibu. Our modest Ramirez Canyon home abutted their vast and lovely seven-mansion complex, which Barbra has since donated as a park to Los Angeles County. Sheri and Barbra were close friends. Jon and I became

In Malibu, CA, with Jon Peters, Cochise of Beverly Hills. January 2001.

inseparable, getting loaded, street fighting, and riding our powerful motor-cycles recklessly through the canyons of the Santa Monica Mountains and along Pacific Coast Highway. We joked about how we had the same trick gene that forced us to push the limits and routinely risk everything.

One unforgettable near-death incident on the bikes happened when both of us were barefoot and wearing nothing but Speedos. We went too fast on a curve on Ramirez Canyon Drive on the way home and almost went off the road, skidding and braking just shy of the cliff and catastro-phe. That was the last time Jon rode his bike. My riding lasted longer, until 2014 when I dumped my old Harley while making an illegal left turn in New Jersey. I was pinned under the heavy bike, but four guys came run-ning to my assistance. When they saw who it was, three of them stopped their rescue efforts and whipped out their cell phone cameras.

Jon made my 1977 ABC *20/20* deal with Roone Arledge, and we fan-cied ourselves standing back-to-back in the barroom brawl of life, often literally. We were constantly punching and jabbing each other, testing who was more macho. He was fiercely protective of Barbra and had a hair-trigger temper, which I saw him unleash several times on intrusive, aggressive, stalker fans trespassing on their Malibu and Aspen properties. Twice I was called on to swear to cops investigating allegations of assault that the other guy had started it.

I was an amateur boxer for about twenty-five years, beginning in the early 1970s. For six of those years, I owned a gym called Broadcast Boxing on West Fifty-Seventh Street, a block from Carnegie Hall. To raise money for my Willowbrook-related charities during that period, aside from con-certs and golf tournaments, I would fight whichever Wall Street broker bid the most money. Jon was in my corner when I won one particularly vio-lent three-round brawl before a packed house in Madison Square Garden, and we have stayed friends to this day. If he is the last man standing, Jon Peters will be among my pallbearers when the time comes. I won some and lost some of the charity bouts, including one unforgettable, Howard Stern–sponsored (instigated) three-rounder against Sylvester Stallone's brother Frank. I was game, but Frank was better, bigger, and younger. You can still find that near-death match on the internet.

When you think of the men who mentored me—Fred Friendly, Jerry Weintraub, Roone Arledge, Jon Peters, and until the summer of 2016, Roger Ailes—it is clear that whatever you think of the student, his teachers were all legends in their own right. In Roger's case there was apparently something else going on that I did not know about until his world dissolved in scandal and shame, but his travails aside, he was also a historic innovator.

Before I get into Roger's personal Armageddon, as I recognize those responsible for giving me the skills and opportunity to stay on television for so long, let me thank the deeply impressive ex-chairmen of the Tribune Co., Dennis FitzSimons, and his predecessor, the late Jim Dowdle. They ran the vast Chicago-based media conglomerate, which during its 1980s and 1990s glory days owned dozens of big-city newspapers, major market television stations, and the Chicago Cubs. They not only produced my long-running daytime talk show, but also cut me and several other prominent minorities in as partners on a deal to buy local television stations in Atlanta and New Orleans. Our partnership, which included Quincy Jones, the eminent songwriter and philanthropist, and the late Don Cornelius, the charismatic host of *Soul Train*, sold the two stations a few years later. The sale came at the top of the market, and to this day the money made is, as I said, a hefty portion of retirement stash.

Like almost every executive at Fox News, from Rupert Murdoch on down to Ailes's protégé Bill Shine and his co-president, Jack Abernethy, my partners at Tribune were also self-made Irishmen. For that matter, so was their sometime rival, sometime ally, the gregarious Roger King, founder of King World. He was another roaring, larger-than-life media giant who was the boisterous syndicator of my talk show late in its run, and more consequentially Oprah's. I want to give props, too, to Jack Welsh, another Irishman and the legendary GE chairman, who gave me the sweet 1997 NBC News deal that I will soon describe. And, love those Irish, their ranks include the leading prime-time host at Fox, my amigo Sean Hannity. Megyn Kelly is also a notable member of the tribe, but now she belongs to another network. Bill O'Reilly, as emerald green as they come, has joined the ranks of Irish exiles, now ignominiously banned from the network he led to prosperity for two decades, until running afoul of sexual politics, exacerbated by bad judgment and lavish settlements.

A last note on the Irish thing: For the twenty-plus years Fox News has been on the air, but especially following the Trump triumph in the 2016 presidential election, observers and critics of Big Media, including former President Obama, have pointed to the difference between Fox and the

With my improbable dear friend Sean Hannity, June 2016.

other networks as being basically ideological. Essentially, they say, there is the conservative network, Fox, standing alone against an array of liberal news networks, principally MSNBC and CNN.

Which is true, but there is something much more basic going on. Those Irishmen are mostly Catholic. Hannity was an altar boy, and like O'Reilly went to parochial school. Many of their beliefs and attitudes are forged from that identity, which helps explain their feelings about hot-button issues like abortion, racial and sexual politics, immigration, and gay marriage. They are just as sharp and smart as any high-flying liberal. They have an opposing worldview, not reactionary or dumber, just different. They are what they were raised, people who believe, for example, that all life is sacred and begins with conception. Their sincerity and intellect aside, I do think O'Reilly's obsession with the imaginary "War on Christmas" was excessive, but better than, say, War on North Korea.

Many mainstream, Big Media pundits who are generally more liberal, Blue State and New York/Los Angeles–centric than Fox, shudder to talk about the fact that a disproportionate percentage of editorial management is, like me, Jewish. Still, as ABC News titan Roone Arledge, a WASP, once suggested to me, in crude, broad strokes, the allegation is true. If you want a list of all of us Jews in news and entertainment, listen to Adam Sandler's Hanukkah song or Google it. What makes the age-old complaints about Jewish people "controlling" the media anti-Semitic is the implication that religion skews our presentation and professionalism, which is not true.

The truth is subtler. Although we come in all ideologies, the bottom-line truth is that Jewish people, like the Fox Irish, are partly what we were raised. How could that not be true? Jewish folk are more progressive than not, urban or at least suburban, seldom rural or gun-toting, relatively cosmopolitan, usually college-educated, and slightly superior, or even smug, regarding folks from the great red working-class heart of Middle America—you know, the "Deplorables." That is why so many of us missed the 2015–16 Trump phenomena happening from Michigan to Miami to Maine.

What changed with the coming of age of Fox News, is that there is now a major news network that reflects a bundle of personal, educational, professional, and religious experiences different from what many were used to seeing in charge of a news network. Despite its recent agonies, and the loss of both Ailes and chief anchor O'Reilly, the network's basic identity remains intact, a testament to Roger's enduring vision.

He made a network in his self-image. Whatever else he was, or became, he was also a born-again Irish Catholic who passionately believed in the basic tenets of his church. He saw in its underrepresentation on television news and in the disdain with which age-old Catholic traditions and teachings were viewed by the mainstream the vast opening for his often embattled but undeniably successful creation, Fox News.

EXPOSING MYSELF, 1990

My personal controversies predate my move to Fox. In 1990 I wrote the vastly controversial memoir the Vonnegut family hated. It combined a gritty recounting of my early career as an investigative reporter uncovering injustice, with a steamy, sexploitation tell-all of the wild and crazy 1970s. A minor best seller, *Exposing Myself* named names, condemning me to both the literary junk pile and the Tackiness Hall of Fame. It came back to bite me badly in 2017. Truth is no defense for bad manners, and I continue to apologize for writing it.

Exposing Myself described the devastating chink in my character that had plagued me from the beginning of my fame: ego-gratifying lust. The inability to remain monogamous became the central fact of my serial divorces. I am speaking about promiscuity, not predation; romance, not rape. Any man who uses his power, position, or prestige to force himself on a woman deserves punishment ranging from shame to castration. Weinstein and his ilk are loser sadists. I'm just a retired Romeo who has seen the light. In the happiest of coincidences, I met Erica and went straight just before public life became a harsh place for aging playboys. Finally I have personal values that match my professional ethics; I have been clean and sober in that regard since my marriage to Erica in 2003. I have never cheated on my wife. Monogamy is now the central tenet of my secular religion.

About seven years ago, at a black tie event at the Manhattan Club on Fifth Avenue, one of the prominent older women exposed in the book, one with whom I had a ten-year illicit relationship, confronted me as we stood in line waiting to enter the formal dining hall. Nineteen years older, she was then deep in her eighties, her noble husband long gone. We had not seen each other for at least a quarter century. After a double take, I recognized her and gasped her name out loud. She approached until we were almost nose-to-nose. "Yes, it's me," she replied in a strong, pained voice.

Having drawn the attention of everyone around us, including her current partner, a dignified older gentleman, she said sharply with a measure of hurt, "You ruined my life." It is a condemnation I shall take to the grave. "And he hates you too," she added indicating her courtly friend, who nodded. "Indeed." The grande dame passed away in February 2017. She was ninety-two.

ELAINE'S

For four years, 1994 to 1998, I taped the syndicated *Geraldo!* show, later re-branded *The Geraldo Rivera Show*, during the afternoons at CBS Studios on West Fifty-Seventh Street. Then, I would drive up the West Side

Highway and take the George Washington Bridge to CNBC headquarters across the Hudson River in Fort Lee, New Jersey, to do *Rivera Live*, at 9 PM. The pair of programs represented the two sides of my personality: tabloid ringmaster by day, sharp-tongued, progressive lawyer-advocate by night. The grueling schedule was mitigated by the money and posh lifestyle. With the family happily ensconced at our lovely home in Monmouth County, New Jersey, about fifty miles south, I was a weekday bachelor living in a suite at the Parker Meridian Hotel. Aside from an ample show staff, I had a tough ex-Marine driver and bodyguard I called Tommy Guns, and a personal assistant, Tommy Roles, a dedicated Deadhead who took care of everything else.

We had a post-show ritual, going out every night after I got off the air at 10 PM. If I felt like keeping it low key, we would go to Ms. Elle's, a dive bar on the West Side, which plays a bigger part in this story later. Usually, I would have one or more of my studio guests with me. Ms. Elle's never saw so many celebrities and public officials, including New York's great three-term governor, Mario Cuomo. If I wanted something higher profile, we would head to Elaine's, the celebrity haunt in uptown Manhattan on Second Avenue, where I had been a fixture since my Vonnegut period.

As Woody Allen once said, Elaine's was perfect for someone with a disorganized social life. I had dinner with the reclusive and increasingly embattled Woody and spouse Soon-Yi in June 2017 and reminded him of that sage assessment of Elaine's. If you were welcome there—a big if—there was a ready-made party waiting. From the Beatles and Rolling Stones to Willie Nelson, Jackie Kennedy, Joan Rivers, Frank Sinatra and Mia Farrow to Clint Eastwood and Truman Capote, every star of stage, screen, literature, politics, and public life on the New York scene during that forty-five-year era eventually went to the relatively dumpy bar, with its barely edible menu, presided over by its gregarious, backslapping, sharply judgmental and opinionated owner, the late Elaine Kaufman. She loved her smoky, throwback joint. She even loved the fact that I had two late-night, tequila-fueled brawls there, one of which ended with a broken window. Dragging my entourage of that night's guests and favored staffers, we would also make a stop every week or so at China Club near Times Square, a late-night spot also favored by Donald J. Trump.

Rivera Live on CNBC was not an instant success, but was close enough. The show went on the air in April 1994. After two months of middling performance, which did not move the ratings needle, and my growing regret that it was not worth the effort of working two jobs, lightning struck when something really bad happened to a pretty celebrity mom, Nicole Brown Simpson. Her famous ex-husband slaughtered her and a friend, and then tried to escape to Mexico on live television.

On monitors throughout the network on the day of his bizarre attempted escape, every station was broadcasting the slow-speed Bronco chase involving former football great O.J. Simpson riding in a white Bronco on California's 405 Freeway with a phalanx of cop cars in slow pursuit. "That's our show," I exclaimed to my staff, excitedly pointing at the incredible scene unfolding before the eyes of uncounted millions around the globe. "Stick with it. Drop everything else."

O.J. SIMPSON AND ME, JUNE 1994

Evolving on the spot from a straight-up public affairs program into television's first show devoted to intense legal analysis of a single case, *Rivera Live* pioneered wall-to-wall trial coverage of the subsequent Simpson double-murder trials, criminal and civil. Much later, watching the excellent 2016 ten-part FX series re-creating the murders and the trial was like a rewind of my 1990s life. As a function of my insistence that O.J. did it, some in the black community complained that I acted more like an advocate for the white victims' families than an objective reporter.

Working the case nightly, I also got to know Simpson's attorneys, his Dream Team. As high-profile lawyers typically do, they were attracted like moths to O.J.'s peculiar flame, basking in the extraordinary attention. The brilliant Johnnie Cochran became leader of the pack that included the social butterfly Robert Kardashian, who fathered the infamous clan and through them posthumously invented reality television. As Simpson's private attorney, and maybe the only person in L.A. who thought the Juice was innocent, Kardashian brought smooth local ace Robert Shapiro into the case, and then gnarly veteran F. Lee Bailey. The eminent, peripatetic Harvard Law professor Alan Dershowitz came too, armed with the brilliance of his army of students, and also the potent Barry Scheck, who pioneered the use of DNA and invented the *Innocence Project*, which works to free the incarcerated innocent.

The sincere but otherwise pedestrian prosecutors Marcia Clarke and Chris Darden never had a chance against those titans. They were not only outgunned, but also on the wrong side of the racial divide. I openly sided with the prosecution, and their de facto clients the Browns and the Goldmans. It wasn't just sympathy, but anger at the defense for playing the race card from the bottom of the deck. They cracked our country in half to beat an easy conviction for a barbaric double-murder.

There was no question that the affable, universally known former football great, actor, and pitchman slaughtered, slashed, and butchered his ex-wife, Nicole, the mother of his children, in an insane jealous rage. Simpson killed her friend Ronald Goldman, a waiter, because he was in the wrong place at the wrong time. Ron was returning Nicole's sunglasses that she had left behind in his restaurant, Mezza Luna, at a dinner earlier that evening. Maybe Ron also wanted to hook up with Nicole, but that is not a crime punishable by double decapitation.

When the downtown jury later acquitted the former football great, I led the way in blaming their obviously distorted judgment on the fact most of the jurors were urban and black. To me it was clear that the nation had fractured along racial lines, and that Johnnie Cochran, the clever and dynamic African American lead defense attorney, had correctly perceived that divide and driven a train through it.

Again, timing is everything in life. The Simpson trial took place in the wake of the savage 1991 videotaped police beating of Rodney King, a black man, and the April 1992 L.A. riots, which I covered following the acquittal of the four white cops captured on tape doing the beating. Two years later, there was no way a predominantly black L.A. jury was going to convict a famous black man of killing two white people. They certainly were not going to convict him on the testimony of white cops, especially not cops like Detective Mark Fuhrman, who had been caught on tape detestably referring to African American suspects as "n*ggers."

Among the celebrity guests I brought on the daytime talk show to comment during the Simpson saga were Donald Trump and his then-wife, Marla Maples. Aside from about an interview a year, Trump and I sometimes hung out. In June 1995, I had joined the couple ringside at the Atlantic City Convention Center to watch local boy Vinny Pazienza overcome a broken neck to beat up a worn-out Roberto Duran to retain his super-middleweight boxing title. The Trumps were the

Kanye/Kim, Jay Z/Beyoncé of that era, marrying after first wife Ivana caught him seducing the younger woman with what Marla described as "the best sex I ever had."

Marla and Donald married in 1993 in New York's grand Plaza Hotel, which he owned at the time, along with dozens of other trophy properties, including the Empire State Building and Mar-a-Lago in Palm Beach, Florida, which he described to me with typical immodesty as, "Maybe the greatest house in America. It's been rated and ranked the greatest house in America, beyond San Simeon, which is in California, and the Breakers, which is in Newport, Rhode Island." Among the guests at his wedding was O.J. Simpson, who attended the lavish affair with bombshell girlfriend Tawny Kitaen. His ex-wife Nicole, whom O.J. was still dating when he allegedly killed her the next year, in June 1994, was at her home in Brentwood, California, with their two children.

It turned out that Trump's take on the case was much more in sync with the jurors' than my own. In an episode of my daytime show that featured Donald and Marla, and aired in February 1995 after Simpson's murder trial had begun, I asked Donald to explain how he could describe O.J. Simpson as "a nice guy," given all the testimony about O.J.'s domestic brutality before the murder of Nicole.

Donald Trump: Well, now, I can only say O.J. as I know O.J. I'm not saying O.J. is guilty, innocent, or anything. What I see is appalling, and what I see certainly doesn't lead to . . . from my viewpoint, if I were a juror, I'd have a real, real hard time with this one. I can only tell you from a personal standpoint, as somebody that knows O.J. well, I found it really incredibly hard to believe that he could do an act, a violent act like this. He's just a very different guy.

Geraldo Rivera: May I ask Marla?

Marla Trump: Hi.

Geraldo Rivera: Was he always pleasant to you?

Marla Trump: I only met O.J. on a couple of occasions in passing, and he was very pleasant on those occasions. But you know, in life you never know what really happens on the other side of things, in any personal relationship.

I always thought Marla wise beyond her stereotype, and that impression was reinforced during the weeks we spent together doing *Dancing with the Stars*. She was calm and dignified in the midst of the tumult of her ex-husband's improbable run for the White House. Her marriage to Mr. Trump ended in 1997. *Rivera Live* lasted longer, successfully anchoring CNBC's prime-time schedule for a total of seven years, 1994 to 2001, spanning the Clinton impeachment and the investigation into the disappearance of Democratic congressman Gary Condit's intern/girlfriend, Chandra Levy. (When the intern's skeletal remains were found in a DC park and her murder was pinned on an undocumented Latino immigrant, the congressman was cleared. By then, however, after his harsh exposure on programs like mine, his political life was ruined. A decade later, on a live edition of my weekend Fox News show *At Large*, his adult son angrily confronted me. I let him slide, understanding that his family had suffered, though not nearly as much as Chandra's.)

To give you an idea of the powerhouse *Rivera Live* became, remember there were two Simpson trials, the murder case in which he was acquitted in October 1995, and the civil case, decided on February 11, 1997. The night of the civil court verdict, which found Simpson civilly liable for the wrongful deaths of his ex-wife Nicole and her friend Ron Goldman, the once-tiny cable channel CNBC outperformed the mighty CBS broadcast network, achieving a 6.4 rating. That was more than thirty times higher than the 0.2 rating the network averaged when I took over the time slot; it was a ratings record for the network that lasted eighteen years, until CNBC hosted a Republican presidential primary debate starring Donald Trump in October 2015.

SEMEN-STAINED DRESS, 1997–1998

After the Simpson saga had run its extraordinary course, I inserted myself into the heart of President Clinton's lurid impeachment and defended him as if he were a member of my own family. At a time when it seemed every other reporter and commentator in the country saw him as guilty of perjury and on the verge of inevitable resignation, I took the opposite view, telling skeptical commentators such as his former press secretary Dee Dee Meyers, a frequent guest, "I like his chances." A sharp, smart, battle-hardened Washington insider, she answered, "I'm eager to hear why you think that."

Clearly, like Dee Dee, almost everyone in and around government thought Clinton was toast. Coming from outside the Beltway, I saw it differently. My angle was that President Clinton would soon be forgiven by most Americans because all spouses lie when caught getting blowjobs from secretaries, flight attendants, trainers, pool boys, family friends, or neighbors. Such matters are best left to the aggrieved spouse or signifi- cant other to settle. At least that was the prevailing thought back in 1998. Times have changed. It is no longer the conventional wisdom. We are much more judgmental and politically correct now than we were before the turn of the century. Thanks to men like Bill Cosby and Harvey Wein- stein, Bill Clinton's sins feel much sleazier today than they did back in the old millennium.

Representing the hawkish House Republicans in the Clinton impeach- ment proceedings, Kenneth Starr, the prudish lead prosecutor, became the target of my nightly wrath. I scolded him mercilessly for hunting down the president for lies prominent Republicans were routinely caught tell- ing. The GOP Hypocrites Hall of Fame then included Congressman Buz Lukens, Republican of Ohio, who was caught having sex with a 16-year- old; Dan Crane, Republican of Illinois, who did the dirty deed with a congressional aide; frisky senator Bob Packwood, Republican of Oregon, who kept a diary he denied having, which listed twenty-nine conquests. Representative Helen Chenoweth-Hage, Republican of Idaho, was one of the first to call for Clinton's resignation. She was later embarrassed by the revelation of an affair with a married rancher.

As bad as President Clinton's behavior was, it was reflected also in the seedy lives of cheaters like fiery representative Bob Barr of Georgia; Speaker of the House Dennis Hastert of Illinois, who later got caught paying a hunk of hush money to a boy he'd abused; Dan Burton of Indi- ana; Bob Livingston of Louisiana; Mark Foley, who specialized in House interns; Newt Gingrich of Georgia, who was also House speaker; Henry "No Abortion" Hyde of Illinois; Senator Pete Domenici of New Mex- ico; and Representative and later Senator David Vitter, who before being revealed as a hooker connoisseur said, "President Clinton having had a workplace affair with an intern in the Oval Office complex . . . some meaningful action must be taken against the president."

It was on *Rivera Live* that the world learned that Monica's semen-stained cocktail dress had tested positive for Bill Clinton's DNA. Here is how I found that out. A close friend of the Machiavellian President Clinton leaked that information to me exclusively, as he did other less liquid details on an almost nightly basis. This unimpeachable source stood shoulder-to-shoulder with the embattled president every day, and every day I would get a message from the White House guiding and advising my coverage with a specificity that invariably turned out to be true. For that period, Bill Clinton was my news director.

The revelation that an ejaculating president deposited the semen stain on Monica's pretty blue dress was received skeptically. The White House knew it would be. Coming from anyone at the *New York Times* or the *Washington Post*, the scoop would have been explosive. Coming from me, a non-Washington insider with a limited following inside the Beltway, the news made only a slight bump.

In leaking the story to me, the White House made the following calculation: Geraldo puts it out there, where it is received with high skepticism. But because it is out there, it blunts the impact of the shocking news when it will be ultimately confessed to and confirmed by more reputable, reliable sources. That confirmation did not happen for three interminable weeks. With my neck stuck way out because I was the only reporter making the positive-DNA results claim, that three weeks was the longest of my professional life.

President Clinton modestly rewarded my unfailing loyalty with a couple of phone interviews following his February 12, 1999, acquittal by the Senate. He later invited Erica and me to the VIP celebration of the opening of the Clinton Library in Little Rock, Arkansas, on a rainy day in November 2004.

That occasion was memorable because we sat between Barbra Streisand, the idol of every Jewish woman on the planet, especially my wife, and the late Robin Williams, who was hilarious, making fun of everything and everyone. Barbra could not have been nicer, inquisitive about how George W. Bush's recent reelection would affect the country and how our lives had changed since the days when we were neighbors in

Malibu. Having dumped Jon Peters and married actor James Brolin, she was already much more politically engaged than she was back in the Diva Days. Twelve years after the library opening, she remained a prominent and loyal friend to the Clintons throughout Hillary's disastrous 2016 campaign.

I also had a chat at the opening with a wan-looking Senator John Kerry, who had just lost the 2004 election to Bush 43. In the connected world, Kerry went to Yale with my lawyer, Leo Kayser III, and the senator's family was active in the charity I founded to deinstitutionalize the care and treatment of the emotionally and intellectually disabled like the kids in Willowbrook.

Until mid-campaign, Kerry had been favored to beat Bush, already an unpopular incumbent, having started the disastrous war in Iraq. But Bush chopped him up and the senator was smarting from the vicious "Swift Boat" attacks that denigrated his heroic service in Vietnam. He still could not believe he "lost to a loser" like Bush 43. In a quiet, somber, and sincere conversation off to the side at the VIP reception, Kerry confided that the reason he thought he lost was an unfortunately timed terrorist attack in Europe that happened the final weekend before the vote. His pollsters had just explained to him how many voters decided only in that final weekend to stick with the incumbent, as Americans often do in war, deciding not to change horses in midstream.

President Clinton has also been exceedingly gracious when we run into each other in public. The problem is that his people never acceded to my many requests for a sit-down interview. His wife, the former first lady, senator, secretary of state, and two-time failed presidential aspirant Hillary Clinton, has never really given me the time of day, at least not professionally. In fact, she has often given me the brush-off.

One snub I remember clearly was when I tried to grab a quick interview on the airport tarmac in Port au Prince, Haiti, in the aftermath of the ruinous 2010 earthquake; she physically turned her back on me in a reporter scrum. I got the interview anyway, but only by elbowing my way around her favored reporters and the gaggle of aides and security guards that surrounded her.

More to the editorial point, Secretary Clinton was asking the outside world for governmental and private aid to the stricken island nation. I wanted to know how she could be confident Haiti's notoriously corrupt ruling class would not hijack that generosity. Most of the aid was indeed stolen by phony charities like Wyclef Jean's *Yéle Haiti*, and the poor people victimized by the earthquake received precious little of it. The Clinton Foundation foundered in Haiti as the greedy sponge of corruption sucked up much of the money raised, as I knew it would.

Her failure to embrace me is one reason I did not mourn her loss to Donald Trump, who, as I mentioned, is unfailingly cordial. I know that sounds petty, especially since her politics are much more in sync with mine than President Trump's are, but at my age, the little things mean a lot. Besides, I am stubbornly hopeful that President Trump will in some-way get over the Mueller investigation, which cast a shadow over his first three years in office, probing collusion between then-candidate Trump and Russian interference with the election. No collusion was found by the stern special counsel, but many Trump loyalists went down mostly for lying to the feds. Trump told me and Fox pal Sean Hannity the inves-tigation equated to a coup attempt. He is thin-skinned and impetuous, but he did not collude with the Russians and is not the right-wing rabble rouser he seems.

Incidentally, when Erica heard me on television making that charge of Secretary Clinton's alleged disrespect, my wife reminded me how nice Hillary has been to us on the several occasions we have met socially in recent years, including running into the Clintons at Barbetta, the elegant northern Italian Theater District restaurant on West Forty-Sixth Street. And in fairness, by the time of the Haitian encounter, I was working for Fox News, Hillary's archenemy. That Fox affiliation also soured Presi-dent Obama, despite my record of having been generally supportive. He was cordial when we saw each other at the White House correspondents' dinner, but never once agreed to be interviewed. I used to joke on my old radio show that Obama would grant an interview to the Dog Food Chan-nel before he said yes to me.

Despite the lack of a personal relationship, I came to Hillary's defense time and again during what I considered the phony-baloney Benghazi scandal and its toxic cousin, the utterly stupid email scandal. However illegitimately, those hyped-up nonissues, fueled by well-placed Russian hacks, put a nail in the coffin of her presidential aspirations. She hastened her political demise by lazy-scolding campaigning and lecturing coal min-ers on their imminent irrelevance.

$30 MILLION MAN, 1997

Although my daytime talk show was never as bad as its reputation, it made me a punch line, draining whatever was left of my reputation as an investigative crusader. Following the on-camera studio brawl with the skinheads, *Newsweek* ran a cover picture of me with my nose bleeding and the caption, "Trash TV." The footage of the brawl, definitely the wildest and most violent in the colorful history of daytime television, is available on the internet. Its notoriety has outlasted the print edition of *Newsweek*.

As the owner and producer of the show, as well as its host, I reaped crazy money, which did soothe the cruelty of critics and my occasional hurt feelings. Besides, there is something culturally significant in being mocked, mimicked, and imitated in five different decades on *Saturday Night Live*.

By 1997 I had been doing both the syndicated afternoon talk show and the CNBC evening show *Rivera Live* for four years, and the NBC show had become so important to the network they offered a six-year, multimillion-dollar deal if I would give up daytime and work just for them. That made it lucrative enough to walk away from the money tree growing in the backyard. I wanted out anyway. Eleven years was enough, both financially and spiritually. I had no debt and there was enough in the bank to live comfortably, get the kids through college, and still be reasonably endowed. At least it was until I got divorced for the fourth and final time a few years later.

Chapter 3

9/11 CHANGED EVERYTHING

My decision to leave daytime TV was cemented by a 1997 incident during the taping of a show involving DNA testing. The easy, inexpensive test to identify a baby's daddy was about to change the genre and breathe new life into the careers of long-running hosts Jerry Springer and Maury Povich. But I was the first to use the technology to create dramatic moments of raw revelation. There are few canned dramas as fundamental as solving the mystery of fatherhood on live television.

As we crafted the DNA segments, the show had a redeeming social value in that we provided a safe space for abused spouses to confront their abusers under the cover of getting them counseling. During one episode, after confronting an insanely jealous husband with his battered wife's allegations of abuse, I took great satisfaction in telling the arrogant slug, "By the way, you're not the baby's father."

The shocked young man looked at me with contempt. "Thanks, Geraldo," he spat out as he punched a hole in the set and stormed off, as the audience gasped. I looked at my longtime stage manager, Mike Jacobs, and told him I had to get out of the business or go straight to hell.

My first instinct was to go back to Roger Ailes, who had made an informal pitch for my services in 1996, when he was creating Fox News. This time, he honored me with a formal multimillion-dollar offer. I initially accepted, but NBC had the right to match any outside offer, which it did. When I inked that pact, the *New York Times* ran an oversized picture of me on the first page of the business section with the caption "$30 Million Man." Said the story: "NBC moved aggressively to keep Mr. Rivera after he accepted an offer from the Fox News Channel last week. NBC had a right to match the Fox offer and did so rather than lose his *Rivera Live* program, which has been the most successful show on CNBC, an increasingly important corporate asset to NBC."

"This is something I need for my honor, for my family, for my own self-image," I told Bill Carter, the new media writer for the *Times*. Referring to some of my most criticized moments in the years since leaving ABC, I continued, "A lot of the problems people have had with me have been of my own creation. But I want to go down as doing something to open up TV news to being more human, not as someone who opened up Al Capone's vault or had his nose broken on TV by some skinhead."

Being embraced by a major network news organization appealed to my ego. It signaled respect. "Andy Lack [once again the president of NBC News, and the man who negotiated Megyn Kelly's big deal when she left Fox in January 2017 and survived the Lauer dismissal in November 2017] sat down with me and said, 'I want you to be an NBC News correspondent,'" I told the *Times*. "That was the most important thing to me." I was a rare media creature, a former news correspondent allowed back into the rarefied ranks of the network-news profession after leaving thirteen years earlier to go into show business.

Also included in the deal was a monthly appearance on the then-dominant *Today* show, at the time hosted by Katie Couric and Matt Lauer. Katie was an ebullient star and a rival to Barbara Walters for preeminence among women in broadcasting. She and I had an emotional bond because of my relationship with her husband, John Paul (Jay) Monahan III, a lawyer and NBC News legal analyst. Dashing and handsome, Jay at the time was battling the cancer that would kill him less than two months later at age forty-two. To show him my love and support, I insisted that my new contract contain a clause in writing naming Jay as my permanent substitute host on *Rivera Live*.

It was an important role because beginning earlier that year, in July 1997, I was taking big chunks of time away from the show to skipper my sailboat, *Voyager*, around the world, on an odyssey I will describe shortly. Jay hosted the show every Friday night during that important time when

With friends Marianne Bertuna and her future husband Arthur Aidala on board *Voyager* off Martha's Vineyard. Summer 2014.

the O.J. Simpson civil trial still commanded enormous attention, also covering the Unabomber and Timothy McVeigh trials.

Jay was so touched by the gesture of being written into my contract that for a time he carried the letter around with him to show people how highly he was valued by CNBC and me. A couple of weeks after I signed the deal, he asked to see me about a personal matter, which I figured was bad news about his health. We dreaded the possibility that his heroic treatments at New York-Presbyterian Hospital had come too late to save him from the ravages of the disease. He and Katie had been very public about his battle with cancer and were already crusading for men to get colonoscopies as soon as they hit age forty. The couple had two little girls who later attended school in New York with my daughters Isabella and Simone.

After playing phone tag, Jay and I caught up outside a car dealership in the Chelsea neighborhood, where I had come to buy a Bentley to celebrate the signing of the NBC deal. "What's up?" I asked, fearing the answer. "I almost died last week," he told me. "Things don't look good. I wanted you to know."

Katie asked me to deliver one of the eulogies at his grand funeral service in January 1998 at a packed Park Avenue church, St. Ignatius Loyola.

Everyone in the news business attended. He was beloved. A Civil War reen-actor, Jay always assumed the role of a heroic Confederate cavalryman. In my corny and overwrought eulogy I put him in character from those long-ago days and spoke of how he and Katie were soul mates through the ages. Thanks to Katie's generosity and fundraising there is now a Jay Monahan Center for Gastrointestinal Health at New York-Presbyterian Hospital.

The last part of the NBC deal was for four prime-time, network-news specials a year, one of which, "Women in Prison," won the 2000 Robert F. Kennedy Award for Journalism, my third. In those days before *Orange Is the New Black*, it was a stark and revealing exposé on the exploitation and abuse that was endemic to the privately owned women's prisons through-out the South.

"HE DOES WHAT HE DOES," JUNE 1999

There was no love lost between me and anchor Tom Brokaw. He was a news snob and I was an outlier. Knowing that bad blood simmered, David Corvo, the excellent NBC News executive who supervised my work, arranged to make my office two feet wider than that of the network's principal star. Of course, as befitting the anchor and managing editor of *NBC Nightly News*, Brokaw's office overlooked the skating rink and elegant Rockefeller Plaza in Midtown Manhattan, while mine in Fort Lee, New Jersey, looked out at the extensive King's Plaza parking lot, a gas station, and a Korean market.

While I enjoyed regular appearances on the *Today* show and *Dateline NBC*, the only NBC News program I could not get on was *Nightly News*, helmed by Brokaw. In those days before humbled by father time, he was still the NBC News god and had strict say over which correspondents could appear on his broadcast. I was not one of them.

In spring 1999, I volunteered to cover the Balkan Wars for the *Today* show and CNBC's *Rivera Live*. That conflict resulted from the breakup of Yugoslavia in the post-Soviet era. Serbia, an Orthodox Christian country, was vying to become dominant, but had just lost Bosnia, a Muslim region, after a bitter war marked by Serbian genocide of Bosnians, who were bur-ied by the thousands in mass graves.

In 1999, Christian Serbia was still fighting to hold onto another majority-Muslim region, Kosovo. Kosovo was supported in its independence bid by neighboring Albania and much of Europe and the United States. Ethnically, Muslim Kosovars and Muslim Albanians are virtually indistinguishable, a people divided by an invisible line on a map.

I had great contacts within the Kosovo Liberation Army (KLA) in New York. Some worked at Elaine's. Little-known fact of Big Apple life: Many of the suave Italian waiters at the best restaurants are actually Muslims from Albania who learned their Italian by listening to RAI, Radiotelevisione Italiana S.p.A., Italy's national public broadcasting company. Italy is separated from Albania by just forty-five miles of water across the Strait of Otranto, which connects the Adriatic to the Ionian Sea.

This Italianization of Albania happened from 1945 to 1992, when the country was a repressed, cloistered communist dictatorship run by the Soviet Union. Now it is a free country and like Kosovo, its little brother republic, sends its children to America where they also control New York City's roofing jobs, and make up most of Manhattan's porters and doormen.

The KLA had a rough reputation for mobsterism in the United States, which I thought was not relevant to their countrymen's struggle for nationhood and independence in Europe. I chose to trust them, and they trusted me. To this day, they are among my favorite folks, along with the Lebanese. In May 2012, Albanian president Bamir Topi awarded me the "Medal of Gratitude," Albania's highest honor accorded a foreigner, for my work during the war and since in support of Kosovo and Albania.

During the bloody conflict in the Balkans, in June 1999, like true friends, the Albanians rolled out the red carpet for me when I flew into Tirana, the Albanian capital. They also provided transportation and armed support to the front lines across the border into Kosovo. We got behind Serbian lines, had some close-up, on-camera encounters with Serbian artillery, snipers, and mortars, and gained exclusive access to a Serbian position that had been overrun by the KLA.

Aside from the drama of nearby explosions, our foray was newsworthy because we discovered Russian Army identification on the dead, which proved that Russia, led by Vladimir Putin, its pugnacious prime minister and once and future president, was assisting its Orthodox cousins the Serbs in the fight against Muslim Albania.

The problem was with NBC News. Though Jeff Zucker, the wunderkind executive producer of the *Today* show (and now president of CNN), made extensive use of my reporting from the front lines, Tom Brokaw's *Nightly News* ignored the dramatic reports.

Syndicated television columnist David Bauder wrote in the *Philadelphia Inquirer* on June 18, 1999, that "It's not hard to find NBC's $5 million man, Geraldo Rivera, on television. You just have to know where to look.

"Try the *Today* show, where Rivera's action-packed reports on the Kosovo Liberation Army first aired this month. But don't try the NBC *Nightly News*, where a Rivera report has never been shown. Better yet, try cable, where MSNBC repeatedly ran the Kosovo reports.

"A year and a half into his lucrative new contract with NBC, the former syndicated talk-show host still doesn't feel completely accepted at the Peacock Network. He may get more camera time than anyone else in the company, but he yearns for the time he doesn't get. It's a strange dynamic.

"Since signing his NBC deal in November 1997, Rivera has been rankled at not having any reports aired on NBC *Nightly News*, the network's flagship show anchored by Tom Brokaw. In December 1997, Brokaw said of Rivera: 'He does what he does, and I do what I do. There's very little common ground between us. That doesn't mean he doesn't have the right to do what he does.' Brokaw hasn't talked much about his colleague since then.

"Yet Rivera's feelings were hurt anew by the treatment of his Kosovo reports. He hoped they were good enough for *Nightly* to seek them out. 'The writing is on the wall, the sky, and the ground,' Rivera said. 'It's just not going to happen. I don't think it will ever happen. If that piece didn't get on, I don't think they'd use anything. I know that *Dateline* and *Nightly* are like the country club in my neighborhood. I'm not allowed in.' The network's only comment was that 'each NBC News program makes its own editorial decisions,' said spokeswoman Alex Constantinople."

SAIL TO THE CENTURY, 1997–2000

My marriage to C.C. was already on the rocks by the time of my NBC News disenchantment in 1999. We were estranged but not yet formally separated as the world approached the new millennium, anticipated around the globe with a mixture of superstitious awe and more-grounded fears of computer malfunctions and systemic technology breakdowns. We were commemorating that historic New Year in January 2000 with a monumental sailboat journey around the world. It was an awesome experience that checked a key item on my existential bucket list.

With the permission of NBC, through my personal company, Maravilla Productions, I sold the Travel Channel a four-hour series documenting the once-in-a-lifetime journey on board *Voyager*, my classic, vintage ketch. Designed by Sparkman & Stephens Naval Architects, she was built in 1972 in Lemwerder, Germany by famed shipbuilders Abeking & Rasmussen. Seventy feet long, with two soaring masts, *Voyager* is a graceful beauty. She is also rugged, with a hull made of half-inch-thick aluminum, and four watertight compartments. She was purpose-built for Tom Watson Jr., who was retiring as CEO of IBM. A world-class sailor, Watson wanted to take her farther north than any cruising sailboat had ever gone. He achieved that goal, taking the sturdy vessel through the ice-bound seas north of Greenland.

I bought her third- or fourth-hand in 1995, in bad shape, but her peerless lines and sailing soul remained intact. I rebuilt her in Howdy Bailey's Boatyard in Norfolk, Virginia. Together, *Voyager* and I sailed tens of thousands of miles, around the world, and up the mighty Amazon River. When my age and lifestyle no longer favored grand sailing adventures, I still could not bear to sell her, so I gave her away. In 2014, nineteen years after setting foot on board, Erica and I donated the beautiful boat to the Maine Maritime Academy in Castine, appropriately close to the Watson family compound in North Haven, Maine.

The grand journey around the world started at Rough Point, my home on the Navesink River in New Jersey, through New York Harbor to Marion, Massachusetts, on Buzzards Bay, down east off New England, into the great circle route across the Atlantic Ocean to the mid-ocean Azores archipelago, and on to Lisbon, Portugal, on the European mainland. Then it was through the Strait of Gibraltar, gateway to the Mediterranean Sea. We stopped in Tangier, Morocco; Malaga and Palmas, Spain; the South of France; Corsica to Sardinia; Italy to Sicily; Malta to Santorini, Greece; Crete, Turkey, and Cyprus; and then across to Tel Aviv, Israel. From there, it was through the Suez Canal, up the Gulf of Aqaba, dreaming of Lawrence of Arabia, to Eilat, Israel,

At the helm of *Voyager*, which I sailed around the world and
1,400 miles up the Amazon River. January 2000.

then after an unpleasant encounter with an Egyptian Navy frigate, it
was down the Red Sea, around the pirate-infested Horn of Africa to the
Seychelles Islands, and Kenya. From Africa, we headed to the island
nation of the Maldives, across the Indian Ocean to Saba, Indonesia;
Singapore, Bali, Australia, and New Zealand; and into the vast Pacific to
the island nation of Tonga, which is located directly on the International
Date Line.

There, after doing a live shot for NBC, which was broadcasting
around the clock as the various time zones hit the historic Y2K marker, we
held our collective breaths hoping that our computer-driven navigational
systems would not crash along with every other computer in the world.
When that did not happen, we celebrated the Once-in-a-Millennium
New Year at a party at the rotund and gregarious Tongan Crown Prince's
lavish home. From those long-dreamed-of festivities, it was on to Tahiti,
and the other islands of French Polynesia, including Bora Bora, across
the broad Pacific to the miraculous Galapagos. We dry-docked *Voyager* in
Guayaquil, Ecuador, to repair a broken propeller shaft, then headed up
the northwest coast of South America, through the Panama Canal, passing the east coast of Central America and Mexico, through the Florida

Straits, riding the swift, strong Gulf Stream current up the Atlantic coast of the US, past Cape Hatteras, and home to North Cove Marina in Lower Manhattan. There, in the shadow of the World Trade Center's Twin Towers, which still had a year of life left, we jumped overboard to celebrate our circumnavigation.

Called *Sail to the Century*, the 30,000-mile journey took several years, from 1997–2000. I managed to do it and my job by taking six weeks off every six months. As I mentioned earlier, Jay Monahan was my semi-permanent substitute host, and after he passed, Dan Abrams, now the skilled legal analyst for ABC News and a dapper internet entrepreneur, filled my chair.

Typically as we sailed east through the Mediterranean, I would leave New York after *Rivera Live* on a Thursday evening, catching an overnight flight to either London or Paris. Then I would fly from that European or Asian airport on Friday morning to wherever *Voyager* was waiting, arriving on board by Friday afternoon.

We would spend the weekend on the move, always sailing easterly. Then on Monday morning I would take an early-morning flight back to London or Paris from wherever we had docked, in time to catch the noon flight on the supersonic Concorde back to New York.

With a cruising speed of Mach 2 (1,354 mph), Concorde got me home in less than three hours. Since there was a five- or six-hour time difference, the ride outraced the sun, getting me back to New York two or three hours earlier than when I'd left Europe. Sadly, months later in July 2000, Concorde stopped flying after an awful Paris crash, which killed all one hundred passengers and nine crewmembers aboard.

In grand style, we achieved the Travel Channel series' big idea to be astride the International Date Line at midnight, January 1, 2000, but along the way I lost my marriage. Chastened and abashed by decades of self-indulgence, I swear I am transformed, faithful during my entire marriage to Erica, and as proud of that as I am ashamed of the earlier philandering that diminishes me. But that is now. Back in 2000, I was getting that fourth and final divorce. I kept the boat and to escape dealing with my shortcomings, kept sailing.

FROM ROOTS TO RAIN FOREST, 2000–2002

Upon returning from Tonga and the Date Line, I was asked by the Travel Channel for another *Voyager*-based, four-part series. We called it *From Roots to Rain Forest*. It documented a second grand journey onboard the old sailboat, this time from Puerto Rico (my "roots") across the Caribbean Sea and down the Atlantic Ocean off the bulge of South America, across the equator, entering the gigantic delta of the enormous Amazon River, then heading 1,400 miles up the big river, across the entire nation of Brazil (hence the "rain forest"), touching Amazonian Colombia, all the way to Peru, farther up the river than any ocean-faring foreign sailboat had yet gone.

This journey began in February 2001 when I brought Erica to a huge family reunion in San Juan Harbor attended by scores of local relatives, who despite the impressive number of guests, still represented a mere fraction of the Rivera clan. My dad, Cruz Rivera, was one of seventeen children. We partied with my cousins and uncles and aunties and reminisced for the cameras. Then we set sail on the tough upwind journey a couple of hundred miles to the Windward and Leeward Caribbean Islands en route to South America's great river.

From the special: "Our short and easy first leg of our journey hasn't turned out that way. We have been battered for the last hour by the wet and driving wind. And now this squall; when it hit, packing rain blown as if by fire hose at forty-plus knots, *Voyager* was soaked and pummeled. Nothing, certainly no synthetic amusement park thrill ride, can match the terror and the satisfaction of riding the wrath of elemental fury. We don't sail the oceans looking for trouble. But we're reasonably competent to deal with it, and relish the glow of flamboyant survival."

A Travel Channel executive who wanted to be hands-on joined us, but he was puking so badly after the first few hours we had to drop him off on Vieques Island, a mere forty choppy miles from our starting point in San Juan Harbor.

As I did for the original 1997–2000 around-the-world voyage, I flew back and forth during this Amazon River odyssey, balancing my day job at CNBC with long weekends and scattered vacations in the jungle. From that February 2001 through the late summer, usually with Erica, I would join the big boat as her crew steamed and sailed her up the legendary river, reporting from the special: "Having sailed *Voyager* over six of the Seven

Seas, in the spring of 2001, we began our exploration of one of the world's most mighty rivers. So vast is the Amazon that its fresh water can be found two hundred miles out in the ocean.

"Home to three thousand species of fish, including the piranha, one of the world's most terrifying; three hundred species of mammals, including these magnificent cats (jaguars, leopards, and mountain lions); and a billion acres of rain forest, there is peace here—and war. Harmony and conflict, and the lure of the jungle and its river, proved irresistible.

"Welcome to the Amazon. Of all the world's exotic destinations, few rival the Amazon in mystery and allure. It is the world's mightiest, largest, and at 4,200 miles, the longest river on the planet. It is a watery highway through an adventure land that stretches the distance from New York to Los Angeles and halfway back again. The journey up the incredible waterway will pass through the immense jungles of Brazil, touch the corner of Colombia, and travel up into the Andes Mountains of Peru."

We met indigenous people, saw boundless rain forest and abundant critters, from monkeys to piranha to pink river dolphin. We wondered at the bizarrely ornate opera house in the jungle capital of Manaus and often ran into stern-faced police and local military forces on and around the river. During our jungle adventure, the vast expanse of the Amazon through Brazil, especially where it gets close to neighboring Colombia, was heavily patrolled to curtail rain-forest and wildlife poachers, battle the endemic ordinary crime, and most urgently, to deter or catch the dope smugglers who were running rampant.

Aside from the four-hour Travel Channel documentary, I also sold my real employer, NBC News, on an hour-long network *Dateline* special using the river journey to probe the huge extent of drug production and distribution surrounding the Amazon River basin. In those days before the Mexican drug lords took control, we were sailing right through the dark heart of the most important cocaine and heroin production and transport artery in the New World, and the adventure made for compelling television.

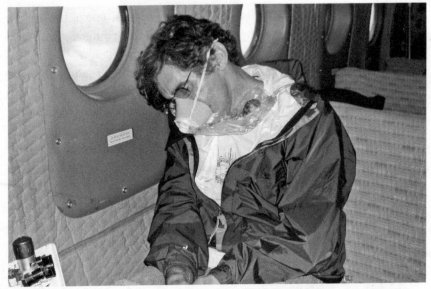

An oxygen-deprived nap on small plane flying over the Andes Mountains. July 2003.

PLAN COLOMBIA, MAY 2001

Voyager docked for the duration of the NBC News shoot in hot, humid, seedy, scary Leticia, Colombia's southernmost city and principal Amazon River port. It was a scene torn from a *Casablanca*-style movie. The shady riverfront was filled with nefarious characters, the majority of whom were ne'er-do-wells engaged in aspects of the drug trade. From Leticia, I chartered small planes to various locations in the region to document the extensive coca and poppy fields and accompany authorities in their raids on production laboratories.

We taped an interview with US Marine General (and later Chairman of the Joint Chiefs of Staff) Peter Pace at the splendidly exotic, semi-secret US jungle base where hundreds of our GIs were deployed. They were there for the now largely forgotten military effort called Plan Colombia. The goal was to counter narcotics production and transport, as well as direct the fight against leftist guerrillas who were facilitating the drug trade and destabilizing regional governments.

As extraordinary as it sounds today, the terrorists had their own mini-country within a country, and in our own hemisphere. In one hairy

With US-trained paramilitary, Plan Colombia. July 2003.

Covering Plan Colombia. July 2003.

sequence, we made contact with and gained access to FARC-landia, the quasi-official chunk of Colombian territory that had been ceded to the Revolutionary Armed Forces of Colombia, known by their Spanish initials FARC. Frantic to get to our rendezvous before the nighttime curfew, the violation of which was death, we drove our borrowed vehicle hard into that rebel-held territory, past numerous checkpoints manned by edgy boy soldiers bearing big weapons.

FARC's leadership was made up of vicious, extreme-leftist revolutionary drug barons responsible for decades of kidnapping and murders that presaged ISIS, only without the artifice of religion. We reached our predetermined jungle clearing just as night fell. The next morning, we were thoroughly searched before being introduced to the boss, Raúl Reyes. Wearing jungle camo, short, bespectacled, and bearded in the Che Guevara mode, he was known as El Comandante and was wanted around the world, including in the United States. I questioned him hard about FARC's dope-dealing ways. He answered calmly. Denying the allegations of drug dealing, he claimed his group only collected taxes on those who were the actual cocaine producers. Seven years later, after peace talks with the government failed, Reyes was killed in a massive US-Colombian assault on his camp. When my brother, Craig, and Greg Hart told me the news, there were high fives all around.

Called "Drug Bust: The Longest War," our NBC special aired in June 2001. I thought it would be a big award magnet, like "Women in Prison." By awards season, though, I was gone from NBC News, and the world's attention was focused on another menace, Osama bin Laden.

PICKING UP THE PIECES, FEBRUARY– SEPTEMBER 2001

The rest of that summer of 2001 was taken up sailing the old boat back down the Amazon toward home. The awesome power of the river flow is fascinating. While we struggled on the way in as if going up a steep hill, averaging just two knots against the mighty current, we virtually flew on the way out, sometimes hitting fifteen or even twenty knots (twenty-three mph) as we were swept downriver toward the Atlantic Ocean and the two hundred-mile-wide delta of this incredible stream.

Out of the river, our most notable stop on the way up north was Devil's Island, France's remote and notorious former prison colony off the northeast coast of South America. It once held Capt. Alfred Dreyfus, the Jewish artillery officer whose trial and conviction came to define institutional anti-Semitism. The brutality and inhumanity of the penal colony are brilliantly described in Henri Charrière's classic memoir *Papillon,* which became a great 1973 movie starring Steve McQueen and Dustin Hoffman.

By staying on the move, I was also postponing dealing with the upheavals in my personal life, especially the divorce from C.C. Our estate was large and complicated, so the process was drawn out, and Isabella and Simone were whipsawed as a result. Born during the flush times, they spent their early childhood helicoptering between our two homes. Rough Point, a 105-year-old Victorian home on eight acres on the Navesink River in leafy Monmouth County, New Jersey, was our principal residence. When we sold it to a newly minted hedge-fund millionaire, he knocked down the old but meticulously maintained landmark the same day in an act of civic vandalism, replacing it with a McMansion.

Our second home was Sea Gate, which C.C. still owns in her sweet hometown, Marion, Massachusetts. It is another lovely landmark, which I try to visit by boat each summer. Built in 1926 on a bluff on Buzzards Bay, it is bordered on the landward side by the seventeenth hole of the world-famous Kittansett Club. Incidentally, neither the Navesink Country Club in New Jersey nor Kittansett in Massachusetts allowed me to become a member. A Jewish Puerto Rican (who is 10% Native American, according to Ancestry.com) was more than either club could abide. These rejections just fueled my drive to succeed.

In late summer 2001, C.C. and the girls moved to Manhattan, into a homey brownstone near their new school. They were there on 9/11 when the planes crashed into the World Trade Center towers downtown. It was a Tuesday and their first day of school. When the authorities sealed the island of Manhattan, even closing the bridges and tunnels, it was temporarily impossible for some of their fellow students from the outer boroughs to get home. Two girls stayed with Simone and Isabella in their brand-new home. Five miles from Ground Zero, the terror of the attacks still reached them. The brownstone has an elevator, but when Simone heard on the news that people were trapped in elevators in the Twin Towers when they collapsed, she refused from then on to use hers.

Reunited in Paris with daughter Simone after a close call in terror attacks, November 2015.

Fourteen years later, Simone had a closer, more personal encounter with terror. She was studying abroad in Paris in November 2015 and attending a high-profile soccer match, Germany vs. France, in the *Stade de France*, when three suicide bombers blew themselves up outside. French president Francoise Hollande was also at the game. Like all the spectators, he was unhurt by the blasts. Some of Simone's school friends were trampled and injured in the stampede that followed the evacuation of the stadium. Other Parisian venues suffered far worse. There were scores of casualties in coordinated attacks that stunned the world.

It is ironic that Simone's near miss from terrorist violence happened in Paris. There was a standing joke in our family. I traveled to and from desolate, violent Afghanistan so often that a flamboyant friend of ours, real estate broker to the stars Robby Brown, once told C.C., "Geraldo must like it there," (in Afghanistan). "I prefer Paris," was C.C.'s punch line, always getting a laugh when she repeated the story. "But Geraldo doesn't because there's no war there."

Then Islamic extremism reached even the City of Light, twice in one year, 2015. In January, seventeen were killed in and around Paris during an attack on the offices of the satirical magazine *Charlie Hebdo* and the three-day murder spree that followed. Then, in November, it happened again, when our own daughter was nearly touched by the horror.

Despite various close calls over the years as a war correspondent, nothing rattled me as much as the uncertainty and helpless feeling of having a child in distress. Simone and three of her friends were marooned outside the stadium, located in a shady part of Paris, after the bomb blasts. The stadium doors were locked once the frantic crowds were emptied out. The Metro subway was shut down, and all the hotels and restaurants in the area locked their doors. The bodies of 132 innocent civilians lay in street cafés and in the landmark Bataclan Theater.

Paris was reeling and it took us an hour of frantic calling around before we got in touch with a savvy Parisian friend of friends who managed to extricate my darling girl and her companions. I was on the air live with my friend and colleague Shepard Smith during the ordeal, and millions watched as my terrified family dealt with the crisis of uncertainty in the midst of the panic and chaos of the massive attack. Few stories generated more statements of concern from viewers than Simone's plight

My three daughters on holiday in London after Simone's close call in Paris, November 2015.

in Paris; total strangers taking time to email or otherwise let us know they were relieved she was safe and unharmed.

CHASING THE FOX, SEPTEMBER 2001

Roger Ailes created Fox News in 1996, asking me early on to come over to see what he was doing, which I did as a courtesy. It did not look like much. In a huge empty basement space that used to be a discount drug store, he used his arms to describe what would be where in his world news headquarters. There were disconnected wires, unassembled desks, and eager, bleary-eyed kids running around, and I told him maybe later. I was in the middle of reporting the O.J. Simpson murders, the crime story of the century, and ratings at CNBC were soaring.

Despite that success, by 2001, a broad range of issues from patriotism to nepotism, pride and hubris, and the periodic need for chaos in my life fueled the decision to leave NBC News and join Roger at Fox News. By then, his headquarters had been built, and he was in the process of making the conservative news channel a competitive force. CNN was clinging to its status as the number-one-rated cable news channel, but barely. Fox was in second place, coming on strong.

Smoldering from the refusal of NBC News in that pre-9/11 era to count me among its top correspondents, I felt that the big money the network was paying me did not seem enough. The stage set, the immediate catalyst to leave came on the day al Qaeda attacked the United States, crashing hijacked airliners into the Twin Towers in New York, the Pentagon in Arlington, Virginia, and into a field near Shanksville, Pennsylvania.

The events of that day were shocking and traumatic for every American in different ways for different reasons. My trauma was nothing compared to so many others'. Still, it left a scar. Erica and I were in Malibu. Longtime sidekick Greg Hart called shortly after 6 AM Pacific Time and told me to put on the *Today* show. As soon as I saw the horrifying sight of the towers burning, I tried frantically to arrange travel back to New York to the girls, but nearby airports were all closed and would remain so for days.

Commentators were speculating on the probability of further attacks, and the world was coming to grips with the fact that everything had just changed. Usually paradise, Malibu was hell on this wrenching day.

Initially unable to reach my daughters on the phone or to get back, I felt as if God was punishing me for every sin I'd ever committed, including leaving our family behind. Frustrated, I was desperate to hear from Isabella, then age eight, and Simone, almost seven, both stuck in stricken Manhattan. I tried repeatedly to get through, but the phones were either disabled or overloaded.

I called the NBC News desk, suggesting that since I was stuck on the West Coast I should go to LAX to report on the situation there. The airport was the intended destination of the four doomed planes, and it made sense to report on the grieving families of passengers and crews. They noted my volunteering ("Thanks, Geraldo, we'll keep it in mind"), but told me lead anchor Tom Brokaw was personally managing all NBC coverage.

Riddled with guilt, I was fuming and about to blow. It got horrifyingly worse when I heard from my sister Sharon, who told me what had befallen our New Jersey neighbors. She was head of ad sales for the local weekly newspaper I published there, the *Two River Times*, based in Red Bank. Sharon told me that when the towers went down, the calamity took many of our friends with them. Our Middletown, New Jersey, area was devastated. Many of the dead were executives from Cantor Fitzgerald, the big financial firm headquartered on the top floors of the North Tower of the Trade Center. Cantor Fitzgerald lost 658 of its 960 New York employees. Some had kids in Rumson Country Day School, the New Jersey school the girls had left before their move to Manhattan. At least six school dads were missing and presumed dead.

When the smoke and rubble cleared and the bodies at the Trade Center were counted, the area had the highest per capita toll of any community outside Lower Manhattan; 135 of our friends and neighbors lost their lives in the attacks. Later I was proud to join two other dads from the school, Bruce Springsteen and Jon Bon Jovi, in helping host a benefit concert at Red Bank's Count Basie Theatre.

Aside from their boundless talent, these two men were stalwarts of the community, often performing for surprised fans and worthy causes, usually unannounced. That night at Count Basie and in many subsequent events, they helped steady the community and build its resolve to help one another. Bruce's song "The Rising" became America's anthem of recovery and resolve to right this terrible wrong.

"DADDY, I KNOW KIDS WHOSE DADDIES ARE DEAD!" SEPTEMBER 2001

I wrote in the next week in the *Two River Times* about how the attacks destroyed everyone's peace of mind, including little Simone's:

"'Daddy, I know kids whose daddies are dead!' she told me when I finally got through on the phone. How do you respond when a statement so fraught with anxiety and alarm bursts from the lips of your kid? What do you say to comfort your child under these circumstances?" Feeling that I had deserted my children in their time of need, I felt guilt wash over me.

I do not mention my two sons in this context because they were spectators to this particular chapter of our tumultuous family life. Cruz, who was born in Dallas and educated at St. Mark's School of Texas there until tenth grade, was with his mom and stepdad living in Portland, Oregon, when 9/11 happened. Gabriel, then twenty-two years old, was commuting between his mom's home in Los Angeles and mine in New Jersey, trying to decide on a career path involving computers. He was with his friends in Brooklyn when the world changed, watching the tortured Lower Manhattan skyline from across the East River in Williamsburg, as shocked and disoriented as the rest of us.

As I wrote at the time: "Now the Two River community and Americans everywhere will have to deal with the awful reality that people we knew and loved and laughed with and attended parents' day with and went to cocktail parties with and stood on the sidelines watching soccer games with are gone.

"They are gone before their time. They are gone despite all the sit-ups and jogging and annual check-ups and careful estate planning and the kids' college funds and the clear career paths and the retirement dreams. Our hearts cannot bear the thought of the pain and loss of those children. Their fathers or mothers are gone with the wind of terror and dismay."

My anger, anxiety, and frustration got worse because there was to be no *Rivera Live* from L.A. or anywhere else on September 11. Shortly after my conversation with the assignment desk offering to go to LAX, I got a call from my Fort Lee staff telling me Tom Brokaw's newscast would be airing simultaneously on all three NBC channels, preempting all programming on both MSNBC and CNBC, including mine.

It was clear the network's coverage of the war on these terrorists was not going to include me in any significant way. I was cut out of the biggest story of our time. Over the next few weeks, as other enterprising war correspondents were already making their way to the battle zones, I paced, filling with impatient rage.

A message I wrote during that week to my dear friend Kevin Overmeyer, then captain of *Voyager*, sums up my emotions. The boat was in dry dock being refitted in Trinidad, West Indies, for its journey back to her Hudson River mooring off my new home in Edgewater, New Jersey.

I wrote Captain Kevin: "The losses are wicked bad for NYC. 343 firemen alone! It's fucking awful. So many funerals and memorials, it's like the Blitz during WWII. I hate the mother fuckers who did this and so does the whole country. Everybody's also scared things will never be the same again. The view from the dock here in Edgewater feels amputated now. Remember, the towers used to be framed by the kitchen window. Now it feels like a gravestone."

MS. ELLE'S, NOVEMBER 2001

To its credit, the Peacock Network agreed reluctantly to let me leave. I told NBC I was leaving one way or the other, but the network was reasonably gracious. Because the show was so important to CNBC's prime-time lineup, they asked for more time to produce a substitute. I resisted, but Roger insisted that I leave NBC on good terms and with a signed release, so I stayed two more months, deep into November. It was a long goodbye that ended on the day of my farewell party at Ms. Elle's.

The city was shaken and smoldering in the wake of the 9/11 attacks. The mass grave of nearly three thousand friends and neighbors was still being exhumed a couple of miles downtown. And I was heading off to Afghanistan to cover the just and popular war to punish the perpetrators and impose restorative justice.

On the social scale of hipster New York, my November 2001 going-away party at Ms. Elle's Restaurant on West Seventy-Ninth Street was a career high point. In a life that was no stranger to parties, this was a milestone. It had a seriousness of purpose that made it more important than other rowdier but less-focused celebrations.

The ambience at the party was somewhere between kamikaze fatalism and Irish wake. I vowed to bathe in glory or die trying. I conflated various clichés, invented others, and came up with my own epitaph:

Evil Heart's Bane
Wild Song Sustained
No Pain, No Gain
No Guts, No Glory.

I told Erica, brother Craig, and all my confidants that I wanted it inscribed on my tombstone. Still do, although at this last stage of an increasingly enfeebled life it seems silly and pretentious. Erica joked that it sounds like a stoner's epitaph, more Stan Lee than Joseph Conrad. Back then, a grim, dramatic time, the whole country was in my corner. It felt like everyone I had ever known from ABC, NBC, and the talk-show days packed my favorite joint that night, that dim, usually gloomy dive on West Seventy-Ninth Street off Broadway.

The place has since closed, but at the time, three lesbians, who took turns cooking and tending bar, owned it. What their joint lacked in flash or décor, it made up for in vibe that night. It was exactly the place, and exactly the emotion-laden moment, I craved and envisioned when giving up the CNBC job. Professional respectability beckoned, and even the possibility of a martyr's death covering righteous combat was a small price to pay for immortality.

As in the Willowbrook days of my youth, everyone was cheering. In this normally cynical, skeptical town, for ten minutes New Yorkers suspended disbelief. Mocking chatter about my tabloid excesses was replaced by reluctant acceptance that I was leaving a safe, lucrative job to risk life and limb for God and country. The *New Yorker* magazine ran a cartoon showing two mujahideen fighters ducking bullets in an Afghan foxhole, one saying to the other, "I hear Geraldo Rivera is coming."

Not everyone was applauding. Speaking for the snots on *SNL*, Tina Fey said, "I hope nothing bad happens to Geraldo in Afghanistan or I'll have to pretend to be sad." I hated it, but it was a funny line, and she is in the business of making fun of people. Her impression of Sarah Palin during the 2008 presidential campaign is among the best ever of anybody. Still, in 2016, when her Afghan-set war movie *Whiskey Tango Foxtrot* bombed, laying a rotten egg at the box office, I experienced a few seconds of gloating, thinking that what goes around comes around.

Roger hired me as a war correspondent for $2 million a year, plus the nice Fort Lee office. I also got to take my two long-time, skeptical, eyebrows raised, take-no-prisoner secretary/assistants: JoAnn Torres Conte, a loyal, street-smart Bronx Puerto Rican who was married to a Bronx Italian cop, and Sharon Campbell, a competent, confident, don't-mess-with-me-either African American. Plus, I got first-class travel. I know that's a sweet deal in real life, but it was just 40 percent of the money I was making at NBC and a fraction of the fat talk-show years. I told Roger that the opportunity to go to war against the 9/11 terrorists was worth the sacrifice, but asked if he couldn't sweeten the pot a bit to ease the pain. He said he could not give me any more cash because in the time since he had first offered me a job several years before, he had "given all the money to O'Reilly."

Chapter 4

AFGHANISTAN AND THE DEVIL'S WORKSHOP

In the two months following the September 11th attacks, allied air forces were pounding al Qaeda and the Taliban government of Afghanistan, pushing them everywhere in retreat. The pro-American Northern Alliance was advancing under the cover of those withering coalition air strikes, and Kabul, the capital, was about to fall. A Taliban commander was quoted as saying the American planes were "destroying everything metal."

My highly anticipated, widely hyped Fox News job finally began on Friday, November 16, 2001, but modestly and close to home. It required just a trip over the George Washington Bridge to the big Sunni mosque in Paterson, New Jersey. The story focused on something that had irked my old/new boss, Roger Ailes, since the attacks: what he saw as the disturbing lack of mainstream US Muslim outrage at al Qaeda and 9/11.

Many conservative Americans especially could not shake the suspicion that in millions of Muslim living rooms around the world, including a handful in the United States, viewers cheered as the towers fell. Later, as a presidential candidate, Donald Trump alleged that "thousands" of American Muslims had done exactly that, cheered as the towers fell. No videotape ever surfaced to prove it happened, because it never did. Candidate Trump was widely disparaged for insisting he saw it on TV, but if you were inclined to believe it happened regardless of the lack of videotape, then Trump was just telling it like it was.

That is the real point. Whether it is factually accurate to say there is relatively little mainstream Muslim outrage at acts of terror committed against American and other Western, Judeo-Christian targets by Muslim extremists, there is no doubt that is the perception held by many, and not just nut-job racists. Truth or fiction, race loyalty continues to be a gnawing, if distasteful and generally avoided, issue leading to the vilification of millions of innocent Muslims who just want productive, peaceful lives. Every attack committed by a Muslim who seemed an otherwise integrated member of society in the United States or Europe drags the issue back to center stage. In the US it is most often brought up in conservative Christian or Jewish circles, and by iconoclastic, button-pushing TV hosts like Bill Maher or Sean Hannity, although it is fair to say that the underlying sentiment probably helped fuel the Trump rebellion and led him to the White House, and his attempts to ban Muslim immigrants

Have Arabic-speaking, American-based Muslim leaders been sufficiently critical of extremism in their Arab-language sermons or speeches? I have not seen any deep study that revealed divided loyalties, neither do I recall intense public Muslim American outrage and condemnation. The election in 2018 gave us our first two Muslim American women members of Congress, Rep. Ilhan Omar of Minnesota and Rep. Rashida Tlaib of Michigan. Both are fervent and sometimes controversial supporters of Palestine and see and speak of terrorism in more guarded and even-handed tones than we are used to, but that is a good thing, the fruits of diversity.

I have many Muslim friends from all walks of life who express acute distress to me at how the various terrorist attacks negatively affect their lives, from the World Trade Center to the mass murders committed in the name of Allah by Muslim maniacs at Fort Hood, San Bernardino, Orlando, Paris, Nice, Berlin, Istanbul, and much more recently in Manhattan and on Easter Sunday in Sri Lanka, where hundreds were killed in retaliation for an earlier atrocity committed against two mosques in New Zealand. It is not fair to question all Muslims for the acts of the few, yet that is our new reality.

Several friends fret and fear reprisal by jerk-offs who blame the entire religion for every Islamist attack. The fear and loathing is so widespread, some relatively secular friends tell me they want to convert, just to avoid the communal blame. One mom wants her twelve-year-old, blond, blue-eyed son to convert at least nominally to Christianity because "it is just too much of a burden for a child to carry," which is disturbingly reminiscent of other waves of religion-blaming in the previous century. President Trump's executive orders sixteen years later, which, after court challenges, were ultimately allowed to ban some refugees from seven majority-Muslim countries, renewed their 2001 angst. It reminds me of how my father, Cruz Rivera of Bayamón, Puerto Rico, worried that we would be sullied and blamed every time a Puerto Rican committed a notorious crime.

A prominent Muslim-American businessman named Mansoor Ijaz accompanied us on that first Fox News assignment to the Paterson mosque. Hardly typical of the mosque's congregants, Mansoor is a highly connected, politically conservative, bon vivant, hedge-fund entrepreneur with a natty mustache and snappy suit, and he is not ambivalent about extremism, which he vigorously condemns. Erica and I later attended his lavish wedding at a seaside villa in Monaco.

We entered the New Jersey mosque in time for the religious service. It was filled for Friday prayers by a kneeling, shoeless sea of obviously devout parishioners. There are more than four million Muslims in America, many of whom are African-American, either converts or families belonging to sects like the Nation of Islam. The crowd in this mosque was pure South Asian, mostly young Pakistanis, many of them cab/limo driver/working class.

After commenting on camera about the lack of communal outrage, Mansour began his ritual prayers as Craig and I taped the service. We were being watched and were cordially but cautiously welcomed with the combination of warmth and hesitancy that has characterized my relationship with scores of Muslims overseas, east of Suez in the years since the clash of civilizations began. The congregants seemed wary and worried about what I was thinking. Was I painting them with the broad brush of collective guilt? In any case, I did not find anyone at that New Jersey mosque who cheered the 9/11 attacks. Instead, it was their discomfort and fear of guilt by association that was the angle of my unremarkable premiere report.

KILLING REPORTERS, NOVEMBER 2001

We flew out the next day, Saturday, November 17, flying United Airlines to London, where we rendezvoused with more Fox personnel heading to the war. Staying at the old Conrad Hotel near the Thames River, we ate fish and chips at a neighborhood pub and got drunk on endless pints of beer, figuring it was for the last time in a long time. Pakistan Airways, my least favorite, is dry all the way to Islamabad.

We arrived in the Pakistani capital Monday morning, greeted by the news that several Western reporters had just been killed in Afghanistan. It was the subject of my first report from the field for my new network, from a satellite set up on the roof of the relatively upscale Marriott Hotel near the US Embassy in what is called the Blue Zone of the capital. It is a super-secure neighborhood that was nevertheless eventually penetrated by suicide bombers later in the war.

The appearance was live at 4 PM local time, 6 AM in New York, for *Fox & Friends*, the long-running number-one-rated cable morning show, which later became President Trump's favorite. I have been on every Friday of every working week since that November 2001. In that first appearance, I followed a report from the White House quoting President Bush as saying, "The noose is beginning to narrow" around our enemies.

After being welcomed to the network via satellite by hosts Steve Doocy, Brian Kilmeade, and E.D. Hill in New York, I told them the shocking news. "We are receiving confirmed but sketchy reports that a convoy of journalists has been attacked on the road between Kabul and Jalalabad, Afghanistan. We believe four are dead." We had learned that the four slain reporters were taken out of their vehicles, robbed, beaten, and murdered.

I reported:

Here's what we know about the journalists' murders. A roving band of brigands, [who were] probably defeated local Taliban soldiers desperate for money and filled with rage, have added homicide to their existing long list of war crimes.

A gunman boasted to a survivor, "You think the Taliban are finished. We are still in power and we will have our revenge."

Afghanistan, November 2001.

We traveled in a caravan of journalists and security
guards into Afghanistan. November 2001.

The murders of the reporters early in the Afghan War are a forgotten precursor of better-known atrocities involving journalists later. They set the stage for the videotaped butchering of Daniel Pearl, Steve Sotloff, James Foley, and the other reporters tortured and beheaded by al Qaeda, ISIS, and other Sunni Muslim extremists.

The World Association of Newspapers condemned the Taliban attacks as "outrageous and barbaric," as Reuters confirmed that two of the dead and defiled were their own, Harry Burton and Azizullah Haidari. The others were Julio Fuentes of Spain's *El Mundo* newspaper and a woman, Maria Grazia Cutuli, who was reporting for Italy's *Corriere della Sera*.

Coming as they did a week after five other Western journalists were attacked by the Taliban while riding a tank up in Bamyan Province, leaving three killed, it looked like an all-out war had been declared on journalists.

Those three dead were Pierre Billard of Radio Luxembourg; Volker Handloik, a German freelancer; and another intrepid woman, Johanne Sutton of Radio France International. Female war reporters in my experience are gutsy and skilled, and Islamist extremists cut them no slack. The two journalists to survive that earlier attack were Australian Paul McGeough and another woman, Véronique Rebeyrotte of France.

Craig Rivera in our first Afghan hotel, where the talk
was of slain journalists. November 2001.

Because none of those killed was American, these war crimes gained little attention in the States. But their deaths weighed heavily on our minds, heading up that same bad road. After months of anticipation, horror and glory were finally close at hand.

WAR-ZONE HOTELS, A RISKY BUSINESS, NOVEMBER 2001 TO 2012

Since there were no flights landing in war-ravaged Kabul in those early days, the Islamabad Marriott was the staging place for correspondents heading by land convoy through the Khyber Pass into Afghanistan.

What I remember most about the hotel from my various stays over the years was that, like Pakistan Airways, it was dry except for infidels like us who were allowed to drink in a small, windowless hotel lounge that felt like an asylum. On the lone lounge TV, a satellite channel from India continuously ran an R-rated version of Fashion TV, featuring scantily clad lingerie models, heightening the feeling that our hosts considered us perverts.

Any Muslim attempting to use the wet room was reported to the police. This strict prohibition gave me an outsized bad feeling that this was a brave new incarnation of Islam that was further from Western civilization than ever. I cannot say the anti-modern drinking ban foreshadowed everything bad about the Islamic world, from improvised explosive devices to beheadings, but it was quick proof they play by different rules out east.

Even the hotel's professed sobriety for Muslim guests was not protection enough. A truck bomb blew it up in 2008. Fifty-four died and 266 were wounded in that attack when the façade was torn off in a tremendous explosion that left a crater where the front entrance had been.

In fact, many of my favorite hotels have been blown up or shot up over the years, some multiple times. I have considered doing a guidebook of high-end places to stay in wartime, such as the Commodore or Phoenicia Inter-Continental, both savaged in fierce fighting in Beirut 1975–76, and the five-star-rated Serena in Kabul, which was attacked in 2008 and again in 2014. The Inter-Continental in Kabul got savagely hit in January 2018. Americans, including Glenn Selig, a former investigative reporter for Tampa's Fox 13, were among the twenty-two slaughtered when five

Craig and I on the banks of the Kabul River, scene of historic massacres. December 2001.

With Manny, keeper of the Fox News safe house. Kabul, Afghanistan, September 2002.

gunmen dressed as Afghan government soldiers gained access. Security was so shaky in some of our hotels that I often slept with a chair wedged against the room door. Ultimately, we gave up on hotels altogether, preferring our own network safe house.

Fortunately, none of our accommodations was ever attacked with me in it. Still, I have a recurring dream of being caught in bed by a nighttime attack. The only hotel invasion dreams that end happily are those when I am packing a weapon, which is prohibited by the one ethical rule of journalism that I consider dopey and out-of-date.

KHYBER PASS, NOVEMBER 2001

We joined a caravan of journalists and security guards from various media outlets, heading first to Peshawar, the last outpost of relative civilization in Pakistan, before entering the lawless Tribal Territories and then the Khyber Pass, doing satellite reports along the way. I say relative civilization because Peshawar to this day exists on the edge of anarchy. In 2014, terrorists killed 145 people in an attack on a school there. Most of the dead were children.

My urgent worry that Tuesday, November 20, 2001, was the same as at my farewell party at Ms. Elle's earlier in the month: Would the war be over before I got there?

Organized Taliban resistance was collapsing all across Afghanistan. In a phenomenon unique to warfare, Afghan forces were allowing most Taliban fighters to just go home if they promised informally to stop fighting. It was one reason we failed then to catch Osama bin Laden or his closest allies in the senior Taliban leadership.

As I reported: "Mullah Omar, the Taliban supreme leader thought about to yield power in return for immunity, now says he had a prophetic dream in which he's been told he'll remain in power for as long as he lives. Of course that could be five years or five days." (It turned out to be twelve years. Omar outlived his pal Osama bin Laden, dying in hiding in Pakistan in April 2013 of tuberculosis, according to various Afghan and Pakistani sources. The $10 million bounty the U.S. State Department had placed on his head in 2001 went uncollected. Because Omar had become so central to the Taliban resistance to the American occupation, his death was kept secret until 2015.)

I continued that report from the field in 2001: "Elsewhere in Afghan-istan it is painfully clear now that our military successes have left a huge and dangerous power vacuum. Chaos rules the countryside. Roving bands of defeated Taliban troops are reportedly turning to freelance murder and robbery," as evidenced by the killings of the four journalists the day before.

"Anti-Taliban fighters from the Northern Alliance are reportedly pur-suing the perpetrators of that hideous crime."

On the road from Peshawar to the Khyber Pass we got word from Nancy Harmeyer, then coordinating producer, via satellite phone from Islamabad that in response to President Bush's announcement of a $25 million dollar reward for the capture "dead or alive" of Osama bin Laden, the Taliban had placed a $100,000 cash bounty "on the head of each journalist."

The news we were being targeted stirred fear and impatience. I urged our team to hurry toward the pass. Like caviar or champagne, Khyber is one of those realities that lives up to our imagining. It inspires anxiety and awe no matter how many times I have driven through. Part of the Silk Road, one of the ancient world's most important trade routes, the pass itself is a steep cut in the Spin Ghar Mountains, foothills of the mighty Hindu Kush. It consists of a narrow, curving, mostly dirt road with often deadly drop-offs into the abyss.

Aside from invaders, smugglers, refugees, and drug dealers, "jangle trucks" crowd the narrow roadway. They are usually battered but gaily decorated cargo and tanker vehicles festooned with bells and jingle-jangles. Pashtun tribesmen drive them hard and fast, seemingly oblivious to the impossibly dangerous cliffs and curves.

But getting through the pass did not mean we were out of Pakistan. We drove uneventfully through Landi Kotal, the town at the summit, but at the bustling border town of Torkham, a substantial Pakistani military presence prevailed. Heavy Soviet-era tanks, armored personnel carriers (APCs), and combat troops were everywhere arrayed. All was vigilance and bureaucracy.

To schmooze us through, we hired a Pashtun tribesman, a member of the Shinwari clan, which holds sway along much of the ordinarily porous border. Akbar Shinwari, who became my friend for life, was then twenty-two years old. He guided me in negotiations with local border authorities, an ordinarily easy task he had done dozens of times before the war. But even his efforts on our behalf were in vain this first time. We were informed that the road was too dangerous, and that since the deaths of the journalists, Pakistan was no longer permitting foreigners to cross.

We were further informed that the decision to close the border had been made at the highest levels of the Pakistani government. I was frantic. After all the hype and buildup, to be turned away from Afghanistan now would be a crushing blow. We spent hours in panicked communications with our base in Islamabad, trying to finesse ourselves across. It took thirteen hours of cajoling and about $4,000 in payments to various authorities to buy our way in. Buying our way to the scene of the slaughter, how sick is that? The money was officially a "fee"; still, in the far reaches of the civilized world, cash and muscle often talk louder than legitimate process. When the reach of order and government fades into chaos and savagery, you sometimes have to pay for protection and access.

We were relieved to be finally on the Afghan side. Once we got there, everybody else was leaving. A miles-long line of refugees was waiting, desperate to escape from Afghanistan into Pakistan. In disasters natural and man-made, this is a common occurrence. Journalists are a kind of first-responders, going in when everyone else is trying to get out.

I reported: "Once through the border area, the pass widens into parched plains that show the ravages of years of drought and war. The

Driving the dusty road from the Khyber Pass to Jalalabad, Afghanistan, November 2001.

two have conspired to create a nation of refugees scratching out a meager life on the side of the road."

Later, "Closer to our first destination, the recently liberated Afghan city of Jalalabad, we saw something even more melancholy than the refugees fleeing the war. It was the Red Cross convoy carrying the bodies of three of the four journalists killed by Taliban thugs on Monday morning." New York told us we were the first to confirm the atrocity on the air; our first sad scoop, such as it was.

SPINGHAR HOTEL, NOVEMBER 2001

We arrived at Jalalabad on Wednesday morning, November 21. Working for Fox News for just five days, I was already at the end of the earth, a swaggering, mustachioed Walter Mitty. Walking through the main bazaar, I found it surprising how little time it had taken for the city to return to market bustle. Just a week before, the Taliban held sway here.

I also reported triumphantly how their collapse appeared nearly complete. "We made a monkey of their promise to fight to the last man," I gloated in mixed metaphorical splendor. Their military camps "must have looked like a big fat cherry pie from our satellites in space."

Heavy weapons were still as common on the streets of Jalalabad as Citi Bikes in New York. But something else was going on. While higher-ranking Taliban officials had disappeared into the parched and unforgiving Afghan landscape, many of their ordinary soldiers were simply switching sides, shifting allegiance with breathtaking suddenness. Sorting the good guys from the bad in that place is problematic to this day, as the bloody January 2018 attack by extremists wearing Afghan Army uniforms on the Inter-Continental attests..

We checked into the rundown Spinghar Hotel, a rambling, ramshackle building set in a dusty garden in the middle of a town where Osama bin Laden just weeks before had lived in comfort and relatively out in the open. Feeling like a movie set in the World War II era, the place was filled with gloomy, agitated war correspondents waiting to convoy up to Kabul. Ashleigh Banfield and Mike Taibbi of NBC News, both solid reporters, were the only ones I recognized in the group.

There was great urgency to get to Kabul because of the general feeling that the deadline was coming for the ultimate fight that would end the war.

At this point it was thought to be just days away. But no team wanted to go it alone on that blood-soaked road.

The fact that four of the slain journalists were caught and killed just three days before, and on the exact same route we were about to travel from Jalalabad to Kabul, was deeply unsettling. Mullah Omar's bounty payable to any gunman who killed a Western journalist also weighed heavily. So did survivors' accounts that vividly recounted how the four killed were dragged from their vehicles and marched into the surrounding hills, where entire AK-47 magazines were emptied in each of their bodies.

The hotel was buzzing with dark tales of how the bodies had been defiled, some of them skinned, a horror that made me again wish I carried a gun. There was a makeshift memorial plaque mounted on the hotel wall nearest the garden, acknowledging the seven line-of-duty deaths. The murder of Maria Grazia Cutuli felt especially barbarous. The thought of the lovely Italian newswoman being dragged from her vehicle by fanatic brutes was enraging. It was another reason I wanted the Taliban and their terror masters to pay.

THANKSGIVING, NOVEMBER 2001

This was just the first of two dozen or so War on Terror–era holidays spent overseas in Afghanistan, Iraq, or some other desperate corner of the world during my eleven years as Fox News Senior War Correspondent. On another Thanksgiving two years later in 2003, I interviewed Senator Hillary Clinton at the Bagram Air Base in Afghanistan. When Hillary later got into a jam for allegedly exaggerating the danger she experienced visiting our troops in war-torn Bosnia, talking about snipers shooting at her and so forth, I came to her defense, saying that at least she had the guts to put herself in harm's way, unlike the vast majority of her safely desk-bound critics.

As much as I missed my family, especially the little girls, who, as I later wrote in my diary, "always hugged me so sincerely and sweetly when I went away," I did not mind missing holidays in the early years. From 2001 to 2012, contrary to my critics' assessment that I was borrowing reflected glory from our GIs, I considered myself a quasi-service member, representing another branch of the Armed Forces of the United States of America: war correspondent. There were deep personal reasons I sought this calling. Having dodged the draft during the Vietnam era, first getting married, then enrolling in law school, I had a gnawing guilty conscience that others went to war in my stead. I only assuaged that guilt in later life by getting as close to combat as possible. Beginning in Chile and Israel in 1973, then across battlefields in Asia, Africa, the Balkans, and Central and South America, I became what Ernest Hemingway in covering the Spanish Civil War called a "whore de combat," or war tourist. Actually, there was more to it than either guilt or glory. When the real warriors are on your side and need your editorial and emotional support, running into battle with war fighters is a virtuous undertaking. I used to revel in presenting live shows from forward-operating bases featuring scores of happy GIs beaming and sending messages home to loved ones watching. I just wish we had had some of our own GIs around at this crucial early time in Afghanistan, November and December 2001.

On this first Thanksgiving on this first assignment in Afghanistan, everyone staying at the Spinghar Hotel chipped in on a communal dinner featuring two winged creatures that were not turkeys. Whatever they were, the Fox News crew got screwed out of our share of the scrawny birds because we got back late from working our contacts in town.

Our first stop was to pay respects at the provincial palace to the recently installed Governor Haji Abdul Qadir, a courtly middle-aged gentleman dressed in traditional Afghan tribal garb.

Newly designated as my right-hand man, Akbar Shinwari advised me that Governor Qadir was an important man to know. After watching Akbar negotiate our way through Pakistan's impossible bureaucratic maze to get us across the border and into Afghanistan, I was learning to trust the young Pashtun implicitly, even with my life. But at the time, I had no idea how important Governor Qadir would be to getting me as close to Osama bin Laden as any American got until ten years later when the Navy SEALs killed the son of a bitch.

The governor was the brother of a renowned anti-Taliban fighter, Abdul Haq. Captured and executed by the Taliban during their desperate retreat in late 2001, Haq had been a border bandit and drug runner. Like most Afghan warlords fighting against the Taliban, Haq had done so for commercial rather than ideological reasons.

Tumultuous Afghanistan's what's-in-it-for-me nationalism even extended to the family that would soon rule the country, the Karzais. Hamid Karzai was little known outside his native city of Kandahar, but this scion of the most important Pashtun clan had the personal good fortune of being from a family opposed to the Taliban, probably for the same reason as Abdul Haq: The religious fanatics were bad for the drug business.

Karzai always struck me as an almost folkloric, though slippery, character. The one question I never asked him was who came up with the brilliant idea of wearing the green robe, which made him look like a Marvel superhero and gave him instant ethnic credibility. That personal style harkened back to the glory days of Afghan royalty. He was our golden boy at the moment, authentic and yet modern, symbolic of our evolving ambition regarding Afghanistan.

I have seen no proof directly linking him to drug trafficking. But after serving two terms, he is said to have left office in 2014 the richest man in the country, worth tens of millions. His brother Ahmed Wali Karzai was notorious, more American than Afghan, a hustler from Chicago with a stable of children and ex-wives left behind in the United States when the American-funded gold rush began in his native country. By the time a trusted bodyguard finally killed him in Afghanistan in July 2011, Wali had survived eight assassination attempts and was worth millions from drug dealing, bank looting, and CIA payoffs.

Before America declared them our enemy for harboring al Qaeda, the Taliban were the good guys. In early 2001 their religiously conservative, rigidly Islamic government won a United Nations citation for suppressing the opium trade, having reduced production from 4,500 tons before they took over in 1996 to just fifty tons in 2000. Six months before America began bombing the Taliban government of Afghanistan back to the Stone Age, our State Department awarded them $43 million as a reward for their anti-drug efforts.

The Taliban are nastier today than they were back when they were merely a savage and regressive government. They continue to host violent extremists, have totally embraced global Jihad and domestic barbarism, and have also abandoned that once-admirable abhorrence of drug trafficking. These days, it is how they fund their insurgency. The Taliban ranks now among the planet's most prolific dope dealers.

It is also true that our forces have been put in the painful and embarrassing position of effectively defending the opium crop. As I reported doing a "show-and-tell" years later in April 2010, from a gigantic poppy field in Helmand Province:

So the deadly harvest has begun. The idea is they scrape these poppy bulbs, then the sap starts coming out and the sap that they collect, that is the opium paste. Then they package it in larger clumps. It looks like cow manure. But obviously it's much more deadly than that. It will soon be made into heroin for the junkies of Europe and the United States.

It is the most unintended and awkward consequence of our military offensive here in Afghanistan: The rout by our Marines of the Taliban from their former stronghold here in Helmand Province, has put us in the position of being protectors of the largest crop of opium in the world.

Geraldo Rivera: And how much is this field worth in Afghani money?

Afghan man (speaking in native language): Like a hundred thousand Afghanis.

Akbar Shinwari (translating): So about two thousand dollars.

Geraldo Rivera: So this field, when harvested, will reap for these farmers two thousand dollars?

Obviously there is no way on earth that this amount of wheat or cotton in a patch this small would reap that kind of money. That's the obvious economic incentive. That's why they plant the opium poppies, because of the value.

Ninety percent of the world's supply comes from this one Afghan province, enough poison easily to supply America's half a million junkies, and the almost three times that many in Europe.

Our Marine and allied bases have been located literally in the middle of poppy fields. When the plants bud prior to harvest, the deceptively pretty flowers carpet entire valleys. No beauty on earth is more evil.

Our commanders are ordered not to mess with the growing season for fear of further alienating the local populace by interrupting or interfering with their principal cash crop. It is depressing to see our young GIs camped in fields of opium that will soon be harvested and on its way to junkies everywhere.

ENEMY ON THE RUN, NOVEMBER 2001

In 2017, sixteen years after 9/11 and seven years after my exposé of the tragic and ridiculous proliferation of the poppy fields, the Marines would be dragged back into Helmand Province to suppress a resurgent Taliban, but in November 2001, the fresh, optimistic, early days of the war in Afghanistan, the enemy was everywhere on the run. Then acting governor Abdul Qadir granted us an immediate audience in his large, darkened office, which when the wall rugs were removed, overlooked the surprisingly resilient and orderly city of Jalalabad. Like the Karzais, the governor was just returned from five years' living in exile across the border in Pakistan.

He expressed misgivings about the prospects for long-term peace. What concerned him was that Taliban forces still loyal to their fugitive leader, Mullah Omar, were going underground and becoming either guerilla fighters or anarchist bandits motivated by greed or rage. This concern turned out to be prophetic.

The governor assigned two of his top military aides to show us around al Qaeda's abandoned facilities in Jalalabad. Both men could easily have been mistaken for enemy combatants. One was a rough-hewn veteran fighter named Misrullah, the other a tough-guy commander named Sohrab Qadir, who may have been related to the boss.

One apparent al Qaeda safe house was littered with personal items such as clothing and Jordanian passports. We also saw an abandoned grade school for the children of the terrorists. One of the most interesting extracurricular activities for the little tots was practice firing on their AK-47 target range, which I reported via satellite to the horrified Fox News audience.

The commanders and governor were of the opinion that bin Laden and his most hard-core Arab fighters were hiding out near the Afghan town of Asadabad, about forty-five miles from our current location and only eight miles from the Pakistani border. They told us his fighters were hard-pressed because winter weather was closing in on that mountainous region in Kunar Province, and they lacked warm clothing and appropriate footwear.

En route to Tora Bora, December 2001.

The commanders also mentioned reports claiming that on or around November 13, about ten days before we got to Jalalabad, Osama bin Laden hosted a dinner for his Pakistani, Arab, and other foreign volunteers in a place not far from Asadabad, nestled in the White Mountains, a place called Tora Bora.

TORA BORA, I wrote the name in caps in my reporter's notebook, not realizing how much it would affect the rest of my life. Tora Bora, my recurring nightmare.

THE DEVIL'S WORKSHOP, NOVEMBER 2001

Back at the Spinghar Hotel, just after midnight on Thanksgiving night, we were all jarred awake by several huge explosions nearby. Every reporter in the building rushed outside to see the action. I reported via satellite that Friday, November 23:

> Just after midnight this morning, we were all jarred awake by a couple of nearby explosions. One of our guides [Akbar] who was awake at the time of the blasts reports seeing flashes of what seemed

American fighter bombers firing two missiles each at bases bin Laden operated about three or four miles from here. The other strike was about twice that far away.

The story behind those attacks got really interesting when the Pentagon announced later that morning that they had targeted a chemical and biological weapons factory in our area the night before. As America tightened the grips on al Qaeda, finding their weapons of mass destruction (WMD) was our obsession—and this was way before Saddam Hussein stole their spotlight two years later. In the case of Afghanistan, the WMD were real. I know because we found them.

I noted, "Earlier the Associated Press reported that at an agricultural ministry lab they had found concentrated anthrax spores. Well, we found the rest of the Devil's Workshop."

Continuing: "The big fear with bin Laden has always been his pursuit of weapons of mass destruction: chemical, biological, even nuclear. So when the Pentagon announced that those nearby air strikes on Thanksgiving night were against a chemical and biological weapons factory, we decided to try to find the target ourselves."

With Akbar and several locals leading us toward the sounds of the explosions the night before, we found the area hit. Close to a vital dam being guarded by a lone anti-Taliban fighter, bomb craters showed the way to a medium-size al Qaeda safe house. Abandoned but undisturbed, it was filled with boxes of documents, including what could only be described as how-to-commit-terror manuals. Everything was intact, and aside from the doors being forced open, it was truly a complete Devil's Workshop.

Because it contained so many manuals for using the components to make weapons, we also called the place "Bomb U." Aside from the incriminating documents, I made a list of what we found jammed in vials, bottles, and cans inside the small wooden-framed building:

- potassium iodate, a treatment for radiation poisoning
- cyanide
- sodium hydrochloride, used to treat exposure to nerve gas
- highly concentrated hydrogen peroxide and lime, used for basic bomb making
- pure potassium, which explodes when it touches water

- hydrazine hydrate, also known as rocket fuel
- concentrated sulfuric acid, useful for poison gas, plus nitric acid, hydrogen, charcoal acetone, calcium carbonate, menthol, talc, dimenthylaniline, urea, dichloromethane, and ammonium nitrate

The find was significant for several reasons. First, and most obviously, it proved that al Qaeda was working actively to procure, manufacture, and deploy weapons of mass destruction for use in the region or abroad. The attacks of September 11, three months before, were obviously not intended as a onetime event, and the terrorists were working hard to get more bangs for their buck.

Second, the aerial assault intended to destroy the facility missed its target by a hundred meters or more. Worse, there was no follow-up on the ground. During the hours we spent there, no allied personnel came by to see if the target had been hit or even what it contained. It was shocking negligence on our part, bordering on incompetence. How could the Pentagon target a suspected chemical- and biological-weapons facility and then not send someone to see if they'd hit it?

Third, clearly by choosing not to commit ground forces to the fight, the Pentagon was missing a lot. Fighter-bombers zooming at 400–500 mph don't make the best collectors of data. Remember, this was before today's drone-centric warfare allowing remote pilots to read the color of a target's eyes.

This specific lapse, vaguely correct intelligence followed by a near miss on an announced target, was my first clear example of why the minimal boots-on-the-ground strategy devised by Defense Secretary Donald Rumsfeld and Commanding General Tommy Franks for the tediously named Operation Enduring Freedom was flawed. The worst example came later in Tora Bora with bin Laden's great escape, but there were miles to go between then and that.

It was hard for a reporter to be critical of or even less than enthusiastic about the way the Bush administration was waging this wildly popular war of revenge. In the super-heated, righteously patriotic, pro-war environment in the days following the Trade Center attacks, any correspondent, but especially a high-profile celebrity Fox News correspondent like me, quickly learned to stifle doubts about the war effort.

For example, I told the anchors debriefing me during the safe-house scoop that I just wished the Pentagon would send someone to my location to investigate the treasure trove of terror we had discovered. I wished out loud that we could take a duffel bag of the stuff we found here to someone who knew the score, who could define and describe the havoc that could be wreaked on America with these toxins and poisons. The only audience feedback I got were angry calls demanding to know why after just a week with Fox News I thought I could criticize the war effort or tell the Pentagon its business.

Because the story seemed so important, I was shocked when no other media picked up on it. This leads to my familiar refrain: If a *New York Times* reporter had found exactly the same stuff in the same place at the same time, it would have ignited a national discussion, and a special mention at a Foreign Correspondents Association award dinner.

The AP reporter mentioned it in passing to the others at dinner that night at the Spinghar Hotel, but that was it. Except for our video, the incident went unremarked, at least until other journalists found what was left of the safe house a day later. By then it had already been ransacked by the local people, debris strewn everywhere.

I am convinced that prejudice against the network and me personally played a role in that story being ignored. The barely contained hatred and jealousy directed at Fox News for years was laid bare much later, when the mainstream media machine led by CNN, MSNBC, and the *New York Times* unleashed their crusade to destroy the network, after the 2016 Ailes scandal. It angers me now, and it angered me then. Damn it, this discovery of the weapons factory was pure journalism, and it should have attracted positive attention and respect.

BLOOD ROAD, NOVEMBER 2001

The ride out of Jalalabad was tense as we drove the chewed-up main road as it follows the storied Kabul River, snaking through the harsh, drought-riddled landscape of high desert desolation. I am a history aficionado, so it was hard not to think of the countless ambushes and monstrous butchery that has happened along this narrow stretch over the ages.

In this land, Alexander the Great in 330 BC watched his veteran army be destroyed and scattered piece by piece by guerilla warfare, which the chronicler Plutarch described centuries later as a hydra-headed monster.

Much like with the Taliban today, as soon as Alexander's formidable veterans cut off one arm of the beast, three more grew in its place. Aside from the ruins of many fortified communities all named Alexandria and strategically located throughout the region, the only lasting monument to the otherwise most successful military commander in history is a scattering of blue- and green-eyed Afghans.

Genghis Khan and his horde came conquering down from the northeast reaches of the Asian continent in 1219, and though they engaged in widespread slaughter, the Mongols didn't stick either. Khan's acolyte, the fearless Tamerlane, invaded in 1383, but even his mighty empire could not suppress the ferocious local tribes over time.

In the golden age of Queen Victoria's empire, on this same road between Jalalabad and Kabul, a British army was massacred in 1842. Afghan tribesmen wiped out Major General Sir William Elphinstone's entire column of 16,000, leaving only one Brit alive and free to tell the tale of cruelty, murder, and enslavement of survivors. Here too, the Soviet Union committed suicide in a disastrous 1979 invasion, which cost so much in lives and treasure that the fifteen-nation communist empire split apart under the stress.

Like Empress Victoria in the nineteenth century and Soviet General Secretary Leonid Brezhnev in 1979, President George W. Bush in 2001 should have read more Plutarch. More to the point, the descendants of the hydra-headed beast the Greek philosopher had aptly described two thousand years before were alive and slaughtering Western journalists, among many others.

Following in the literal footsteps of those dead reporters, it was hard not to be preoccupied with the threat. Our ten-car convoy had several vehicles filled with armed guards, mostly Pashtun tribesmen, like the Taliban, but with a sprinkling of Tajiks, the minority ethnic group, who mostly sided with our friends, the anti-Taliban Northern Alliance.

We had one Tajik fixer, a schoolteacher we called "Teacher." He and Akbar, who is Pashtun, hated each other. They were constantly squabbling, Hatfield vs. McCoy. Teacher even tried to get us to fire Akbar for disloyalty or incompetence, I forget which.

I would not hear of firing Akbar, of course. He had morphed in my mind from Gunga Din to honorable peer, competent and totally trustworthy sidekick, translator, and editorial, historical, and geographical

On the road in Afghanistan, November 2001.

guide. And while you might think that Rudyard Kipling reference demeaning, or worse, racist, Akbar would not. He is my brother from another mother, good-luck charm and friend for life. I was not going anywhere without him. He is of that brutal land and its demanding religion and fierce tribal loyalties. But I worried at the time that if his and Teacher's mutual antagonism was representative of the nation writ large, then it was hard to see how their respective ethnic groups would ever be able to work together.

Naturally, we were fearful of a military attack during the drive from Jalalabad to Kabul, but we also worried about robbery. Cash was king in the early months of the Afghanistan war. We were carrying over a hundred grand US in small bills. There was so much cash that some of it literally blew away. It happened when Alistair, our mannered British coordinating producer, a brave and resilient but clumsy chap, opened his stuffed sack to pay off some locals selling produce. It was like the scene in Woody Allen's *Annie Hall* when he sneezes and blows away his host's precious cocaine. Money blew everywhere, swirling inside the car, some of it blowing out the windows to be lost in the dust.

We also carried a bag full of Afghan currency, which had been plummeting in value since Operation Enduring Freedom began. It took years to recover, but back then it was trading at even less than the official rate of 73,000 Afghanis to one US dollar. At various giddy times during this initial odyssey, I tossed huge handfuls of bills to children begging by the roadside.

FREE KABUL, NOVEMBER 2001

When we got there, Kabul was a dusty beat-up typical medium-size South Asian capital city with a sprinkling of recent high-rises towering over badly constructed two- and three-story adobe buildings. The shabby, hazy city is surrounded by sharp peaks, snow covered and breathtaking 15,000-foot giants that are mere half-sized foothills leading up to their awesome cousins, the Himalayas, a thousand miles east. The frightened town was barely stirring back to life after the Taliban retreat in the face of a short but withering aerial assault from the US-led coalition.

Actually, the enemy did not put up a fight for the capital. There was no heroic rearguard action, nor was there even an invading army. The bad guys just left one night, disappearing into the countryside. It gave the profoundly false illusion that this was going to be easy.

We were staying at the Intercontinental. Set on a small rise overlooking the city, it is far and away the biggest building in town. It had no electricity, but it did have running water. I met CNN's admired foreign correspondent Christiane Amanpour at the front entrance. At the time she was the news network's ace and a rarity. Now, as I mentioned, with Arwa Damon and Lara Logan and others, brave female foreign correspondents have near parity in the overseas news business, often proving more enterprising and gritty than their male counterparts.

Christiane was their role model, and she was sincere and elegant at our meeting, despite the attempts by media writers to stir up trouble between us. During the long wait for my announced move from CNBC to Fox News to take effect, some columnists had tried to instigate an anticipatory rivalry. I was intent on showing her respect. We had a nice conversation and went on to report the Afghan War our own ways, never crossing paths until Baghdad, Iraq, and another war two years later.

Checking into the disordered, barely functioning hotel, our crew met up with our Fox News colleagues, reporter Steve Harrigan and his intrepid cameraman, Joel Fagan, already on location.

Steve had been covering Afghanistan for CNN when his contract ran out that October. In his typically bold and clever fashion, Roger Ailes then out-hustled CNN, recruiting and signing Steve on the spot, thus giving us an instant, experienced presence at the heart of the story in these dramatic early days of the war.

Atlanta-based Joel, Steve's cameraman partner, incredibly had hiked in from the neighboring country of Tajikistan, in a heroic, grueling, dangerous five-day test that involved bumming rides on any available transport and literally walking much of the way through war-shattered countryside. He had been working nonstop since the first weeks of the war and welcomed us as necessary reinforcements. CNN, on the other hand, had a massive presence, with at least five crews in-country already.

The one meal I remember the battered hotel cafeteria staff preparing was an omelet. I was pleasantly surprised by the presence of eggs but was grossed out along with everyone at our table when I started eating my omelet, cooked in the filthy kitchen, and bit into something hard. I drew the thing out of my mouth the way you would draw out an offending but not particularly gross piece of pasta. Eyewitnesses report how I did not realize what it was until the bitter end when my mouth exploded, spitting frantically in disgust. It was a giant rat tail.

AL QAEDA POWs, NOVEMBER 2001

In Kabul, the most gut-wrenching story was the prisoner-of-war camp on the outskirts of town. In a cluster of perhaps a half dozen otherwise empty shipping containers, at least a hundred or more non-Afghan prisoners, mostly Arabs, were packed shoulder-to-shoulder inside. They were slowly baking. With no light, fresh air, or water, the foreign captives from Jordan, Chechnya, and elsewhere were bedraggled, beat up, hot, and thirsty. It was clear that the Afghans considered these foreign fighters dead already, grist for the savage mill. Their treatment was a mini-version of the 1915 Armenian Christian Death March; in a matter of days these prisoners would all be dead.

Rather than complain to someone in authority about the inhumane conditions under which the condemned prisoners were being kept, I instead yelled questions into their dirt-caked faces about why they killed our innocent civilians on 9/11.

A few defiant ones angrily tried to answer, which gave me a bad feeling about the war not ending anytime soon. The hatred inside these doomed fighters portended an enemy committed to a long struggle. Willing or not, the Afghan people were in for some major suffering, and so were our GIs and taxpayers.

That Saturday night, November 24, in Kabul, the interim government consisting of the Northern and Eastern Alliances and other regional and ethnic forces, and now calling itself the United Front, paraded out a former Taliban minister, a turban-wearing cleric named Mullah Khaksar, who was changing sides.

At a packed address to gathered tribesmen, the mullah announced that America's campaign against terror was "a good thing" and that he was throwing his support to the Front "to save" Afghanistan. As I noted at the time, "The news wasn't that the rat was deserting the sinking ship, but that the United Front was letting him."

Resistance was crumbling as the Front surged everywhere. The Taliban and its extremist allies were in total retreat. Sunday morning, November 25, we walked around dirty, exhausted Kabul. Much of its former bustle was back, "but street bustle aside, this is a ruined city in a wrecked country," I reported.

Winter was coming, food was scarce, shops and schools were closed. Highlighting the devastation, I reported, "Look what Osama bin Laden has wrought. To kill four thousand of us he has cost his allies the Taliban their country. He has led his thousands of loyalists to grotesque deaths or harrowing imprisonment, and he has made himself the world's most hunted man."

At this late stage, pockets of violence continued only around Kandahar in the west and Kunduz in the north, where the end of fighting seemed near. In addition, there were those persistent, unconfirmed reports of al Qaeda making a last stand back down near Jalalabad. With the option of heading anywhere, we chose Kunduz.

Joel and Steve bent over backward to help us prepare to chase whatever remained of the active fighting in the north. At my request, Joel hooked me up with a local guy who sold me a loaded Soviet-era Makarov 9mm semiautomatic pistol with a shoulder holster and bandolier filled with extra ammo. After all, my hero Ernest Hemingway carried a submachine gun during World War II's Battle of the Bulge. This fight was a fraction of that epic, existential struggle, but it was dangerous enough. We were just getting word of another murder earlier that day of another journalist,

A local guy sold me a Russian-made Makarov 9mm, which I carried
after eight reporters were killed. November 2001.

Swedish TV4 cameraman Ulf Strömberg, right where we were going in
Kunduz. He was the eighth Western journalist killed in two weeks.

In that tense climate and heading north toward the scene of the crime,
I mused on the air about wanting "to go down fighting" if someone tried
to jack us. "It's going to be a gunfight, not a murder," I half-jested during
one live shot, thus beginning a controversy that would fester from Kunduz
to Tora Bora.

HEADING NORTH, NOVEMBER 2001

From Kabul it was a haul to get to what was left of the active ground
combat several hundred miles north of the capital. We left on a beat-up,
1970s-era, Soviet-built Mi-8 helicopter provided by the Tajik-dominated
Northerners in the United Front. We were heading for the fighting just as
it was reaching its climax around Kunduz.

If we had had GoPro or iPhones in those days, we could have been
a Nat Geo reality show. Aside from courage, drive, equipment, connections, and sources, war reporting requires logistical enterprise. You need
stamina and initiative. Sometimes the journey to get to the story is the
most interesting part of the job. Over the years, brother Craig, Greg Hart,

and I have come to the conclusion that we are far more likely to die at the hands of our own overenthusiastic pilots or drivers than from enemy fire. You have not lived until a buckaroo at the controls of a hot-rod Black Hawk helicopter does flips trying to impress or scare you.

But the rule is that you can never show fear to those pilots or drivers, or get sick. That just encourages the swashbucklers. What you do is whoop and holler joyfully at their maneuvers until they realize you are just as willing to go down with the ship for a thrill as they are. We all got to go sometime.

Our two-man chopper crew flying out of Kabul was not into aero-nautical antics. Russian, maybe Chechen, I did not check, they had their hands full just making the drooping old bird fly. Their aged helicopter was so shabby and overloaded we thought our odyssey had an excellent chance of ending before it began.

In addition to the crew, the chopper was stuffed with eight of us, plus our massive pile of gear and a huge, leaky canvas bladder bursting at the seams with several hundred gallons of fuel, which dominated the cabin, sloshing back and forth in tandem with the chopper's maneuvers.

After taxiing past the remains of bombed-out, busted-up planes littering the city airfield, our old bird labored to take off, squeezing through narrow mountain passes because it did not have the power or oxygen to fly us over the surrounding peaks. I reported: "Flying from Kabul Airport on

With villagers in Kunduz, Afghanistan, November 2001.

With the first team, Greg, Craig, me, Pat Muskopf, and Pat Butler, boarding an old Soviet-era Mi-8 helicopter, November 2001.

In the Hindu Kush. If we had had GoPro or iPhones back then, we could have been a *National Geographic* reality show. November 2001.

Piled into a Black Hawk helicopter: me, Craig, Greg, Carl
Glogg, Brian Donnelly. Iraq, March 2003.

Craig Rivera and I stand by a huge cache of rockets abandoned by
fleeing Taliban. Near Kunduz, Afghanistan, November 2001.

board one of the Northern Alliance's banged-up, bald-tired, patched-up old Soviet-era helicopters, we flew past the remnants of the Taliban Air Force, wiped out by our precision strikes. Then over the devastated Afghan capital and countryside up into the foothills of the Hindu Kush."

THE PANJSHIR, NOVEMBER 2001

Before getting to Kunduz, we stopped in the Panjshir Valley. "We have landed briefly near the home of America's greatest ally in the war, even though he was already dead by September 11," I reported as we landed at the mountainside hamlet that had been the home base of the late, great anti-Taliban leader Ahmed Shah Massoud. "This village is still the center of the revolt against the Taliban. This is their Lexington, Concord, or Bunker Hill," I reported as our helicopter set down on a snowy field.

Set in a part of the rugged Panjshir Valley that was green, lush, and partly snow-covered and could be the model for Shangri-La, the hamlet was lit by chilly, misty sunshine and was far from idyllic. Fierce, edgy Alliance fighters were everywhere. These ethnic Tajiks look much different from the desert Pashtun tribesman—sharper featured, more Macedonian than Mongol or South Asian.

"This lovely spot is the top of the Panjshir Valley. It is from here that Ahmed Shah Massoud, the legendary resistance fighter, held off first the Soviet Union in the 1980s, then the Taliban and its terrorist allies in the 1990s."

We stopped here for a couple of reasons. One was to pay homage to the fallen Massoud, the "Lion of Panjshir," who was killed in September 2001 by a Taliban suicide bombing that presaged the attacks on the United States.

"Massoud was assassinated by suicide bombers posing as journalists two days before the World Trade Center attacks," I reported. "Osama bin Laden knew the US would come looking for him so he killed Massoud to prevent him from helping us in the war on terror."

A pair of extremists had masqueraded as journalists to stalk the fearless but vain Massoud. He granted their request for an interview, disregarding pleas from advisers to keep a low profile. When he got close to them, the ersatz interviewers ignited the bomb hidden in their camera, killing Massoud as they gave praise to Allah and also died.

Happening just two days before the planes struck the Trade Center and Pentagon on the other side of the globe, the assassination of Sheik Massoud was the opening salvo in the war meant to cripple the fierce Northern Alliance. Indeed, without their charismatic leader, the Alliance was staggered, its future dark. But that near-mortal blow was undone just two days later when al Qaeda's attack on America dragged the mighty United States into the Alliance's war against the Taliban.

Far from being defeated by the death of Massoud, the reborn Alliance fighters were filled with rage. They were strengthened by American muscle and also sought revenge against our common enemy.

"The much-revered Massoud's Northern Alliance survived his assassination to provide us the ground troops, which now hold twenty-eight of Afghanistan's twenty-nine provinces," I reported.

Aside from respecting Massoud, we were in Panjshir more practically to meet and interview Dr. Abdullah Abdullah, at the time one of the most powerful men in Afghanistan. I had been corresponding with him for weeks before arriving in Afghanistan, knowing that we would need local contacts once we got there. And he proved the perfect source, reliable and totally connected.

With the shattering of the Taliban, he was running half the country as Alliance foreign minister. Later to be cheated out of the presidency twice by a process rigged by supporters of his rival, Hamid Karzai, Abdullah always put his country ahead of his personal ambitions. Part Pashtun, part Tajik, he was the perfect person to bring the nation's two dominant ethnic groups together.

Dr. Abdullah has a deceptively gentle manner, more doctor-like than warrior, but it masks tremendous courage and resolve. He is a fighter and more courageous than many combat veterans. He has stared down would-be assassins and despite his nation's patent dysfunction, he remains true to the probably unattainable ideal of a redeemed Afghanistan ready to play its part in the modern world.

In 2001 the war was new for the United States, but Dr. Abdullah had been fighting for decades, first with the mujahideen against the Soviets, then against the Taliban in his convulsed nation's twenty-five-year-long civil war. Filled with despair over the death of his hero Sheik Massoud less than three months before, Abdullah had feared all was lost.

I asked him, "You must have been relieved in a way when you heard two days after Massoud was killed that al Qaeda attacked New York,

My urgent worry was that the war would be over before
we got there. Afghanistan, November 2001.

knowing America would come seeking revenge against the Taliban,
against your enemy."

He shook his head no, giving me a small, sincere smile that is his
trademark. "We had no idea who attacked New York. It could have been
some cowboy militia like Oklahoma City. Once we knew it was Osama
bin Laden, then everything changed."

KUNDUZ, NOVEMBER 2001

We left Panjshir heading north early on Tuesday, November 27, on our
belabored old Mi-8 helicopter, burdened by our satellite equipment, entourage, and a new load of fuel. "Once over the Hindu Kush we've arrived at
the Alliance's new prize, the city of Kunduz, the last Taliban stronghold in
Northern Afghanistan," I reported. "Kunduz fell Monday morning after
a siege that cost the Taliban and its terrorist allies well over a thousand
dead, most killed by our air strikes."

With live satellite reports filed every several hours, I was being propelled to the front rank of correspondents covering the war. Fox News was

surging in the ratings, and that rapidly expanding audience could not get enough of our work in the field.

"You're looking at first pictures of the newly liberated town of Kunduz. As you know, this was the scene of a very bitter siege. The city is swarming with soldiers. Now remember, this was Taliban territory until yesterday and there's been this profound power change. Every vehicle commandeered by the army."

As often happened over the last four-and-a-half decades of high-profile reporting, my every step was being stalked, my reports igniting fierce controversy and smoldering resentment. The corps of mainstream journalists was just waiting for me to screw up, which I did, but that was later. Now I was flying high and certainly didn't care if my warrior-journalist style bugged my fellow reporters.

In Kunduz I broadcast from what was then a relatively rare live satellite hookup from on top of a moving armored vehicle. Just ten days on the job, I cut a dashing figure during that period, an Afghan scarf called a *shemagh* (or *keffiyeh* by the Palestinians) wrapped around my neck, gaining arrogant confidence that I alone among many reporters knew the score and how to tell it.

"As you can see, things are chaotic in Kunduz now. With fifteen thousand heavily armed troops in town, many of them young volunteers from

With General Baryalai Khan. Kunduz, Afghanistan, November 2001.

the countryside, the local commander, General Atiquallah Baryalai Khan, told me they represent the biggest threat to public safety now and they've been ordered out of town and back to their homes. They'll be arrested if they don't comply by Wednesday [November 28]."

Thanks to General Khan we had a front-row seat for the action, such as it was. The problem from our point of view was there was not much of it. The most urgent development was the need to control those raucous volunteers. These were unsophisticated country kids who had rallied to the banner of the Alliance in the days following the start of the intensive American-led bombing campaign on October 7.

As I reported:

The twenty thousand Taliban fighters who once held this town are all gone, allowed to melt back into the countryside, granted an informal parole. The hard-core and the imported terrorists—Arab, Pakistani, Chechen, and other foreign fighters—have either been taken to the big prison in nearby Mazar-e Sharif or have escaped and are believed headed for Kandahar for a last stand.

I was right about their gathering for a last stand, but it was not to be in Kandahar, but in Tora Bora the following week.

Working the town and surrounding area after the retreat and disappearance of the once-fearsome enemy, we were introduced to a solitary US special operations soldier. Almost two months into Operation Enduring Freedom, he was our first glimpse of an American GI on the ground in combat in this war.

He was wearing undecorated camouflage and looked like every deer hunter in the Pennsylvania woods. Thin, bearded, dignified, and steely eyed, he told us to forget we'd met him. His commanders were not keen on our telling the world of the specific role special ops guys like him were playing in directing the war, although afterward some of them decided to write about their adventures.

There should have been a lot more of our fighters on the ground in more places a lot earlier in Afghanistan. It was certainly the fault of policymakers, not our troops, but a huge mistake nevertheless. While the 2003 invasion of Iraq two years later is recorded as the most serious failure of the Bush administration, the failure to deploy our army to take down the al

Queda and Taliban militants in Afghanistan in 2001 is another historic strategic mistake. It gave Osama bin Laden ten more years to kill and maim us.

Because we came bearing Dr. Abdullah's endorsement, the swashbuckling General Khan guided us for the next several days through the territory under his control. Later military attaché to Afghanistan's embassy
in Canada, the general was then a wiry, shaven-headed, total warrior committed to capturing or preferably killing Taliban.

One of those combat commanders who seem at ease, competent, and
confident without being cocky, Khan had strong views on how to conduct the war against the Taliban. He was hard-core against trusting any
turncoats, especially Pashtun Taliban. Scornful of his better-known Tajik
commander General Daud Daud (Afghans often carry double surnames),
Khan felt deserving of more credit for holding the northeast of Afghanistan in the early days of the fighting, and then leading the United Front,
or more honestly the Tajiks of the Northern Alliance, on the offensive
against the Taliban, once the American air strikes began.

Khan felt that he alone, or at least he primarily, had led the ground
forces that pushed the assault on the enemy's strongholds, demonstrating
the vulnerability of the once-feared Taliban foe and its inability to hold
territory against a determined assault.

"Where is the genius?" General Khan fumed. "Daud masses artillery
and kills everybody. How does that make him a military genius?"

My Fox News crew and I had the field pretty much to ourselves around
Kunduz and the nearby city of Taloqan for this last week of November.
With the fighting over, an uneasy peace, punctured by rampant criminal-
ity, prevailed.

The chaos was unnerving, even before word of Swedish cameraman
Strömberg's Sunday-night murder. Troubled by thoughts of the three
dead reporters in Bamyan Province and the four killed earlier, flayed by
machine-gun fire on the road to Kabul, many news organizations pulled
their reporters out of the unsettled and dangerous Kunduz area. In this
gap between the Taliban's fleeing and the imposition of order by General
Khan and the Alliance, gangsters and disorder were the real threats.

On Tuesday, November 27, I reported that:

Kunduz on its second day as a liberated city seems a town out of
the old Wild West. Heavily armed men and boys, the army of the
Northern Alliance, are everywhere. To the local commander, that is

the most urgent problem. They sit around bored and intimidating, or drive through town, a dozen or more packed in their banged-up Toyota pickups, all packing AK-47 machine guns or rocket-propelled grenade launchers.

Half these guys are volunteers from the surrounding countryside who've never been in a city. And their scary presence has caused most shops to stay shuttered. And one shudders to think how all these hungry mouths are going to be fed when winter comes.

The other big question in Kunduz is, where have all the Taliban gone? They're certainly not in the vast and empty prison. The town's airport is a busted and broken place littered with debris left by our precision strikes. In their desperation to hide their last working chopper, the Taliban nestled it alongside a small airliner. Our bombs incinerated both.

KUNDUZ, 2009 AND 2015

The Afghan War, the longest in our history, is largely an exercise in futility. The fate of Kunduz is a raw example. In 2009, eight years after its initial liberation from the Taliban, the United States had to re-bomb the city.

Kids with guns. Kunduz, northern Afghanistan, November 2001.

Our pilots were trying to stop the next generation of Taliban from robbing two of our fuel trucks. Because of bad intelligence, we instead killed about ninety civilians.

It happened again in November 2015, when the Taliban reoccupied Kunduz. It was the first time since America had gone to war in Afghanistan that a major city fell back into the hands of our enemy. They were driven out only after fierce fighting and US air strikes that lasted two weeks. In the intense US military bombing, a civilian hospital being run by Doctors Without Borders was destroyed by one of our planes. It was the worst single incident of friendly fire in the entire war. Carried out by an AC-130 gunship, the attack caused a confirmed death toll of at least forty-two civilians, mostly doctors and patients.

Belatedly, President Obama personally apologized to the victims and to the head of Doctors Without Borders. It was a rare gesture that came only after our fine commander in Afghanistan in 2015, my friend for life, four-star general John F. Campbell, gave graphic testimony before Congress.

Rejecting the usual excuse that the responsibility for the attack lay with the enemy or with our Afghan allies who mistakenly identified the structure as an enemy facility, the brave general testified that the devastating attack by the AC-130 gunship was "a U.S. decision made within the U.S. chain of command."

His frankness was one reason he was not promoted to head up all-important Central Command (CentCom) or even be appointed Chairman of the Joint Chiefs of Staff, which he deserved. Instead, he chose to retire rather than accept a lesser command. Though friendly fire is the curse we brought the Afghan people, the United States is reluctant to acknowledge and apologize, citing the "fog of war" or inconclusive intelligence or theories that maybe it was the enemy's fault. For many reasons, including domestic politics, the USA does not like to say we are sorry.

It is tough politically. Former vice president Dick Cheney has been among the many hardliners critical of any appeasement-like apology that makes us look weak or inept. Former presidential contender Mitt Romney even wrote a book called *No Apology*, which the *New York Times* said was a "not so subtle dig at Mr. Obama." The forty-fourth president was at least somewhat open-minded about admitting error. Republicans particularly have an institutional reluctance to acknowledge that in the hell of war even the good guys sometimes inflict pain and suffering on innocents and allies. The almost-automatic denials of responsibility for friendly casualties are relevant to this story.

THE MAKAROV 9MM, NOVEMBER 2001

In the tense twenty-four hours between hearing about Strömberg's murder while still in Kabul and then heading up to Kunduz and the hot zone where he was killed, I vowed to go down fighting if someone tried to jack us the way they did the Swedish reporter. I carried the pistol I got in Kabul in the battered shoulder holster for the rest of the war. It led to the first of my Afghan War disputes, setting the stage for the bigger, more destructive controversy later.

Our friend Laurie Dhue, who later incurred the wrath of Roger Ailes, was, at this early stage of the war in 2001, the "Belle of Fox News," widely adored. She was anchoring from New York, while I reported via satellite from Kunduz. During one report, Strömberg's nearby murder was noted. The trouble for me started when Laurie brought up that offhand comment I had made on the air earlier in Kabul about "not going down without a fight." Laurie asked me straight out if I was "packing."

I answered, "If they're going to get us, it's going to be in a gunfight." When Laurie asked me again and specifically whether I meant I was carrying a gun, I did not answer, but finally half-nodded yes, enough to set me up as a giant target for competing reporters.

"If word gets out that a journalist is carrying a gun, it makes it difficult for everyone," Peter Arnett, the veteran NBC reporter, sourly told the Associated Press in a widely circulated interview.

Arnett got into big trouble of his own a couple of years later during the 2003 invasion of Iraq for seeming to give aid and comfort to the enemy, the regime of Saddam Hussein. But on this issue he was on firmer ground, voicing a rule that governed journalists.

The ethos at the time was that we reporters are noncombatants, neutral, impartial observers who deserve to be treated as civilians if snared in war's embrace. I knew I was in trouble when in its February 2002 magazine the NRA weighed in. Calling me a "so-called" reporter, the magazine posited that I was a hypocrite who once I arrived in Afghanistan had changed the pro-gun-control views I expressed after the mass murder of twelve students and a teacher in Columbine, Colorado, in April 1999.

The magazine called the article "The Two Faces of Geraldo Rivera" and said, "Rivera, who has made plenty of noise in the past by promoting various anti-gun proposals, revealed recently that while covering the war in Afghanistan, where he does not feel quite so safe, he's conveniently jumped to the other side of the fence . . . Hopefully, Rivera will remember that experience when he comes home to the United States, where law-abiding unarmed citizens in some neighborhoods are argu-ably in more danger than he ever was while traveling with bodyguards in Afghanistan."

I put aside as asinine that comparison of a Colorado high school with the barbarism of the unstructured Afghanistan battlefield where eight reporters had just been killed, four of them mutilated in the process. In the ongoing world war against radical Islamists, whether Taliban, al Qaeda, ISIS, or al Nusra, it is impossibly idealistic for reporters to feel they can still demand a sort of amnesty if captured.

The fate of the dead journalists in the early days of the Afghan War, like the later savage beheadings of Daniel Pearl and Steve Sotloff, and all the other reporters killed, belies that naive notion. To any journalist cling-ing to the old ways, the ISIS beheadings in Iraq and Syria are undeniable proof that, if it ever existed, the quaint notion that reporters are somehow beyond the fray is baloney.

Speaking of baloney, the PR guy for Fox News explained somewhat lamely to reporters seeking comment on my gun controversy that what I really meant to say was that we had armed guards traveling with us, who would handle any necessary gunplay. Nobody believed him, and the great gunslinger controversy set the stage for my career apocalypse at Tora Bora, but that was still a week away.

SALANG TUNNEL, NOVEMBER 2001

After a busy several days, we tried to leave Kunduz on December 3. All of northern Afghanistan was in the hands of the Alliance. The rout of the Taliban, which had begun three weeks before, was over. It started with a now-legendary cavalry charge, probably the last in the history of mod-ern warfare, in which six hundred or so anti-Taliban horsemen accom-panied by a handful of our special operators took the big northern city of Mazar-e Sharif. The battle is described in Doug Stanton's terrific book *Horse Soldiers* and the current movie *12 Strong*. The rout of the Taliban ended with the artillery barrages at Kunduz two weeks later and about a hundred miles away.

Since bad weather and the unavailability of aircraft prevented us from flying out, the most direct way to get to Kabul from Kunduz was through the Salang Tunnel. In peacetime, it is the main artery connecting north and south in Afghanistan. Burrowed through the ancient rock of the Hindu Kush Mountains, Salang was the world's highest tunnel when built by the Soviets in 1964. But when we needed it in December 2001, the tunnel was a postapocalyptic mess. Long closed to vehicle traffic, it looked like something straight out of the world of *Mad Max*.

As I reported:

The mighty Hindu Kush Mountains cut across Afghanistan, dividing north from south. To facilitate the movement of their troops and tanks through those mountains during their ill-fated occupation, the Soviets built a mighty tunnel. But fifteen years later their broken tanks litter every highway and byway in Afghanistan. This tunnel they built is a wreck now, and if you want to pass through it, as we do, the only way is to walk.

Wrecked in savage fighting in 1997–98 between the Afghan Taliban and the Northern Alliance in their war before our war, it was impassable for vehicles. Gigantic fragments of cement from exploded and collapsed

At entrance to Salang Tunnel, elevation 11,200 ft. November 2001.

walls, blasted stone, and twisted metal blocked the roadway. Even on foot, the passage through the tunnel was a high-risk obstacle course, the approaches especially prone to Taliban ambush.

Desperate to move men and supplies, the anti-Taliban Alliance used Salang by driving to a loading zone about a half-mile from the tunnel entrance, off-loading, then hand-carrying cargo, first between the mine-fields on both sides of a narrow road to the tunnel entrance, then through the 1.6-mile chokingly claustrophobic hump to the other side. We had the added challenge of having to carry our two tons of television and satellite equipment.

We were anxious to meet Akbar bringing a Kabul-based team we had arranged to rendezvous with us on the other side. He had fresh vehicles and drivers waiting. Everybody and everything was awaiting our reemergence. The war was not waiting. Impatient to get through, I assumed the role of work boss, aggressively supervising the task of mounting our wartime safari.

Hiring two dozen local tribesmen on the spot as porters, I was a hurricane of horse-trading, rapidly sorting the fittest of those available, as Craig and the rest of the team worked hard to parcel our load into manageable bundles. It was a surreal experience; it was one of those "Damn, I am alive" existential moments.

Not believing in God or an afterlife, I am nevertheless a deeply spiritual man. Schooled in both my mother's Judaism and my father's Catholic faith, I am fatalistic about being a fleeting part of the great cosmos. As I mentioned, I feel we all spend our allotted days on Earth, and then we go back to where we were before we were born, nowhere, at least not anywhere physical. But before we go, we taste life, and live as long as someone living remembers us. Then, our essence is recycled, "dust to dust," even in death remaining part of the world.

On this deeply lived evening, we were 11,200 feet above sea level on a cold, dark, wintry night dominated by a harsh cutting breeze driving light snow perpendicular to the ground. The blacker shadows of the massive Hindu Kush peaks loomed up on each side. The valley below was a sharp, steep pit, those minefields on both sides waited hungrily for a misstep, and we faced a badly broken tunnel in front. I roared into the black night, alive and formidable, a fifty-eight-year-old Jew-Rican Tarzan.

We repacked everything down into the smallest units. There were about two dozen suitcase-sized, heavily built cases weighing between thirty and fifty pounds each. The toughest problem was the bigger of our two generators. The way through the tunnel was too tight and tortured for two men working together to carry a single heavy machine.

Momentarily stymied, the project was rescued when the biggest of the local guys said he would carry the generator through the tunnel alone. He rigged a canvas sling on his forehead, staggered momentarily, then gaining his balance, humped that two-hundred-pound beast through hell. This guy could easily have competed in one of those *Strongest Man Alive* shows.

The grueling two-hour transit accomplished, we set up a pay station in a recycled school bus our team had delivered to the other side. Giving each porter the grand sum of $40, about two weeks' salary, I made sure that nobody got paid twice by drawing a star on each man's hand with a Magic Marker.

A couple of guys tried double-dipping by washing my mark off and getting back in line, but a clean hand in that filthy place was a dead giveaway. I gratefully paid our Superman his promised double share. Even Akbar was impressed. Having kept his side of the deal by delivering the vehicles to the Kabul side of the tunnel, he was a whirlwind, urging his guys to get the vehicles loaded so we could get back to the capital as soon as possible.

Nightfall at wrecked, heavily mined Salang Tunnel, Afghanistan, November 2001.

THE *LOYA JURGA*, DECEMBER 2001

Events were rolling. In Kabul, everything was still shabby and broken, but there was a sense that the end was in sight. Bin Laden was uncaught, but the bad guys were everywhere on the run. We met again with Dr. Abdullah Abdullah, the suave, composed representative of the Northern Alliance, this time for dinner at his modest compound in Kabul. By then, December 3, less than two weeks after our first meeting, he was acting foreign minister of the entire de facto post-Taliban United Front government.

With the Taliban gone from the capital, entrepreneurs or their agents already crowded the now opened but dusty and barely functioning airport, bearing ambitious schemes ranging from establishing cell-phone networks to rare-metal mining to selling debit cards.

If that seems like putting the cart before the donkey, given the fact that bin Laden was still at large, consider that most Afghans viewed this conflict differently from the way we in the West did. The carnage of September 11 was our trauma, not theirs. Afghans are not a progressive bunch. Many still consider Christianity a capital offense and believe women should be confined to perpetual, invisible subordination. In Kabul, then and now, what is most revealing is that so many women completely hide their face and body, dressing in ugly blue burkas. They are invisible and indistinguishable from one another and have no public persona.

The ruling and educated class, at most 10 percent of the total population of 30 million, had been suppressed by the Taliban and understood that America's powerful military intervention was creating commercial opportunities, some involving sticky fingers. As I reported as I walked through a bazaar filled with contraband US military uniforms, canteens, endless boxes of rations, knapsacks, and other equipment:

> America is a great and generous nation, but sometimes our good intentions don't always end up helping those most in need. To get an idea, for example, of just how much US aid has been siphoned off or just plain, flat-out stolen, all you have to do is take a quick shopping excursion in Kabul's main bazaar. It's the Mall of American Aid.

Most knowledgeable Afghans saw this current turmoil as just another chapter in Afghanistan's long-running civil war, which had raged since the

"Afghans are not a progressive bunch. Many still consider Christianity a capital offense."

overthrow of the last monarch, King Mohammed Zahir Shah, by his own brother-in-law in August 1973.

But now in this heady time, the frail but revered ex-king came out of his long exile in Rome and returned to Kabul to preside over a *Loya Jurga*, a summit of the various tribal leaders. Later, my meeting with his former highness in his faded but still-grand palace in Kabul was a high point of my Afghan coverage. Living a good, if quiet, life in Italy, he was roused to answer his country's call as a symbol of continuity and order. He was too frail to make a difference, but America and our European allies liked the idea of the Return of the King. He died, still in Kabul, in 2007. He was ninety-two.

But in that December 2001, two energetic younger men had the inside track. They were hand-picked by the US State Department and appeared to be a match made in heaven to break the cycle of violence and lead Afghanistan to a new age.

With his powerful and deeply connected family and tribe based in the southern Kandahar region, Hamid Karzai was designated by the US to lead Afghanistan and unite the nation's various factions, now that the Taliban was beat up if not yet defeated. The fact that his brother would turn out to be a crook and a drug dealer was not yet known. The

With his majesty King Zahir Shah. He was overthrown by his
own brother. Kabul, Afghanistan, December 2001.

talk was that Dr. Abdullah would be Karzai's second-in-command in
a permanent postwar government. It was the Afghan equivalent of the
"Dream Team."

As I mentioned earlier, with a Tajik father and a Pashtun mother,
Dr. Abdullah was what the West hoped a "new" Afghanistan would be:
educated, secular, or at least tolerant, inclusive, and democratic. But our
trying to apply contemporary political science in the context of Afghanistan shows how hapless and ignorant we were of this pit of social regres-
sion. In this fifteenth-century environment where sect and tribal hatred is
instinctive and ingrained, the dream hatched at Foggy Bottom, the State
Department's headquarters in Washington, was impossible.

Dr. Abdullah is a noble soul, and at our dinner in Kabul on December
4, he gave me the scoop that changed my life, mostly for the worse. He told
me about Tora Bora.

"You have to get down there. It is near Jalalabad. We think bin Laden
is there." The news electrified me, as he knew it would.

"How do I get there?" I asked, my mind racing between panic and
exhilaration.

Meeting local leaders en route to Tora Bora, November 2001.

He gave that familiar small smile again. "I can arrange a helicopter to Jalalabad. Your team can prepare your supplies and security there. Tora Bora is just a few hours' drive away."

It was the biggest story of the war, and we had a head start. The killer of all those friends and neighbors, the man I had exuberantly, but sincerely, vowed to kill with my own hands if I had the chance, was within reach, making a last stand in a rugged valley not far from the Pakistan border.

JALALABAD, LATE MORNING, DECEMBER 5, 2001

We landed the banged-up chopper at the beat-up Jalalabad Airport on December 5. In a double irony, we were back in the city where we had begun our Afghan adventure two weeks earlier, and at the same airport from which SEAL Team 6 would launch the raid that finally brought back bin Laden's dead body from Pakistan. It would take almost a decade of fighting and dying.

Dr. Abdullah gave me a letter of introduction addressed to Hazrat Ali, a local anti-Taliban fighter who, as commander of a militia we were calling the Eastern Alliance, was leading the assault, such as it was, on bin Laden's redoubt in Tora Bora. We also benefited from our established relationship with acting governor Abdul Qadir, who, at the time, was Ali's ally in the fight.

We met at the Spinghar Hotel, the same one we stayed at on the way into Afghanistan in November. Like most semi-bandit militia leaders, Hazrat Ali played the angles, surviving by allying himself with whichever force had the upper hand at the moment.

Ali and other local leaders had coexisted with al Qaeda for several years. Indeed, a few years later he was sacked from his job as police chief because he was considered too close to the Taliban. But before al Qaeda took on the United States, alliances in that neck of the woods were fluid; everybody was hanging with everybody. The Arab and other foreign fighters living in the Tora Bora valley often owned their property and intermarried with the Afghans in the area. Bin Laden even had a home in Tora Bora, as well as the one in Jalalabad.

By this first week of December 2001, it was obvious to everyone that al Qaeda's time living in the open was over. The real issue was when, rather than whether, bin Laden himself would be killed or captured, that is if he was still there at all.

Morning bath. Base camp, Tora Bora, Afghanistan, December 2001.

First meeting with Afghan foreign minister Dr. Abdullah Abdullah, who became a great friend and ally. Panjshir Valley, November 2001.

Like most semi-bandit leaders, Hazrat Ali played the angles. December 2001.

Watching smoke plumes rise over the White Mountains
of Tora Bora from intense bombing raids.

The Americans had begun our intensive bombing of Tora Bora. We were using high-level, heavy B-52 and B-1B bombers based on Diego Garcia, an island 2,885 miles away in the Indian Ocean, and from about half as far away, more nimble F-15E fighter bombers, based on aircraft carriers cruising the Arabian Sea. We were pulverizing the valley and surrounding area, killing fighters and civilians alike. Raining death from above is often a messy and imprecise business.

As I scrambled to put together our convoy, my smartest move was hiring Hazrat Ali's son-in-law as head of our Afghan security force. Tall, slim, Omar Sharif–handsome, and obviously connected, he proved a perfect conduit for ensuring that Ali gave us the inside story as the climactic battle approached.

Chapter 5

MISTAKE IN TORA BORA

Our convoy made its way through a series of mud-walled villages until at the end of the winding road we reached the approach to Tora Bora and the first checkpoint, at midafternoon of December 5, 2001. Afghan mujahideen fighters, the good guys who were allied against the primarily Arab and Chechen fighters of al Qaeda, manned it.

The fighters belonged to Hazrat Ali's rival here in Nangarhar Province, a hustler of low repute named Haji Zaman Ghamsharik, who had just returned to Afghanistan from exile in France. Putting aside their differences for this final push against al Qaeda, Ali and Zaman were co-commanders of the anti-Taliban militia, which was now more grandly known as the "Eastern Alliance." Unlike the scene in Kabul or Kunduz, we were not too late to see action here. In fact, we were the first reporters on the scene of the biggest story in the world.

As we spoke with the militia leader, out-going cannon fire roared a short distance away. Farther off, we could see the smoke and flash of aerial bombs striking, and then hear the delayed blasts from the chains of explosions, perhaps five miles away.

We were in a valley looking south toward Pakistan. The area being targeted was at the base of the White Mountains, which separate Afghanistan from Pakistan, on the far side of the snow-covered ridges.

With militia fighter near Tora Bora, Afghanistan, December 2001.

At this junction, several country roads and trails come together and merge into the single dirt road running straight into the hamlet of Tora Bora. With a clear view of the action, bin Laden finally in our crosshairs, and no other reporters around, I was elated and spoke excitedly with the militiaman about the beast's finally being cornered.

His reaction was deflating. With fierce beard and demeanor, he lectured passionately about the deaths that morning of three of his fighters to friendly fire. Akbar translated as he complained of the imprecision of our air strikes and the fact that his men and innocent civilians were being killed by our negligence. He pleaded with me. I wrote down what he said in my reporter's notebook:

"First you do reconnaissance. Then send in the planes. We have no radio coordination with the aircraft. Can you help us speak with the aircraft?"

It was at that moment that I came to grips with the inescapable fact that as we killed our enemy, we were also killing our friends. Later accused of helping bin Laden escape Tora Bora, Commander Zaman survived this fight only to be assassinated by the Taliban in Kabul in February 2010.

Expressing my regret at the time for the losses to friendly fire, but indelibly committed to cheering from a front-row seat America's pursuit of bin Laden, the man who killed our thousands at the World Trade Center, I ordered our caravan down the road toward Tora Bora. The danger from friendly fire was firmly in my head. It would later tear out my heart.

FRIENDLY FIRE AT TORA BORA, WEDNESDAY, MID-LATE AFTERNOON, DECEMBER 5, 2001

We drove past scattered houses perched on the side of the valley as it dipped down to our left. Akbar told me these homes belonged to the foreign fighters of al Qaeda, mostly Arabs. Although most of bin Laden's troopers came from outside Afghanistan, many of their wives were local women, Sunni Muslims like them, with whom they had settled comfortably with their families into this lovely spot nestled at the base of the White Mountains, now just a mile or two away.

Smoke and dust plumes from aerial bomb drops erupted in plain sight in the valley in front of us. Driving down the road, we were soon close enough to see the orange-red flashes, not just the dark smoke plumes generated by the blasts. The time between flash and bang was less now, down to a second or two. It was like sailing toward a lightning storm at sea, the crack of thunder catching up to the searing bolts of light.

The main road dipped left toward the base of the mountains and in the direction of the action. A dirt trail split off to our right. We could see that the trail led up to a large plateau. On this inaugural journey, we drove past it until we reached a bend in the road beneath, curling under the plateau now rising a hundred feet or so up on our right. I made note of the plateau as a possible campsite. Leaving our crew and vehicles, we made the long walk toward the front lines deeper down in the valley.

Both Craig and Greg were shooting with their handheld DVD cameras. As we got closer to where the bombs were exploding just over the next ridge, our Afghan security and the mujahideen fighters nervously warned us that the gravest danger was not al Qaeda, but getting too close to the bombs impacting.

Akbar told me that bin Laden's summer home was farther down the road nearer the base of the mountain, but in an area still controlled by the bad guys. Unable to go farther because of the ongoing bombardment, and losing light, I ordered us back up the road to rendezvous with the satellite crew and find a suitable place to camp and set up our gear.

When we reached the trail going up off the road, we turned up to explore that big plateau overlooking the battlefield. Maybe two city blocks wide, it dropped off on the far side into another valley. About a half-mile long, it jutted toward Tora Bora. It was good ground, safe from direct fire from below, and vulnerable only to mortar or indirect rocket attack. At the far end, the plateau overlooked the battle like the front row of the mezzanine section of an outdoor theater.

FRIENDLY FIRE AT TORA BORA, WEDNESDAY EVENING, DECEMBER 5, 2001

We want to believe that America always fights clean, that only evil perishes by our sword. Modern war, especially from the air, is neither so clean nor precise, especially not in Afghanistan. The consensus number is that from 1,000 to 1,300 civilians and friendly fighters died countrywide in Afghanistan in the three-month-long Operation Enduring Freedom aerial campaign, from October 7, 2001, to January 1, 2002.

Chris Tomlinson, a solid, brave correspondent whom I ran into several times in Afghanistan including at Tora Bora, wrote for the Associated Press on December 3, 2001, "Afghan village riddled with bomb craters; 155 villagers said killed."

Philip Smucker, an excellent adventuring reporter, whom I also ran into at the wildest stretches of the Tora Bora battlefront, wrote in the *Daily Telegraph* on December 4, 2001, "Villages pay price as U.S. bombs go awry."

John Donnelly wrote in the *Boston Globe* on December 5, 2001, "Unintended Victims Fill Afghan Hospital."

Richard Lloyd Parry wrote in the *Independent* on December 5 that, "Civilians Abandon Homes after Hundreds Are Casualties of U.S. Air Strikes on Villages."

In the late afternoon of December 5, we set our camp on our big plateau overlooking the battlefield, choosing a location near an old Soviet-era tank the mujahideen were using as an artillery piece to lob shells in the direction of the enemy. In the fading light, our terrific satellite operators, Pat Butler and Pat Muskopf, finished setting up the generators and the big dish. The rest of us, including security personnel, worked to complete our base camp, rigging the tents and so forth.

In communication via satellite phone with New York for the first time since leaving Kabul and Dr. Abdullah about twenty-four hours before, we learned that earlier on December 5 there had been a tragic incident of friendly fire. One of our bombers mistakenly hit a large party of Afghans, including some of the anti-Taliban leadership. More painfully, we were told several of our US special operations personnel were also killed in the accident.

The names of the fallen GIs were released, but for reasons of security, the location of their deaths was not. With no word yet on where exactly the incident had taken place, I assumed this tragedy was the same one we had been warned about there in Tora Bora.

LIVE FROM TORA BORA, THURSDAY MORNING, DECEMBER 6

Our first live shot from Tora Bora was on the *Hannity & Colmes* show. Afghanistan is a weird nine and a half hours ahead, so for us it was 6:30 Thursday morning, but Wednesday night at 9 back in the New York studio. As I stood on the edge of the plateau where bombs had begun falling again at first light, Hannity introduced me:

"We're now joined by Fox News war correspondent Geraldo Rivera. He's reporting from a place in Afghanistan where very few journalists are willing to go, Tora Bora. Geraldo, I understand there's actually bombing going on right behind you."

"There is, Sean. If you just pan the camera over here, it looks like mist in the mountains. That's actually what's left of the—the impact from the bombs that dropped not more than six or eight minutes ago . . . The bombers have been coming over, I'd say at the rate of about every twenty minutes. At this rate, you know, during the course of your program, I'm sure they'll be back . . . We're actually on the outskirts, where we stand here, of Tora Bora. Tora Bora, the cave-and-cavern complex where Osama bin Laden has, with his hard-core fighters, set up what will be his—his last stand . . .

"There, another explosion! There! You can see it off on the—on the ridgeline. Can you see that? Another one. You'll hear the sound . . . There it is. There's the sound now. So we're—we're giving him hell. We're given him hell, Sean."

Cohost Alan Colmes was a wonderful colleague and fierce defender of liberal values on Fox News who passed away in January 2017. He asked the next question:

"Geraldo, it's Alan. We've heard reports that it's difficult for some reporters to get access to the front lines, a paucity of information. What was it like for you to get there? What was the process like? And are you one of the only reporters in that area?"

I answered, "We are the only—we are the only—here come the planes, right over us! Here they are. Alan, we are the only reporters here, Western or otherwise, as far as I can determine."

It was the answer I had left the plush, safe, high-paying NBC job to be able to give. We were ahead of the pack. Proof is in the pudding. Data talks, bullshit walks. Tora Bora was getting blown up, and we were the only ones to record and report it. Not only was my team on the front lines of the most important battle of the new twenty-first century, we were there alone. Then it was my buddy Sean again:

"Geraldo, just—just to be clear here—who's dropping those bombs there? And by the way, we see it very clearly. And the second part of my question is there—there's been a lot of press coverage, Geraldo, of you

"We are the only reporters here…" Tora Bora, Afghanistan. December 2001.

being over there, most of it very positive, an article in the *New York Post* today. I doubt you got your coverage while you were there, but —"

"B-52s coming! B-52s coming, Sean," I interrupted excitedly. Then addressing his first question, "It looks to us like you have naval air and the United States Air Force. You have both—you have the fighter jets coming in, tactically. They drop the one, the two, and the four. Then you have the B-52s. They're coming in. They're carpet-bombing."

At this stage I walked off the career cliff, conflating our local friendly-fire casualties with what we had heard from New York about the incident involving several of our Green Beret warriors killed the day before:

"I mean, that, of course, is—is how the three poor guys, Master Sergeant Jeffrey Donald Davis, Sergeant First Class Daniel Henry Petithory, and Staff Sergeant Brian Cody Prosser, got killed yesterday [December 5, Afghan time] in an incident of friendly fire from the B-52s. They're courageous guys. They called the big bombers in right on their own positions.

"So you've got the whole combined air might—you know, that tragedy, that awful warrior's nightmare of friendly fire aside, you've got the combined air might of the allied—allied forces striking at Tora Bora. And then on the ground, you've got four thousand of these mujahideen massed for the attack."

For whatever reasons, it never occurred to me that there were massive bombing and friendly-fire casualties going on anywhere else in Afghanistan. Without checking with my local sources, I had decided without even mentioning it to Craig that the three special operators who died by friendly fire must have been killed at the scene we witnessed in Tora Bora. In fact, they were killed three hundred miles away, in Kandahar.

It is not uncommon to assume in battle that the action you are seeing is the entire war. The ultimate conceit of war correspondents is that nothing important happens unless we are around. Reporters like me have the dangerous tendency to believe we are at the center of the universe and everything revolves around us. We aspire to be more Ernest Hemingway than Ernie Pyle.

Speaking of which, I then addressed the second part of Sean's question. Although I obviously had not read the *New York Post* story he was referencing, I was sure it concerned my earlier scandal about carrying a gun.

"As to the coverage about me . . . I'm just one of those lightning-rod kinds of personalities, and people like talking about what it is that I wear, or what my personal habits are, how I feel about the Second Amendment to the United States Constitution.

"All I say is I'm here doing a job. I'm reporting the facts as I see them. No one's criticized my reporting factually. And if they want to, you know, talk about whether I'm wearing a gun or not wearing a gun or wearing a six-shooter or a cowboy hat or whatever, you know, that's their problem."

What I should have said was that I was aware there was a big bull's-eye on my back and that every armchair reporter back in the States was ready to pounce on any misstep. In reporting about friendly fire, I had just given them a doozy. But for now, I was bathed in glory. Hannity concluded:

"Geraldo, you deserve a lot of credit. You've gotten closer than any other journalist there, very close to the bombing. You do have to arm yourself. We wish you Godspeed. Get home safe, buddy."

"Thanks. Thanks, man," I replied, the humble, six-gun-packing hero-in-his-own-mind.

LONG AND WINDING ROAD, THURSDAY MORNING, DECEMBER 6, 2001

The next live appearance, which is called a "hit," was about a half-hour later on the 10 PM show hosted that night by Rita Cosby. It was just past 7:30 AM locally, and full daylight bathed the contested battlefield.

Rita started her show with a sound bite from Pentagon spokesman Rear Admiral John Stufflebeem, who said, "Well, they're trying to determine locations of al Qaeda, and specifically, al Qaeda leadership and the remaining Taliban that might be in the area. The reports from that region are that many of these forces may have or have taken up refuge in caves and tunnels. So we're working to determine where these bad guys are and then to bring strikes on them."

Rita followed by assuring her audience, "And where those bad guys may be is Tora Bora, the suspected location of bin Laden's cave hideout and home to some of the most fanatical members of his murderous al Qaeda network. It's perhaps the most dangerous place in the world tonight, and you won't find any journalist with the guts to stand their ground and get the story. That is, any journalist except for Geraldo Rivera, who is standing by now in Tora Bora."

"We are standing here on the newest front line in the war against terror," I said, confident that we were where every war correspondent and daydreamer in the world longed to be. "You mentioned Tora Bora and you mentioned the cave complex, and I heard the admiral and the defense secretary mention it. It's right over here. You see the snow-covered mountains. The other side of these mountains is Pakistan. So you see strategically why bin Laden, the world's most-wanted criminal, wanted to locate here."

Then I compounded my earlier error about friendly fire, saying, "The mujahideen here really are very motivated. You know, that tragic friendly-fire incident that we had yesterday losing three of our own—three Special Forces—they lost a couple of their own guys in that same incident. Still, they're filled with a fire in their belly. They're amassing their infantry. We expect a big push that could come as early as today."

I referenced another of our scoops, soon obscured by the coming scandal. As far as I know, we were the first to confirm that bin Laden's mostly Arab foreign legion were in Tora Bora. We did it by intercepting their communications. On our handheld VHF radios we could hear them speaking to each other in Arabic, rather than in Pashto or Urdu, the indigenous Afghan languages. Fluent in all, Akbar translated.

"They have these very short-range walkie-talkies, Rita, and the amazing thing is that we can hear Arabic being spoken on their walkie-talkies. In other words, the bad guys—al Qaeda and these Arabs, the other foreign nationals fighting—are communicating in Arabic and using the same frequencies.

"So these guys who do not speak Arabic really hear that. They hear these foreigners in their turf. They get really motivated, very angry . . . they're ready, four thousand of them massed for an assault. I doubt they'll take the whole redoubt today, but they're certainly going to begin.

"It's going to be cave by cave, one against one, eyeball to eyeball, bayonet to bayonet. It's going to be brutal. It's going to be ugly, but it's necessary, because if they don't root out the approximately twelve hundred hard-core Arab and other foreign fighters that he's got up there, it's going to be a cancer that metastasizes and comes right back down infecting this valley all the way down into eastern Afghanistan. So, we're standing, I think, at a real hinge in history here."

It would have been "a hinge in history" if bin Laden had been caught there or killed. Instead, the words Tora Bora just became a shorthand, at least in my mind, for my deconstruction. Like Hannity, Cosby was generous with her sincere on-air goodbye: "All right, Geraldo Rivera, please stay safe, my friend, the only reporter tonight from Tora Bora. Thank you so much. Amazing pictures there."

Imagine if you were the news director of CBS, NBC, ABC, or CNN at that moment, watching the rival newscast up on the monitors, as they all do. Here I was, alone with my capable crew, live and right where they all wanted to be. To suggest they were frustrated is to understate the obvious.

For Fox News, the insurgent cable news channel charging down the right side of American society, it was a heady moment. All the publicity about my defection from CNBC led to this. Their man Geraldo was kicking butt. Ratings were soaring. Roger Ailes's gamble was paying off, big-time.

INTO THE ABYSS, THURSDAY MID-MORNING, DECEMBER 6, 2001

After the live shots were wrapped, we got ready for our real job, getting close enough to see if all the sound and fury of our bombardment was doing anything to win the war. Craig, Greg, and I, accompanied by Akbar and one of the local mujahideen bodyguards, put on our body armor and helmets, ready to hike down toward the action. That became our ritual for the next ten days. Home-base cameraman Pat Butler helped me tighten the straps on my vest, checked my rig, and wished me good luck as we marched toward the firing.

Getting near an ongoing battle in these circumstances is unforgettable. Every step you take toward close-in combat summons dread and elation. Your antenna is sharp and you are focused, at your best, and every veteran of combat knows what I am talking about. The battle and bombardment of Tora Bora dragged on so long that the odds of something bad happening to us kept increasing. My emotions went from eager confidence to resignation.

Pushing through physical fear is easy if you don't mind dying heroically in a good cause. I was filled with confidence. Despite being late to the war, I managed to bring my intact, competent, well-equipped, and now combat-tested team to the scene of the pivotal battle first. Even death could not defeat me now. If it did, my name would live forever bathed in the warrior ethos. Death would lead to secular sainthood, complete with a photo on the wall behind the bar at Elaine's or Ms. Elle's. This is why I took the Fox job, revenge and glory, and I was going to push even harder to stay in front of the pack.

As we advanced into no man's land that Thursday late morning, December 6, I wrote my script: "The frontlines are a deadly, dangerous place where weapons ranging from the giant B-52s to the AK-47 machine guns used by both sides are most evident by their ferocious sounds, from the big booms of the bombs to the rat-tat of the machine guns. The sounds of death are writ big and small.

"As mujahideen fighters filed past us, one was being carried on a stretcher, wounded by either shrapnel or a sniper's bullet. Another was bleeding, injured less seriously. At the base of the mountain, we tread more cautiously, aware that we were both in range and in sight of enemy sharpshooters."

Making our way up the first hill, we were acutely aware of enemy snipers on the ridge beyond. Leaving Craig and crew shielded behind a slight rise, I crawled out on my belly into the open to do an on-camera report about how the enemy was being pressed against the mountains. As I reported later:

We were alone in front-row seats for the biggest story in the world. December 2001.

Later in the afternoon, it appeared as if the Alliance lines were breaking under a counterattack by al Qaeda forces. But the commanders explained to me that they have called in additional US air strikes and were vacating some of their hard-won ground to avoid any more incidents of friendly fire. Whatever the reason for the withdrawal, it was temporary and the outcome here is inevitable, although as you're about to see, this rat can still bite.

As I do my on-camera stand-up, a sniper's round cracks right over my head, interrupting me in mid-sentence. For a war correspondent there is no more unnerving or exhilarating sound in battle than the whistle of small arms fire breaking the sound barrier as it zips past, especially when all the sound and fury is caught on camera and nobody friendly gets hurt.

As the bullet zings by, I make a sound like, "Ohhh!" and then press closer to the ground. I continue with the stand-up: "It can't last—it can't last much longer. It can't last much longer. Their backs are literally to the wall. They can keep sniping. They can—they can put up—they can put up a fight, but they've got no place else to go."

My intense caught-on-tape near miss at Tora Bora on December 6, 2001, should have been the headline for posterity, the takeaway memory of my undeniable walk on the wild side. Instead, it was investigated and pored over for authenticity by skeptics, cynics, comics, and haters who grabbed the legitimate controversy about my confusing two separate incidents of friendly fire, and perverted it into a nearly successful and enduring attempt to destroy an example of unflappable courage.

BREAKING THE FAST, THURSDAY
SUNSET, DECEMBER 6

Back at our plateau base, an extraordinary scene was playing out as the sun went down. Below us, jogging mujahideen fighters were retreating in scattered bunches.

"Where are they going?" I asked Akbar.

"It is Ramadan," he answered matter-of-factly. "They've been fasting all day because of the holiday. They're going back to their homes to break the fast with their families."

It was a revelation. I had covered war for decades, but this was the first where the warriors went home for prayer and dinner after work. Imagine if the Israelis had chosen to commemorate Yom Kippur instead of fight when they were attacked in October 1973. It seemed too casual for serious soldiers in all-out combat. The fire I saw in their bellies only burned from about 9 in the morning to 5 in the afternoon.

My near-miss moment at Tora Bora captured on tape made it on all the Fox News shows around the clock and beyond. It was a viral moment that had a huge impact commercially, one that helped reorder the cable-news hierarchy. By the end of this evening of December 6, insurgent Fox News reached a new plateau with a 2.0 rating that passed longtime leader CNN. (With rare exceptions, Fox News has stayed ahead of CNN ever since, faltering only temporarily when Bill O'Reilly got fired fifteen years later. That didn't last long, Sean Hannity soon retook the lead for Fox News, displacing MSNBC's Rachel Maddow whose brief reign on top during Summer 2017 featured a constant barrage of negative attention on President Trump's flaws, real and imagined. She was particularly obsessed with his purported collusion with Russia to rig the 2016 election. As of this writing, there has not been credible evidence implicating the president in any such plot. Conversely, as far as I know Ms. Maddow has never given Mr. Trump any credit for the economy, which has so far boomed under his watch). Back to Tora Bora.

NO ELITE WARRIORS, DECEMBER 7, 2001

At the beginning of our third day on the battlefield, at 5:30 AM Friday (8 PM Thursday back in the States), I was live on *The O'Reilly Factor*, which was beginning that generation-long run as the dominant, number-one show in all cable news. Bill expressed sincere concern for our safety as he introduced me on his broadcast.

Then O'Reilly asked about US special operators in our vicinity. I started to answer, then stuttered because we had seen only one, and he was the fellow up in Kunduz. We had pledged him confidence. We had not seen, nor would we see, any of the other elite warriors said to be directing the fight in Tora Bora. Nevertheless, I had leapt into the incorrect narrative that this was where three special operators died by friendly fire, and I was mentally stuck there, repeating the error for the next two days, obviously not realizing how destructively wrong I was. No one corrected me.

Bill O'Reilly: All right, how many US special ops are around you, and do you have any contact with them? Or what are they doing?

Geraldo Rivera: . . . I don't want to say, I tell you truth. I promised I wouldn't, and I won't. But I will say this, that yesterday we did walk over what I consider hallowed ground—yesterday my time, today your time—that area where the friendly fire hit. And it was—you know, it's just breathtaking, it's just so awful, the whole area kind of vaporized, little tatters of uniform everywhere.

Who would make this stuff up? Nobody would create that picture out of whole cloth. It was the truth. We saw and videotaped obviously fresh bomb craters, incinerated circles of scorched earth that the assembled fighters and our trusted guides told us was where our US aerial bombs had killed several mujahideen, anti-Taliban fighters.

"It was the saddest place I've ever been in my life. I stopped and I said the Lord's Prayer. It's just—it's the warrior's worst nightmare to be killed by friendly fire, to be killed by your own. Accidents happen in war, especially when it is as fluid as this conflict is here."

I saw the devastation and the carnage. I said the prayer out loud. I reported it, mistakenly thinking it was the same incident being reported near Kandahar. It was a stupid mistake. There were no Americans killed at the scene I saw. In fact, there were no Americans in Tora Bora on December 5, except us and, presumably, the sprinkling of special operators farther up the hill directing the aircraft. There were Afghans killed there, by our bombs.

Remember the now famous bullet whizzing through the air? After a series of widely viewed live appearances, everybody in the world knew my real location. Whom could I fool? Why would I want to? What glory is there in observing the remnants of a tragic friendly-fire incident? Did I just make it up because, as some later wrote, I wanted people to think I was in the midst of every substantive action for some psycho reason, that I cannot stand anything happening that is not happening to me?

At Fox News, it didn't seem to me that we cared much about Afghani friendly-fire casualties anyway. At least that was my impression especially then, just three months removed from the September 11 attacks. Fox was not unique in that regard. Three weeks later in a January 2002 FAIR (Fairness & Accuracy in Reporting), the progressive media watchdog group published a major article critical of war correspondents for omitting or downplaying reports of friendly casualties in Tora Bora and elsewhere. It stated, "When media portray reports of civilian casualties as an attack on America, it's hardly surprising that serious reporting on the issue [of friendly fire] is scarce. It is crucial that news outlets independently investigate civilian casualties in Afghanistan—not only how many there have been, but how and why they happened."

On *Hannity & Colmes* an hour later, Sean broke into his in-studio interview with a military expert, Robert S. Bevelacqua, to go to me at the front.

Sean Hannity: Bob, I got to stop you right there. We're going to go live to Tora Bora right now with Fox News Channel war correspondent Geraldo Rivera, who is there. Geraldo?

Geraldo Rivera: Sean, a B-52 coming in live. You see it right now. We just had one of the fighter-bombers come in and drop one of the precision munitions. Now comes the big B-52. This guy's going to unload big-time on the Tora Bora terrorist base right behind us in the White Mountains. We're watching virtually from underneath the bomb bay, actually, happily just clear of it. He's going to drop any minute. He may have already dropped.

This is now the second day of a ferocious assault on Osama bin Laden's terrorist base there in the White Mountains. You can hear—go back to the contrail (I instruct cameraman Pat Butler). Just show the—where the B-52—they should be impacting any second here.

The bombs were exploding right in front of our camp. Glamorous and just dangerous enough, this aspect of Tora Bora was also easiest. Up on high ground overlooking the pivotal battleground, our live cameras rolled as the action unfolded. And we were alone in front-row seats for the biggest story in the world.

Those other news networks with live capability were arriving in the area from Kabul and elsewhere, but initially they were not getting this close. Trailing us by almost two days, they were choosing to settle in the village we passed through at the entrance to the Tora Bora valley several miles farther from the action. To that point, Sean's sidekick Alan Colmes complimented me later in the show that I had scooped the world: "Geraldo, you have brought us the best pictures I've seen anywhere of this war, the backdrop day after day. You've really had some incredible graphics for us here."

As the Afghan War wore on, President Hamid Karzai would complain constantly about friendly fire and civilian casualties. He said the uncounted acts and many thousands of friendly casualties showed disregard for his people. But at this time, before his triumphal arrival in Kabul as the anointed face of the new Afghan government, like us Americans, he did not make a big deal out of what would later become his biggest issue with us. To me, because of the scandal that ensued, the terms "friendly fire" and "Tora Bora" have become obscenities, accusations, and attacks on my character.

THE BATTLEFIELD GRANDSTAND, DECEMBER 8–9, 2001

For the next several days we settled into an exhausting routine, up early enough to do the morning satellite hits, then donning body armor and venturing off the plateau toward the front line. Craig, Greg, Akbar, and I marching down into the scary unknown, shooting video all day then feeding the material via satellite to New York; grabbing a few hours' sleep between the 8 AM *Fox & Friends* hit at 5:30 PM local Afghan time; then up again before dawn for the live hits for evening prime time back home, beginning with O'Reilly at 8 PM, 5:30 AM local.

Aside from guts, in war reporting the three most important things, as with real estate, are location, location, and location. Ours was perfect. We were a mile or two from where gigantic explosions at dawn announced the start of the day's battle, on cue for the evening newscasts back in the States.

With the exception of a single barrage of RPGs—rocket-propelled grenades, i.e., shoulder-fired rockets—that were shot at us as we stood on the edge of the plateau looking down on the action below, our broadcast plateau was never directly attacked. Still, the constant threat of enemy infiltration initially kept the crowd of incoming journalists down to the hard-core.

For most of that first weekend, December 8–9, before the wave of the international press corps broke on Tora Bora, we patrolled farther up the ridge than even most mujahideen. Wearing our bulletproof vests and helmets, we marched into the unknown, dreaming of finding bin Laden's mangled corpse and returning with it before dark, in time for the next morning's hits.

The fact that the terror mastermind still had another decade to live was partially the result of our incompetent or at best unimaginative leadership's not committing ground troops and trying to run the Tora Bora air battle from far-off Central Command HQ in Tampa, Florida, nine and a half time zones away.

In the predawn dark as I prepared to go on live, tremendous explosions shook the earth around us. There was another, newer noise. The whooshing sound of Gatling guns hosing the area with deadly machine-gun fire let us know that close-in air support was also, finally, in action. How effective those attacks were in killing bad guys was another matter.

I was passing on resistance leader Hazrat Ali's casualty estimates, but needed proof, a Vietnam-style body count. By that point, several days into the aerial campaign, what was missing were dead bodies. A lot of bombs had been dropped, but not many human remains found, except for the shards of flesh at the friendly-fire killing field, the hallowed ground we had walked on December 5. Historians say that about two hundred al Qaeda fighters were killed in and around Tora Bora over the two weeks of bin Laden's last stand, but it was nothing like the pitched battles and fields of dead Egyptian and Syrian soldiers I reported on during the Yom Kippur War in 1973, in places like the Sinai desert and Kuneitra in the Golan Heights. Although the point is seldom made, during bin Laden's last stand in Tora Bora and environs, our bombing probably killed as many innocent civilians and friendly fighters as enemies.

I also wanted some news on whether the US-led coalition had managed to put a blocking force on the high ridges to prevent bin Laden from using the obvious escape route over the White Mountains into nearby Pakistan, a three-hour walk away.

Akbar got permission to accompany one of the forward-most mujahideen patrols to assess close up some of the damage wrought the night before. Taking a camera, he went up the mountain to see if any real damage was done.

He returned with footage of several dead terrorists apparently killed by the bombings, but told me there was no evidence of a substantial contingent of US special operators in front of us. If they were there, none of our Afghan good guys knew about them.

Subsequent books and testimony before the Senate Foreign Relations Committee in 2009 revealed that from December 3, when the aerial bombing campaign really began, until about December 10, the total US ground force in Tora Bora consisted of just "20 U.S. CIA NCS [National Clandestine Service] and Fifth SFG (A) ODA572 [Special Forces Group] team members, code name Jawbreaker," all inserted by helicopter; twenty against al Qaeda.

There were almost that many security personnel and techs working for my Fox News team. Adding in the CNN, NBC, and other crews who were arriving, the media clearly outnumbered the US Special Operations forces during the first crucial week of Tora Bora. Of all possible explanations as to how bin Laden was allowed to escape, the fact that only twenty GIs were assigned to trap him in Tora Bora is the most glaring explanation. However skilled or courageous they were, those twenty were obviously not able to do much on the mountain other than presumably spot targets for the warplanes.

It was a pitifully small number and insufficient to surround the al Qaeda positions. The notion put out by the Pentagon that we had skillfully inserted a substantial contingent of black-clad, bearded gringo warriors unseen even by friendly Afghans in the relatively confined Tora Bora valley as it was being pounded by B-52s turned out to be folkloric nonsense.

Another of the Afghan commanders, Muhammad Musa, later said, "There were six American soldiers with us, U.S. Special Forces. They coordinated the air strikes . . . My personal view is if they had blocked the way out to Pakistan, al Qaeda would not have had a way to escape. The Americans were my guests here, but they didn't know about fighting."

When they did finally arrive in force, some came by chopper, others more conspicuously in a convoy of SUVs on the one road into the valley, in plain sight of reporters. By the end, the force still consisted of only about seventy fighters from Delta Force, Navy SEALS, and Air Force STS, later supplemented by a handful of British commandos and even a sprinkling of Germans.

WHY THE FUCK DIDN'T SOMEBODY
TELL ME? DECEMBER 11, 2001

Six days into the Tora Bora campaign, I did something rare: I checked some of the stateside reports of the war's progress that our techs had printed out. As I read one of the wire-service accounts, my throat constricted with the realization that I had been misreporting our friendly-fire incident, or rather that I had confused ours with a far more notorious event involving three US special operators and members of the Karzai family, which actually happened on the other side of the country in Kandahar.

Perhaps typically, my first thought was defensive, "Why the fuck didn't somebody in New York tell me?" That was followed by the less-savory notion that maybe nobody in New York had noticed, and that I could just correct myself without making a big deal of it. More than on most stories, war reporting is typically amended and rewritten on the fly, minute-by-minute, as facts replace initial impressions. Five died; no, ten died; no, it was thirteen, etc.

No such luck.

Preparing for the Hannity hit, I walked past our little equipment tent crammed with satellite gear. One of our two Pats, Pat Butler, innocently delivered my career death sentence. Looking up from his gear after reading the same report I had, he said, "You know they're saying that the friendly fire incident was in Kandahar, not here." A highly competent, thirtysomething, prematurely bald, solid-as-a-rock cameraman and technician with a wonderful temperament, Pat had no malice in his voice, but he was clearly concerned.

"I know," I muttered flatly as I took my mark for the live shot now two minutes away. As I stood next to the ancient mujahideen tank, which had become my signature shot at Tora Bora, explosions were shaking the valley below us. The high-altitude bombers were resuming their runs anew as daylight spread through the valley. They were right on cue.

The bombing was not my angle, though. However dramatic, it was already old news. My emphasis was going to be the arrival the night before of the Special Forces cavalry. It was Monday evening, December 10, in New York, about 6:30 AM Tuesday, December 11, local time. Hannity cohost Alan Colmes asked, "What's it been like the last 24 hours?"

The two Pats with Allister, our gutsy but awkward money man.
Craig, Allister, Pat, Pat, me, Greg. November 2001.

Geraldo Rivera: Well, Alan, let me start with the latest news, and I'm not talking about the bombing raid that just happened a minute ago because that's basically more of the same. Let me tell you what woke me up about three, four hours ago.

We heard the unmistakable sound of choppers, helicopters . . . It had the distinctive sound of American Black Hawk helicopters. And put that in conjunction with what sounded to us a lot like AC-130 gunships, not only AC-130 gunships, but that unmistakable sound from those Gatling guns that the AC-130s have.

I would submit to you, when you combine that information, what we heard with our own ears three hours ago, with information from local sources, that suggests that American military personnel are finally in the area here in eastern Afghanistan. To me, the conclusion that I get is that they mounted some kind of major special operations raid last night.

Now, let me tell you something else, Alan, that I find of great interest. Last night, a couple hours before we were awoken by the helicopter sounds, we got a call from Hazrat Ali. Hazrat Ali is the man who is in charge of the . . . Hear, another strike! Just got another strike up on the hill. You'll see the plume soon. We missed the flash . . . Haz-rat Ali called me to say . . . There it is! There's the plume.

They are convinced now that Osama bin Laden himself is up there, that their radio intercepts on the—you know, the short-range walkie-talkies and their human intelligence. They are—they tell us that they have—they have people inside. They have people who are pretending to be with the foreign legion of Osama bin Laden.

They are—they are telling us that the world's most wanted criminal himself is leading the defense with perhaps one thousand hard-core fighters, one thousand or more, many of them still, inter-estingly enough, Alan, with their families, certainly, at least with their wives.

They say that twenty-five of the terrorists were killed over the weekend, including one woman, in fact. So at that butcher's bill, how long can they sustain? We don't know. But it all suggests a tightening of the noose around Osama bin Laden, Alan.

Alan Colmes: So every time we see one of those plumes, as you call it, there is the hope that beneath that plume might be Osama bin Laden. The Pentagon, by the way, is saying that US special opera-tions forces are being resupplied, and that's what the helicopters are all about, and there's nothing more going on at this point with those helicopters.

Sean Hannity: Hey, Geraldo, it's Sean. Listen, I want to ask you about this. There you are in Tora Bora, and Fox News on its website has reported that within the last thirty-six hours that they dropped one of these fifteen-thousand-pound "daisy cutter" bombs. For those that don't remember, it's about the size of a Volkswagen beetle. That had to be fairly close to where you are. What can you tell us about that?

Geraldo Rivera: All I can tell you is my brother, Craig, and I awoke simultaneously last night, and Craig said to me—and I'm quot-ing—"That felt like a daisy cutter." I can't say that I felt what Craig did. I was half a second behind him in waking up. But Craig's pretty reliable and pretty conservative, so I would not at all be surprised if one of those, at least, was dropped maybe four hours ago . . .

IT HITS THE FAN, DECEMBER 11, 2001

After the live shot, I walked back past the equipment tent. Pat had a pained look on his kind face. "They want to talk to you. Rob Zimmerman, the PR guy. He's on the line," Pat said, handing me the bulky satellite phone.

Another competent new colleague, as the network's spokesman Zimmerman was riding the bucking bronco those days. A studious yuppie who left Fox News a few months later, Rob was the network's spokesman to the world during this heady, tumultuous period when the five-year-old news organization was rocketing to the top of the cable ratings.

Rob apologetically, almost sheepishly, explained that a reporter for the *Baltimore Sun* was aggressively inquiring about an "anomaly" in my reporting. He went on to explain the disconnect between my having reported on multiple occasions that I had walked the "hallowed ground" of friendly fire, when the actual incident being discussed back in the States happened three hundred miles from my location.

As my stomach dropped, I shot back defensively something like "but we had one here too." He listened sympathetically and then asked reasonably if I wouldn't mind talking to the *Sun* reporter, a guy I had never heard of, named David Folkenflik.

With about forty-five minutes until the next hit, I agreed, confident that I could quickly clear the matter up. As I recall, Rob punched in the reporter's number and conferenced us. In any case, I was soon explaining the innocent error to a gleefully skeptical representative of the most loathsome class of journalist, a newspaper media critic who had never actually covered war but who was an expert nevertheless. Here is how he described our encounter:

> Yesterday, in a twenty-minute interview peppered with profanity, Rivera railed against those who would question his work.
>
> "It's time to stop bashing Geraldo," Rivera said. "If you want to knife me in the back after all the courage I've displayed and serious reporting I've done, I've got no patience with this [expletive].
>
> "Have you ever been shot at?" Rivera demanded. "Have you ever covered a war?"

By this point the interview was clearly going badly. Pat listened as I railed against the smug reporter safe back home in Baltimore. In his initial account, Folkenflik paused in his written narrative about the friendly fire incidents to criticize my career shifts, characterizing my move as "a kind of pilgrim's progress from muckraker for a local station, to network reporter, to war correspondent, to syndicated showman, to liberal talk show host," to man with a mission. He wrote:

Now, he has returned to the coverage of war. From the day of the terror attacks, Rivera, 58, spoke fervently of his anger with a nationalistic bent. He said the many deaths in his small New Jersey town led him to quit his anchor's desk at CNBC in November. He took a pay cut to travel to central Asia for Fox News. Since then, the television star that conservatives once loved to hate for his unabashed defense of President Clinton [during impeachment] is now featured as a leading example of how patriotism has resurfaced in American life.

The veteran television war reporter angrily listed many of the hot spots he has reported from over the years. He also noted that he had won the Robert F. Kennedy award, a prestigious national journalism prize, last year for his reporting on conditions of women in jail.

So far in Afghanistan, he said, he has been the first television reporter to have covered the fall of Kunduz and the fighting in Tora Bora . . . Here's what Rivera said last Thursday, a bit past 8:30 AM Eastern time [December 6, 6 PM local time], in a report filed from Tora Bora:

"We walked over what I consider hallowed ground today. We walked over the spot where the friendly fire took so many of our, our men, and the Mujahedeen [anti-Taliban fighters] yesterday," Rivera said. "It was just—the whole place, just fried, really—and bits of uniforms and tattered clothing everywhere. I said the Lord's Prayer and really choked up."

Although he had shown video footage from the Tora Bora ranges in other stories on Thursday, he did not identify where he had seen the site of the so-called "friendly fire" incident.

A few minutes earlier, Fox News had run captions across the bottom of its screen describing the previous day's events, with some details about the deaths Wednesday of the three American special operations troops. The captions said they had been killed outside Kandahar.

As Rivera had been seen live on the air from Tora Bora both Wednesday [December 5] and Thursday [December 6], journalists, Defense Department officials, and international aid workers expressed skepticism that anyone could make a round-trip across such treacherous, distant terrain in that time.

It would take twenty hours to thirty-six hours by car across ravaged roads each way, people with knowledge of the region said. They said helicopter flights were almost unheard of and would have afforded dubious safety.

Because he was hell-bent on screwing me, Folkenflik spun the most obvious evidence that my mistake was innocent to make me both guilty and stupid. Does anyone reading this believe that I would be so dumb as to try to pretend I was three hundred miles from where everyone in the world knew I was?

Everyone knew my location because I was on live television, telling viewers hourly where I was. Precisely because of the logistical impossibility of being on two sides of Afghanistan at once, no one, however arrogant or dishonest, would try to pull off what he suggested I tried to pull off. Did he think my editors and news directors were ignorant of my travels?

I was with a team of twenty, including security. Were they all in on my fraud? What about the Fox News assignment desk in New York? Is the supposition that they were all part of a conspiracy to deceive the public?

Later, in anguish, I asked our lead technician, Pat Muskopf, why no one at Fox warned me that I was making a big mistake in conflating one friendly fire incident with another hundreds of miles away. He suggested, "You know, you are Geraldo. Maybe they were just afraid to contradict you."

Even as I write this more than a decade and a half after the fact, my blood boils. I made a damn mistake, innocent, however devastating to my life and career. The reason the entire press corps eventually seized on the allegation that I was a chiseler is that they wanted it to be true.

THE CORRECTION, TUESDAY MORNING, DECEMBER 11

By the time of my next hit an hour and a half after the shouting match, as I reported to Fox News host Jon Scott, I paused to clear up my transparent error about the friendly fire incident and cover my ass by setting the record straight:

But hopefully, with the news that I reported before the break, Jon, of the special operators on the ground, there'll be some land-air coordination. You know, I know that Kandahar is the place that suffered that dreadful friendly fire incident involving our special operators and some of the mujahideen.

But we had one here as well. You know, I walked that hallowed ground. At least three mujahideen fighters killed by our bombers because of the fluidity of the front line. One day, one side has the hill; the next day, the other side has the hill. And they're desperate to avoid repetition of those two friendly fire tragedies, the warrior's nightmare.

So hopefully, with our guys on the ground now—and I really do expect an escalation, a notching up of the quality of the combat. If our people are there, they have not—these Eastern Alliance fighters, God bless them—haven't gotten close to the cave complex yet. I would say we're at least a mile—three-quarters of a mile—away from getting there.

Confident that I had nipped any controversy in the bud, I swaggered from the live-shot location past the equipment tent and said smiling to Pat Butler, "That should take care of that. I was born at night, but it wasn't last night."

Pat nodded, but was otherwise noncommittal, clearly not as confident as I was that bygones were bygones. That was the last I heard about the friendly fire controversy for the entire time we were in Afghanistan.

GERALDO AND HAZRAT, DECEMBER 11, 2001

It is impossible to exaggerate the role Sheik Hazrat Ali played in my reporting. Unlike his double-dealing co-commander Haji Zaman, he was the military arm of the effort to capture or kill Osama bin Laden. Many later reports, written from far away, minimize Ali's stature and significance in the battle of Tora Bora. Some accuse him of being just another dope smuggler looking for an inside angle. I don't know about his other activities, but on the role he played here, the critics are wrong.

We had bin Laden in Tora Bora before anyone else. Our information was so razor-sharp, our access to the front lines so complete, it eventually created another near-scandal. A few days into the Tora Bora battle, as the broader press corps finally descended on this corner of Afghanistan, a reporter for the *Boston Globe* accused me of paying for information. The encounter came during a media gangbang, one of a handful of events staged by the authorities, such as they were, for the gathering press corps. The mujahideen put several al Qaeda prisoners on display. At the site of the sad mini-parade of POWs, a scrawny reporter from the *Globe* asked me to respond to "the charges." I said, "What charges?" Rather than answering, he asked straight up, "Do you deny paying for information?"

I said out loud in a voice full of attitude, "I deny it," and came close to punching his preppy face. We did not "pay for information." We got information from local people, some of whom we were paying for doing legitimate jobs like transporting and protecting us. In this world's most perilous place, our folks were doing the crucial job of keeping us alive.

We paid salaries. We did not pay in the way other news networks, desperate to catch up to us at Tora Bora, were throwing money around "to buy documents" (their lame excuse). I could name the reporters and the producers here and now, but what is the point? They know who they are.

It is impossible to exaggerate the role Sheik Hazrat Ali
played in my reporting. September 2002.

DAMNING COINCIDENCE, DECEMBER 2001

Stateside pundits far from Tora Bora jumped on the *Sun* bandwagon. They were also exclusively men who had never covered combat. They included Tunku Varadarajan, then a cultural critic for the *Wall Street Journal*, who was quoted as mocking "another Rivera report last Thursday in which the correspondent ducked in the face of apparent sniper fire. Rivera is 'really the subject of the story,' Varadarajan wrote Monday [December 10], 'Lest you thought, in a moment of stupidity that it was about Afghanistan.'"

"I think he is a clown, basically," *New York Times* columnist Frank Rich, at the time the ruling effetist, said about me on CNN. "His stories, with clear-cut morality tales of 'good guys' and 'bad guys,' reflect 'Rivera's self- aggrandizement,'" Rich is quoted as saying. "It's not about patriotism or anything else. It's about him trying to basically have reflected glory from the American military."

In truth, I did become enamored of my own sagacity and wisdom. If a thought occurred during one of my unscripted monologues, then it must be true. Once I started down the road to self-confirmation—and again, it's important to note, not being contradicted by my editors in New York—I became increasingly confident, and later paid a disproportionate price. I will never forgive myself the hubris, which led to my disgrace.

MAN-MOUNTAIN CRAIG, DECEMBER 12, 2001

As we traversed the bomb-gouged and cratered mountainside, Greg Hart and I found discarded Pakistani Army–style helmets that had recently protected the heads of now dead or missing al Qaeda fighters. I attached one to my belt. For one of our roaming patrols on the mountain, journalists from CNN and the Associated Press joined us. We began taking fire from snipers up the hill. Craig joked macabrely that he was most in danger because he towered over everyone else. Wearing combat boots and an old-style WWII US Army helmet, he was a mountain standing at least six feet four inches, a walking tall target for the snipers above.

The good news is that Greg Hart's camera was rolling as the volleys of shots began whistling past. The bad news is that Craig and the AP reporter got separated from the rest of us. They were farther up the hill on the upside of a dirt berm. The sniper rounds were either zipping past us or were thudding into the berm or the bomb-damaged adobe walls of the wrecked buildings behind which we had taken cover.

I kept calling out, "Craig Rivera!" worried about my intrepid brother up the hill, exposed to fire from above. As the rest of us crouched behind the berm, we were shocked and delighted when first the AP reporter, then Craig, tumbled over the berm to crash beside us. I was never happier to see my big lug of a kid brother.

As I described it later to Hannity: "It wasn't easy getting to the front, another one of those days where the snipers were obviously targeting foreigners, targeting Westerners like us. The bullets were zinging through the air all day long. My brother, Craig, the producer, had an incredibly close call, bullets whistled past his ear. All the journalists gathered there had to take cover, real salvo after salvo, fusillades fired at us."

During the time between when we taped our intense encounter with the snipers the afternoon before and the live hit with Hannity the next morning Afghanistan time, there had been the first political development of the Tora Bora fight. The Eastern Alliance had made a surrender demand.

As I reported,

They [al Qaeda] have until eight o'clock [AM] our time, ten-thirty PM Eastern time in the United States tonight . . . an hour and fifteen minutes from now, to surrender. If they don't surrender, then—the attack will recommence, and I fully expect that we'll be in the cave network today . . . And for any al Qaeda fighter—the reason two hundred to three [hundred] of them are said to be trying to flee to Pakistan on the other side of the White Mountains—the reason two hundred or more of these so-called suicide fighters are parlaying about surrender today is they know that they are a nineteenth-century army against a twenty-first-century Air Force and Army. They stand no chance.

I have no doubt that bin Laden, if he survived that attack, is deep in the caves. He's not going to give up. He's going to be Hitler in the bunker at the end of the Second World War. But we'll get him, too. By "we" I mean our guys.

At that point, with a flourish, I whipped out my confiscated helmet.

I have . . . a little token from yesterday—you know, I would never disgrace a warrior, but these guys were trying to kill us for no reason.

This was on the head of an al Qaeda fighter just twenty-four hours ago. Now I intend to give it to my friends at the firehouse at Sixty-Fifth Street and Amsterdam Avenue. They lost so much on September 11. I want to show them that . . . the guys that did this to them are now paying the price.

At this exact moment, my living, honest-to-goodness dream was me sitting alongside Erica on top of the backseat of an old Cadillac convertible for a World War II–style, confetti-showering victory parade through downtown Broadway's Canyon of Heroes. The only thing my glorious war story needed was a happy ending. I hinted to the anchors that one was just over the horizon.

I saw the ranks of the mujahideen, the good guys, swell yesterday as word of the victory, of the offensive, as the advance went forward. They came from everywhere. They seemed to come out of the woodwork, the volunteer army, as often happens when momentum shifts their way, so charged, so energized, that where I was watching two hundred, three hundred, four hundred guys fighting, suddenly there were a thousand.

But they do feel charged. They do seem energized . . . you should have seen the road up to the front lines yesterday. It was bumper to bumper with would-be volunteer warriors coming out of the woodwork to be part of the last big push against Osama bin Laden and what is left of his terrorist army.

I would estimate that there are less than five hundred of them left around him, if he still survives. It might have been that he's already incinerated, but my guess is that he's deep down in those caverns . . . he's someplace in some last bunker reserved for the boss. But it won't be long. The world's most hunted man is about to be—about to be nabbed, killed, or in some other ways, eliminated, guys.

THE FAKE SURRENDER, DECEMBER 11, 2001

The focus of the world during this tense day was the surrender deadline, which anchor Jon Scott brought up as soon as my next hit began.

"We want to get more now on that looming deadline for Taliban fighters in Tora Bora," said Scott. "Fox News war correspondent Geraldo Rivera is on the front lines in Tora Bora. Geraldo, we're twenty-five minutes away, any signs of surrender?"

And counting. I'm about to leave this position, Jon, as soon as I finish this broadcast to go back down the valley to the actual front line about three miles from this current position. If I were them, I would definitely take Hazrat Ali up on his offer. They have been pounded to smithereens. And it's—it couldn't happen to a nicer bunch, and it couldn't happen on a better day, the third-month anniversary of what the al Qaeda terrorists' network did to us on September 11.

Then, as we showed video, beginning with the cave, and later making special note of the tremendous bomb dropped during the night:

The scene of the daisy-cutter devastation: utter, utter destruction. It looks like a lunar landscape or a World War I battlefield. They're saying now that Osama bin Laden might have been in the area when this monster was dropped, and it was unbelievable what happened. This had to have, if it didn't kill them, oh, it had to shake their resolve and let them understand that there is no escaping, no escaping now from the firm resolution of the United States and our allies to perpetrate justice against those who perpetrated violence and mass murder against us . . . So, Jon, I think the end is in sight. It's D-Day, man. It's the beginning of the end. Back to you.

Every Johnny-come-lately reporter with or without credentials was arriving at the outskirts of town. Most were setting up camp at the entrance to the valley, but a dozen or more teams eventually found their way to our plateau overlooking the battlefield, which was filling daily with the arrival of the international press corps.

CNN was now there in force, with several correspondents and a score of technicians; NBC had also arrived in considerable strength, joining the French, German, Japanese, British, Canadian, Swedish, and other journalists on our plateau. We bought a half-pint of rum from a French team for fifty dollars US. Despite the steeply marked-up price, we were more than glad to pay it.

Anchor Brit Hume led into the taped version of my overview report that evening on *Special Report*: "Al Qaeda soldiers are cornered in a mountain canyon, and the US has been pounding the area with air strikes. Our war correspondent, Geraldo Rivera, is there."

(voice-over) The B-52s withheld their fire until the deadline for a negotiated surrender came and went this [Wednesday] morning. But when the forces of al-Qaeda did not turn up to turn in their weapons, the lumbering giants unleashed their fury on the remaining terrorist positions.

But even as the United States waged war from the skies, the mujahideen fighters, who yesterday had so successfully swept the enemy before them, withheld their fire, sealing off the front lines from fighters and journalists alike, as they attempted to salvage at least a partial surrender. Tense peace talks were held, we are told, in the same adobe huts where we had taken such intense sniper fire from just yesterday.

Based on another conversation with Akbar and the mujahideen around us, I concluded this report with an on-camera analysis of what was happening strategically, the big picture, and how a nonnegotiable demand had sabotaged the entire surrender process.

So essentially, the mujahideen agreed to allow two hundred of the rank and file al Qaeda members to go free. Their insistence, though, in the most important condition to accepting surrender, is that Osama bin Laden, if he is in there—and they don't know, but they suspect he might be—Osama bin Laden and twenty-two of his top lieutenants, all named and known in Washington, must surrender. Otherwise there will be no truce. If these conditions are not met by tomorrow morning, the war starts again.

Because it is extremely unlikely that they ever intended to turn over bin Laden dead or alive, in retrospect it seems al Qaeda used the negotiations as a ploy to gain a day off from yesterday's furious infantry assault. That ends at daybreak tomorrow. The B-52s are not stopping at all. From Tora Bora, Geraldo Rivera, Fox News.

SOCKS FOR THE SOLDIERS, DECEMBER 12, 2001

We arranged for a truckload of socks to be brought up to Tora Bora from Jalalabad for distribution to the ill-equipped mujahideen fighters. When Alan Colmes asked me what was going on, I told him how we were doing our humanitarian part.

Well, Alan, let me start with the small things first. I know how concerned you've been about the condition of the—of the mujahideen, the Afghan freedom fighters and their really—their clothing, so thin, so shabby, so ill-equipped for winter.

Well, the "Fox Patrol" [us], it's not much, but we've started our socks distribution. We had a truck come up from Islamabad bringing a hundred pair of socks, so we're going to start clothing these warriors from the bottom up, so they'll be—here's a couple more—so we can rest easy at least that their feet will be warm when they go into battle. So it's not much, but it's the beginning of our—our private, compassionate, you know, help for our allies.

These guys, the enemies of our enemies, they're fighting a wonderful fight here against a much more modern army. They're helping us. They're saving American lives by sacrificing their own. So it's the very—the very least I could do.

Recounting this incident more than a decade and a half later and remembering the audience response to this simple gesture of kindness, I am still impressed with the sincere patriotism of the Red State audience that is at the soul of Fox News. Over the years, they have reminded me that a vast, unjaded heartland lies between America's coasts. Denigrated and dismissed as deplorable rubes by some political and media elite, it is the population from which much of our armed forces hails. They are the crowd that fifteen years later saw something in Donald Trump that political pros missed, and elected him president.

Sean Hannity: Geraldo, Sean here . . . My great interest and the interest of many Americans is finding Osama bin Laden. After, as we've been reporting the last two nights, after they dropped the daisy cutter bomb, there apparently were numerous communication breaches on their part that gave every indication that Osama bin Laden was there, very close to where that daisy cutter blew up; any confirmation of that?

Geraldo Rivera: No confirmation yet, Sean, because that would really require, in my view, my eyeballs seeing the six-foot-five-inch Saudi lurking around back there, and I can't say that either mine or any other Western pair of eyes have actually spotted him. But I must say you're absolutely correct. The reports are consistent, sketchy if consistent, that bin Laden himself is still in there.

This was pretty ballsy reporting at the time. Pundits on television back in the States, especially beat reporters in the Washington-based defense establishment, were divided on whether bin Laden was ever really in Tora Bora. Eight years later, the US Senate Foreign Relations Committee confirmed that the best intelligence showed bin Laden to be in Tora Bora when I said he was.

Geraldo Rivera: When you think about it, maybe the easiest answer is the simplest answer. And maybe after preparing this last stand, this formidable cave and cavern complex, this last redoubt, he hightailed it there, thinking that he could buy temporary sanctuary, in the same way he underestimated American resolve and our anger—he underestimated, one, how successful he would be on September 11; two, how angry and how stirred to action the United States would be; three, how formidable our staying power and our invincible armed forces. And finally, he underestimated what his nineteenth-century fortifications could withstand against twenty-first-century munitions . . . I think that if it's not this afternoon, then it's tomorrow. We'll know what the hell and who the hell is in that—that Devil's Workshop.

Alan Colmes: Geraldo, thank you. Good reporting. Stay safe. Thank you for caring about the well-being of the soldiers, as well, and . . . keeping them warm.

AL QAEDA HOME MOVIE, DECEMBER 13, 2001

With the latest surrender deadline approaching in Tora Bora that Thursday evening, December 13, a sensational hour-long home video surfaced back in the States of bin Laden appearing to take credit for the 9/11 attacks.

Apparently not intended for public consumption, the tape records a meal shared by bin Laden and several key aides, including Ayman al-Zawahiri, the Egyptian surgeon widely regarded as bin Laden's principal deputy. If al-Zawahiri survives today, he does so despite the ravages of war, age, and a $25 million bounty, dead or alive.

In the video, an adoring radical Saudi cleric is shown serving the group sitting on the floor around a low table filled with food. A sheik, he is shown respectfully kissing bin Laden on the forehead as bin Laden describes watching the aircraft smashing into the Twin Towers at 500 mph, killing 2,606 innocent civilians, collapsing the structures, shaking American complacency, and ending the New World Order declared in 1991 by President George H. W. Bush after the end of Gulf War I.

US intelligence officers found the tape in a residence in Jalalabad on November 9, about fifty kilometers (thirty miles) from where I was standing and just three weeks before we got to Tora Bora. Hannity led his show with the bin Laden video, with the terror mastermind saying he underestimated the devastating force of the planes' impact.

Osama bin Laden (US government translation): "We calculated in advance the number of casualties from the enemy, who would be killed based on the position of the tower. We calculated that the floors that would be hit would be three or four floors. I was the most optimistic of them all. Due to my experience in this field, I was thinking that the fire from the gas in the plane would melt the iron structure of the building and collapse the area where the plane hit and all the floors above it only. This is all that we had hoped for." (End video clip)

Sean Hannity: Unbelievable. Joining us now from Tora Bora is Fox News war correspondent Geraldo Rivera. Geraldo, what's happening today?

Geraldo Rivera: Well, you know, it's so fitting when you hear . . . Osama bin Laden so coolly describing what he expected his body kill to be, so appropriate that, although it's not exactly accurate to say, "It's all over but the shouting!" because there's still some killing and some dying to do, Sean—I think it is fair to say that virtually every source here in and around Tora Bora suggests that when the Muslim holy month of Ramadan ends this weekend, there is a joyous celebration . . . There is a feeling Osama bin Laden is finally cornered in a place where he has no exit whatsoever. They have him surrounded . . . There is a feeling here of nervous expectation, a feeling here that this thing could be over by the weekend.

As I spoke with silly confidence in a happy ending, New York rolled video we had fed them earlier of a dangerous excursion Craig and I had taken that morning to work our way around the mujahideen roadblocks set up to prevent press access to the front during the crucial negotiations. As I reported to Sean that morning, "We decided to hike it. It was six miles uphill, very steep, with body armor and our packs, but it was well worth the walk."

What we saw was awesome devastation, chewed-up ground and gaping craters. There were also numerous caves bored deep into the mountainsides. What we did not tape, however, was a confrontation Craig and I had with the two local guys who were guiding us on this hump in the hills to get around the roadblocks. With Akbar off on another errand, the pair had convinced me that they could get us close to the surviving members of al Qaeda and the fight.

At one point, after taking us deep into no man's land, as I sat on a rock to catch my breath, both of them started shaking down Craig for cash. I watched as my brother excitedly argued with these two armed desperados, who were demanding $200 each.

They were gesturing with their weapons and getting red-faced pissed off. So was Craig. I fingered the pistol I was now carrying in the outside pocket of my coat. These were desperados and we were miles from Akbar at our home base. Finally, Craig agreed angrily to give them $100 each. As he stormed past me beginning the march home he spat out, "I wish you shot the motherfuckers."

On the air later with Sean, my live narration was interrupted by a bomb blast nearby.

> Oh, we just had a strike, just a strike over there, a strike just this second. We found what those strikes are doing . . . huge chasms in the ground, huge craters, and house-sized craters left by those B-52s. One of them destroyed absolutely a defensive position. It revealed in the destruction a small opening in the earth. When we peered inside, lo and behold, it was another one of those caves for which the Tora Bora camp in the White Mountains is so infamous.

As I spoke, producers were rolling the dramatic video of me inside the cave.

> Poked inside. It looked like a small cave. However, once inside, it was apparent it was a huge vault, at least a twelve-foot ceiling, maybe higher, the room itself at least twenty by twenty. I did not find any connecting tunnels in my very brief examination, my inspection. We couldn't stay long there. But it was again, I think, very characteristic of what we have been up against in our assault on this final stronghold of Osama bin Laden.
>
> But by the look of the concussion outside that cave entrance, it was pretty apparent that whoever was inside was also concussed at least to death, maybe even incinerated, the way so much outside the cave entrance had been.
>
> Now, again, Sean and Alan, we hear the small-arms fire now, to go with the artillery and the aerial bombardment. It is pretty clear that if they're not eyeball-to-eyeball yet, they soon will be. And I think today really is the day, tomorrow at the latest.

That Friday morning in Afghanistan, I spoke on camera with Hazrat Ali the mujahideen leader, as Akbar translated. The late, great Tony Snow hosted from Washington, saying in his lead-in to my taped report, "Opposition forces in Afghanistan say they've advanced toward cave and valley hideouts in the mountains near Tora Bora. The US continues to support their mission with bombing raids aimed at forcing al Qaeda loyalists into the open. War correspondent Geraldo Rivera is there."

(Videotape of the Hazrat Ali interview begins.) Rivera: Will tomorrow bring victory?

Hazrat Ali (Akbar translating): I hope that at five o'clock, six o'clock, we will finish them.

Geraldo Rivera: Finish them—finished?

Hazrat Ali: Yeah.

Geraldo Rivera: Free Afghanistan?

Hazrat Ali: Yeah.

Geraldo Rivera: No Arabs?

Hazrat Ali (Akbar translating): He says he hopes that we will finish them tonight.

Geraldo Rivera: Evening time tonight?

Hazrat Ali: Yeah, tonight.

Geraldo Rivera: But maybe tomorrow?

Hazrat Ali (Akbar translating): No, tonight. He said he hope one hundred percent for tomorrow, twelve o'clock.

Geraldo Rivera: High noon tomorrow [Saturday, December 15]. As they say in Afghanistan and Brooklyn, "From his lips to God's ears." As far as bin Laden's whereabouts, the Alliance is saying they found evidence that he's occupied one of these recently discovered caves, but would not be more specific. But how much more specific than high noon tomorrow can you get? From Tora Bora, Geraldo Rivera, Fox News.

By sunset Sunday, December 16, and the end of Ramadan, the fighting was over. As the Senate report later said, "On or around December 16, two days after writing his will, bin Laden and an entourage of bodyguards walked unmolested out of Tora Bora and disappeared into Pakistan's unregulated tribal area. Most analysts say he is still there today." Issued on November 30, 2009, the Senate report was correct, as events leading to bin Laden's eventual takedown two years later would reveal.

I was the lead story on *Fox News Sunday*. Sadly, my news was not very good. Anchor Tony Snow began the broadcast network show with a reminder of Osama bin Laden's mocking tone on the captured video, and then cut to Defense Secretary Donald Rumsfeld.

Donald Rumsfeld: It is frightening and shocking to sit there and listen to him invoke the name of an Almighty to defend murder, to defend evil.

Tony Snow: . . . Good morning. We'll talk with our guests in a moment, but first there are major developments in Afghanistan. And for that we turn to Fox News war correspondent Geraldo Rivera live in Tora Bora. Good morning, Geraldo.

Geraldo Rivera: Tony, how you doing? Big news here, good news and bad news, a story of victory and disappointment; the victory first: The war in Tora Bora, therefore the ground war in Afghanistan, is over. Tora Bora has fallen to the forces of Afghanistan, the mujahideen, the freedom fighters. The army of the Eastern Alliance has captured the cave-and-cavern tunnel complex where Osama bin Laden was making his last stand here in Afghanistan.

The disappointment, the gross disappointment, is that the world's most hunted man, the world's master terrorist, is not there. When I asked the Eastern Alliance military commander in a world-exclusive interview, his first live interview, fresh from the battlefield, as Akbar translated he told me of this curious mix of elation and disappointment over these mixed results. Here is Hazrat Ali, the Eastern Alliance commander.

(Video clip begins)

Disappointment, happy, both today? He won the war but Osama bin Laden is not there.

Hazrat Ali (Akbar translating): We are very happy today because we finish our—the terrorist from our own homeland. But we are very disappointed because we didn't capture the Osama. Therefore, this is a day of both happy and—we are happy and also unhappy.

Geraldo Rivera: As to Osama bin Laden, when did he get out of here? According to Hazrat Ali, the commander, he said that it was during that phony cease-fire, during those thirty-six hours when the political wing of the Eastern Alliance insisted on giving the al Qaeda fighters the chance to surrender. They were asking, begging, for a chance to surrender over their short-range walkie-talkies.

Where are they now? They think either in the high passes of the White Mountains or that they've already made it successfully some-place into Pakistan, although, as you know, President Musharraf of Pakistan has mobilized a substantial chunk of his army on the Paki-stan side of this very porous border. So now is the time to ask Pakistan for results. Back to you, Tony.

IT WAS OVER, DECEMBER 16, 2001

It ended with a whimper on that sleepy Sunday morning in the States. All of the buildup, the bombs, the tension and attention had come to this. Tora Bora was conquered, but so what? Bin Laden was gone. In those days, many questioned whether he was ever really there.

Despite my reporting, commentators and pundits argued passionately on that crucial point. Although he would later waffle, General Tommy Franks's second-in-command during the war, Lieutenant General Michael DeLong, was convinced that bin Laden was at Tora Bora, until he was not.

In his memoir, *Inside CentCom*, DeLong describes the massive, three-week bombing campaign aimed at killing al Qaeda fighters in their caves at Tora Bora. "We were hot on Osama bin Laden's trail," he wrote. "He was definitely there when we hit the caves. Every day during the bombing, Rumsfeld asked me, 'Did we get him? Did we get him?' I would have to answer that we didn't know.''

Subsequent accounts were filled with scenarios under which an appropriate blocking force could have been placed between Tora Bora and the Pakistan border. On the question of whether bin Laden was in Tora Bora, there should be little doubt. Remember when bin Laden was discovered nearly ten years later, he was barely a hundred miles away in Abbottabad, Pakistan. Everything I heard, saw, and reported during that volatile period put him in Tora Bora. And as far as I know, every commentator with actual experience on the ground in the Tora Bora fight concurred.

For example, in his 2005 book, *Jawbreaker*, Gary Berntsen, a national-security analyst, who as a CIA officer based in Kabul in December 2001 directed a team charged with finding bin Laden, claimed that his operatives pinpointed the terror mastermind in Tora Bora.

"We needed U.S. soldiers on the ground!" he wrote emphatically. "I'd sent my request for eight hundred U.S. Army Rangers and was still waiting for a response. I repeated to anyone at headquarters who would listen: We need Rangers now! The opportunity to get bin Laden and his men is slipping away!!"

CNN National Security Analyst Peter Bergen, who produced the first interview with Osama bin Laden in 1997, wrote reliably in *The New Republic* in December 2009, in what the magazine called the definitive account of what really happened at Tora Bora: "At least five Guantánamo detainees have given eyewitness accounts of bin Laden's presence at Tora Bora."

Dalton Fury makes a similar claim in *Killing bin Laden*, in which he recalls how one of the CIA operatives at Tora Bora picked up a radio from a dead al Qaeda fighter.

"The CIA had a guy with them called Jalal, and he was the foremost expert on bin Laden's voice," Fury wrote. "He worked on bin Laden's voice for seven years and he knew him better than anyone else in the West. To him, it was very clear that bin Laden was there on the mountain."

In the words of the Foreign Relations Committee 2009 Report, "Fewer than 100 American commandos were on the scene with their Afghan allies, and calls for reinforcements to launch an assault were rejected. Requests were also turned down for U.S. troops to block the mountain paths leading to sanctuary a few miles away in Pakistan. The vast array of

American military power, from sniper teams to the most mobile divisions of the Marine Corps and the Army, was kept on the sidelines."

BIN LADEN IS GONE, DECEMBER 16, 2001

If not for the friendly fire mistake, I might have been honored when I got home by that ticker-tape parade I dreamed of, if not in downtown Manhattan, then at least at the VFW Hall in my modest New Jersey river town of Edgewater. None of that mattered on that Sunday evening, December 16. The chicken had flown the coop. Bin Laden was gone, disappeared into the White Mountains and into the belly of Pakistan to live almost another decade as Americans fought and bled in Afghanistan, and Iraq, expending trillions and alienating a huge hunk of the Muslim world. The mass killer upon whom America had sworn vengeance had escaped.

With adrenaline hemorrhaging, a deflating anticlimax gripped me. I wanted to get back to the States. I missed Erica and the kids and yearned for that hero's welcome and the beginning of a new career at Fox News. The big game was over, and although our home team played well, the match ended in a tie. I shed the gun and we headed home.

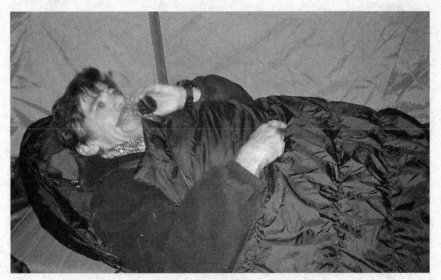

"I missed Erica and the kids and yearned for that hero's welcome and the beginning of a new career at Fox News." December 2001.

COMING HOME, DECEMBER 19, 2001

We caught a rickety (and dry) Pakistani Airlines flight to London and civilization. The initial inkling of utter career disaster came hours later, shortly after we settled into the lush first-class seats of the United Airlines flight from London to New York.

Over my long career as a roving reporter coming home from faraway places, that moment of first-class airline embrace is always the Big Sigh. The lush seat, the smiling attendants, the stiff drink . . . I had survived peril and discomfort, burnished the legend, and was heading back to applause and romance.

Given how big a deal it became in my life, it is surreal still that no one had even mentioned what was going on with the scandal brewing back home. It was about to blow up my life.

Having heard nothing about it for almost two weeks, I was stunned when I looked at the newspaper handed out by the flight attendant just before takeoff. There it was on the day-old front page of the *International Herald Tribune*:

GERALDO RIVERA DRAWS CONTROVERSY IN
AFGHANISTAN

Dec 18 (Reuters)—It didn't take long after arriving in Afghanistan as a war correspondent for maverick broadcaster Geraldo Rivera to do what he is best known for—generate controversy.

Days after nearly having his hair parted by sniper fire while filming a report for the Fox News Channel near Jalalabad, Rivera found himself the target of criticism in journalistic circles for carrying a gun on assignment, despite long-standing taboos against correspondents packing heat in war zones.

Now the *Baltimore Sun* is challenging Rivera and Fox News on a dispatch Rivera filed about a deadly "friendly fire" bombing incident Dec. 5 . . . The apparent contradictions have raised questions from news executives and journalistic ethicists.

"I believe that Geraldo Rivera and Fox News owe their viewers a substantive explanation of what this means, journalistically and ethically," Bob Steele, director of the ethics program at the Poynter Institute in St. Petersburg, Florida, told the *Sun*.

My first reaction was apoplectic horror. My head was about to blow off. I was being accused of the most hideous offense imaginable, perpetrating a wartime hoax on the American people. I was outraged; how dare they? I had explained the confusion. It was a classic "fog of war" mistake.

Thankfully we were back in the land of cell phones. Frantic, I called Roger Ailes before the airplane doors closed. With raised voice that alerted everybody in the first-class cabin to my distress, I explained what was going on. He told me to calm down and keep my mouth shut. His argument was that it was a minor flap that would soon blow over, and if I argued too loudly, I would only make matters worse. It was the worst advice he ever gave me, creating a breach that never totally healed.

DADDY IS HOME, DECEMBER 20, 2001

C.C. and the girls met me at JFK. I wept tears of relief at the sight of the children, who ran into my outstretched arms. "Daddy's home!"

In their eyes I was a returning hero. During their entire childhood, we had a routine whenever I was heading into danger. "Daddy always goes away," I would say. "But he always comes back," they would answer in unison, relieved and smiling through their tears. Over the years, parting from my children got harder, not easier.

On this original return from the front as a Fox News correspondent, I slunk through the airport. I remember being grateful that no one brought up my disgrace, which apparently had not yet made much of a splash in New York. I could not bear to look at the newspaper stands, for fear of what I would find. In those few days before my shame at Tora Bora became more widely disseminated, I could still picture myself the warrior journalist returning triumphant. Except, I was not.

Erica was waiting for me later at our small penthouse apartment on the West Side of Manhattan. In a minor historic coincidence, we lived in a Trump-branded building on Sixty-Second Street and Riverside Boulevard. As soon as the door closed behind us, we made love in the entrance alcove, not even waiting until we could reach the bedroom ten feet away. At least this part of my homecoming played out the way I had dreamed it a dozen times during the rugged journey just completed.

If only that passion was the enduring "coming home" memory of that first Afghan assignment. Instead, there is another tortured image from that first weekend home. It is a photo of me, a day later, standing in front of our home in Edgewater. By then the impression that I had faked the Tora Bora story was spreading all the way to late-night television. Conan O'Brien and Jay Leno were having a field day, mocking what they portrayed as my seemingly obvious misrepresentation.

Wearing an embarrassed, fake smile in the photo taken over the weekend of December 22–23, I am standing in front of our New Jersey house. It is festooned with an oversized "Welcome Home Geraldo" banner.

It was put there by our local contractor, a giant ex-cop and retired Marine named Tom McNiff, who had cheered my leaving NBC and going to war for Fox News and country. It was a gray, overcast day, and the banner had been soaked in an overnight rainstorm. Thinking we were coming back to the house, Tom hung the banner two days earlier, but I had opted to hide out in the New York apartment instead.

Whether in New York or Edgewater, by putting my head under the pillow I aggravated a disaster. Many of the same friends who just a month before had crowded Ms. Elle's celebrating my brave sacrifice were

With NYPD Marine Unit at my Edgewater, New Jersey, dock. Summer 2016.

now part of the chorus of ridicule, which was bounding and rebounding through the news business at lightning speed.

One incident I still remember vividly was running into Linda Sittenfeld, one of my closest, longest-running CNBC producers, so close that I considered her part of my brain. She asked me incredulously, "What happened?" I answered with a pained shrug, "I made a mistake."

"That was some mistake," she said almost contemptuously, her voice dripping disdain as she walked away, never to be heard from by me again.

With every media writer in the country choosing to focus on my dilemma instead of on the war itself, I was getting more ink than Osama bin Laden. Toby Harnden of the *London Telegraph* accurately saw what was happening in his story filed December 20.

GUN-TOTING GERALDO UNDER FIRE FOR THE STORY THAT NEVER WAS

. . . Sensing his difficulties, the American media has swooped with a vengeance. Having already had to defend his decision to arm himself, he is now being peppered with questions about the veracity of his reporting. The usual obscure academics and journalism tutors have been wheeled out to do him and Fox News down.

Geraldo's main crime, his defenders say, is his overnight switch from left-wing defender of Bill Clinton to a gun-toting, uber-patriot who warned that, if he found Osama bin Laden, he'd personally "kick his head in, then bring it home and bronze it." Critics hope Geraldo will be recalled in ignominy for crimes against journalism, while his application for a Pulitzer Prize is filed in the bin.

Steve Murray of the *Atlanta Constitution* was similarly evenhanded.

RIVERA IS EASY TARGET FOR CRITICS

These days, he doesn't have to get his nose busted by a white supremacist or open Al Capone's empty vault to grab attention. No, Geraldo Rivera—former tabloid journalist-turned-self-styled war reporter—has been grabbing headlines lately. But not the kind he'd like . . .

Geraldo "fessed up to [Folkenflik], it was a mistake," Fox News spokesman Robert Zimmerman says, referring to a follow-up interview Rivera gave a reporter at the *Sun.* He adds, *"The Baltimore Sun is trying to advance a story that was dead on arrival."*

Here reporter Murray made a fair point that it effectively took me years to follow up on.

The story doesn't end there, though. The only officially recorded incident of friendly fire casualties in Tora Bora happened three days after Rivera's report, when Afghan fighters were killed by a bomb. But that doesn't necessarily mean Rivera fabricated what he says he observed.

"It may well have been Taliban or al-Qaida guys he saw," says Lt. Col. Dave Lapan from the media office of the Department of Defense. "I have no way of telling what he may or may not have witnessed."

Which was fair enough as far as it went. The problem was that aside from my reporting and commentary, I had presented no hard, objective evidence that there had been friendly fire casualties in Tora Bora during that first week of combat. We never showed on air the video we had shot that day of the carnage in Tora Bora.

Murray concluded,

Rivera couldn't be reached for comment: On Wednesday he was en route from Afghanistan to spend the holidays back in the States. No, he isn't being called home early. Zimmerman says the seasonal furlough was always intended, and Rivera will return to report on the war later. "Right now the man has to come home and shower," Zimmerman adds. "He hasn't showered in three weeks." So it's official: Rivera stinks. But not the way his critics mean.

For days after returning home, I simmered with rage and embarrassment, wanting to fight back to prove my innocence.

At one point during that period, Jay Leno invited me on *The Tonight Show.* I was delighted and relieved finally to have a forum during which I could put the whole controversy to rest. But Roger refused my request to go out to the coast to do the show.

"Aren't you supposed to be on vacation?" he asked, coldly dismissing my frantic request just as he had earlier dismissed my distressed phone call.

CORPORATE RECKONING, FRIDAY, DECEMBER 21, 2001

There is another scene that aches. On Friday, December 21, my first full day back in the States, there was a meeting in one of the big conference rooms on the second floor of Fox headquarters on Avenue of the Americas, six or seven men in ties and shirtsleeves assembled. Lawyers and news executives present, this was my formal hearing to determine if the staging charges were true.

Did I intentionally misrepresent my location to make it appear that I was in Kandahar to walk "hallowed ground"? Did I lie to put myself near those slain by friendly fire incident? Faking news was utterly unacceptable.

News chief John Moody chaired the meeting. Short, with slicked-back black hair and a taut frame, Moody was Roger's powerful number two. In the post–Roger Ailes era he has been moved from the second-floor executive area to the seventeenth floor. Ironically, he is now next door to me. He was no friend at the meeting in December 2001. It was in a darkly lit, tastefully decorated conference room. I told my story as I have here, explaining my alibi to him and the other Fox News executives seated around an oval table.

There had been an incident of friendly fire in my location, I told them. We saw the aftermath. It was easy to confuse that Tora Bora incident in our location with the incident in Kandahar that everyone else was talking about back here in the States. Cut off from outside news sources, I explained how I made a flawed but innocent assumption.

Moody responded coldly in low, dramatic tones that rattled my nerves. "Our sources in the Pentagon say they know of no other incidents of friendly fire near your location on that date."

"I can't believe that," I responded defensively, my gut dropping out. "Every Afghan at Tora Bora was talking about the danger of friendly fire from the American bombers. Besides, it only matters that I thought sincerely that they were talking about friendly fire at my location."

Fox News cleared me of any intentional wrongdoing after considering the lack of communication with the outside world and the fog of war. "Based on Geraldo Rivera's thirty-year track record, Fox News has full confidence in his explanation and journalistic integrity," said the statement from Fox News. "This is not the first, nor will it be the last, mistake made in a war zone."

That boilerplate statement of support aside, I thought Moody's main goal was to make sure that I took the fall for the embarrassing blunder. Nobody wanted to confront a basic question: Why no one at the News Desk told me I was making a mistake.

Roger was not at the meeting. He had an expanding empire to run, and later said he sincerely believed that my flap would die down, like so many public relations crises he had steered his clients through in his political career. He ordered me to keep my mouth shut, and let the network handle it, which was the worst advice he ever gave me.

"LOOK, THEY'RE TALKING ABOUT YOU," DECEMBER 2001

Reporting on the Fox News statement, and no doubt empowered by my public silence, the *Baltimore Sun* attacked me again, this time more viciously. On Thursday, December 27, David Folkenflik reported that according to the Pentagon it was essentially impossible for me to have been confused. He added that although there was indeed a friendly fire incident in Tora Bora, it happened on December 9, three days after my mistake.

Most damningly, he wrote, "No journalist, international aid worker or Defense Department official interviewed could confirm the existence of another 'friendly fire' incident on December 5."

Note how carefully he couched his damnation, writing only that no one *he interviewed* could confirm the existence of another friendly fire incident on December 5. I tried to be indifferent, but it was impossible to ignore. Mainstream pundits were crawling over each other to appear on cable news decrying my blatant dishonesty. Wolf Blitzer devoted an entire hour-long program to the scandal; worse, it was on the monitor the first time I visited Roger alone in his office. "Look, they're talking about you," he said, his voice dripping disdain.

No one understood the depth of my humiliation, but I remained silent, becoming an obsession for reporters who chose to overlook the groundbreaking truth of my reporting from Tora Bora. Aside from being the first in the caves, as I said, I was also the first to report with confidence that Osama bin Laden had escaped, probably during or immediately after the phony truce engineered by local fighters.

Throughout 2002, I would spend half my energy making the case that the *Sun*'s reporting was based on a false accusation. Yes, I made a mistake. No, it was not intentional. Not many establishment types believed me, and the story continued to haunt everything I did. At one point Roger said to me, "I had no idea you had such a big bull's-eye on your back."

What I took away from that first meeting was that he regretted hiring me from CNBC, but as a loyal friend he was stuck with me. Like every executive and reporter in the building, he wanted my controversy to fade away to protect the network.

The pain it caused me could not be understood by anyone except Erica and Craig. By New Year's Day January 2002, Fox News had achieved ratings preeminence over CNN, a ranking that would run uninterrupted for a decade and a half. The last thing the flourishing operation needed was a credibility-draining controversy like mine.

NOWHERE TO RUN, JANUARY 2002

I thought of disappearing to escape the ridicule and even thought of suicide, but decided not to let my accuser off the hook that easily. The thought of critics remaining on Earth after me, garnering credit for revealing the shame that led me to take my own life, was what kept me alive. I could just see the nerd absorbing the quiet congratulations from the Geraldo-haters. "Oh I'm sorry he felt so ashamed that he killed himself to escape the truth." Bullshit.

Instead, I took a two-pronged approach to life after Tora Bora: one, to ignore the slings and arrows, vowing eventually to clear my name; and two, to fight the charges on their merits by proving there had been friendly fire deaths in Tora Bora during that first week of December 2001.

On December 12, an article had appeared on the website of FAIR, which billed itself as "the national progressive media watchdog group challenging corporate media bias, spin and misinformation." In other words it is an organization as ideologically far away from Fox News as possible. In the article, writer Rachel Coen did a survey of friendly fire incidents during the air campaign in Afghanistan.

Quoting the *Independent* newspaper, dated December 4, 2001:

From all over the countryside, there come stories of villages crushed by American bombs; an entire hamlet destroyed by B-52's at Kili Sarnad, 50 dead near Tora Bora, eight civilians killed in cars bombed by U.S. jets on the road to Kandahar, another 46 in Lashkargah, 12 more in Bibi Mahru.

. . . After U.S. bombing near Tora Bora destroyed two villages and killed over 100 people—reporters seemed surprised at Afghans' negative response to America's war on the Taliban and al Qaeda. CBS's Randall Pinkston reported that "at least 100 people" had been killed . . . He noted that the Tora Bora killings had provoked criticism of U.S. policy, and called this "a troubling new reaction." *CBS Evening News 12/1/01.*

Over the long years of this endless conflict, those friendly fire deaths strained our relations with the emerging Afghan government and put at risk all the blood and treasure that we shed there. The fact that our forces accidentally killed thousands of innocent Afghans in this longest war in our history is undeniable.

WALKING DEAD, DECEMBER 2001–JANUARY 2002

I kept myself crazy busy, seeking to prove with reckless courage that I had not deceived, because I was the bravest celebrity war correspondent ever to wield a microphone. It became my ambition to die in combat. Emotionally crippling, professionally, the flap destroyed my road to glory. On a fast track to being regarded as the preeminent combat correspondent of the age, I instead became a punchline. One cruel January 2002 television sketch on *Late Night with Conan O'Brien* cut deep. In it the character representing me is reporting an incident on a shipwrecked vessel. Because the faux Geraldo is far from the sea at the time of his report, a sidekick helpfully splashes "me" with water to make the scene more authentic. When Craig brought up the skit in the office the next day, saying I had to admit it was funny, I didn't speak to him for weeks. My team knew forever after they could not talk about Tora Bora. However vivid and important our memories of the caves, the bombs, the bodies, or the sense that we had been at center stage of living history, no one was allowed to mention the place in my presence.

As I wrote in my diary at the time: "Spent the entire month almost making history in Afghanistan only to watch it all turn to shit with the stupid story about friendly fire. It should have been great, but as Al Pacino said, every time I seem on the verge of a breakout 'they drag me back in.'"

Leaving Erica, who traveled home to Cleveland for the holiday break, I visited the girls at their seaside home in small picturesque Marion, Massachusetts. It was painful. The girls were still traumatized by my breakup with their mom C.C. the year before, and it did not help matters that I was damaged goods. A widely syndicated *Washington Post* article by Howard Kurtz appeared on Christmas Day, based on an interview I had given him before Roger Ailes shut me down. The headline was: "Geraldo Rivera is offering to resign from Fox News."

> Rivera acknowledges that he made an "honest mistake" by saying he was at a "friendly fire" incident in which three American soldiers were killed in a U.S. bombing raid. He was hundreds of miles away, near what he maintains was a second such incident in which two or three Afghan opposition fighters were killed.
>
> *Sun* writer David Folkenflik "has slandered a journalist who is an honest person and has contributed arguably much more to American society than he has," Rivera said. "This cannot stand. He has impugned my honor. It is as if he slapped me in the face and challenged me to a duel. He is going to regret this story for the rest of his career."
>
> Folkenflik said he was very careful in framing the story and could find no military official or journalist in the region who could confirm Rivera's account. "I don't know how many bites of the apple he gets to get a version that works," Folkenflik said. "There may be an explanation for this that bears up to scrutiny, but we haven't seen it."

Living in a semi-permanent funk, I became reckless, pushing as relentlessly toward danger as possible. Tora Bora was a low-grade fever, or a stain that could only be cleaned with glory. Time did nothing to alleviate the misery because the harder I tried to forget, the worse the memory got.

It felt impossible to walk the halls of Fox News. Although I had been in the news business for decades, these were people I hardly knew. With great fanfare, Craig and I had gone off to war within the first week we came to work with them. I could not meet anyone's eyes. They were strangers and I was notorious. My arrival was supposed to help bring the young network the credibility of long experience. Instead, I had brought ridicule and embarrassment to myself and, undeservedly by extension, to Fox News.

After a New Year's week with my sons, then twenty-two-year-old Gabriel and fourteen-year-old Cruz, and with Erica, spent mostly hiding out at our rented Malibu beach house, which felt like an enforced exile, we finally got back to New York from the coast during the second week of January 2002. Bill O'Reilly had me on his show first. In fact, he never faltered in his loyalty to me, always finding a once-a-week spot for me on his show throughout the fifteen years we shared at Fox News. Sometimes socially awkward, he was nevertheless a pillar of friendship, putting me on his show, and the two of us together making smart, tough, good TV. On this fraught occasion, he reverted to the Long Island blue-collar accent the network's first crossover star sometimes affected, blurting out the question I yearned to answer. "So what happened?"

I told the story as well as possible in the few minutes allotted, which satisfied the hometown Fox audience, but could not compete with the scorn being heaped by the outside world. It felt like the whole journalistic establishment was wagging its finger. They hated the ascendant Fox News Channel anyway, and I had given those critics the ammo they craved to attack and nearly destroy me.

Chapter 6

TOUR OF TERROR

The year 2002 became my year of living ever more dangerously. Stuck with me by contract and apparently still thinking the Tora Bora scandal would blow over before it destroyed my career or killed me, Roger made me senior war correspondent and host of a weekend show then called *War Zone*. The designation of *senior* correspondent was a letdown. The understanding I had with right-hand man John Moody was that if I returned home bathed in glory, I would be named the network's *chief* war correspondent.

Always with brother Craig and/or Greg Hart in tow, I vowed never to let any reporter out-risk me. Chasing institutional terrorism became my mantra and raison d'etre. After saying goodbye to Erica and the children, the crew and I headed for Kenya. I had not been there since 1998, just weeks after al Qaeda destroyed two of our embassies in East Africa, in its first major attack on US interests.

After doing a series of interviews with military and political experts in Kenya, the crew and I flew on to bordering Somalia. On Saturday, January 12, we landed in a pair of small, chartered twin-engine aircraft on a rolling grass field outside Mogadishu.

The trip was unusual even for that relatively free-spending era in foreign news coverage. We were lavishly equipped. We had a nimble airplane, a King Air, with us the entire time, and a second, less-elegant twin-engine cargo airplane available whenever we had to move the two tons of satellite gear needed to make television when we found something newsworthy. Nowadays, crews in the digital era need far less equipment to do the same job. I am convinced that eventually some tech genius will figure out a way to make our eyes able to transmit stories directly to home base with a coded blink.

Our King Air was owned and operated by a supremely knowledgeable and impressively connected black African pilot named John Mohammed. With him, we could fly confidently to every dusky, dangerous enclave around the Horn of Africa, secure that we had both local knowledge and a trusted go-between to negotiate access with whomever the power players happened to be at the moment. This man could have run a major airline or a big import/export firm.

The main Mogadishu airport, like the harbor and most of its infrastructure, had been destroyed by constant, careening, often-mindless violence. We drove into the lawless, ruined capital where no real government had existed for nine years. Back then, in 1993, our first military intervention into Africa, which was designed to prevent Somalia from dissolving into ethnic/tribal/religious factions, was ill-advised, short-lived, and tragic in its ending. The military disaster is now known by the radio call that signaled catastrophe to our commanders, *Black Hawk Down*.

Craig dresses down during a satellite hit from Kiwayu, Kenya,
February 2002. Later the scene of a deadly terror attack.

The supremely knowledgeable and impressively connected
pilot, Captain John Mohammed, January 2002.

We landed in Mogadishu in a pair of chartered twin-engine aircraft. January 2002.

It ended when President Clinton brought the troops home. We should have stuck it out, despite the disastrous loss of that Black Hawk helicopter and eighteen GIs. When Clinton and our international partners lost their nerve in 1993 and ordered our forces to pull out precipitately, we left a vacuum in East Africa that sucked law and order out of that corner of the continent, allowed anarchy free rein, and made room for al Qaeda, and later al Shabaab, the main Islamic militant group in the region, to take root.

The remains of the helicopter were still there when we arrived in 2002. Covered in street scum and dirt, it is a sick sort of tourist attraction. Any Mogadishu cabbie can take you to the half-buried, garbage-strewn remains. Ironically, the movie *Black Hawk Down* was playing in US theaters at the time we arrived at the actual scene of the crime. That coincidence was very much on the minds of Somalis. As I reported at the time:

"We visited the site of the real *Black Hawk Down* crash site over the weekend. It's all overgrown with cactus and covered with barbed wire now. And what the government here fears is that the movie will encourage American military planners to believe that Somalia is still an enemy of the US and make more believable the charge that Somalia is harboring al Qaeda."

In downtown Mogadishu we stayed in the bunker-like Central Hotel. With the constant rat-a-tat of gunfire outside the sturdy wall that surrounded the compound, the hotel was protected by huge iron gates and patrolled by heavily armed guards. For many years, it was a speck of stability in Mogadishu's cascading turmoil, frequented by what remained of Somalia's business and political elite and visiting media, who all treasured its security. That aura of safety suffered a blow in 2015 when al Shabaab militants blew it up, killing twenty-five.

WITH SKINNIES CHEWING KHAT, JANUARY 2002

After visiting ex-Somali president Hussein Mohammed Farrah Aidid, a former US Marine who was living in exile in Ethiopia, we flew to Luuq, an Italian colonial town on the Juba River in Somalia's western desert. We stopped there to spend some time with Western aid workers, part of the heroic crew of true humanitarians, who unlike the flabby poolside UN officials we had just seen at the hotel in Addis Ababa, really work selflessly for the greater good. In the next few years, many aid workers

With guides and bodyguards in Mogadishu, Somalia, February 2002.

would suffer abuse, kidnapping, and even murder at the hands of Somali extremists.

Less disciplined than the Afghan mujahideen, but just as fierce, Somali fighters are badasses. They are ebony stick figures, none tall, most around five and a half feet. They are kids with heavy weapons and extra ammo slung over bony bare shoulders, and are known locally as Skinnies or Technicals.

One of the reasons they are so lean, mean, and crazy is that most chew the narcotic leaves known as *khat*. These local extremists who came to be al Shabaab use khat to fuel their aggression. In fact, the leaf has been a fixture in the Horn of Africa for a thousand years. I confess to trying some. I am a sucker for local flavor. Chewing it numbed my mouth, increased my heartbeat, and reminded me of the times I had chewed coca leaves when covering another crusade, the War on Drugs in the South American Andes during the 1970s, '80s, and '90s, while working for ABC and later NBC News.

The main ingredient in cocaine, coca grows almost everywhere in the Andes. At 14,000 feet in Bolivia, it is all around you. Running hard to get the story, you can either chew the leaf or gasp for breath in the thin air of the High Plateau. I chewed and ran.

Less disciplined than the Afghan mujahideen, but just as
fierce, Somali fighters are badasses. January 2002.

Banned by the United States and Canada, khat is legal and widely
traded in Somalia. An amphetamine-like stimulant, in my case it ampli-
fied and aggravated my already reckless state. The leaf juice made me feel
bulletproof, had me running toward the gunfire rather than away from it.
I was snarling like an animal and belittling the concerns of my crew that
we lacked body armor or even basic security.

After "Black Hawk down" in '93 and the withdrawal of all US forces,
the fighting in Somalia turned stupid. Young men were getting their guts
ripped out by .50-caliber machine guns in daily gunfights in and around
Mogadishu.

By 2017, most Skinnies had become political and were fighting for
or against militant Islam in the jihad with the West. Back in 2002 these
kids were anarchists, not particularly religious, and fighting for nothing
more than bragging rights over which warlord controlled which block of
abandoned buildings in one of the world's most battered and bloodied
capital cities. Mogadishu is an aggravated, apocalyptic African version
of *Mad Max* gone truly crazy.

I have been in the company of scores of honored war dead, soldier
and civilian. During this 2002 trip we taped a guy dying in front of us.

In his midtwenties and dressed like a bank clerk, he was on a stretcher in a rudimentary field hospital and our camera rolled as his brains dripped out from a devastating head wound until he gasped and his heart finally stopped pumping blood onto the dirty floor.

Young men were getting their guts ripped out by .50-caliber machine guns in daily gunfights in and around Mogadishu, Somalia, February 2002.

ALPHA MALE SEEKS HONORABLE DEATH, JANUARY AND FEBRUARY 2002

That January and February 2002, I was a psychologically wounded man seeking an honorable death. There was gunfire and death everywhere in Mogadishu, which, as I said, I made a practice of running toward. During this malignantly obsessive, post–Tora Bora phase, I was self-centered, deeply hurt, and half-crazy enough to seek guns and gore to restore glory.

When heavy firing broke out as we were interviewing a local official near the wreck of the US Embassy, not far from our hotel in Mogadishu, I urged our crew to rush with me toward the sounds of gunfire even though we were unprepared. Our bulletproof vests and helmets were still in our rooms, precious minutes away. When Craig and Greg, who never refused to go into action, counseled that we should at least be properly equipped, I snarled, "If you're afraid, then go back to the hotel."

Needless to say, everyone followed me toward the action, although one of the members of the crew was so shaken by the tumult he left Africa as soon as we could arrange transport. The incident itself provided some of the most dramatic combat footage since Tora Bora. In one sequence, what must have been a .50-caliber machine gun blasted apart a street lamp just as Craig ducked under it.

Here's part of my report on Fox News:

We saw something today that provided us with a tiny glimpse of the horror and violence our GIs faced on the battle-scarred streets of Mogadishu in 1993. It was a bloody street fight between two sub-clans that ended with two militiamen dead and at least half a dozen innocent civilians seriously wounded.

Making a mockery of the government's call for the Mogadishu militias to disarm, the two sub-clans engaged in a fierce morning-long firefight, which began about a mile from the former American embassy.

By the time we reached the scene, it had escalated into a raging street battle, cutting down civilians and passersby alike with no regard for whether they were in one of the warring sub-clans or had any dog in this fight.

We later found that the origin of the violence was an absurd dispute over which group controlled a single ruined building in the devastated neighborhood. We discovered something even more distressing, that one of the dead was a driver for our hotel who had been caught in the crossfire.

At the hospital, the only working hospital in this city of one million, we saw the full extent of the grim reaper's tally. At least a half dozen were seriously injured, one was dead and one was dying right before our eyes. Chaotic, senseless, it was a bloody mess.

Later, I had nightmares of having to explain to Craig's wife, Cordelia, and his kids, Austin, then eight, and Olivia, age four, or to Greg's parents, that my recklessness had killed their loved ones.

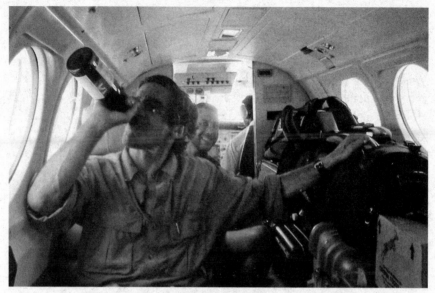

Celebrating when we left Somalia in one piece, February 2002.

BEIRUT, RUINED OASIS, JANUARY 2002

From the Horn of Africa, our next stop on the Tour of Terror was back in the Middle East. The crew and I arrived in Beirut, one of the planet's most unique cities, on January 27, 2002. It is five thousand years old, an ancient yet modern multicultural metropolis sitting at the rocky nexus of the Christian, Druze, Sunni, and Shiite worlds. Here East meets West, disco meets belly dance, and sharia meets sexy. How could it be otherwise given that the city has been held in turn by Phoenician, Greek, Roman, Byzantine, Arab, Crusader, and Ottoman rulers until fracturing along religious lines.

Still, until the mid-1970s, Beirut sported a wide-open, tolerant, cosmopolitan air that was a favorite of travelers from jet-setters to backpackers. The American University still attracts scholar/adventurers from throughout the Old and New Worlds. But beginning around 1975, a vicious, ten-year-long, sectarian civil war shattered the façade of harmony, probably forever.

I had covered Southern Lebanon from the Israeli perspective since Operation Litani, the 1978 Israel Defense Forces invasion whose purpose was to eliminate raids from Lebanese territory against Israeli coastal communities such as Haifa. Editorially, almost all my early reporting in the region was from an Israeli-American Zionist perspective.

Those were the Israel-can-do-no-wrong days, Israel as bastion of Western democratic ideals. Created by the scrappy underdog survivors of every persecutor from Goliath to the pharaohs, the Romans to the Nazi Holocaust, the Zionists were the underdog victors of desperate wars in 1948, 1956, 1967, and 1973, and worthy stewards of the Holy Land, protectors of the sacred ancient places and irrigators of the desert. The local Arabs, on the other hand, whether Sunni, Shiite, or Druze, were always portrayed by me and most others as shady, primitive, and generally up to no good.

I was totally wired into the Israeli government in those days, often getting editorial guidance from their powerful intelligence community, including the Mossad. That preference for Israel extended to their New Testament cousins, the Christians of the Mideast, whom I always described as "beleaguered" or "embattled." One vivid 1978 ABC News 20/20 piece, done with extensive Israeli editorial guidance, featured Major Saad Haddad. He was a gritty Lebanese Army officer who had formed his own militia of Christians and announced a military alliance with Israel.

Haddad occupied Southern Lebanon's strategic Beaufort Castle, which dates to the twelfth century Crusades. With Israel's logistical help, his forces were holding the castle's still-sturdy stone ramparts against a much larger Hezbollah militia in the midst of Shiite territory. In one vivid scene, my cameraman, old friend Anton Wilson, taped from a hilltop as I rode in one of Haddad's armored vehicles as it ran the gauntlet of Hezbollah gunfire, making the perilous supply run from Christian lines down a contested valley and then up to the castle. The audio of the ride is punctuated with the sound of small arms fire pinging as it hit the armored vehicle.

Curiously, Major Haddad also ran an American-funded Christian radio station out of the stronghold. The Voice of Hope played gospel and American country music. I scored the Haddad 20/20 profile with recent Christian convert Bob Dylan's just-released song, "Gotta Serve Somebody." It is a great tune about how he surrendered to the faith, although he has since returned to Judaism.

LEBANON'S GEORGE WASHINGTON 1980-1983

When I went to Beirut for the first time in 1980, ravaged by the savage, ongoing civil war, it was with the specific guidance of Israel's Mossad. An Israeli spymaster and former journalist named David Kimche put our team in touch with an up-and-coming Lebanese leader named Bashir Gemayel. A Christian warlord, Gemayel was promising to lead Lebanon away from confrontation with Israel once his faction won the war and he got elected president.

I came to love the guy. Sheik Bashir, as he was universally known, was dashing and courageous. He spoke effortless English (plus Arabic and French), orating expansively of a New Lebanon, one that would regain its central position in the Mideast and coalesce beyond its internecine cataclysm.

I had profiled him for an action-packed, bullet-whistling, April 1981 *20/20* hour-long special, "The Unholy War," which was more propaganda than journalism. As Jack G. Shaheen wrote in his book *The TV Arab* (1984):

> Consider the opening of the program in which host Hugh Downs says, "Geraldo Rivera goes behind the lines with PLO (Palestinian Liberation Organization) terrorists" and "the PLO has made the world its battleground." *War* continually calls Palestinians terrorists. There are over fifty references to terror, terrorism, and terrorist in all.

Given the strong, institutional, pro-Israeli bias that still exists among mainstream American media, the piece would not be out of place today, and certainly not on Fox News. My deviation from that Israel-can-do-no-wrong school of advocacy journalism would later get me into serious hot water and undermine my standing in the company, perhaps as egregiously as Tora Bora.

In one sequence of 1980's "The Unholy War" I follow as Sheik Bashir jumps from closely packed Beirut apartment buildings rooftop to rooftop, directing intense urban combat. Later, he speaks intensely on camera of his vision of a US-allied Lebanon helping moderate the region in cooperation with Israel.

With Lebanese journalists. Weeda, Ghassan, and team, Beirut, Lebanon, February 2002.

A charming, crafty leader, Bashir had a grand scheme, that if elected president, he would encourage Israel to invade Muslim-held areas of South Lebanon, humble Hezbollah, and force their Syrian and Iranian allies out. He was then going to use his relationship with the United States, enhanced by his personal connections with Americans like me, to encourage Israel to withdraw from Lebanon. To that end, he spent time in the United States to rally support, especially with the influential Lebanese community. He and I hung out socially in Washington, DC, and New York.

Sheik Bashir was indeed elected president of Lebanon on August 23, 1982. Having become a dear friend, he had promised me his first interview and, true to his word and despite the fact that I was four thousand miles away and he was in Beirut surrounded by the international press corps, he took my phone call from the United States and gave me his first interview.

Bashir was killed by a massive bomb blast along with twenty-six others three weeks later. The Syrians were later declared the culprits. They did not want a Lebanese leader friendly with Israel. His death enraged the embattled Christian community he had helped save and touched off an atrocity that foreshadowed the savagery of al Qaeda and ISIS.

A week after his murder, outraged Christian militiamen loyal to the slain sheik slaughtered as many as 3,500 Palestinians and Lebanese Shiites, including women and children, in what came to be known as the Sabra and Shatila Massacre, named for the village and refugee camp where the blood-letting took place during a night of wanton butchery. Since by that time the Israeli Army had invaded and occupied a huge chunk of Lebanon, the IDF and especially its legendary commander and later prime minister, Ariel Sharon, did not escape at least tangential blame for the atrocity.

The Mossad-inspired scheme of installing a pro-Israel, Christian-dominated government in Lebanon was in ruins. Instead, 850,000 Christians have emigrated, leaving the country forever. The Christian Lebanese diaspora is an underreported story. This proud and enterprising culture has spread its élan and enterprise throughout the world. Despite its travails, like the Jews and Jerusalem, they knew Beirut is their eternal home.

PISS OFF, FEBRUARY 2002

We ended this Part One of the 2002 Terror Tour in Sudan, where officials were as unhappy to see us as local officials had been earlier in Somalia. Dealing with the cancerous influence of foreign extremists, as well as homegrown Black tribal versus Arab, Christian versus Muslim civil strife, the Sudanese weren't eager for the international spotlight.

That has been one side story of my entire career. When I show up, it is generally bad news for the hosts. If they have anything to hide, I am the last person they want to see, and they frequently react accordingly. When we were trying to film the Nile River from a strategic bridge in downtown Khartoum, we were swarmed by fidgety, heavily armed soldiers who seemed on the verge of killing us as infidel spies. Briefly detained, we were released after a pledge to leave the country. Before flying out, we managed a brief visit to Osama bin Laden's onetime compound on the edge of the capital city, and another side trip to the aspirin factory President Clinton ordered destroyed in 1998, after mistakenly thinking it was a bomb factory connected to the African embassy bombings.

THE MURDER OF DANIEL PEARL, FEBRUARY 2002

After our 2000–2001 journey up the Amazon River onboard *Voyager*, I brought the old boat back from South America in stages. One of the last cruises I managed to squeeze between combat assignments was sailing her from Trinidad the six hundred miles to St. Thomas in the beginning of February 2002. Then it was back to real life, broadcasting the latest episode of *War Zone* from our New York studios. The weekend show on Fox News was now a regular part of the schedule and doing well in the ratings. I was already planning our next trip back to the conflict zone in Afghanistan when the awful news broke: twenty-eight-year-old *Wall Street Journal* reporter Daniel Pearl had been beheaded and otherwise mutilated in neighboring Pakistan.

He had been kidnapped by al Qaeda a week before, and the leaked video of his subsequent execution was chilling and infuriating. Years later, and only after waterboarding, Osama bin Laden's key terror aide, Khalid Sheikh Mohammed, confessed. He claimed at a closed military hearing in Guantánamo that he personally beheaded the journalist and cut him into ten pieces. Before he was brutalized, Pearl was forced to confess his Jewishness:

> My name is Daniel Pearl. I'm a Jewish American from Encino, California, USA. I come from, on my father's side, the family is Zionist. My father's Jewish, my mother's Jewish, I'm Jewish. My family follows Judaism. We've made numerous family visits to Israel.

His murder was dramatized five years later by the 2007 film *A Mighty Heart*, starring Angelina Jolie as Mariane Pearl, the crusading wife of the slain journalist. Aside from admiring the resolve of groups like Reporters Without Borders, which benefited from the gala New York opening of the film, and the thrill of meeting the glamorous yet down-to-earth Jolie and then-husband, Brad Pitt, at the premiere, I took Danny Pearl's death personally.

Remember how I got into major hot water for asserting that if the bad guys came for me, "it would be a gunfight, not a kidnapping"? With a Jewish Star tattooed on my left hand, I had chilling visions of what extremists like ISIS or al Qaeda would do if they had the chance.

The slaughter of Danny Pearl reaffirmed my decision three months earlier, in November 2001, to carry the pistol in Afghanistan, which came after the kidnapping, mutilation, and murders of the eight other Western reporters covering the early months of the war. Reporters have to protect themselves with deadly force if necessary. The fiction that reporters are above the fray and therefore a protected class, as I said, is naive and dangerous. I remember arguing with Jeffrey Gettleman of the *New York Times* at Baghdad Airport in the early days of the Iraq War about what to do if detained by extremists. I told him I was resolved to go down fighting.

At the time, an earnest, quietly daring thirty-three-year-old reporter, who five years later in 2006 became chief of the *Times'* East Africa Bureau, Gettleman replied passionately, "No, no, no . . . " before recounting how he had managed to extricate himself by talking his way out of just such a jam. He was adamant that a reporter should be neutral and not otherwise engage.

Those days are gone. This war on terror and Islamic extremism is way too dirty to expect rules to be followed by the bad guys. Just remember "Jihadi John" and his brutal beheadings of American journalists James Foley and Steve Sotloff and so many others beginning in 2014 with the ISIS reign of terror in Syria and Iraq.

In retrospect, while it was arguably practical for me to carry the gun in those chaotic early days of the war in Afghanistan, especially after the Taliban massacre of our colleagues there, I should have kept my mouth shut and quit the verbal swaggering. Nowadays, specifically on the issue of carrying a weapon, my rule is that if you do not have armed good guys watching your back, you do not go into the abyss. Let the pros carry the guns. If there are none available, don't go.

Chapter 7

WARRIOR JEW HEADS TO
THE UNHOLY LAND

Despite Danny Pearl's grotesque and outrageous murder, given the strain and tension I was feeling at Fox News' home base in New York because of the smoldering Tora Bora controversy, it was a relief to travel back to the Mideast war zone. Going first to Israel and Palestine, I wrote in my journal, "The warrior Jew heads for the Unholy Land."

Our hotel in Palestine sat on a ridge overlooking their de facto capital, Ramallah. On March 9 we had a front-row seat from the hotel balcony restaurant as an Israeli missile hit, with pinpoint accuracy, a vehicle in a convoy carrying Palestinian militant leaders. Like a lightning bolt it cut through the night sky. We later found it was righteous retaliation for a suicide bombing earlier that evening in Jerusalem, which killed eleven Israeli civilians and wounded scores of others in and around the Café Moment coffee shop near the prime minister's office in downtown.

During that time, provocations from both sides were constant. A couple of days after the Café Moment bombing, in one of the most poignant, painful incidents I have ever witnessed in a conflict zone, I watched as a Palestinian father and mother in traditional Muslim garb who had just given birth in an East Jerusalem hospital were prevented by soldiers at an

Israeli checkpoint from returning with their newborn to their West Bank home.

On this chill night, the new mother held her crying, swaddled newborn tightly in her arms. The parents had the appropriate identification and were pleading unsuccessfully to be allowed through to get their baby home out of the cold.

The inhumanity of the scene was exaggerated by the infuriating nonchalance of the IDF soldiers, who were brushing off the woman as if she were trying to sell them a bad watermelon. Witnessing it began a kind of emotional chain reaction. If it did not turn me against Israel and the side I had always taken, then at least it sowed doubt. I never felt the same about Israel after that night.

On edge because of the spreading anarchy and violence, the IDF was using quick-trigger muscle to quiet discord. We were heavily tear-gassed one afternoon outside Ramallah at Checkpoint Kolandia, and as we approached another checkpoint, shots were fired close over our heads from about a block away.

Aside from making you want to rip your eyes out to stop the burning irritation, tear gas does not bother me. A heavy dose of water usually does the trick, easing the irritation. Anyway, if you do not get gassed from time to time, you are not getting close enough to the action. What accelerated my doubts about Israel's moral supremacy at the time was a more troubling tactic. The soldiers had begun using magic markers to write identifying numbers on the forearms of the hundreds of young Palestinians being rounded up.

It reminded me of my Uncle Phil, a Holocaust survivor. Related to me by marriage, Phil was built like Popeye. He was a butcher with bulging forearms. What fascinated us kids growing up on Long Island was the faded but still readable numbers the Nazis had tattooed on the inside of Phil's arm. I remember running my fingers over the tattoo in disbelief at the inhumanity of it. The fact that Israelis had adopted an obviously more benign but arguably similar technique for keeping track of detainees made me sick.

I got understandably reamed for agreeing with Arafat's condemnation of the technique as "Nazi-like." Nothing compares to the Nazis, and shame on anyone, including me, who uses the comparison to make a point. But I have not changed my mind about the branding. Interestingly, the IDF dropped the technique soon after the controversy blew up.

My subsequent commentaries about Israel's oppressive occupation of Palestine had a profound effect on my standing at Fox News. My views were extremely unpopular, in a practical sense, affecting me almost as negatively as Tora Bora, although not in the same soul-rattling way.

Make no mistake, Israel, frightened, frustrated, and angry, was suffering abundant Palestinian provocation during what was becoming a full-fledged uprising. The Second Intifada was beginning. Civil order was being challenged. There were dangerous demonstrations, and insurrection was widespread, including suicide bombers. Most of the worst was still to come.

I remember how sincerely unapologetic Palestinian intellectual Hanan Ashwari was at dinner one evening in East Jerusalem, defending the suicide bombings. A high-level PLO official, she and I have known each other for decades. Usually I am sympathetic to her family's struggles with occupation and to the plight of her people. She has spoken to me of the humiliation of living in a territory totally controlled by an occupying force, and how not having a real passport caused complications for her family, involving everything from college to marriage. That night, though, she startled me when she told me with chilling frankness, "They [the suicide bombers] are our F-11s, our strategic bombers." Here, she used two-fingers walking to make sure I got the reference that the number eleven represented human bombs on legs; suicide bombers were Palestine's answer to Israel's superior weapons. As President Trump frequently trumpets, Israel's Great Wall, sitting astride Israel's version of the 1967 border with the Occupied West Bank, has virtually ended the practice.

Marine General Anthony Zinni, President George W. Bush's peace envoy, was visiting the region when I again appeared on *Special Report*, the network's signature show, Tuesday, March 12. Having heard my condemnation of the hideous new IDF practice of painting numbers on the arms of Palestinian detainees, Fox News principal anchor Brit Hume debriefed me after we resolved some technical problems.

Brit Hume: Earlier in the broadcast before we were rudely interrupted by satellite problems, Geraldo Rivera and I were talking about the change that some journalists undergo when they experience covering the Middle East firsthand. Geraldo, himself part Jewish, has been feeling some of that and he was telling me about that. Please continue.

Geraldo Rivera: The most insidious thing about evil, the most insidious evil about terrorism, I should say, is that because it is sometimes difficult to fight, you become something like the thing you are fighting.

You become someone who violates some of the basic concepts of your own fundamental democracy; who you are. That is the danger in the United States and a danger being realized in Israel.

When you use tanks and F-16s and these sledgehammers against thickly populated civilian towns and cities, that's not fighting terrorism; that is inflicting terrorism.

You may get some of the bad guys, but I walked down the streets of Bethlehem the other day. There were fifty-nine Palestinians killed, 367 injured by the Israeli action, and many were women and some were children.

You remember that infamous video of some months ago that showed a Palestinian father huddled with his nine-year-old son against the wall, caught in a crossfire between the Israelis and Palestinians, who were throwing rocks and shooting, and before it ended, the boy was dead and the father severely injured.

I would die for Israel. But watching the suffering of the Palestinian people, the real suffering, I've become a *Palestinianist* in a sense.

Like our president, like President Bush's stated United States policy, I believe the only solution is two states, living side by side with internationally recognized and maybe United States–guaranteed borders.

Brit Hume: When you come to see a certain equivalency, and you even used the word terrorism to refer to what Israel does, Israel inflicting terrorism. Do you really think that Israel is intentionally killing civilians or are they in a sense collateral damage?

Geraldo Rivera: I think that—it's more than collateral damage. There's an expectation when you use a jet fighter they're flying at five hundred miles an hour to get a terrorist nest, although the Israelis are the best at it, as precise as any of our guys, there is an inevitability that there will be civilian casualties.

They do not intend to hurt the Palestinian civilians. I don't mean to suggest that at all. That's not the case. The tactics they're employing, that Prime Minister Ariel Sharon over the severe objections of his defense minister, as we at Fox News broke the story of the secret argument about the incursion into Ramallah on the eve of General Zinni's visit. You cannot do those things. You cannot round up Palestinian young men and put numbers on their arms to make it easier to identify them in the future.

What does that remind the world of? That reminds the world of what Hitler and the Nazi pigs inflicted on the Jewish race during the Second World War. Maybe the comparison is not precise or exactly parallel, but the echoes of it are unmistakable. It's indefensible.

These people, the Palestinians, they bleed just like we do. They suffer just like we do. They have the same aspirations. They want to make a living. Yes, there are terrorists among them. Yes, there are young people who would strap explosives to their body and on the promise of something in heaven, blow themselves up. We cannot become the thing we loathe. That is indefensible and non-Jewish.

Brit Hume: Geraldo, very interesting. Great to have you. Geraldo Rivera, having a change of heart on this issue not unlike that which many other journalists have had in that region. It is striking.

THE WRATH OF THE JEWS, SPRING 2002

Roger Ailes later told me how he and our boss of bosses, Rupert Murdoch, watched my Brit Hume interview together, and how at one point Murdoch asked him incredulously, "Is he [meaning me] pro-Palestinian?" Roger told me his reply was, "The Israelis think so."

The viewer reaction to my remarks was much more intense. It blew up the Fox News audience email system and main switchboard in New York, as supporters of Israel heaped scorn and outrage. It was not just that Israel was being criticized, but that in the midst of another Intifada someone who had consistently supported the Jewish state was criticizing it and doing it on the most conservative news network in America.

Doing a live shot later outside the Café Moment bombing site, I was berated by a middle-aged, potbellied, gold-necklace-wearing Russian Jewish cab driver who pulled over to lecture me about being dangerously naive. "Do you see what these people are doing?" he said, gesturing dramatically at the scene where eleven Jews were murdered three days before. He gave me a disdainful sneer as he got in his cab, slammed the door, then spun his wheels leaving rubber as he sped off.

As is my custom, I stayed at the King David while in Jerusalem. Built in 1931, the deeply historic five-star hotel overlooks the walls of Old City and hosts endless conventions by the JCC, B'nai B'rith, ADL, Federation, countless aliyahs, bat and bar mitzvahs, weddings, class trips, and reunions.

The hotel was not immune from violence, the deadliest attack coming from militant Zionists. In 1946, when it was being used as a headquarters by occupying British forces, it was severely damaged in a bombing that killed ninety-one people. Future prime minister Menachem Begin's Irgun Gang carried out the lethal attack. Its aim was to terrorize the British authorities and make them eager to end their rule, called the Palestine Mandate, which the League of Nations granted Britain following World War I. The Irgun and its similarly violent adversaries wanted them to leave and let the Jews and Arabs fight it out among themselves, which they have predictably done for seventy-five years and counting.

Over its long reign as the best hotel in the country, the King David has housed everyone from the dowager empress of Persia to the emperor of Ethiopia and virtually every world leader who has ever visited modern Israel. The 1960 film *Exodus* was shot there, and if it was good enough for Hollywood royalty Paul Newman and Emperor Haile Selassie, it is good enough for me. And, because I use my hotel room as both road office and VIP interview location, my suite tends to be among the best in the building.

On the weekend following the Brit Hume eruption, I was visited in my room by once and future Israeli prime minister Benjamin Netanyahu. Bibi and I met during the taping of the 1980 "The Unholy War" special for *20/20*, getting along great, hanging out in New York and Israel over the years, before drifting apart as his career soared and mine soldiered on.

Even though he was not formally in the government at the time, I had the distinct impression when Bibi showed up in my room on short notice that he had been dispatched as part of a charm offensive by the Israelis. The government seemed to be operating on the assumption that if it just treated me better, my reports would be more favorable to Israel's position.

Skiing at an unlikely resort outside Beirut, Lebanon, April 2002.

A few years earlier, Netanyahu had been Israel's youngest-ever prime minister and the first to be born there. At the time of our meeting at the King David, he was no longer in the top job, having been crushed by former IDF commander Ehud Barak in a reelection bid in 1999. When Ariel Sharon defeated Prime Minister Barak a few months later, in November 2002, Bibi was appointed Sharon's foreign affairs minister and later finance minister. Bibi later returned to the premiership, getting reelected a record three consecutive times. As of this writing, he is still prime minister, although various corruption controversies swirl around him and his wife, Sara.

More than any Israeli leader in history, Bibi is an inflexible hard-liner against independence for the Palestinian territories. He calls the West Bank "Judea and Samaria" in deference to their Old Testament roots as Jewish states, and his mental map of Israel includes them as a biblical imperative. An MIT and Harvard graduate, he is hugely popular among American conservatives. He also became the first Israeli leader to choose sides in terms of American politics, bluntly and boldly campaigning for Mitt Romney in the 2012 presidential election against Barack Obama. Arrogant and self-assured, Bibi also had the audacity to come to Washington, DC, uninvited by President Obama, to receive the adulation of the Republican-led Congress in 2015.

I feel about Bibi the way I feel about President Trump as I write this. Both are undeniably powerful, charismatic, and charming, while both propose policies I sometimes detest. Perhaps the Trump administration will have more success in promoting peace between Palestinians and Israelis. Early signs are not encouraging—the announcement that President Trump is moving the U.S. embassy from Tel Aviv to Jerusalem seems fraught, but you never know with Donald Trump; he may pull off another miracle.

When I opened the door to my big duplex suite in the King David, Bibi sailed in, lit a big cigar, pulled up a chair, which he spun around, sat down, gestured to a second chair, and said bluntly, "We've got to talk."

He then lectured me for the next hour on the impossibility of the two-state solution, and more generally, on trusting the Palestinians on anything. Remember, at this time the Intifada was escalating dangerously, and day-to-day life in Israel was being profoundly disrupted by horrible acts of mass violence. Fear stalked Israel's streets.

Bibi was scornful and dismissive of the current, frantic, and ultimately fruitless efforts of the Bush administration to get traction on the peace process. Bush 43 had taken to referring to the territories for the first time as *Palestine*, which took guts. President Bush also dispatched Vice President Dick Cheney on a diplomatic offensive to the region, having already appointed Vietnam War hero Zinni as special envoy to Israel and the Palestinian Authority.

"Do you know what the sum total of my concessions to the Palestinians was when I was in office?" Bibi smirked, as he gestured broadly with his lit cigar in our hotel room confrontation.

"A casino in Jericho," he said, barking a short laugh. He went on to explain that his sole concession to the peace process was allowing the Palestinians in 1998 to open The Oasis casino in Jericho, the world's oldest city. Located deep in Palestinian territory and frequented mainly by Israelis, the casino was closed two years later as a security risk.

Bibi was pushy in suggesting that I resume backing Israel unambiguously, but he was not unpleasant, granting me a formal sit-down interview on the security situation the next day, Sunday, March 17. Unlike Bibi, many of those phoning my room that week were intensely disagreeable, even threatening my job. Some were leaders of various Jewish groups in the States, others just regular civilians, and they were barraging my suite at all hours, until I put a do-not-disturb order on the line, something a foreign correspondent on assignment abroad rarely did in those days before reliable international cell phones.

We pulled out of Jerusalem for Tel Aviv the next day, ultimately making the difficult border crossing into the Gaza Strip to do several confrontational interviews with assorted radicals, including the leader of Islamic Jihad. One of their terrorists had just killed seven more Israelis, including four IDF soldiers, while injuring twenty-seven others when he blew himself up on a bus going from Tel Aviv to Nazareth in northern Israel.

Despite the Intifada's accelerating descent into full-scale religious warfare, newly elected warrior prime minister Ariel Sharon was struggling to maintain some semblance of a peace process, and the government wanted me to know that.

Their relatively liberal defense minister in the new and still-shaky coalition government, Binyamin Ben-Eliezer, an Iraqi Jew, gave me an intimate briefing suggesting that if only the Palestinians would toe the line of civility, peace was still possible. He also told me there was some positive stirring in the Arab world that I should watch, in Beirut.

PASSOVER MASSACRE, MARCH 2002

With little advance planning, but now informed that the Arab League was meeting in the Lebanese capital to propose something dramatic to resolve the Israeli-Palestinian conflict, we set out immediately.

It is only 125 miles from Tel Aviv to Beirut, but you cannot get there from here. There is no direct air, sea, or land traffic between Israel and Lebanon. You can fly to the island of Cyprus and then change planes to fly to Lebanon. Or, since Israel's heavily fortified northern border is impassable, closed tight, you can drive the long way around through Jordan, which is what we did this trip, driving across Israel and Palestine, across the tightly guarded Allenby Bridge spanning the Jordan River, across the desert to the capital city of Amman, where we caught the short Royal Jordanian Airlines flight to Beirut.

I was thrilled to be back for such an auspicious occasion. The summit conference marked the first time the Arab nations were officially throwing their weight behind a comprehensive peace plan that recognized Israel's right to exist as a nation. They were scheduled to vote on the Saudi-sponsored resolution the next day, which coincidentally was the first day of Passover, March 28, 2002.

Certain to have unanimous support because of its Saudi imprimatur, the resolution coming out of the summit called for Israel to withdraw from Syria's Golan Heights and from the Palestinian West Bank and Gaza Strip in return for normal relations. It was to be "Land for Peace," and I was practically dancing in the streets of Beirut.

During that groundbreaking conference, I met and interviewed the most reasonable Sunni Muslim leader in the Middle East of the era, Lebanon's prime minister, Rafik Hariri. There will never be peace in that troubled region without the help of people like him. Though a devout Sunni Muslim who specialized in building mosques for the faithful, he was another confident, self-made billionaire businessman. This one, though, wanted to help steer the Arab world into the modern era.

Hariri, always dressed in sharp, shiny business suits, black-gray hair slicked back, and sporting an ample mustache, reminded me of an Arab Prince Rainier, Princess Grace of Monaco's husband. The prime minister's opulent palace in Beirut, personally refurbished by him, made him seem royal despite his humble birth.

Prime Minister Hariri told me that the Arabs were ready to take a chance for peace. But he complained bitterly that the Israelis were "stealing Palestinian land" with their continued expansion of settlements in the West Bank. Still, he told me passionately, the Arabs were ready to make their historic proposal, if only Israel was ready to compromise.

Then hell was unleashed back in Israel by a Palestinian suicide bomber. Disguised as a woman, Abdel-Basset Odeh entered a big Passover Seder celebration in the Park Hotel in suburban Netanya outside Tel Aviv. Inside were 250 guests, many of them elderly Jews in Israel without family. The Seder was a hotel tradition for the lonely who gathered for conversation and company at its annual party on this festive holiday.

Detonating his powerful explosive vest, the bomber ripped apart twenty-eight of the innocent old folks and injured 140 others, many of them Holocaust survivors. The Palestinian terror group Hamas claimed responsibility. The fury in Israel was raw and understandable. My lesson for then and now is clear and indelible. Never bet on a happy ending in the Mideast. Violence always wins.

"ARE YOU JEWISH?" APRIL 2002

With this mass murder, Hamas killed the peace process for my lifetime and beyond. I was bereft. It was the end of hope, the last best chance for peace in the Mideast. Even today I look back on that singular atrocity, the Passover Massacre, as the moment disorder finally routed hope. It is over. We will never get that close again. Trust me, never.

The next day, after reporting at a Palestinian refugee camp in Beirut, I cornered the highest-level Hamas official attending the Arab summit. I fired off a rapid-fire series of angry, condemning questions about the immorality of slaughtering innocent elderly civilians. The smug creep responded coldly with a question, "Are you Jewish?"

I was flustered. To say yes would be to make my righteous anger parochial, as if only a Jew would think the bombing was a disgusting atrocity. So I picked the middle road, avoiding the question.

"What the hell difference does that make?" I responded angrily. "Why did you ask me if I was Jewish?"

"Just a question."

"Why?"

"Just a question."

"Why?"

"Because you were talking about them as if they were innocent people."

"They are innocent people."

"No, they are not."

The next evening, I was on with Sean Hannity and cohost Alan Colmes.

Sean Hannity: We continue now with Geraldo Rivera reporting from Beirut tonight. This is why—I got to tell you something; it's your reporting that—and I'm an optimist by nature—that causes me not to be optimistic.

When you have people sworn to the destruction of the State of Israel like the leader of Hamas you showed us last night—I want to remind our audience—I don't know how there could ever be peace . . . They're not going to be happy even if we went back to the pre-1967 borders. They won't be happy with that mind-set until Israel is pushed into the sea. Correct?

At which point I made a pitch for Palestinian sovereignty, if only to have a political entity that could be held responsible for atrocious acts of violence. Alan, a sharp observer, brought me down to earth.

Alan Colmes: Geraldo, he wanted to know if you were a Jew because he clearly felt that you had an agenda. That was a very scary question.

At this point in the live shot I described and demonstrated how the Hamas confrontation had unfolded.

Geraldo Rivera: This is what happened—we did the interview here. Right where I'm standing. We started walking over here. And it was over here where I finally got the kind of rage in me where I said, "Why in the world would you ask me if I was Jewish?"

By the time we got to this light-stand over here, Craig and I are united [indicating my brother as the camera panned over to show him]. You know, we're Jewish, our mom, our dear mom is watching right now in Sarasota [Florida], Jewish, our dad Catholic. And right here, both of us wanted to thump that guy. Both of us wanted to give him a couple of overhand rights and say, "How dare you? You're a pig, you're an animal, and you don't deserve to . . ." And then I bit my tongue at the very end because I didn't want an international incident. I didn't want to fight my way out of Beirut.

I understand that these are devilish, terroristic kinds of people. But Arafat can—listen, the sainted former prime minister of Israel blew up the British in the King David Hotel in 1946. He was then considered a terrorist, and then he became a statesman. Give the guy [Arafat] a chance. He's a better—it's better to make friends with these people. You can't—Palestinian and terrorist are not synonymous. That's my basic point.

Sean Hannity: Alright. We'll give you the last word tonight. I say he's still a terrorist. I hope you're right. Great reporting.

THE ELEVENTH COMMANDMENT, MARCH 2002

I left Beirut for JFK via Paris on Air France the next day, flying to meet Erica and her family in her hometown of Cleveland for Friday Seder dinner. During the long flight, I penned a blog to my Jewish viewers explaining how hurt I was by their continuing rage.

It was a weird and troubling experience. In the thirty-two years I've been in the television news business the response to my work from viewers of the Jewish faith has been unswervingly positive. The walls of my den in Rough Point were lined with plaques, a large percentage of which were given by Jewish organizations for work like my 1980 ABC News documentary *The Unholy War.*

After my televised battles with neo-Nazis and skinheads, and with the Star of David tattoo on my left fist, I've been one of America's most highly visible, tough-guy Jews.

Now, all I'm getting is hate mail from my old admirers, 18,000 angry emails and still counting. The problem is that I broke the 11th Commandment: I publicly criticized Israel. The issue is Palestine.

On the eve of Gen. Anthony Zinni's peacekeeping mission to the region, in February I traveled there with my TV crew. It was clear even then that the administration of George W. Bush had become convinced that America's strategic interests required it to resolve the issue, and that the resolution required nudging the parties into meaningful peace talks.

For Yasser Arafat and the Palestinians, that meant at a minimum stopping the suicide bombing. For Ariel Sharon that meant negotiations the end result of which would be the creation of an independent (Palestinian) state. Over the bloody weeks and months that followed it became clear that neither side was willing or able to do it. The result was more chaos and violence and an escalating conflict, despite the further visits of Vice President Dick Cheney and Secretary of State Powell.

My break with my traditional Jewish allies came when I began warmly endorsing America's calls for an Israeli withdrawal from the West Bank and the Gaza Strip, territories Israel has occupied since the 1967 War.

While constantly hammering the Palestinians for their hideous use of suicide bombers and the targeting of innocent civilians, I also criticized Israeli abuses of Palestinian human rights. One specific tactic I found particularly offensive was the rounding up of all men between the ages of fifteen and forty-five, stripping them, and then painting numbers on their arms to better administer the incarceration and interrogation process. When I commented about the world seeing this kind of thing before and that if the roles were reversed, can you imagine Jewish reaction? The stuff hit the fan.

First there was the deluge of angry phone calls, hundreds of them, followed by the email avalanche. My new bosses at Fox News were soon shell-shocked. When I refused to back down, citing the fact that I was merely stating support for express U.S. policy as set forth in a recent U.S.-sponsored UN Security Council resolution, the situation calmed, only to flare whenever I pointed out that Israeli-occupation of the territories had to end.

No amount of lobbying can change that fact. Occupation and terror are organs of the same beast. They feed off each other. Arafat may be the savage Ariel Sharon portrays him as. Still, as long as Israel remains one of the few countries occupying the land of another, the violence and misery will continue. It might continue in any case. But at least Israel will be fighting from the moral high ground, as a democratic nation intent on protecting its people and its recognized borders. Not as a military occupier intent on inflicting its will on others. Please, keep your cards and letters.

WE'RE MAKING ALIYAH! MARCH 2002

I came up with a flamboyant fix for my specific "Jewish Problem" on my way to Seder in Cleveland. The brilliant idea was that Erica and I would marry ASAP and resettle in Israel. Here is the good part: Having established residence, I would then run for the Knesset, Israel's parliament, from Herzliya, an upscale neighborhood on the north side of Tel Aviv, popular with expat American Jews. How better to prove that I loved the Jewish State than to move there and become part of the government?

After my hotel-suite confrontation with Bibi, and after many long phone calls to Erica in New York, I went so far as to apartment-shop in Herzliya. My dear friends Hanani and Naomi Rapoport live in Tel Aviv. She was a real estate agent, he an Israeli television-news executive who worked with me as a producer on *20/20* when the couple lived in the States.

Our families are still close. They provided the ten men or minyan for my son Gabriel's bar mitzvah in Jerusalem in 1993. Their baby daughter, Dana, grew up to be a producer of mine at Fox News. We have known and loved each other since Hanani's dad, Azaria Rapoport, was Israel's consul general in New York. Consul General Rapoport was instrumental in getting me embedded with the IDF during the 1973 Yom Kippur War.

Holding public office was something that always appealed to me. My dream growing up was to be mayor of New York. As a representative of two of the big city's most important ethnic groups, Jewish and Puerto Rican, I felt born for the job. In 2000, when two-term mayor Rudy Giuliani was set to leave office, I went so far as to commission a poll to determine my chances running as an independent. It would have required moving my voter registration back into the city from New Jersey, where I was still living at the time, but I was keen on making the race.

As expected, the poll showed the probable Democratic candidate, a lifelong politician named Mark Green, winning easily, with me as the independent tied with the probable Republican candidate, Michael R. Bloomberg, a little-known rich guy from Boston. When Bloomberg announced that he would spend up to $50 million to win the office in City Hall, I pulled out. Now a billionaire and one of the world's richest men, Bloomberg spent that $50 million and about $950 million more in winning three full terms in City Hall.

The political bug kept buzzing in my ear. Years later, in 2013, I came within minutes of filing to run as a Republican against then-mayor Cory Booker of Newark for the US Senate seat vacated by the death in office of long-serving senator Frank Lautenberg. In contemplating making the long-shot run against a powerful celebrity Democrat in a hard-blue state, I consulted various, very connected experts, beginning with Roger Ailes, who was skeptical. I also spoke with Kellyanne Conway, the brilliant pollster and frequent guest on my CNBC *Rivera Live* show, who later became President Trump's mouthpiece and White House consigliere.

Mayor Booker is a camera-ready media darling, well known for frequent appearances on Bill Maher and other celebrity talk shows. A tireless
self-promoter, he got a ton of press for getting Facebook's Mark Zucker-
berg to donate $100 million to Newark schools. The money was squan-
dered on thousand-dollar-per-day consultants, changing next to nothing
in the school system. The mayor also attracted attention driving around
Newark searching for crime, and for running into a ghetto house fire to
rescue a family pet, like an action hero. Kellyanne advised me to tape my
campaign spots in the wrecked heart of ghettoized Newark, where Mayor
Booker had long held sway. "Your spot could say, 'In the Senate, Corey
Booker will do for New Jersey what he did for Newark.'" Ouch.

I pulled out of that Republican primary race literally a few minutes
before a midnight deadline for filing. Again, it was about the money. The
immediate reason was the just-announced support for my primary opponent, a hard-right-wing, small-town mayor named Steve Lonegan, by the
fabulously wealthy Koch brothers. They were said to be willing to invest
$5 million to back Lonegan, the truly conservative candidate, which I was
obviously not. Running against him would have busted me in the primary
alone. My argument that a rigidly conservative GOP candidate had no
chance in relatively left-of-center New Jersey fell on deaf ears. Booker
won easily, as expected.

In 2002, the possibility of the far more exotic run for Israel's Knesset
did not even last as long as my Jersey US Senate dream. When we arrived
at the Levy home in suburban Shaker Heights, Ohio (where we now live),
a distinct chill was in the air, and it was not all coming from the notorious
lake-effect snow on the lawn. Although her parents had been remarkably
accepting of Erica's and my relationship despite the enormous difference
in our ages, they were firmly opposed to our moving to Israel, especially
as an Intifada raged.

Erica's dad, Howard A. Levy, was an excellent labor lawyer who handled discrimination cases and did precedent-setting work on the limits of
electronic discovery. Discovery in this context is what opponents during a
lawsuit are permitted to see of the opposition's emails, text messages, and so
forth. He was also a highly regarded official in the Anti-Defamation League,
the ADL. Her mom, Nancy, taught preschool and English to immigrants
and was active in the heavily Jewish east-side Cleveland community where
Erica was born and raised and that, fifteen years later, we now call home.

Both a couple of years younger than their notorious son-in-law-to-be, they were invariably kind, defending me to their close-knit group of friends in Shaker, many of whom were following our very public romance. Afflicted by the prostrate cancer that would kill him five years later at age sixty-two, Howard was not remotely amused by the prospect of his daughter's moving to violence-torn Israel. Usually deferential, he dismissed this notion and refused to hear another word. Eventually, I felt foolish enough that I dropped the subject. Over the years, Erica and company have had a few laughs at my expense over that Knesset scheme.

RUNNING BACK TO WAR, APRIL 2002

Having celebrated the tail end of Passover with my future in-laws in Cleveland, and soon to celebrate the Catholic confirmation of my then-fifteen-year-old son, Cruz, in his hometown of Dallas, I completed my ecumenical family travels when I went to ultra-Episcopalian Marion, Massachusetts, to be with the girls and their mom, C.C., on Easter Sunday.

Like every man who ever left his family, I was weighed down by guilt, but I was soon heading back to the Middle East. That is one of the fringe benefits of being a globe-trotting correspondent. Whenever dealing with real life gets uncomfortable, you leave. Before returning to the Intifada, though, the immediate plan was to sail *Voyager* to New York Harbor from her current berth in picturesque Beaufort, North Carolina, where she had spent the 2001–2002 winter getting a new engine installed after the grueling trip up the Amazon and back. She was coming to the new home I was building on the Hudson River just south of the George Washington Bridge in Edgewater, New Jersey. Designed as the ultimate bachelor pad, it was being converted in a hurry to a family home now that Erica and I had fallen in love and planned to marry.

The trip on board *Voyager* did not go as planned. What I hoped would be a pleasant early-spring sail up the coast instead turned out to be a crashing, smashing several days of fighting a full gale on the nose in the area known as the "Graveyard of the Atlantic." I described it at the time as "Cape Hatteras fucks us again, freezing, awful, true shit, but nonetheless a vivid experience."

After we had passed the cape, slowed by the wicked weather, the much-longer-than-expected journey was aborted after I was summoned to New York to do a special episode of *Warzone*. I left *Voyager* with the crew in Norfolk, Virginia, and flew home, before heading back to the Mideast on April 16, 2002. Israeli forces had just occupied the biblical city of Bethlehem in the Palestinian West Bank, and the region was on the brink of all-out war.

As the Israeli Army (IDF) continued to sweep up thousands of suspected Palestinian militants, dozens took refuge in the Church of the Nativity, the traditional birthplace of Christ. When they sought sanctuary, the Franciscan monks had no choice but to grant it. The church was surrounded, IDF snipers were in place, and a tense standoff was attracting the attention of the world.

Gambling that the situation at the church would hold, we went first to Southern Lebanon, where I planned to meet with bitterly anti-Israeli UN Special Envoy Terje Larsen. As I reported, "With escalating exchanges of fire coming on the eve of Secretary of State Colin Powell's scheduled visit here to Lebanon and to neighboring Syria, the fear is of a second front in a full-scale shooting war."

Ground zero in Southern Lebanon was an area called Shebaa Farms, a disputed hamlet-sized pocket of land located in the border corner where Lebanon, Syria, and Israel meet. Israel claimed that the farm was under its control as part of its occupation of the Syrian Golan Heights since the 1967 War. The Lebanese, led by Hezbollah militants, claimed Shebaa Farms as its historic territory and had mustered their army, threatening war, if necessary, to get Israel out.

"On a day as stormy and miserable as the current political situation here in the Middle East," I began my live show from the edge of a minefield on a black, wet night.

The sign says it all, "Danger, Death, Minefield." I'm standing right now on the border between Lebanon on this side of that fence and Israeli-occupied (Syrian) territory on the other. And between here and there, as the sign says, is a minefield that promises to kill anyone foolish enough to tempt it. Less than a week before, fierce fighting between Israelis and Lebanon's Hezbollah guerrillas ripped through Shebaa. The fighting was so intense it seemed on the verge of becoming a second front in an expanding Arab-Israeli conflict. The fact that it has not yet happened is one of the few bright spots in this tortured region.

BEIRUT, MARCH–APRIL 2002

On this trip, I interviewed Lebanese prime minister Rafik Hariri for the second time. Welcoming me to his palace like an old friend, this gregarious man was beset by melancholy, holding little hope that a pending visit to the region by Secretary Powell would do any good. Although he was deeply concerned about the standoff at Shebaa Farms in his own country, events in Palestine were foremost on his mind. Bloody fighting in the West Bank town of Jenin horrified the prime minister, and he was fearful the incendiary standoff in Bethlehem would explode in full-scale war.

Underlying his pessimism, Hariri told me on camera, was the fear the Israelis had been emboldened by the 9/11 attacks on the United States, with Americans now regarding all Muslims as enemies. Long before the advent of Donald Trump on the political scene, the prime minister said woefully, "Now to American eyes we are all terrorists. If President Bush doesn't step in, things will get worse."

The next day the crew and I flew from Beirut back to Amman, Jordan, en route to Bethlehem and the standoff at the Church of the Nativity. As it entered its fourth week, Israeli snipers began picking off Palestinian militants foolish enough to poke their heads out the windows of the old church.

ALLENBY BRIDGE, APRIL 2002

I was anxious to get to the action, which brought the region back to the front page, leading news shows in the United States. But the tension in the region made getting across the historic Allenby Bridge over the Jordan River into the Israeli-controlled West Bank more difficult and interminable than usual. Even in the best of times, Israeli security is not like our TSA. They are humorless, ruthlessly efficient, and meticulous, going through every crevice and wrinkle of every bag. Rather than waste time waiting for stern-faced IDF reservists to sift through our two tons of stuff, I wrote a short essay based on my conversation with the Lebanese prime minister.

Allenby Bridge, Jordan River Crossing, Occupied West Bank, 22 April 2002

An old rabbi once described the Middle East as a dark basement in which all kinds of horrors were being perpetrated: human rights abuses, torture, suppression of women and ethnic minorities, etc.

Israel, he said, was the one small corner of that basement where the light of democracy, free speech, and freedom of the press shined. But because it was the only place in that dark basement light enough to see anything, critics were always saying, "Look at this problem or that with Israel."

I relate the old rabbi's story to suggest that since its creation in 1948, Israel has suffered unfairly from criticism made possible only by its open and democratic nature. And that virtually every other country in the region experiences far worse abuses.

But Israel's relative goodness is no longer enough to shield it from being raked over the coals of public disapprobation. Her harsh and unfocused military response to the suicide bombings has made sure of that.

"How can any Arab ignore what is happening in Jenin and the West Bank?" asks Rafik Hariri, the Lebanese Prime Minister, his voice cracking with emotion, his arms spread wide. "It's on every television station, American, British, Lebanese, and the Gulf States. You can't avoid the images of destruction and suffering. My daughter called me from Paris. She heard that I had arrested four Palestinians trying to cross our southern border to attack Israel. 'Dad,' she asked me. 'How can you arrest people trying to struggle for their freedom?' I explained how Lebanon has laws and that they were breaking our laws and if we don't follow the law, how can we criticize the Israelis for their illegal acts in the West Bank?"

In this anecdote, more of a loving father and his daughter, than of a political figure explaining policy, I found some scant hope in an otherwise bleak landscape.

Lebanese prime minister Rafik Hariri, the most reasonable Sunni Muslim leader, later assassinated by Syrians. Beirut, Lebanon, 2002.

A consistent voice for reasoned accommodation in the Middle East, Hariri was murdered in a massive February 2005 bombing in Beirut, engineered by the Syrians. The longer I live the more alarming becomes the number of dead friends and the prospect of joining them. The explosion wiped out his motorcade, claiming twenty-two lives, wounding hundreds of others. Rest in peace, Rafik Hariri, a fine man.

CHURCH OF THE NATIVITY SIEGE, APRIL–MAY 2002

The Israeli offensive in the West Bank and the subsequent siege of the Church of the Nativity were making a mess of the ancient city of Bethlehem. While driving to the scene past destroyed buildings, burned vehicles, and garbage-strewn, smoke-filled streets, I reported:

> Given the awful provocation of the murderous suicide bombing attacks against innocent Israeli civilians, when you look at the widespread damage and devastation here in Bethlehem, it is hard to avoid the conclusion that a kind of collective punishment has been meted

out on the Palestinian people, and it is hard to avoid the conclusion that the seeds are sown for future conflict.

The Church of the Nativity and its host city of Bethlehem are an island of Christianity in a Muslim sea, unique in Sunni-majority Palestine. For various reasons including religious intolerance, as in Lebanon and throughout the region, the religion of Jesus is fast diminishing in this land. Holy places are profaned and antiquities destroyed, especially with the coming of al Qaeda and later its savage progeny ISIS and al Nusra. Religious oppression threatens to make Christianity a relic, like the ruins of past civilizations that dot the ancient landscape.

I have Palestinian friends in Bethlehem, families I have known for generations. I met Joseph and his family in the 1970s. Long-established in Bethlehem, his dad was my fixer when I worked at ABC News during and after the Yom Kippur War. His namesake son worked with me at Fox News despite the obvious bias of my network in favor of the Israeli point of view.

A couple of years ago, we put together a mini-rapprochement when I brought my assistant, Israeli-born Dana Rapoport, to a family dinner in Bethlehem. Although her parents' home in Tel Aviv is just fifty miles from his, it was the first time Dana had ever been in the "Territories," which is the sanitized way Israelis reference occupied Palestine. I am convinced that if native-born Israelis, known as Sabras, and native-born Palestinians spent more time together, they would see how close they are, cousins really, at least genetically/DNA-speaking.

The situation is worse, and the future bleaker, today in 2018 than it was in 2002. Nowadays there is not even a legitimate attempt to bring the sides together. Outsider peacemakers have given up. President Trump openly and enthusiastically embraces Benjamin Netanyahu and his hard line. The Palestinians simmer and can burst into another full burn at any time. When President Trump made the announcement that he will move the US Embassy from Tel Aviv to Jerusalem, and that we recognize Jerusalem as Israel's capital, the world condemned it as one-sided and unproductive. Worse, the US is tacitly allowing Israel to continue expanding settlements in the West Bank. If there is no land left for a viable Palestinian state, what will happen with the Palestinian people? Will they be vassals of Israel forever, living in isolated enclaves in a Greater Israel?

In 2002, the ancient Church of the Nativity was plunged into this heart of Muslim discontent when Palestinian rebels occupied it. The church lies at the end of a broad, tree-lined plaza across from a town square lined by two- and three-story buildings, with restaurants, small hotels, and shops selling Nativity trinkets on the ground floors, Palestinian Authority and other offices above. During Christmas and Easter celebrations, Manger Square is traditionally filled with Christian celebrants, although because of the Intifada it was not in 2002.

The sacred church structure is a patchwork that reflects the changing fortunes of the region, going from pagan to Christian to Islamic, back to Christian, then back to Islamic. Built during the Roman Empire, and then lost to the Muslim conquest of the seventh century, the original building sheltering the manger was largely destroyed. But some of the fortress-like, massive stone walls and towers have stood since the very beginning of this formal church in the fourth century.

The European Crusades of the Middle Ages liberated this traditional birthplace of Jesus for eighty-eight years, from 1099 until 1187, when the conqueror Saladin recaptured Palestine for Islam. Now, during this siege of April 2002, 815 years later, Muslim militants protected by Christian clergy sought refuge behind its walls as a Jewish army laid siege. All eyes were focused on "Humility Door," the main entrance, a single heavy wooden door clearly visible across the empty square.

As I reported:

According to various sources, the negotiations for ending the impasse at the church, now in its fourth week, while stalemated over the larger issue of what to do about the Palestinian militants wanted by Israel, have agreed on something.

While the standoff and siege of the 1,700-year-old Church of the Nativity promises to drag on, today the expectation is that the Israelis will allow the two dead bodies inside to be removed. They've been inside now for days, and are said to be decomposing.

We're told that the teenagers inside the building, or at least some of them, will also be coming out. The young people have been a point of considerable controversy. The Israelis allege that they're being held by the Palestinians against their will, the Palestinians countering they're in there because they want to be.

BE NICE TO GERALDO, APRIL 2002

Defying bitter complaints from journalists gathered from dozens of the world's news networks, the commanders of the besieging Israeli forces, including IDF spokesman General Ron Kitrey, gave us preferential treatment. The Be Nice to Geraldo – So He'll Be Nice to Israel strategy was clearly still in place.

All press, including us, were kept at a distance of about a football field from the church door, but even though we had just arrived in Bethlehem and our rivals had been covering the siege for four weeks, we were taken to the head of the line and given the best vantage point, on the second floor of a building called the Peace Center, a sweet spot from which we could broadcast Humility Door on live television.

Remember, in those days, spring 2002, to be live on TV required a cable from the camera to a satellite uplink, which requires substantial equipment. It was neither easy nor convenient, not like today's lightweight, handheld wireless devices. In any case, we were in the perfect spot to watch the excruciatingly slow surrender process take place. On Sunday, April 28, I reported:

> Now in its second month, the bitter and bloody standoff here at the birthplace of Jesus seems headed for a conclusion sooner rather than later. Another melancholy, empty Sunday for what has become the most watched entrance in the world, Humility Door, the Church of the Nativity's main entrance facing Israeli troops occupying Manger Square.

On May 1, the sanctuary seekers finally began emerging in a steady stream, twenty-six of them, but as they were leaving, American and European peace activists were using the commotion to sneak past the Israelis and join the besieged inside the church. The damn standoff seemed endless. Even the kindness shown me by the IDF could not alter the fact that the stalemate went on long enough that we were forced to move when the Peace Center closed for security reasons.

At our new location, we found ourselves spending a cold night clinging to a slippery steep roof overlooking the church square, not knowing when the siege would break. This waste of time is why I hate stakeouts.

They are the hardest part of original reporting. You wait around for something to happen, and if you take a bathroom break or grab a bite, you might miss the money shot.

The hang-up prolonging this crisis was the ultimate fate of the militants inside. All were required by Israel either to go to jail or at least be exiled from the Middle East. Would they get asylum in friendly countries or be deported to the Gaza Strip?

SHARING HUMMUS WITH ARAFAT, MAY 2002

Under intense pressure from America and Britain, the Israelis lifted a weeks-long blockade of Yasser Arafat's Mukata walled compound in the West Bank city of Ramallah. As I reported:

> That would pave the way for the Palestinian president to be released from his house arrest, and for the Israeli army to release its iron grip, its siege of the devastated compound as early as tonight. The fear among all the parties is that the sort of fighting we've been tracking from that fierce fight we witnessed last night that lit up the sky over Ramallah would spread even wider.
>
> Emerging from his 34-day-long confinement under Israeli siege, Yasser Arafat is one of the most enigmatic people on the world stage. Branded a terrorist by the Israelis and those who support them, he is hailed here as a hero by most Palestinians, a kind of Founding Father.
>
> The 73-year-old Arafat has been part of the public dialogue on the Middle East for most of the last four decades. Credited with giving the Palestinians a national identity, he also stands accused of consistently choosing confrontation over conciliation. But who is this frail strongman whose face has been featured on so many front pages and so many cartoons?

To answer that question, I used sharp elbows and a determination not to be beaten to scoop an exclusive interview with the Palestinian chairman, beating every other reporter crowding around him. Apparently impressed by my aggressive performance, Arafat, through an aide, later invited me to spend time inside his still-surrounded West Bank compound.

"Yasser Arafat was one of the most enigmatic people on the world stage." April 2002.

What he did not seem to remember was that this was actually our second encounter. I had first interviewed Arafat nineteen years earlier in June 1983 in Tripoli, Lebanon, as his encircled followers were being forced to surrender to a dissident Palestinian faction backed by a surrounding Syrian army. It was a low point in his life. He was being deported from the Holy Land. As he emerged from a bunker in 1983, I asked him if this was "the end of the Palestinian Revolution."

"Of course not," he replied curtly, his eyes bulging in anger and frustration, as he headed under heavily armed Syrian escort by convoy to Damascus and from there to be flown to exile in Tunisia, where he would spend the next decade.

Flash forward to May 2002 as he was released from confinement in his compound in Ramallah. But in any case it was a compound no more. The Israelis had torn down the adobe wall that long encircled his headquarters and were driving their military vehicles around it like Apaches attacking a wagon train in our Old West.

Arafat seemed unperturbed by the provocation. He was just relieved to be free from house arrest and able to speak to comrades and the gathered world press. In a buoyant and reflective mood, he shared a lavish Lebanese mezza consisting of heaps of tabbouleh, hummus, and kebabs with Craig and me. I didn't bring up the fact or the circumstances of our first meeting in Tripoli, and he didn't mention it, either. At one point, he was so keen on making friends he hand-fed us an elaborate pita sandwich piled with cucumber and hummus.

"Taste this," he insisted as he daintily put the food in our mouths.

We took pictures, and he quietly reflected on his greatest disappointment, making news when he confessed that his biggest mistake was not accepting the 1999 Clinton two-state peace initiative, which came closer than any other to resolving the intractable Israel-Palestine conflict. Arafat balked because he did not feel an impeachment-wounded President Clinton could deliver on his promises. When I later shared with Prime Minister Ehud Barak after he was out of office and visiting New York what Arafat had told me about the near miss of the Clinton peace process, Barak, a former fighting general, replied earnestly, "I wish he [Arafat] had told me that."

As I reported from Ramallah:

In a wide-ranging interview with the Palestinian president on the very night he regained his freedom of movement, we spoke of many things, including his willingness, indeed his eagerness, to have an international peacekeeping force inserted between his people and the Israelis.

Conducted before Israel released its latest intelligence claiming Arafat personally approved acts of terror against Israeli civilians, I did press him during the interview to denounce suicide bombing.

It is doubtful that Chairman Arafat's statements will change any minds, certainly not [then-prime minister] Ariel Sharon's. The Israeli leader is scheduled to meet with President Bush this weekend.

From that day, I felt more sympathetic to Arafat than almost any of my colleagues. He should have trusted President Clinton, regardless of Monica Lewinsky. The deal Bubba proposed was so specific it defined the exact borders of the proposed "two states living side-by-side in peace" down to named streets and landmarks. Arafat did not take the offered deal, in my opinion, because he had no faith given impeachment that Vice President Al Gore could win the 2000 election and be able to implement the fragile deal.

Meanwhile, the Church of the Nativity siege finally broke a week later when the remaining militants, and various civilian sympathizers, slowly began emerging to go either into exile abroad or a local prison, or to be released. We were there as it happened. Fox News interrupted a taped episode of the *O'Reilly Factor* to go to me live.

I reported,

> The negotiators accompanied by the monks have just come out. Eight men have just come out of the Church of the Nativity. They are gathered at the lower left of your screen . . . There you see them. They are apparently waiting.
>
> It seems as if they are waiting for the others to come out of the church to leave Humility Door, the main entrance of the 1,700-year-old building built over the birthplace of Jesus. We understand the two groups to be coming out with the civilians—the seventy-five to eighty or more people who are relatively innocent and of whom the Israelis said they will be able to go home, go free. It seems inevitable now. This is Geraldo Rivera standing by live at the Manger Square at the Church of the Nativity.

ABE MEETS GERALDO, SPRING 2002

In the right place at the right time to record the historic moment of surrender, I noted at the time, "We kicked CNN's butt." But the Arafat/Nativity scoop was a small triumph in the scheme of things, and had no enduring impact either on this highly charged saga or on my career.

Rather than propel me to greater heights inside the Fox News hierarchy, this April 2002 trip was essentially the end of my uncensored criticism of Israel. Like former president Jimmy Carter, whose 2006 book *Palestine: Peace Not Apartheid* made him a pariah among Zionists, for years after Bethlehem, like so many other commentators who do not toe the pro-Israeli line, I too was intimidated into silence. It's one thing to stare down Islamist terrorists or gangbangers or ghetto muggers. It is another to take on the Jewish establishment, which truly never forgets.

Hoping to repair my rift with the pro-Israeli world, my future father-in-law, Howard Levy, later arranged a dinner with Abe Foxman, the fiery head of the Anti-Defamation League, the ADL. As I mentioned, Howard was a ranking ADL official representing the Midwest from his base in Cleveland. The lunch in New York's Plaza Hotel did not go well.

During an afternoon none there will ever forget, all conversation ceased when red-faced and veins-popping Abe exploded at me, demanding to know who the hell did I think I was to criticize Israel? How dare I? And so forth. I responded calmly, knowing by this time that I was not going to change his mind on the subject. The Levys, although they generally agreed with Abe's position, were mortified by his rudeness and ill manner. We made up years later, when Abe and I shared a stage doing a marathon reading of Eli Wiesel's *Night* to benefit the Museum of Jewish Heritage in Lower Manhattan.

Abe won our battle in 2002. After Bethlehem, Arafat, and the Intifada, I did not allow myself to speak of Israel's transgressions on the air with the same courage and frankness that I showed that spring 2002. For one thing, Fox News stopped sending me to the Middle East. In the August 2006 war between Israel and the Lebanese-based Hezbollah, I was not asked to go, and chose not to volunteer. I knew that almost everyone assigned would cover the war from the Israeli side, and that because the IDF made access easy and relatively safe, many desk-jockey anchors would jump at the chance to play war correspondent.

In any event, the fierce border skirmish between Israel and Hezbollah ended inconclusively. One hundred eighteen IDF soldiers were killed in combat in Southern Lebanon. About thirty-five Israeli civilians also died, killed by Hezbollah rockets. The number of casualties on the Lebanese side was far larger, but in no sense was this battle a victory for Israel.

Despite having a force numbering 20,000, the vaunted IDF's failure to destroy Hezbollah led to the collapse of the government of Prime Minister Ehud Olmert and a shakeup in the Israeli army command. If anything, it revealed how powerful the Shiite militia had become, and how vulnerable Israeli civilians living in the north were to attacks by cheap, easily handmade, unguided missiles.

By 2014, in the similarly vicious mini-war in the Gaza Strip against Hamas, the Sunni militia widely considered a terrorist group, Israel was ready for those unguided terror rockets, deploying the American-supplied "Iron Dome" anti-missile system. I covered that deployment of the Iron Dome in Gaza, but that assignment was an exception.

For the ten years beginning in 2002, I focused on the wars raging in Iraq and Afghanistan and seldom visited Israel, except to pass through coming and going from Jordan. I avoided Israel to avoid the "Palestinian Problem" and my conscience. From the encounter with Abe Foxman until relatively recently, the last couple of years really, I muted my public criticisms of Imperial Israel in a way that now feels cowardly.

Chapter 8

FACING TORA BORA

By April 2002, Tora Bora was back in the news. Some of it was good, as several reports and quickie books confirmed our scoop that bin Laden had been there, and had been allowed to escape under the guise of the phony cease-fire.

Unfortunately, I was not getting the credit for the original reporting of his escape, and, worse, I was still getting reamed for faking the friendly fire incident. By avoiding the issue, I had made the situation worse. To the journalistic ruling class, my name was now synonymous with cheater. Sitting in Royal Jordanian Airlines's modest first-class lounge at the Amman Airport, and having just been asked for the umpteenth time by a radio correspondent who was there from another network what "really happened" at Tora Bora, I decided I had to face it.

I went outside and, taking advantage of the fact that Jordan had something Afghanistan and most of the Mideast at the time did not, cell phone service, I called the Chicago home base of the Tribune Company, which owns the *Baltimore Sun.*

Although we had not spoken for a year, my former partner on the successful syndicated talk show and Tribune's chairman Dennis FitzSimons was a trusted friend, and was sympathetic. "What took you so long?" Dennis asked when he got on the line, his voice kind and concerned. He explained that the public pummeling I had been receiving from one of his newspapers troubled him. I made my case to Dennis over the phone that I had made an innocent mistake. He promised to have his corporate ombudsman check out the *Baltimore Sun*'s account, and to do the right thing.

At the urging of that Tribune corporate official, the editors of the *Sun* agreed to hear my side of the Tora Bora story when I returned to the States. I eagerly looked forward to confronting my accusers at the paper. To help prepare my case, I hired Charlie Thompson, one of my best producers from our days together at *20/20*, as my investigator. A gun-toting Vietnam War veteran, Charlie did some great reporting with me for ABC News. He produced our giant hour on Elvis and a series of reports on the lingering effects of Agent Orange on our Vietnam GIs.

We had some rollicking times together, near and far, including a blockbuster fistfight with a mean-spirited Missouri cowboy who was trying to prevent our reporting on the use of Agent Orange as a defoliant on his dioxin-contaminated ranch. When he smashed my camera, I punched him so often in the teeth that my fist got infected. I did the voice-over narration for our subsequent special report on the prevalence of toxic human carcinogen with an IV of antibiotics attached to my arm in Lenox Hill Hospital on New York's Upper East Side.

Our team strode into the conference room at the *Sun* confident that the half dozen or so newspaper executives gathered would soon declare my mistake about the friendly fire incident an innocent one. We were greeted coolly but politely and were allowed to screen our videos, but we may as well have been speaking Pashto. They were not budging. Also, I confess to being disappointed that the video evidence we brought with us did not specifically show the "hallowed ground" where I alleged the friendly fire had happened in Tora Bora.

Although I was sure we had taped it, the scene was not among the tapes we showed the newspaper people. Having only arrived the night before from Israel, and having spent the morning before this confrontation at my daughter Simone's piano recital in New York, I did not have a chance to screen the videos, which Craig and Greg had hurriedly put together upon their arrival home. Of all my self-inflicted wounds, this one takes the cake. My video vindication would wait another fourteen painful years.

We had been refused the chance to talk directly to the *Sun*'s TV critic David Folkenflik, but Charlie Thompson had earlier spoken with Steve Proctor, the paper's assistant managing editor for features and the reporter's immediate superior. Charlie told Proctor that, according to Major Brad Lowell, the spokesman for CentCom, Central Command down in Tampa, there had been between twenty and forty civilian and mujahideen fighters killed by friendly fire on or around December 5, 2001. "We won't agree to the hundreds some are claiming happened that day, but are willing to live with twenty to forty," Charlie quoted Major Lowell, but to no avail.

"DEAR BILL," JUNE 3, 2002

In the case against me, Folkenflik had a single military source, a Pentagon spokesman, Marine Lieutenant Colonel David Lapan, who said there was no friendly fire incident in Tora Bora until December 9. In other words, I could not have confused the friendly fire incident I reported on December 5 with the friendly fire incident in Kandahar that day because there was no friendly fire in Tora Bora until several days after my report. *Sun* editor Bill Marimow wrote me that, "Marine Lt. Col. David Lapan said he did not recall any friendly fire incidents in Tora Bora around December 5, the day before your report."

In a Dear Bill letter pleading my case to Marimow, I wrote on June 3,

> Without belaboring the point, it is crystal clear in retrospect that the *Sun* television critic's reliance on the Pentagon's denial of a specific friendly fire incident in the midst of a raging conflict was at best naive . . . Pentagon denials [of friendly fire] were as routine as they were later proven inaccurate.

There have been many hundreds of friendly fire tragedies in Afghanistan, some documented, some not, that have inflicted widespread death and destruction, straining our relations with the government and putting at risk all the blood shed and treasure spent there. The AC-130 gunship's destruction of the MSF hospital, killing scores in Kunduz in November 2015, was the worst recent example. In my letter to Marimow, I laid out some specific reports concerning Tora Bora during our intensive bombing campaign. This one, from Paul Salopek at the *Chicago Tribune* from December 28, 2001, is typical:

U.S. BOMBS LEAVE WASTELAND . . . FIERCE ATTACKS
ANGER VILLAGERS, RAISE QUESTIONS

According to death tolls gathered from elders in four communities
in the area in recent days, at least 87 farmers *and anti-Taliban soldiers* appear to have died in intense U.S. airstrikes on Tora Bora, the
cave-riddled mountain stronghold of Bin Laden ... For its part, *the
Pentagon at first categorically denied the bombing reports* (emphasis added).

An unnamed Pentagon source told reporters earlier this month
that the attacks "*never happened.*" More recently, however, the U.S.
military has softened that view. "It is certainly possible that there were
civilian casualties who were not Taliban and Al Qaeda that we're not
aware of in Tora Bora," said Colonel Rick Thomas, a spokesman
for the U.S. Central Command in Tampa, the headquarters of the
Afghan campaign.

After reviewing the available articles and screening the videotapes
we provided, editor Marimow did write me privately praising my "courage and grit" getting "to the front line at Tora Bora, and under those
extremely difficult circumstances, I can understand how any reporter
could make a mistake." Further, he assured me that he did not believe I
intended to deceive our audience. Adding, "I personally do not believe
that, despite the erroneous foundation of your story, you intended
to deceive your viewers," but he refused to say so in the pages of his
newspaper.

There was also another piece of evidence that the editor and his folks
chose to ignore as irrelevant. While Greg Hart was taping the killing zone,
he spotted a longish piece of metal in the scorched earth. After he finished shooting, he retrieved the metal shard, which turned out to be shrapnel. It bore US identification, and was later identified as being part of a
two-thousand-pound bomb, clearly dropped by a B-52.

THE *SUN* NEVER RISES, MAY 2002

After a month-long review process, the paper decided not to retract or clar-
ify its report publicly. The paper also insisted that, while it might be unfortunate, it was not responsible for the fact that other critics and journalists

were inferring from the *Sun*'s reporting that I willfully misrepresented the facts, rather than just got the story wrong.

As a result, critics kept piling on. Contrary to Roger Ailes's confident prediction that the story would eventually go away, it showed no signs of doing so. An article in *Variety* in June 2002 tore into me. As I wrote to Kevin Magee, who was Roger's number-two administrator at the time,

> I understand what a pain in the butt my obsession with this Tora Bora controversy is, but it is like cancer to me. My silence on the issue will not help it disappear. In retrospect, I only wish that I had followed my initial instinct to challenge the slanderers earlier. My continuing frustration with the story is that everyone who repeats it, like today's *Variety*, writes as fact that I had been "charged with and found guilty of unethical conduct." Not only is that false, but my principal accuser now says for the record (but not in his newspaper) that I am innocent of it.

The *Variety* story was the type that editor Marimow supposedly found regrettable, but brushed off. "I know that we disagree about whether [our] stories were 'fair' and I believe that we agree that some of the stories in other publications, which followed the *Sun*'s stories, were not fair." But too bad.

Reporter Folkenflik's career flourished, much of it at taxpayer-supported National Public Radio. He was the man who successfully cut Geraldo Rivera and Fox News down to size. In June 2002, he got $10,000 for his efforts, winning the Paul Mongerson Prize for Investigative Reporting on the Media, administered by the Center for Governmental Studies at the University of Virginia.

Adding insult to injury, I found out about the ten-grand prize from Roger, who told me as a "by the way" one afternoon in his office, saying, "Did you hear your boy won an award?" I didn't even know Folkenflik was up for an award. The stay-at-home critic who risked nothing gets the cash prize, while the swashbuckling hero who gave up so much, risking life and limb, gets ridicule. I complained bitterly to Professor Larry Sabato, the well-known television pollster who runs the UVA program, that they could have at least reached out to me for my side of the story. He never responded.

After I simmered down, I had a Eureka! moment. The pending award to Folkenflik was why the *Sun* refused to say publicly what editor Marimow was saying to me privately. It was the fact that their reporter was up for the Mongerson award in the first place that kept editor Marimow from publishing in his newspaper the mitigating words he put in his letters to me. The editor denies the charge.

"A GOOD GIRL?" JUNE 2002

Professionally and personally, I stayed busy after the *Sun*'s devastating 2002 decision. Roger's affection and loyalty to me seemed undiminished by the scandal. Linked at the hip, he named me to the cast of a new, though short-lived, Fox Broadcast Network show called *The Pulse*, hosted by Shepard Smith. It failed after a few episodes, but it got me back on the publicity circuit promoting the program. After I made several appearances, Craig referenced how cheerful I was on tour in comparison with my dour mood since Tora Bora. "I forgot how charming you could be," he said.

On the personal side, Erica and I were swooning over each other hot and heavy, as our improbable relationship careened toward marriage. I used appearances on Jay Leno's *Tonight Show*, Billy Bush's *Access Hollywood*, as well as visits with the funny and charming Regis and Kelly, irreverent Howard Stern, along with Carson Daly and Dennis Miller to introduce Erica—and the notion that we had fallen in love and were going to be spending the rest of our lives together—to the American people.

The only personality to scoff publicly was Joy Behar on *The View*. She was openly scornful and said as much on the air, essentially accusing me of being just another old man who dumps his age-appropriate mate to troll for naive postgrads. Cohost Star Jones was also cold. I do not blame either. Judging from appearances, I was the stereotype. Seventeen years later, no one is skeptical. Joy always remembers Erica's name, and is totally respectful. We love her and Star, cohost Whoopi Goldberg, and, of course, the one and only Barbara Walters, who has withdrawn from the show she created after an incredible career spanning more than sixty years. Dear, diamond-tough Barbara was also passive aggressive when I first brought Erica around. Barbara simply refused to look at my shining star in the green room, even though just a few feet separated them. Nowadays, whenever we see any of them in public, our encounters are marked by kindness and caring.

Those few exceptions aside, even back in the day, most commentators were supportive of the relationship. *Tonight Show* host Jay Leno was especially loving and welcoming. He was so protective that he went so far as to edit out something I said on the show that offended Erica. When he asked on the air about my feelings for her, after telling him how I adored her and bragging on her professional competence, character, looks, and quality, I clumsily said, "She's a good girl."

After the show I found Erica in angry tears in the green room. "What's the matter?" I asked. "A good girl?" was her sharp, pained response. "I'm not your child!" It was our first crisis. I had put my foot in my mouth. Worse, the statement made credible the old man/young lover stereotype. Leno saved me. Back in the Bel Air Hotel as Erica and I watched the taped show airing later that night, we realized that the excruciating scene did not appear. Unprompted by me, Jay had cut the offending phrase out of the interview. He got me off the hook, and I will always appreciate it.

Whenever possible, I used our downtime to bring Erica and the girls together, often on board *Voyager*. On one cruise, I wrote in my journal: "The sail was great. I just love being out there with the crew and the structured casualness and the magnificent vessel. It's the best life. The family reunion went OK once I profusely apologized for breaking the news of our engagement on television, which really was déclassé."

At this point inseparable for twenty-one months except for my travels, Erica and I were hurtling toward permanency. We spent a week with all four kids at our Malibu beach house. Cruz, then fifteen, and Gabriel, twenty-two, were more or less blasé about the unfolding soap opera. Isabella and Simone were OK with Erica, but cautious, skeptical, and embarrassed by the age-inappropriate match. Many of our old friends were regularly ridiculing the age difference, and the preposterous possibility that I was going to add a fifth notch to my tally of marriages. Then stuff really hit the fan when *Page Six*, the notorious gossip column in the *New York Post*, ran the following item:

> You'd think that a cynical old journalist like Geraldo Rivera would
> be out of the marriage stakes after four attempts. But Geraldo, who

covers war and mayhem for the Fox News Channel, is heading for the altar again. His former assistant Erica Levy, 29, is the lucky girl, according to the upcoming issue of *Star* magazine. The supermarket tab says Rivera popped into Harry Winston the other day and put down $280,000 for a five-carat ring. Erica is apparently unaware of what's coming her way because Geraldo is waiting for the right moment in the next week or so to make his formal proposal.

The right moment came on board a flight to Edinburgh, Scotland, on August 21, 2002, where I was to make a major speech about advocacy journalism at the historic city's Fringe Festival. As we snuggled, shortly after takeoff from JFK, I handed Erica the complimentary toilet kit. It contained the big ring, which cost almost ten times more than my modest first home on Avenue C in New York's Lower East Side.

"I just love being out there with the crew and the structured casualness and the magnificent vessel." Winter 2007.

FIFTH TIME'S THE CHARM, AUGUST 2002

When we got home from Edinburgh and our formal engagement was announced, I was distraught. The persistence of the Tora Bora issue convinced me that I would never be free of the emotional load until I proved my innocence of that charge of fakery. Contributing to my fragile emotional state was the fact my accountant was near panic.

From the journal:

> Another emotional rollercoaster all centered around the very public engagement of Erica and me . . . Then there was my psycho breakdown in Scotland over money and age and Erica, then the buildup to the house and party, and the revelation of our finances all going to hell in a hand basket. The nightmare scenario is ending up old and broke. Won't happen of course, but the thought of it is still very unsettling.

Statistically speaking, our coming marriage faced an actuarial bump down the road. At the rate I was spending money, how was I going to provide for my life after television, and for a wife who would survive me by half a century? Putting doubt aside and a smile on my face, I acted the Puerto Rican–Jewish Great Gatsby for the engagement party of the summer. Along with the tents and decorations, I temporarily added two hundred feet to our dock so that a deep-draft ferry could shuttle guests from the West Seventy-Ninth Street Boat Basin in Manhattan across the Hudson to our newly refinished home in Edgewater, New Jersey. It was unfortunately a dark and stormy night, the wickedest August weather in memory. Nevertheless, hundreds attended, including our families and numerous friends and friends-of-friends. Many of my former colleagues at NBC News came, as well as Roger Ailes and the entire Fox News crew, who improbably mixed with Reverend Al Sharpton and others from our earlier lives. I left shortly after the party, bound for Afghanistan.

AKBAR REUNION, SEPTEMBER 2002

Despite my chronic self-indulgence as a younger man, nothing is more important to me than family. My wife, siblings, and children command my unshakeable loyalty. Akbar Shinwari, about five feet seven inches with a mustache over a perennially smiling face, is de facto family, and seeing this cherished friend again was like seeing a too-long-absent brother or son.

I put my life in his hands during the first battles of the never-ending Afghan War and would many times over the years. He came to stay with us in New Jersey, and I knew he could be trusted to keep us safe anywhere on earth that his Sunni Muslim Pashtun cousins held sway.

Akbar gave me a deep and abiding respect for the sincere power of his faith. He had proudly made the Hajj, the ritual pilgrimage to Mecca, several times, and regardless of the state of combat raging, sometimes with bullets zinging around us, he dutifully prayed the requisite five times facing toward his holy city.

On this journey back to Afghanistan to mark the first anniversary of the 9/11 attacks, the worst sneak attacks on America since Pearl Harbor, he knew I had two goals. One was to prove Osama bin Laden could easily have escaped the ridiculously imperfect trap our forces tried to set for him at Tora Bora in December 2001. The other, more personal, was to prove that there were friendly fire casualties where and when we said there were.

We drove the depressingly familiar thirty miles of bad road from Jalalabad, arriving back in Tora Bora, scene of bin Laden's great escape and where my fate as a war correspondent was sealed. It was exactly as we had left it nine months and a lifetime ago. The Arab fighters, their wives, and consorts were gone, but everything else was the same.

The next morning we broke camp and set out first to visit bin Laden's home in Tora Bora. A gigantic bomb had leveled the one-story cement structure, but you can still see how nicely the property is situated, with a swimming pool looking out at the majestic snow-peaked White Mountains and Pakistan beyond.

With widespread doubt still attached even to the issue of whether bin Laden was here when and where I said he was, and how and why he was allowed to escape, my goal on this return as I said was to confirm my reporting once and for all. Using footage from December 2001, I reported:

Not many observers had a better front-row seat to the fight at Tora Bora than we did. We were close enough to get shot at [video showing

With Greg, Craig, cameraman Carl Glogg, and Akbar, who gave me a deep and abiding respect for the sincere power of his faith. March 2003.

ducking and grunting] . . . We were close enough to watch the sound and fury of U.S. airstrikes [video showing boom booms]. We were close enough to witness the advance of our Afghan allies [video] and we were close enough to watch their occasional retreat [video]. And if he was there—and we have still heard no reliable evidence to the contrary—then we think we know when, how, and to where Osama bin Laden escaped.

It is the second week in December 2001 and al Qaeda is on the ropes. We hear them on the radio speaking in Arabic about laying down their arms and surrendering. The U.S. strongly suspects the obvious, that the requested cease-fire is a hoax, a hoax to allow the beaten terrorists some breathing room in which to escape . . . Yet over the objections of Hazrat Ali, the brave Afghan military commander on the scene, local Afghan politicians grant a twenty-four-hour cease-fire, later extending it to thirty-six hours.

So even as our mighty B-52s circle overhead cutting back on their bombardments, and honoring a cease-fire that the U.S. had warned against and does not believe in, many Afghans believe the al Qaeda chief escapes.

Militia commander Hazrat Ali met us on this return to Tora Bora and granted a new interview at the scene, with Akbar translating: "When I found out about the cease-fire, I said to my commanders they just want to betray us."

Here is what the Senate Committee on Foreign Relations reported in November 2009, eight years later: "On or around 16 December 2001, two days after writing his will, bin Laden and an entourage of bodyguards walked unmolested out of Tora Bora and disappeared into Pakistan's unregulated tribal area. Most analysts say he is still there today (2009)."

OSAMA BIN LADEN'S ESCAPE ROUTE
REDUX, SEPTEMBER 10, 2002

If partisan-cheerleader war correspondents like me had had the courage or insight to report it, we would have said that the war in Afghanistan started unraveling almost immediately with bin Laden's escape. As our high-altitude bombers pounded the bunkers and caves thought to be hiding the architect of the 9/11 attacks, he snuck out the back door. As we boasted of "America Triumphant" on live TV, showing the world what real resolve looks like, the mastermind, the world's most-wanted man, just walked away unscathed.

It should have been vexing news, but its impact on American self-esteem was muted by the prevailing "we can do no wrong" patriotism that followed the brutal attacks on the Pentagon and World Trade Center; and by the newness of this war, wars always being popular in the beginning. Buoyed by our counterattack, no one wanted to view bin Laden's escape as anything more than a temporary setback. We will get him. It is just a matter of time.

In my return to Tora Bora in 2002, it was with great pleasure that I pissed on what remained of bin Laden's residence in the rugged but lovely valley. Then, as the crew filmed from the valley floor, I frantically scaled several cliffs, sometimes with Akbar by my side, to peer inside to see whether there was any evidence left behind. I was manic the entire time, restlessly tracking down every lead as to the whereabouts of bin Laden. Here is how we solved the mystery of bin Laden's disappearance in 2002, almost eight years before Congress came to the same conclusion:

"We follow a small river coming down out of the White Mountains of Tora Bora on the lookout for yet-undiscovered al Qaeda hideouts. In a Fox News exclusive we find something else instead. After a three-hour march we discover an ideal escape route out to Pakistan."

If you were around to follow the news from Tora Bora, you heard the refrain on countless talk shows: How could a caravan led by bin Laden, a six-foot-five-inch Arab on kidney dialysis, traveling with his extended family, walk out from under the noses of the world's most formidable military? It was easy. The most formidable military in the world had virtually no soldiers on the ground.

We had that handful of special operators but, as I mentioned earlier, no plan for creating a blocking force, and were utterly incompetent in our plan of action. The United States endured the consequences of bin Laden's escape for years to come. It emboldened his fellow Sunni Muslim extremists and proved that even the vilest crime could be committed against the United States and (for too long) go unpunished.

After our march, I ended the report by reading our location from our handheld GPS device. Our coordinates proved that in just three hours we had walked from the Tora Bora battlefield in Afghanistan across the unmarked, undefended international border into the tribal territory of Pakistan. We could have easily kept marching deeper into Pakistan until we reached a town or city or railroad station and disappeared into the teeming populace, as bin Laden manifestly did. I showed the reading on the GPS to the camera. We were live on *Fox and Friends*.

That would make our position right about here, 070 degrees 11 minutes east longitude, 34 degrees 05 minutes north latitude; that would put us right about here. This white [on the map], this is Pakistan. If we could make it into Pakistan, certainly Osama bin Laden could.

Although the crucial question of Osama's current whereabouts is impossible for us to answer, he clearly had the means and opportunity to make good an escape to Pakistan.

Tora Bora was and remains a rough neighborhood for outsider infidels. As far as I know, no other reporter replicated our relatively simple exercise, exploring the immediate environs. No one picked up on either our original December 2001 reporting of bin Laden's probable escape date or on this September 2002 report of his likely route out. Though every historical account now confirms that our reporting was accurate, even groundbreaking, critics were less interested in bin Laden than they were in taking shots at me, and, through me, at Fox News.

Returning home to the United States, I wrote,

Coming back from Afghanistan, I head home with an almost perfect performance under pressure and duress. It is unusually low pressure, really. Danger is not pressure. Getting close enough to danger is pressure. Weird how Tora Bora still rankles. If only. Yet the only way to remove the stain is by consistent brilliance under fire. And surviving.

In presenting my case to friends and colleagues at Fox News once I got back from this second trip to Afghanistan, I chose a letter addressed basically to all the reporters and producers at our bureaus across the country and abroad.

Despite risking everything in many violent encounters from Afghanistan to Somalia to the Palestinian territories, for the first time in my thirty-two-year career I stood publicly accused of combat chiseling. For war correspondents, there is no graver charge. It has been a humiliating and frustrating experience.

But because we saw what we saw in Afghanistan and taped it, I knew the truth would eventually clear us. And here comes the truth.

Then I described our return to Tora Bora.

RETURN TO HALLOWED GROUND, SEPTEMBER 2002

It was relatively simple to track down eyewitnesses to the widely remembered friendly fire tragedies, including the one that happened during the first week of the critical offensive in December 2001. On the same "hallowed ground" where tragedy struck, I interviewed a twenty-five-year-old fighter named Sheer Ahbad, who described three of the victims on camera with Akbar translating. "They were mujahideen [anti-Taliban fighters]," Sheer Ahbad says on tape.

After taping the interview and doing several live shots during our dramatic hike from Afghanistan to Pakistan, we pulled out. Resentment over the bombings and the disruption from the war, along with a general lawlessness and opposition to authority, made it too dangerous to hang out. But as a trusted insider and member of the dominant Shinwari clan, Akbar had free rein, so I left the task of further evidence-gathering to him, our Afghan brother.

Akbar taped several more interviews with eyewitnesses. One was with another mujahideen fighter with the regal name Sultan Mahmood, a member of the provincial military commander Hazrat Ali's staff. Sultan was one of our guides at Tora Bora during the original December 2001 trip.

The interview was conducted at the Jalalabad Airport where Mahmood was the head of security for the US Special Forces base there. As the tape shows, his US-issued identity card reads, SULTAN/ALPHA COMPANY/1st CORPS/RANK: COMPANY XO/No. 86.

Mahmood told Akbar on tape that he remembered the incident of the mujahideen fighters accidentally killed and injured on the first day of our coverage of the assault on Tora Bora. "They were mujahideen from our side," he recalled. "These people were killed by the B-52 bombing on Tora Bora." Mahmood recommended that Akbar then visit the nearby village of Agam, near the Pakistani border, to speak with other eyewitnesses.

In Agam, Akbar found and later interviewed several, including Sayed Alam and Abdul Sapar, both twenty, and both mujahideen fighters near the front line at the time of the bombing. Sayed recalls during the videotaped interview done at the scene, "This was the front line where we were fighting against Taliban and al Qaeda and we were here when a B-52 dropped a bomb here and three of our mujahideen were killed here and more of them were injured."

Forgive my obsession with this incident, but understand that it is the only time I have been formally accused of faking a wartime report, the one persistent stain on my reputation. It changed my life.

SHOCK, AWE, AND DRINKING HUSSEIN'S BOOZE, BAGHDAD, MARCH 2003

The world's attention was about to leave Afghanistan, despite my feeble efforts to keep it in the headlines. We missed the beginning of the March 2003 Iraq invasion because my team and I were 1,645 miles away in Kandahar, Afghanistan. We were with the First Brigade Combat Team of the Eighty-Second Airborne Division when the Iraq War started with the massive "shock and awe" bombing of Baghdad. I had committed to then-Colonel John F. Campbell, my war buddy and the commander of the Fort Bragg, North Carolina–based First Brigade, that we would cover a major offensive his fighters were waging in Afghanistan against the Taliban. When he was forced to retire in 2016, Campbell had leaped five ranks and was a four-star general, having received the fastest promotions of any other flag officer in decades.

General John F. Campbell retires after a brilliant career that saw him rise from colonel to four-star general in record time. April 2016.

We knew the Iraq invasion was coming, having covered the run-up to the war from nearby Turkey and Cyprus, including the frantic efforts of the International Atomic Energy Agency (IAEA) investigators to prevent it. We gambled that we could wrap the Afghan assignment before the Iraq battle began, but were a week off. The administration of President George W. Bush was beyond eager to launch the Iraq invasion despite only sketchy evidence that Saddam Hussein had weapons of mass destruction. The WMD were only just an excuse to oust the Iraqi dictator, anyway.

Colonel Campbell arranged to have us flown from Kandahar in one of his C-130 cargo planes heading to Kuwait, the staging area for the Iraq invasion. At the sprawling base outside Kuwait City, we loaded our gear onto a flight of Black Hawk helicopters, embedding with the First Brigade of the 101st Airborne Division, Air Assault, the famed Screaming Eagles, at their front-line base in the blowing sands of Iraq's western desert. From there, the Apache attack choppers of the Air Wing of the division were launching furious attacks against Saddam's rapidly deteriorating forces, but not without casualties. Three of the warbirds were lost trying to land in the intense, blowing sand of Iraq's desert.

Preparing to embed with the 101st Airborne Division during
an Iraqi missile attack. Kuwait, March 2003.

As the division and the rest of our massive invasion force swept unstoppably into an upscale suburb of Baghdad, our unit made its camp in the abandoned estate of a cousin of Saddam Hussein. The lush compound had a swimming pool and a private helicopter hidden under a camouflage awning. It also had a full bar, which made the two-day stay particularly luxurious. The Hussein family thus bought this correspondent a few drinks. Funny how many supposedly devout Sunni Muslims, from Morocco to Saudi Arabia, Kuwait, and the Persian Gulf, are some of the biggest party-hearty players on the planet.

As we rested after the grueling sprint across the desert and into the outskirts of the city, then two-star Major General David H. Petraeus, code-named "Eagle 6" and commanding the 101st, visited our company. What I remember most about his demeanor was that he was all business. He led the division into battle from the front, issuing the stirring battle cry of the Screaming Eagles when the war began:

"Guidons, Guidons [Battle Flags, Battle Flags]. This is Eagle 6. The 101st Airborne Division's next Rendezvous with Destiny is north to Baghdad. Op-Ord Desert Eagle 2 is now in effect. Godspeed. Air Assault. Out."

You do not want to mess with this war-fighting man. Despite the suffocating heat and choking dust, General Petraeus's uniform was immaculate, and we watched as he chastised several troopers for not being shaved and for having their uniforms out of order. When one NCO stated mildly defensively that they had just finished a long, hot march, the general shot back, "So have I."

It was clear that Petraeus was going places, and as with eventual-General Campbell, it was an honor to track his meteoric rise from two- to three- to four-stars. In my cluttered Fox News office, which is festooned with memorabilia from far-flung assignments, right next to the dead al Qaeda guy's helmet from Tora Bora, which I never got around to donating to the firehouse because of embarrassment over the controversy, I have an array of signed pictures taken with battlefield commanders I have had the honor of covering, including General Petraeus after he engineered the Surge, which, for a time, vanquished our radical Islamist enemies in Iraq.

The photo was inscribed, "20 October 2010, For Geraldo—With respect and with thanks for sharing hardship and risk with our troopers over many campaigns and many years. Air Assault! Dave Petraeus."

With honored war buddy General John F. Campbell,
"America's Spartan." Baghdad, Iraq, 2007.

Another photo is with the indefatigable warrior I by then had dubbed "America's Spartan," General John F. Campbell. We are standing outside Saddam Hussein's parade grounds in the Green Zone in the battered Iraqi capital, where the general had command during hard, ugly fighting that claimed many GI lives.

Petraeus retired first, leaving the military in 2011 to assume the directorship of the CIA. A year later, our generation's greatest general got into the much-hyped scandal that ended his career. It involved an ill-advised affair (aren't they all?) during which he told tales out of school to his biographer-mistress, Lieutenant Colonel Paula Broadwell. It was stupid and shortsighted on his part, but having often thrown caution to the wind under similar circumstances, I can relate. Boners make boneheads out of the best of us. Petraeus is a great patriot, and his forced resignation was a tremendous loss for the country.

Speaking of hype, let me tell you a bit about my second wartime scandal, the infamous "Line in the Sand." This one generated far more negative press than Tora Bora, but did not bother me nearly as much because

It was clear that Petraeus was going places. Brilliant war fighter. Baghdad 2007.

it was an attack on my judgment, not my character. In broad strokes, as I explained the state of the battle during a live shot from our desert base, I used a stick to draw a map of Iraq in the sand. The purpose was to demonstrate generally where our unit was relative to Baghdad, the Iraqi capital.

Check out the tape of the incident. There was never any actionable intelligence in that crude, stupid map. I would never give away military secrets or put our beloved troops in the field at risk, two of the most frequent and annoying charges at the time. Military experts in studios in New York and Washington, DC, were using far more detailed electronic maps of the unfolding action in real time.

As I said at the time, aside from my dopey drawing of the dumb map in the sand, grossly aggravating my dilemma was the fact that Fox News was engaged at the time (2003) in a publicity war with our desperate cable-news rivals at CNN and especially at then-fading MSNBC, whose parent network, Big NBC, came after me with all PR guns blazing. Remember, I had jilted them by leaving my top-rated show to jump to Fox two years earlier.

It was, as several key participants later admitted, an organized, network-sanctioned "Get Geraldo" campaign, for which, as I said at the time, they used their "neo-Nazi ex-congressman [Joe Scarborough] and psycho ex-sportscaster [Keith Olbermann] as their hatchet men." I promised to beat the hell out of both men when I caught up with them, but never got around to it, although I came close with Scarborough in a Washington, DC, bar while in a tequila haze after one of the White House Correspondents' dinners.

In fairness, their attacks on me were a tit-for-tat for our attacks on them. At the time, our guys were mercilessly mocking NBC's Pulitzer Prize–winning war correspondent Peter Arnett for "giving aid and comfort to the enemy." His sin was granting an unauthorized interview to Iraqi state television in the first few days of our invasion, in which he questioned US policy.

"It is clear that within the United States there is a growing challenge to President Bush about the conduct of the war and also opposition to the war," Arnett told the interviewer. "So our reports about civilian casualties here, about the resistance of the Iraqi forces, are going back to the United States. It helps those who oppose the war when you challenge the policy."

Despite the fact that he was technically correct, the timing and the venue of his interview were indefensible. One of the few Western correspondents reporting live from Baghdad, Arnett was soon cable-news history. Fox News and most congressional Republicans came after him. Former New York senator Al D'Amato accused Arnett of treason in wartime, for which the penalty can be death. Unlike my crude line in the sand, Arnett's sin was not forgiven, and he was summarily fired by NBC.

In June 2005, in describing the overreaction to my incident to Sridhar Pappu, the fine writer for the *Atlantic* magazine, I said,

Attacks like this are more illustrative of the people who hate me than they are in any way of me—because action talks and bullshit walks. That's why I said [then-CNN anchor] Aaron Brown would shit in his pants if he had been in some of the places I was. That's true. That's absolutely true. It's the same way about all of them—every one of those Geraldo detractors. How many times have you been shot at?

Reporter Pappu wrote in that issue of *Atlantic* what I consider the most intellectually honest biographical summary of me, saying,

He is a cultural phenomenon and often, it seems, the punchline to some pop-culture joke. He broke major stories as far back as thirty years ago, and there is no more fearless war correspondent around. This is hard to remember, however, when seeing footage of him having fat from his buttocks injected into his forehead, or contending with brawling neo-Nazis on his talk show, or vainly searching "Al Capone's vault" for two hours on live TV, or promising to personally kill Osama bin Laden, or simply strutting and preening and boasting the way he does.

Some smart, prominent people (Harvard professors, high-powered lawyers, distinguished journalists) who know Rivera well call him brilliant—and yet he can't seem to escape the larger-than-life circus act that is "Geraldo."

Guilty as charged. But there is much to be proud of in the last five decades, like the Willowbrook crusade, which changed the fate of so many of the disabled; my work on behalf of migrant farmworkers, the urban poor, the drug-addicted, the wheelchair-bound, cheated consumers, storm victims; the many televised confrontations with the KKK and racist skinheads; and the fact that few high-profile correspondents have spent more time marching into harm's way alongside members of our military.

I doubt any correspondent has taken more pictures with deployed service members, attended more memorials, fundraisers, and promotion ceremonies, or has pictures alongside GIs later killed in combat sent to me by their families after the tragedy.

WARRIOR JOURNALISTS, NOVEMBER 2003

It has taken several years, but the cynical attitude and skeptical vibe toward me has definitely diminished as I evolved toward senior citizenship. Still, it remains a wound on the body of my career, not the whole run as a larger-than-life persona, but the war reporting specifically. In my case, every accusation of dishonesty is baseless. Whatever you think of my style or grandstanding, no one can deny that over the last four-and-a-half decades I have been around more hostile gunfire from closer up than any other "celebrity" reporter.

In Israel, Egypt, Gaza, the West Bank, the Golan, Sinai, Syria, Egypt, Mexico, Lebanon, Somalia, Sudan, Afghanistan, Pakistan, Iraq, Kosovo, the Philippines, Colombia, Bolivia, Peru, Venezuela, Guatemala, Nicaragua, Libya, and elsewhere, I have always behaved admirably under fire or extreme duress, as gutsy as any war correspondent in the half century beginning in 1973.

I am not alone. In the late War on Terror era (2013–2017), which I played no role in, there were brave beat reporters who matched my earlier exploits, while getting a lot less attention. More recently, women like CNN's Arwa Damon and Clarissa Ward have taken the lead in covering the fight against ISIS in occupied Iraq and especially in the bloody Syrian Civil War, which began in 2014. Because not many American forces were initially involved on the ground, the reporters' superb efforts under fire attracted far less intense public interest than the giddy early days in what we called the War on Terror.

Despite the relative lack of attention, those conflicts are still grinding out death, misery, and refugees as I write three years later, although the end, or rather the latest version of the end, may be in sight. All of Iraq, including Mosul, has been retaken from Islamic State, as was the "capital" of their self-proclaimed Caliphate, Raqqa, Syria, which fell to a U.S.-backed

My fierce face. Iraq, 2007.

alliance in October 2017. There were still scattered pockets of resistance along the Euphrates River, but ISIS no longer exists as a geographic entity.

Let me further amend my statement about having been Top Gun among celebrity reporters, which I define as public personalities whose fame exists beyond the boundaries of the news business, men like Hemingway and Ernie Pyle in WWII, and Dan Rather and Morley Safer in Vietnam. In that exclusive crowd, there is a gutsy chick who is the heir to glamorous World War II icons Oriana Fallaci and Martha Gellhorn. Even after she got brutally assaulted in Tahrir Square, Cairo, in 2011, CBS *60 Minutes*' Lara Logan, a sharp, smart, beautiful woman, also had the biggest balls in the modern war-reporting business, gender ceiling notwithstanding.

I saw her courage up close in Afghanistan. Craig, Greg, and I were riding a few vehicles back in the same military convoy as Lara and her CBS team on November 23, 2003. She was in the lead truck because the military loved her, a lioness's heart with a face from *Vogue* magazine. Our convoy was driving along a desolate dirt road close to the Pakistani border, just below a trouble spot called Lozano Ridge, outside the Shkin base in Paktika Province.

Embedded with the 504 Brigade, 82nd Airborne Division.
Paktia Province, Afghanistan, March 2003.

The ridge had been the scene of several fatal ambushes in recent months. Everybody was on edge, GIs scanning the ridge, fingers on their triggers, when all hell broke loose. I watched as the lead truck Lara was riding in hit an IED. She and her cameraman, who were both riding in the bed of the truck, got tossed as the vehicle was rocked and overturned in the violent blast. The soldier riding in the front passenger seat of the truck lost his leg as the wrecked vehicle rolled and twisted.

Cameras rolling, Craig, Greg, and I ran toward the truck; the GIs that formed a protective circle around the wreckage were unleashing furious suppression machine-gun fire aimed at the ridge above. Lara, her cameraman, and David Rohde, a *New York Times* reporter who had been traveling in a second vehicle, were sheltering in a huge hole blown in the road by a previous explosion. (A two-time Pulitzer Prize winner, Rohde was later captured by the Taliban, and dramatically escaped after nine months of captivity.) As we taped the wounded GI being evacuated by helicopter, I interviewed Lara, who gave a breathless, but otherwise incredibly calm, professional account of what happened when the bomb blew up under her. When it became apparent that her camera had been smashed in the blast and that she had no tape of her own near-death experience, I offered to provide her all the footage we shot of

At Shkin Base, "The evilest place in Afghanistan." Paktika Province, November 2003.

her harrowing ordeal. She accepted gratefully, later using our video in
her report for CBS News.

As long as I'm acknowledging ballsy colleagues, there's also ABC's
Pentagon correspondent Martha Raddatz, who broke the news in 2006
that bin Laden's main man in Iraq, Abu al-Zarqawi, had been killed; and
CBS correspondent Kimberly Dozier, who was brutally wounded in an
IED attack that same year in Baghdad. She fought her way back to health
and work. She reports now for the *Daily Beast* and I ran into her when we
shared a military C-130 relief flight down to hurricane-stricken Puerto
Rico in 2017. Others include NBC's excellent Richard Engle, who came
to fame by getting to Mesopotamia as a freelancer and sticking it out as
war started all around him in Iraq in 2003. Now he's the network's chief
foreign correspondent. CNN's Ben Wedeman, like my excellent Fox News
friends and colleagues Steve Harrigan, Christian Galdabini, and Rick Leventhal, is cool, unflappable, and deeply impressive. Ben also speaks Arabic. I give kudos as well to CNN's Anderson Cooper, who despite his
status, high style, wealth, and fame, often went the extra step toward peril
to get the story, as in the Cairo uprising of 2011.

In front of a Humvee severely damaged in an IED attack.
Paktika Province, Afghanistan, November 2003.

A THOUSAND MILES OF BAD ROAD, MARCH 2004

Having covered war during five different decades, I subscribe heartily to what British prime minister and serial war hero Winston Churchill said about surviving close combat: "Nothing in life is so exhilarating as to be shot at without result."

That is why soldiers go to war. Everyone thinks the other guy is the one who is going to get shot, not you. To quote perhaps our greatest World War II fighting general, George S. Patton, who said before leaving North Africa to begin the invasion of Nazi-occupied Sicily in 1943, "I want you to remember that no bastard ever won a war by dying for his country. He won it by making the other poor, dumb bastard die for his country. We want you alive!"

Thankfully, while my brother, Craig, and other brothers-in-war like Greg Hart have endured hardship, loneliness, and danger at my side in combat, in my forty-eight years as a television correspondent, my crewmates suffered only a single combat injury. In 2004, one of my drivers was wounded when our convoy was ambushed outside Mosul, Iraq.

Ambushed in Mosul. Our driver Hussein took a bullet in the arm. Probably a ricochet. Iraq, 2004.

We were taping an action-packed, hour-long Fox News special report called *A Thousand Miles of Bad Road*, which chronicled a perilous tour of war-ravaged Iraq from south to north, bottom to top. We began on the Kuwait border in the southern city of Basra and made our way north through the tense Shiite strongholds of Najaf, Karbala, and Sadr City, to the Sunni Triangle towns of Ramadi and Fallujah.

In Fallujah, we videotaped a pickup truck filled with dead bodies in the same community where eleven years later bloody battles were still being fought. As I reported on February 15, 2004, "Tension was razor sharp near the embattled Fallujah police station. Evidence of day-old violence was everywhere, following a guerrilla raid that took the lives of twenty-two cops, left others wounded and dazed, and resulted in a jail-break that freed dozens of anti-government prisoners . . . Still, they put up a hell of a fight, as indicated by the four dead attackers piled in the back of a police pickup truck, bound soon for coalition headquarters in Baghdad. This is the grim carnage, the reality of what happens, this is what Iraq looks like far too often."

Few journalists saw more death than our team in those years 2001–2012. Because I saw my role as part goodwill ambassador, I gave these battered Iraqi cops in Fallujah a pep talk. As I noted at the time, "Because under those circumstances it took guts and grit to stand and fight and not to cut and run, I let these men know how they earned my enduring respect." I exhorted the dispirited government cops through our translator: "Tell them we appreciate their courage. They are brave fighters, fighting for a free, independent Iraq. Don't be discouraged by this, don't let them frighten you away."

After a few days of high-tension work in and around then deadly, dangerous Baghdad, we continued north, making a stop in Saddam Hussein's hometown of Tikrit on the historic Tigris River. There we met General Ray Odierno for the first time. Big, bold, bald, and confident, he was then the newly anointed two-star commander of the Army's Fourth Infantry (Iron Horse) Division, the crew Hemingway attached himself to in the fighting around the Ardennes in 1944, submachine gun in hand.

Odierno was an aggressive war fighter in the heartland of the Sunni resistance in the early days of the Iraq War, and he was a far more realistic administrator than our charismatic ambassador-dud, Paul Bremer, a Yale-educated Yankee who made the disastrous decision to dismantle the Iraqi Army after the invasion, thereby destroying the one integrated Iraqi entity that might have prevented the nation's vicious spiral into chaos and anarchy. As Bremer scrambled desperately to keep Iraq from unraveling, I was in his office when he handed a shady-looking Sunni sheik a suitcase jammed with Benjamins, as in fresh, stacked $100 bills. I did not see him get a receipt.

General Odierno, on the other hand, had supervised the efforts of his First Brigade Combat Team to capture Saddam hiding in a rabbit hole near his hometown of Tikrit. We watched, over the years and through many interviews, as Odierno ultimately became the four-star Army chief of staff before his retirement in 2015.

Leaving him, we headed up to the Kurdish communities of Kirkuk and Erbil, until we finally met our near-death experience in Mosul, the northern Iraqi city that is a perfect example of how frustrating the wars against militant Islam have been for the United States. Even back then in 2004, I said of the city, "Mosul is a former Saddam stronghold, overwhelmingly Sunni Muslim. Former regime elements are still strong here." They were strong enough to capture the city and surrounding countryside. Between 2014 and July 2017, thirteen years after the incidents described here, ISIS controlled Mosul. Iraq's second-largest city was recaptured from the militants only after months of ferocious fighting that left much of it in ruins.

General Raymond T. Odierno, retired chief of staff of the Army. June 2015.

Our destination in 2004 was the big base in the city that had recently headquartered the legendary 101st Airborne Division (Air Assault) when it was under the command of one of our best-ever warriors, the afore-mentioned General David Petraeus. After he received a big promotion to three stars and the division was redeployed back to Fort Campbell, on the Kentucky-Tennessee border, the Mosul base was taken over by a smaller and much less effective fighting force out of Washington State called Task Force Olympia, centered on the relatively new and untested Stryker Brigade.

We were en route to an interview with the task force commander, Brigadier General Carter F. Ham. Later in his career, General Ham was commander of all our forces in Africa during the time of the tragic 2012 attack on our consulate in Benghazi, Libya. He is a good guy, charming and charismatic. Back then he was working hard to get the kinks out of his just-deployed unit.

Among their Herculean tasks was to make sense of the new multi-wheeled, but lightly armored, Stryker combat vehicle, from which the brigade took its name. Ultimately, it proved not up to the task of deal-ing with the wickedly powerful improvised explosive devices, the IEDs that wreaked havoc on our forces, and which required the much heavier Mine-Resistant Ambush Protected (MRAP) vehicles to defeat. Ham had the additional task of getting the Sunni tribal leaders to respect him. Unlike Petraeus, who exerted a tremendous authority over the wily sheiks, Ham had no such status among the tribesmen, many of whom would later turn on the United States and support the ISIS occupation.

As we approached the base, Craig and I were riding in the backseat of a hardened SUV that was just behind our security guys leading our four-vehicle convoy. Hardened means it was armored strongly enough to deflect most bullets, but not anything bigger. A rocket-propelled grenade (RPG), for example, would tear it to shreds.

Picked by a bushwhacker as the highest-priority target, our vehicle was suddenly hit by fourteen shots on Saturday morning, February 28, 2004. Each shot from what was probably an AK-47 felt like a hammer blow on the armored doors and bulletproof windows. We got most of the incident on tape. In those days Craig and Greg both drove around holding a digital camera in their laps, fingers on the trigger.

"Roll tape!" I yelled to Craig, unnecessarily. He was already rolling as the rounds smacked into the SUV. Then I said breathlessly to Craig's camera:

Craig caught the attack on camera. "Roll tape!" I yelled to Craig, unnecessarily.
He was already rolling as the rounds smacked into the SUV. Mosul, Iraq. 2004.

"We've been hit. Ladies and gentlemen, we have just been attacked. We've just been sniped. We've been hit! Go, go, go! We've been attacked. We've been hit."

After scrambling a few blocks to reassemble our convoy, I got through on the security guard's radio to the US base, "We've been hit as we were about to enter your base. We have a wounded man. Our driver has been wounded. We're going into the university area; can you give us instructions?" Not getting a reply, we pulled into what seemed a safer area. As I reported, "Seeing the four-man security detail guarding the university hospital, we pulled behind their strong gate to await help from the Army base nearby."

Then on camera: "Now, we're inside the grounds of the university hospital. There are cops here, situation relatively stable. Actually, we've got a good place because we've got that injured driver also. He's been hit in his left shoulder and hand. Right wrist possibly fractured."

Aside from tending to our wounded man, the first thing we did when we were safe was to screen Craig's tapes. "He got the shots," Greg confided with quiet jubilation after seeing that Craig had captured seven of the fourteen bullet impacts on tape. As I said quoting Churchill earlier, there is no greater sense of satisfaction for a war correspondent than surviving close calls. I reacted by smoking a cigar offered by cameraman Carl Glogg and strutting around like I was General Patton.

Protected by fate, our armor plating, and good luck, we suffered just that lone casualty, our longtime driver and friend, forty-year-old Hussein Ali Farhan. He was driving the unarmored equipment bus behind us when he was hit by a single shot, maybe a ricochet off the side of our vehicle. The round pierced his right shoulder, running down his arm and fracturing his wrist before exiting his body.

"Who loves you, baby?" I kidded Hussein, as our security guys stopped the bleeding and stabilized his wound. Then after puffing on that celebratory cigar, I did a show-and-tell describing how the rounds had struck our vehicle.

They [the bullets] came sweeping down, obviously on this side. The shot—this is the first shot. I heard the first shot. It hit here—then the bullets—got in front of us, turned back, sprayed us again—then he—then he went to the next vehicle. Which has—the glass is not bulletproof, it punctured his [Hussein's] window and put the rounds into the glass. We're OK. Thank God. Thank God.

Pointing where bullets struck our armored vehicle, which
likely saved our lives. Mosul, Iraq, 2004.

We later pried out the crushed bullets and kept them as souvenirs. Hussein was fine after being treated at the then-still-functioning university hospital, never losing his good nature as we completed our taping at Task Force Olympia and eventually made our way out of Iraq via Turkey, eighty long miles away.

I personally drove our SUV for the rest of the journey, resolved that if we came under fire again I would use our hardy, now-tested bulletproof vehicle to squash any attacker. Typically, no other media picked up the story of the breathtaking, caught-on-tape ambush. I said bitterly at the time, "Imagine if this had happened to any other network correspondent?"

After a few days home, I wrote in my journal, "Coming back from Iraq after that violent trip, filled with death and still stunned by the attack in Mosul, I went through an unprecedented decompression. I was in shock, my bravado stripped, nerves shaken. It was deeply unsettling." Again, in retrospect, I am fortunate that my wild post-9/11 reporting did not get Craig or Greg or somebody else killed along the way.

NEW YORK HARBOR, SEPTEMBER 2004

A steadfast friend from our initial meeting in Afghanistan in November 2001, Dr. Abdullah Abdullah, a man of impeccable character I described earlier, is one I continued to rely on to get a firm, fair idea about the war and his nation's progress. Sadly for him and Afghanistan, neither has gone well. In fact as I write this, more than sixteen years after our war in Afghanistan began, the nation totters on the brink. The Taliban is resurgent and the future bodes ill. President Trump has authorized a mini-surge to reverse the downward slide, but I don't expect his efforts to do more than prolong the endless fight.

Several years after we met in Panjshir Province, I had the pleasure of hosting Dr. Abdullah in New York. By then representing his nation as foreign minister, which is comparable to our secretary of state, he was in town to attend the United Nations General Assembly of 2004.

I picked him up by boat at the West Seventy-Ninth Street Boat Basin in Manhattan, and, with brother Craig and Greg Hart, took the foreign minister on my well-practiced tour of New York Harbor. It is a boat ride I have done so many times, I consider the harbor my backyard and

buoy and navigational marker. Tugboat crews and police and
.rd personnel wave friendly greetings when they see my familiar boat *elle*, an old thirty-six-foot Hinckley, a stylish but modest vessel,
which is a cross between a traditional Maine lobster boat and a classic,
varnished-wood runabout.

In *Belle* I gave Dr. Abdullah my "Why We Fight" harbor tour, which
since 9/11 includes stops at the Statue of Liberty and Ground Zero in
Lower Manhattan. I later gave an on-camera version of the same tour
during *Celebrity Apprentice*, narrating the highlights and capping the task
by yelling, "Screw the terrorists! We have rebuilt the Trade Center bigger
and bolder than ever!"

The NYPD freaked when we told them the Afghan foreign minister
had accepted my invitation to tour the harbor. They assigned a police
boat to shadow our cruise after reminding me that Dr. Abdullah was a
"Class One Target" for terrorists. Our boat ride ended with dinner with
Erica at our home on the Hudson River near the George Washington
Bridge. We catered it from the local Afghan restaurant on nearby River
Road.

After being twice cheated out of the presidency of his country, Dr.
Abdullah has served as chief executive of the Islamic Republic of Afghanistan since 2014. The position is a kind of co-presidency. He, at the highest
level, and more modestly, other solid friends like Akbar in the middle, represent the best of Afghanistan. Unlike the more outwardly sophisticated
Iraqis or Iranians, the down-to-earth Afghans I have met are fiercely loyal
and reliable friends, but they are captives of their history.

Despite Abdullah's unfailing honesty, courage, and patriotism, political cronyism and endemic corruption, plus the spreading cancer of Sunni
Muslim extremism and the undefeated Taliban's eternal war on women
and modern life, all conspire to keep the country stuck in the fifteenth
century. The population rejects outside ideas instinctively. That cultural
and now harsh religious intransigence drained the energy of Alexander,
and of the Persian, Sikh, British, and Soviet empires, and will do the same
to ours if we over-commit to trying to change it. Afghanistan will break
President Trump's heart as it has all the others'.

PETER JENNINGS'S LAST PATROL, IRAQ 2005

Because of my own experiences with the Tora Bora controversy and the "line in the sand" in Iraq, among other professional crises, I had some sympathy for NBC anchor Brian Williams when he got into that jam for puffing war tales. As I mentioned earlier, he spoke repeatedly about how his helicopter had been hit by enemy rocket fire, when the RPG had actually hit another helicopter from the unit. Despite that obvious unforced error, you should know that Brian is a brave reporter. Notwithstanding his unfortunate exaggeration, he had the guts to be in Iraq during the most dangerous period, pre-Surge, when we were losing three or four or more GIs a day.

We shared a flight on a C-130 military transport plane from Baghdad to Mosul during 2005, a really violent year when the insurgency made flying truly perilous. Our aircraft was forced to execute extreme evasive action, banking sharply to the left after takeoff following an incoming missile alert. We were fine, but I am just saying those were bad times, and he was there, unlike most of his critics.

Also on board that flight, coincidentally, was ABC News anchor Peter Jennings, who at this point in his distinguished career rarely made his way to the front lines. As senior men, Peter and I sat in the cockpit jump seats. Brian sat with the crews and GIs in the main cargo compartment. Before boarding, Brian and I had a whispered conversation about how nice Peter was behaving to everyone, signing autographs for the crew and being extremely gracious to all the soldiers and to us. Since he was often overly formal and stuffy during the fifteen years I worked with him at ABC News, his egalitarian behavior now was as refreshing as it was unexpected.

Not long after that trip, back home in summer 2005, Peter died of cancer, and I wondered if he knew he was sick while in Baghdad, and whether that influenced his mellow mood and gracious conduct.

Hopefully, by the time you read this, Brian Williams's career will have been restored. Although he necessarily lost his big anchor job at *NBC Nightly News* to Lester Holt, who by the way is terrific, Brian made a good start at rehabilitation at MSNBC with his skilled, professional election coverage in 2016. Subsequently, in 2017 Brian got his own show on MSNBC called *The 11th Hour* (and his scandal became small potatoes compared to what happened to Matt Lauer and the other men drummed out for sexual harassment), but everyone makes mistakes. It is easy to puff, brag, and misremember a y, especially in a barroom retelling. But the shaming that accompanies innocent puffing in this one area can be disproportionately egregious.

One extreme example from 1996 involves the Chief of Naval Operations, Admiral Jeremy Borda. The first CNO to rise from the enlisted ranks, he killed himself after a *Newsweek* reporter questioned why he was wearing two Combat Distinguishing Devices from Vietnam that were not earned. I mention Borda's suicide because, at times during the Tora Bora scandal, as I said, I contemplated my own. If you hear some snot savaging someone you trust, remember what Teddy Roosevelt said: "It is not the critic who counts; not the man who points out how the strong man stumbles, or where the doer of deeds could have done them better. The credit belongs to the man who is in the arena . . ."

VINDICATION, THE LOST TAPES, MAY 11, 2016

As I was about done writing an early draft of this book in May 2016, before the harassment furor at Fox over Ailes and O'Reilly, I asked Greg Hart to have one more go at our video libraries to see if there was anything from Tora Bora that we might have missed. Although nowadays most news cameras are digital, with archives stored in the cloud, we still keep a vast archive of all the pre-digital field tapes. The storehouse also contains random memorabilia, such as the studio chair the racist skinhead used to break my nose in 1988.

Now fifty-two, Greg has worked with me since the day thirty years ago he graduated Fordham University in the Bronx. Erica, Craig, and I attended his wedding to Andrea at their new home on John's Island, South Carolina, in June 2017. As his brother said during his wedding toast, "Here's to the last never-married straight guy in South Carolina." With the tightly built body of a jockey, Greg is a perpetual-motion machine who has an understated way of delivering good news, like when he told me that Craig had captured on tape the bullets hitting our car during the Mosul ambush of 2004.

This time, Greg told me that he had found previously untouched outtakes from Tora Bora from the days in question, December 5 and 6, 2001. It was like the past decade and a half of cloudy skies parted and the glorious sun shone through. My life was redeemed. On May 12, 2016, I sent the following email to former *Baltimore Sun* editor William Marimow and former Pentagon spokesman Colonel David Lapan, to then Fox attorney Dianne Brandi, Fox executive Bill Shine, and to my immediate Fox supervisor back in 2001, John Moody. Later that day I sent it to television critic David Folkenflik himself.

From: Rivera, Geraldo
Sent: Thursday, May 12, 2016 9:14 AM
To: Marimow, William; David.Lapan.com; Moody, John; Brandi, Dianne
Cc: Shine, Bill; Rivera, Geraldo
Subject: Urgent: Lost Tapes Found

Gentlemen and Lady,

In vetting the final draft of the manuscript for my war memoir, we found the raw tapes in storage from Tora Bora from 5–6 December 2001. Those tapes belie the then *Baltimore Sun* reporter David Folkenflik's destructive characterization of my work as fraudulent. They also disprove then Pentagon spokesman Lt. Colonel David Lapan's statement that there were no incidents of friendly fire until 9 December 2001 in Tora Bora. Obviously in the heat of combat Pentagon statements on friendly fire have been wrong before, at least until corrected by the facts. I herein offer you the facts of what I saw and reported.

In your defense, it does not appear that we presented these tapes to you when we visited the offices of the *Baltimore Sun* on 15 May 2002 in the vain attempt to prove to you that I made an honest error rather than intentionally reported that I was somewhere I wasn't. What we presented to you that day 14 years ago was what we *aired* on Fox News. The following on camera statements were *never aired*. Obviously, since I present them to prove my statement that I witnessed the immediate aftermath of an incident of friendly fire in Tora Bora on 5–6 December, the fact they never aired is irrelevant.

Since we had two cameras rolling, the incident is captured on both the camera operated by Greg Hart, and a second camera operated by Craig Rivera.

Late on 5 December local time, as the tapes which we have now recovered and which are available for viewing show, I reported on both cameras as we walked across a battlefield in No Man's Land:

(51:25 in on HART #16 tape)
(12:18 in on CRAIG #22 tape)

That smoke over the rise is from our air strikes, you can tell that these guys are a little edgy about getting on the other side of this thing (indicating the nearby ridge. A bomb hits nearby as I speak, the explosion is caught on tape). They don't want another repetition of friendly fire, the forces are so fluid, they are moving so quickly it is almost impossible I would imagine for U.S. Central Command to know exactly where the good guys are. They are moving. They are sweeping.

Early on 6 December local time (and before the appearances that doomed me to a decade and a half of ridicule), I report the following graphic scene on both cameras:

(22:14 in on HART #17 tape)
(47:58 in on CRAIG #22 tape)

This devastated moonscape here is where at least one incident involving friendly fire happened. There are the bits and pieces of Mujahedeen uniforms, even body parts. It's obvious that some American bombs were dropped here, inadvertently. I told you how fast the Mujahedeen were advancing. The intelligence back at the Central Command simply could not keep up with it. This is the result, a tragic accident of war; a warrior's worst nightmare, death by friendly fire.

The shards of body parts and the shreds of clothing are clearly visible in the huge bomb craters. Then, on tape, I said the prayer, the reporting of which I was widely mocked as being fraudulent.

(48:49 in on CRAIG #22 tape)

Our Father who art in heaven hallowed be thy name. Thy kingdom come, thy will be done, on earth as it is in heaven. Give us this day our daily bread and forgive us thy trespasses as we forgive those who trespass against us. And lead us not into temptation, but deliver us from evil, for Thine is the power and glory forever, Amen.

It is on tape. Then I do another on camera, which says,

> *(57:55 in on CRAIG #22 tape)*
>
> So the butcher's bill is in for today's fighting, three Muja-hedeen fighters killed, two wounded, but they ended up killing nine, they killed nine of their enemies, al Qaeda. Now they have come down off of the mountain. They have called in air strikes to get rid of some of the Rats Nest up there, so they have come down off of the mountain to avoid any of those terrible friendly fire incidents. So from Tora Bora, the Rats Nest itself, and the battle raging around it, I'm Geraldo Rivera, Fox News.

It is on tape. We are ready, willing and able to show these tapes to anyone you suggest. I will follow any timely instructions you have to allow you to view these tapes. I want you to admit what these tapes prove, that you made an honest mistake in portraying me as dishonest.

Please pass this message to David Folkenflik. I await a response from all of you. If you would like to designate anyone, including a forensic expert, to come to Fox News to screen these tapes please so indicate as soon as possible.

Thank you,

Geraldo Rivera

Neither of them answered, not former Pentagon spokesman Colonel David Lapan nor editor Bill Marimow. Speaking for Fox News, attorney Dianne Brandi was generally supportive, but cautioned against my counting on my antagonists suddenly reversing themselves. Folkenflik, to whom, as I said, I sent his own copy of the message, and much of whose career since December 2001 has been based on this lie, did say he was interested in seeing the lost video from Tora Bora, but has not been heard from since.

Marimow and Folkenflik gave lame statements to *Page Six* of the *New York Post*, standing by their stories, but have otherwise remained silent and have not responded to my request to have our grievance arbitrated by a panel of journalism-school students.

The awful irony is that I am bringing this long-dead incident back from the grave of obscurity. My obsession with it is probably more interesting to most than whatever happened at the time. But I could not let this black mark go unchallenged for the obituary writer at the *New York Times* or Wikipedia to gloat over when I'm gone.

Chapter 9

GERALDO OF ARABIA

Although it hurts worst, my work as a war correspondent was not the only aspect of my long career subjected to ruthless criticism and unfounded allegations. Hurricanes Harvey, Irma, and Maria raked Texas, Florida, and the Caribbean in 2017, causing uncountable misery and devastation, but the granddaddy of them all was Hurricane Katrina in 2005. It was the deadliest, most-costly natural disaster of the modern era. Sent down to New Orleans five days after the Category 5 killer storm crashed ashore, we arrived to find a city flooded and many of the 1,245 dead still uncollected.

Craig, Greg, and I set out into the flooded, ruined Ninth Ward of the city, where we watched as rescue workers evacuated stranded residents. We later set up our live shot in front of the otherwise ruined Convention Center, which was at least on higher ground with an intact roof under which the refugees from the storm were seeking shelter. I remembered the center from the glory days of my talk show when it hosted the NAPTE (National Association of Television Program Executives) conventions, during which I did deals and partied with syndicators. Remembering those extravagant times in this building in this city made this horrible, grim time even worse. The other intact structure, the Louisiana Superdome, was similarly ravaged, wet, and inadequate in the chaotic aftermath of the epic storm.

The shocked and shattered residents were not being fed. There was no child care, no medical supplies. The situation was desperate. The worst thing was that the mostly black and poor residents were being prevented from leaving the city. There were roadblocks on all the main bridges and highways leading out. The white suburbs were insistent that this poor, black, hungry horde not be allowed to enter their towns and neighborhoods.

The reaction to the relief effort in New Orleans broke down along strictly partisan lines. Republicans and many of my Fox News colleagues publicly supported the Bush administration. Democrats were vehement in their criticism of what was clearly an unfocused, incompetent, even racist response. But those who expected my friend, Fox News anchor Shepard Smith, or me to toe any political line were to be quickly disabused of the notion.

Standing astride the blockaded elevated highway out of town, Shep was wickedly critical of the grossly inept FEMA, Federal Emergency Management Agency, and the Bush administration. My criticism was equally blistering. Choked with emotion and surrounded by destitute mothers and children, I said to anchor Sean Hannity:

Geraldo Rivera: Sean, I can't emphasize what Shep just said enough. He said it exactly right. There's no earthly answer that anyone can understand to why these people after six days are still in this filthy, filthy miserable Convention Center. Why are they still here? This is the freeway here. I tell you what I would have done. And what I would still do. I would say let them walk out of here! Let them walk away from the filth. Let them walk away from the devastation; let them walk away from the dead bodies in here.

I'm telling you, Sean and Alan, this is . . . you cannot deny that it is six days since this natural disaster befell New Orleans. What has happened since is as bad or worse than what Mother Nature did. It's just . . . I mean I can't understand it. I've only been here in Louisiana for less than a day. I left New York yesterday, but coming to the Convention Center, it is as if time stopped. It's as if I'm back and it's Wednesday.

I saw Fox News on Wednesday and people were here at this building, the Convention Center, saying, "Get us outta here. Help us; help us," and now it's forty-eight hours after that and the people are still here . . . They're all still here. Why is that? God, I wish I knew. I wish someone would tell me. Where are the buses? There are so many buses but they're all still here.

Why is that? Look at this . . . look at this little baby. So many little babies. [I pick up a baby.] How old is this baby?

Mom: Sixteen months, okay.

Geraldo Rivera: Sixteen months, okay . . . I got a baby. [My daughter Sol was one month old at the time. I start crying as I hold the child.] You know, I have a baby. You see, there are so many babies here . . . it's just not . . . I mean it's just not . . . it's not, you know . . . it's not a question of objectivity; it's a question of reality. This is . . . how do . . . I don't, I don't know, man.

Let them walk out of here. Let them walk the hell out of here. Let them get on that interstate and walk out, walk someplace. Walk to the Wal-Mart on the other side of the river. Walk to some other town. Walk someplace where you can help 'em. What you got here is thousands of thousands of people who have desperate, desperate needs six days later. These people are still in the same clothes. Where do you think they go to the bathroom? They don't wash their hands; they don't wash their face . . . these babies. What the hell? It's, it's, it's . . .

Shepard Smith: They won't go anywhere because I'm standing right above that Convention Center, and what they've done is they've locked them in there. The government said you go here and you'll get help, or you go to that Superdome and you'll get help and they didn't get help. They got locked in there. And they watched people get killed around them and they watched people starving and they watched elderly people not get any medicine. And now they know it is happening because we've been telling them.

At that point, enraged that Shep and I were excoriating the Bush administration's bungled response to the crisis in New Orleans, Roger pulled the plug on my coverage for the night. He later told me, "Passion is one thing. Incitement is another." I suspected Roger's reason was bogus, and my passion totally appropriate under the extraordinary circumstances of Hurricane Katrina. He was being protective of his longtime friend President George W. Bush. "We did a 4.9 rating that night," Hannity recently confided, "but Roger hated your coverage." I kept my mouth shut until the next morning when I was allowed back on the air to celebrate the arrival of the US military into the city. They began mass evacuations and bailed out the grossly incompetent FEMA and its administrator, the hapless Michael Brown, who soon resigned.

The otherwise pleasant and engaging president failed utterly in his role as Healer-in-Chief. To add insult to injury, Bush 43 did not cut short his vacation on his Crawford, Texas, ranch. His only visit to the devastation wrought by the worst hurricane in US history was to overfly New Orleans in Air Force One en route back to Washington, DC.

Cruel comparisons were soon drawn between his apparent lack of compassion for the poor black folks of New Orleans, compared with his lavish generosity toward the more upscale victims of the hurricanes that had hit his brother Governor Jeb Bush's Florida the year before. Kanye West sealed the Republicans' defeat in the next year's midterm elections when he said, "Bush doesn't care about black people."

By not following the company line, and with our unflinching coverage of the meteorological, human, and political disaster in New Orleans, Shep Smith and I saved the honor of Fox News.

After our tour of duty ended in New Orleans, Craig, Greg Hart, and I drove up to Baton Rouge, the battered state capital, to assess the belatedly mobilizing rescue effort. During an interview with Hannity for his radio show, my friend Sean blindsided me, asking about an article in that day's *New York Times,* which I had not yet read. Sean told me the article alleged I had staged my coverage. It was devastating and outrageous. Specifically, the paper's chief television critic, Alessandra Stanley, wrote that I had "nudged" an Air Force rescue worker out of the way so I could appear a hero, carrying an elderly nun to safety from the storm.

Here is what Stanley wrote: "Fox's Geraldo Rivera did his rivals one better: yesterday, he nudged an Air Force rescue worker out of the way so his camera crew could tape him lifting an older woman in a wheelchair to safety."

I was furious, sputtering as I told Sean it was a total lie. And I was hellbent on proving it. As soon as our team returned to New York, we made all the video from the incident available to the newspaper's editor,

Bill Keller, and demanded a retraction. Despite the unequivocal video evidence, Keller and company refused to correct their patent error. That did not sit well with the paper's own public editor, Byron Calame, however, who decided after receiving dozens of complaints from readers, some of whom were not particularly fans of mine, that the paper was being unfair.

In a column headlined, "Even Geraldo Deserves a Fair Shake," after saying that "one of the real tests of journalistic integrity is being fair to someone who might best be described by a four-letter word" (which is a hell of a way to begin a correction), Calame concluded that "the *New York Times* flunked such a test in rejecting a demand by Geraldo Rivera of Fox News for correction of a sentence about him in a column by the paper's chief television critic.

"My viewings of the videotape—at least a dozen times," continued Calame, "including one time frame by frame—simply doesn't show any 'nudge' of any Air Force rescuer by Mr. Rivera . . . a nudge is a fact, not an opinion. And even critics need to keep facts distinct from opinions."

The bottom line is that even the newspaper of record has its own good guys and bad guys when covering people in the news, and it is willing to abandon any pretense of objectivity and fairness when it suits its political agenda. The distorted way the paper covered Donald Trump during the 2016 presidential election and the way it covers him now that he is president proves beyond a doubt the *NYT* is exactly what it criticizes Fox News for being: partisan. They hate the 45th president, and the feeling is mutual.

The paper and its rival the *Washington Post* also hated Richard Nixon. The difference between Tricky Dick and The Donald four decades later is Fox News. If Fox News had been around in 1972–73 to defend Nixon and savage his critics, the thirty-seventh president would never have been forced to resign. Just as I helped save Bill Clinton during impeachment by berating his nemesis Ken Starr night after night on CNBC's *Rivera Live*, formidable Sean Hannity would have wrapped his arms around Nixon and battled Woodward and Bernstein to a draw.

INCONVENIENT TRUTH, 2006

In the early years at Fox News, I was often asked whether I regretted leaving NBC to go to work for a network whose politics and philosophy are so different from my own. My answer was and remains that I am the same person, true to the same values I have always had. Some remain skeptical. One particular incident still rankles.

In the summer of 2006 as I was entering the Fox News World Headquarters on Avenue of the Americas, I ran into former vice president Al Gore and former *Saturday Night Live* comic Al Franken, who had not yet announced that he was leaving comedy to run for the United States Senate from his home state of Minnesota. Franken would narrowly win the race despite the best efforts of Bill O'Reilly, who absolutely hated him.

The ultraliberal pair had just screened Gore's controversial Oscar- and Nobel Prize–winning documentary, *An Inconvenient Truth*, in one of 21st Century Fox's screening rooms upstairs. It seemed an ironic incongruity, these two high-profile Democratic activists viewing a film widely derided and ridiculed in that particular building, which housed perhaps more skeptics on climate change than any other, your humble correspondent excepted. To them, it must have felt like going into the heart of darkness.

When I greeted both men, whom I had previously met and interviewed, and both warmly responded, Gore with a smirk asked me, "How can you possibly work for Fox News?"

I gave him my standard answer about being the same man, just in a different building. Gore shook his head, never losing the smirk, and added, "I guess you can't bite the hand that feeds you." When I protested his cutting remark, he kept that maddening smirk, saying goodbye as he walked through the security gate with soon-to-be-senator Al Franken in tow.

The vice president's air of moral superiority was insufferable, especially when you consider what a hypocrite he later became. In January 2013, it was announced that the former presidential candidate had sold his principal business, a cable network called Current TV, to Al Jazeera, the Qatar-based broadcaster owned by the Qatari royal family, for about $400 million. So here is smug Mr. Gore, who pinched me for working for Fox News, making a cool profit selling his network to an oil-soaked emirate, which makes its billions pumping and selling dirty oil, the use of which is warming the planet and causing the very "Inconvenient Truth" the former vice president rails about.

Senator Franken had worse karma. In his second successful term he was forced to resign when the infamous photo surfaced of his pretending to grope the bullet-proof protected breasts of a sleeping radio talk show host with him on a USO tour in 2006. His presence is missed by many progressives who worry about losing sight of the big picture.

LOSING MY SWAGGER, SPRING 2010

Aside from its emotional baggage, by 2010 a decade of hard-marching war coverage had taken a toll on me physically. I was in a spiraling funk. The cause was severe complications following surgery on my lower back. The devastating aftermath of that surgery was made painfully clear one weekend afternoon in 2010. I remember looking out at trusty old sailing vessel *Voyager* riding comfortably on her mooring in front of my home in Edgewater. That was the moment when it hit me that I was not working.

For the entire nine years I had by then been at Fox News, Saturday and Sunday was "show day" for my Fox News program, first called *Warzone*, later *Geraldo At Large*, and still later *Geraldo Rivera Reports*. This was an especially pretty April day on the big river, and I was feeling guilty about missing work because I had done something unthinkable: called in sick.

Sick days are not part of my nature. In four-plus decades of hard marching, field reporting out beyond the wire from some of the grimmest places on the planet, plus the often nerve-jangling experience of doing studio and location shows by the thousands, I honestly do not remember ever taking a sick day. I had never been so incapacitated that I could not drag myself in and get the job done, all the while being secretly scornful of weaker souls who beat it out of the office at the first sign of a sniffle.

Generally fearless and combat-tested, I described myself with clichés, as a damn-the-torpedoes personality always ready to answer the bell, and if push came to shove, able to handle crises with confidence that I could still kick most asses. Until that moment in 2010, that is, when excruciating pain from my otherwise dead foot rendered me incapable of working—wounded, mortal, and a shadow of my former self.

The experience of forced inactivity yielded some undeniable truths. First, that getting old sucks. Even if you're not sick, vital moving parts are wearing out. My left knee was replaced in October 2009. That irksome recovery was nothing compared with this complication following back surgery I felt compelled to undergo.

The catalyst for the surgery was my poor performance on the ground earlier in 2010 in southern Afghanistan. That was two tough weeks in mid-February, when I could hardly keep pace with the rugged young Marines patrolling the dangerous, opium-poppy-laden, IED-plagued, Taliban-infested, semi-ghost town of Marja and similar dusty shitholes up and down Helmand Province, the world's heroin capital.

On foot patrol with the Marines, I had to bend over every hundred meters to stretch my weak back or even sit down for a minute or so to relieve the pain and catch my breath. Walking at the rear of the column, I tried surreptitiously to touch my toes unnoticed, but out of the corner of my eye, caught the surprised, concerned glances of the young war-dogs shocked by the surprisingly fragile icon in their midst. As I wrote at the time in Afghanistan, "To be so handicapped after being so active is deeply upsetting. All the Marines saw it. I had to sit and/or stretch every hundred meters. Only sitting down relieves the symptoms. No more marches for me."

It happened all of a sudden a couple of days after the surgery. The recuperation from the back operation was going smoothly, and I strutted around the sixth floor of New York's elite Hospital for Special Surgery at a crisp pace, climbing and reclimbing the steps in the physical therapy room, demonstrating my flexibility and growing strength to the fine rehab staff. At that point disaster struck.

Late one Saturday, my third night in the hospital, I was surprised by an unwelcome guest, an ex-con doctor who insisted on staying to talk about his legal problems involving insurance fraud until the last second of visiting hours. To show him through body language that I was not pleased with his persistent presence, I slammed the room's refrigerator door closed with my foot, while leaning over still attached to the IV on my bed. The result was a popped sciatic nerve that was painful and debilitating and wrecked my right foot, leaving it as numb as a peg-leg pirate's. Something neurological had been busted.

Despite shooting pains that were like a Taser shot, after I got home I did drag my lame, sick-day ass and numb foot off the couch and out of the house to make a little speech to a big group of local kids marching against breast cancer. Then I spent another post-op day back in the hospital trying to figure out what was going on with my broken body. But I was clearly screwed, and it would affect the rest of my life.

In the days following his own hobbling heart condition, former president Bill Clinton increasingly referenced our cycle of life, that journey from youth to puberty, maturity, old age with its escalating infirmities, and death. Among older Baby Boomers, it is common to infuse any conversation with updates on the various maladies afflicting us. "How's it going?" we quietly ask those with heart problems or prostate or colon cancer, perhaps finding comfort in the struggle and triumph of others. My rule is to limit such discussions to the first two minutes before moving on. Otherwise it is all we talk about.

Here is my two minutes: The complications following my back surgery are not life-threatening, but the busted sciatic nerve adds a dimension of physical and emotional discomfort and vulnerability that I have been unable to purge. To add insult to injury, my back pains are back, worse than ever. My sidekick, brother Craig, younger (by eleven years), taller (six foot one to my five foot nine), better looking (check Wikipedia), laughingly encourages me with mock seriousness. Playing on the unwaveringly upbeat rhetoric of the rehabilitative community, he says, "You're not handicapped. You're handicapable."

LIMPING IN LIBYA, APRIL 2011

As a kid in the 1950s I loved a TV series called *Gunsmoke*, which featured actor James Arness as the understated but nevertheless dependably competent and courageous hero, Marshall Matt Dillon. In the days of my youth, I identified with his wise, brave character. Now, I more resemble his loyal sidekick, Chester, played with wry humor by Dennis Weaver. Like Chester, I limp now, but that did not stop me from dragging my sorry foot through some final hairy combat assignments, including one in eastern Libya in April 2011, memorable for the intensity and proximity of the combat we captured on tape.

The fight involved some of the same double-dealing, low-life Sunni Islamist scum, which the Obama administration sixteen months later tragically entrusted with keeping safe our diplomatic compound in Benghazi, Libya, resulting in the death of our ambassador and three other American heroes on September 11, 2012.

The violence I recount here happened a year before the ambassador's death, just after the United States and France militarily intervened to oust the dictator Muammar Gaddafi. He fled Tripoli, his capital in the western part of the country, and was on the loose. His loyal forces in eastern Libya were outnumbered. Far from their home base, they were fighting against a ragged and undisciplined group of rebels. Supposedly the good guys, the rebels sucked in every regard: competence, motivation, honesty, and morality. In broad strokes, we were supporting the scum of Libya, lowlifes worse than Gaddafi ever was. With North Africa in chaos and turmoil from Tunisia to Libya to Egypt, I dragged my crew and myself into a fierce gunfight, which turned out to be my last.

THE FIREFIGHT AT BREGA UNIVERSITY, APRIL 2011

Our team got caught in the crossfire between what was left of Gaddafi's army and the unprincipled Islamist militiamen who would replace his despotic rule with vengeful anarchy. As a result, we got some of the most vivid, high-intensity, close-up combat footage of the modern era. You can still see it on Geraldo.com.

Outside the town of Brega, west of Benghazi, along the North African coast, I reported:

> Most of the "freedom fighters" are a ragtag hodgepodge of civilians that has less discipline, training, experience, and organization than a Chicago street gang. They are hapless, clueless, and frequently seen retreating at the first shot. They cannot even tell the difference between incoming or outgoing fire; they shoot with little or no idea of what they are aiming at; and they are as dangerous to themselves or to civilians in the area as they are to Gaddafi's forces.
>
> Driving through the old section of Brega early Sunday morning, I was surprised at how lightly manned the road was. Where was the rebel army? Later, I learned that they usually show up for work after breakfast in Benghazi. Then they call it a day in time to get home for the evening meal.
>
> After a series of rolling hills, we could see the University of Brega on the next rise. There was a small group of rebel fighters

crouched by the side of the road, maybe four of them, lightly armed with AK-47s and an RPG. "Gaddafi! Gaddafi!" they said, urgently pointing toward the university.

Because they tend to see Gaddafi soldiers under every tree, I discounted their shouted warnings. We got out of our vehicles, and I started walking up the slight rise toward the university buildings, Greg Hart walking alongside, camera in hand, taping everything.

Then the first shot whistled over our heads. What followed was a cacophony of firing from the Gaddafi forces holed up at the crossroads less than a half-mile ahead. They started firing at us with everything from RPGs to heavy machine guns. The shots cut through the air with that zinging sound that terrifies the soul. The worst part came when enemy mortar rounds started landing behind us. Retreat then had to go through that zone already bracketed by their firing.

On our side, opposing the Gaddafi forces, were the rebels.

The Libyan rebel army is the most ill-disciplined, inexperienced, and unreliable I've ever seen in a combat situation. Their level of incompetence is so shocking the very notion of heavily arming them gives me nightmares of dudes walking around with machine guns, looking to settle personal scores that have nothing to do with their revolt in the desert.

On this eastern front in Libya, the rabble rebel army roars with bravado until confronted. They fire their weapons wildly, and shout *Allah Akbar* as if Allah cared about their macho posturing. Then, at the first sign of a determined counterattack, they run. Their whining incompetence makes them unfit to wear the title "freedom fighter"; even "rebel" sounds too grandiose for these poseurs. These gangsters should not be armed by NATO; they should have their asses kicked into shape by French, Italian, and British noncommissioned officers who can teach them not to run away when fired on, but to dig in, form a defensive line, send forces out to the flanks, and scouts up forward, and to shoot horizontally, not vertically.

When we got caught in that crossfire, it revealed that what this mob needs is a few good Marine Corps drill sergeants, not more or heavier weapons. Picture this: In front, a fortified enemy position; Gaddafi loyalists have dug in behind the brick or cement walls of the town's university. Actually, it's more of an oil-related trade school, called Bright Star Petrochemical University.

What deeply impressed me was how much more admirable Gaddafi's forces were than the rebels opposing them. They are outnumbered and far from home; they know that if they surrender their fortified positions and attempt to flee westward toward the remaining Gaddafi stronghold of Tripoli, they will be exposed to harassing attacks and possibly more allied air strikes. So they are not going anywhere, and they have no choice but to fight.

Coming down the road from the eastern side is the vastly larger rebel force of at least 1,500 or 2,000. They are armed with rocket launchers, RPGs, heavy machine guns, twenty-millimeter anti-aircraft guns mounted on the backs of Toyota pickups, and other assorted lethal weapons.

The rebels drive toward the fortified position essentially in single file. In other words, only a few of their formidable arms can be brought to bear on the target they are attacking. No effort is made to spread out the line. No effort is made to protect either the north or south flank. No scouts are sent ahead to pinpoint potential targets within the Gaddafi stronghold.

Instead, the lead elements begin firing wildly. In vehicles back farther in the line, weapons are also let loose. Rounds fly dangerously close to the heads of the rebels in front. To avoid killing their comrades, the rebels aim high. Clearly the fact that they are shooting the sky does not occur to them, as they are made euphoric by the sheer power of their weapons igniting, however harmlessly. Many shout *Allah Akbar* as they fire.

The Gaddafi forces endure this assault for several minutes before letting loose their own barrage, better aimed. Several rounds land among the rebel column. This sets off one of their typical mad dashes to the rear, the entire column rushing incoherently to retreat back up the hill and out of range of the incoming rockets and mortars. Some keep going all the way home to Benghazi, 135 miles away. The gravest danger of the day is that of traffic accidents as they careen away, many still firing their machine guns as they swerve up the road.

In forty years of war reporting, I have never seen so disgraceful a performance under arms. Granted, just a few weeks ago most of these rebels were students and clerks and gas-station attendants, lawyers, teachers, and thugs released from prisons. Still, didn't anyone think to look up a basic training manual before they set out to make war?

The lack of discipline also manifests itself in behavior that is sometimes larcenous, as weapons and vehicles are snatched and stolen from fellow fighters, presumably because the snatcher believes he can do a better job than the snatchee. Besides, who wouldn't want their own AK-47?

When Greg Hart and my calm, hard-as-steel former British SAS commando bodyguard, Scott Board, and I were walking up that road toward the campus, not expecting to be met by the fusillade that came, we took cover off the road, beginning the running commentary that formed the basis for our special report, *The Firefight at Brega University*. As we did, several Gaddafi rockets and mortar rounds landed right where we had been standing minutes before.

My second cameraman, Greg Khananayev, who along with Mohammed Ali, our local stringer, had literally just physically fought off a larcenous rebel trying to steal our vehicle, watched in horror as the rounds landed right where we had been standing. Terrified that we had been killed, Khananayev drove our Toyota down the hill toward the firing to retrieve us. He thought we had been killed, but was determined not to leave us behind, dead or alive. His courage allowed us to avoid the walk back up that long hill through the cluster of fire coming from both sides. He probably saved our lives, and I will never forget that.

At one point, the vivid video shows me visibly limping as the crew vehicle mistakenly drives off without me in it. They came back for me, but the incident was so unimpeachably harrowing that Jon Stewart on Comedy Central did a mash-up that fell between mild ridicule and unmistakable compliment.

Sarcastically comparing me to the title character in *Lawrence of Arabia*, he superimposed my face on some of the iconic scenes from my favorite movie starring the great Peter O'Toole in his film debut. Then Stewart intercut sound and video from the movie with our real-life battle footage, calling it *Geraldo of Arabia*.

Stewart tagged the piece saying, "Whatever you think of Geraldo Rivera, dude's got major sack," indicating his genitals, as in big balls. Geraldo of Arabia considered "major sack" such high praise that I took Stewart's joke as homage, and thought hard before rejecting *Major Sack* as the title of this book.

Chapter 10

TRUMP, BIN LADEN, AND

DANCING WITH THE STARS

Nine years, seven months, and nineteen days after the 9/11 attacks that changed all of our lives for the worse, Erica and I attended the White House Correspondents' dinner in grand style. We sailed up the Potomac River to Washington, DC, in *Voyager*.

We had previously attended several of these glitzy occasions, amused by how star-starved Washington-based journalists react to famous guests, who are usually gracious. As a semi-celebrity, I usually got a warm welcome from the younger staffers, had fun sitting next to prominent guests such as the late Supreme Court Justice Antonin Scalia and astronaut Buzz Aldrin, the second man on the moon, and enjoyed some belly laughs at jokes from the president and the comedy host, who this year was an unusually acerbic Seth Meyers.

The target of the ruthlessly barbed jokes by Meyers and the president was my old friend Donald J. Trump, who had it coming after joining maliciously xenophobic Sheriff Joe Arpaio in resurrecting the long-simmering "birther" movement that sought to prove President Obama, who was seeking reelection in 2012, was really born in Kenya and was thus disqualified from occupying the Oval Office. However twisted, a straight line can be drawn from Trump's involvement in the birther crap and his election to the presidency. No one else running knew how potent the bogus issue would prove to be.

The dinner came just a week after President Obama released his long-form birth certificate, substantively putting the silly issue to rest. That night, with Trump in attendance, Obama enjoyed twisting the comic knife. He queried whether Trump's next probe might be whether the moon landing actually happened. Obama also showed a video of his own birth, which turned out to be the iconic clip of Simba being born in the cartoon movie *The Lion King.*

Trump would have better luck using the birther issue later against Ted Cruz in the Republican primaries. Since the Texas senator really was born abroad, in Canada, the argument could be made with a semi-straight face that Senator Cruz technically was not the "natural-born citizen" the Constitution requires of presidents.

The billionaire businessman-who-would-be-king was also in the bull's-eye at the correspondents' dinner because for several weeks he had been talking up another wacky idea: He was running to succeed Barack Obama in the White House. The forty-fourth president launched a string of stinging jokes about how Donald as the forty-fifth president, clearly a laughable idea to most of those smarty pants gathered in the cavernous Grand Ballroom, would convert the White House into a casino with a jacuzzi on the South Lawn.

The president mercilessly mocked Trump's inexperience for high office, pointing out that on that week's installment of *Celebrity Apprentice* Trump had just fired Gary Busey rather than Meat Loaf. The president deadpanned, "These are the types of decisions that would keep me up at night. Well handled, sir."

The man who would improbably become president was fuming. I am certain the mockery that night helped persuade Trump, after years of pondering, finally to make the run for the White House.

President Obama was in fine form, relaxed and funny. He and First Lady Michelle Obama gave Erica and me a warm greeting, waving and smiling broadly from their seats on the dais. Twenty-four hours later, when Erica and I realized what must have been going on in the president's head at the time of his wisecracking, we decided he was the world's best actor. If the weather had been better that same day in Afghanistan, he never would have made it to this Saturday party. He would have been concerned with the far-weightier matters that he dealt with on Sunday night.

THE GREATEST NIGHT OF MY CAREER, MAY 1, 2011

That Sunday night, May Day 2011, the White House announced that the president of the United States would be addressing the nation at around 10 PM. The prevailing wisdom was that he was going to tell the American people that the fugitive Gaddafi had been caught.

But even that dramatic premise caused major head-scratching. Gaddafi dead or alive, captured or free, did not warrant a presidential prime-time address to the nation. So as our live 10 PM show approached, we pondered what the hell was up.

At the Fox News Washington Bureau, Craig, Greg Hart, and a team of the bureau's young staffers were frantically calling sources and checking social media and the AP wires knowing that it was probably something connected with the military. On the other hand, it was not a major act of war like an atomic explosion because we would have heard about it by now. I was on the air speaking via remote with Fox News's White House correspondent, Mike Emanuel, when it hit me.

"Wait a minute—hold it. Ladies and gentlemen, something I just thought of," I interrupted Mike. "What if . . . what if it's Osama bin Laden?" When I said it, the words just out of my mouth, I knew that it was true. I sensed a gasp, then a wave of affirmation sweeping the nation.

I doubled down, cautioning the audience that I was not reporting the death of Osama bin Laden as fact, but saying, "This is a reporter relying on his experience telling you what my surmise is." Then I asked viewers and specifically my studio guest, retired Air Force Lieutenant General Thomas McInerney, "Is it possible that the terror mastermind who killed so many Americans, that striking from bases in Afghanistan, something may have happened to him?"

Was it too good to be true? Bin Laden, captured or dead? I promised high fives and cheers all around if that were the case.

At 10:40 PM ET, five minutes before CNN, my voice cracking with emotion and joy, I reported the confirmation from senior Capitol Hill producer Chad Pergram. I read a note from Chad out loud, saying over and over, "Osama bin Laden is dead. Osama bin Laden is dead. Can it be? Can it be, ladies and gentlemen? The man who caused so much misery and pain? Osama bin Laden is dead!"

Then, as I read the AP wire from my desktop computer, my voice filled with rising excitement, I said, "Hold it. Hold it. Hold it. Hold it. Hold it. Bin Laden is dead! Urgent confirmed! Bin Laden is dead. Multiple sources. Happy days. Happy days, everyone. This is the greatest night of my career. The bum is dead. The savage who hurt us so grievously, and I am so blessed, I am so privileged to be at this desk at this moment."

Beginning with a typically snotty headline, here is how the important website Mediaite described what happened:

GERALDO RIVERA'S FINEST MOMENT: HOW THE MUCH-MALIGNED ANCHOR BROKE THE BIN LADEN NEWS BEST

In breaking the news, no one could top Geraldo Rivera's pure euphoria. Rivera, who was on deck to anchor his regular program *At Large*, appeared as confused as all of Twitter around 10 PM, when the White House announced the news that the President would speak about an unknown topic within the hour. After about a half hour of errant speculation on the life and health of Muammar Gaddafi, a light bulb went off in Rivera's head.

It was true. Bin Laden was dead, and I was never more alive. When Fox News anchor Brett Baier and his impressive team of staff and experts took over the channel at midnight, at the urging of Darla Shine, wife of FNC's then-senior vice president and later co-president, Bill Shine, I hurried to join Craig and a live camera crew outside the White House, where a huge and boisterous crowd of college students had spontaneously gathered. They were cheering and high-fiving, and I was with them, "dancing on bin Laden's grave."

A funny story that I have never told . . . When I first got to the White House, I could not find Craig and the crew. In a panic, I asked to be admitted to the White House on the assumption that he and the rest of the media were somehow inside. The Secret Service guys at the heavily fortified gate reluctantly let me into the president's residence. They were as euphoric as I was, and they understood that I needed to find my crew. To make a long, silly story short, Craig and crew were not in the building. So after running through its historic halls I came out the other side, asked breathlessly to be allowed to exit, was permitted out, where I finally found them, and immediately went live, ebulliently reporting the news and the jubilant crowd reaction.

Amidst the raucous celebration, I somehow noticed that I had a text message from Afghanistan. My dear friend, then-two-star Major General John F. Campbell, was watching our coverage with a large contingent of his soldiers of the 101st Airborne Division (Air Assault). His command was having a very tough time on this deployment, having just lost six soldiers in a vicious firefight with the Taliban. The division would lose 245 soldiers killed in action by the end of the year's deployment when I joined them in Afghanistan in 2012.

But this night, they were cheering and celebrating along with the rest of the Free World. The monster was dead, and I was honored to bring the nation the news for which we had waited for so long.

It was as Mediaite further described, "The most significant and joyous national security announcement of the past several decades," and here is how I described the significance of the moment the next day in a column for Fox News Latino:

> He haunted my life since that crisp, clear September day almost ten years ago, when Osama bin Laden sent four hijacked airliners to inflict mass murder on innocent men, women, and children.
>
> When the twin towers fell on 9/11, among the business people, visitors, and first responders who died were several dads from my girls' former elementary school in Rumson, New Jersey.
>
> The loss of those fathers sent a tsunami of grief and disquiet through all of our children. The horrors and grief of war had come to the shore of America.
>
> At the time anchor of CNBC's highest rated show, I begged to be allowed to go into the field to chronicle the hunt for the mass murderers who killed those fathers. Refused permission, I quit my plum job and signed on as a war correspondent with Fox News, the spunky new network created by old friend Roger Ailes.

I started at Fox on a November Friday. By the following Tuesday, I was in Pakistan en route to the Khyber Pass and Afghanistan, reporting on the burgeoning effort to catch or kill bin Laden, and to punish the Afghan Taliban who had given al Qaeda sanctuary.

Ten difficult assignments in that war-torn region since brought little advance to the story. We marched, we searched, and we watched our soldiers, sailors, airmen, and Marines fight, kill, and be killed. Still bin Laden eluded us.

My secret fear was that he would outlive me, or that he would simply stay vanished and invisible, sending an occasional taunting or threatening video, mocking us: "Catch me if you can!"

Now Osama bin Laden is dead, killed in a hail of gunfire from an elite team of Navy SEALs raiding the terror mastermind's absurdly lavish compound in Pakistan.

We were there when he escaped our clutches in Tora Bora in December 2001. And we were on the air Sunday night when the news was confirmed that he was dead. In between those monumental events, life has gone on for my family, my country, and me. But the long shadow of the world's most wanted man darkened the sky and chilled the air. Now he is gone. Sure there are more storms ahead. But today the sky is again crisp and clear.

Mediaite's Frances Martel, whom I don't know, wrote the piece grudgingly praising my performance that fateful night, admitting,

It's difficult to give props to Geraldo Rivera. Building a legal career out of militant Puerto Rican separatism only to hop on TV and spend decades highlighting the absolute worst in America—from local news reports on crack houses to his *Jerry Springer*-esque talk show to the Milli Vanilli of journalism, *The Mystery Of Al Capone's Vault*—few can challenge his reign as America's most prominent media punch line.

That's not to be overly harsh on Rivera or to undermine the role he played to Americans last night, but only to emphasize how much more unexpected it was to see him rise so strikingly to the occasion. He is the last person one expects to accurately speak for all America on a serious issue, but he was the only journalist on the air that night with his heart sufficiently placed on his sleeve to stop being an anchor for a little bit of time and just react like a human, specifically, a New Yorker.

Sure, many will refute that a journalist getting emotional is the proper decorum for someone privileged with such a responsibility . . . But last night was unquestionably the best broadcast of Rivera's life; he said so himself. No one better captured the breathless, unadulterated relief of knowing a man who had caused so much suffering had finally reached his end after a life that will go down as one of the most repulsive in human history, and for that, at least part of the debt of good reporting Rivera owes to his viewers has been paid.

"FOR GOD AND COUNTRY, GERONIMO, GERONIMO, GERONIMO," MAY 2011

Rob O'Neill, the member of SEAL Team 6 who killed the terror mastermind, has described how the corpse of bin Laden was first brought to Jalalabad Airport for tentative identification. The team was also waiting for a second aircraft ferrying the remaining members of the team, whose helicopter had been left behind and destroyed after crashing as it attempted to land in the bin Laden compound in Abbottabad, Pakistan. I interviewed Rob about it one day at Fox.

Rob O'Neill: It was neat because we were with the entire team. We are all obviously elated for a number of reasons: One, we just killed bin Laden; two, we lived. We are gonna live. We are gonna be best friends for the rest of our lives. This is so cool. We were part of this team that will be legendary. We didn't expect them to say SEAL Team 6, but the more we heard it, we were like, this is a bigger deal than even we thought. And then you were on the air and then I remember you started speculating the first time we heard bin Laden and then you confirmed, "bin Laden is dead, bin Laden is dead!"

And I was eating a sandwich as the president came out. And finally, 'cause what was happening before that was we were watching you on television and most people I am assuming were wondering why it was taking so long, but behind us, my boss is on the phone with probably the White House or the CIA and they are just trying to get a head count on what happened in the house; how many are dead; how many were wounded; how many women and children; what is the total head count; 'cause we always want that after a mission.

So they are just trying to straighten that out before they tell the president. Then the president comes out and I remember watching him and he said, "Tonight I can report to the American people and to the world, the United States conducted an operation that killed Osama bin Laden, the leader of al Qaeda." And I remember that so vividly because I hear him say bin Laden, Osama bin Laden, and I look at Osama bin Laden, like he is right there and just everything kinda flashes through all the missions, that "We are never gonna find him." "The guy is a ghost." "I will never be on that mission"; and realize, Oh my God, how in the world did I get here from [his hometown] Butte, Montana? [Laughs] And I killed him.

The melancholy side of the triumph is that the death of bin Laden did not end the War on Terror. In a pessimistic appraisal that was widely reported in February 2016, the director of national intelligence, James Clapper, told a Senate hearing, "There are now more Sunni violent extremist groups, members, and safe havens than at any time in history." Matthew Henman, head of the Terrorism and Insurgency Center, which analyzes international security risks, told reporters, "Five years after the killing of Osama bin Laden, it is not wrong to be fairly pessimistic in our outlook on the world."

It did not take long for Henman's pessimism to be realized. In June 2017, Tora Bora was back in the news for the worst of reasons. It had fallen back into the clutches of radical Islamists. Only this time it wasn't the Taliban or al Qaeda, it was ISIS. After gaining and then losing territory in Iraq, Syria, and Libya, this malignancy spread to Afghanistan. Smaller than the other extremist groups, ISIS in Afghanistan had been more or less contained in a network of tunnel hideouts in the Achin District, near the Pakistan border.

Our air forces found them there and attacked their refuge in April 2017, dropping the so-called Mother of All Bombs, a 20,000-pound giant said to be the most powerful nonnuclear weapon in our arsenal. By all accounts, the gigantic explosion inflicted scores of casualties and led to rejoicing among our military leaders. We had landed what seemed a killing blow. Rather than being wiped out, however, the terror organization simply regrouped and moved, choosing a sanctuary less vulnerable to our air strikes. According to my old friend Hazrat Ali, who is still in the area, a thousand surviving ISIS fighters attacked Tora Bora. As of this writing, ISIS occupies the infamous cave and tunnel complex that bin Laden built, and our side spent so much time, money, energy, and reputation trying to destroy.

I am almost tempted to let ISIS alone to discover the same sorry fate as every other would-be occupier of Afghanistan. Let them exhaust their blood and treasure trying to outmaneuver the Pashtun tribesmen and alter their brutal society. ISIS will not find the fertile ground they found in the Sunni heartland of Mesopotamia. However they fare in Tora Bora, there is no end in sight to their brand of terror. The peril posed by Sunni Muslim extremists will be just as bad or worse on the tenth anniversary of bin Laden's death as it was on the fifth, but at least he is dead. The United States did what we pledge to do to those who attack us. We tracked him down and took our revenge on the perpetrator for his terrible crime. I was not in New York when the planes hit the towers, but I was on the air almost a decade later when we learned justice had been done. And SEAL Team 6 and the world were watching.

LAST DANCE, DECEMBER 2011

Bin Laden's death did not end the War on Terror. Like President George W. Bush's preposterous "Mission Accomplished" banner eight years earlier, 2011 turned out to be President Barack Obama's year of cockeyed optimism. Six months after we celebrated bin Laden's death in Afghanistan, Obama told us our war in Iraq was also ending.

America was eager to move on, and bring our troops home. I had the privilege of being on what we all thought was the last US combat convoy out of Iraq in December 2011. As we left, bound for Kuwait, there was an omen of bad times ahead in the rearview mirror. It was a mob scene happening at the base behind us. Instead of the valuable assets we left behind being handed over to proper authorities, as we pulled out of the base, a mob of civilians poured over the fence, grabbing and stealing every piece of equipment they could get their hands on. Among the loot was row upon row of brand-new Ford F-150 pickups, symbolic of all the billions of American taxpayer dollars wasted on that sorry excuse for a country. I left apologizing for not opposing the Iraq War in the first place.

As I reported at the time, "For someone who considers himself a patriot, as I do, it is extremely difficult not to rally behind a president when he beats the drums of war. So it has always been. We can disagree about domestic policy, but when the nation's leader says we are threatened from abroad, the majority of Americans suspend misgivings or even gnawing disbelief and give the man in the Oval Office the benefit of the doubt.

Our war against Saddam Hussein's Iraq was the classic example. It was funky from the get-go, and I should have known better. Instead, I concentrated on chronicling the heroic efforts of our stressed Armed Forces as they followed goals that vacillated from attempted conquest, to force protection, to nation building, to finding a respectable way out.

We didn't go for the oil. We didn't go to establish a strong base in a dangerous, strategically important part of the world. We went as an act of national self-defense. But was it really?

Invading Iraq to find weapons of mass destruction that we had only flimsy evidence ever really existed required an act of willful blindness. That lame dog-and-pony show that Secretary of State Colin Powell put on in the United Nations in 2003 to prove our case that the Iraqi dictator was really attempting to build a nuclear weapon and then to rally international support for the invasion, showed how pathetically thin our proof was. For good reason, Secretary Powell's longtime military adviser and chief of staff, Colonel Lawrence Wilkerson, later called his own involvement in that UN presentation "the lowest point of his life."

Our proof then was a thousand times less convincing than the evidence today that neighboring Iran is heading down the road to nuclear weapons. And yet in 2003 we all nodded sagely when Powell, the hero of Gulf War I, spoke, and I dusted off my body armor and packed my bags, eager to follow our troops into action in the sands of Mesopotamia.

I had plenty of company in the pro-war camp in February and March 2003 during the inexorable run-up to the war, including Bill and Hillary Clinton. But that doesn't take me off the hook for enthusiastically backing a bloody conflict that turned out to be as unnecessary and costly as its critics predicted.

I don't for a second want to imply that what I experienced was even a fraction of the trauma endured by our deployed warfighters, but my experiences still rattled and deeply unsettled my soul.

The only salve to my conscience is that I always put my own ass as far out on the line as the GIs who fought and died in this God-forsaken place. After our vehicle got shot up outside Mosul in northern Iraq in 2004, I was convinced I was going to die there. On some trips I would come home and sit on my porch overlooking the Hudson River, staring in a kind of dark trance, drool leaking from the edge of my mouth, thinking about all the death and destruction we were seeing.

Two images haunt me to this day; both involve pickup trucks. The bed of one Toyota truck outside Baghdad in 2005 held the torn-up body of a woman killed because she wanted to vote. The bed of another pickup outside Fallujah in 2004 held a pile of dead insurgents piled one on top of the other like they were bloody lumber headed to the mill.

During the war's darkest days before the surge, between 2004 and 2007, we were losing two, three, or four GIs every single day. The line from the Sting song, "every step you take . . . " played in my brain every time we went out on foot patrol, because every step contained the possibility that the ground would explode in our faces.

All those images crowded my mind this past Saturday as our C-130 military transport aircraft landed at Camp Adder, our last Iraqi base. I was there at the beginning of the conflict. This was my eleventh and final trip into Iraq.

At the height of the war, this sprawling base in southern Iraq held 12,000 of our troops and airmen. It is a vast, dusty place, far larger than, say, JFK or LAX. Now it was almost deserted, save for the visiting brass and journalists gathered to mark the occasion of the withdrawal of the last US military unit in Iraq, 480 officers and enlisted personnel from the Third Brigade of the First Cavalry.

After speeches and interviews, the brass left on the aircraft, and I was privileged to be among five reporters given the high honor of making the four-hour drive out of Iraq and into neighboring Kuwait. And so the long war that claimed the lives of 4,487 GIs, spread so much pain and suffering, and cost a trillion US taxpayer dollars, ended not in victory, but with a profound sense of relief. It was over, and I survived.

Some of the friendships made with members of our fighting forces will endure forever. Having seen so much tumult and death together, we are friends for life. My heart aches for those who fell or were wounded or otherwise scarred by the grim experience. But the next time the president calls, they and I will be there again, however heavy it weighs on our hearts and minds.

HOORAY FOR HOLLYWOOD, 1990–2017

My final combat assignment was Afghanistan in 2012, where General John F. Campbell was by then the four-star commander of all our forces. As I arrived at the US Embassy for an interview with our brave and highly skilled ambassador Ryan Crocker, the compound came under Taliban mortar attack. The fortified building was immediately locked down, and to my dismay, I was trapped inside as the action raged outside.

Refused my urgent requests to be allowed to leave, I was comforted by the fact my brother, Craig, was outside the compound with a second camera crew. I knew that because the embassy had the TV on a live, local news broadcast reporting the action, and there was Craig doing his thing.

As the attack in Kabul and around the nation fizzled with minimal casualties, I had a life-affirming moment during a live broadcast of my own show the next morning. Akbar set up a phone interview with the spokesman for the Taliban, and I asked him, "How does it feel to get your ass kicked? All those dead Taliban and no US casualties?"

My most vivid recollection of that eleventh and final assignment in Afghanistan was a lot less macho. I was accompanying our forces on a pre-dawn helicopter raid on a suspected Taliban compound. The choppers landed in a tilled field about a quarter mile from the compound, and the troopers charged ahead. By then a limping gimp, I was humiliated when the sergeant in charge had to come back to ask me to hurry it up, because I was falling too far behind.

I twice tried to get back to war reporting in 2014, after ISIS invaded Syria and Iraq. But after initially being approved, the trips got canceled. The first time was when ISIS, the scourge that replaced al Qaeda, captured Iraq's Mosul Dam. Fox canceled that trip because it said there was no money in the budget.

As for the second cancellation, during the siege of the Syrian city of Kobani by ISIS, I was told it was the unavailability of appropriate insurance. By then James Foley and several other journalists had been beheaded by ISIS and all the networks were becoming reasonably very concerned about reporters' getting caught, tortured, and killed.

To stay busy during that long dry spell, I did mostly Hollywood true-life post mortems like *Elvis at 80*, *The Sad Life and Death of Anna Nicole Smith*, and *The Mysterious Death of Joan Rivers*. On the tenth anniversary of Scott Peterson's being sentenced to death for the murder of his eight-months-pregnant wife, Laci, and their unborn child, I did a special one-hour report on the surprisingly privileged life Scott was enjoying on death row in San Quentin prison.

There was also Hollywood. Many reporters have done cameos in films and television series over the years. I have done more than most. Most proudly, I appeared as myself in the finale of *Seinfeld*, directed personally by mad genius Larry David, and in the last season of *The Sopranos*, where I heaped a faux investigative reporter's scorn on James Gandolfini's fabulous Tony Soprano. Speaking of great mobsters, I joined Robert De Niro and Harvey Keitel in Sylvester Stallone's *Cop Land*, which was shot in and around my home in Bergen County, New Jersey, home to many NYPD officers. A couple of times, I related to Jerry Orbach's Lennie Briscoe in *Law and Order*, and got literally knocked out by Jane Lynch's wonderful Sue Sylvester in the finale of *Glee*.

Storm-tossed sharks ate me limb by limb in Ian Ziering's *Sharknado V, Silver Shamrock*, in a gory bit reminiscent of the bridge scene in *Monty Python's Monty Python and the Holy Grail*; remember, "It's just a flesh wound," the Black Knight says as he loses body parts. Creator and producer Greg Garcia put me in several episodes of his long-running hit comedy, *My Name is Earl*, starring funny, cool Jason Lee. I take an artiste's pride in having guest-starred as Alfred the Nerd in the highest-rated episode ever of *Baywatch*, bulking up opposite perennially hunky David Hasselhoff. I appeared, again as myself, in the Jody Foster film *Contact*; the John Travolta-as-Bill Clinton mash-up movie *Primary Colors*; and with Bruce Willis and Tom Hanks in the 1990 bomb *Bonfire of the Vanities*, directed by the otherwise great Brian De Palma.

One of my movies, *All About Steve*, a widely panned road romp starring Sandra Bullock and Bradley Cooper, was honored with two Golden Raspberry Awards, given to films the critics feel are the year's worst.

I hit the soaps back in 1991 with a smoldering performance in *The Young and the Restless*, which had a kissing scene. Speaking of passion, I was also murdered that year in the title role in the Perry Mason movie *The Death of the Tattletale Romeo*, starring Raymond Burr. *Tattletale Romeo* was a not-too-subtle play on what should have happened to me after I published my unfortunate tell-all autobiography earlier that year. The fun part of the film mystery was discovering which of the many infuriated women whom I "exposed" was the real perpetrator.

The assorted cameos keep my Screen Actors Guild card active, and while my acting resume is not exactly Hollywood Walk of Fame material, it has certainly been colorful. If only I could do *Game of Thrones* or *Star Wars* or maybe a remake of *Up in Smoke*, my acting career would be complete.

PRESIDENT TRUMP AND ME, 1976–2017

I have known him for decades, through various phases of life in the big city, including more than a dozen interviews, clubbing, and prominent attendance at pro fights at Madison Square Garden, and in Atlantic City. We met around 1976 when I was engaged to marry Francine LeFrak, the elegant daughter of another powerful real estate mogul, Sam LeFrak, a friendly rival of Donald's father, Fred. Both magnates hailed from the borough of Queens and came up at roughly the same time. The families remain close. Francine's billionaire brother, Richard, is one of President Trump's close friends.

We were class flirts during high school, and, while always working hard, were also fixtures on the New York scene. He kept zig-zagging to success, accumulating power and money, while I went from local reporter to network correspondent to talk show host and back again.

Beginning around 2000, we often discussed on camera and off the possibility of Trump's running for president. He brought up the topic so often I finally lost patience with the question. When he asked Sean Hannity and me after the *Celebrity Apprentice* finale in February 2015, whether he should "go for it?" I told him, essentially, put up or shut up. Still, I was shocked when he did, more for the platform he choose than the decision to do it. I thought he would run as a pro-choice, pro-immigration, pro-business, independent, Reform Party, fiscally pragmatic, social liberal, not unlike Hillary Clinton. Instead, I watched along with the rest of the world as he evolved from the flamboyant billionaire showman I knew, into a wildly unconventional, deeply conservative Republican candidate. I hold out hope that he will remember his core New York values on issues like the social safety net, choice, and health care, although his ideological transformation seems deep and permanent.

By steering hard right, he won the election, but not the affection of most women. My wife and her friends hate him. The scope of their alienation became apparent on the day after his January 2017 inauguration, when hundreds of thousands marched on Washington and in scores of other cities, here and abroad. The biggest day of protest in American history was specifically motivated by the fear that President Trump will stack the Supreme Court with pro-life justices, who will abolish a woman's right to choose. Their fears are exacerbated by the president's late-in-life conversion to the anti-abortion side of our divided society. He managed, by the day after his presidency began, to frighten, alienate, and motivate an entire gender.

The college-educated, more female and minority half of the country professes disgust and alarm that a chauvinist is our president. Yet, among the whiter, more male, less-educated half, he is beloved. Despite the hubris and chaos of his early presidency, many of his supporters are healthy traditionalists, old-fashioned, and politically incorrect. I am none of those things, yet I cling to the promise that Trump has it in him to be a great, or at least a good, president. As I will shortly argue in closing this book, I believe he is a good man, and I lament that saying that infuriates the Hillary Clinton/Erica Rivera half of the American electorate.

Whatever your feelings about the man, there is no denying that his election has jolted awake the economy. He is a cheerleader for capitalism and so far, it is paying off for everyone with a 401-k.

SEVENTY IS THE NEW FIFTY, JULY 2013

Aside from the physical battering of my life rigorously lived, now three-score and fourteen years, there has undoubtedly been an emotional toll. I have a form of post-traumatic stress, the most dramatic symptom of which is sitting more or less comatose for long stretches, immobile. As I mentioned, there were times after particularly grueling combat assignments, the ten or so during the really bad pre-Surge, Iraq War years, 2004–2008, when I would come home, sit on my porch, and simply stare.

After years devoted to staying fit, plus the blessings of good genes from long-lived ancestors, veneers on my teeth, the knee replacement and medicines, sprays and ointments focusing on but not limited to hair loss, high blood pressure, cholesterol, and wrinkles, I am holding my own. My workout regimen is not rigorous, but it is regular and frequent. I love old-fashioned newspapers, but refrain from reading them until I'm on the stationary bike. It is a reward that makes the pedaling easier. Then I do some medium weights and lots of abs. I do it four or five times a week, unless I am on assignment, when I just do the best I can in the hotel room.

When I'm in New York, I routinely take my real bicycle everywhere. From the Upper East Side of Manhattan to Fox News in midtown is twenty minutes tops, usually through Central Park, which is mostly closed to vehicles other than pedaled or horse-driven. During daytime traffic, on the always-jammed streets and avenues, a cab, Lyft, or Uber could take twice that long. The only impediment is weather; I do not ride in the rain, snow, or when it is below forty degrees. Biking is risky enough; there is a near-death experience almost every time out, and it may eventually kill me.

Despite the risk, the alternative to staying fit is too grim to bear. Dying slowly is bad enough. Do not go gentle; go kicking and screaming. Plus, I enjoy working out. Being physical sometimes leads to drunken self-confidence, as on the late night I sent a nude selfie out to the world to mark my seventieth birthday. As I said at the time, "70 is the new 50."

It became a big deal, going viral and hitting every entertainment news show. It later topped *Rolling Stone* magazine's list of "2013's Most Mind-Blowing Selfies." Happily, nobody got hurt and I didn't get fired. Roger was snide but not riled whenever it came up. Erica de-escalated the crisis by joking, "This is exactly the kind of thing that happens when I fall

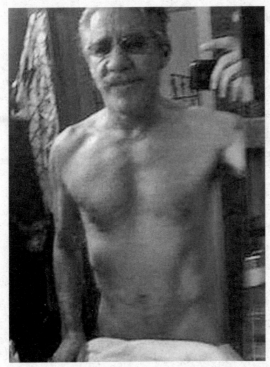

"70 is the new 50." July 2013.

asleep first. Thank God we have towels in the bathroom. (One was placed strategically.) But I'm proud my husband looks so hot."

I later tweeted, "Note to self: no tweeting after 1 AM." Having been initially critical of my impetuosity, several friends and business advisers later told me that the buffed nude shot was great promotion, especially for the Millennial viewers who do not usually watch cable news, certainly not Fox, and instead caught the septuagenarian strongman on the internet.

The only negative selfie feedback was the cancellation by Duquesne University of a July 2013 speech and panel discussion I was going to lead to mark the fiftieth anniversary of the assassination of JFK. As the first reporter in the United States to broadcast the Zapruder home movie of one of history's most significant murders, I had an undeniable connection to the story. That did not matter in the end. In announcing the cancellation of my appearance, the college called my selfie "inappropriate and not in line with the school's values as a Catholic University."

I launched a Twitter storm in response:

Duquesne's cancellation of my JFK panel appearance is pretentious censorship. Do students agree with administration? Am I banned for life? Are all prospective speakers similarly scrutinized, or is my sin receiving special attention? Does the selfie outweigh my Peabody, Emmys, RFKs, and other professional achievements on Duquesne's scale of morality? Are the students of Duquesne so sensitive and protected that they will be unable to concentrate on the topic being discussed because they cannot un-see the image?

Most of the internet agreed, criticizing the school's rigid policies regarding social media etiquette. Columbia University professor Marc Lamont Hill tweeted, "They did the same to me last year."

I posted another nude selfie a year later, but the picture was neither as salacious nor as widely disseminated. By then, around the time of my ominous and cautionary meeting with Roger about getting old, my tight bod began deteriorating. Running my hands over wrinkling alligator skin and atrophying muscles, I see an old man in the making, in slow motion. The camera may not blink or lie, but makeup and good lighting help create an illusion that I am more or less the same swashbuckler you grew up with. No longer cute like during the rock 'n' roll newsman days, I cling to being marginally appealing in a reminiscent way, still recognizable, at least to women over forty. Looks are only skin deep, but most days it feels like an old man lives inside.

Sitting on a bar stool, cigar-smoking and boozy, I maintain the illusion of toughness, relatively big shoulders and biceps; but that illusion only lasts as long as you don't ask me to take it outside. Too gimpy now for real street fights, I would limp into the alley as my opponent laughed. Adjusting to this new reality, I am in the late stages of making the television transition from roving bare-knuckled reporter to wise/faded/Ancient Mariner/Veteran Correspondent/Stoner Uncle.

As I mentioned in the prologue, my operating philosophy is pragmatic idealism, the need to deal realistically with the moral imperative to be good, do well, and be happy. Essentially it is "love the dream," but always remember that dreams do not put food on the table or pay college tuitions, charitable contributions, or make good on your wife's or kids' shopping and doctor bills.

FIGHTING FATHER TIME, 2014–2017

My hair color is probably fading brown over spreading white, but I cannot say for sure because it has been color-corrected ever since Roger Ailes went on a rant to our mutual old friend Woody Frazier, then Fox News coordinating producer. Woody has been around so long, he was my producer at *Good Morning America* in the mid-1970s. In the early 1990s he was my older son Gabriel's Little League coach in Brentwood, California.

One morning out of the blue, Woody asked why I was letting my hair go gray. "No wonder the younger demo [ratings demographic] sucks," etc. Since Bill Shine, then Roger's executive sidekick, asked me the same question that same morning, I knew it was Roger doing the asking and reached immediately for the Just for Men. When I failed to get the color right, at times looking cartoonish-dark brown or shoeshine black, I hooked up with Kirsten, a clever stylist at Truman's Hair Salon for Men on Madison Avenue, just happy I had hair left to color.

It may not have much to do with "fighting Father Time," but my generation was the first to embrace recreational drug use as a lifestyle. I smoked my first joint as a junior at the University of Arizona in 1964. The only semi-gringo playing in the intensely competitive Tucson intramural soccer league, composed mostly of Mexican and other Latin American university students and workers, I was introduced to *Reefer Madness* and have probably averaged a modest joint a week since. My pro-pot position has been consistent for the half-century since college. In the 1970s I was on the board of the National Organization for the Reform of Marijuana Laws (NORML).

With some notable exceptions (Bill O'Reilly and Donald Trump), virtually everybody I have ever known has at least tried pot. If you are reading this, the odds are that you have tried marijuana, which is why surveys consistently show that a majority of Americans, across a broad ideological spectrum, favors medical marijuana, broad decriminalization, or even total legalization, as in Colorado, Washington, Massachusetts, California, and a half dozen other states and counting.

Several stubborn holdouts, like Alabama, still treat pot possession as a felony, which is dumb. One of my deep fears is that in appealing to his right-wing base, President Trump will become a throwback to the bad old days of Prohibition. His pick of old-line, conservative, former

Alabama senator Jeff Sessions as attorney general is worrisome in this regard, although with Russiagate, a revolt by so-called Sanctuary Cities, and a fight over the border wall on his hands, the new AG may not have the energy to go after potheads.

As grass spreads, it needs personal regulation. As with booze, the rule is never to get high when you are trying to do anything except making love or chilling out. I agree with former president Obama that pot is less destructive than alcohol, but when you get high on your supply before you have fulfilled your duties as a responsible student, teacher, or parent, you are destined to be a lethargic dope-smoking dope. People who start smoking as young teenagers, and then try to go to school or work stoned, are the generation that makes up the slacker class of underachievers.

Pot isn't the only drug of choice among my age group. Baby Boomers now use an array of pharmaceutical weapons in the losing war against Father Time: Rogaine, Propecia, statins, Lyrica, medical marijuana, chin lifts, liposuction, eyebrow lifts, and other life-enhancing, penis-enlarging, artery-expanding, mental-health-extending therapies that have changed the social pecking order to an extent that is not yet fully appreciated.

FIRST (SENIOR) CITIZEN TRUMP, JUNE 2015 TO NOVEMBER 2016

Sexual capacity and a firm body are just two measures of vivacity. Internal health is still the ultimate arbiter. Seventy may be the new fifty, but a seventy-year-old neck still aches. Billy Crystal's classic *SNL* character Fernando says, "It is better to look good than feel good," and I do look better than I feel. Which brings me back to President Trump, and the extraordinary stamina he displayed during the grueling campaign.

A large man at six-foot-three inches tall and weighing anywhere from 230 to 250 pounds, he refuses to show any signs of wear and tear over the year and a half of nonstop campaigning, and now a year as the nation's chief executive. Despite a diet that was often composed of fast food, and a less-than-stressful exercise regimen that consists primarily of playing golf at Mar-a-Lago (sixteen times in the first hundred days) or at another of his fabulous resorts, he physically dominated the long campaign, behaving like a prime-of-life Energizer Bunny. At every stop along the way, he bounded onto the stage, enthusiastically greeting his swelling crowds of devoted followers, throwing kisses, waving his arms in triumph, and pumping his fists.

Then already seventy, fully five years past the traditional, sanctioned retirement age, Trump was more vibrant and energetic than his "low-energy" rivals for the nomination. In a funky appearance on *The Dr. Oz Show* two months before the election, he was hailed as "the healthiest person ever to run for president" by his colorful personal physician, Dr. Bornstein. When I asked the president in a conversation on board Air Force One in October 2017 to what he credited his extraordinary stamina, he said it was his parents and their "good genes."

Whatever his secret, there is no doubt Trump ran circles around Hillary Clinton, out-campaigning her every step of the way. When she faltered, wilting in the heat at the World Trade Center memorial service on September 11, 2016, stumbling as she entered her limousine, Trump pounced, ridiculing her frailty and saying bluntly that she lacked the stamina and energy to be president. She later disclosed that she had been secretly diagnosed as suffering from pneumonia. It was a plausible explanation, but that she kept it from the public just added fuel to the notion that she was a sneaky secret-keeper.

Love him or hate him, First Senior Citizen Trump on the campaign trail displayed amazing physical prowess. It could be a function of the fact that, unlike me, smoke-free President Trump never drank, either, reserving his body for his crusade to accumulate enormous wealth and then capture the White House.

CELEBRITY APPRENTICE, FEBRUARY 2015

In the months before the official beginning of the 2016 presidential campaign, I was shocked that Roger allowed me to do *Celebrity Apprentice*, my first reality show. In retrospect, my loving ex-boss, who was not yet laid low by scandal, probably wanted to give his aging, unpredictable, still explosive and ideologically suspect fading star reporter something to do as far away from Fox News as possible. I have a way of sometimes offending the conservative sensibilities of our audience, as I did, for example, asserting confidently during the campaign that there was zero chance Hillary Clinton was going to be indicted for the phony-baloney email controversy.

Celebrity Apprentice turned out to be a blast. I did well and spent quality time with soon-to-be president Trump and his family, whom I hold in high regard. I have spent time before and since with his older children, who were deeply involved in the show. Their dad and mother, businesswoman Ivana Marie Trump, did a great job raising them. As the campaign made clear, daughter Ivanka is enormously poised and impressive, and could well be our first female president. I lament the fact that hatred for her father has rebounded so negatively on Ivanka and her businesses, which should have nothing to do with politics. Her brothers, Eric and Donald Jr., are also solid citizens, and have theoretically taken full control of his far-flung business empire.

Until his father's run for the White House, Don Jr. and I shared the added connection of being dads with daughters in the same school. I ran into his wife, Vanessa, in the school elevator and told her a couple of months before the election that her father-in-law still had a shot. Stately, in a tall, blonde, stylish way, she joked, "He'd better, after all this work." Thirty-four-year-old Eric is nothing like the doofus portrayed on *Saturday Night Live*. A tall, good-looking, thoughtful young man, he and his wife, Lara, raised a ton of money, north of $15 million, for St. Jude Children's Hospital, an effort I was delighted to support.

On *Celebrity Apprentice*, the Trump kids were tough judges, but they gave me every benefit of the doubt. My journalism background and legal chops also helped immeasurably in outmaneuvering rivals like *Sharknado* star Ian Ziering, rocker Kevin Jonas, and helicopter-pilot-to-the-stars, *Falcon Crest*'s Lorenzo Lamas, who all conspired to get me fired. Despite his machinations with the other two plotters, I had a soft spot for Lorenzo. His dad, Fernando Lamas, was my dad Cruz Rivera's favorite actor. Pop loved the way Fernando represented the ideal Latin man—suave, sharp, and sexy.

SHE'S HIRED, FEBRUARY 2015

My stint on his *Celebrity Apprentice* required six weeks of taping, eight months of waiting for NBC to schedule the series, and a month and a half of highly rated, nail-biting, two-hour taped broadcasts, followed by a two-show live finale in February 2015. Beginning with an eclectic collection of sixteen strong personalities, the show went through incidents of backstabbing, phone looting, clothes shedding, shouting, and buckets of crying, finger-pointing drama.

The idea is that the two teams are assigned business-related tasks that are taped one day, and presented to boss Donald in the boardroom the next day.

One task was fairly typical, to compose and present a jingle for Budweiser's new wine coolers. My "Team Vortex" triumphed even as rival "Team Infinity" collapsed, and we easily won the competition, which featured our rapping to my memorable catchphrase for the wine-cooler commercial *Nice over Ice*.

To set up the final showdown between longtime television host and producer Leeza Gibbons and me, Trump fired everybody except Vivica A. Fox, the feisty and impressively talented actress. At that point, the lovely star of *Empire* and *Independence Day* graciously conceded that she could not match either Leeza's skills as a producer or mine as a fundraiser. It was a humbling moment for both Leeza and me, and we both love Vivica for bowing out with such grace.

The task for the finale began when Leeza and I were flown down to Universal Orlando Resort onboard one of the private jets in Donald Trump's aerial armada. Our task was to produce and shoot a new commercial for the theme park. At the same time, we were told there would be a finale fundraising gala for which we would be responsible not only to raise as much money as possible, but also to provide entertainment for the event.

The show began with the introduction of the teams brought together to help Leeza and me complete the complex task. It was like a class reunion. Her "Team Leeza" was buttressed by previously "fired" celebrities Brandi Glanville, the fiery and underrated *Housewife of Beverly Hills*; baseball great and man of deep integrity and soul Johnny Damon; and my arch-nemesis, former boy-band guitarist Kevin Jonas.

My squad consisted of Vivica and the two actors who had unsuccessfully conspired with Kevin to get me fired earlier on, Lorenzo Lamas, who starred in the soap operas *Falcon Crest* and *The Bold and the Beautiful*, and Ian Ziering of *Sharknado* and *Chippendale's* fame, whom I really did not like at the time. I have subsequently changed my mind, and now admire

Ian's work ethic and resolve. When he was conspiring with Lorenzo and Kevin Jonas to sabotage me, I called them out in the boardroom in a dramatic confrontation. Faced with firing either Ian, Kevin, or me, Trump gave the young rocker the heave-ho. President Trump later told me how NBC executives lobbied him to fire me instead of Kevin because he was a bigger draw for the younger demo coveted by television advertisers. The boss declined because, as he said, "It was the right thing to do."

In the final task, after Universal executives briefed both teams about the parameters of the commercial they were looking for, we set out to plan. As presented on the program, Leeza's team had a rocky start when Brandi and Johnny wandered off to have hot dogs and beer, as Leeza and Kevin strove to get the commercial scripted and cast.

Distracted by the need to raise even more money than the almost $600,000 I had already brought in, I reached the day of the commercial shoot with many loose ends still unresolved, as usual. I was the front man for our spot, which emphasized the adventurous aspects of Universal and the need for kids to have courage to experience it fully. I decided to focus on the new Harry Potter theme park, dressing as a caped wizard, wand and all.

When the time to shoot the spot came, we discovered that no one had taken responsibility to get our child actors gathered where we needed them, when we needed them. The episode ended with me charging off to find our crew, even as I muttered that from this point on I was taking full control of our production. As we faded to black and teased the next week's huge live finale, the odds seemed to favor my rival, Leeza, who despite her crew's partial desertion announced that she had landed Olivia Newton John to perform at the finale's big gala.

At that point, I had secured neither a performer nor enough donations to secure a victory. It was a nerve-wracking week, struggling to pull off a long-shot, come-from-behind win. Anyway, I tried mightily but fell short in fundraising because my generous donors were by that point tapped out. I did put on a great show, though, landing live performances at the celebrity-studded gala from Jose Feliciano and Tony Orlando, both friends of more than forty years.

The challenging competition culminated in a rousing, highly rated live finale, in which I lost to the formidable talk-show host and philanthropist Leeza Gibbons. When Trump declared Leeza his latest Apprentice, despite the fact that I raised more money, most of the cast members reacted favorably.

Leeza was much more popular than I during the taping. She was a soothing presence who kept her head below the line of fire. I was more sharp elbows and bare knuckles, earning the loyalty of just six of the sixteen contestants, including Kate "Plus 8" Gosselin. I have a soft spot for Kate because of all she was forced to cope with in her life before television, and was protective of her during the competition. Most responsible adults would be respectful of any woman who could successfully nurture that many kids, including surprise sextuplets, with such a lame husband.

After another task, which was to sell wedding dresses, Kate and I dressed as a newly wedded couple. She wore one of our dresses. I was in black tie and tails. In the boardroom scene that followed, Kate told the world that her ambition was to "be Geraldo's next ex-wife," a funny line that my straight-shooting, plain-talking, gorgeous wife, Erica, did not particularly appreciate.

What I appreciated beyond Erica's unvarnished and loving support was her donating $25,000 of her own money to my cause. My Fox News crowd also came through impressively. Because the show rules say no checks, and given the short notice that a particular task was a fundraiser, nobody had the chance to get cashier's checks.

Sean Hannity, who really has become one of my best friends, showed up with $10,000 in hundred-dollar bills. He still talks about how I planted a big kiss on his cheek during the network TV broadcast. In October 2017, Sean donated another $25,000 to the charity I designated for Puerto Rico's hurricane relief. He really has a heart of gold. Another generous conservative not given credit for his philanthropy (he could give away his fortune and liberals would say it was ill-gained anyway), Bill O'Reilly came through during *Celebrity Apprentice* with $15,000. Morning show cohosts Steve Doocy and Brian Kilmeade, both stand-up guys and terrific pals, came by with $5,000 each. Joseph Abboud, the famed suit maker, just happened to be walking by. He emptied his pockets, donating the $800 he had on him. Supermarket billionaire businessman and perennial mayoral candidate John Catsimatidis and his wife, Margo, brought more than $20,000 cash. They are among New York's most generous philanthropists, and I really like them.

Best of all was party-boy billionaire Stewart Rahr, better known as Stewie Rah Rah, who actually has an office in Trump Tower. In one of my earlier fundraising drives, Stewie had donated $50,000 through my radio show to help rebuild the Rockaways on Long Island after the devastation wrought by Hurricane Sandy. For *Celebrity Apprentice*, Stewie gave me another huge donation, a whopping grand total of $150,000. This man is a treasure and so much fun to be around. Short and stylish, a caricature of a Jewish entrepreneurial perpetual-motion machine, he made hundreds of millions when he sold his family's generic drug business. Now he's party central from the Hamptons to St. Tropez. When he and the other high rollers gave me all that money, Trump complained that my fundraising consisted of taking money from all our mutual friends.

At the announcement that Leeza had won the competition, my daughter Sol, sitting with Erica in the studio audience, began sobbing. She was bereft. Trump did something then that made him a friend for life. He was compassionate and grandfatherly to my then-ten-year-old, comforting her and even allowing her to sit in his big red chair to see what it felt like to be boss.

Also at the Leeza announcement, what was noteworthy to me was that Trump did not say that I was "fired," his signature line. Instead, on the last *Celebrity Apprentice* of his life, he said that Leeza was "hired." The distinction is important. He told me later that he informed network executives that despite their desire for him to "fire" me, he wanted to make it clear that Leeza and I were both winners.

After the dust settled and we were off the air, I confessed to the future president of the United States that I was relieved that he picked Leeza. Given the strong women on the show, and their majority preference for Leeza, I told him that he and I would have been reamed if he had picked me over her. "Those dames would have kicked our butts," I whispered.

He agreed, giving me a knowing glance and saying quietly as he looked around, "You're telling me." He said it shaking his head as only a man who understands contemporary gender politics would shake his head. When Hillary Clinton later played the "woman card" against him, I was relieved that she did not have a *Celebrity Apprentice* arrow in her quiver.

Reacting to being fired on *Celebrity Apprentice*, February 2015.

When I lost *Celebrity Apprentice*, Donald Trump "was compassionate and grandfatherly to my then-ten-year-old, comforting her and even allowing her to sit in his Big Red Chair." February 2015.

BIG MONEY FOR A GREAT CAUSE, MARCH 2015

Even though I lost in the end, doing *Celebrity Apprentice* was a terrific, positive experience. I outran and outlasted fifteen of the sixteen younger competitors and thus became the first Peabody Award winner to be a finalist on *Celebrity Apprentice*. That was almost as cool as when I was on the covers of both *Newsweek* and *Playgirl* magazines in the same year, an earlier (1988) distinction. I also renewed my friendship with the charismatic host, the man who would soon become our forty-fifth president.

The show brought me back to the prime-time mainstream television audience, which had followed the talk show but usually does not watch Fox News. Black and Latino young people seemed especially delighted to see me again after such a long absence, given their reaction on the street or in airports.

I also made a new friend in fellow cast member Sig Hansen, the star of Discovery Channel's *Deadliest Catch*. A chain-smoking, hard-drinking free spirit, Sig is my kind of guy. He is bold, brave, and exists on a diet of coffee, cigarettes, and chocolate.

After the competition, I repaid his efforts on my behalf during the show by traveling to Alaska to attend a benefit for his charity, the US Coast Guard Foundation. At a gala in Anchorage attended by Coast Guard Commandant Admiral Paul Zukunft, since retired, and Senators Lisa Murkowski and Mark Begich, Erica, Sol, and I were pleased to be able to present a $40,000 gift to the foundation in honor of Sig.

Putting aside the usual ebb-and-flow melodrama of reality television, I was responsible for one discordant note. It began when former NFL great Terrell Owens, one of the best receivers in the history of football, a six-time Pro Bowler and future Hall of Famer for the Dallas Cowboys, was fired when his *Apprentice* team failed to generate any meaningful money during one of the fundraising challenges.

During the taped post-task analysis, after Terrell was fired and had left Trump Tower, I said casually to no one in particular that since Terrell was famously broke at the time, he should never have appeared on a program that was basically a fundraiser for charity. Just the week before, my daughter had shown me a tape of Terrell on an episode of *Dr. Phil* in which mothers of his children were demanding unpaid support.

Unbeknownst to me at the time, Kenya Moore, the devious star of *Real Housewives of Atlanta*, took it upon herself to snitch to Terrell, who later that night called me demanding to know how I could do something so unnecessary. I begged forgiveness and lobbied the NBC producers to keep the obnoxious sequence off the air, which to their credit they did. Terrell was right. It was low, and the telling of it embarrasses me.

By the way, speaking of low, this was the season the treacherous yet charming *Real Housewife* Kenya Moore got thrown off *Apprentice* for stealing Vivica A. Fox's cell phone and posting bizarre, obnoxious tweets in sweet, religious Vivica's name. I would pay top price for an MMA bout between Kenya and her idol Omarosa, who, after terrorizing several seasons of *The Apprentice*, similarly rode roughshod for a year in the White House as an aide to President Trump.

Reunited with the entire cast at the show's live finale, Terrell could not have been nicer or more friendly and forgiving. I also lament that this fine fellow, indisputably one of the best NFL pass-catchers ever, has not yet made the Pro Football Hall of Fame. Hopefully, he'll join the class of 2018.

That sad story aside, *Apprentice* had a positive impact for me professionally, regenerating some of my old-school cool and leading to roles in shows such as the *Glee* finale and *Law and Order*, not to mention *Dancing with the Stars*, another reality show adventure in 2016. All my on-camera *Apprentice* feuds ended amicably. In 2017, my best frenemy, Ian Ziering, called personally to encourage me to do the hilarious *Sharknado* movie.

Celebrity Apprentice helped me raise $725,000 for Life's WORC, a charity founded in 1971 by parents of disabled children living in the squalor and filth of Willowbrook. Leeza raised just $464,000, but then won the $250,000 bonus from the show for a grand total of $714,000. Raising money is harder than earning it. I hate asking people for money even for a good cause, but these are great causes. Leeza's money went to a center dealing with Alzheimer's disease. Mine was used to open the Family Center for Autism, a service for stressed families dealing with autistic children in Nassau County outside of New York.

BEAUTY AND THE BEAST, FALL 2015

The funniest coincidence in my entire, modest show-business career came when I played myself in a Puerto Rican–themed version of the classic Christmas tale *Miracle on 34th Street*. The film was called, perhaps unsurprisingly, *Miracle in Spanish Harlem*. In limited theatrical release in 2013, it did better on video.

Since the lead actress was not in any of my scenes, what I did not realize until recently when I finally watched the entire film is that it costarred Kate del Castillo, a notorious Mexican-American actress. Her notoriety is not based on her celebrity. It is based on the fact that the biggest fan of her biggest hit show was a real-life Mexican drug lord, Joaquin Archivaldo Guzman Loera, otherwise known as El Chapo.

Three years after *Miracle in Spanish Harlem*, in spring 2016, I wrote and reported a Fox News special called *Beauty and the Beast: When Kate Met Chapo*. It documented how El Chapo, the savage head of the Sinaloa, Mexico, drug cartel, called by the DEA "the bin Laden of the drug trade," was undone by his need to see Kate del Castillo, at the time Mexico's hottest actress, in the flesh, in the jungle.

I was drawn to the story, even identifying with the drug dealer. Not with his cancerous business, obviously, but with the absurd peril in which he put himself and his empire, just to be with the woman of his searing dreams. Remember in the movie *King Kong* when the giant gorilla is lying dead on Fifth Avenue? As the crowd gathers in wonder, a bystander speaks glowingly of the pilots of the military aircraft that have just knocked Kong from his perch atop the Empire State Building, congratulating them for killing the lovesick monster. Overhearing the conversation, the man who captured Kong, the promoter Carl Denham, played most recently by Jack Black, shakes his head and utters the movie's unforgettable line, saying it was not the pilots, "No, it was beauty killed the beast."

In my Fox News special on the drug lord's recapture, El Chapo is the beast. Kate del Castillo is the beauty. He was captured because of his burning need to see the sultry actress whose character Teresa Mendoza in the wildly popular Mexican prime-time soap opera *La Reina del Sur (Queen of the South)* became Chapo's destructive obsession.

The fictional Teresa was a ruthless, though charismatic, drug dealer. El Chapo identified with her and he was crazy about Kate. My in-depth special report chronicled how Chapo and Kate became pen pals, exchanging highly suggestive text messages both while he was in prison before his second escape, and later when he was on the lam.

So desperate was the world's most-wanted fugitive to see the object of his fascination that he risked everything to meet her face-to-face in a

With Kate del Castillo, the woman of El Chapo's searing dreams. May 2016.

jungle rendezvous. Kate brought Oscar-winning actor Sean Penn with her for the high-stakes meeting.

Penn ended up screwing her businesswise, but that is another story. Mexican and American authorities agree that El Chapo's recapture was the direct result of the Beast's need to see his Beauty.

With reporting from Beverly Hills and from Altiplano Prison in Mexico, my Fox News special chronicled the obsession; the rendezvous; the semi-sleazy role actor Sean Penn played both during and after the steamy jungle meeting; the role of the Mexican government; the extradition of Guzman to the United States; his obsession with then-candidate Donald Trump, whom he threatened to kill; and finally, what impact (not much) Chapo's incarceration would have on the terrible drug scourge his Sinaloa cartel unleashed on the United States.

Before his recapture I was spry enough, barely, to climb down a dark, hundred-foot-long rickety ladder to gain access to the fugitive's remarkable mile-long tunnel, which should be the envy of civil engineers everywhere.

I joked at the time of the escape in July 2015 that he should be hired to finish Manhattan's Second Avenue subway. It was approved in 1929 with a whopping budget of $86 million. Predicted to open between 1938 and 1941, the subway was finally inaugurated on New Year's Day 2017, seventy-six years late and about $4 billion over budget.

At Kate's request, before he was recaptured after four months on the run, the diminutive billionaire doper provided a tape to Sean Penn in lieu of the interview they never got around to doing in their October 2015 jungle rendezvous. In the tape Chapo deadpans that he is merely providing a service by distributing a desired product to a needy clientele and that if he did not, somebody else would. Then the lovestruck tough guy got caught in a shootout with Mexican Marines and extradited to the US, and now awaits trial in Brooklyn on several capital offenses.

THE *NEW YORK TIMES* LIES ABOUT ME (AGAIN), APRIL 2016

Roger had taken me off the bench to cover the rioting in Baltimore, which followed the death in police custody of a young man named Freddie Gray. Two days into the upheaval, the boss was unhappy with the network's coverage and ordered Bill Shine to order me down. Frustrated with being ignored by the Fox News producers, I welcomed the assignment. We got down there in a hurry and produced some important reports, including dramatic encounters with community members and rioters.

My team continued to monitor the situation in Baltimore until the riots simmered down with the indictment of six cops for the death of Freddie Gray, and a massive $6.4 million civil settlement to his family, which to me smacked more of a blackmail payout than reasonable compensation. The West Baltimore neighborhood remains in ruins.

My brother Craig produced a report that proposed a partial solution to what ails the racially fractured, half-wrecked city. He profiled a team of architects encouraging a massive rebuilding of West Baltimore by transferring ownership of its tens of thousands of derelict buildings to the residents in exchange for "sweat equity," their agreement to rehabilitate the ruined and abandoned structures with private and public help. If only the local and state politicians were interested in solving their problems rather than just complaining about them.

But for the rest of the year and beyond, the big news out of hapless Baltimore was the orgy of bloodshed in the wake of Freddie Gray's death in police custody. Most of the victims of the escalation of violence were young, black men shot to death by other young, black men at a rate that on a per-capita basis made 2015 the deadliest ever in the city, with 344 homicides. Although the city is one-thirteenth the size of New York, more were killed that year in Baltimore than in the Big Apple.

There have been no marches protesting the bloodshed in Baltimore. Instead, during the 2016 election campaign for a new mayor to replace Stephanie Rawlings-Blake, I was somehow made the issue. The *New York Times* blamed (credited?) me for providing the pivotal moment for the winning candidate for the Democratic nomination, which is tantamount to being elected in that overwhelmingly Democratic town. (Mayor Catherine E. Pugh was forced to resign the office after being caught secretly using city funds to buy thousands of children's books she wrote but never delivered.)

Here is my blog protesting the wretchedly false characterization:

In a story appearing in the Thursday 28 April 2016 edition headlined *Victor in Mayoral Primary Is Ready to "Get Baltimore Working,"* reporter Sheryl Gay Stolberg writes that the apparent winner in the hotly contested Democratic primary for mayor, State Senate Majority Leader Catherine E. Pugh, "stared down Geraldo Rivera, the Fox News anchor, and berated him on national television for 'inciting people,'" during the devastating 2015 Baltimore riots.

Ms. Stolberg concludes that it was the defining moment for Senator (now Baltimore mayor) Pugh's successful primary campaign. It is a total fiction.

As the videotape Fox News has provided the *New York Times* makes clear, Senator Pugh and I were united in trying to report honestly and professionally about the chaos in West Baltimore a year ago, following the tragic death in police custody of Freddie Gray. We spent hours together during the urban turmoil and violence, the senator making several appearances on camera.

As the tape shows, Senator Pugh's disquiet was directed at the trouble-makers who were contributing to the mayhem, not at this reporter. Indeed it was my interview with Senator Pugh that the demonstrators, the most vocal of whom was later arrested, were attempting to disrupt.

In 2005 another *Times* reporter (Alessandra Stanley) wrote a similarly fictional account of my coverage of Hurricane Katrina. That discredited story alleged that I pushed rescue workers out of the way so that I would be seen on camera rescuing elderly victims of the storm.

There is a pattern. New Orleans was a fabrication the newspaper was forced to correct. So is Baltimore. Because the *NYT* wants it to be true doesn't make it true. Your hatred of Fox News and me clouds your judgment and distorts your reporting.

President Trump calls the *New York Times* "a failing newspaper," while still craving its acceptance. His ongoing complaint, particularly after the paper ran a front-page, two-page spread on his alleged exploitation of women, is that the self-proclaimed "Newspaper of Record" consistently exaggerates his failings.

During the presidential campaign, stories abounded in outlets like the *Times* and the *Washington Post* about the Trump University class-action lawsuit settlement, his bankrupt casinos, and his alleged mistreatment of women, most of which he still dismisses as "fake news." Yet nary any stories praised either Trump's civic accomplishments or his admirable family's accomplishments, except to criticize their potential for conflicts of interest. Still, it was a surprise the morning after my April 2015 confrontation with the bullies in the rubble-strewn, tear-gassed streets of West Baltimore to get a congratulatory telephone call from Trump, who tracked me down at a local radio station in that stricken town.

"I loved when you told that punk that he was making a fool of himself," the reality host about to turn formidable presidential candidate told me. Then he railed against urban anarchy and violent activists like Black Lives Matter and Occupy Wall Street and the gangbangers who just want to wreck and plunder.

Demonstrations, protests, and unrest initiated by those anti-police groups were polarizing the nation, fracturing it again along racial lines. When I criticized best-selling hip-hop artists like the highly talented Kendrick Lamar for exacerbating tensions with constant anti-police images in his videos, he retaliated by devoting an entire song on his top-selling album *DAMN.* to criticizing me. When President Obama told the country in his farewell address ten days before Trump's inauguration in January 2017 that race relations "have never been better," I wondered to which nation he referred. Each alleged act of police violence, like Freddie Gray's death in Baltimore Police custody, generated a furious and counterproductive response on the streets. All of it seemed to help Donald Trump's candidacy. Police unions and those sympathetic to law enforcement, and most of the white working class, rallied to him ever more vigorously as supporters of inner-city communities protested the divisive Republican candidate.

With typical moderation, President Obama tried to balance his response, condemning both cops who kill and cop killers, pleasing advocates of neither. Unseen or barely noticed was how street violence began ticking up in cities like Baltimore; Ferguson, Missouri; and Chicago as police began a subtle slowdown. In 2016 it was impossible not to notice that the Windy City had a bloody record 796 murders, more than New York and Los Angeles combined. I have neither doubt nor proof that the cop slowdown was intentional and perhaps even secretly coordinated among law enforcement agencies or constituent unions. "Blue flu" pulled cops back from the fray even as candidate Trump held boisterous rallies against rampant urban disorder in his often-inflammatory primary and general-election campaigns.

When he reached me at the radio station that day in Baltimore, he added that, before calling me, he had first called my boss, Roger Ailes, to praise my reporting in Baltimore. But mostly he wanted to praise the fact that I had not retreated during the confrontation on the street with the provocateur.

"You're a champion," he said, not for the last time. To great impact and mixed reviews, he draws harsh distinctions between champions and chokers.

CHAMPIONS, CHOKERS, CARICATURES, AND CONVENTIONAL THINKERS, 2015–2016

I thought Trump became a caricature to win the Republican nomination. You have to be a hard-right loco to win it. At least that was my conventional thinking. Trump, like any GOP presidential candidate, had to be a harshly conservative, hard-right-wing Attila the Hun to get nominated, and then a moderate-sounding Ronald Reagan or George H. W. Bush to get elected.

What the world and I did not expect was that, after securing the nomination, Trump never pivoted to the center. Instead, the harsh tone that won him the nomination later won him the White House. President Trump made a clear-eyed calculation that if he motivated both the frustrated and vaguely uneasy white working class, and the old, mostly but not exclusively southern, anti-civil rights, and yes, even semi-racist, whites who deeply resented political correctness, multiculturalism, undocumented immigration, and unmistakably, the eight-year tenure of our first black president—if he did all that, he had a shot.

Anyway, the person I thought I knew, my fantasy "real" Donald Trump, was visible when he spoke to the New York Republican Gala in April 2016, days before the Empire State's primary election. This was Trump the builder, speaking at the event in the Grand Hyatt Hotel, which he reminded everyone was once the crumbling, derelict Hotel Commodore until in 1978 he maneuvered to get control of it as a thirty-two-year-old novice developer from Queens.

A magnet for junkies, hookers, and derelicts, the hotel was redeveloped by him, saving the neighborhood and remaking East Forty-Second Street. He sold it twenty years later for a $143 million profit. He then went on to convert the West Side of Manhattan on the Hudson River waterfront from Fifty-Seventh Street to Seventy-Second Street. He overcame decades of neighborhood intransigence to remake a mangled rail yard, rusted tracks, and wrecked piers into a wonderful neighborhood, where Erica and I used to live.

After the city failed for a decade to get it done, in 1986 Trump made the Wollman Rink in Central Park an ice-skating asset for every kid in town, including mine. Twenty years later in 2016, he opened his terrific Trump Golf Links at Ferry Point in the Bronx, in an area that had been a garbage dump for decades as the city struggled to rehabilitate it.

As a mogul of uncertain reputation, he apparently made a habit of stiffing suppliers, some of whom I knew, which I duly reported beginning in 1991. But he also created jobs and made money from enterprise unlike any of his rivals for the nomination and certainly unlike Hillary Clinton. As candidate Trump brutally alleged during the campaign, she and husband Bill got rich, earning roughly a quarter-billion dollars, without ever having a real job in the private sector.

SUNDAY MORNING TRUMP, MAY 2016

Another small example of the president's unfailing friendship came during the campaign on a Sunday morning in May 2016. Trump had just appeared for a remote taping of *Fox News Sunday* with Chris Wallace from our studio on the twelfth floor of Fox News in New York. Chris, who would later receive deserved praise for his masterful moderating of the third and final presidential debate, was in the studio in Washington, DC.

I was downstairs in our first-floor *Fox and Friends* studio to commemorate the fifth anniversary of the killing of bin Laden, but first went upstairs to say hello to my controversial pal. He had not yet sealed the GOP nomination, but was getting close. When Trump finished taping, to prevent any competitive jealousy that I was stealing Chris's guest and scooping him by putting Trump on my show live before Chris's pre-taped show aired, I joked to Trump that I thought it was "Bring Your Friend to Work Day." Rather than ask the presumptive Republican nominee to come downstairs with me, I told him I was going on *Fox and Friends* and would be delighted if he stopped by.

He did, to my surprise, taking a seat on what we call the "curvy couch," for a long, live, newsworthy interview on the eve of a pivotal May 3 primary in Indiana. That friendly gesture is an example of why it is hard not to like him. He has always treated me with respect and affection. Of course, if he moves to deport innocent, undocumented immigrant youngsters or succeeds in banning Muslims or abortion, I will change my mind. But absent the implementation of some draconian policy, I am willing to give him the chance to surprise his critics and bring the country together. Indeed, there were some glimmers of hope. The compassionate way he handled the federal response to Hurricanes Harvey, Irma, and Maria was more like the president I hoped he would become.

To the extent that I can detect, Donald Trump does not have a racist bone in his body, although I certainly wish he had been quicker to condemn the KKK's David Duke during the campaign and the Charlottesville Neo-Nazi rioters after he was elected. Before becoming president, green was his most important color. Other than driving ambition and an irrepressible ego, the president is a down-to-earth, all-around good guy, a player in his younger years to be sure, but not now. What kept me from supporting him was his toxic immigration policy. As I discovered researching two books on the subject, *HisPanic* in 2007 and *The Great Progression* in 2008, we cannot deport our way out of this problem. These immigrant families contain adults who are undocumented, but most are otherwise law-abiding and have been here for decades. Many of their children are US-born citizens. Make all the undocumented get documented by registering, getting background checks, paying a fine, learning English, and getting in line. Don't muster a "deportation force" to round them up as if they are terrorists. They are the pizza deliverers, the babysitters, lawn mowers, poultry processors, and meatpackers. Some are computer whizzes and members of the military. They make America stronger, not weaker.

In that regard, I confess to being totally dismayed when Trump began spewing intemperate words against the federal judge hearing one of the class-action lawsuits pending against him, stemming from his now-defunct Trump University. In criticizing federal District Judge Gonzalo Curiel, Trump went out of his way to label the Indiana-born jurist a "Mexican"—not a Mexican-American, but a Mexican. Can you imagine the chaos if judges were disqualified because they happened to be Irish or Jewish or African-American?

At the time of the controversy involving Judge Curiel, it seemed inevitable that "The Donald" was going down to defeat. This is what I wrote for the now-defunct Fox News Latino website in the days before the nominating conventions. In retrospect it reflects uninspired conventional wisdom.

"Trump's obvious intemperance during this June 2016 controversy shrank the Republican Party, which needs to expand and be more inclusive. A Republican cannot win the presidency on white votes alone. There just are not enough to go around. He must moderate his rhetoric and reassess his apparently dim view of many in the Latino population and assure non-white, or non-Judeo-Christian Americans, that he does not consider us second class or some kind of enemy within. If he does not, then again, he knows that I could not vote for him. He may win anyway, but it is a long shot and he would take office in a nation divided."

Shows how little I know. Trump's long shot obviously paid off. The candidate ignited a movement grounded in white working-class men that uniquely captured the disquiet many Americans feel about our nation's being destabilized by unregulated immigration. The reality is not nearly as daunting as the hype from xenophobic nativists, whose real fear is that the country will lose its white majority. But that is not to suggest that there are not real problems with our southern border.

EL CHAPO'S REVENGE, FEBRUARY 2016

As candidate Trump pointed out in campaign stops from the postindustrial Midwest to stricken New Hampshire, Mexican drug cartels are flooding our towns and cities, particularly in the Northeast, with heroin and its lethal synthetic cousin fentanyl in amounts and potency unseen previously. The Sinaloa drug cartel, formerly run by the aforementioned billionaire drug kingpin and now inmate "El Chapo" Guzman, is responsible for the deaths of tens of thousands of Americans, ranging from the kid next door to the doomed entertainer formerly known as Prince. According to Drug Enforcement officials, the number of US heroin addicts has jumped 135 percent since 2002, about when the Mexican cartels expanded out of the ghetto and began targeting the American Heartland. Heroin deaths in the same period skyrocketed 533 percent.

In the February 2016 week leading up to the first-in-the-nation primary in New Hampshire, I filed a rare series of field reports investigating the impact of the drug scourge on folks in the Granite State. What I saw in New Hampshire was dire. This state of just 1.1 million mostly white, suburban, and rural people suffered four hundred overdose deaths in 2014 and another four hundred in 2015. Then 2016 and 2017 kept the pace with at least an O.D. death a day.

Reeling from that epidemic, authorities in New Hampshire and the Drug Enforcement Administration identified Chapo's Sinaloa drug cartel as the principal supplier of the poison responsible for so much misery in such an unlikely place. El Chapo is in federal prison, as I said awaiting the first of his many trials, but while the head has been taken off the snake, nobody in law enforcement expects the cartel to slither away. In fact, now that they have synthesized heroin with a substance called fentanyl, their body count is just getting higher.

Each of the candidates from both parties picked up on the heroin/fentanyl-abuse issue, but Trump tied it best to border security, and made the biggest impact, easily winning the New Hampshire primary and accelerating his bizarre and historic journey to the White House.

LET'S DANCE, MARCH 2016

From the physical demands alone, Trump's endurance during the campaign was a feat I could not have matched. I did not even get past the first elimination round on *Dancing with the Stars* in March 2016. By then my movements had lost fluidity, my legs were shot, my left knee creaky, having been replaced in 2009 with a titanium device that works well enough, the principal pain in the ass being at airports when the knee invariably sets off the metal detectors.

I no longer do my trademark strolling standups to camera because of the limp caused by the neuropathy in my right foot. Aside from swagger, the dead foot cost me a lost decade of senior tennis, skiing, and jogging. I have a perpetually sore back and wrists, ankles that crackle and pop, and a once-piercing stare that has become watery with age.

My main takeaway from *Dancing with the Stars*, Season 22 is that I probably should not have waited until I was a lame seventy-two-year-old to do the show. The physical challenges of the dance routines are rigorous, the training akin to the buildup to a boxing match. Actually, boxing has the advantage over dancing in that fighting is not as tough, at least not to me. A boxer for twenty-five years, getting punched in the face is nothing compared to the embarrassment of missing a dance step live in front of 12 or 13 million viewers, which I did routinely on *DWTS*.

My performance was lamentable, disastrous esthetically, but not lacking in good humor or charm. It was especially bad during the widely anticipated world-premiere event in March 2016. My partner, who deserved better, was Edyta Sliwinska. A glamorous, classically trained ballroom dancer who hails from Poland, Edyta was making her grand comeback to the program after an absence of five years.

Our dance that fateful premiere night was a Cha-Cha, a Latin number. Since dances on the show are actually thematic mini-musicals, ours needed a story. Returning to an old chestnut, *The Mystery of Al Capone's Vault*, our idea was that Edyta was the long-sought treasure that had eluded me when I opened the Prohibition-era gangster's vault in the

My Trump impression. In the backstage lot with Cheech
Marin at *Dancing with the Stars*, March 2016.

basement of Chicago's old Lexington Hotel in 1986. I blew the door
open onstage, and she slinked out in a cloud of smoke to dance. *DWTS*,
like *Capone's Vault*, is live television. (*Capone's* worldwide audience was
far larger, approaching 40 million in those days before cable and Netflix.)

Back in 1986, the Capone event was a gigantic embarrassment, but at
least I did not have to dance. Here, dancing is the whole point. Aside from
the theatrical aspects, the Cha-Cha demands considerable hip swiveling
and rhythm, which I never had. Infirm, disabled, and lacking rhythm, I
was a dance disaster.

Lack of rhythm aside, there was another reason I had turned down
several earlier requests to appear on *DWTS* when I was more physically
able: backstage romances were en vogue on the show in the early days.
One professional dancer became serially engaged to several of her celebrity dance partners. Clean and sober in regard to fidelity, I no longer stray.
I don't have the track record to judge anybody who does, but I am over it.

With Edyta Sliwinska, my professional partner in *Dancing with the Stars*. She deserved better. January 2016.

To ensure that everybody knew my *DWTS* partner and I were only in it for the dancing, Erica and I invited Edyta, husband Alec, and son Michael to dinner at our New York apartment the week ABC announced the cast and pairings.

Aside from checking it off my bucket list, another reason I wanted to do the show was to send the message to the big Boomer generation coming up behind me that they should get off the couch and shake their booty. Use it or lose it. Everybody our age has something that hurts. But move what you can, for as long as you can, since you will have plenty of time to be still after you die.

During rehearsals, the lame foot led to two body-slamming falls, but with the help of hidden braces on ankles, knees, and back, I got to the point where I felt I could make it through the routine without collapsing. My only beef was that the producers never communicated to the audience that I was an old man overcoming a physical impairment to compete.

Instead, I came off as just an old man who could not dance. The bigger problem was that I choked during the live show. Adding to my physical clumsiness, during the Cha-Cha I zigged when I should have zagged and as a result earned for poor Edyta and myself the lowest score of the twelve couples competing.

When crotchety *DWTS* judge Len Goodman heaped scorn on my inability to point my toes, I laughed since with my ankles immobilized by tape, toe pointing was impossible. In a way, even worse was the post-dance interview with cohost Erin Andrews. The brave and glamorous sports-caster had just won a $55 million jury verdict against parent companies of the Nashville, Tennessee, Marriott hotel, an award she deserved, the hotel having failed utterly to protect her against a stalker who videotaped her naked through the peephole in her room door. To add to her tough slog, she later announced she was battling cervical cancer.

Perhaps because of the enormous attention her case had attracted, she seemed uncomfortable with me, as if she thought I was paparazzo cov-ering her case. In fairness, I may be reading more into that than existed, but when I used an old show-business adage to explain my clunky perfor-mance, she did not get it. I said of my performance, "It is not how well the bear dances, but that the bear dances at all." Her face was blank; then blinking as if snapping out of a mocking trance, she said she had no idea what I was talking about. My attempt at self-effacing humor dropped like a stone.

Anyway, it was ridiculous to think I could compete against the 2016 season's crew, which featured some great, young athletes includ-ing Superbowl MVP Von Miller of the Denver Broncos, and Antonio Brown, the Pittsburgh Steelers All-Star wide receiver. The deaf heart-throb Nyle DiMarco, winner of *America's Top Model*, performed impec-cably, rousing the audience to cheers even as they wondered how he could keep the beat.

Wanja Morris, the charismatic heart of Boyz II Men, performed exuberantly with star dancer Lindsay Arnold, a gorgeous young blonde. Another budding star dancer who can also kick your eye out, UFC fighter Paige VanZant, was very impressive and a crowd favorite. Paige and Lind-say were both graceful and athletic.

Super-sweet Kim Fields, lately of *Real Housewives of Atlanta*, did a great job charming the crowd. So did the ABC Network hometown favorite Ginger Zee, who is the popular *Good Morning America* meteorologist. Ginger had a new baby, but she was trim, ferocious, and wowed the audience week after week.

The scrappy and wonderful Marla Maples, whom I have known since she was the second Mrs. Donald Trump, cartwheeled through the early weeks, easily handling with style the renewed and intense attention brought on by her ex's electoral success. It was impressive to see her keep her poise and balance on and off the dance floor, her daughter Tiffany frequently by her side. The often-forgotten child among her supercharged siblings, Tiffany is also underrated, impressive in her own right, thanks in part to her wonderful mother.

Mischa Barton seemed to have a bad time on the show. The actress who surged to fame on *The O.C.* danced just marginally better than I did and did not seem to enjoy being there. We had a heart-to-heart about how at barely thirty years old she had been aged out of her ingénue phase by the casting directors and was only being offered mother roles. She had a series of well-chronicled controversies later.

Meanwhile, *Full House* and *Fuller House* star Jodie Sweetin did a great job impressing both the audience and the judges. Like Mischa, Jodie had a difficult time dealing with life after youthful stardom, and both Mischa and Jodie saw the dance show as a way back to show-business success or at least heightened visibility. To tell you the truth, that is probably why I did it, even though I was lame and getting lamer.

Heisman Trophy winner and former pro quarterback Doug Flutie was the only other contestant over fifty, and he is almost twenty years younger than I am. Best remembered for throwing the monumental sixty-five-yard "Hail Mary" pass in the rain to bring his Boston College Eagles to victory in the 1984 Orange Bowl over a heavily favored Miami team, he is one of the nicest guys you would ever want to hang out with. I was reminded that among the host of NFL and CFL teams he played for professionally were the New Jersey Generals of the now defunct USFL, a team owned by Donald Trump, who paid $8 million for it before the league went belly-up after failing to merge with the NFL. The Generals were terrific but the league was awful.

Flutie tried hard on *DWTS*, practicing each evening with his daughter Alexa, a professional dancer and San Diego Chargers cheerleader. Calm and sincere, he is a real family man and deservedly lasted on the show far longer than I did. Comparing Doug and the rest of *DWTS* cast to my colleagues on Trump's *Celebrity Apprentice*, I'd say this was a much nicer bunch. They were loving and supportive instead of backstabbing and conspiratorial.

The pleasant vibe did not help my performance. After forgetting key steps during the first routine, I similarly botched an even more flamboyant second routine the next Monday night. That sketch began prophetically with President Donald Trump (me) being interrupted in the Oval Office on a phone call with Vladimir Putin by my drop-dead-gorgeous first lady Melania, played of course by Edyta, another equally gorgeous European import.

For the routine, two other sexy dancers in the troupe rip off my conservative presidential suit, and Edyta and I break out in dance, doing a hot salsa to "Mi Amigo," an upbeat classic by the late, great Tito Puente, who was *mi amigo* in real life. The idea was to stress the comic irony of Donald, the alleged anti-Latino who is hell-bent on building a great wall on our southern border after calling Mexicans rapists and drug dealers, dancing the Latin Night Salsa. We also aimed to ride the wave of attention that the candidates' wives were receiving at the time, March 2016, in the tacky, "Whose Wife Is Hotter" debate mudslinging between Trump and Senator Ted Cruz.

To make a long story short, my dance did not suck as badly as it did on premiere night but was still pretty bad. The score was the same as the first night, a meager 13 out of 30, but it did not matter since, unbeknownst to us, we had already been voted off. They should give scores based on a handicap, like in golf. I joked when Edyta and I were eliminated that if we had *not* been, "I would have demanded a recount."

My supporters in the studio audience included Erica, all five of my children, and Cheech and his beautiful Russian-born wife and brilliant concert pianist, Natasha. Everyone took the defeat fairly well, except then-ten-year-old Sol Liliana, who again, just like when I lost *Apprentice* the year before, started sobbing inconsolably. She loves her daddy and hates to see him hurt.

Since the only star she wanted to meet was Von Miller, I brought the strapping six-foot-three-inch, 250-pound Super Bowl MVP linebacker over to give her a hug, which went far to relieve her disappointment. He and the others, including the production team, were super-considerate, nice people.

At *Dancing with the Stars* with all five kids and Gabriel's wife, Deb. March 2016.

Nyle won the *DWTS* competition. Not only did he dance superbly, he did it without the benefit of being able to hear the music. It was an amazing and deeply impressive achievement. The runner-up was Paige VanZant, who I thought was equally impressive, going from using her feet to kick people in the face as an ultimate fighter to elegant, sensual dancing. She could easily have been the winner of the show's coveted "Mirror Ball Trophy."

Looking back on the experience, I only regret not doing more to keep Edyta on the show's center stage. That aside, having the far-flung kids all in one spot for those several days was wonderful. The girls giggled and shared "GLAMSQUAD On-Demand Beauty" makeup artists (the ones who come to your apartment or hotel room rather than you going to their salon) and tried on different dresses with Erica; the big boys hung with their daddy and I got to play with Desmond, aka Desi, my second grandson. The girls got to see me on a show their girlfriends actually watch. Trump got a kick out of my impression of him. Jon Peters and I hung out, endlessly talking about the good old days and the challenges of getting creaky; I lost five pounds and had a lot of laughs. All things considered, the whole *DWTS* experience was a life-affirming blast.

Chapter 11

FUROR AT FOX

Speaking of explosions, several months after I completed the first draft of this manuscript, in the summer of 2016, all hell broke loose at Fox News, when my boss, Roger Ailes, became embroiled in a catastrophic sexual-harassment scandal. One of my former colleagues, Gretchen Carlson, alleged that he had tormented her throughout her decade at Fox News. I responded to Gretchen's original allegations with extreme skepticism.

Along with all but a handful of my Fox colleagues, I figured Gretchen was motivated by sour grapes. At the time she got fired by Roger, she had the lowest-rated show on the network. She also withheld her allegations that Roger harassed her until she was fired at the end of June 2016, her contract not renewed. In ordinary times, before the #MeToo movement, there was ample reason to be skeptical, if not cynical. It is self-evident that those days are gone.

I am now beyond sorry that I doubted her, but at the time, her case was not a slam-dunk. Nobody knew that Gretchen had secretly recorded Roger being an obnoxiously macho deviant. At that initial point it was a he said/she said, based solely on her shocking allegations, which the monarch of Fox News, through his spokeswoman and ace attorney Susan Estrich, vehemently denied..

Aside from the accuser's motive to exaggerate, there was also the fact that the accused did not fit the stereotype. Roger did not seem the type.

331

While the man I knew was a lot of arguably bad things—brawler, bully, ideological zealot, to name a few—he did not seem a sex predator. For instance, I never heard him say anything sexually suggestive or inappropriate about a female colleague. Don't get me wrong. He was as harsh and insulting to women as he was to men. Remember the scene with Laurie Dhue and the necklace, but he was brutal rather than sexist. "Well, she's as dumb as a bag of rocks." "What in hell does she call that outfit?" Man, woman, straight, gay, he was an equal-opportunity insulter.

I never took his jibes personally, but maybe that was a function of our being roughly the same age, both products of the world before feminism, gender equality, equal rights, and sensitivity training. Now I feel like a sap, a sucker who did not know the score. I always pictured Roger as a hail-fellow-well-met, another backslapping scrapper, more likely to tear your throat out than engage in sweet talk, as my first tweet on the Gretchen scandal indicated:

Geraldo Rivera @GeraldoRivera
I've known him 40 years. He's about as flirty as the grizzly in #TheRevenant. I stand with Roger Ailes

Remembering how Roger always had my back through thick or thin, even as his scandal deepened during the Republican National Convention, and as many editorial writers were writing him off, I fired off this tweet:

Geraldo Rivera @GeraldoRivera
Don't believe the crap about #RogerAiles. Only ones talking dirt are those who hate #FoxNews & want to hurt network that's kicking their ass

Roger resigned two days later when it became apparent that Gretchen was not alone in alleging abhorrent behavior behind his closed doors. Disbelieving the charges against him, I almost walked out alongside him, enthusiastically joining a budding revolt by many of my colleagues. If Roger was forced unfairly to leave, we vowed to follow him.

Like many of Roger's big talent, I had a "key man" clause in my contract that allowed me to leave the network if for any reason Roger was ousted or left voluntarily. Roger encouraged the clause to be inserted in his talent deals to enhance his own invulnerability. If you messed with Roger, you risked having the whole enterprise crumble as the talent loyal to him left with him.

Many of us were fixing to follow him out the door. Under the leadership of an enraged Sean Hannity, with hearty cheerleading from hyper-conservative websites, we decided to join forces and demand that our company stand behind our embattled chief executive. To us Know Nothings, it seemed obvious that Roger was being hoisted on a petard of political correctness. Sure he was grizzled, gruff, and tough, but that was his charm. Like Donald Trump and millions of other old machos, including me, Roger was a 1950s relic of *The Front Page*.

We hail from an era when virtually every executive smoked and drank too much, while often behaving inappropriately with secretaries, female executives, or other men's wives. Necessarily, times, attitudes, and laws have changed, but my sympathy for Roger is based on the feeling that creaky old relics like him should be allowed to die off. He should have known better, but he was too arrogant and entitled to notice that the world had changed. Please note that I do not think that "dinosaur" excuse applies to the disgusting alleged rapist Harvey Weinstein or to pompous pervert *House of Cards* actor Kevin Spacey, the single most unpleasant person I have ever met in show business. Those twenty-first-century predators weren't even around in the 1960s.

When the Roger/Gretchen story broke, I remember vividly being at the Republican National Convention in the makeshift Fox News green room at Cleveland's Quicken Loans Arena, clenching my fists along with Sean and angrily condemning what felt like the railroading of our founder and leader.

Producer/brother Craig stopped me from destroying my own career and reputation. He prevented me from sending a third, even more outrageous tweet, blaming the victims and their co-conspirators in management while celebrating the perpetrator.

During that period of high drama and profound flux, I was especially impatient with Fox News anchor Megyn Kelly for refusing to back the man who had made her a star, thinking that the elegant, ambitious anchor was selfish and in it only for herself. A "Boycott Megyn" movement started within our ranks, with various on-air personalities muttering about how it was all part of Megyn's ongoing and ultimately very successful contract negotiations, albeit at another network, NBC. Many Fox talent

loyal to Roger were vowing never to go on her *Kelly File* show again, and I
was among them, not that I was often asked.

Without naming names, let me say that the older women at Fox were
particularly vicious in their attacks on the soaring celebrity. Thank God
that boycott nonsense never went anywhere beyond a few soon-deleted
references on *Breitbart* and *Drudge*. The next day Sean pulled me aside to
say the revolt was over because the allegations against Roger were true.
"How bad is it?" I asked. "It's bad," Sean replied, shaking his head in
melancholy and disbelief.

The most explosive allegation of Roger's several purported victims of
unwanted advances came from Megyn Kelly herself. When word spread
that he had allegedly sexually bullied and come on to her at the start of her
Fox career, her reluctance to back Roger vs. Gretchen's lawsuit suddenly
transformed from bitchy to heroic.

At that moment, to Roger's malignant misfortune, Megyn was the
most important person at Fox News, maybe in the entire television news
industry. For one thing, her contract was expiring the next summer, in
2017, and the network was desperate to keep her. She had become more

At the Democratic National Convention with *Fox and Friends* friends, Tucker
Carlson, Heather Nauert, Steve Doocy, Ainsley Earhardt, Brian Kilmeade,
me, Major Pete Hegseth, and Clayton Morris. Philadelphia, July 2016.

important than Roger. Her ratings success made her valuable from a commercial standpoint, but that was just the beginning of her appeal. Megyn had crossed over into mainstream recognition and respect. She had become a sought-after celebrity in her own right, separate and apart from Fox.

MEGYN ASCENDANT, AUGUST 2015

Megyn put the nail in Roger's professional coffin with her charges that he had harassed her back in the day. But it was her interaction with Donald Trump fifteen months earlier that almost changed the course of history. By taking on the candidate's past chauvinistic and coarse treatment of women during the first Republican presidential debate in August 2015, also in Cleveland, she both distinguished and distanced herself from others at Fox News.

Led by the unflinching Hannity, the slightly subtler O'Reilly, up-and-comer Eric Bolling (a talented broadcaster who gravely damaged his

Megyn Kelly and her husband, author Doug Brunt, at
Erica's fortieth birthday party, January 2015.

career with a dopey prank allegedly involving intimate pictures of himself to three female staffers), earnest Steve Doocy on *Fox and Friends*, and me, our network was already behaving deferentially to our hometown hero, the flamboyant Mr. Trump. I began trumpeting his certain nomination from the first day of his campaign in June 2015.

During that first debate in August 2015, Megyn embarrassed and infuriated Trump by brutally recalling previous public comments he had made about women generally and the actress-comedienne Rosie O'Donnell specifically. Megyn stuck a knife in Trump's ribs when she famously asked how a man who refers to women as "fat pigs," "slobs," and "animals" could ever be president of the United States.

The question was prescient, a harbinger of scandals to come for the forty-fifth president in his long-shot quest for the White House. Flushing with anger, he sputtered. His stunned response was to criticize Megyn for daring to ask so impolite a question. It was a sin for which he would never forgive her. Trump lamely suggested in response that he did not disrespect women generally, but only one woman, Rosie, who suffered his specific wrath for something she had said while hosting *The View*.

With Eric Bolling, Colonel Oliver North, and Sean Hannity.
Inauguration festivities, January 2017.

ROSIE VS. DONALD, DECEMBER 2006

The friction between Trump and the then-almost-as-large-as-life Rosie O'Donnell had its roots in a controversy ten years earlier. Rosie had the temerity in 2006 to tear into Trump, who was at the time the owner of the Miss USA contest.

It happened after he had held a news conference announcing grandly that he would overlook allegations of past drug and alcohol abuse by his current Miss USA, Tara Connor, and allow her to keep the title. "I've always been a believer in second chances," he told reporters, his tone dripping magnanimity.

As we later learned in the campaign, Tara Connor was not the first pageant winner to incur Trump's wrath for her alleged shortcomings. Hillary Clinton later uncovered another, Alicia Machado, his 1996 Miss Universe, whom he condemned for being overweight, calling her "Miss Piggy." Hillary used Alicia's story to flog her campaign theme that Trump and the Republicans were waging war on women.

The day after he gave Tara Connor a reprieve, Rosie ripped his throat out on *The View*. She ridiculed his hair, his business acumen, and his casino bankruptcies, while asking rhetorically how dare he, a deeply flawed man, pass judgment on anyone.

"He's the moral authority? Left the first wife, had an affair, left the second wife, had an affair, had kids both times, but he's the moral compass for twenty-year-olds in America? Donald, sit and spin, my friend," Rosie fumed. When one of her cohosts brought up that Trump was an extremely successful businessman, Rosie pounced, "He's been bankrupt so many times! The people that he owed money to got shorted out, but he got to try again and again," and so on.

Trump went ballistic in his rage, summoning a few of his longtime friends in the media, including me, to his side at his ornate office in Trump Tower to hear him excoriate Rosie, who is also a friend of mine. He was brutal: "She's a loser. She's always been a loser," and downhill from there. I was tempted to replay my damning 2006 Rosie tape when candidate Trump was on the ropes, embroiled in a devastating scandal involving outtakes from the *Access Hollywood* segment he shot the year before, in 2005, with another mutual friend, Billy Bush.

Three days before inauguration in Trump Tower with the president-elect, January 2017.

As I'll describe, the *Access* scandal almost sank him, and continues to haunt him among many women as the worldwide epidemic of sexual harassment allegations that started when Gretchen took down Roger continues to sweep through politics, media, Hollywood, and beyond. Despite the fact that Trump uttered his grossly inappropriate, politically incorrect remarks a generation ago, they continue to dog him. Almost a year after his caught-on-tape remarks were published, and six months into his presidency, in a widely read July 2017 piece in the *New York Times Sunday Review*, Michelle Goldberg called the president "an erotically incontinent libertine." Coming, though, as the *Access* scandal did, in the heat of the campaign, in October, a full month before the 2016 election, with two debates remaining, and before the FBI's James Comey and the Kremlin's Vladimir Putin/Wikileaks dropped their bombs on Hillary, Trump had just enough time to recover and pull off the greatest upset in recorded political history, bar none. His wife saved him. When Melania characterized the *Access* exchange as "locker-room banter," many men in her husband's and my generation knew what she was talking about.

As the *Access* scandal and the war with Megyn Kelly played havoc with the Trump candidacy, he lashed out at Megyn, condemning and berating her at every opportunity. Roger stared him down, deeply critical of the candidate's obsession with the correspondent. Isn't it ironic that in the same year Roger Ailes rode to Megyn's defense against the wrath of Donald Trump, her allegations of Roger's long-ago sexual harassment ended his career?

The scorn and ridicule from the media industry could not help but contribute to Roger's steep physical decline and death less than a year later. Megyn's damning allegations, as described in her bestselling memoir, *Settle for More*, joined the flood of condemnation from other accusers that swept away what remained of Roger's legacy so totally that these days scarcely a trace remains. Now, it is almost as if Roger never existed, despite the fact that he was one of the most important figures in the history of television news.

Despite the pity and guilt I feel over the circumstances of Roger's death, I am filled with regret for stubbornly discounting the accusations of his various accusers, and apologize for my skepticism. Like victims of sexual assault, those alleging harassment deserve the rebuttable presumption of credibility. Even Gabriel Sherman, Ailes's obsessive pursuer, the reporter who disclosed every sin Roger had ever committed and then some, Roger's personal Inspector Javert, the *New York Magazine* writer I called a "nerd with a grudge," deserves my apology. He was on the right side of history. Roger allegedly used his position to talk dirty to terrified women who worked for him. Might does not mean right. Roger was wrong, and in sticking up for him before I knew the score, I was part of the problem.

Various *New York Times* reporters, including Emily Steel, worked tirelessly for months to prove that the Ailes scandal was the tip of a Fox News iceberg. In a gigantic April 2017 exposé carried on her newspaper's front page for several days running, Steel's thesis was that Fox was Animal House, where horny executives routinely preyed upon vulnerable women. One of her eventual prizes was my old friend, Roger's aide-de-camp, Bill Shine. After being named one of Ailes's successors as co-president, Bill was forced to resign amidst the storm of controversy and swirl of lawsuits spawned by the sexual-harassment hurricane. He was essentially accused of aiding and abetting Ailes, although I believe, as our mutual friend Sean

"The *New York Times*'s real prize, though, was taking down the
giant, Bill O'Reilly." At a Mets game, May 2017.

Hannity does, that Shine never did anything bad to anybody. He is a great
guy, a terrific producer, and is sorely missed at Fox News.

The *New York Times*'s real prize, though, was taking down the giant,
Bill O'Reilly, who was shamed into resigning about three weeks after the
paper's initial exposé. Not the nicest or certainly not the smoothest guy,
impatient and as volatile as an IED, O'Reilly was given to outbursts of
rage. He could be scary and socially awkward, but as far as I knew, not evil.

O'Reilly fell off the cliff when the *Times* revealed that he had settled
several sexual-harassment lawsuits, including one claim dating back fifteen
years, for a total of around $13 million. He said it was all in an ultimately
vain attempt to keep the cases quiet and protect his family and career from
scandal. That news was shocking enough. Six months later, it got worse,
when news leaked that he had bestowed an additional $32 million fortune
on former Fox News legal analyst Lis Wiehl. I can't imagine that kind of
money being paid out unless the underlying secret was undeniably grisly.

Our friend Lis's $32 million settlement almost equals the $33.5 million O.J. Simpson was ordered to pay to the families of Nicole Brown Simpson and her friend Ronald Goldman after being found liable for their brutal murders. Just for context, the $20 million Gretchen got from Fox is more than three times the typical settlement from cities to black families, like Freddie Gray's, whose beloved sons were killed by cops.

I can't say it often enough: sexual harassment is low down and dirty. If you are a senior staffer using your power and position to prey sexually on a subordinate, you should and will get your balls cut off. Which brings me back to the president.

The news that Donald Trump was caught on a hot *Access Hollywood* mic sounding like a filthy old Hollywood pervert hit the race for the White House like an exploding bomb. His unguarded remarks to Billy Bush about how he could physically molest any woman he wanted because of his celebrity nearly destroyed his chance to be president. The remarks were raw, arrogant, and ugly.

Donald Trump: I just kiss. I don't even wait. And when you're a star, they let you do it. You can do anything.

Billy Bush: Whatever you want.

Donald Trump: Grab them by the pussy. You can do anything.

Although the remarks were made in private eleven years earlier, most women cut him no slack. Even some die-hard Trump supporters who had been forced by loathing for Hillary Clinton to stick with him through thick and thin found this latest revelation beyond the pale. Certainly many folks not tuned in to the campaign spectacle found the remarks unsavory. How can we elect someone president when we could not let our children hear his profane remarks?

Prominent GOP senators and governors jammed the doors, jumping off the Trump train in the wake of the revelations. From former Secretary of State Condoleezza Rice to former California governor Arnold Schwarzenegger (who had his own series of similar scandals), some of the biggest stars in the GOP firmament announced they had turned off their already tepid support for Trump.

Speaker of the House Paul Ryan held his nose, indicating he would never appear with Trump again, despite the obvious threat a landslide defeat for the Republican at the top of the ticket posed to Ryan's majority in the House of Representatives.

Gross even in the old days, in today's hypersensitivity to the issue, that 2005 conversation sounds grotesque. I thought mistakenly that the arrogance he displayed talking then about his sexual prerogatives made it impossible for any but his most hard-core supporters to stick by candidate Trump. Remember, in October 2016, with the election just a month away, he was still running well behind Hillary Clinton in most polls.

Going into the second debate, Trump needed a miracle performance to salvage his crippled campaign. He did not quite get it, but did better than expected under the circumstances. His stunt, dragging Paula Jones and the other purported victims of Bill Clinton's predatory sexual behavior to the front row of the audience, was outrageous, ill-mannered, and out of line, but it was just barely plausible and worked to cheer Trump's deflated supporters.

Even though Bill was not running for president, Trump made Hillary the chump. Her husband, President Clinton, was punished for his transgressions with Impeachment by the House of Representatives, only the second in the history of the land to be so humiliated, but Bill beat that rap, winning an acquittal in the Senate. He was not forced from office. Eighteen years later, Hillary paid his old tab.

Trump's obnoxious stunt with Bill's ladies and his implacable attacks on Hillary's essential character and honesty wounded her candidacy. Although most liberal women had forgiven or refused to believe the ring-wing allegations against the progressive 42nd president in 1998, by 2016 his reckless, often low-brow adultery was no longer forgivable. Hillary was Bill's enabler, guilty by association of his sins. It is another reason so many women are angry that Trump is their president. Add to his many transgressions that he made a wife pay for the sins of her husband.

Trump narrowly won that second debate by attacking relentlessly in a way unseen in modern American history. His savage assault, including his pledge to put Secretary Clinton in jail ("Lock her up!"), got gasps from the audience in St. Louis and the millions watching on television, breathing new energy into his deflated followers. Thanks to his swaggering and extraordinarily aggressive performance, he dodged the *Access Hollywood* bullet and rallied his base. I did not think it would be enough to upend the race. I mistakenly believed that no candidate for the highest office in the land could prevail with just the support of high school–educated, low-to-middle-income white folks, many of whom are deeply religious, and presumably offended by his coarse language and stated sexual prerogatives. I was obviously wrong. That base was solid for Trump, of course, but he also did surprisingly well with suburban dwellers and people over forty who quietly cast their ballots for Mr. Us vs. Them Clintons. Trump even attracted 42 percent of the female vote, but not my wife or her friends.

BOYCOTTING THE IOWA GOP DEBATE, JANUARY 2016

His shocking victory was a long way off when Megyn Kelly lobbed her atomic question at candidate Trump ("You've called women you don't like 'fat pigs,' 'dogs,' 'slobs,' and 'disgusting animals' . . .") at the first Republican presidential debate, setting in motion their extraordinary feud. In one fell swoop, Megyn managed to do what no other journalist or candidate did all campaign long. She cut Trump down to size, infuriating him and many of her own viewers of Fox News.

Megyn catapulted herself into the first tier of political journalists. Among the liberal media and mainstream audience, she became that rare phenomenon, a hero, the Rosa Parks, Susan B. Anthony, or Malala of broadcast news, especially among the educated women who despised candidate Trump. She showed strength and courage in the face of bluster and fury, and as she would throughout the campaign, she refused to back down or lose her elegant composure.

He attacked her relentlessly with barrages of negative tweets, which put me in an awkward position. He was being a bully. She was standing against Goliath, reporting fairly on the candidate's various foibles and woes. As he has shown even in his presidency, Donald Trump is not the kind of guy who forgives and forgets. As he typically tweeted:

Donald J. Trump @realDonaldTrump
Everybody should boycott the @megynkelly show. Never worth watching. Always a hit on Trump! She is sick, & the most overrated person on tv.

My less-than-bold response:

Geraldo Rivera @GeraldoRivera
@realDonaldTrump @megynkelly I love you man but basta. This
obsession w @megynkelly is weird & unhelpful. She's doing her job,
you do yours.

Megyn later thanked me, although unlike her, I was not a profile in
courage, but in compromise. Contrast my muted remarks to what Roger
said about Trump, whom he had known nearly as long as I have: "Donald
Trump's vitriolic attacks against Megyn Kelly and his extreme, sick obsession with her is beneath the dignity of a presidential candidate who wants
to occupy the highest office in the land."

That is how you put down someone messing with your colleague.
Whatever his personal feelings about the candidate or his star journalist,
Roger bathed himself and the network in the glory of principle, not that it
helped him when his own shit hit the fan.

I was conflicted throughout. My dilemma was that Trump is a closer
friend than Megyn. In person she is smart and funny, with a terrific husband and wonderful family, but she rarely booked me on her show. In
contrast, aside from my knowing the guy forever, Trump and I had just
done *Celebrity Apprentice*. Together constantly for six weeks, just a couple
of months before he began his run for the White House, he gave me the
benefit of every doubt on the show.

"Trump puts me on television a lot more than Megyn Kelly does,"
I told friends to explain my initial ambivalence and relatively tepid support of what later became clear was an incredibly brave stance by Megyn.
Trump was already a monstrously popular, super-connected candidate
whose past alleged misogynist treatment of women was certainly fair
game at the time she asked her seminal question. In some ways, the divide
it revealed between the old ways and the new are at the heart of our current split nation and of the culture of scandal that is devouring macho
icons on both sides of the divide.

THE WRATH OF ROGER, JANUARY 2016

The morning after the Trump-boycotted Iowa debate, I incurred Roger's wrath for what turned out to be the last time. He had nobly sacrificed an enormous ratings bonanza by refusing to capitulate to Trump's demand to remove Megyn as debate moderator, saying that it would "violate all journalistic standards" to remove her from the panel.

On *Fox and Friends* that next morning, asked who "won" the Trump-less debate, I answered that in my opinion both Megyn and Trump emerged as winners. She won because of her courage in the face of the Trump steamroller, but he won, too, I said, because his boycott and simultaneous telethon to benefit veterans attracted enough attention to overshadow his rivals. Looking back, I was wrong substantively. Trump's absence from the Iowa debate probably cost him that state's primary, which he ended up losing to Ted Cruz, and he barely beat Marco Rubio, who came in a close third.

That night my scheduled appearance on what was then our most important program, *The O'Reilly Factor*, was suddenly canceled, as were scheduled appearances over the next several days on other high-profile Fox News shows. I was on ice. When I confronted O'Reilly's longtime producer David Tabacoff as to why my appearance was canceled, he admitted that the order to take me off, and keep me off, had come from Roger Ailes himself. After an absence that lasted until the next week, I apologized on the air for equivocating and not more vigorously backing the home team.

THE RAT PACK ERA IS DEAD, JANUARY 2017

On the issues of workplace morality and sexual harassment, having worked at all the networks over the last forty-seven years, I can say definitively that the social culture is industry-wide. For lots of reasons, TV news is a flirty business. There is a constant and usually harmless sexual banter that goes on. Men tell women they look good, and vice versa, or at least we did before it became fraught with profound consequence.

When grown-ups of equal status are involved, it is usually the kind of lighthearted fun you might hear on a family-hour sitcom. There has to be room for consensual adults to do their thing without the threat of blackmail if relationships don't work out, which is what I think happened with my Fox News colleague Charles Payne. With its pressure-cooker environment and long hours, the newsroom is sometimes the only place young professionals and old can meet. How do you think MSNBC co-anchors Joe Scarborough and Mika Brzezinski and scores of other happy couples hooked up? After work? Add up all the newsroom romances that have resulted in marriage over the years, including three of my own. Where are busy professional supposed to meet, Match.com or Tinder?

Management's role is to keep the playing field level, professional, and fair. As society evolved from the *Mad Men* era, giant steps have been taken to protect subordinate employees from harassment and unwelcome advances, particularly by superiors. Human resources departments have been enormously beefed up and empowered. Roger got drummed out of the business, and he was king of the world. Bill O'Reilly was also banished from Fox News despite having the highest-rated cable news history for twenty years running. Eric Bolling, Charlie Rose, Matt Lauer, and many other powerful men lost their jobs even though they were hugely popular and had ironclad contracts. At the time of his Armageddon, Tavis Smiley was the most important African American personality on PBS.

Sure, there is far to go, but as the seismic response to Gretchen, Megyn, and the other purported victims of real harassment makes clear, the news business will no longer tolerate loutish conduct by anyone, however powerful. The danger is that in the national reckoning, some few are using the current climate to even old scores with bad boyfriends or despised ex-bosses. Harassers are most often schmucky lowlifes anyway. There is nothing cool about it, and there is no place for them. Perpetrators harass at tremendous peril to their careers and families. Strict policies are in place. Everyone gets mandatory sensitivity training. I had a mandatory session on a Tuesday, which happened to be Valentine's Day, 2017.

I wrote in a widely circulated Facebook post, "To all the victims of sexual harassment, direct and indirect, I am sorry for what happened to you. As the father of three daughters, including one in the news business, I urge all who have been offended to reach out. Similarly, if you see harassment, say harassment, even if the alleged offender is an old friend."

The stern point was made in spades. Rico Suave is dead. No man or woman, however exalted or powerful, has the right to impose him- or herself on a subordinate. As one of the aged poster boys of the era, Roger was shamed, shunned, and stripped of all honors, his legacy despoiled, his legend ruined. He has been erased from television history, his name stripped from schools and civic institutions he endowed, even as several of his alleged and lavishly compensated victims have gone on to celebrity and societal acclaim. When I look back on how severely Roger was punished, I regret helping write his professional obituary with my Facebook post. Maybe he had it coming, but given the harsh justice already imposed, the last thing his family needed was a disillusioned old friend piling on.

As I wrote that line, I paused to call him to tell him of my regret, but he did not pick up the phone. Three months later, on May 18, 2017, I did get a call—not from Roger, but about him. The old lion was dead. A hemophiliac, living in the vast Florida oceanfront estate he purchased with his $40 million settlement from Fox, he died after stumbling in his bathroom and hitting his head. Roger left behind his wife, Beth, and teenage son, Zack, and I feel awful whenever I think of the circumstances of his decline and fall.

EPILOGUE

JANUARY 2017–MAY 2019

Erica, our three daughters, and I went to South Africa on safari at the Mala Mala Game Reserve over the Christmas holidays, December 2016. We hooked up with Kevin and Julietta, our old *Voyager* crewmates. After sailing around the world with us, and up the Amazon River, they live now in Kevin's native Cape Town. It was Sol's first safari; it brought up memories of past African adventures, and a wonderful time was had by all. After stopping in Amsterdam, Holland, on the way back for a visit with my firstborn son, Gabriel, and his wife, Deb, and their firstborn child, Desmond, we got home to an uneasy America about to give a decidedly mixed welcome to President-elect Donald Trump, the longest of long-shot chief executives.

It was a tumultuous transition amidst sharp charges that Trump's presidency was illegitimate. Aside from the fact that he lost the popular vote to Hillary Clinton, who garnered almost 2.9 million more than he did, my friend Donald was being tarred by serial scandals. One included alleged Russian-sponsored hacking of Democratic Party operatives, and the inference that Russian president Vladimir Putin poisoned the minds of American voters with damaging leaks. The hard left was having a field day alluding to the *Manchurian Candidate*–elect who was a stooge for the wily Kremlin boss.

Adding to the toxic atmosphere surrounding Trump's ascendency to the White House were the actions of FBI Director James Comey, who destroyed Hillary's momentum in the last week and a half of the campaign

349

With Erica, Isabella, Simone, and Sol boarding the Blue
Train in Pretoria, South Africa, December 2016.

With Erica, Sol, and Isabella near the Cape of Good Hope, South Africa, December 2016.

with a bogus story of ultimately nonexistent illegal emails. There were also salacious and almost surely false and slanderous allegations of shenanigans leveled at Trump and/or his staffers during the 2013 Miss Universe Pageant in a Moscow hotel room with prostitutes, golden showers, and so forth. True or false, it all conspired to make him the most unpopular president-elect in the history of polling. By midsummer 2017, he was the most unpopular president in the seventy-year history of polling.

As he carried on with his lurching transition, he did something shortly after our arrival home to New York that, despite everything, stirred optimism in my heart. On the night of January 2, 2017, with Congress officially out of session, GOP leaders had voted virtually in secret to disembowel the Office of Congressional Ethics. Some of those voting to eviscerate the office had themselves been investigated and punished for ethical lapses. President-elect Trump would not hear of it, letting Republican congressional leaders know that he opposed the underhanded move. The next morning I tweeted twice:

Geraldo Rivera @GeraldoRivera
Nice move by #PEOTUS Trump putting Republican lawmakers in their place for attempting to weaken #Ethics laws. Strong, significant signal.

Geraldo Rivera @GeraldoRivera
#GOP is about to find out who is in charge. Hint: it ain't them & it won't be business as usual. It is #POTUS45 #draintheswamp

On January 12, eight days before his inauguration, I got an email from Trump assistant Meredith McIver that copied both tweets. Scrawled across it was a handwritten note from Trump: "Geraldo-Miss You-Thanks! Donald"

Worried that my opposition to his policies on everything from Mexican immigration to Muslims to former POW senator John McCain's service had soured our friendship, I was delighted to hear from him. I emailed Meredith immediately, telling her I was honored, and asking if I could stop by to say hello before he left for Washington and the inauguration. She wrote back, "He asks if you are here now? Can you come up? Let us know your schedule. He's here Tues/Weds next week as well . . ."

Glad that I had shaved my scrawny vacation beard, at four o'clock that afternoon I was escorted up the gilded elevator at Trump Tower to his transition office. After waiting a few minutes as he and the first lady–elect met with Missouri senator Roy Blunt and his wife, who were helping organize the inaugural festivities, I was escorted in. As he was leaving, Senator Blunt was helpful, pointing out that I had been among the first to predict that Trump would be the eventual GOP nominee. I was grateful no one asked whom I voted for in the general election; it would have been awkward. As the Missourians left, Melania lingered to ask by name how Erica and Sol were doing. She told me how excited she was about her husband's extraordinary success.

Trump was relaxed and confident, sharing his sincere excitement at the prospect of living in the White House, belying the notion that he would consider it slumming after the luxury of his Trump Tower digs and his winter palace, Mar a Lago in Palm Beach, Florida.

The next day I posted a picture of us, and said on Facebook:

> Great spending time with the President-elect yesterday afternoon. He started by joking that I look better without the beard. But then he went right into a serious discussion about how he is getting the American taxpayer a break on the F-35 fighter jet. The first lady-elect, Melania,

With Bret Michaels, Ainsley, Sean, and friends during the inauguration. January 2017.

was there. She could not have been more gracious. She remembered Erica's name and invited us to the White House. The President-elect joked about *Celebrity Apprentice* and about how Arnold Schwarzenegger is not doing nearly as well as he did.

It wasn't the last time he brought up the subject of ratings with me. He returned to the topic when we spoke on the phone, months into his presidency. He loved talking about how badly his reality-show successor had performed, bizarrely bringing up Arnold's tanking ratings, and comparing them to his own, even during his address at the traditionally dignified National Prayer Breakfast on the day after he was inaugurated. Trump slammed Schwarzenegger again after the former governor was fired from *Apprentice* for low ratings at the end of his first season. What made it bizarre was that it came in the middle of a major controversy that had President Trump accusing President Obama of wiretapping his Trump Tower offices during the campaign and the transition.

That was all ahead for the forty-fifth president, like the endless debate over repealing and replacing Obamacare, building a border wall and banning Muslims, and cancerous Russiagate. At our Trump Tower meeting, he was in a good mood, looking forward to his inauguration, and decidedly annoyed by those calling his election as president illegitimate. I wrote, "That is of course bogus. He is our president, our one and only president, and on January 20th after his inauguration, he will be the 45th person in the history of the republic to have that honor. We wish him well."

At the time of the Trump Tower meeting, still–Fox News executive Bill Shine had asked me to get the president-elect's signature on a printout of an internal Fox News Election Day memo. The document was published around 5 PM on that historic Tuesday, November 8, and spoke of how the polls were forecasting a certain Hillary Clinton victory, which our Fox News experts predicted we would be able to call for the Democrat at 11 PM Eastern Time.

Sitting behind his desk in the transition office, President-elect Trump autographed it with his customary black marker, writing, "It didn't turn out that way. Love, Donald."

During the transition, I commented on how disappointing attempts to delegitimize President Trump's election were, and reacted with humility upon discovering I was one of forty-one people he follows on Twitter, which, for better and worse, is still his go-to method of communicating with the American people. We spoke too on the night of his controversial inaugural address, which I thought was way too militant. At the Freedom Ball in Washington, DC, with Sean Hannity and *Fox and Friends* cohost Ainsley Earhardt, a lovely person inside and out, we were waiting for showtime backstage, hiding from the euphoric crowd gathered at the Convention Center, one of the three official celebrations. Sean was covering the ball with a live two-hour Fox News Special Report, and Ainsley and I were there to give color commentary on the show about the festivities and our take on the day's historic events.

Through his unfailing support and vigorous advocacy during the campaign, Hannity had become the nation's most important commentator, surpassing even Rush Limbaugh and Bill O'Reilly in his prime. By inaugural night, Sean was one of the president's closest unofficial advisers, and he had the president's old cell phone number, which to our surprise still worked. It would be shut down permanently at midnight.

It was so noisy in the cavernous hall, I could not hear what either Sean or Ainsley was saying to newly elected POTUS 45. When it was my turn, I congratulated him warmly, alternating between calling him Mr. President and "Boss," the nickname I used during *Celebrity Apprentice*. At that moment, he was en route to the various balls with the first lady and his ecstatic children and their spouses, in the elaborate presidential convoy.

Surprisingly, he was not merely accepting of my warm wishes, he was combative, angrily criticizing the media for underestimating the size of the crowd that attended his address on the National Mall, ranting about the "dishonest media." It was the beginning of his crusade against fake news. I tried to soothe him as best I could and promised to watch his back. A couple of hours later, he and the family showed up at the Freedom Ball. They danced to Paul Anka's "My Way," which became Frank Sinatra's anthem in 1969, but which was seldom more appropriately used than on that inaugural night 2017.

The next day, the gigantic gender revolt, larger by far than his inaugural crowd, manifested itself on the boulevards of the capital and around the country. The vast sea of mostly women and girls hit the streets to demonstrate against Trump's ascendency to the highest office in the land. It was perhaps the biggest day of protest in American history and an inauspicious way to begin a presidency.

Sean Hannity was covering the presidential ball for a live two-hour *Fox News Special Report*, and Ainsley Earhardt and I were there to give color commentary. January 2017.

The demonstrators used the color pink to symbolize their profound disquiet that the reins of power had been handed to a chief executive who in their minds, among all the other things, views women as sex objects, and their reproductive rights as revocable. Rather than being off-put by the obvious schism in American society, I am heartened that the progressive half of the country, for months before and after the election lethargic and unfocused, that day found its voice. As the massive post-Inaugural protests and another on the president's first anniversary in office made clear, there is now energetic opposition to President Trump, much of it fair-minded and fact-based, though some of it "fake," to use the president's character-ization. Erica at one point asked me to stop supporting him with tweets because I was embarrassing her with her girlfriends.

"Why the implacable hatred directed at Trump?" I asked my loving, but steadfastly feminist wife during one of our kitchen debates that are reflected in millions of politically divided American households. She replied with anguished sincerity, "I feel like, what is it going to take to stop you defending him?!" She paused before firing another volley, "Him not speaking out about hate crimes or white supremacists? Him wrecking Obamacare and not replacing it? Him doing away with the global warming accord?" And so on. Her brother Josh Levy, a well-regarded Washington lawyer and former Democratic staffer whose firm represents GPS Fusion, the group that sponsored the infamous Trump Russia Dossier, has apparently stopped speaking to me because of my tireless effort to find silver linings in the president's actions.

As in my family, the divisions within the country are bad and getting worse. The danger is that the two sides are so scornful of each other, that rather than checking and balancing, we are now at each other's throats, fighting an ideological civil war. Amidst flashes of economic competence and riding a strong stock market and booming economy toward optimism, President Trump doesn't help quell the discord. He still gives ammunition to his enemies, while making life difficult for his friends, careening from Twitter storm to Twitter storm of his own making.

Bottom line, I am dismayed by both his hard head and the unrelenting hatred directed his way. He may not think as you do, but that doesn't make

"Why the implacable hatred directed at Trump?" I asked my lovely, loving wife during one of our debates. December 2016.

him bad. Although his policy choices are sometimes hard for me personally to tolerate, and as he and his administration deal sometimes haphazardly with crises like the Iran nuclear deal or issues like climate change, I am still determined to be the man in the middle. Roger Ailes once warned me that the only thing in the middle of the road was roadkill. Still, I want to be a small voice in the president's ear and the country's that says, "Cool down. Let us work this out. We are in this together." Sometimes the president listens.

And sometimes the president makes it difficult. As we went to press, and just a few days after Mr. Trump had called to tell me he appreciated my defending him and his family against some of author Michael Wolff's more scurrilous attacks in his bombshell book *Fire and Fury*, the president got in hot water again when he reportedly asked, "Why do we want people from Haiti here?" and demanded to know, in reference to Africa, why he should accept immigrants from "shithole countries." It's impossible to excuse this sort of statement, and it's hard to understand why the president makes it so easy for his opponents to paint him as a racist.

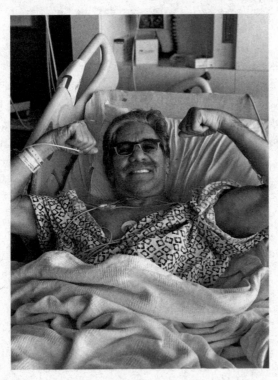

I tweeted him from my bed in the Cleveland Clinic.

Geraldo Rivera @GeraldoRivera
@realDonaldTrump last week I told you on phone that I love you
like a brother. In that spirit I ask you to apologize for your unfortunate remarks. I'm in hospital getting back surgery My skilled compassionate nurse is from #Kenya She told me how you'd hurt her
family's feelings.

But there are times when President Trump gets it right. When historically vicious Hurricane Maria slammed into Puerto Rico in September
2017 with winds in excess of 150 mph, it laid waste to the countryside.
Civil society on my adored but battered Isla del Encanto teetered on the
brink of breakdown.

Assigned by *Fox and Friends* to cover the disaster because of my lifelong ties to the island, limping into action, I spent almost two painful
weeks in rough conditions bouncing between coverage of the general population's suffering and helping my own family members in distress. My
eighty-four-year-old Aunt Eli, youngest of my father's sixteen siblings, and
one of just three surviving, was living in the dark with a tree through her
roof. It was my abuelos' old house in Bayamón, where I lived and learned
Spanish during the summer of 1958, when I turned sixteen years old.

Craig and I got Eli a generator and other supplies, but big picture, I
was frightened by the extent of the destruction islandwide. In terms of the
number of people negatively affected, Maria is the worst natural disaster
in modern U.S. history, and I wrote the following open letter to President
Trump a couple of days before he was scheduled to visit:

Dear Mr. President,

As a concerned citizen with deep personal ties to the Puerto Rican
people, I am heartened by your coming visit to this storm-ravaged
island, home to 3.4 million of our fellow citizens, including members
of my own family. This is a community in dire need of outside assistance after two devastating hurricane strikes in two weeks. As you
know, Mr. President, the entire agricultural crop has been wiped out.
The whole island is still without electrical power. Half the people have

I turned sixteen in the Rivera family home, Bayamón, Puerto Rico, 1958.

My eighty-four-year-old Aunt Eli, youngest of my late father's sixteen siblings,
in the Hurricane Maria aftermath. Puerto Rico, October 2017.

no running water, and the communications network has also been destroyed. Cell phone towers are down everywhere, and numerous streets remain clogged by downed trees and debris from the storm. Hospitals and other vital institutions are also severely damaged and vital staff struggles to get to their jobs because of fuel shortages that require waits of six hours or more at stations lucky enough to have gas. I am concerned that the relief effort up to this point does not seem to reach the scale necessary to alleviate the misery inflicted by the storms. Relief flights have finally started after a distressing delay, but what this beleaguered island needs are giant ships bearing cargoes of fuel, telephone poles, generators, heavy equipment and the like.

My tour of the port of San Juan does not show anything like the effort required to turn this awful thing around. Suspend the Jones Act, at least temporarily, so foreign flag vessels can join an armada of US ships bearing critically needed assets to rebuild and replace the wreck that exists now.

He delivered. The next day, President Trump temporarily suspended the Jones Act, opening San Juan Harbor to foreign flag vessels, and escalating the pace of the relief effort. He selected Lt. General Jeffrey Buchanan, an excellent soldier I met in Baghdad in 2011, to coordinate. Then the president called me. Luckily the operator on Air Force One got through on my cell phone in a rare area along the highway where cell service existed. We pulled over so as not to lose the signal as the operator put through his familiar voice.

He restated our friendship, promised to do all he could to help, and asked me to accompany him and First Lady Melania as they toured storm-ravaged areas. He gave me an exclusive interview when he arrived, the only one he did during this visit, and made news saying that the bankrupt island's crushing $73 billion debt would have to be wiped out at the expense of bondholders like Goldman Sachs and "my friends on Wall Street." Unfortunately, that idea never made it past the drawing board.

When the visit was over, he gave Craig, cameraman Benjamin West, and me a ride home on AF-1. The president and I talked about old times in several conversations on board the gigantic, plush aircraft, and I promised again to "watch his back," as I did when I criticized two reports that were falsely alleging Trump fiddled when Puerto Rico burned. One of

With the Coast Guard during a relief mission. Aguadilla, Puerto Rico, October 2017.

"He gave me an exclusive interview when he arrived, the only one he did during this visit" to the Hurricane Maria aftermath. Puerto Rico, October 2017.

them blamed his alleged neglect for a nonexistent cholera epidemic on the island. Another sought to make him responsible for Puerto Rico's notoriously corrupt, inept, and bankrupt power authority.

We parted at Joint Base Andrews near Washington, DC, he and the first lady to head to the scene of the horrific Las Vegas massacre early the next morning, me to get home to Cleveland to recover from twelve days of nonstop reporting.

The media assessment of Trump's efforts in Puerto Rico was much more negative than mine; in fact, it was brutal. As the FEMA-led relief effort faltered, the president was essentially blamed for the deaths of more than 3,000 islanders who perished in the months following the hurricane from causes like tainted water or the unavailability of dialysis.

I felt the criticism uninformed and grossly unfair. For instance, most of the commentators made no mention at all of the criminal incompetence and corruption of PREPA, the Puerto Rico Electric Power Authority, which had totally neglected the electrical grid, leaving it prone to chronic, system-wide outages.

The bitter irony of the whole debacle was that the more Trump was criticized for inaction, the less inclined he was to help out. What should have been a united effort to fix a broken island became a political pissing match that did no one any good. In any case, the only real way to fix Puerto Rico is to make the territory a full-fledged state of the union.

On the political front, Trump fared far better on the Russia Collusion–hoax. In April 2019, Robert Mueller, the special counsel, issued his long-awaited report. As I had projected with confidence, the president was not a Russian spy or a traitor. After a $25+ million probe in which Mueller employed "19 lawyers, who were assisted by a team of approximately 40 FBI agents, intelligence analysts, forensic accountants . . . 2,800 subpoenas, nearly 500 search warrants" and interviews with approximately 500 witnesses, "the investigation did not establish that members of the Trump Campaign conspired or coordinated with the Russian government in its election interference activities." The Democrats, led by several 2020 presidential hopefuls continued to groan and moan, along with many disgruntled and profoundly embarrassed media pundits, but it was essentially all over but the shouting.

Despite the contempt in which half the country holds him, I do still consider him a friend. Erica thinks I have stopped being objective. In her opinion, the dark side has seduced me, my moral compass overcome. I disagree, and argue that while there is plenty to criticize, the reality is more nuanced. Never, or at least not since Nixon, has any president had a worse relationship with the press. Not the slickest ad-libber, everything President Trump says or does is construed in the most evil, negative way possible. Blessed as I am that many folks still trust what I have to say, I insist that POTUS 45 is not wicked. He has thin skin, but a big heart. He is not his stereotype. Neither am I. Otherwise, how could either of us have defied conventional wisdom for so long?

Everything Trump does or says is construed as evil. San Juan, Puerto Rico, October 2017.

ACKNOWLEDGMENTS

Hopefully I've made clear in this book how much Erica has changed my life and made me a better person. There is perhaps no greater evidence of how important she is than the fact that this native New Yorker to the bone agreed to relocate to her suburban Cleveland, Ohio, hometown. I also want to acknowledge her parents, Nancy and the late Howard A. Levy, for trusting this ancient mariner to marry their daughter, and my kids, Gabriel, Cruz, Isabella, Simone, and Sol, who despite my eccentricities love their dad and are a Modern Family unit despite their varied ethnic, religious, and geographic backgrounds.

I treasure also the friendship of Bernard Carabello, the former resident of Willowbrook, whose life has been an inspiration; Leo Kayser III, my cranky lawyer and former roommate down on Avenue C; Marty Berman who has been there from the first days of *Eyewitness News*, and who, with publisher Glenn Yeffeth, had the grit to bring this book back from the dead; and Jon Peters, who still calls me every week to share memories of the old days. My kid brother, Craig, and our partner in peril, producer/cameraman Greg Hart, are very special to me. Neither man ever said no when I asked them to follow me off the cliff.

General John F. Campbell, retired, was a noble and near-constant presence in my life as a Fox News war correspondent in Afghanistan and Iraq from 2003 to 2012. Tracking the meteoric rise of this hero soldier I dubbed "America's Spartan" as he earned his way up through the ranks from colonel to four-star general was deeply impressive. I hope he runs for high office because he would make a terrific senator. Even more inspiring has been spending long days and nights with our war fighters, young men and women far from home who serve our country with honor and distinction. I cannot walk through an airport in America without one coming up to me and saying we met and maybe took a picture in this or that forward operating base or other deployment.

I want to acknowledge also my boss Rupert Murdoch, who kept me on when so many others bit the dust; the forty-fifth president, who treasures friendship above politics or ideology; my steadfastly loyal Fox News colleagues, especially Sean Hannity, Kimberly Guilfoyle, Ainsley Earhardt, Brian Kilmeade, Liz Claman, Charles Payne, Shepard Smith, Juan Williams, Rick Leventhal, Mike Tobin, Steve Harrigan, Steve Doocy, Bill Hemmer, Dana Perino, Janice Dean, and Arthel Neville; and, finally, the folks who still like to watch what I do, if only to shout their disagreement at the screen. You have kept me on the air for almost half a century.

"Even more inspiring has been spending long days and nights with our war fighters, young men and women far from home who serve our country." Afghanistan, 2008.

ABOUT THE AUTHOR

One of America's most enduring broadcasters, Emmy and Peabody Award–winning journalist Geraldo Rivera is a Fox News correspondent-at-large and host of breaking news specials, the *Geraldo Rivera Reports*. He also provides weekly reporting and commentary for FNC's *Fox and Friends* and *Hannity*. A native New Yorker outraged by the terror attacks of 9/11, he left CNBC's *Rivera Live* to become an FNC senior war correspondent, reporting live from Afghanistan beginning with the initial siege on Osama bin Laden's Tora Bora hideout, and broke the news ten years later that the terror mastermind had finally been killed by SEAL Team 6. He has reported extensively on the Arab–Israeli conflict and other armed conflicts around the globe, including the 2003 invasion of Iraq, one of eleven extended assignments there.

Rivera began his forty-eight-year television career at WABC-TV in New York where he presented a series exposing the deplorable conditions at the Willowbrook State School for residents then described as mentally retarded. These historic reports are credited with helping end the nation's policy of warehousing the developmentally disabled.

Before becoming a member of the original cast of ABC's *Good Morning America*, Rivera presented the first television broadcast of the Zapruder film of the assassination of President John Kennedy as host of ABC's *Goodnight America*. He then began an eight-year association with ABC's *20/20* as senior correspondent. One of his hour-long reports, "The Elvis Cover-Up," was for more than two decades *20/20*'s highest rated. Between 1987 and 1998, he produced and hosted *Geraldo!*, later called *The Geraldo*

Rivera Show, for daytime TV. The winner of the 2000 Robert F. Kennedy journalism award (his third) for his NBC News documentary on "Women in Prison," and the Scripps Howard Foundation national journalism award for another NBC special report, "Back to Bedlam," Rivera has received hundreds of honors for journalism and community service, including the prestigious George Foster Peabody, the Columbia duPont, and three national and seven local Emmys.

An avid sailor who circumnavigated the globe, skippered four Marion to Bermuda yacht races, and took his vessel *Voyager* hundreds of miles up the Amazon River, Rivera is a graduate of the University of Arizona and Brooklyn Law School, and is the author of seven previous books. A philanthropist whose causes include the care and treatment of the disabled, he is married to the former Erica Michelle Levy and has five children, four of them adults. Geraldo and Erica live happily ever after with their fourteen-year-old daughter, Sol, in Cleveland, Ohio. Go Cavs. Go Tribe. Go Browns.

GOVERNORS STATE UNIVERSITY LIBRARY

SO-ARK-656

DATE DUE

JAN 0 5	MAR 2 9 1993
FEB 2 2 1993	
DEC 2 2 1997	

STORYTELLERS
TO THE NATION

□ □ □

PN 1992.7 .S74 1992

Stempel, Tom, 1941-

Storytellers to the nation

284356

Of Related Interest from Continuum

American History/American Film, New Expanded Edition, John E. O'Connor and Martin A. Jackson, eds.

And the Winner Is . . . The History and Politics of the Oscar Awards, New Expanded Edition, Emanuel Levy

The Cinema of Stanley Kubrick, New Expanded Edition, Norman Kagan

The Dead that Walk: Dracula, Frankenstein, the Mummy, and other Favorite Movie Monsters, Leslie Halliwell

FrameWork: A History of Screenwriting in the American Film, New Expanded Edition, Tom Stempel

The French through Their Films, Robin Buss

Hitchcock in Hollywood, Joel W. Finler

Italian Cinema: From Neorealism to the Present, New Expanded Edition, Peter Bondanella

Loser Take All: The Comic Art of Woody Allen, New Expanded Edition, Maurice Yacowar

A Project for the Theatre, Ingmar Bergman

The Screening of America: Movies and Values from Rocky to Rain Man, Tom O'Brien

Screening Space: The American Science Fiction Film, Vivian Sobchack

Small-Town America in Film: The Decline and Fall of Community, Emanuel Levy

Steven Spielberg: The Man, His Movies, and Their Meaning, Philip M. Taylor

Take 22: Moviemakers on Moviemaking, Judith Crist

Teleliteracy: Taking Television Seriously, David Bianculli

Toms, Coons, Mulattoes, Mammies, and Bucks: An Interpretive History of Blacks in American Films, New Expanded Edition, Donald Bogle

World Cinema since 1945: An Encyclopedic History, William Luhr, ed.

For more information on these and other titles on the
performing arts or literature, write to:

The Continuum Publishing Company
370 Lexington Avenue
New York, NY 10017

TOM STEMPEL

Storytellers to the Nation

A HISTORY OF AMERICAN TELEVISION WRITING

GOVERNORS STATE UNIVERSITY
UNIVERSITY PARK
IL 60466

CONTINUUM · NEW YORK

1992

The Continuum Publishing Company
370 Lexington Avenue, New York, NY 10017

Copyright © 1992 by Tom Stempel

All rights reserved. No part of this book may be reproduced, stored in a retrieval system, or transmitted, in any form or by any means, electronic, mechanical, photocopying, recording, or otherwise, without the written permission of the Continuum Publishing Company.

Printed in the United States of America

Library of Congress Cataloging-in-Publication Data

Stempel, Tom, 1941–
   Storytellers to the nation: a history of American
television writing / by Tom Stempel.
    p.   cm.
   Includes bibliographical references and index.
   ISBN 0-8264-0562-2 (Hardback : acid-free)
    1. Television authorship—History. 2. Television plays, American—
History and criticism. I. Title
PN1992.7.S74 1992   812'.02509—dc20   92-12636   CIP

CONTENTS

(Photographs may be found between pages 156 and 157).

ACKNOWLEDGMENTS

You do not do a book like this—especially a book like this—alone, and the appropriate institutions and people ought to be thanked:

At the Margaret Herrick Library of the Motion Picture Academy of Arts and Sciences: Head Librarian Linda H. Mehr and her staff, especially Howard Prouty.

At the Doheny Library of the University of Southern California: Head Librarian Anne G. Schlosser and her staff, especially Ned Comstock in Special Collections and Leith Adams, the head of the Warner Brothers Collection.

At the Louis B. Mayer Library at the American Film Institute's Center for Advanced Studies: Head Librarians Misha Schutt and Ruth Spencer and their staff.

At the Theatre Arts Reading Room in the Graduate Research Library at the University of California at Los Angeles: Head Librarian Brigitte Kueppers and her staff, especially Sharon Farb.

The Writers Guild of America, west was especially helpful in facilitating my contacting writers, as were some writers' agents.

It would not have been possible to prepare properly to do the interviews for this book without Vincent Terrace's three-volume *Encyclopedia of Television* (New York: New York Zoetrope, 1985–6). While the books are not as encyclopedic as one might hope, writers are listed and indexed in enough detail that the basic outlines of a writer's career can be determined. For more recent credits, Lynne Naylor's *Television Writers Guide* (Santa Monica: Lone Eagle Publishing Co., 1989) was very helpful. For television movie and miniseries credits, Alvin H. Marill's *Movies Made for Television* (New York: New York Zoetrope, 1987) was essential.

At Los Angeles City College: George Bowden and two of his students Eugene McCloud and Suzel Bertrand were able to get to some Museum of Broadcasting programs I could not.

Mary Ann Watson and Jonathan Kuntz read the first draft of the manuscript and made many useful comments. Tovah Hollander read the first draft and gave me extensive notes that helped shape the final book, in addition to sharing her pertinent and often wonderfully impertinent observations about television over many years, which is why this book is dedicated to her. Mel Tolkin read and commented on the section of *Your Show of Shows*. Aubrey Solomon, George Bowden, and Joni Varner read the second draft and also made many useful comments and encouraging noises.

The photographs were obtained at the Collector's Bookstore in Hollywood with the assistance of Jake Hughes.

At Continuum Michael Leach started me off on this project, and he and Evander Lomke have been both helpful and encouraging. Copy editor Donn Teal raised several interesting questions, some of which I could answer. Debbie Mills helped set up two of the interviews through her extensive connections.

The late Howard Ostroff started me thinking about television writing when our daughters were in pre-school together, and they are both a lot older now. I regret that Howard died just before we were to sit down for the formal interview we had planned for this book, but those who knew and loved him will recognize his influence. Howard Suber added his usual provocative questions and comments to get me thinking. Donna Woolfolk Cross was nice enough to introduce me to her father, and I hope our sitting off in a corner discussing television writing did not disrupt her party too much.

Needless to say, my wife Kerstin has been her usual observant and supportive self, as have our daughter Audrey and her husband Daniel when I was on the road. My brother John and his wife Susan did not object when I borrowed their typewriter right before their wedding. Susan's daughter Alix took the photograph of me for the book, after I explained to her the difference between her usual nude studies and author photographs.

Finally, there would be no book without the writers interviewed, who gave generously of their time, their experiences, their wit, and their wisdom. In alphabetical order (come on, you don't think I'm going to get into a hassle over billing with them, do you?) they are: Kasey Arnold-Ince, Juanita Bartlett, Eric Bercovici, Don Brinkley, Jay Burton, Richard Conway, Madelyn Davis, Joseph Dougherty, Robert Dozier, D. C. Fontana, Horton Foote, Everett Greenbaum, Roy Huggins, E. Arthur Kean, Christopher Knopf, Charles Larson, Allan Manings, JP Miller, Phil Mishkin, Rick Mittleman, Thad Mumford, E. Jack Neuman, Liam O'Brien, Nat Perrin, Abraham Polonsky, Richard Powell, Larry Rhine, Joel Rogosin, Lou Shaw, Sam Rolfe, Wells Root, Reginald Rose, Sy Salkowitz, Aubrey Solomon, Mel Tolkin, Coles Trapnell, Catherine Turney, Joseph Wambaugh, Robert Ward, Ed Waters, Lydia Woodward, and William Woolfolk.

INTRODUCTION

"Was there any?"

That was the reaction of a film historian when I said I was researching writing in American television. He was only partly joking; he knew 25 years ago, when I started researching screenwriting in the American film, that the reaction I got from other film historians was what I was now getting from him. In those days everybody knew directors made movies up as they went along and writers were semi-amiable drunks who occasionally came up with a good line of dialogue.

Much has changed since then. Screenwriters are interviewed at some length in newspapers and magazines. There are at least seven volumes of collected interviews with screenwriters if not in print, at least available in libraries. There are two recent books on the history of screenwriting, and a 1990 book on Ben Hecht begins with the author announcing that the reason for a biography is not that Hecht wrote Broadway plays or novels, but because he was an important screenwriter.[1] This particular West has been opened; there are roads, towns, schools, and even churches; and the historiography of screenwriting has almost become a fit place to raise young'uns. What else could I do but light out for the territories?

The original plan for my previous book, *FrameWork: A History of Screenwriting in the American Film*,[2] was that it would include a section on writing for television. What I discovered was more than enough material for a book just on screenwriting. What I also discovered as I worked on the book in the mid-eighties was that the volume of good writing was higher in those days in television than it was in film. As I frequently said to my screenwriting classes, "Name me any 11 two-hour feature films this year that are as well written as the 22 one-hour episodes this, or any, season of *Hill Street Blues*. Plus *St. Elsewhere*." They couldn't do it, nor could I. When Mike Leach, my editor at Continuum, asked me what I was going to write for them next, the obvious answer was a book on the history of writing for television.

Unlike the history of screenwriting, however, there is not much previously published material on the history of writing for television. Most writing about television, I discovered, fits into two categories. The first is the academic writing, which tends to emphasize the role of institutions in television (the Federal Communications Commission [FCC], the networks, the sponsors, the pressure groups). The second is the nostalgia industry, which tends to emphasize massive amounts of information, a good deal of it trivial, and mostly about very light entertainment shows (a nostalgia book can generally be identified by its listing the fictional address of the characters in shows). There are so far no collections of interviews with television writers, although some are interviewed for other books, especially the nostalgia books. There is so far only one published biography of a television writer, Joel Engel's excellent *Rod Serling*.[3]

To do this book, then, it was necessary to do what the academics call "original research." By habit, training, and interest, this meant my interviewing television writers. I did do background reading of books and articles, as well as materials at various research libraries, but I thought the best stuff would come from the writers themselves. I think I guessed right about that. I ended up doing 42 interviews, which ran everywhere from a few minutes on the phone to five hours, with one and a half to two hours about the average.

The book therefore tells the story of the history of writing for television very much from the point of view of the writers: their adventures, their fun, their agonies, their passions. It cannot, alas, tell the story from the point of view of the writers I was not able to interview (or whose recollections are not published elsewhere). Certain shows I would like to have written about, such as *The Carol Burnett Show* and *Cheers*, to name just two, are not discussed in detail for those reasons. Because of limitations of space and time, I have limited the book primarily to network prime-time fictional television, but several of the writers interviewed have worked in other areas, so occasional side trips for comparison purposes are made to production for syndication, late-night programming, public television and cable shows, and documentaries. Writing for news shows, daytime drama, and game shows is not included.

One unavoidable question with interview material is: How accurate is it? The people interviewed for this book have had, for the most part, a great deal of success telling the nation stories, so they are very good at it—which is one reason why doing the research for this book was such a delight. The writers I interviewed were very aware, and made sure I was aware, that I was getting *their* version of the story. Several times during the interviews, writers would warn me (as you are warned now) "This is how I remember it. So-and-so [or more likely, that @$#%^&%$#* so-and-so] will remember it differently." In several cases I have two or more sides to the stories; in some cases, just one. As a general rule, though, I have found over 25 years of interviewing and reading other interviews that writers tend to be a lot more accurate and honest than actors, producers, and especially directors.

In addition to the writers' point of view, there is also my point of view, as both a television viewer and an historian. This book is not just a collection of interviews, which would have been easier to do (and don't think there weren't days I wished I had taken the easy way out), but an attempt to weave the material together into some kind of historical perspective. The structure of the book is generally, but not strictly, chronological. Like television itself, it is a pattern of recurring elements: individuals, types of programs, and themes. The structure of the book is also not strictly narrative, but, inspired by the increasing complexities of both how television is written and what is written for television, the pattern of recurring elements becomes ultimately, I hope, richer and more complex than you might have expected of TV. Avoiding the simpler approach should help the reader understand how good television writing can be.

The recurring individuals and types of programs will be obvious to the reader, and to give you a start on the themes, some of them are: the collaborative nature of television writing; writers and actors (especially stars); writers and producers; censorship; reality and fiction, the various Golden Ages of television writing (yes, there was more than one); the process of writing versus the result of the writing; and the maturation of television and its connection with the increasing openness of American society. (I realize many people are under the delusion that America is turning culturally conservative, but a comparison of what was generally, or institutionally, accepted in the popular arts—such as, in this case, television—in the fifties and the eighties or nineties should dissuade them. The cultural conservatives are certainly fighting a semi-gallant if sociologically ignorant war, and they have even won a battle here and there, but their cause is clearly doomed.)

Most academic writing about television deals with the institutions of television, which is perhaps why a major thread in the fabric of this book is the conjunction (at best) or conflict (at worst) between the institutions and the individual writers. Part of the reason for the power of institutions in American television is that they dominated the development of both radio, and (out of radio) television. One reason, and perhaps the most important reason, for the power of the institutions was, paradoxically, the talent of the individuals who worked for them.

·1·

RADIO TO TELEVISION

When Jay Burton returned to New York City in the late summer of 1948, the institutions that were to dominate American television were in place. The television networks grew out of the radio networks, which in turn grew out of corporate giants protecting their control of radio patents. The commercial expansion of television, delayed by the Depression and World War II, began in earnest after World War II. In May 1947, NBC began a regularly scheduled series of dramas, *The Kraft Television Theatre*, although not many people were watching. What television needed was some person and/or show to make owning a television set essential to the American people. Jay Burton was about to go to work for that person and that show.[1]

The Texaco Star Theatre

Jay Burton had started in New York years before as a press agent for the Latin Quarter nightclub, writing topical jokes for Earl Wilson's newspaper column; then he wrote for Bob Hope's radio show in Los Angeles. In 1948 Hope had one of many housecleanings of his writing staff and Burton was fired. Burton returned to New York because he had heard that Milton Berle was going to have a regular television show. He called Berle up and said he used to work for Hope. Berle, who admired Hope, hired him.[2]

Milton Berle was a big star in nightclubs, getting $15,000 per week, and not quite such a big star in radio, where he was getting only $2,500.[3] He had done a radio variety show for Texaco (written by, among others, Nat Hiken and Danny and Neil Simon), and after a summer tryout on television for Texaco was given a regular show Tuesday night at 8 P.M. on the National Broadcasting Company (NBC): *The Texaco Star Theatre*.

Berle's recollections of the writing of the show have changed over the years. In his 1974 autobiography he wrote that for the first three shows in September 1948 he had only Hal Collins, who did not write new material but merely organized old Berle material for television. Berle added that the system only lasted three weeks—until they learned they needed writers.[4] He also admitted in his book that they *eventually* had five writers on the show the first season.[5] By the time of a 1985 interview, Berle was claiming the budget was too tight the first *two* years to be able to hire any writers at all.[6]

According to Jay Burton, there were six writers on the show beginning in September 1948. Burton wrote gags for the opening monologue and five other writers worked on the sketches: Hal Collins, Bobby Gordon, Jerry Sellen (who did the musical material), Buddy Arnold, and Woody Kling. After the first six months, Burton wrote sketches as well, and more writers were added later. Burton says that Berle "liked writers, respected writers. Only he wanted more [jokes]. I used to write eleven pages [of jokes for the] monologues, used to hold out four, I'd give him seven at first. Then I'd say the next day I wrote four extra pages. He always liked those last four better." As for writing the sketches, Burton says, "We all sat in a room and pitched."

From its debut in 1948 to the fall of 1952, the structure of *The Texaco Star Theatre* was that of a vaudeville show, with sketches, musical numbers, and guest acts. The scripts for the shows[7] are casual to the point of sloppiness, befitting the time pressures under which they were written. Often the monologues were missing from the mimeographed scripts, since comedians like Berle, Burton notes, "wanted to keep the monologues to themselves. They wanted it to be fresh . . . They'd often not do it in rehearsal so the crew wouldn't hear it."

The sketches on the show started out at the shorter length of vaudeville sketches, running four to five pages each. By February 1950, the sketches were longer, running fourteen to fifteen pages, similar to the length of sketches from burlesque. Burton attributes this to a combination of more writers on the show and Berle's wanting longer sketches. In spite of the increased length of the sketches, the format runs basically the same. The sketches do not really tell stories, but are primarily collections of gags, many of them used repeatedly. (As are many of the jokes on the show: Berle often asks his guest stars how it feels to be on a comedy show and they invariably reply, "I don't know. Someday I hope to be on one.") There are several slightly changed versions of a parody of *Caesar and Cleopatra*. Burton says the standard sketches were called "Nat Hiken sketches, a sure-fire laugh because the sketch had been tried a thousand times." Hiken had written for Berle on radio, but not on television. The writers were drawn to the familiar material because, as Burton says, "You knew where the jokes were. It's kind of insurance. Milton always liked it if he was going to get squirted in the face." Berle also repeatedly worked in drag. Burton observes: "Milton loved that, what he'd do with his eyes, his very expressive mouth. In drag he looked just like his mother."

Several of the sketches were parodies of relatively recent movies, but none of them are particularly well observed. Supposed parodies of *The Sea Wolf* (November 30, 1948) and *Mutiny on the Bounty* (June 14, 1949) are the same sketch. A December 7, 1948 parody of the Hope-Crosby *Road* pictures has Berle as Hope and Buddy Lester as Crosby, but there is very little specifically Hope or Crosby about anything they are given to do or say. Another variation on Hope and Crosby on March 25, 1952, with Mickey Rooney as Crosby, is a little closer to the originals, but not much.

The language in the scripts is very informal. Burton notes, "They wrote as they talked. Nobody had that kind of literary talent. They didn't do fine-tuning." The writing, even in the introductions of guest stars, includes phrases like "I wanna," instead of "I want to." What might seem to be ad-libs were written into the scripts. In one Foreign Legion sketch Berle is calling roll, and when one man flubs his answer, Berle says, "One line he's got—and he can't remember it." One script notes that Berle and a guest star "do a phony breakup," and another has Berle "breaking up, correcting." Burton says, "Milton was good at that. He could get himself up to laugh in a false breakup."

If the writing of *The Texaco Star Theatre* was not particularly sharp, it did provide an opportunity for Berle to become the first *television* star. The verbal gags were mostly run of the mill, as was Berle's delivery, which is why he was only a moderate star on radio. The material for the TV show provided Berle with very physical and visual humor. The drag scenes and being squirted in the face are only two examples. In a May 23, 1950, sketch, "Suits for Sale," Jerry Lewis as a suit salesman tears Berle's suit off him. In several scripts, there are no specific details of the action, just the note that there would be "business." As Jay Burton remembers, "A lot of the [slapstick] stuff was last minute." Berle worked best as a visual comedian, not in the sense of doing pantomime, but in doing rather vigorous slapstick. This also played to another of Berle's strengths: the immediacy of his live performances—one of the reasons he had been better paid for nightclub work than for radio.

It was that sense of intense immediacy, communicated visually, that made Milton Berle a star on live television in 1948. He quickly became known as "Mr. Television" and is credited with selling millions of television sets. In 1951 NBC signed Berle to a thirty year contract, which guaranteed him $200,000 per year whether he was on the air or not.[8] And by the end of the 1951–52 season his ratings had begun to slip. The most obvious reason was that the DuMont network had put on opposite him *Life Is Worth Living*, a half-hour program of sermons by Catholic Bishop Fulton J. Sheen, which led to Berle's great line that Bishop Sheen had better writers than he did. The first impact of Berle was over and the Bishop was the hot new face on television. But it was more than that. *Your Show of Shows* had begun in February 1950 and was doing consistently sharper sketches, especially in its film parodies. *I Love Lucy* had started in the fall of 1951 and was doing visual comedy better than Berle did. Berle had invented television comedy, but Sid Caesar and Lucille Ball were taking it further than Berle had.

They were also taking it further than Berle could. Berle had a limited range, as the attempts to change the format of his show proved. At the urging of the advertising agency that produced the show for Texaco, the show was changed to something resembling a situation comedy. Each program would deal with the problems "Milton Berle" had renting his apartment, getting acts for the show, etc. Berle would play the character of "Milton Berle." Gags were cut down in favor of "character" comedy, and physical slapstick was almost eliminated. The problem was that Berle was not as good at playing the character of "Milton Berle" as he was at being Milton Berle. The character of "Milton Berle" had never been developed beyond a few superficial characteristics: ego and the reputation for stealing jokes.

The ratings went back up for a while, but Berle was obviously uncomfortable in the new format. In the script for the third show of that season, there are more handwritten notes than on any previous script, and the notes are all jokes to be added. In the fourth show of the season, October 14, 1952, Berle is in the unemployment office, and to identify himself to the attendant he does a complete mini-version of his show:

> Texaco Star Theatre—You know—HE DOES THE TEXACO FIRE CHIEF BELL AND SINGS) We are the men of Texaco, I wipe the pipe, I scrub the hub—and here he is—America's number one—Good evening ladies and germs—Don't laugh, lady because you too—then Pinza comes on: SOME ENCHANTED EVENING—I look ashamed—I fall asleep—Oh, I feel so jazzy, I swear I'll kill you—and then Bobby Sherwood—OH DON'T FORSAKE ME OH MY DARLING . . .—and then Jimmy Nelson—I'm Danny O'Day—Marfak—Havoline—Sky Chief—and then the girls dance—(HE DOES WALK) A PRETTY GIRL IS LIKE A MELODY—and now, ladies and gentleman, Martha Raye—OH BOY . . . Sing a song—CYNTHIA—Precious memories of Cynthia—She wasn't pretty, she wasn't ugly—She was pretty ugly . . . Allen, my little nephews and nieces—There's one place for me—that's near you—(HE DOES SIREN) . . . Texaco Men: Oh, the curtain is descending, the best friend your car ever had! BOM POM BOM POM BOM POM! (SINGS CHIMES) BOM BOM BOM—NBC . . . Well?

The attendant replies, "Yeh, but what do you do?" The routine was in the style of the original show, the one that made him a star, not the revised format, but the original format had worn out its welcome with the audience.

There was also a mismatch between Berle and the new head writer brought onto the show, Goodman Ace. Ace and his wife, Jane, had throughout the thirties and forties done a very successful radio show, *Easy Aces*, which they attempted to bring to television in 1949. The show consisted of Ace's comments on various subjects and Jane's malapropisms. The show only lasted six months on television. It was not so much that it was too literate for TV, as some have suggested, but that there were not enough visual elements to it.

When asked why he joined Berle's staff in 1952, Ace replied, "I worked for 15 years [on radio] writing good stuff (*Easy Aces*) and nobody paid any attention to it. Now I can write for a big audience and still squeeze in some clever material."[9] Berle complained at the time that Ace's jokes were "too intelligent for my audience,"[10] and he later wrote in his autobiography that Ace was wrong for the show and not good for "the sort of comedy that the character 'Milton Berle' made people think of."[11]

The other writers loved Ace. Just a few weeks into Ace's first season, Burton wrote a handwritten note on his copy of the script, "Jay Burton, protege of Goodman Ace." Burton recalls, "I'm crazy about Goody . . . He was the giant. He loved words. He wasn't interested in big sketches. He liked dialogue . . . Sometimes he looked away from the screen just to listen to the dialogue." When Goodman Ace left the Berle show in 1955 to go to write for Perry Como, Burton and several other writers went with him. Berle's show was canceled the following year. NBC continued to pay him on the contract until it was up in 1981.[12] Burton continued to write, primarily for variety shows, trying to avoid situation comedies. He found he "understood variety. Sitcoms are not really show business, singing, dancing. Just 23 minutes."

Jack Benny

Milton Berle was not the only radio performer to move into television. Jack Benny had been doing a regular radio program for 18 years when he started doing a television series in 1950. Unlike Berle, Benny had the advantage of having created, with his writing staff, a distinctive "Jack Benny" character: cheap, vain, cheap, incensed, cheap, etc. Benny not only played the character on radio, but variations on it in his films. The transition to television should have been easy for Benny, but it was not.[13] Benny was not only worried about being seen too often by his audience, he felt the subtlety of his humor might not work as well on television.

There were losses for Benny in the transition from radio to television. His writers had developed several running gags based purely on sound effects, most notably the starting of his old Maxwell car (done on radio by Mel Blanc) and Benny's vault, which was guarded by Carmichael the bear (also Blanc). While these appeared on television, they did not catch the imagination as vividly as they had on radio.

There were also gains for Benny on television. The writers learned to develop material that depended on Benny's reactions to the action around him. (Part of this may have been Benny's concern about being overexposed on the new medium.) The plotting of *The Jack Benny Show* is very simple. In the 1957 "Christmas Shopping Sketch," the sketch is the entire show. Benny goes to a department store to buy presents for his friends. Benny simply reacts to the people he meets. He does as much with an expressive deadpan as anybody since Buster Keaton, and the reactions would simply not work on radio.

The writing process on Benny's show began with the writers kicking around ideas, which they would mention to the comedian.[14] One of the changes in television for Benny was that because of all the time he had to spend memorizing lines, getting costumes fit, and rehearsing, he spent less time with the writers than he had on radio.[15] The writers would write the script and Benny would go over it with them, since he worked best, even in radio, as an editor and reactor. Benny, for all the deadpan of his performance work, was a noted laugher, frequently falling on the floor at something in the script, which led to writer George Belzer's line "If a writer doesn't cause Jack to send a suit to the cleaners twice a week, he's not earning his money."[16]

Burns and Allen

Unlike Benny, his friend from vaudeville days, George Burns was more involved with the writing of his television show than he had been on his radio show. According to one of the writers, Paul Henning,

> In radio George didn't have much of an active hand in the writing. Although he approved the material, he pretty much left it to his writers. When it came to television, you really had to work and use your imagination. This is where George came into his own. He met with the writers on the first day of each episode, worked out the story in detail with them and then went over the completed scripts very carefully.[17]

Burns himself has downplayed making the transition from radio to television: "We talked in vaudeville, we talked in radio, we talked in television. It wasn't hard to go from one medium to another."[18] On the other hand, he recognized at the time that there was a difference, telling the writers, "We can't get by with just funny lines. We have to give them stuff to watch, too."[19]

The problem for Burns and his wife and partner, Gracie Allen, in the transition from radio to television was slightly more complicated than just providing the visuals. Like Benny, they brought over to television the characters they played on radio and before that in vaudeville: George who asked Gracie logical questions, Gracie who answered with her own tortured logic. Their act was primarily verbal humor. If that had continued on television, Burns would have had very little to do, and the balance between them would have been off. Over lunch, William Paley, head of the Columbia Broadcasting System (CBS), suggested that Burns should open the show with the monologue. Burns thought about this and came up with the idea that he would be like the Stage Manager in the play *Our Town*: not just doing a monologue, but explaining the story, making transitions.[20]

In the television shows this gives Burns a chance to react, both visually and verbally, to what is going on. In the movies the team made, he showed limited kinds of reactions, mostly exasperation. Burns's reactions get so complicated later in the series that he is also commenting on the show as a television show. In the 1956 "Missing Stamp" episode, he decides not to return the stamp because, he tells the audience, ". . . if I do, our show will be fifteen minutes short." In the same episode, he is later watching a scene from the show on the television set in his son, Ronnie's, room.

While the characters of Burns and Allen and their neighbors the Mortons were brought over into television, none of the scripts or plots from the radio shows were used on television. The plots of the television shows are much more complicated than the radio shows (as well as more complicated than the plotting in the Benny television shows).[21] In a two-episode story in 1958, "Hypnotizing Gracie"/"Gracie Is Brilliant" Gracie's trying to find a designer for her dress, gets involved with a hypnotist who hypnotizes her, which makes her mentally brilliant. In an effort to get her back the way she was, the hypnotist inadvertently hypnotizes her neighbor, who ends up with Gracie's brain.

Given the plot complications and the need to maintain a balance between Burns and Allen, it is not surprising that Burns was more involved in the writing of the television shows. Burns and the writers would sit around the office Monday and not leave until they had worked out the story. The "Hypnotizing Gracie" shows came from the writers' wondering what would happen if Gracie were the smartest woman in the world.[22] The writers would then write the episode while the current episode was rehearsed and shot on Tuesday and Wednesday (unlike the first years of Jack Benny's show, which were done live with an audience, their show was shot on film but without an audience, so they could have more scene changes the complicated plotting called for). On Thursday and Friday Burns would work with the writers. On Saturday he would put together all the material they had developed during the week.[23] There are constant changes in the scripts, often simply in the wording of a joke, and in some cases optional versions of the lines are given in the scripts. The changes are generally to cut and simplify the material. The pauses that are an integral part of Burns's timing are all written into the scripts.

The Lone Ranger

Not only were performers like Berle, Benny, and Burns and Allen making the transition from radio to television, so were many dramatic programs. *The Lone Ranger* began as a local radio show in 1933 and quickly became a nationwide hit.[24] It was created by George W. Trendle and written by Fran Stryker, who also wrote such series as *Covered Wagon Days*, from which several *Lone Ranger* stories were taken.[25] In the late forties Trendle went to the sponsor General Mills and suggested they underwrite a half-hour television show. Trendle kept control of the property, and Charles Larson, who wrote several *Lone Ranger* TV episodes, remembers that Trendle was "the greatest limitation. Trendle was a kind of old-fashioned gentleman with old-fashioned ideas about protecting the youth of America. He was very strict on language, which was very stiff. He would not allow contractions. We had to use 'shall.' " Among the other limitations Larson mentions were that they could not have the Lone Ranger unmasked, but when he was captured by the bad guys, Larson recalls it as "the agony of the damned" trying to figure out how not to unmask him. One solution was, "We had Tonto being knocked out and captured a lot."

Some of the differences in writing for radio and television can be seen in a comparison of the 1938 radio episode "He Becomes the Lone Ranger" and the 1949 first TV episode, "Enter the Lone Ranger," both of which deal with how John Reid became the Masked Man. The radio program is shorter, only eight minutes of story, while the television episode is 26 minutes. The radio program begins with a sound montage of the Cavendish Gang attacking wagon trains, towns, and ranches—which suggests an epic scope. The beginning on television is a Building-of-the-West montage made up of stock shots (general shots purchased from a film library or studio). The TV story begins with Collins, who will lead the Rangers into the Cavendish ambush, telling the story of the attack on the trading post. With a budget of approximately $15,000[26] there was no way to show the attack. The ambush is shown, as is a long scene of the wounded Reid dragging himself to water, which is not in the radio play at all. There are only a few lines of dialogue in the television version from the radio version.[27] There is also not in this television episode, nor in the others, the incessant "Whoa, steady, big fellow," jingling of bridles, and clopping of hooves that are in all the radio shows. On television we can see Silver.

Other Transitional Programs

While Trendle insisted that the Lone Ranger be as wholesome on television as he was on radio, Marshal Matt Dillon on *Gunsmoke* became more wholesome on television. The radio version of *Gunsmoke* began in 1952, the last days of network radio drama. Dillon on radio, played by William Conrad, was a bit shorter-tempered than on television and not as infallible, which James Arness insisted on for television.[28] Miss Kitty also became less hardened in the television version. The character could be suggestive on radio simply because audiences could use their imagination. The network, CBS, wanted to clean up Miss Kitty for the television show, and after the first episodes audiences did not see men going upstairs at the Long Branch.[29]

Gunsmoke, however, did use scripts from the radio show for the television program in the first few years. Norman MacDonnell and John Meston had created the radio program, but when the series first went to TV, it was put under the control of Charles Marquis Warren, who had done considerable work in Western films. In the first season, 32 of the 39 episodes were based on scripts from the radio show; Warren specifically told his writers to select stories from the radio scripts.[30] This worked so well that in the second, third, and fourth seasons, all 39 episodes in each season were based on radio stories. Of the radio episodes that were *not* done on television, many were not done for obvious budgetary reasons. Most stories about the cattle trail that ended at

Dodge City, such as "Brothers," which is about a herd of 2,000 head, were not done on television, nor was "New Hotel," about a hotel that is built and burnt down in the episode. Some of the tougher-edged radio stories were not done, such as "Square Triangle," which portrays a three-way love affair, and "Kitty," which deals with the town's dislike of Kitty.[31] Programs done on both media were often softened for television. In "The Guitar" a mule's ear is cut off on radio, but on television the mule is merely painted with white stripes.[32]

Death Valley Days, which had started on radio in 1930, also used radio material for its television series. Ruth Woodman, who had created the series for radio, supervised the early television version of it, beginning in 1952. On radio the narrator was The Old Ranger, and on TV, as Woodman noted, he "mellowed a bit, of course. No more tobacco juice dripping off his chin, not quite such a hardbitten desert rat. And we could no longer depend as heavily on narration as we did in the old [radio] days."[33]

My Friend Irma, on the other hand, did not use its radio scripts.[34] Part of the reason may have been that the radio show was mostly characters dropping in with five minutes of jokes—which worked well enough on radio (several radio shows worked in similar ways, such as Jack Benny's and Fred Allen's), but for television stories were needed.

Writers who worked in radio found they had to make the adjustment to television, some of them reluctantly. Sam Rolfe began writing for both radio and movies and he liked writing for radio because he found it "the perfect writer's medium" because "you had to get character and definition out of the dialogue." He recalls the advice of an old radio writer who pointed out that in a script that the name of the character speaking was on the left side of the page and the dialogue on the right. The old writer told Rolfe to put a ruler on the left side to blot out the names, and "then read the stuff on the right. If you don't know who's talking, you're writing shit."[35]

Richard Conway, another writer who made the transition, wrote 120 episodes of *The Life of Riley* when it moved from radio to television. He tried to

think sightwise. You felt you could do a lot of sight gags. You could be less verbal. In radio you had the narration that connected the scenes, and you also had to explain the sound effects so people would understand them. [In television] you went more for sight gags, but we found you couldn't bring it off in the short amount of [production] time, so we went back to verbal gags. They had to shoot 45 pages of script in two days, it was a burden on the director and we were limited on the sets. On a *Riley*, we had a scene of Riley going to a jewelry store to buy a present for Peg. Peg was at the store, so we had some sight gags. The director said we haven't got the time, so we had to do the scene on phone, with Riley ordering the jewelry on the phone.

Richard Powell got this succinct piece of advice from writer Charles Issacs about the difference between writing for radio and television: "When you have someone writing a letter on TV and they finish it, you don't have to write [the dialogue] 'There.' "

The Ones Who Didn't Make It

Not everyone managed the transition from radio to television. On radio Fred Allen was as popular as Jack Benny. Allen was in many ways the quintessential radio performer. Allen's radio show depended not merely on verbal wit, but literate verbal wit (even to the point of satire), very little of which found audiences in the early days of TV. When Allen tried television in 1950, he appeared to be at ease in front of the cameras,[36] but he was not, just as he had not been in front of the movie cameras in Hollywood.[37] Unlike Benny, he was not particularly good-looking, and he was not a visual performer in the way Benny and Burns came to be on television.

Duffy's Tavern was a success on radio but not on television. Ed Gardner, the star and creator of the show, had, unlike Benny, Burns, and even Fred Allen, no experience performing before a live audience and did not think visually. When Larry Rhine, who wrote for both the radio and television versions, tried to think of the show in visual terms, Gardner replied, "Just give me the jokes. I'll stand there and do them." Gardner wanted to do what he did in radio: stand with his hat in his hand and read the jokes. The show only ran from April to September in 1954.

The radio writers as well as performers had trouble with the transition. When Catherine Turney, a stage and screen writer, went to work for a show called *Cavalcade of America*, she was assigned to do a show based on a radio play for the series on Eli Whitney, the inventor of the cotton gin. She re-thought it for the limitations of early television. The radio script had Whitney looking out the window at a large crowd, but Turney realized the set would only allow for three to four people. When the writer of the radio play read Turney's script, "He loathed me. He was so upset. He was an ear writer. He didn't think in visual terms." Turney saw that the radio writer understood television was going to take over but did not want to learn the new technique.

·2·

EARLY FILMED TELEVISION

*I*n 1950 Chicago radio writer Don Brinkley decided to try writing for the movies:

> Actually I came out here to bring the industry to its knees. I found it was already on its knees. It was that panic time when the movie studios were in terrible trouble. Television was just beginning to rear its ugly head . . . there was a lot of confusion. So what I had to do was take what was available and I started doing radio again.

Writers already doing movies had it just as bad. Charles Larson, who had started as a junior writer at MGM writing short subjects, says, "The whole Hollywood closed up. Hollywood just died." Even Wells Root, whose credits included such big pictures as the 1937 *The Prisoner of Zenda*, saw that "There was an active market for writers in television, more than there was for the screen."

The active market Root refers to was not live television, of which there was very little in Hollywood in the late forties and early fifties. There was yet no coaxial cable connecting the coasts, and no regular coast-to-coast live telecasting until 1951. There was also virtually no filmed production for television by the major film studios, who generally hoped television would just go away. The television market was smaller production companies producing some programs for the major networks, but mostly for the syndication market. Many local stations, to fill up their programming hours, bought shows from syndication companies, which would sell them filmed shows that the stations could then sell to local advertisers. By 1955 local advertisers were spending $150 million on 150 syndicated programs.[1] Inevitably the budgets for such programs were less than network budgets, which created opportunities for film producers, and writers, experienced in low-budget film production.

One of the first producers to get involved in television film production was

Hal Roach, Sennett's rival in making short comedies in the silent films. In 1949 his son, Hal Roach, Jr., suggested doing half-hour films for television. Their company started that year with a half-hour situation comedy entitled *The Stu Erwin Show*, which they sold to the fledgling American Broadcasting Company (ABC) network. Subsequently they produced *My Little Margie* (which started on CBS and became a radio show *after* it was a success on television), the ill-fated *Duffy's Tavern*, and *Racket Squad*.[2] Hal Roach, Jr., told *TV Guide* the keynote to his work was "Quality. Give them good entertainment, and you stay in business. But it's not the movie business. It's an entirely different proposition."[3]

Racket Squad was originally produced in 1950 for the syndication market, but in 1951 was picked up by CBS for a two-year run on the network. Probably because it was written and shot cheaply ($25,000 per episode[4]) and quickly (44 pages of script shot in two days[5]), an interesting stylistic touch in the writing of *Racket Squad* was dropped after the first few episodes: The stories dealt with various cons run on unsuspecting citizens, which were foiled by Captain Braddock of the Squad. In the first episodes, Braddock narrates the stories, but in the second person, addressing the victim of the con. This supposes Braddock knows everything about the con before the victim tells him, which makes him rather obnoxious. Eventually the narration was changed to Braddock telling the story in the third person—a more conventional approach and therefore less demanding of writers.

Westerns and Jack Chertok

Television audiences very early grew used to filmed Westerns. In 1948, WATV in Newark began running old B-picture Western movies seven nights a week and continued to do so through 1954. Part of the reason was that the films were cheap programming, available for between $25 and $500 per showing.[6] Actor William Boyd bought up the television rights to his Hopalong Cassidy B-Westerns and syndicated them as a series for between $1,000 and $1,250 per film.[7] By 1949 Boyd was a millionaire and NBC picked up the films for network showings. Boyd made additional films for network and syndication.

George W. Trendle's selection as the television producer of *The Lone Ranger* was Jack Chertok, who had produced low-budget features for MGM in the early forties. Chertok hired George B. Seitz, Jr., who had written shorts for MGM, to write and direct the first *Lone Ranger* filmed episodes. Seitz worked with Fran Stryker, adapting the latter's radio scripts for the television series.[8] The budgets for the *Lone Ranger* episodes in the first few years were $15,000 per episode, raised to $18,000 by 1953. Writer Charles Larson remembers the writers were very aware of the budget limitations:

> At the end of one season, we were at the end of the budget. Tom Seller said to Chertok, "I can write one with only two people in it." He did one where the

Lone Ranger and Tonto were following the villains. They fall into all kinds of traps but we never see them being set. We were all so dazzled to see how he did it.

According to Larson, the writers would not directly adapt the radio plays but would look at them for ideas for stories. Often story ideas came from material already shot. Before the season would begin, all the exterior scenes would be shot. This footage would be shown to the writers, who would decide who would get to use what, and then the writers would write stories with interior scenes, in cabins and mines, to match the exteriors.

Larson describes Chertok as "a wonderful man to work for. He loved writers." One reason Chertok loved writers is they could save him money. On one of his non-Westerns, *Private Secretary*, Larry Rhine wrote a seven-page scene that could be shot in one take, which cut shooting time and expense. Chertok loved the scene. Chertok had a group of writers he used, although they were not officially staff writers. Larson started at $250 per week and later got up to $300. Sam Rolfe remembers getting "Five hundred bucks a pop [for *The Lone Ranger*] and I could knock one of those things out in a night." He adds:

> I found them [the early shows, not only *The Lone Ranger*] very easy shows to write. . . . It's like you're grunting and groaning, like a train starting up to get that first page going. Once the characters start talking to each other, they take off on their own, and I was always trying to catch up. I had second and third pages beside me, writing notes on what's coming ahead because it would all flash in while I was working and I didn't want to forget it. But it would write itself, particularly the half-hour television.

Chertok was producing other shows as well as *The Lone Ranger* and "his" writers wrote for them as well. One was *Sky King*, a modern Western in which the hero gets around in a plane. As Larson describes the format, "It was extremely rigid. You had to have him in the plane. Something exciting had to happen with the plane." Once the plane was out shooting aerial footage and came across a plume of smoke. It was a cabin on fire. The cameraman shot it, and Larson was instructed to write a story to fit it. Chertok also produced a couple of seasons of *Cavalcade of America* when it was finally done on film, and Charles Larson managed to set one on an ocean liner even though they did not have the sets for an ocean liner. Larson found the writing process familiar: "We all came out of B pictures. It was kind of like writing B pictures: hurry, rejection, frustration."

Ziv

When Don Brinkley came out to Hollywood and found it on its knees, the radio production company he started writing for was Ziv, a radio syndication company. The success of *Hopalong Cassidy* pushed Ziv to try its hand with *The Cisco Kid* in 1950.[9] It was the first of many successes, all of them made on the cheap. Brinkley describes the company as "really a rinky-dink organization." The half-hour shows were shot in one and a half days, and they had to be written half exterior scenes and half interior scenes so that all of the one could be shot the first day and all the others shot the second day. Brinkley, who also wrote for the *Highway Patrol* series, relates: "We ground those out like popcorn. The format was easy; you could put him [Broderick Crawford] anywhere." For the series they tried occasionally to use stock footage of events such as fires, but found it looked cheap. Which was in keeping with the look of the show, because, as Brinkley notes, "What went on film, stayed on film." One *Highway Patrol* episode was shot near an animal park. In one take, as Broderick Crawford was on the phone, a llama walked by in the background. There was no retake.

Ziv also produced two service-academy series, *Men of Annapolis*, which was syndicated, and *The West Point Story* on CBS. Both were supposedly based on real stories, but writers for the series deny it. Sy Salkowitz got on *Men of Annapolis* because he met the producer, William Castle, at a party. He gave Castle several story ideas for the series, all of them made up. Annapolis did have control over the story content, and writers were not allowed to do stories on events that might tarnish the reputation of the Academy, such as midshipmen going AWOL.

Sam Rolfe wrote for *West Point* and his stories were not based on true cases either. His story editor on the series was a former film editor for Ziv named Quinn Martin, who later produced *The Untouchables* and *The FBI*. Also on the series was a cop moonlighting as a writer, Gene Roddenberry, who went on to create *Star Trek*. Rolfe himself went on to develop *The Man From U.N.C.L.E.* As Rolfe says, "We all seemed to be moonlighting on that show."

True and Semi-true Stories

Allan Sloane wrote *Navy Log*, which unlike the Ziv shows, was based on actual stories,[10] and when *Death Valley Days* came to television in 1952, its original creator, Ruth Woodman, still insisted each story be based on fact.[11] Nat Perrin came on the show as producer in the late fifties, and he says McCann-Erickson, the advertising agency producing the show, insisted that "When a writer came in with a premise, he'd have to bring in the documentation."

Crime shows also based episodes on true stories, notably *Dragnet*, from Los Angeles Police Department cases, and its San Francisco rip-off, *The Lineup*. E. Jack Neuman wrote for the latter. The producer was Jaime del Valle, and when Neuman came on the show he found he had to rewrite eighteen scripts del Valle had bought from other writers. The stories were based on actual cases, but Neuman recalls he "angled them differently. It was very valuable to me because I studied the San Francisco Police Department. And I wore a wire [recorder] while I was doing it. They didn't even know I was wearing a wire. So that was how I got all the cop talk right." Neuman adds that doing the show, "was hard, hard work, because I had to take all of Jaime's responsibility too." Neuman became Associate Producer of the show because del Valle was busy entertaining the cops and not doing his work.

There were other producers for writers to deal with as well. Frank Wisbar produced a half-hour anthology series titled *Fireside Theatre*. It was also cheaply done. Catherine Turney says, "It wasn't too much different [from live television]. You still had the limitations of the set. It was like the early days of talkies, the actors all worrying about the mike boom." Sam Rolfe says Wisbar offered him "Little pieces of crap and he'd make them sound so great." Once he tried to get a writer to do a full adaptation of James Fenimore Cooper's novel *The Spy* to fit into half an hour. Turney adds: "They all had grand ideas like that," and that the writers were all reading de Maupassant to see what they could steal. Two indications of the industry attitude toward television writers at the time: Turney says the writers on the show were put in the old B-picture writers' offices and her agent refused to come down to that office.

There were also shows filmed elsewhere. One, done for a New York–based company, was *Captain David Grief*, based on stories about a South Seas islands schooner captain written by Jack London. The show was shot in Mexico when Sy Salkowitz met the New York story editor (there was also one in Mexico to do rewrites). The New York editor took it as his right that of the $1,300 fee paid the writer, he would get a kickback of $200. Salkowitz was incensed and went to his agent to complain. His agent told him he should have taken the deal. The New York story editor was later fired and the one in Mexico wired Salkowitz that he had read the first draft and asked, "Where the hell's the polish?" Salkowitz was baffled, and when the Mexico editor returned to New York he told Salkowitz they had paid him for the story. Salkowitz replied, "You never paid me anything." After they did pay him, Salkowitz wrote three more episodes.

I Love Lucy

At CBS radio in the mid-forties Madelyn Davis[12] formed a lasting partnership with Bob Carroll Jr. In the summer of 1948 they joined the staff of radio's *My Favorite Husband*, whose producer was Jess Oppenheimer and whose star was Lucille Ball.[13] In 1950, CBS wanted Ball to do a television series of *My Favorite Husband*, but Ball, for personal reasons, wanted to do a series with her husband Desi Arnaz,[14] and enlisted Carroll and Davis to help them. Ball liked their writing for radio, she told Davis, because they wrote "visually,"[15] which Davis took to mean, "We had written gags *and* situations, not just written gags." To help persuade CBS that audiences would like Ball and Arnaz as a couple, they put together a vaudeville production. The centerpiece was a routine Ball learned from the clown Pepito. Davis says, "He did the routine for her with the props, and then we adapted to it and wrote the dialogue." The routine—about Ball trying to get into Arnaz's act—became the basis of the first pilot for what became *I Love Lucy*.[16]

The first pilot was done before an audience, like a live television show, recorded by kinescope (filming the show off a television screen). The ad agency for the sponsor, Philip Morris cigarettes, wanted the show broadcast live from New York, while Arnaz wanted to do it live from Hollywood, with kinescopes for the East Coast. Most of Philip Morris's customers lived in the East, and since kinescopes were very bad copies, the sponsor turned Arnaz down. Arnaz broke the impasse by working out a system to film the show with three cameras while performing it in front of an audience.

What has become the standard method of filming situation comedies was born. For the writers, the three-camera system had distinct advantages. They could include costume and set changes that could take more time to do than could be allowed for in live television. Given the amount of physical comedy Ball was going to do in the series, it was almost essential that it be filmed.

In the beginning Carroll and Davis borrowed storylines from their old *My Favorite Husband* scripts, but learned that television was different. They had to move the characters around and not depend on the sound effects as much. Primarily, they had to learn to think visually, which Davis says they did not have "any big agonizing trouble with . . . because she [Ball] was so visual and lent herself to it so much." Davis describes the working pattern for making a show a week that soon developed:

> We'd get the story line [in a Monday meeting with Jess Oppenheimer]. He started out dictating it in front of us, then later I would type it. Then we would do the story line and then we wrote what we would call the first draft and then we would give it to him for a second draft or a polish. Then we'd have a meeting and then we'd go on and get another story, and then meanwhile while we were working on the next one, he was doing a polish on the one we'd finished. So there wasn't a lot of this "We need a whole new second act" and "Let's throw the script out." Believe me, we would have been off the air. Like they do today, they really push and pull the script a lot, go through a whole massive redrafting over the weekend. We just didn't have time. We had two weeks off at Christmas, and by the end of the season they were building sets from the storylines. The first season we did 38 shows, because that's how we did radio. That's what we thought you did.

What Davis calls the polish, Oppenheimer described as "redictat[ing] the entire script from start to finish into my dictation machine . . . because that way each of the characters consistently spoke the same way. It didn't have to be *me*, necessarily, but as long as it was filtered through one person's senses."[17]

Davis and Carroll "did sit down once and tell him we didn't like that. In a very nice way. We had worked very hard on it. We talked the script out loud, and acted it out. So we didn't feel that was necessary." Davis adds, "We worked well together. He taught us a lot. He really taught us how to plot."

The storylines came from the writers asking themselves each week, "What does Lucy want this week? What does she want and who's going to keep her from getting it and what's she going to get into?"

> Every once in a while we wrote backwards. We had an idea for a physical routine, and then we wrote out how we got her there. One time we went to a pizza place in Hollywood and the man was making pizza in the window. He'd throw it up to get air in it, and he was very good at it, throwing it up and catching it, and then he'd put it in the oven. So we said, "Ah ha." We got Lucy to come there, and she practiced. She made pizza in the window. Of course she collected a crowd. And then we worked to how we got there.

Davis found that she, as the one woman writer on the show, got to try out the physical gags they thought up to see if they could be done: "You didn't want to be on the stage with seventy people all hired and then it didn't work. Then you had to come up with something in fifteen minutes. Also, we found that by acting it out, we found funnier things than if we had just imagined it." Once they decided to roll Lucy up in a carpet, but when Davis tried it the rolled carpet was impossible to roll out the door, which made the scene even funnier. On the other hand, they wanted to put Lucy into an office chair on rollers, but discovered it tipped over. They dropped the idea, because they already knew that if the audience thought the gag was really dangerous, it killed the joke.

They wrote down the physical humor in detail. Because it was written all in capital letters, it was known as "The Black Stuff" (a term still used, although some writers refer to it as "The Block Stuff," referring to the block of prose on the page). The writers worked closely with Ball, letting her "embroider" on the material, with the writers in turn suggesting additional bits. Nor was the dialogue always delivered as written. One of her most famous routines was a supposed commercial for Vitameatavegamin. Davis recalls, "I can remember I was so young then. She was marvelous, but something got a little different in the middle, just by accident and I thought, 'Well! She changed it.' I was furious. . . . We had worked so hard on it. I think it took us all day, at least."

Ball later remembered the physical humor as more ad-libbed than it was, such as one gag in the "Hollywood at Last!" episode. Davis says,

> She somehow remembered that as her nose caught on fire accidentally. And that's not true. We got the idea of that, and all screamed with laughter and all hoped to heaven we could do it. And then they built this marvelous nose. She

had the nerve to set fire to her own nose, which I don't think I would have. . . . I didn't try that stunt. But she did put her nose in the coffee cup. That was her ad-lib, I think in rehearsal or on the show. But it was planned to set fire. That's one of those things I wanted to set straight because it was such a wonderful gag and it worked so well. But it wasn't an accident.

From as early as the unaired kinescope pilot of *I Love Lucy*, it is clear the writers' instincts for what to write for Lucille Ball for television were right. Beyond the slapstick in the imitation of Pepito the clown, the script gives Ball a chance to react comically. Ball's reactions, even in her radio days, were so striking that the writers gave them names, such as "The Spider," which came from Ball's reading a commercial on radio about Little Miss Muffet. In the unaired pilot Ricky gets out of bed first and we see the back of his pajamas have the face of a mule on them. He leaves them hanging over the mirror, so when Lucy gets up she sees them and does a reaction thinking that it is her. She then takes the pajamas off the mirror, gets a look at her real face, and her reaction tops the first gag. In episode five, "The Quiz Show," she is repeatedly squirted in the face with a seltzer bottle. Milton Berle would have simply left it at that, but Ball gives us different reactions to each squirt and varies the pace of squirting the water out of her mouth.

The writers were not, however, only writing for Lucille Ball, but also writing for Desi Arnaz, both as a producer (Davis says he let them wander around the studio prop department to find props to do shows about) and a performer. Arnaz had not shown any great acting skills in the movies he had done. By giving him reactions to Lucy's antics, the writers provided Arnaz the opportunity, as early as the unaired pilot, to show how charming a straight man he could be.

They also had fun with his Cuban accent, again as early as the unaired pilot, although, as Davis remembered in 1990, they never went beyond that:

> It never occurred to us to do an "issue." Lucy and Desi wouldn't have known what to do with it. For instance, in all that time we never brought up the fact that he was Cuban and people may not have cared for her being married to a Cuban, because we never discussed that. We never discussed that. It just occurred to me now that we never did. Nowadays you would.

Davis continues, discussing other issues the show did not deal with:

> Maybe now you would deal with the fact that she had the baby and they'd been married quite a while. They hadn't had children. You'd probably get into that. Which of course was their real life. But that never occurred to us then. It was enough to have a child on the air, let alone get into the fact of why they couldn't conceive, couldn't have them. We had the public reeling. [Imagine what Philip Morris would have said if we were] talking about how smoking is bad for pregnant women.

In 1952, the second year of the series, Ball became pregnant. On radio the pregnancy would not have been apparent. On television there was pressure to avoid dealing with the pregnancy by "hiding" Ball behind the furniture. There were concerns on the part of the network and the sponsors over the question of "taste." Fortunately, when Arnaz told Jess Oppenheimer of the pregnancy in the spring of 1952, Oppenheimer's reaction was that this would give them new material to write about in the second season. Fortified by this reaction, Arnaz became determined to include it as part of the show. To protect themselves, Oppenheimer arranged for a Catholic priest, a Protestant minister, and a rabbi to read the scripts.[18] According to Davis, the advisers never changed a thing. The writers had not written anything offensive in the first place.

In the fall of 1954, the writers sent the Ricardos and the Mertzes on a trip to Hollywood, which enabled them to have several guest stars. The writers made fun of this themselves by beginning their first scene in the Brown Derby Restaurant with Lucy and Ethel pointing out all the stars they are seeing, but which we cannot see. The payoff to the joke is William Holden, in person, sitting down in the next booth. In episode 124, Ball does the classic mirror routine with Harpo Marx. The writers did not even look at *Duck Soup*, in which the mirror routine first occurred, and they did not write out all the detail because Marx knew the routine by heart and taught it to Ball.

In 1956 Jess Oppenheimer left the show and Carroll and Davis became the senior writers, although, as Davis says, "The pattern was set. We were used to doing the full script." In the middle of the 1956–57 season, the Ricardos moved out of their New York apartment and into a house in Connecticut because the writers found they had run out of stories to do in the apartment.[19]

In the fall of 1957, the Desilu company stopped making half-hour episodes of *I Love Lucy* and turned to doing one-hour episodes that appeared once a month. Davis notes how this affected the writing:

> It changed it because we didn't know what we were doing. We wrote the first hour, and we put in musical numbers. It turned out to be way over an hour. We didn't know how long to do it. We sound rather dumb but we were breaking precedent. To my knowledge there had not been an hour situation comedy. To that point. So, by the time we put commercials in it, our first show ran an hour and fifteen minutes. Desi didn't want to cut anything, and of course cutting fifteen minutes is a lot. So that's when he went to the show that followed us, *United States Steel [Hour]* and asked to buy fifteen minutes of their time. He talked to CBS and they said, "Fine." I think we're the only hour-and-fifteen-minute show that was ever done.

Davis adds that it took Arnaz to have the nerve to even try to persuade U.S. Steel and CBS to do that.

The other hour episodes do seem overextended. The second episode, "The Celebrity Next Door," plays like two half-hour episodes, the first half being a mismanaged dinner Lucy throws for next-door neighbor Tallulah Bankhead (played by herself), and the second half the rehearsal of a PTA show Lucy has hustled Bankhead into appearing in. The half hour was the best format for the Lucy and Ricky characters.

Bob Carroll and Madelyn Davis continued to write for Lucille Ball after the demise of *I Love Lucy*. They wrote for *The Lucy Show* (1962–68), *Here's Lucy* (1968–74), and Ball's last show, *Life with Lucy* in 1986. They also wrote Lucille Ball specials and even contributed to one of her films, the 1956 *Forever Darling*. According to the script, Ball was not playing "Lucy," but Desi Arnaz asked them to write a scene and it came out "Lucy." Madelyn Davis is still amused by the sequence where Ball starts out in the house in the film's character, goes outside and turns immediately into "Lucy." Neither Ball nor the writers could escape their creation.

·3·

EARLY LIVE TELEVISION

Abraham Polonsky, who moved from writing movies to writing live television,

> kind of liked live television, but live television is a form that makes great demands on the people who make it. You write dialogue a bit differently, because you can't rehearse it as often. And then they have to learn it quickly. And very complicated things get to be difficult to do, whereas in film nothing's too complicated. So you search for other ways of doing things.

Kraft Television Theatre

The Kraft Television Theatre was the first regularly scheduled drama anthology on live television, and it was also the longest-running, beginning in 1947 and ending in 1958. When it premiered in May 1947, it was seen by 32,000 viewers only in the New York area. By 1953 the audience had grown to 22,570,000 in 46 cities.[1] It was so successful in its regularly scheduled Wednesday nights on NBC that Kraft ran a second night on ABC Thursday nights from October 1953 to January 1955. The programming done on Kraft Television Theatre show both the strengths and the limitations of early live television drama.

The show produced 650 scripts from 18,845 submitted to it.[2] Ed Rice, script editor on the show from its beginning, has described the early days: "I was the entire script department for the first year and a half. I had to write one act a day for three days each week, leaving me four days to seek out what would be the next show."[3] Since there were no summer replacement programs, the show did 52 productions a year (104 when on ABC as well). Understandably, Rice tended to use previously written material. In its first six years, Kraft produced 169 adaptations of Broadway plays, 53 London stage plays, 27 plays not produced elsewhere, 22 classics, and only 40 original television plays.[4]

Another practical reason for selecting theatrical plays was that they were written to be performed in a limited time and, especially, a limited space. *Kraft* did its first few years in NBC's Studio 3H, then moved to its famous Studio 8H, which had heard Arturo Toscanini lead the NBC orchestra on radio and would later see the production of *Saturday Night Live.* Studio 8H was nearly twice as large as 3H, but it was still only 128 feet by 76 feet.[5] A play with three sets could fit into the studio with a little room to move the cameras, but anything more was generally beyond the scope of the facilities.

"Double Door," the first *Kraft* production, was a broadcast play, all taking place in one room. "Alternating Current," the first original play done on the program (in January 1948), was set entirely in the kitchen of a Senator's house. The 1953 production of "Rip Van Winkle" was based on the acting version Joseph Jefferson toured in during the nineteenth century, and is hurt by the limitations of the stage and studio. The long first act takes place in the town, and the second act takes place up in the mountains. Rip does not fall asleep until the end of the second act, waking up 20 years later in the third. The second act is as long as it is so that changes can be made in the town set during that act.

The limitations of live television are particularly apparent in plays with material that could easily be shown on film. This is especially noticeable when *Kraft* tries to do documentary material, such as the 1956 production "I Am Fifteen—And I Don't Want to Die," based on the true story of a 15-year-old girl who lived in Budapest in 1944. The program begins with filmed inserts of the German bombing, but most of the play takes place in the cellar where the girl's family is hiding. The single set does give a sense of claustrophobia, but actions outside the cellar are talked about rather than shown.

As the series continued, writers learned how to use the limitations of the sets effectively. Meade Roberts's 1953 "The Rose Garden" works well within the confines of a Hollywood garden apartment house. Ben Radin's 1954 "Edie and the Princess" cuts very effectively between several different rooms in one apartment and even between apartments in one building.

There were also limitations in terms of subject matter. Typical of the time, the show was produced not by the network but by the J. Walter Thompson advertising agency. Ed Rice worked for the agency, and unsolicited scripts were read by an agency reader, who would pass on to Rice or his assistant, Charles Jackson, at the most only three or four of the twenty scripts submitted each week, so the weeding out of unacceptable material began early.[6] The agency's tendency was to be cautious in order to protect the sponsor. A look at the kinds of plays done on *Kraft* demonstrates that it was never an adventurous show in terms of subject matter. "Double Door" was a 1933 stage play described in a review of its Broadway production as a "grim melodrama . . . after the pattern of the well-made gasping thriller."[7] "Alternating Current" is a tepid satire of politics, second rate Hecht and MacArthur. Victor Wolfson's 1956 "The Sears Girls" is the same kind of melodrama the movies did in the forties with such films as *Now, Voyager.*

Rod Serling's 1953 play "Long Time Till Dawn," about an ex-con who tries to come back to his hometown seems reminiscent of many Warner Brothers films of the thirties and forties, enlivened by having the leading role played by a not-yet-famous James Dean. But the director may have felt Dean was too intense for the gentility of *Kraft*. One of the director's handwritten notes on the script reads: "Jimmie—too frantic and too high a tension—psychopath schizoid." Only a few months before that production, Ed Rice told *TV Guide* "We can deal with any subject but it must be about people you believe in and not case subjects from a psychiatrist's notebook. We look for matinee-type plays—believable incidents that might happen to people who live down the street from our viewers."[8]

The kinds of plays *Kraft Television Theatre* did changed. In the first year they were mostly adaptations, and in 1949 the show turned to the classics. In 1952 character studies became popular, and in 1953 the show started doing "slice of life" plays.[9] Here again, the show was running behind the time line of the cutting edge of television drama, since the show was obviously reacting to the success of writers such as Paddy Chayefsky on other shows. Rice said in 1953, "What we plan to do is find more short stories and novels we can adapt for TV. We'll actually be on the lookout also for original plays, and that may eventually become our chief source of story material." He added that the agency might hire writers to work only for *Kraft*, which other producers, such as Fred Coe, had already done.[10] The difference was that Coe was willing to take chances that *Kraft*, because of its institutional nature, was not able to do.

The one exception to this in *Kraft's* history is Rod Serling's 1955 play "Patterns," a corrosive study of ambition and office politics. Ironically, one of the reasons for its power was that the office environment, which was not "authentic" in Serling's original script, was developed based on the J. Walter Thompson agency, the producers of *Kraft*.[11] On anything more volatile than office politics, however, *Kraft* was more cautious. Allan Manings wrote a play for the show about the first black family to vote. Writers were not allowed at rehearsals, and while the show was supposed to be in rehearsal, Manings ran into an actor who had been cast in it. The actor said it was a shame it had been canceled. Manings replied, "They can't cancel a show in rehearsal."

The actor said, "Yes they can. The agency decided. You cannot do anything this controversial." J. Walter Thompson and *Kraft* went back to more genteel programming, much in the same way that twenty years later the Public Broadcasting System would be able to get corporate underwriters for uncontroversial drama on their *Masterpiece Theatre*.

Filmed Inserts and Time Stretchers

Kraft Television Theatre was not the only early live show to use filmed inserts. *Man Against Crime*, a detective show starting in 1949 starring Ralph Bellamy, also used filmed inserts in its first years, and in 1952 went entirely to film. When it was live, the show also found an inventive way to make sure it came out at exactly the right time. The writers were required to write a "search scene" for late in the show. Bellamy would be told before he went on the set whether he needed to stretch the scene. If not, he'd go straight to the clue. If he did, he could spend however much time was needed in the room.[12]

Roscoe Karns, the star of another live detective show, *Rocky King, Detective*, found another way to fill out the time, if necessary. When one show ran short in rehearsal, Karns, whose wife Grace Carney was playing a role in the show, came up with a phone conversation at the end of the show between King and his wife Mabel. Carney played the wife off-screen, and the character stayed offscreen the run of the show.[13] The final conversation also became a way for the writers to tie up any loose plot points.

Your Show of Shows

In 1945 a young writer named Mel Tolkin came to New York from Canada; his parents had immigrated there from Tolkin's birthplace in the Ukraine. The following year Tolkin, who by now was writing songs, was hired by Max Liebman, producer of the weekly shows at Tamiment, a summer resort in the Poconos.[14] By the summer of 1948, Liebman realized the Tamiment shows were preparation for a different kind of television. Most TV variety shows, he thought, were based on vaudeville or radio, but he was more influenced by the theater, especially "the element of sophistication . . . The show [at Tamiment] was performed in a manner that didn't patronize people."[15] Sylvester "Pat" Weaver, then at an ad agency, saw a Tamiment show and asked Liebman if it could be done every week. Liebman had him see the next week's show.[16] As Tolkin describes what happened next, Weaver "just about lifted it, bodily, for *The Admiral Broadway Revue*," which began in January 1949 as a one-hour weekly show on NBC.

The *Admiral* show was to use some Tamiment material, but also to use "classical material" written by people like Moss Hart and George S. Kaufman for previous Broadway revues. According to Tolkin, there was simply not enough Broadway sketch material to keep a weekly television show going. The star of the show was Sid Caesar, and the conventional revue material was also, the semi-official biographer of *Your Show of Shows* Ted Sennett writes, "too diffuse, too vaguely focused for his [Caesar's] very special talent."[17] What Caesar needed in order to take off was material written for his talents.

Liebman kept the staff of *Admiral Broadway Revue*, and on February 25, 1950, *Your Show of Shows* premiered.[18] Some Tamiment material was used on the new show, but it was mostly new material. The writers were Liebman, Lucille Kallen, and Tolkin, who describes how working on the new show varied from the previous one: "Basically because we wrote the whole frigging show." In keeping with Liebman's idea that the show should be like theater,

Your Show of Shows included music, ballet numbers, and even some opera. What made the immediate impact and lives on in the hearts of the show's fans was the comic material.

Mel Tolkin and Lucille Kallen were the head writers, and shortly after the show began Mel Brooks, a friend of Caesar's, and Tony Webster were added to the writing staff. As Tolkin remembers, he and Kallen did not have much time to supervise as head writers:

> First of all, when you write an hour-and-a-half show a week, four or five sketches, three, four, or five songs, there's no luxury of rewriting a whole show. So you just do your best. An idea can be thrown out [discarded] at the very beginning. That goes without saying. It's got to be acceptable to all. Whoever gives it, somebody else can say, "It's only a one-joke idea. It's good, but where do you go? There's no force to it, no kinetic push to develop." Then it's a matter of fixing. I can't think of a whole full sketch being thrown out after it was written.

As the ideas were developed, they would be shown to Liebman and Caesar if they were not in the meeting. Eventually Tolkin and Kallen would read the finished sketch and then, "Everybody dived in and a good sketch became a brilliant one, occasionally."

Lucille Kallen has described the writing sessions this way:

> Sid boomed, Tolkin intoned, [Carl] Reiner [who joined the show as an actor but worked with the writers as well] trumpeted, and Brooks, well, Mel imitated everything from a rabbinical student to the white whale of *Moby-Dick* thrashing about on the floor with six harpoons sticking in his back. Let's say that gentility was never a noticeable part of our working lives. Max Liebman was fond of quoting what I think was a Goldwynism: "From a polite conference comes a polite movie." [19]

In other words, the conferences were not unlike those of Mack Sennett's "gathering of badly deranged lunatics" in the silent film days. [20]

Mel Tolkin has been quoted as saying that "with one writer different, it wouldn't have been the same show. Or with one actor different." [21] He thinks it helped that the writers were all in some way "outsiders": he was from the Ukraine, Kallen was a woman, Brooks was from the Bronx, and Webster was a Catholic. "Most writers are outsiders, if I may talk pretentiously. The result showed: it was an outsider's look at Earthlings' foolish, absurd behavior. We were all a little offbeat. We did have a fresher look." There were differences in the writers as well, which also helped. Tolkin compares Kallen and Brooks:

> Basically she would sit with a long yellow pad writing in ink and very often say "No." In addition to being creative, of course, she was a powerful editor. And she'd type it out while we'd walk around. I think Mel Brooks was more in adding

[bits later] rather than sitting in a room, but he was a very brilliant guy, a wild sense of humor.

The great challenge in writing for *Your Show of Shows* was that the performers could do anything. Tolkin says, "When you write for Sid you write old, young, fat, short, any language in the world. Because there was no limit. It was as simple as that."

The writing then for *Your Show of Shows* combined those elements: theatrical sophistication, writers with a wide variety of backgrounds working in collaboration, both brilliant imagination *and* editing skills on the part of the writing team, and writing specifically for talented comic performers with wide acting ranges. The writing went well beyond the simple gags and gag sketches Milton Berle's writers provided for him. The sketches, monologues, and pantomimes gave Caesar, Imogene Coca, and the others not only something to do, but attitudes to play. In the first *Your Show of Shows*, Caesar's monologue is the thoughts of a man going down the aisle to be married. Mel Brooks specialized in creating the interview sketches, where Caesar played a German professor who thought he knew everything, but didn't. That dichotomy provided Caesar with differing reactions to the questions his interviewer, usually Carl Reiner, asked him. Recurring sketches on the show were about Charlie and Doris Hickenlooper, a married couple. The couple did not generally engage in the physical slapstick that Lucy and Ricky did, nor did they generally yell as much as Ralph and Alice Kramden did on Jackie Gleason's program. As Ted Sennett points out, however, "they were truer, more honestly observed, and funnier," than Lucy and the Kramdens.[22] Part of what made them seem that way was the attitudes the writers gave them: she was something of a snob, particularly about culture, and he was something of a slob, particularly about everything.

For many viewers, the best of the sketches were the parodies of movies. It is a mark of the sophistication of the show that not only did it parody American box-office successes, but foreign films such as *The Bicycle Thief*. The show felt it could take these on because not only were those films shown in New York theaters, local New York TV stations were filling up their schedules with telecasts of recent foreign films. Tolkin notes that in writing satires of foreign films the idea was that the takeoffs must be funny in themselves, whether the viewer had seen the original or not. The foreign film parodies gave Caesar a chance to speak in a variety of accents and made-up languages. The writers would not try to write out themselves the fractured languages, but would just write "doubletalk," or let Caesar himself dictate it to a secretary (if you think the secretary had it easy, listen to one of Caesar's routines and try to transcribe it).

Mel Tolkin has admitted[23] the writers were a little more malicious in their satires of contemporary films because they felt superior to them. The film satires were especially popular in New York, which then tended to look down on films.[24] Tolkin admits, "There was a certain snobbishness. I felt it. You walk into a restaurant and you hear people the next morning after the show talking about it." He remembers talking one day about a movie they'd seen and the writers saying, "Movies? I just saw a movie. What a piece of shit it was." Tolkin says today, "We were talking about *Shane*. Actually we thought it was a good movie. We did do a good job on *Shane*" which in the *Show of Shows*' version became *Strange*, where the basic joke was, as Tolkin remembers: "What idiot, what schmuck, will risk his life to protect a family of total strangers?" They also did a parody of *From Here to Eternity* called *From Here to Obscurity* featuring the best of many takeoffs on Lancaster and Kerr kissing in the surf. In their version Caesar and Coca are nearly drowned. It not only makes fun of the scene, but as Tolkin is proud to note, "That scene has a brilliant satirical point: that you can't fuck right near the waves." The same kind of honest observation that helped the Hickenlooper sketches helped the movie parodies.

As the success of the show grew, more writers were added to the staff, including for one season only in 1952, Danny Simon and his younger brother, Neil. It has also become a legend that the young Woody Allen worked on *Your Show of Shows*, but he did not.[25] Shortly after the demise of the program in 1954, Allen did join some of the writing staff, but for a new show.

Caesar's Hour and *The Imogene Coca Show*

Ted Sennett in his book is not clear exactly why *Your Show of Shows* was canceled in 1954.[26] He notes that some critics felt the show had begun to get a bit stale. He discounts rumors of friction among the cast and staff, as does Mel Tolkin today. Tolkin thinks the network simply believed the show was "too rich, too expensive," and wanted "to give Max a show, give Sid a show, give Coca a show. They made three. It had to be [the] network. I don't know of any reason of a split [among the people on the show]. I didn't feel that." Max Liebman went into producing what were then called "spectaculars" for the network, but they were not on a par with his previous work.

Sid Caesar got the best of the division of talent. In addition to actors Howard Morris and Carl Reiner (who, as noted, also wrote), he got custody of Tolkin, and the Simon brothers, and added Larry Gelbart, Selma Diamond, Michael Stewart, Sheldon Keller, and later Danny Simon's protégé Woody Allen. Because the writing staff was bigger than it was on the early days of *Your Show of Shows*, the writing process was slightly different. Tolkin describes it:

> Well, there'd be a story conference in which everybody came with ideas, or the staff worked out some ideas. Then the [writers] split up in teams. I was with Shelly [Sheldon] Keller. Then it was brought back and read to Sid. Of course Sid was in the story conference when the ideas were decided. He certainly had

to have a powerful veto. Everybody can prove that a sketch stinks. "It's no good," or "We saw that somebody did it," or whatever it is. But Sid, in a way, did not have to have a reason for veto—for a very good purpose: He has to be the guy sticking his ass out on camera. Now and then you'd insist, "It's a good idea, Sid," but if he didn't like it, you would kiss it good-bye. You can't afford the time to fight it.

Many of the writers who worked on both shows tend to describe the writing on *Your Show of Shows* in this same way,[27] but as Tolkin slyly says, "These new ones remember *Caesar's Hour*" (or the specials that came later). Two of the later well-known writers were not particularly vocal at the story conferences. Tolkin says that Neil Simon "seldom opened his mouth, but when he did, it was perfect, whatever he would say."[28] As for Allen, who did not work with Caesar until a 1958 special,[29] "He almost didn't open his mouth, but when he and Larry [Gelbart] went to their corner somewhere, they came back with fabulous stuff. That goes for the material Gelbart and Neil Simon brought in. I don't recall Woody speaking a lot at story conferences. Gelbart spoke for them."

Instead of Imogene Coca, the leading lady was Nanette Fabray, and the edgy domestic sketches of the earlier show became more conventional situation comedy. The wilder humor was left to Caesar, Morris, and Reiner, and often the movie parodies. The October 25, 1954, show[30] opens with a sketch in which Reiner and Caesar are parents of two kids who got into a fight. In the school principal's office, the parents re-create the fight, both kicking and pushing the principal, then ripping his suit. The movie parody in this show is of a World War I flying movie in Caesar's version of German. The setpiece of the sketch is Caesar's description of the aerial dogfight in which his friend was shot down. It is such a tour de force of what Caesar does best that the audience applauds at the end of his speech.

Caesar's Hour ran from 1954 to 1957, while *The Imogene Coca Show* only lasted the 1954–55 season. Coca got Lucille Kallen, Mel Brooks, and Tony Webster from *Your Show of Shows*, and added to the writing staff Ernest Kinoy, who later wrote for the major live dramas, as well as Allan Manings, who had written a few sketches for *Your Show of Shows*. Manings had written satirical revues in college, directed in summer stock, and worked as a standup comic in strip joints, where he did "Freudian analysis of nursery rhymes while ladies with blue veins were ripping their clothes off."

Allan Manings describes the writing process on *The Imogene Coca Show*:

> On Tuesdays we used to go to burlesque shows. We used to get in a car and go to New Jersey. Things were intriguing. Being new, I would get there bright and early every morning and Bob [Van Scoyk, my partner, and I] would start to work on something. Then Lucille would work and Tony would work. Mel would come in later and say, "Nothing is working." Because of his relationship with her [working on *Your Show of Shows*], I guess Coca had more faith in him. The

reality was she didn't want to do a show. She wanted to rest. I think NBC wanted her to do a show, badgered her to do a show. The show never really had a focus.

The show also never really had a firm hand from a producer or director, since they seemed to change every few weeks. One new director came in and started assigning jobs, saying, "Now, Mel, you're the belly-laugh writer. You and you, you're the constructionists."

Brooks started screaming, "You mean I don't know how to construct?" The staff was so discouraged about the show that when the producer gave Coca a live fox for Christmas and the fox bit either Coca or the producer, the writers felt that in either case it was "politically correct."

Neither Caesar nor Coca had the same kind of success later on television that they enjoyed in the early fifties. Partly this was the death of variety shows. Mel Tolkin notes of the one-hour stories used on *Caesar's Hour*, "It didn't work because he wasn't using his full talents. He was mostly just the middle-class character of [the] Sid and Coca [domestic] sketches, and for an hour it didn't pay off as well." Caesar himself may have understood his limitations, or he may just have been spoiled by the collaborative process with the writers willing to shape material only for his talents. In the early eighties he was offered a part in a new situation comedy. He wanted to be part of the process of developing the character and the scripts, but was told he could not. In an interview at the time he said, "I told them, 'Fine. You know what you can do with your script,' and I walked out. Twenty-five-year-old boys who were brought up on *Gilligan's Island*." [31]

The show he turned down was *Cheers*.

Mr. Peepers

In 1952 one of the small jewels of early live television was created by producer Fred Coe and writer David Swift. NBC liked the letters of response it got to a quiet young actor named Wally Cox, who had appeared in a Swift one-hour comedy on *The Goodyear TV Playhouse*, so they asked Coe and Swift to create a show for him. As Swift recalled in 1989, "What could you do for Wally Cox? You write *Mr. Peepers*. It's the only thing he could do." [32] The show, about a gentle high school science teacher and his friends and associates, was put on as a summer replacement. When it was replaced by another series in the fall, the audience complaints were so vocal (and the ratings of the replacement were so bad) that *Mr. Peepers* was brought back and stayed on the air until 1955.

Unfortunately, by the third or fourth show of the summer, a "schism" developed between Coe and Swift. [33] Jim Fritzell, who had written another comedy series about a teacher, *Our Miss Brooks*, was brought in as an "anodyne" [34] between Coe and Swift and the summer's episodes were completed. When the show was picked up in the fall, Julian Claman of Talent

Associates, the company producing *Mr. Peepers*, decided Fritzell needed some help. He assigned a radio writer he knew to work with him. Fritzell and Everett Greenbaum remained partners for thirty years, until Fritzell's death.

Greenbaum remembers that there was no script coming in from an outside writer the first week he was there, so he recalled an incident from his youth in Buffalo in which the schools were closed because of snow. It became an episode in which, because of a school closure, the lessons would be taught by the teachers over the local television station. Peepers's friend, Harvey Weskit, who always seems to be on top of things and who tries to be cool about it, freezes on camera, while Mrs. Gurney, who in the person of actress Marion Lorne would raise fluttering to a high art, worries before the broadcast but sails through it without trouble. Greenbaum thinks that "probably most of" the shows were based on personal experience.

Swift, who liked physical humor (his disagreement with Coe was how physical the show could get: Swift wanted more, Coe wanted less), still told Fritzell what the show was about: "No jokes—just a nice, soft, easy, show." [35] There was still physical humor. One running gag was Peepers's opening his locker: he taps a radiator with a hammer, measures the last locker in the row with a yardstick, kicks at the point measured, and his locker opens. The physical humor was a holdover from David Swift. As Greenbaum notes, "David was the teacher of Jim in the way that Jim was my teacher. So a lot of that physical stuff seemed important to Jim to continue." It did cause problems in live television, as Greenbaum remembers:

> We took terrible chances. A lot of time things didn't work. I remember we did a show where Peepers's mother wanted him to clean under the bed because there were dust bunnies, and they were supposed to move. Well, on the show they looked like rats running around. We had that kind of disaster. . . . There was one show that had a dog in it. In live television, you simply ran from one set to the next and had to cover it with something else. We didn't realize that on the actual show people would be running faster than they were in rehearsal, and the dog starting chasing every one of them on the show, and barking. You never saw the dog but you heard the barking. There was a disaster.

The problems were not always on such a large scale. The show was live, with a studio audience, which meant that the laughs often lengthened the show, which in turn meant that cuts had to be made as the show was in progress. Tony Randall, whose performance as Harvey Weskit made him a star, recalled why he got the cuts, "They couldn't give the cuts to Wally because he never knew his lines that well anyway. And they couldn't give them to dear old Marion Lorne, because her whole approach to comedy was that gasping, panting, uh-uh-uh thing, and it would have ruined her timing." Randall added that the cuts were never in one place in the script and they were generally given to him right before air time. [36]

With all the changes in lines, it is not surprising that lines got missed. In "Mrs. Gurney Learns to Drive," Peepers is riding with his Aunt Lillian (in a car with the passing scenery done with rear projection—unfortunately the action on the rear projection screen does not match the action in the car). She guns her car to pass three cars, with Peepers looking out at each car as they pass. When they go by the last one, Peepers says, "You passed them like they were standing still." His next line is obviously supposed to be "They were," but Wally Cox says instead, "We were"—which produces almost no laugh from the audience. Fortunately, his befuddled look at messing up the line fits right into character.

Greenbaum and Fritzell wrote for the show for three years. Greenbaum said in 1989, "It was three years of actual terror, Jim and I wrote forty shows a year. Nobody knew how long it took to write a show. Now they have five or six writers on staff and free-lancers, and they only do 22 shows a season."[37]

In the second full season of the show, the ratings for *Mr. Peepers* began to decline and it was decided, probably from a suggestion by Fred Coe,[38] that Peepers should marry his girlfriend Nancy. The wedding episode was shown May 23, 1954, and the ratings went up the following season, then declined, and the show was canceled in 1955, replaced by a Western. David Swift, who was brought back as a consultant when Peepers was married, said, "It's possible, though, that *Peepers*'s quiet humor doesn't appeal to the average viewer,"[39] and Fritzell and Greenbaum said at the time, "You might say ours is an intelligent humor, or humor that makes intelligent people laugh."[40]

Unlike filmed shows such as *I Love Lucy*, which have been in syndication since their creation, *Mr. Peepers*, which survives only on kinescopes, has not been seen outside of archives since its original showings. Michael Wilmington, writing about an archive screening of several episodes, suggests that one reason it has not been picked up for syndication was that its look (minimal sets, live television bloopers, not being in color) was dated.[41] Its look is dated, but not the characters and their emotions. In the wedding episode there is a brief moment when Mrs. Gurney comes to see Nancy before the ceremony. In a close-up we see both a sweetness and a strange sadness Mrs. Gurney feels. It is the kind of sudden, vivid moment so affecting in live television.

·4·

A GOLDEN AGE

" "*T*he writer was the star."

That is the recurring refrain from television writers talking about their experiences with live television. Charles Larson, who wrote for both filmed and live television in the early years, says of writing for live drama, "Even when they were out here [in Los Angeles], they still had the 'Broadway feeling' [that] they were the heirs of the Broadway stage. The writer was the star. The filmed shows were the direct descendant of the B picture. The writer was sloughed off."

Robert Dozier wrote for live television drama in the fifties. He was the son of film producer and former agent William Dozier, and the younger Dozier remembers growing up in a house that was often filled with writers, all of whose "peculiarities were tolerated, such as their drinking and their madness and their insanity, and I think that's really why I decided that writing was a terrific thing to do, because it was obviously something that would gain you great approbation."

Living in New York in the fifties, Dozier was impressed with the quality of writing on television and got in to it:

It was a very exciting time. There were maybe fifteen hours of live anthology television drama each week in New York. There was an enormous need for material and there were very few writers. So you would sit down and write something with the almost sure knowledge that if you wrote something halfway passable you would sell it.

You would hope to create a bidding situation, perhaps jack up the price. The prices were not large in those days. I think the most I ever got for a live television show was $5,000. I could live for a year on $5,000. My rent was $85. I had no children and my wife didn't eat much.

They did not own the material. What they bought in those days was the right to produce it once and rerun it once on kinescope, so the material resided with you. And if they bought the script and wanted to do it and wanted to change anything that you really objected to, you could say, "Listen, if you wanted to do another story, why didn't you go buy another story? If you want to give it back, I'll give you your money back and I'll take it somewhere else." So the writer had a great deal of strength in those days.

We got fan mail. That was very seductive too. Writers got fan mail. The fan mail I got was very sophisticated. It was intelligent mail written by literate people. And it probably sounds kind of snobbish, but in those days, not many people had that many television sets. They were expensive, and because of that fact, the people who owned them tended to be a better-educated class of people and a more articulate group . . . They enjoyed the anthology dramas.

There was a very healthy competitive thing at that time among writers. Now there were a whole bunch of us, Howard Rodman and myself, Gore Vidal, Ernie Kinoy, Paddy [Chayefsky] was the champ, and Bob Aurthur and Manny Rubin and Mayo Simon, a whole bunch of guys. You would see something on a television show, and you would be incensed by it, and you would sit down and rebut it. You'd write your own version. It fed on itself.

We all hung out together at a saloon called Downey's in those days in New York, on 8th Avenue and 41st Street, where you could get an open double cheeseburger and a beer for 90 cents. And none of us had a lot of money in those days. That was a welcome place to be. So it was an exciting time.

The Philco/Goodyear Television Playhouse

From the writers' viewpoint, the best anthology drama to write for was *Philco Television Playhouse*, which ran from 1948 to 1955, and *The Goodyear TV Playhouse*, which alternated weeks with *Philco* from 1951 to 1955. Both shows were produced by Fred Coe, who was the reason writers liked the show.

Coe had worked in professional theater in New York and elsewhere before going to work in the mid-forties with NBC.[1] In 1948 he started *Philco* with a season of adaptations of classic plays, such as *Cyrano de Bergerac*. Coe eventually hired a staff of writers who were to write almost exclusively for him and his productions, which was unheard of in television drama at the time.[2]

Coe was producing *Mr. Peepers* during the time he was doing *Philco/Goodyear*, and *Peepers* writer Everett Greenbaum compares Coe to MGM's Irving Thalberg, in that both loved writers and neither hogged the credit. Greenbaum says, "We would just talk quietly. He was always very calm, and he'd say, 'Well, now that could be a story.' And we'd always come out with something."

Coe may have been calm with writers, but he was not with secretaries, publicists,[3] and certainly not with sponsors or sponsors' representatives. JP Miller, one of the *Philco* writers, remembers Coe coming into the control room once and finding the sponsor's representative there making comments about the show. Coe screamed at him, "What the fuck are you doing here?" and threw him out. Miller says, "He was a producer. He was not a sycophant. He was not a hired altar boy. He analyzed a script with brilliance."

One of the best and most distinctive writers Coe collected for *Philco* was Horton Foote. Foote, born in Wharton, Texas, was an actor and playwright. Foote got into television "through the back door," as he puts it. His friend, stage director Vincent Donehue was in New York to direct *The Gabby Hayes Show* on television. Donehue asked Foote to write for the show, and Foote wrote Hayes's introductions to stories about American history. When Donehue moved to *Philco*, he brought Foote with him. Foote found Coe "marvelous to work with," and that on the show, "Everything was kind of done for the writer." Unlike some other dramatic shows, the writer was always involved in rehearsal.

Coe "had the courage to do" Foote's plays, says Foote, which were all set in and around the fictional Harrison, Texas, for what was then mostly an East Coast audience. (Foote was what is called in literary circles a "regional writer," which generally means that he does not write stories that are or could be set in New York.) His plays were enormously popular on television. "A Trip to Bountiful," broadcast in early 1953, was such a success that it was transferred to Broadway in the fall of that year and ran 39 performances. It has been performed often on the stage since, and 32 years later was made into a theatrical film. "A Trip to Bountiful" on television managed to overcome the limitations of space (Foote says, "You just used your wits") to suggest a bus trip with only a few bus seats and inspired acting by Lillian Gish and Eva Marie Saint. Foote says, in his courtly manner, "It was a great privilege to work with people like that."

Foote's 1953 play "A Young Lady of Property" also worked around the limitations of live television. In the opening scene the characters stand and talk in front of the Harrison post office in 1925 instead of walking down the street, as they would in both real life and a film. The story builds to a confrontation between the fifteen-year-old Wilma and Sybil, her widowed father's fiancee, but Foote does not show us the scene. We only hear Wilma's description of it later to her aunt. Foote explains, "That [scene] was the obligatory scene, but it was cliché. Fred [Coe] asked about that, then defended me [and] my right to do it my way. I wanted to avoid the cliché. I think it's a more interesting way to do it." Foote's method maintains the quiet and nostalgic tone of the play. Foote was also establishing his very distinctive voice; none of the other writers on the show could have written this speech for Wilma:

Well, it's a long time ago now, but I still remember it [the house]. My mama and I used to play croquet in the yard under the pecan trees. We'd play croquet every afternoon just before sundown and every once in a while she'd stop the game and ask me to run to the corner without letting the neighbors know what I was doing, to see if my father was coming home. My mother always kept me in white, starched dresses. Do you remember my mother?[4]

Foote eventually, like many writers of early live television, shifted into writing for stage and films. He avoided writing weekly series television, saying, "It would be death. You'd be churning things out, week after week after week. You're just bound to go crazy."

JP Miller was another Texas-born writer of Coe's. After attending Yale Drama School, he wrote Broadway plays nobody would read, let alone produce. He did not even have a television set until a friend who was a TV repairman gave him just the picture tube and the tuner of a set. Miller put it in a cardboard box and painted the box purple. Miller watched *Philco* and thought, "Jesus Christ, these people are for real. If I could write for that show, I'd condescend to write for television." Through a friend he got a script to Coe, who liked it and said, "Listen, pappy, you got any other stories?" Miller told him one and Coe said, "Pappy, go home and write it." So he did.

Miller's best-known *Philco* play was "The Rabbit Trap," shown in February 1955. Miller had originally conceived it as a half-hour show, but it did not sell. He then saw a way to do it as an hour show and pitched it to Coe, who liked it. While Miller was working on it, Coe called him up and said a script that had come in from another writer was not working and could he finish "The Rabbit Trap" in ten days. Miller protested that he couldn't, but Coe replied, "Write your ass off, pappy." Coe and Delbert Mann, the director, asked him as he was writing it whom he had in mind for the parts. Those actors were cast before the script was finished. When he brought the script in, its first reading ran exactly the 53 minutes the one-hour program ran minus commercials. There were no changes in rehearsal.

The play deals with Eddie, a young executive, and his wife and their eight-year-old son. On a vacation in the Vermont woods, they build a rabbit trap. Eddie is called back to town by his boss. He goes, but later he tries to tell his boss he has to go back to the trap. The boss says if he does, he's fired. Eddie and his wife find the trap, with signs the rabbit caught in it has escaped. The story is more of an anecdote than a full story, and the writing shows the lack of space for sets. Eddie tells his wife he has been fired only after they are back in the Vermont woods set. We never see the car. Eddie says he did not tell her before because she would have made him turn back, but it seems artificial.

The public's response was, according to Miller, "the most incredible thing that's happened to me in show business. Nobody expected it. It was a nice little show, no car chases, no sex. Everybody saw themselves in it. The phones started ringing off the hook."

In the later film version of "The Rabbit Trap," Miller thinks the casting, different from the perfect casting on television, was off, and the whole film became too slick and glossy. Miller also let the play be done on Italian television. Because of its success in Italy, it was picked up by the Eastern European countries, which played it often but never sent Miller any royalties.

Gore Vidal, by this time the author of several published novels and plays, also wrote for *Philco*. Vidal discovered to his surprise that he liked writing for television, "that it could be taken seriously, and that in spite of the many idiot restrictions imposed by those nervous sponsors who pay for plays, it was possible to do a certain amount of satisfactory work," [5] and that television was "a wonderful place to experiment. A writer can tackle anything if he learns how to dodge around forbidden subjects." [6]

At least once, *Philco* was more hospitable to Vidal's stinging wit than Broadway or Hollywood. In his 1955 television play "Visit to a Small Planet," the second-act debate is between Kreton, a visitor from another planet, and the head of the World Council as they exchange Vidal's witticisms about arms and man. The play was turned down by three sponsors before *Philco* put it on. As Vidal described it later, "With some anxiety we waited for the roof to fall in; to our very real surprise it did not, and most people were pleased with my gentle heresy." [7]

To make the stage version work for the Broadway theater audiences later, however, he had to dull down the satire and play up the farce. [8] The head of the World Council is eliminated completely and the story turns on Kreton's efforts to help two young lovers. The television and stage versions starred Cyril Ritchard. The 1960 film version starred Jerry Lewis—and even the French don't like it.

Paddy Chayefsky

Paddy Chayefsky was as much a regional writer as Horton Foote, but his region was his native Bronx. After the war he went to Hollywood, where he wrote stories for films, then nightclub routines. His first television work was writing gags for Danny Thomas, but as Chayefsky later described it, "He threw me out." [9] After writing some radio drama, Chayefsky's first television dramatic works were half-hour scripts for *Danger* and *Manhunt*. In 1953 he met Fred Coe and for two years wrote for *Philco/Goodyear*. [10]

From the beginning Chayefsky saw the differences between live television and film. For his first hour show, "Holiday Song," Chayefsky "approached the script as I would have approached a movie," and the story he came up with was "not a good one for television. It is much too complex and mechanically active [several scenes take place in the subway] and is better suited for a movie." [11] Chayefsky thought another of his scripts, "The Big Deal," would have been better on the stage because "its sheer weight and power are too much to be handled to television's fullest advantage." But he found television gave him a mobility he would not have had in the theater,

> I was not confined to a one-scene set, nor did I have to write unnecessary lines of dialogue to justify characters being on the set when they would not naturally be there. I was able to concentrate the action of my story on the people

directly involved. I was even able to catch more literal reality than I could have caught in a stage play.[12]

In both "Printer's Measure" and "The Mother" Chayefsky is able to use the confines of a few sets to give vivid details about the lives of the characters. In the latter, a sixty-six-year-old woman gets a job briefly in a sewing room at Tiny Tots Sportswear, and we get a sense of the community of workers, who include black and Puerto Rican women.

Chayefsky's most famous play came out of the poverty in which the shows were produced. As David Swift remembered, "There were no [rehearsal] studios, no offices, no limos. We worked out of hotels. We rehearsed in dance halls."[13] The rehearsal space for *Philco* was a room in the old Abbey Hotel used for meetings of a lonelyhearts club. Director Delbert Mann was running the rehearsals of Chayefsky's "The Reluctant Citizen" when the author wandered off and noticed a sign on the wall that said, "Girls, Dance With the Man Who Asks You. Remember, Men Have Feelings, Too." Chayefsky told Mann he thought there might be a play about a girl in a place like that. Mann, busy with rehearsals, tried "to get him off my back" by agreeing. Chayefsky wandered back a little later and said that, no, it should be about a man. Mann sent him to see Fred Coe, and all Chayefsky said was, "I want to do a play about a guy who goes to a ballroom." Coe's response was typical: "Go write it, pappy."

Some time later, Mann told Coe on a Monday the next script he was assigned was not very good. Coe called Chayefsky to see how his play was coming. He said it would be done in a couple of weeks. Coe told him they needed it sooner. Chayefsky brought the first two acts in on Thursday and the last act in after the show had started a week's rehearsal. The show's original title was "Love Story," which NBC for some reason objected to. It was shown on May 24, 1953, on *The Goodyear Television Playhouse* with the title "Marty."[14]

Chayefsky was right when he wrote that "Marty" was "the sort of material that does best on television," and that the play deals "with the world of the mundane, the ordinary, and the untheatrical"—adding in a much-quoted line, "I tried to write the dialogue as if it had been wire-tapped." He "tried to envision the scenes as if a camera had been focused upon the unsuspecting characters and had caught them in an untouched moment of life."[15] The play opens on Marty Pilletti, a thirty-five-year-old butcher. The neighborhood women ask when he is going to get married. Marty and his friend Angie go to the Waverly Ballroom, where Marty is sympathetic to Clara, a rather dowdy schoolteacher, who has been dumped by the man who brought her. The next day, when Angie and Marty's other friends give him a hard time about being seen with a "dog," Marty explodes and tells them

You don't like her. My mother doesn't like her. She's a dog, and I'm a fat, ugly little man. All I know is I had a good time last night. I'm gonna have a good time tonight. If we have enough good times together, I'm going down on my knees and beg that girl to marry me. If we make a party again this New Year's, I gotta date for the party. You don't like her, that's too bad. When you gonna get married, Angie? You're thirty-four years old. All your kid brothers are married. You ought to be ashamed of yourself.

What we get throughout the play are those "untouched moments" of Marty's life. Rod Steiger brings striking intensity to his performance as Marty, particularly in giving us Marty's pain. The small scale of the production and Delbert Mann's use of close-ups give us a sense of the heat of the emotions between Marty and his mother and his friends, and Chayefsky's writing gives us a sense of the world in which they live, which is beyond the physical limitations of the production. We believe as viewers that we are in the middle of the story.

"Marty" was the first television play bought by Hollywood and made into a theatrical film. The television play and the film, also written by Chayefsky, shows the differences between the two media. The film is approximately twice as long as the play, and there are several subplots added. The relationship between Marty and Angie has been developed, and we get more of Angie being upset that Marty would rather be with the "dog" than with him. Shooting the film on location gives us more of the local atmosphere.

What is lost in the film is the intensity of the emotions. Ernest Borgnine's excellent performance in the film does not have Steiger's pain. Borgnine is more open and charming, his pounding on a stop sign in delight after he's taken Clara home could only have been done by Borgnine's Marty and not by Steiger's. Clara is made much more engaging in the film than on television. Partly this is the casting of Betsy Blair, but it is also the extended scenes in the film. Nancy Marchand's television Clara is much less open and not an obvious charmer. There is no question that Borgnine's Marty will be happy with Blair's Clara; it is not such an easy call with Steiger's Marty and Marchand's Clara.

Chayefsky also turned his 1955 television play "The Bachelor Party" into a 1957 film. He recognized early that "The material is more suited to the movies than to television," but thought the television version "came out excellently."[16] The director and actors in the television version gave a consistency to the characters that Chayefsky had missed in the writing,[17] but in the filmscript he was able to reorganize the material and keep the focus on the attitudes of the main character, Charlie, through the night of the party. As a result, Charlie's final speech to the groom-to-be, Arnold, which is the same in both versions, plays better in the film because Chayefsky has shown us the feelings that lead up to the speech.

When Chayefsky went back to New York after doing the film of *Marty*, he thought "there was no television anthology left,"[18] but that was not entirely true. *Philco* had stopped, but others continued. What he had learned was that he could make a lot more money in films than in television. He had been paid $900 for the television "Marty" and $13,000 plus a percentage for the film. In one year he had written nine one-hour shows, for which he had been paid a total of $17,000.[19] Movies had their appeal.[20]

Studio One

Studio One began on CBS as a radio drama in 1947 and a year later it was brought to television under producer Worthington Miner. Like many early dramas, *Studio One* first did public domain material, such as *Julius Caesar*, which was done twice in the spring of 1949.[21] Miner could not afford writers to adapt stories and did 39 of the first 44 scripts himself, or so he claimed. Catherine Turney, who did adaptations of Graham Greene and Somerset Maugham, discovered Miner "easy to work with," although, unlike Coe, "he was inclined to take credit for everything." In 1952 Miner moved on to other shows, most notably *Medic*, and *Studio One* was taken over by Herbert Brodkin.

The major television writer to come out of Brodkin's regime at *Studio One* was Reginald Rose. Rose had been a camp counselor and a publicist for Warner Brothers.[22] In a 1982 interview Rose recalled that he had been trying to sell short stories and a novel without success, but: "The first time I wrote a TV script I sold it and when I sold that first one they said, 'More, More, More!' and I haven't stopped since."[23]

For almost two years after that first 1951 sale, Rose wrote mostly half-hour original scripts and hour adaptations, which he described as "uniformly mediocre."[24] In November 1953 he showed *Studio One* story editor Florence Britton an outline for a one-hour original, and she urged him to do it. He had been struggling with the outline for some time, but completed the script in two to three weeks.[25] The play was "The Remarkable Incident at Carson Corners," in which a group of school children try their school's janitor for murder for pushing a child off the fire escape. Over the course of the trial we learn the fire escape was faulty because the community did not want to pay to fix up the old school. The public response was strong, and kinescopes of the show were shown for years thereafter at schools and civic groups.[26] Rose could give up his current job writing advertising copy and write for television full-time. He found television much less stifling than advertising, where he had to use the more genteel term *derrière* in lingerie ads.[27]

In late 1953 Rose read of reactions of white people in Cicero, Illinois, to news that some new tenants in the neighborhood would be blacks. Rose was appalled. "The inhuman, medieval attitudes of those free, white Americans had so disturbed me that I decided to do a play about them in an attempt to expose the causes behind their mass sickness."[28] Rose wrestled for a time with how to condense the story into an hour play. Then: "I woke up one morning and had the entire idea in front of my eyes. It was complete." His idea for

"Thunder on Sycamore Street" was to tell the story by focusing each of the three acts on a different house on the block during the same period of time. In the first act we go into the house of Frank and his wife, Clarice, who are discussing whether the neighbors are with them. In the second act we see Arthur and his wife, Phyllis, who are not as sure as Frank that action ought to be taken. In the third act we meet Joe Blake, the object of the neighborhood action, as he faces up to the crowd.

The problem with the idea, as Rose says now, was that "Everybody knew [you could not do a story about blacks moving into a white neighborhood], except me. Oh, I knew, but I thought I could maybe get it by." Florence Britton took him to lunch and explained the facts of network life: the hero of such a story could not be black because the South would object. (This was the same year the *Brown v. the Board of Education* decision that outlawed segregated schools.) Rose "felt that a compromise would weaken the play but I decided to make one anyway, hoping that the principle under observation was strong enough to rouse an audience."[29]

Blake became an ex-convict but, as Rose rewrote the play, we only learn this in the middle of Act II, so before this we can only imagine what Blake's "sin" might be. And imagine audiences did. In the mail that poured in after the show's broadcast on March 15, 1954, viewers felt that the ex-con was a symbol for a black, a Jew, a Catholic, a Puerto Rican, an ex-Communist or fellow-traveler, a Japanese, a Chinese, a Russian, an anarchist, and/or an avowed atheist. Rose wrote, "Not one single person I spoke to felt that he was actually meant to be an ex-convict," and he thought "perhaps 'Thunder on Sycamore Street' had more value in its various interpretations than it would have had it simply presented the Negro problem."[30] A week after the show, Rose got a letter from ten married couples in the West saying events like that could never happen in America.[31]

Later in 1954, Rose served on jury duty in a manslaughter case in New York's General Sessions Court. Like most people, he grumbled about getting stuck on jury duty, but then

> It occurred to me during the trial that no one anywhere ever knows what goes on inside a jury room but the jurors, and I thought then that a play taking place entirely within a jury room might be an exciting and possibly moving experience for an audience.[32]

The outline for the play took a week to do, and it was 27 pages long (as opposed to his usual five-page outlines) because he had to work out the dramatic and emotional movements between all the jurors. The script was written in five days, less time than the outline, and the only reason it took that long was that the first draft, done in four days, was fifteen minutes too long and Rose had to cut it.[33] The play, "Twelve Angry Men," was shown on

September 20, 1954, and like "Marty" effectively uses the limitations of live television to present the emotional intensity of the situation.

Not all of Rose's live television plays were done for *Studio One*. "Crime in the Streets," a tough play about a juvenile delinquent, was turned down by all three networks because, according to Rose, "It dealt sympathetically with juvenile delinquency at a time when juvenile delinquents were considered to be eminently unpopular,"[34] particularly by sponsors trying to appeal to middle-class audiences. The Elgin company picked up the show for its *Elgin Hour* drama series, where it was shown on March 8, 1955.

Both "Twelve Angry Men" and "Crime in the Streets" were bought for the movies, as was a third play, "Dino." Rose had relished being treated like a star playwright in live television ("The writer got the reviews and the publicity"), but, as he notes, when the movies "got over the shock of television being invented," they went after the writers the same way they had always gone after Broadway playwrights. For the movie rights and for doing the script for the film *Crime in the Streets*, Rose got $25,000 plus 10 percent of the profits, whereas he had only received between $1,800 and $2,000 for the television version.[35]

Live Drama Moves West

Not only were the writers moving to Los Angeles, so were the shows. Ten years after it started in New York, *Studio One* moved to Los Angeles. Some people thought that CBS was buckling under to the sponsors of the show, who wanted more stars on it. Harry Ommerle, a CBS vice president, told *TV Guide* it was important to get "top box office names in sufficient numbers" and thought stars would get bigger audiences, which would please sponsors.[36] There was another more practical reason: As the movies had discovered forty years before, there was much more space available in Los Angeles. In 1953 CBS had opened its eight-square-block Television City at the corner of Beverly Boulevard and Fairfax Avenue in Los Angeles. The building, and a similar one built by NBC in Burbank, had studios designed as television studios, not just remodeled radio studios. There were other amenities. No longer would actors have to rehearse in ballrooms of old hotels.

Diehard New Yorkers screamed in pain. Producer David Susskind was the most outspoken, describing Hollywood as

> a world of lotus blossoms, swimming pools, smog, and indifference, [lacking] the electricity, the tang [of New York]. Even writers and actors who go to Hollywood from New York to do a show fall into the smug attitude. I don't know why.
>
> It's a tired self-satisfaction caused by their tired way of life. We could be at war and they wouldn't know it because all they read is *The Hollywood Reporter* and *Daily Variety* [as opposed to *Weekly Variety*, one supposes, which was of course published in New York]. Their entire horizon is motion pictures and TV.

It induces a torpor, a retreat from creative ideas. . . . Don't be surprised to see a trend from Hollywood back to New York, from film shows back to live.[37]

Producers were concerned they would lose control of their shows, but that did not happen. Sam Rolfe was a film writer who wrote for *Studio One* and other live shows in Los Angeles. He says it was, "A very simple process. There was one person you worked with. That was the producer. And you did your script." If there were other people, such as a story editor or a network representative, Rolfe worked one-to-one with him as well.

Robert Dozier wrote for live television drama both in New York and Hollywood and found that in California "We were working basically with all the same people, the same directors, the same actors." Dozier even thought the network people helpful:

> The people at the networks were not like the people we have who are in the networks today. They were basically a more mature generation. They were showmen. They were not actuaries and accountants, and they didn't have Master's Degrees in Communications from Montana Normal and know everything. And they weren't 24. And they did things just simply because they thought it would be nice to do that. They didn't have 18 people making their decisions for them.
>
> They were people with track records, who had been through the creative experience and understood it, and were sympathetic to it and did not want to hire you for your talent and then pay you enough money to put your talent aside and do what they wanted you to do. They wanted you to exercise your talent.

Playhouse 90

One hour was rather restrictive. Chayefsky and Rose both added material for the film versions of their teleplays. The obvious solution for television was to go to a greater length, which CBS did in 1956 with *Playhouse 90*, produced in its Hollywood Television City. As the name implies, the program was an hour and a half each week. Martin Manulis, its first producer, told *TV Guide* in 1957, "On *Playhouse 90* we're trying to keep that standard [of excellence in the theater]—we're trying to bring theatre into the home."[38] Because of the running time and the budgets, Manulis and the producers who came after him (John Houseman, Herbert Brodkin, and Fred Coe, among others) were able to get many of the best writers of American anthology television, including Tad Mosel, Robert Alan Aurthur, Horton Foote, Reginald Rose, and Rod Serling.

After graduating from Antioch College, Rod Serling wrote for radio and in 1950 made his first television sale to a show called *Stars Over Hollywood*.[39] He wrote for several dramatic shows, but scored his biggest success with the January 1955 *Kraft Television Theatre* production of "Patterns." After that play he was able to sell many scripts "out of his trunk," that he had written before but had not sold.[40]

Serling wrote the first two plays produced on *Playhouse 90* when it debuted in the fall of 1956. The first was "Forbidden Area," an adaptation Serling had already written. The second was an original he wrote especially for the series, "Requiem For a Heavyweight." The play deals with the end of the boxing career of Mountain McClintock and his corrupt manager Maish, who has lost money to gamblers betting McClintock would not go three rounds in his last fight. Maish wants to get McClintock to try wrestling to make enough money so Maish can pay off his debts. The writing of the characters of McClintock and Maish is strong and vivid, as is the atmosphere of the boxing world.

The production values also help create that atmosphere because, for all the increase in the space available, the sets still look like something from a cheap B movie, which corresponds to the cheap world of boxing. As in other live drama, there is the intensity of the performances, helped no doubt by everybody's concern as to whether Ed Wynn, playing an old trainer, was going to remember his lines.[41] There is also, as with other live presentations, a lack of precision in the acting that is noticeable in comparison with filmed television, or with film.

Two years later JP Miller wrote another famous *Playhouse 90*, "The Days of Wine and Roses." Miller was working again for producer Fred Coe and just went in and told him the idea: two people love each other, but they come to love the bottle more. Coe's reaction was the usual, "Sounds fine. Go write it, pappy." Coe was still very much on the job. The stars were Cliff Robertson and Piper Laurie, and the director was John Frankenheimer. Miller was distressed as rehearsals progressed to see the actors, under Frankenheimer's encouragement, playing it drunker and drunker. When Coe called him up and asked him how it was going, Miller suggested Coe attend a runthrough, which he did. When it was done, Frankenheimer asked Coe, "Isn't that great? Isn't that great?"

Coe replied, "John, you've got the wine, now get the roses." And then he left the room. Frankenheimer understood and pulled the actors back.

The End of Live Drama

The first season of *Playhouse 90* was done live, but beginning in the second season there were occasional filmed shows to relieve the pressures of doing a live show each week. At the beginning of the fourth season, the show was cut back from weekly to every other week. In January 1960, the show was reduced to irregular showings, with the last telecast in September 1961.[42] Live drama was dying out, replaced by filmed series.

The obvious reason for the decline of live drama was that filmed production values were so much better than live television could provide. The filmed shows also tended to be series, which the sponsors loved because the audience got involved with recurring characters, which would encourage them to tune in again the following week. Perry Lafferty, a producer and network executive, has suggested that the filmed shows killed off live dramas like *Playhouse 90* because the live shows were anthologies, with a different story each week and a different set of characters, and Lafferty thought "The writers were simply unable to provide that much material."[43] The problem from the writing point of view is that each anthology show had to get the audience involved in the new characters each episode, whereas a series developed audience involvement in the same characters over the life of the series. The hour length also limited the writers in establishing the characters and getting the audience involved as deeply as a longer show could. The anthologies, both live and film, died out in the late fifties and early sixties, to be replaced a decade later by the television movie.

Not all television writers have the same feeling of nostalgia for what television historians like to call the Golden Age of live drama. E. Jack Neuman says

> The best of it was really a third-rate movie, the very best. [On] *Playhouse 90* I was always thinking about what I could do on a movie set, and how terribly limited and awkward [it was]. The people who were running it at the time, mostly New Yorkers, [had theatrical] aspirations or actual theatre background. They wanted to preserve that "spontaneous" horseshit. I had no use for them. Marty Manulis and John Frankenheimer I thought were both assholes. I had to deal with them all the time. There were several others.
>
> Ann Roberts Nelson, a good old pal of mine at CBS, pulled out one I'd done in '54 or '55. Ugh! It looked just fucking awful. It was embarrassing. And it was supposed to be a huge success at the time. I mean, it was something you pin together on film in one day and make it look five times as good. It's just bad.
>
> No, it was a boring medium, in my estimation. I only had a couple of years of it before I began writing for movies again and then filmed television.

Perhaps it was only "a" Golden Age, not "the" Golden Age.

·5·

ENTER THE MAJOR STUDIOS

The Black Market

*T*he reason Abraham Polonsky moved from writing movies to writing live television was that he was blacklisted in Hollywood. Since Polonsky took the Fifth Amendment in his April 1951 appearance before HUAC,[1] he was unemployable in Hollywood. Even while writing in California, he'd kept an apartment in New York and felt, "I'd rather be in New York if I'm going to be blacklisted than out here. This is a company town."

The blacklist also existed in New York and the broadcasting industry. In 1950 the pamphlet *Red Channels* listed 151 people who were supposedly subversive. Shortly after it was published, the Korean War broke out, and as historian Erik Barnouw puts it, "Broadcasting executives were suddenly thumbing the pages of *Red Channels* against a background not of peace but of war."[2] Those executives then used the book and other sources to keep potentially subversive people from being involved in their shows. The executives' fear was that people such as Laurence S. Johnson, a New York supermarket owner who became a leader in the blacklisting, would create boycotts of the products of sponsors who allowed blacklisted people to be involved in their productions.

As in Hollywood, a black market grew up for blacklisted writers. Abraham Polonsky had two writer friends, Arnold Manoff and Walter Bernstein, who were already working on the black market. Bernstein was working on the program *Danger* when he was blacklisted. The producer of the program was Charles Russell, who was, according to Polonsky, "opposed to all this blacklisting. He had no political position in a positive sense. He just thought it was a nasty, shitty thing to do to people." Russell continued to employ Bernstein and hired Manoff and Polonsky as well.

The three writers agreed that since they were officially unemployable, their best solution was to take over a show. Eventually CBS decided to turn their radio show *You Are There*, which presented historical events as if being covered by contemporary news reporters, into a television program. Russell was the producer and the three blacklisted writers wrote for it. Polonsky says that, while "working with friends on *Danger* was pleasant, working on *You Are There* was more than pleasant," since doing their own research into the historical events was educational for them.

There were of course limitations on their activities. They were not allowed at rehearsals, and it varied from show to show as to who knew they were writing. Polonsky again:

> David Susskind knew, because we'd go to his office and meet with him. And everybody in his office knew. Charlie Russell knew. Sidney Lumet [the director] obviously knew. He was a close friend of Walter's [Cronkite, the show's host and narrator]. But he knew less than he thought he did. Bill Dozier [then a CBS executive] was not supposed to know, but after we had been working some time, there was a screenplay Charlie had given to Dozier. He had a discussion of the script with Dozier, and Dozier said to Charlie, "Tell Polonsky it's a damned good script."

Dozier was then transferred to the West Coast and wanted to take *You Are There* with them. When the network refused, he told them he thought there were blacklisted writers working on it, and they sent the show to Los Angeles with him. Dozier then called the writers and asked them, "Can I get you to write the show out here?" Polonsky says, "We wouldn't have anything to do with it," adding: "It's so typical of the elaborate personal betrayals that happened as a matter of course in this industry. I suppose in all industries, but more here. I suppose the only other place where it's taken with the same nonchalance is Washington. Most places people aren't like that."

During the first years of the black market, the network was willing to accept pseudonyms for the authors of the scripts, but then, as Polonsky says,

> The studios [Sic. Polonsky means the networks, but old Hollywood habits die hard] got suspicious. The rumors go around. So you had to have real people who could show, which is how the fronts came to operate in the business.
>
> I think we were pretty lucky with the fronts, at least we three were, in [terms] of these people we got to help us. . . . With the exception of Leo Davis, who later on became an associate producer, and was a writer by himself, the fronts were not necessarily in the same business we were. Sometimes they were advertising writers.
>
> The most famous one was Walter Bernstein's front, whom we borrowed from time to time. His name was Leslie Slote. Leslie Slote was a p.r. guy for Governor Rockefeller and then for the Mayor of New York, and he finally became a vice-president of RCA over in England. He was the only one I know who enjoyed it. When they called, he said, "I'll meet you at '21.' " and they'd get the bill. He'd been a commander in the Navy. You know he had the attitude. He was the greatest of all fronts.
>
> I began to feel sorry for our fronts. It's embarrassing to have someone say, "I

saw your show last night. It was marvelous." It's even more embarrassing to have someone say the opposite. . . .

Polonsky's usual front did not have Slote's panache. After a particular *Danger* episode, the front got a call from a producer wanting him to turn it into a play. The front called Polonsky in a panic and Polonsky said to him, "You go down, tell him you'll do it, get an advance, and then we won't write the play." To avoid meetings, producer Charles Russell made up excuses like: "He's in Florida." "He's got cancer." "He's living in Oklahoma."

Manoff, Bernstein, and Polonsky were not the only blacklisted writers working in New York.[3] Allan Manings, after writing for *The Imogene Coca Show*, got a call one day from his agent, who said, "You're in trouble." Manings's name had shown up on one of the lists. Manings prefers not to talk in detail about work on the black market, saying only, "I fronted for some, others fronted for me." He eventually went to Canada to work, then got back into American filmed television in the early sixties. While the "Un-American" writers of *You Are There* were writing episodes for that show that were winning a variety of citizenship awards, Manings came back to write for the quintessential American sitcom, *Leave It to Beaver*.

In Hollywood the black market existed in the early television film production. As with motion pictures, some of the blacklisting came out of the fights among writers over control of their guilds. Richard Powell, a former radio writer, had been active in the Television Writers of America, a guild for television writers organized by former radio writers who felt the Screen Writers Guild did not understand their problems. In the bruising political battle between the two guilds, Powell and others were "red-baited."[4] Powell wrote on the black market for two seasons on *Topper*, with either the name of the producer or the name of a partner on the script. Powell got off the blacklist by 1958.

There were, of course, writers and writer-producers who were helping writers and actors get off the blacklist. Roy Huggins, who had been a friendly witness before the congressional committee, made a point of hiring blacklisted writers later. When Sam Rolfe was writing and producing *Have Gun—Will Travel* in the late fifties, he discovered that the blacklist was falling apart:

> I had one experience I still don't believe. I can show you how absurd that period was. I got one writer, who was on the list, and in those days they cleared certain names on writers, directors, and actors. They called me on this guy and I said, "What's he supposed to have done?"
>
> They said, "Well, he's on this list." He signed for some black cause and they nailed him on it as a Communist.
>
> I said, "Obviously you got the wrong guy because this guy is white."
>
> He said, "Are you sure?"
>
> I said, "Yeah."
>
> The guy at CBS, I could hear him smile, said, "You know, you're right.

O.K." He was looking for any excuse not to follow these things. The guy's off the list like that.

Just as the major studios made some anti-Communist movies to try to pacify the right, the smaller television companies tried anti-Communist programs. Ziv had had a success on radio with *I Was a Communist for the FBI* and developed a similar program for television, *I Led Three Lives*, based on a book by Herbert Philbrick, who had reported to the FBI about activities in a Communist cell. An executive at Ziv told *TV Guide* they were "not a corporate knight in shining armor" delivering a message, but: "Our chief purpose is to find good story properties, turn them into good films and sell them. We think *I Led Three Lives* is good, exciting entertainment, and we know durned well we're selling it." Not surprisingly, the regional sponsors buying the show included oil and steel companies, utilities, and banks.[5]

The writers who worked on *I Led Three Lives* do not remember it with any fondness. Don Brinkley had written for the radio version of *I Was a Communist for the FBI* and was asked by Ziv to do the pilot for *Three Lives*. He did, but did not like writing for the show. He says it had a "sameness to it. They always seemed to be meeting out on a lake in a rowboat." Gene Roddenberry, an ex-cop who wrote for the show, had even stronger feelings: "It was fiction. I hate myself for having written two episodes. It was entirely trumped up."[6]

Movie Stars

When television first started, the major movie studios shunned it, as did the major movie stars. Writer Catherine Turney recalls that on the early anthology shows, "Most of the actors they were getting to play in them were not top drawer, so they were happy to get the work."

Some big stars did turn to television early and were just as difficult as they had been in the movies. One of Sy Salkowitz's first jobs was working on a syndicated series made in England called *The Errol Flynn Theatre*. Because of his production experience, Salkowitz was hired originally as a technical consultant, but to deal with all aspects of the production, including Flynn. "A real bastard. He was as unpredictable and terrifying as anybody has ever said." Once Salkowitz wrote an episode overnight to keep Flynn from flying off to Majorca while the show was in production. The story editor felt he could not come up with the material for Flynn's introduction until the scripts were complete, but Salkowitz wrote several general introductions they shot to be used if Flynn later wandered off.

Salkowitz also became the unofficial American story editor for the show. The British writers not only took too much time to write episodes, but told their stories at a much slower pace. Salkowitz added two or three scenes per episode, condensing the other scenes and picking up the pace. He says, "I kind of Americanized it, or internationalized it."

Bette Davis, Flynn's stablemate from his Warner Brothers days, could also be difficult on writers. In 1957 Lou Shaw got a script for Davis to do as a pilot for a series at Revue, the filmmaking organization of the giant talent agency Music Corporation of America. Davis called him over one time and pointed to a four-page scene (in a half-hour script) between the two young lovers. She told him it was a great scene, then added, "But where in the hell is Bette Davis in those four pages? This is the Bette Davis show and they're tuning in to watch Bette Davis and not two young little shits making love or whatever you have in mind." Shaw says now, "That was ingrained in my mind," so that when he later did other star vehicles, "My lead was always on the screen."

One of the early anthologies using stars was *Four Star Playhouse*, produced by a company owned by Dick Powell, Charles Boyer, Ida Lupino, and David Niven.[7] The function of the story editor on the show was to find scripts for the stars. One story editor, Coles Trapnell, explains, "In some respects it was easier to find stories for them for the half-hour television form than it would have been for making a movie feature, because they would be reluctant to take a chance on a big picture, but they'd try anything that appealed to them on [this]." Boyer, for example, did not care what kind of image he projected as long as it was an image of authority, so Trapnell had him play a fascist in several episodes.

Trapnell said to David Niven one day, "You know, you really have quite a resemblance to Robert Louis Stevenson, if we let that mustache droop down, and put on a fall on the back of your head." Niven liked the idea and it became an episode about Stevenson's last days in the South Pacific. Niven also played a barroom drunk in "The Answer" and an Episcopal priest in the Old West in "The Collar."

In addition to Hollywood veterans like Coles Trapnell and Wells Root, Dick Powell also made room for younger television writers such as Christopher Knopf. Knopf, the son of MGM producer Edwin Knopf, wrote one theatrical film, *The King's Thief*, which he says "almost ruined eight careers," then turned to television because he thought that was where the best and the brightest of the younger writers were. He had a point. His fellow writers at Four Star included Stirling Silliphant, Robert Towne, Sam Peckinpah, and Bruce Geller. By this time (the late fifties–early sixties), the live anthology dramas had died out and Powell was keeping filmed anthologies going by casting stars in them. He could provide not only himself, Boyer, and Niven, but also Loretta Young, Van Heflin, Robert Ryan, and Jack Lemmon.

Powell was politically conservative, but would let the young writers write any story if they fought for it with enough conviction. As in live drama, the writers had one-to-one relationships with the producers and the sponsors' representatives,[8] and if necessary Powell would run interference with the sponsors and the sponsors' representatives for the writers. No wonder Knopf says of Powell that he was "the greatest guy I ever wrote for."

The Majors

It was inevitable the major Hollywood studios would get into producing films for television. Columbia, one of the smaller majors, began to sneak into television as early as 1949, although not under its own name and not on its own lot. In that year it formed an experimental television subsidiary company called Screen Gems. Irving Briskin, a film executive, was put in charge of it in 1950, and his offices were two rooms in an old two-story apartment building. In 1952 *Ford Theatre* was its first show to air, and the following year *Father Knows Best* was the second. By 1956 Screen Gems was spending $40 million a year on television films and was using between 40 and 60 television writers.[9]

The next well-known studio to get into television was Disney. As historian/critic Richard Schickel points out, "Disney alone of the moguls—and he was not, at the time, a very big mogul—found a way to use the new medium to his advantage."[10] Disney made a deal with Leonard Goldenson, the head of ABC, that involved ABC in helping to finance Disneyland, in return for which Disney was to make an hour weekly program for the network.[11] Disney shrewdly used the program to promote Disneyland, with one of the hours a documentary on construction of the park. The *Disneyland* program was, like the park, divided up into different lands: Frontierland, Fantasyland, Adventureland, and Tomorrowland. The Fantasyland and Adventureland programming came from the Disney vaults, and the Frontierland programs were made for the series, the most famous being the three-part "Davy Crockett" shows, which were so popular they were cut into one feature film and released theatrically.

The problem section of the *Disneyland* show was Tomorrowland, since Disney had little experience making science films. He called in Ward Kimball, who had been at the studio since 1934, and gave him a blank piece of paper and a pencil, a gesture indicating he could do anything he wanted. Kimball contacted rocket scientist Werner von Braun and they worked out ideas for the shows based on a series of articles in *Collier's* magazine in the early fifties outlining the possibility of space travel. When the first orbital flight around the moon was made, von Braun called Kimball and said, "They're following our script exactly."

The most spectacular of the Tomorrowland shows was created in a very un-Disneylike way. For "Mars and Beyond," Kimball and the people on the show looked at various books on what life on other planets might be like, then went to a bar across the street and got drunk on stingers. They came back to the studio, drew as many drawings as they could. When they sobered up the next morning, they created out of the best drawings an animated sequence of what life on Mars might be like. The actual photographs of Mars many years later disappointed anyone who saw the film.[12]

The success of the Disney show, which started in the fall of 1954, paved the way for the other majors to get into television. The autumn of 1955 brought shows from three major studios to television. *The MGM Parade* and *The 20th Century-Fox Hour*, both anthologies, lasted one season and two seasons, respectively. Otto Lang, the producer of *The 20th Century-Fox Hour*, told *TV Guide*, "Our main problem is the shortage of story material and the pressure of the time element to meet air dates." Lang added that a movie producer has months to develop a script, but a television producer has only minutes.[13]

Warner Brothers

The third studio was a bit more successful, eventually. After Goldenson made the deal with Disney, he had a four-and-a-half-hour dinner with Jack Warner. Warner was reluctant to get into television, telling Goldenson, "Leonard, I made those quickies thirty years ago, and I'm not going to make them again."[14] Warner put his son-in-law, William T. Orr, in charge of the program, called *Warner Brothers Presents*. Instead of making an anthology, Orr and his staff made one-hour series that rotated from week to week based on two very successful and one moderately successful Warners films: *Casablanca*, *King's Row*, and a Western called *Cheyenne*. As if to demonstrate that television was different from films, both *Casablanca* and *King's Row* died rather quickly. *Cheyenne* became a series on its own, and if it had not been for Roy Huggins it would probably have flopped as well.

Roy Huggins was born in the state of Washington, grew up in Portland, Oregon, and was graduated Phi Beta Kappa from UCLA. He missed out on a graduate fellowship in political science because he was thought to be a Communist, which he was not, but he was so incensed at losing the fellowship he joined the Party. He left the Party over the Russian-German non-aggression pact in 1939 and later testified before the HUAC investigators. Huggins wrote magazine stories and novels in the forties, as well as films in the forties and early fifties.[15]

Huggins says he

> had got to thinking that the future was in television, especially for people whose basic talent was writing. . . . I thought—and I turned out to be right, by the way—that in television the people running the networks were so new at it that they would find someone who could do it and leave them alone. I had long talks with friends of mine in television and they agreed with me that was the way it was working, so when Warner Brothers asked me to come over and talk to them about becoming a producer, I said yes. I took a 50 percent cut in what I was earning per week in order to get into television, because I thought, "I'll be maybe making ten times this in no time." All of which turned out to be true.

Huggins was assigned to *King's Row*, but knew from the beginning that a dark adult drama would not work in its 7:30 P.M. Sunday time slot. When the sponsors of the show sent a long telegram to the studio complaining about *Cheyenne*, all of which Huggins agreed with, the studio asked Huggins to take over the show. He did, but only after he got Warners to "grant me three wishes." The first was to get rid of the comic sidekick of the hero, which he felt was "Republic['s] C Westerns." The second was to get rid of the hero's occupation (he was a mapmaker) on the grounds that "Western heroes do not have occupations" unless they are cowboys or lawmen. The third wish was, "You've got to let me tell stories for adults, because the kids are going to watch it anyway because it's a Western." Warners agreed, and the series ran until 1963.

Huggins's theory on *Cheyenne* was that "A television series can be a series of short movies. That's why I didn't want him to have an occupation. You mustn't put anything into the series concept that narrows the scope of story-telling." This is why Huggins believes that 1955 was "a key year in the history of television. It's the year they not only moved to Hollywood and started using film [there's a certain hyperbole in that, as can be seen from previous sections of this book], but it's the year they started doing the one-hour series on film." The filmed series, with the exception of Disney (and his program was more an anthology), were all half-hour before Warners's series. Huggins credits Leonard Goldenson with realizing that "Television is not radio, and we're doing it like radio [with the half-hour series, which was standard in radio], and it's time we do it like it should be done."

Maverick

Huggins did not last very long on *Cheyenne*. Even when he started on it, he was seeing twists on what he recalls were the

> simpleton stories where they would come across some old people in a covered wagon, weeping because someone had stolen all their cattle. Cheyenne would say, "I'll get them back for you." And he would get them back, and that would be the end of the story. You said, "Wait a minute. In the first place, this would be an interesting story if when it was over these old folks went off chuckling with their cattle following them, saying, 'Well, we got those guys' cattle, Ma. What'll we do next?' "

After doing a year of the show, Huggins was "so sick to death of the classical Western, I began to yearn to do an anti-Western." He found the key:

> On *Conflict* [a Warners anthology show] I did a show in which I used Jim Garner in a small part as a con man. He was under contract to the studio. I didn't discover Jim. What I discovered was something Jim could do that no one

knew about, and that was to play a very wily and funny confidence man. He read lines that were only mildly funny on paper and were *very* funny in the dailies.

I said, "My God, there's the guy I've been looking for. I'm going to a Western with him. And we're going to make him a bad guy in every way. He's going to dress in black. Bad guys always dress in black. He's going to be outwardly a coward, because he will genuinely avoid trouble and especially gunfights and fistfights.

"He's going to be a gambler; nobody likes gamblers. And he doesn't really gamble. He takes advantage of people. He won't get into a game with true, good poker players." I did that in *Maverick*. People would say, "Hey, you want to join this game?" He'd look at them and say, "No, I don't want to join the game. That's gambling. I don't believe in gambling."

There are rumors that *Maverick* did not start out to be a humorous show because the first episode shown did not have as much of the humor as the later episodes. This had more to do with Jack Warner than it did Roy Huggins. The first script for *Maverick* that Huggins wrote, "Point Blank," had the Maverick humor: Maverick turns in the girl he loves for the reward, then haggles with the sheriff over the size of the reward. The problem, from Warner's point of view, was that if that was the first episode shown, then Huggins would get creator royalties from the series, and according to Huggins, Warner had laid down the law to William T. Orr: "No royalties will be paid. It will open the door to those goddamned miserable writers. We won't have that." So Huggins found a book Warners owned called *The War of the Cooper Kings* and adapted it into "The War of the Silver Kings," putting as much humor as he could, but not as much as in "Point Blank." "Silver Kings" became the "official" pilot for the series, Warner was happy, and Orr kept his job. After that everybody was willing to let Maverick be Maverick.

In addition to Huggins, there were other writers on the show, who enjoyed writing for it as much as Huggins. Wells Root, who had been in films since the late twenties, loved Westerns but got few opportunities to write theatrical Westerns. He'd toured the West for many years, keeping a notebook with ideas for Western stories that he was now able to use on *Maverick* and other Warner westerns. Like Huggins, he speaks highly of James Garner: "He was a joy to write for [on] *Maverick* because you know what he'd do with it. He took a joke and gave it extra life and vigor. You sort of patted yourself on the back [when you heard how he read it]."

Another writer on the show as Marion Hargrove, who had written the World War II best-seller *See Hear, Private Hargrove*. He not only wrote funny dialogue, but funny stage directions as well, which Huggins says "helped the mood." Huggins rewrote Hargrove's material, which was "six feet off the ground. I had to bring it down and make it real. It isn't funny if you can't believe it. It's only funny if it's true. Comedy has to be truer than drama."

Not surprisingly, Huggins says he and Hargrove had "a falling out after every show." Sometimes they would have a falling out while the show was in the making. In the second season, Hargrove came up with the idea of a parody of *Gunsmoke*. Huggins wrote the story, Hargrove did the script, and Huggins did the rewrite—which Hargrove did not like. Hargrove kept trying to get the director, Leslie Martinson, to add bits, which Huggins kept trying to keep out, such as the marshal patting the saloon woman on the arm every time he saw her. Huggins let Hargrove supervise a cut of the episode, but it did not play well and Huggins had to recut it. Huggins still thinks there was too much of Hargrove's "shtick" in it, but it is a funny episode that lives in the minds of *Maverick* fans both then and now. It also so upset the makers of *Gunsmoke* that there were rumors they were going to name a villain Huggins, but they did not.

It took eight days to make a *Maverick* episode, which meant that even if they started production in the early summer, it was next to impossible to do a full season of 39 episodes all starring Garner. Huggins's suggestion was that the network preempt the show from time to time, but the network people were afraid that if it did, people would not come back to watch it. The solution arrived at was to give Bret Maverick a brother Bart and have several episodes a season featuring only Bart. Eventually there was also a cousin Beau, and even the Maverick brothers' Pappy, who was mentioned and quoted in the first seasons but not seen. The problem, and the solution, was that Jack Kelly, the actor hired to play Bart, was not the gifted comic actor that Garner was, so the Bart Maverick episodes did not have the kind of witty writing the Bret episodes did. On the other hand, Bart made it possible to do more conventional dramatic stories.

Roy Huggins left *Maverick* after two years, and he was replaced by Coles Trapnell. Trapnell found Huggins "extremely obliging and helpful to me when I came on board [in June 1959]. We talked story ideas over. We had absolutely nothing to shoot and we were going on the air in September." Trapnell eventually brought over writers he had worked with at Four Star, but the show was beginning to run short of cons for the Mavericks to do. Warners had purchased the rights to a book on cons called *Yellow Kid Weil* in 1958 and Huggins used those classic cons, as well as ones he had learned as a student at the Hill Military Academy. They also used ones from the book *Con Men and Con Games*. Trapnell and his writers started stealing from elsewhere, such as "Maverick and Juliet," which borrowed an episode from *Huckleberry Finn*, in which Tom Sawyer gets Huck involved with two feuding families. Trapnell figured if Mark Twain could steal from Shakespeare, he could steal from Twain. Some stories were original. One day, writer Leonard Praskins came in and told Trapnell he wanted to do an episode entitled "The Resurrection of Joe November." Trapnell said, "Fine, what is it?"

Praskins replied, "I don't know, but isn't that a hell of a title?" Trapnell agreed and they came up with a story. Trapnell, like Huggins, came up with many stories, but unlike Huggins, who got story credit, Trapnell "had one of those delightful contracts where I got no residuals and no extra credit, no nothing, so they were welcome to anything they could get."

Unfortunately Garner left the show after the third season, and the writers were left with Kelly and Roger Moore, who played Beau. They were good at what they did, but they were not Garner.

77 *Sunset Strip* and Its Clones

Roy Huggins was coming up with another show for the studio. He was going to do another one-hour pilot for a private eye show (previous shows in the genre were half-hours) with Marion Hargrove doing the script. The story Huggins gave to Hargrove had a standard villain, but Hargrove came to Huggins one day and said, "You know, Roy, something's gone wrong with the younger generation. They're crazy. They are absolutely, totally, frighteningly immoral." He quoted sociologists about the postwar generation of kids, and told Huggins he wanted to make the killer a young middle-class boy who kills in cold blood. Huggins loved it and Hargrove started on the script.

Huggins then got a call from Bill Orr, who asked him if they could expand the script from the 54 minutes of an hour pilot into 75 minutes to make a theatrical feature. Huggins and Hargrove were happy to do it, although Huggins was suspicious of Orr's motives. He told Hargrove, "Bill Orr's up to something. I don't know what, but this is not on the level. But you're going to get paid more. So let's do it." The film became *Girl on the Run* and got enough of a limited release that the studio could claim it was a film. When *77 Sunset Strip* was spun off from it, the studio did not, once again, have to pay "those goddamned miserable writers" creator royalties.

Because the film was made as a theatrical film, it was sneak-previewed in the Los Angeles area, which is when they discovered what Huggins calls "the accidental factor in success." He explains:

> The one thing we never ever predicted in our wildest dreams was that this character [played by Edd Byrnes], who was new and who was interesting, was anything except repulsive. After he killed people in cold blood, he combed his hair. At the preview, everyone in the audience under the age of twenty came out, took a look at Efrem Zimbalist Jr. over here and Edd Byrnes over here. And they wanted Edd's autograph. I never saw a man so shocked, surprised, pleased, flabbergasted, in my life.
>
> Efrem, Bill Orr and I stood there across the lobby and watched this without any understanding. We were absolutely baffled. Now Bill was thinking, "Jesus Christ, we've got something." He was happy. It did prove Marion was right. We don't know what we're doing when we're writing. The audience tells us.

For the series, the character was changed from a killer into a parking-lot attendant who constantly combs his hair and Byrnes became the first teen cult star of television.

One advantage ABC discovered in getting programming from a major studio was being able to clone a hit show. When *Cheyenne* became a hit in 1955–56, Warners followed on ABC with *Sugarfoot* in 1957 and *Bronco* in 1958, both Westerns using young, untried male players in the leads. The success of *77 Sunset Strip* in 1958 brought even more spin-offs: *Bourbon Street Beat* (set in New Orleans) debuting in 1958, *Hawaiian Eye* in 1959, and *Surfside 6* (set in Miami Beach) in 1960. Hubbell Robinson, a producer of the declining live dramas, described the structure of these shows accurately in 1961, when he said:

> The ingredients are three or four handsome young Hollywood men, one of them a shocking blond; a busty and beautiful girl; a succession of violent encounters with the not very bright "bad guys," and a title that involves a number like *Crocodile 8*. Run them all together and you've got a hit. Whether you've got entertainment that people look at or just stare at is something else again.

By 1959 Warner Brothers was providing eight hours, or 40 percent, of ABC's prime-time schedule, and four of those shows were in the top twenty.[16] What ABC had discovered in researching its efforts to beat NBC and CBS was that advertisers preferred the younger audiences that were attracted to the action-adventure shows. The younger audiences were not as set in their ways and were more willing to change the products they bought, especially the products television advertised.

Having a major studio and its resources and ruthlessness could be useful in other ways. When the Writers Guild of America struck in 1959–60, the shows that were clones of each other could provide story material. Scripts used for one Warners private-eye show could be used for another, and even scripts for Westerns could be adapted for the private eye shows, and vice versa. Huggins, who was by this time making another attempt at writing feature films, recalls that it was William Orr, Hugh Benson, and one other person who did the "adaptations," but there were other writers willing to work as long as their names were not used. On many of the adapted scripts, and non-adapted ones as well, the writer credited was W. Hermanos. Hermanos is Spanish for brothers; you can guess what the W. stands for.[17]

Huggins left Warners, and after some years he ended up at Universal, which like Warners in the late fifties was a factory. Huggins felt more comfortable in a studio setting. Likewise Coles Trapnell also went to Universal in the sixties, getting "one of those contracts where they could use me as a producer, an associate producer, a story editor, a writer, and I think in the small print it said I could be used to get in early to sweep out the office." Joel Rogosin, who had followed Huggins on *77 Sunset Strip*, also moved to Universal in the sixties, since Warners television was diminishing at the time. Universal had by then been taken over by MCA, which folded its Revue operation into

Universal. Universal was making a big move into television, where it has remained a force ever since.

Major studios producing television could provide other elements writers could take advantage of. When Everett Greenbaum did an episode of the later-fifties series *How to Marry a Millionaire* at 20th Century-Fox, he remembered Fox had a large computer set from their film *The Desk Set*, so he wrote an episode to use it. Charles Larson wrote and produced for the same studio's series *Twelve O'Clock High* in the middle sixties, and the studio had so much stock footage of airplanes collected for the 1949 theatrical film of the same name that the writers could come up with any situation and be confident there would be footage of it. When Sam Rolfe was making the series *The Man from U.N.C.L.E.* at MGM in the mid-sixties, he would get on a bicycle, ride around the backlot, and come up with stories to fit the standing sets. He also used to "scout" sets for movies in production to see what he could use. At the time of *U.N.C.L.E.*, MGM was just beginning to get into television on a big scale and Rolfe found that the craft departments were eager to show what they could do so that they could keep their jobs.

One of the best, and in some ways most bizarre, uses of the resources of a major studio came in a second-season episode of *Maverick* called "The Brasada Spur." The story makes no sense as Bart Maverick finds himself dressed up not in his usual outfit, but in a large coat with a big white hat. He gets involved with railroad men and finds himself on a train that is headed for a collision with a train coming the other way on the same tracks. It is only when the trains crash that Warner Brothers fans can make sense of the plot: it has all been a lead-in to the crash and the brawl that follows, which is from the 1945 Warners release *Saratoga Trunk*. Maverick is in this outfit so that he will match Gary Cooper's stunt double in the film. The train wreck sequence gives the episode a spectacular element that neither live television nor small-scale film production could provide.[18]

·6·

REALITY/DOCUMENTARY

Reality

When the American fiction filmmakers who made wartime documentaries returned to theatrical filmmaking after World War II, their films tended to be more realistic. Many early television writers were World War II veterans themselves. Chayefsky, Rose, Serling, and JP Miller all served in the military during the war, as had Richard Powell, Everett Greenbaum, Allan Manings, E. Jack Neuman, Christopher Knopf, and Sam Rolfe. Even Gore Vidal was first mate of an army ship in the Aleutians Islands from 1943 to 1946.[1] So it is not surprising that early television made attempts to be as real as possible in its fiction. These attempts took three forms.

The first was stories based on facts, such as *Navy Log*, *The Lineup*, and *Dragnet*. *Dragnet* boasted it was based on actual cases from the Los Angeles Police Department. *TV Guide* tried to explain in 1953 how Jack Webb's approach worked on *Dragnet*: "[T]here is no dramatic license taken with the cases. Each is related factually, but in such a manner that even the criminal would not recognize his own case. Webb is dedicated to the idea that the show should do nothing to harm a man who has paid legally for his misdeed."[2] The magazine does not make clear how the show can be factual and at the same time present the case so the criminal would not recognize it.

Medic was created and written by former *Dragnet* writer James Mosher. Mosher also tried to have it both ways, saying, "It's not a documentary. Each story is based on a number of case histories."[3] Each story idea for the show was discussed with a three-man committee from the Los Angeles County Medical Association, and the completed scripts were checked by a representative of the association.

The second form of getting at reality was seen in Paddy Chayefsky's attempt to capture the texture of real life, particularly in his use of dialogue that could have been "wiretapped." This goes beyond Webb and Mosher's "Just the facts, ma'am" approach to begin to suggest the rhythm of real life, not just the surface facts.

The third form was seen in Reginald Rose's attempts to deal with contemporary social issues. Rose was not alone in this, since many of the other writers wanted to write about contemporary issues as well.

The institutions of television, particularly the sponsors and the networks, were happiest with the first of the three forms. The factual approach seemed real and was not particularly controversial, especially if the cases had been disguised enough so the participants would not sue. Chayefsky's approach was acceptable as long as it brought in the upper- to upper-middle-class audiences who owned the sets in the fifties, but as the audiences expanded, the sponsors and therefore the networks wanted shows with wider appeal, and went to the more glamorous, less realistic filmed adventure shows. The most troublesome, from the viewpoint of the sponsors and the networks, was the third form.

The sponsors were concerned with the question of public taste, especially since there was generally a single sponsor for a show, often with his name in the title. Audiences could be antagonized, and they did hold it against the sponsor, according to one director of television for a large cosmetics company:

> You'd be surprised how many people complain to us directly when they don't like a show, and threaten never to buy our product any more. Evidently they believe the program is produced right here in our executive offices. If the public makes us responsible for our shows in that way, then we must retain complete control.[4]

Needless to say, the writers of television in the fifties and early sixties remember some of the more idiotic attempts of the sponsors to protect themselves and their interests. Jay Burton recalls that J. Carroll Naish could not guest-star on *The Buick-Berle Show* because there was then a car called Nash. Don Brinkley once wrote a script about Dr. Samuel Mudd, the doctor who set John Wilkes Booth's broken leg after the assassination of Lincoln, but *Climax!* passed on it because the show was sponsored by Chrysler and there was too much mention of Lincoln in it.

The sponsors involuntarily brought about their own withdrawal from the production of television shows. By July 1957 five of the top ten shows on television were quiz shows,[5] but the shows were rigged: certain contestants were given the questions and answers before the show. The public scandal over the rigging in 1959 led to sponsors' no longer being allowed direct control over program production. The networks took control of production, and the most stupid of the sponsor restrictions were lifted. However, the networks still had to sell the shows to the sponsors, and the sponsors were still interested in shows that did not offend, so the institutional pressure on the makers of television continued, only now focused in the network censor. The network censor's office has gone under many names: Standards and Practices, Programming Practices, Continuity Acceptance, and others. The function is still the same: to protect the public image of the network and the companies sponsoring shows on it.

Even in 1956, when the sponsors still controlled production, Stockton Helffrich, the director of NBC's Continuity Acceptance, listed the special interests that shows on his network had to avoid offending: gas interests, meat interests, florists, bowling and billiard interests (gangsters were not allowed to be shown in pool halls), warehouse interests (night watchmen could not be shown as dirty and warehouses could not be the locations for murder); as well as regional, social, philosophical special interests, such as physical and mental afflictions. Helffrich noted his office was "very active in censoring of racial stereotypes, religious oversimplifications, unkindness toward the physically handicapped, ignorance regarding the emotionally disturbed."[6]

Needless to say, the writers fought back, sometimes at full voice. Charles Larson describes having "long screaming sessions on what we could say or do. A good censor can see filth anywhere." When Richard Conway was writing on *Leave It to Beaver*, he and his partner wrote in a joke that ended with the clean punch line from a very old dirty joke. The lady censor was upset, but the producers, Bob Mosher and Joe Connelly, persuaded her that the only people who would understand that it was the punch line of a dirty joke were those who already knew it. The line was kept. (Unfortunately Conway cannot remember the punch line. Drat.)

One writer used his own instincts about a lady censor to liven up a show. In the script for an action-adventure show in this period, the writer wrote in an implied lesbian affair between the villain's girlfriend and another woman. The studio told the writer he could never get it past the network censor, but he pointed out that he thought the censor was gay herself and would probably think it was a normal affair. Whether the censor was or not, the script was approved, shot, and went on the air.[7]

By 1968 the censorship role had shifted so much to the network that writer-producer Bill Froug could write,

> It is always the network *program* department that says that the *sales* department says that the *sponsor* says that they will withdraw their support of any segment containing such-and-such a theme. But sponsors are never consulted. Sponsors simply stand in line like everybody else.[8]

That was a drastic change from the heyday of sponsor influence the decade before. It was also part of an opening up of American television that has some of its roots in documentary film and especially documentary film for television.

Documentary

It is all John Grierson's fault that the first thirty years of network documentaries were so humorless. Grierson, the first great theorist of documentary film, thought documentaries should be educational, but never anything so trivial as amusing. Educational documentaries appealed to television networks for several reasons. From the beginning, network television was a commercial, but the networks and their stations still had a responsibility, under the FCC, to use the airwaves responsibly. What better way to do that than to present something educational? The network insisted upon control of what went out on their air, so Grierson's authoritative point of view was matched by the networks' view of themselves as the authoritative source of entertainment, news, and information.

The documentary units at the networks were originally put under the control of the people running the news divisions, most of whom had come to television out of radio news, so they were used to their work being primarily the printed or spoken word; and Grierson's approach depended very much on narration. In Edward R. Murrow's first documentary series, *See It Now* (1952 to 1955), Murrow is the authority figure telling audiences what they should think about such subjects as Senator Joseph McCarthy. As strong and important as some of these programs were, in terms of technique they were not much more than illustrated radio.

Murrow's tradition continued at CBS. When producer Irving Gitlin started a series called *The Twentieth Century* in 1957, he brought in writers not usually associated with television. For his program on Winston Churchill, Churchill's biographer John Davenport co-wrote the script with producer Burton Benjamin. Hanson Baldwin, the military editor of the *New York Times*, wrote the program on the V-2 rocket.[9]

Robert Drew

In 1954 a picture editor for *Life* magazine was on a Neiman Fellowship at Harvard thinking about whether it was possible to make documentary films that had the informality of the still pictures in *Life*. One night he turned the sound off on Murrow's *See It Now*. The picture alone made no sense. When he turned off the picture and listened to the sound, the show still made sense.[10]

Drew began to realize that "The kind of logic that does build interest and feeling on television is the logic of drama. Dramatic logic works because the viewer is seeing for himself and there is suspense." Drew was drawn toward storytelling, but also wondered "what, if anything, all this stuff about storytelling had to do with journalism." From his reading of Walter Lippmann and John Grierson and their observations of the need for education of the masses in a democracy, Drew came to the conclusion that "Television had gone Grierson one better [in terms of delivering large audiences], and now what were we going to do about it?"

Drew spent the next five years trying to work out the technical problems of his approach. The first time most of the lighter-weight cameras and lighter-weight sound recording equipment worked most of the time was in *Primary*, Drew's film of the 1960 Wisconsin Democratic Presidential Primary between John F. Kennedy and Hubert H. Humphrey. Drew and his filmmakers followed the candidates in and out of cars, walking down the streets, through crowds, and even into their hotel rooms. Drew and the filmmakers collaborated on the editing process. The result was a film that with only three minutes of narration in its 54-minute running time tells the story of the election by putting the viewer into the action and cutting between the candidates. The viewer was not lectured to, or nudged to think one way or the other about each candidate.[11]

Drew's new documentary storytelling style was what many would come to call *cinéma vérité*, but is more accurately called direct cinema, since it records experience directly.[12] (*Cinéma vérité* uses the same portable equipment, but by the filmmaker asking questions provokes the subject into revealing him- or herself.)

Primary was shown to the executives at the networks and Drew sums up their reaction by quoting one as saying, "You've got some nice footage there, Bob." In other words, "Come back when you have a strong narration and music that tells the audience what to think." The film was shown in a shortened form on several local television stations owned by Drew's boss, Time Inc., and syndicated to other stations.

Drew's direct cinema technique was too striking for the networks to completely ignore it for too long. Later in 1960, ABC commissioned Drew to do a film about Latin America *(Yanki No!)*, and in 1963, after Drew's unit was released by Time Inc., a film they were working on was financed and picked up for broadcast, again by ABC. Drew kept in touch with the Kennedys after *Primary* and wanted for some time to do a film about a presidential crisis. In June 1963 he got his wish as his camera people followed Attorney General Robert Kennedy through the attempt to integrate the University of Alabama. Drew's associate James Lipscomb also talked Alabama Governor George Wallace into letting a crew film his side of the crisis. The resulting film, *Crisis: Behind a Presidential Commitment*, was again documentary as storytelling.[13] Documentarians at the networks understood what Drew was up to. Burton Benjamin, the CBS producer of *The Twentieth Century*, said, "It is obvious to me that they could get closer to the essence of the truth through this technique than you could get through the conventional technique. It just seemed to be a breakthrough."[14]

It was not, however, a technique that was picked up generally by the networks. Direct cinema was too free and informal to appeal to the men who controlled, and wanted to be seen as controlling, network programming. Direct cinema was simply too democratic in letting the audience make up its own mind about the subject. The people running the networks were more comfortable with the older, authoritarian style.

The longer form of documentary eventually gave way on the networks to the magazine shows, although when a documentary is done at the longer length, such as CBS's *48 Hours*, which does use some of the observation technique of direct cinema, there is still the narration to tell the audience what to think.

Frederick Wiseman

If there is little room on the commercial networks for the direct cinema approach, there is slightly more room for it on public television, which is more willing to speak with several voices rather than a single one. One of those voices is Frederick Wiseman, a lawyer who turned to documentary filmmaking in the mid-sixties. His first films, *Titicut Follies* and *High School*, were financed independently, but his films since have been financed at least in part by, and shown on, public television.

Wiseman works in the direct cinema mode, although he prefers to call what he does "reality fictions."[15] Unlike Drew, however, he does not organize his films in a conventional dramatic structure, which is why Drew's dramatic conflict structure was more quickly adapted to fiction television, and Wiseman's influence is more apparent in the multi-character dramas of the eighties. Wiseman's films generally deal with institutions both public and private, and are made up of sequences showing how the people of the institution deal with their "clients," with recurring connecting material showing the operational details of the institution. The meaning of the films comes not from the story or a single crisis situation, as do Drew's films, but from the thematic connections between the scenes.

Wiseman's films often deal with institutions that fictional television dealt with before and after his films, and by placing his films in their historical context one can begin to see the influence not only of Wiseman but also of the direct cinema style in general on American television and particularly on the writing for American television.

Wiseman's fourth film was the 1970 film *Hospital*, shot at New York's Metropolitan Hospital. In the earlier medical shows on television, the doctors never made mistakes, nor did the hospitals. Early in *Hospital* we see Dr. Schwartz on the phone complaining to another hospital that they have sent over a patient to Metropolitan without the proper paperwork. He goes through the entire situation and then has to repeat much of the story when it becomes clear the person on the other end of the phone has not been paying attention. Later on Schwartz, who is the closest to a star the film has but who only appears in a few scenes, is helping a young man who has overdosed on mes-

caline. The doctor is caring, but in a cool, professional way, and he is repeating, almost like a mantra, "You will not die." The man vomits. And
vomits again. And again. And when you think he cannot have anymore left,
he vomits again. Network television of the time would obviously not show
the vomiting as casually as Wiseman does, but network television would also
not let a medical show have the loose structure of Wiseman's film, since part
of the reason for a medical show is to provide a dramatic structure for stories.
And a network documentary would not let the vomiting scene go on so long
that it becomes funny, as Wiseman does.

Wiseman's third film, *Law and Order*, was shot in 1968 in Kansas City.
The film is not dissimilar to *Dragnet*, in which the citizens Sgt. Friday deals
with tend to be, if not completely criminal, at least slightly off-center. In one
of *Law and Order's* opening scenes, Wiseman shows a man who has come
to the police to get them to arrest his brother-in-law. The man had mentioned to someone that he was going to take the brother-in-law and "throw
him in the river," but the other person said, "The cops are paid to do that."
Wiseman's cops tend to be more human than Webb's, and unlike Sgt. Friday
they cannot always settle the cases. Wiseman puts at the beginning and end
of *Law and Order* two different domestic dispute cases in which the cops are
unable to provide any solution. In the one at the end of the film, the cop
tells the man involved that he will have to get a lawyer to help settle the
situation.

The law, in Wiseman's view of the world, may not be able to help. In his
1973 *Juvenile Court*, the entire film is summed up by a scene at the end of
it in which one of the teenagers brought before the court keeps asking if he
can get justice. Wiseman deliberately does not tell the audience the outcome
of one case we spend some time watching, in contrast with the law shows of
the time, such as *Perry Mason*, where the case is always solved. What *Juvenile Court* looks forward to are the law shows of the eighties and nineties, in
which the practice of law is seen as more complex.

The Raymonds

Alan and Susan Raymond first broke into the public eye as filmmakers on
producer Craig Gilbert's 1972 direct cinema/soap opera/miniseries for PBS,
An American Family, in which American family life was not seen as slapstick
farce as in *I Love Lucy* but as slapstick drama; not seen as simple problem
solving as in *Father Knows Best* or *Leave It to Beaver* but as virtually unsolv-
able in its emotional complexity; and not seen as emotionally intense as in
conventional afternoon soap operas but as a combination of intensity and
languidness. *An American Family* caught the rhythm of U.S. family life that
would not show up in American fiction on television until, in a slightly different but just as well observed manner, *thirtysomething*.

In the mid-seventies, the Raymonds moved into Wiseman territory and made a documentary about the police. In *The Police Tapes* the locale is not Kansas City but the 44th Precinct of The Bronx, an area known as Fort Apache. The style is partly direct cinema. In one scene the police have to break down a door to get a barricaded suspect. They try. It does not give. They try some more. More cops try. Everybody stands back for a bit, then they try again, and they finally get the door open. It generally does not take this long for television police to get through a door.

The film is also partly *cinéma vérité*, in that the Raymonds listen to the police talk about their work. They even directly interview on camera the Police Commander of the precinct, Antony Bouza, who becomes a benign authority figure giving the audience the benefit of his expertise and his sympathies for both the cops and the citizens in his precinct.[16] He is less rigid than Jack Webb's Sgt. Friday, and he looks forward to police in later series.

As does the film as whole. In a scene near the beginning, a sergeant is handling the roll call of the officers on the watch. The camera, in hand-held direct cinema fashion, watches the police, and at the end of the meeting we hear the sergeant say, "Let's be careful out there."

The Influence of Fiction on Documentary

The influence of fictional structures can be seen in television documentary, where documentary filmmakers try to work in patterns TV audiences expect. Aubrey Solomon, a young filmmaker and film historian from Canada, got his first job in television through his work as an historian of Twentieth Century-Fox. In 1976 he was hired as a researcher for the pilot for a syndicated documentary series called *That's Hollywood*, and later was an associate producer on the series. Solomon describes the process:

> Well, we followed a format because it was a TV episode: we had a tease (a glitzy, slam-bang first 60 seconds), and then we go into the credit sequence, then we would open up the show. By the end of the first act we had to come up with a big production, or a big explosion, or a big action scene, which holds the interest until the second act, and then come up with another socko ending.
>
> We would do a rough outline and say approximately what we wanted to say. Then we would do our best to find a clip that illustrated [that], but then in the writing of the show, we would finesse the script as we found the clips to find the proper lead-ins and lead-outs, and gag lines that we could make to counterpoint what we'd seen or what was coming up or whatever.

·7·

COWBOYS AND OTHER
SIXTIES PROFESSIONALS

Westerns

*I*n the late fifties and early sixties, there were still the formula Westerns. Revue, both before and after MCA took over Universal, made filmed Westerns both for syndication and the networks. The writers working on them had to be aware which market the show was headed for. D. C. Fontana wrote for two Revue Westerns, *The Tall Man* for NBC and *Shotgun Slade* for syndication. Fontana notes that the limitations on these half-hour shows were established by Ziv, and since Ziv was successful, other companies followed Ziv's rules. On *Shotgun Slade* a writer was limited to only four major speaking parts, including Slade, and three sets. On the one episode Fontana did, no exteriors were allowed since it was raining and the company could not hold production until it stopped. On the network shows writers could go further in terms of characters and sets, although not much.

There were also several westerns that appealed to adults in varying degrees. *Have Gun—Will Travel* did not start out as a Western. Sam Rolfe received an Academy Award nomination for his first produced screenplay, *The Naked Spur*. According to Rolfe, most movie people thought of television as a "sort of second cousin that you kept in the attic," but he saw television as "a field for exploration, an adventure." He met Herbert Meadow, the creator of *Man Against Crime*, who announced he had a great title, *Have Gun—Will Travel*. Rolfe told him, "It's a great title to create something out of, but it will never go on the air with a title like that. *Have Gun—Will Travel*, what does it mean?"

They developed an idea for a modern adventure series about a man who lives in New York, gets the out-of-town papers, and clips out stories of people in trouble, to whom he sends his card, which says, "Have Gun—Will Travel. Cable Paladin." They pitched the idea to Hunt Stromberg, Jr., at CBS, who loved the concept but told them to make it a Western. As soon as they got out in the hall they began to think: In 1870 how is a guy in a cave surrounded by Indians going to get a timely message to Paladin and what's going to be left of him by the time Paladin gets there? They went back into Stromberg's office, and Rolfe says that, "Hunt said the one thing that solved the problem: 'Dissolve to:' . . ." They could just fade from the man in trouble to Paladin and back. Because of the time period of the show, they also had to change "Cable" to "Wire." Rolfe says, "The first thing that made me a little afraid of the great American public . . . was 50 percent of the mail we got started out 'Dear Wire.' "

Rather than doing simple action stories, Rolfe did "things that guys said you can't do, but I put it in the west." He wrote an episode where a teacher was teaching that Quantrill of Quantrill's Raiders was a bad man, and a Southerner pulls a gun on her to make her stop. Paladin comes to town and makes it clear you cannot tell teachers what to teach—an risky idea to promote at the end of the McCarthy era.

Rolfe was helped, or at least not hurt, by the sponsor's representative on the show. The representative read the scripts and would send long memos tearing them apart to both Rolfe and the sponsor. The representative then would tell Rolfe to ignore his comments and that he was just writing the memos to persuade his boss he was on the job. Rolfe left the show after a year, but *Have Gun—Will Travel* continued to do more than conventional western stories continued under his replacements, Frank Pierson and Al Ruben. Lou Shaw did a first draft script for them they rejected, but when they explained what was wrong with it, Shaw got the concept of the show as a "little morality play" and persuaded them to let him do the second draft, which they used.

Have Gun—Will Travel was not the only Western to put political material into the context of the West. Christopher Knopf wrote an episode of *Wanted: Dead or Alive* about a sheriff who was a nice man, but not up to the demands of the job. Knopf says it was based on "My view of Eisenhower at the time. I'm sure I'm wrong, but that was how I saw it as a kid at the time."

Unlike Sam Rolfe, who by his own admission loved the "mythical history of the West, not the real West," E. Jack Neuman wanted his Westerns to be accurate. In 1957 NBC began the series *Wagon Train*, which ran until 1965. Neuman thought "It was a great, swaggering, Western idea," following a wagon train for a season as it winds its way from St. Joseph, Missouri, to Oregon. Neuman wrote the first three episodes after the pilot, and he "wanted to write it the way it was, not the way everybody thought it was." The first episode he wrote dealt with the whole wagon train having to stop because a spanner nut on one of the lead wagons broke. The studio and network "never thought that we should really do anything authentic. It was Never-never Land. I said, 'No, no, no. The real thing's a lot more fun.' " Neuman had his preference between the two stars of the series. He says that with Ward Bond "You couldn't discuss anything. Also, he wasn't too bright anyhow," but Robert Horton was "very literate" and even wrote a background sketch for the character he played, Flint McCullough, which Neuman used.

One advantage of the *Wagon Train* format was that it lent itself to guest stars, although as D. C. Fontana notes, "If you counted as many guest stars as there were in the season, the wagon train would have stretched from St. Joe all the way to San Francisco in the first place."

Charles Marquis Warren followed his year on *Gunsmoke* by creating *Rawhide*, which began in January 1959. Warren found George C. Duffield's diary of his 1866 cattle drive from San Antonio to Sedalia, and as Warren told *TV Guide*, "We are following Duffield's diary literally and exactly. When he crosses a river, we do. When he is stopped three weeks by rain, we are. When he doesn't encounter Indians for three months, we don't."[1] Warren bridled at the suggestion his show was similar to *Wagon Train*: "No. The *Wagon Train* people come across their exploits and suddenly the wagon train disappears while they tell their story. With us the herd is primary. We're always up against the elements—flood, fire, dust, thirst—and we never leave them entirely behind."[2] Lou Shaw, who wrote on the show in its early years, thinks it was "Basically the same premise as *Wagon Train*, with people coming in and out with a group of people on the move and they have to keep moving, so they had a *raison d'être* for doing the show every week."

The lead in *Rawhide* was nominally Eric Fleming, who played Gil Favor, the trail boss, and his second-in-command was Rowdy Yates, played by a young actor in his first major role, Clint Eastwood. Shaw says he was told, "Don't give him [Eastwood] too many lines because he can't talk. He just looks good in profile when he rides." Shaw was called in once specifically to rewrite Eastwood's dialogue and give it to somebody else. Shaw says, "There wasn't a great deal of respect for Clint Eastwood on the show in terms of being the lead actor." That changed over the course of the show. By the time Charles Larson was writing for the show,

> We thought Eastwood was better than Fleming. We tried to throw things to him. Eastwood could do drama, he could do comedy. Fleming was stiff. We were always told not to make the speeches in his scenes with other people too long. We had to write in short breaks in the other person's speech so Fleming would have a line. If he just had to stand there and react, he felt jumpy. He didn't know what to do.

Don Brinkley also thinks Eastwood was much more interesting to write for than Fleming on *Rawhide*, and believes it was partly because of their characters: Yates was young and learning things, while Favor, like the actor, was stolid.

Sy Salkowitz was brought reluctantly onto *Rawhide* in its next-to-last year, 1964–65. Writer-producer Bruce Geller and director Bernard Kowalski had been asked by CBS to do less obviously Western, more "human," stories, which is why they approached Salkowitz, who admitted he did not know how to do Western stories. He did two scripts for them, one of which was filmed. Then William Paley, the head of CBS, looked in on an episode of the new, improved *Rawhide*. He immediately called his executives and asked, "Where are the cows?" only to be told "Oh, we don't do cows anymore on *Rawhide*." Paley's response was, "The hell you don't. Fire everyone." As Salkowitz points out, "But Mr. Paley didn't fire his people. He fired our people." Geller and Kowalski were fired and Salkowitz's second script was never done.

When Fleming left the series in the fall of 1965, Eastwood's Rowdy Yates was moved up to trail boss, but William Paley preferred to have older men as the authority figures in the series on his network, so he canceled the show in January 1966,[3] and Eastwood disappeared from television into Italian westerns.

In addition to the "trek" Westerns, there were also Western shows set on ranches, where the guest stars either came to the ranch or had the stars come to them (which got them off the ranches). E. Jack Neuman wrote a few episodes of *Bonanza:* "You had the almost stock scene of all four of them [the Cartwrights] riding somewhere, or kicking the shit out of an Indian or something, then you separated them. That made it a lot easier. That was the format." Neuman was brought onto the series by the producer, David Dortort, who was, according to Neuman, "exhausted because they [the leading actors] were all becoming big stars." Dortort particularly needed an episode for Pernell Roberts, who "threatened to quit each week and so on. David asked me if I could do anything with him and I said, 'Sure.' " Neuman suggested an episode where Adam Cartwright would "love and lose." This was not an uncommon storyline on the show, and the sons avoided permanent relationships with women so often that dirty-minded viewers began to get suspicious.

A problem on *Bonanza* was not only the stars, but the network's protection of the franchise. Catherine Turney once pitched a story to the show that called for the father, Ben Cartwright, to have a minor character flaw. Both the producers and Lorne Greene were more than happy to do it, but NBC took the attitude that Ben was "a minor deity," and could not have what Turney calls "one foot of clay."

To get out of his contract at Four Star after Dick Powell died, Christopher Knopf agreed to do the pilot script for a CBS ranch Western, but only if he could bring into it the characters from a similar project of his CBS that had rejected. Knopf wrote the pilot and one episode, then left the company. Nobody was more surprised than Knopf when *The Big Valley* ran for four years.

By the early sixties, one-hour was the standard length for dramatic series. In 1962 Universal created the ninety-minute *The Virginian*, in theory if not in fact based on the Owen Wister novel and its two previous film versions. Writers like Sy Salkowitz had no objection to the greater length, since the first drafts of his hour scripts tended to run an hour and fifteen minutes. With a ninety-minute script, Salkowitz "used to stretch my muscles and write an hour-and-three-quarters script and then squeeze it down into an hour and a half." He felt the longer format gave him time to develop some characters.

To create a weekly show of that length, it was necessary to have an executive producer and three producers, each of whom were responsible for an episode every three weeks. Joel Rogosin, who thinks of himself as a producer-writer more than a writer-producer, was with the show for five years, most of which was spent rewriting material for Lee J. Cobb, who played Judge Garth, the owner of the ranch. Cobb would call Rogosin at 8:30 at night to complain about the scripts, and Rogosin would go in about 5:00 A.M. and rewrite the material, taking it to Cobb when he came in. Rogosin recalls, "And he would say things in those wonderful dulcet tones like, 'Spare me from embarrassing you by publicly saying this shit.' Which of course it wasn't. It wasn't deathless prose, but it wasn't the other either."

The Virginian was not the only ninety-minute Western series. In the mid-sixties, CBS wanted a series on "the end of the West," and asked Christopher Knopf, late of *The Big Valley*, to create it. He selected the Cimarron territory of Oklahoma as the locale, where as he puts it, "The cowboys had it and the farmers wanted it." Knopf became the Supervising Producer of the show and dealt with the forty writers they used. He thinks the show was

> uneven. We had some wonderful, wonderful material and some that was not very good. . . . We always tried to do something wonderful each week. We got our head handed to us sometimes, and sometimes we pulled it out like crazy. . . .
>
> I did not recognize there are certain things you can't do every week. You have to find a certain level. I was always going for irony. I was going for something where I could flip the story upside down, and at times it was almost too much for the audience who wants to watch Westerns to keep track [of]. It's not like watching *The Defenders*. Different audience. People who watch Westerns don't want to have to concentrate, think, and be tested, and we were doing that. *Gunsmoke* did it right. They took one little idea and ran with it.

There were also problems with the network on *Cimarron Strip*. The programming executive at CBS that season was Mike Dann, who, according to Knopf, "liked absolutes." Knopf wanted more shades of gray. At one point in the season Sy Salkowitz did a script for the show that started out with three enlisted men capturing a sergeant we first think is bad. As the episode progresses, we discover he may not be that bad after all. Dann disliked the episode and Albert Aley was brought in to rewrite it to make the sergeant more "hateable," in Salkowitz's phrase. What happened was that the director and the actors "read past the rewrite," as Salkowitz puts it, and came close to the original idea. Salkowitz had already taken his name off the script and put on a pseudonym, and now Aley did the same thing. Perry Lafferty, then an executive at CBS, saw the episode, called Dann and told him, "They did what they wanted to do, not what you told him to do."

Dann said, "What are you going to do about it?"

Lafferty replied, "Well, I can't fire them."

"Better them than you."[4] And the staff was fired.

One reason CBS may have been thinking about an "end of the West" series in the mid-sixties is that it was the time of the end of the Western. In 1959–60 nine of the top twenty shows in the ratings were Westerns. By the season *Cimarron Strip* premiered, 1967–68, there were only two.[5] Like live drama the decade before, Westerns had gone through a cycle and begun to fade, replaced by more urban shows.

Cops

The Naked City began as a 1948 theatrical film, one of the more notable attempts at using location shooting to make films more realistic. In 1958 the film became the basis for a half-hour cop series filmed on location in New York. The next year the series followed the trend of dramatic shows and became an hour show, still filmed in New York. The problem was that many of the best writers had moved to Los Angeles with the change from live to filmed television. The show was then written (and edited) in California, but shot in New York. This usually meant there was great pressure on the writers from the producer Herbert Leonard.

Lou Shaw calls it "a mad show to work for." He once turned in a story idea to *The Naked City* and for several weeks did not hear back from the show. Then one morning at eleven he got a call from Leonard, who said, "We're shooting your show next."

"You are? I thought it was dead."

"Oh, no. Oh, you mean nobody's called you?"

"No."

"Well, start writing it. I'll send a messenger by later tonight to start picking up the pages, because we have to prep it in New York." Shaw told Leonard he had other things going on in his life, but Leonard and his story editor, Howard Rodman, insisted, so Shaw started writing and every three hours a messenger would arrive to collect the pages.

In spite of that, Shaw thinks the episode came off "incredibly well." He calls Leonard an "old-time producer. He was always ill-prepared. He was always going off the cuff, but he had a great flair." Shaw suggested to him an idea for a scene involving thirty people on a fire escape, thinking it would be prohibitively expensive and time-consuming, but Leonard told him to write it and the scene went into the show.

In theory the leading characters were the police officers, but Sy Salkowitz notes that one reason the show was so good was that

> *Naked City* wasn't a cop show. It was a criminal show, because the way you wrote a *Naked City* was to get inside the head of the criminal and tell why he

committed the crime. He usually was not a bad guy. You had at least sympathy for the victim if that guy was being manipulated into being a crook. You had to be careful about your police work, because you had to make it real. You had to bring your action so that it was like a V, [the police and the criminal] starting from opposite points, and met at the bottom, and the criminal was apprehended.

The man who became story editor for the one-hour *Naked City* was Howard Rodman, whose credits in live television included *Studio One.* Sy Salkowitz calls Howard Rodman "probably one of the most gracious and giving men who ever lived. He was known as the writer's rabbi. If you had a problem, you talked it over with Howard. A problem about anything. But Howard always listened. He was a big bear of a man, a little crazy, and we all loved him."

Rodman was such a good and distinctive writer that, as Salkowitz says, "Howard made it difficult because you had to live up to Howard." Because of Rodman's skills and the chaotic nature of the production of the show, Rodman ended up rewriting many, if not most, of the scripts. Salkowitz says

> Bert [Leonard] would say, "It's a damned fine script [from the assigned writer], now Howard, put it through your typewriter." Now normally when somebody says that what they mean is they'd like to have the flavor of the writer.
>
> Howard had a problem. Howard might write a line, but the answer to that line was two steps away from what the answer had been in the original script, and the rejoinder to that was another two steps away, so Howard would end up writing his own story, which Bert would shoot because the phrase there was, "We were writing with our backs to the camera." That's how tight the schedule was. [They had no scripts done] in advance.

Rodman's work eventually led to a change in the Writers Guild credit rules. Previously a story editor on a show could write 35 percent of the show and get a writing credit, which meant producers could hire story editors for less money and promise they would make it up in residuals for shows they got credit on. The rule was changed so that a story editor had to write 50 percent to get a credit. The new rule was known informally as the Howard Rodman Clause, although as Salkowitz points out, "This didn't mean anybody disliked Howard. Everybody loved Howard." But credits meant money, and credits on *The Naked City* meant even more. Salkowitz again: "Years after, I would get calls saying, 'We're looking for a *Naked City* writer. Are you available?' That was the phrase. Not just me, but all the guys who wrote it."[6]

One of the shows that Salkowitz then wrote for was *The Untouchables*, which like *The Naked City* was a "criminal show," and in which "the real color and the real excitement from the show came from the criminals: who were they? what were they doing? what did they want? who were they trying to screw?"

Salkowitz, being from South Philadelphia, did not find the show difficult to write:

> I came from an area where "Heyyouovertherecomehere" is one word. So the dialogue was easy for me to write. I grew up with those people. I understood their mentality and their attitudes. I understood their families were sacred. Long before you ever saw *The Godfather* I knew what "Go to the mattresses" meant. And I wrote it. It was fun.

For E. Jack Neuman, who was from Indiana, *The Untouchables* was not fun. He found the show's format "very cumbersome. Remember you had Eliot Ness and his five dwarfs and then you had Al Capone and his ten dwarfs." Neuman also objected to the studio's insistence on using the same stock footage of the truck crashing into the brewery on what seemed to him every episode. He tried to write new action into his scripts. The show was criticized for its violence and Neuman notes that the producers would come to the writers and verbally ask for "All the violence you can give us," but never put it in writing.

The show was criticized just as heavily for its portrayal of the gangsters as Italian-Americans. Salkowitz remembers that the studio said they would not make changes in the names, "and of course we immediately did. So we started using German names, some Jewish names, Irish names." On the other hand, "We took our guys into spaghetti joints, drinking red wine, asking about 'Momma, howsa Momma?' Two guys, ready to kill each other, talking about when they were kids in the street, the priests used to chase them. They were Italians, no question."

The Untouchables was produced by Quinn Martin, who also produced *The FBI*, which ran from 1965 to 1974, and the writers again found the criminals were the most interesting characters to write, because as Ed Waters says, the FBI agents were "stick figures." The reason for this was the involvement of the Bureau itself in the series, the most intensive involvement of any organization in a series based on its exploits.

The Bureau was protective of the image of its agents to an absurd degree. Don Brinkley wrote an early show in the series in which the lead, Inspector Erskine, came down with a cold and had to decide if he would let his assistant handle the case. The script went to the Bureau for approval. It came back with the instructions that FBI agents do not catch colds. They had to disable Erskine some other way. Agents were not allowed to be shown in anything other than a jacket and tie, were not allowed to have their sleeves rolled up, and they were never to be shown drinking coffee or eating doughnuts.[7] As Charles Larson, a writer and producer on the show, recalls, their objections were usually over "some damned thing that wasn't important." While the Bureau did have a rigid view of itself, Larson says, "They let us get away with things. They allowed us to have black agents, which they did not have at the time. We told them it would be good for their image. They agreed."

The stories were, in theory, based on real cases. E. Arthur Kean remembers that Charles Larson would give him a case, then tell him to change it as much as possible. Apparently there was a fear the criminals might sue if it was too close. Kean says, "We changed the names to protect the guilty." Don Brinkley recalls that the Bureau was more flexible later on and that sometimes the writers would work backwards. They would come up with a story, take it in to Charles Larson, and he would rummage through the FBI files to find a case it was close to. Until the last year of the series, the Bureau had to approve every storyline.

The scripts were not only shown to the Bureau, but went up to its head, J. Edgar Hoover. In one first draft script E. Arthur Kean made a typographical error that had Erskine taking a "parting shit" instead of a "parting shot." Kean, knowing the script was going to Hoover, left it in. Larson, also knowing the script was going to Hoover, had him take it out.[8]

Just as Roy Huggins saw the flip side of Westerns with *Maverick*, he also saw the flip side of cop shows. His inspiration was to try to put a Western in contemporary form, i.e., have a hero who moves around from place to place and has no commitments. He realized audiences would probably think the man was a bum. Then it occurred to him, "But what if he was a fugitive from justice for a crime he had not committed?" He wrote up a three-page treatment called *The Fugitive*, but everybody who read it[9] thought it glorified a criminal, even though Huggins explained that the voice of the "all-knowing narrator" told you each week that he was innocent. Everybody disliked it but Leonard Goldenson, the head of ABC, who said, "Roy, that's the best idea for a television series I've ever heard," and it went on the air.

Some years later Huggins ran into Goldenson, who asked him if he had any trouble selling *The Fugitive* before he sold it to ABC. Huggins asked him why he asked, and Goldenson said he had "nothing but trouble" over the series from his network people and from the public, such as the letters the American Legion wrote "saying it was Un-American" for suggesting the American justice system might not work.

Don Brinkley thought at the outset of *The Fugitive* that it was a "one-joke" show, but later, writing for it, he came to appreciate what the situation gives the writer: "The hero wakes up in the morning and he's in trouble. There's always Lt. Girard somewhere."

Lawyers

The most traditional, even conservative, lawyer show was *Perry Mason*, which was based on stories written by Erle Stanley Gardner. Protective of his franchise, Gardner wrote three- to four-page letters on each script complaining of holes in the plots. Sy Salkowitz remembers checking out the original stories and finding the same plot holes in Gardner's stories. Part of the plotting problems was from *Perry Mason* being what is called a "closed mystery" in which the identity of the villain is not known at the beginning. Salkowitz finds writing this kind of show "probably one of the most difficult techniques in television." He compares it to "peeling back the onion. You unearth the clues, you have to see where they lead, then you peel back another layer, you see what it looks like."

One of the best lawyer series, *The Defenders*, came out of live television. Reginald Rose was sitting around the beach one day with his friend and lawyer Jerome Leitner (who later was the technical advisor for the series), who said that no play, TV show, or movie about the law and the courts had ever been accurate. Rose could not resist the implied challenge and suggested, "Suppose I write a courtroom drama that is accurate. Will you go over it for me?" Leitner agreed, and Rose wrote "The Defender," which was broadcast as a two-part *Studio One* episode in 1957. Jack Gould, a former court reporter who was then the television critic for the *New York Times*, reviewed the first part and criticized the show as inaccurate. Rose wrote a reply, and Gould wrote back, "Dear Reginald Rose. You may be right." Rose cannot recall ever getting a good review from Gould after that.

A series based on the father–son defense team from "The Defender" was pitched to CBS and a pilot was made on film. CBS turned it down. Then in May 1961, John F. Kennedy's new head of the Federal Communications Commission, Newton Minow, made a speech to the National Association of Broadcasters in which he described television as "a vast wasteland." When William S. Paley met with the FCC and was asked what he was doing to improve television, he told them he had a series coming up he thought they would like. It was *The Defenders*, which premiered in the fall of that year.

Even though the pilot had been shot in Hollywood, *The Defenders* was both written and produced in New York. This gave Rose access to writers from live television and the New York stage who did not wish to go to Hollywood. The producer of the show was Herbert Brodkin and Rose was officially the story editor, but everybody agreed it was Rose's show. Brodkin said of Rose, "He created it. He lives with it. He provides a consistent point of view."[10]

The writers who worked on the show also spoke highly of Rose's individual contributions to their work. Peter Stone said, "He sends you back and back and *back* for rewriting. My first draft never has human beings in it. He is always telling me, 'Go back and put the *conflicts* in.' " John Vlahos said, "In my case, I get so involved with the people, I have practically no story. He's always sending me back to put the *story* in."[11]

Rose found working with the writers had "its ups and downs. Except for a very few scripts, we had to rewrite everything. They weren't good enough." Rose tried to get the writers to do their best, but often after a first reading with the cast (something often done in live television, but seldom in filmed drama at the time), it was necessary to rewrite. Rose, in the first season, or David Shaw or William Woolfolk in later seasons, would then start to rewrite scenes not in their order in the script, but in the order in which they were going to be filmed. Rose figures that he wrote sixteen episodes and rewrote most of the others.

William Woolfolk and Rose had been friends since Rose's early days in television when Woolfolk would read and comment on his scripts. Woolfolk was not primarily a TV writer but had written for comic books (*Captain Marvel*) as well as published magazines. Rose talked him into story editing on a part-time basis for the show, then fulltime. Woolfolk and Rose would discuss a story idea with a writer over lunch. Sometimes the idea came from the writer, more often it came from the two of them, and then the writer would do an outline and up to three drafts of the script. Woolfolk was amazed at how many writers came in with outlines and scripts that were totally different from the story that had been discussed. He also had trouble getting writers to turn in material. They kept insisting it was "not right" yet. Woolfolk told them, "Do you want me to go on television Thursday at eight and tell the audience we don't have a show because the script is not right?"

Woolfolk says the actors were sometimes intimidated by the substance of the material. On one show about a phony minister E. G. Marshall, who played the older lawyer, objected to lines given the minister on grounds that they were things his minister had said. Robert Reed, who played the son, was so afraid of this episode that he left for the week of its production and went to Oklahoma. Reed's lines were rewritten for Marshall, and Reed later apologized. On another occasion, Marshall called Woolfolk and said, "I have a scene where I come in a door and I don't have any lines. What do I do?"

Woolfolk replied, "Say, 'Hello.' "

While *Perry Mason* did conventional murder cases, *The Defenders* took on a variety of social issues. Edith Efron wrote in *TV Guide* that the standard Rose script for the show deals with a man who has the law on his side, but who usually turns out to be a bad person, while the person who has broken the law is usually a good person with "noble motives."[12] As the producer Herbert Brodkin told her, "It's a *liberal* show. I'm a conservative Republican in my personal life, but I'm a reeking liberal in my artistic life. Maybe I do it to shock. I'd call this the most liberal show on the air."[13]

The show was produced not by a sponsor, but by the network, so Rose and Woolfolk had to deal only with the network censors. Woolfolk says Rose found the best way to deal with the censors was make them write down a list of what they did not want. The first thing that would happen was that the censors would realize how ridiculous some of their requests were and drop them. Then it became a matter of negotiating with the network.

These negotiations led to one of the best shows. Rose had an outline for a story in which a black District Attorney turns out to be the villain. The network people were afraid audiences for *The Defenders* would be upset the villain was black. Rose's attitude was, "What the hell, anybody can be a bad guy." The network stood firm, and Rose finally said, "I'll drop this if you let me do a show on the blacklist."

The three network executives said, "O.K. If you do it with taste."

Rose shot back, "You mean the way you did the actual blacklisting with taste?" There was no reply, but they let him do the show. Rose himself was working on another script, but he called up Ernest Kinoy and asked him if he wanted to do it. Kinoy did and won an Emmy for himself and the star, Jack Klugman, for the 1964 episode.[14]

Both Rose and Woolfolk agree Kinoy was the best writer on the show. His scripts came in ready to shoot and in need of very little rewriting, if any. One of his scripts was "The Non-Violent," which was shown on June 6, 1964. The Prestons are called in to defend a young, rich, white man who has participated in a civil rights demonstration led by a black minister. The young man is perfectly willing to spend time in jail, but the minister eventually agrees to the compromise the Prestons work out. The young man is disillusioned by the minister's action. The strengths of the script are that it deals with what was a very hot issue at the time and that it gives the actors, especially E. G. Marshall, James Earl Jones as the minister, and Ivan Dixon as a black lawyer, good scenes to play. Some of the secondary character writing is also good, such as a municipal court judge who says he's not used to hearing the names of Brandeis, Holmes, and Jefferson in his court. The weaknesses of the script include an inevitable didactic quality. Some of the characters are obviously drawn and their dialogue is too "on the nose," too much an obvious statement of how they feel or what their positions are. The episode also suffers from typical early sixties television direction: many big close-ups of the actors as they make their speeches, usually with very simple lighting. The most realistic-looking sequence is the opening sequence of the demonstration, shot with a hand-held camera in the early direct cinema style.

After *The Defenders* Rose decided never to do a television series again. He simply found it "too hard," especially since he, Woolfolk, and David Shaw were doing 35 or 36 shows a year with a staff of three. When Rose left the show, he asked Woolfolk to continue it. Woolfolk told him he was only doing the show because of Rose, and said, "I couldn't survive doing it without you." Woolfolk left television and turned to writing novels. Rose moved into theatrical films and occasional television movies and miniseries.

With several cop shows on the air, and several shows about lawyers, it was natural that somebody would try to combine the two. One bizarre attempt was the 1963–64 ninety-minute series *Arrest and Trial*. In the first 45 minutes Sergeant Nick Anderson (Ben Gazzara) would track down and arrest suspects, then in the second 45 minutes Attorney John Egan (Chuck Connors) would prove they were innocent. Don Brinkley says, "It probably sounded great in the room" when it was pitched to network or the studio, but Sy Salkowitz would not even go that far. He thinks the show was obviously conceived by a Universal executive who had not thought it through. Salkowitz thinks the executive probably just said, "*Arrest and Trial!* We'll arrest 'em and then we'll try 'em," and everybody at the network said, "Yeah." Salkowitz defines the problem of writing for the show: "If Ben Gazzara made a good arrest, Chuck Connors couldn't get him off. If Chuck Connors got him off, it made Ben Gazzara look like a stupid ass." Salkowitz's solution was to have the suspect a fugitive from another jurisdiction, so all Gazzara had to do was catch him and not have to prove anything against him, and Connors could get him off.[15]

Doctors and Other Professionals

Writing about television in the years of the Kennedy Administration, broadcast historian Mary Ann Watson calls *The Defenders* "clearly the jewel of New Frontier character dramas," which she defines:

> They were programs based on liberal social themes in which the protagonists were professionals in service to society. This new breed of episodic TV hero struggled with occupational ethics and felt a disillusionment with the values of the past . . .
> Unlike the action-adventure series in which the heroes settled their problems with a weapon, the problems of New Frontier character dramas were not always resolved. Poverty, prejudice, drug addiction, abortion, capital punishment, and other issues of public policy did not lend themselves to tidy resolutions. The loose ends of the plot might get tied together, but the world was not necessarily a better place at the end of the story.[16]

Among the other series she fits into this category are *Dr. Kildare* and *Ben Casey*, both of which started their runs in 1961 (the same season as *The Defenders*).

Dr. Kildare was in theory based on the older MGM film series of the same name. E. Jack Neuman, who wrote the pilot, looked at one of the films and thought it bore no resemblance to medicine at all. He went to the L.A. County General Hospital to do research and found it crawling with screenwriters: Walter Newman was doing research for the film *The Interns* and James Mosher was researching for *Ben Casey*. The staff used to ask Neuman, "Which screenwriter are you?" He did live like an intern for three months at the hospital, doing "the scut work, and they used to think I was an intern. I learned the feel of what it was like to be a doctor. And that's how I got the idea for really making it very authentic."

He thinks the series got off the track by concentrating too much on the diseases of the week. He suggests, "It's the story of Dr. Kildare, not the story of the disease. They just couldn't get it through their head. They would rack their brain for some great exotic disease or something." Because of this search for diseases, *Dr. Kildare* became what Lou Shaw calls "more gimmicky," in the sense that the stories depended on the disease. This meant, however, that the show could do stories that brought to light little-known medical conditions.

David Victor, the series producer, once approached Sy Salkowitz and asked him for "something really unusual." Salkowitz came up with the first network medical show on sickle cell anemia, a disease that strikes primarily blacks. As Salkowitz puts it, "In a sense I integrated Blair Hospital," with guest stars Ruby Dee and Ossie Davis. Salkowitz got no negative reaction from the network: "It seemed that everybody kind of thought maybe it was time, but nobody had done it yet." He was also pleased to read several years later about a young researcher working toward a cure for the disease who developed his interest in the subject from having seen that episode.

The network, NBC, was not always so lenient. President Lyndon Johnson called up Neuman and asked him to do an episode on venereal disease. Neuman wrote it but the network would not do it. Neuman did another story about the birth control pill, but the network again would not allow it. Neuman complained to the *New York Times*, and he got a call from the president of NBC, Mort Werner. Werner told him, "Go after them. Chew their ass. Tear them apart." Werner had been in favor of the show, but it had been shot down by the Board of Directors.

Neuman thought the other medical series, *Ben Casey*, was "run a lot better than *Kildare* eventually, because Jim Mosher produced it and stayed with it. *Ben Casey* always gave you that hard grit and substance of reality." Lou Shaw, who wrote for both medical series, says, "In some ways I think *Casey* was a better-plotted show, a better-developed show." He thinks it had a "much stronger lead" character in Ben Casey, whom Shaw calls a hero "unique for television at that time." Although Richard Chamberlain had both strength and charm as Kildare, Vince Edwards is, in Shaw's words, "a very intense, inward kind of guy. He hulks, and I think that's his persona that he's never gotten away from, really." With an actor with those qualities playing Casey, it was then easier to get him involved in conflict with his boss or his patients, such as the story D. C. Fontana did in which Casey is sick and put in a room with a patient who thinks he, the patient, is a leprechaun.

The year 1962 saw the first dramatic series about psychiatry, *The Eleventh Hour*. Sam Rolfe created the series for NBC, and the network insisted on having the American Medical Association seal of approval on the show. Rolfe went to the AMA, and they assigned him a medical doctor to head a panel of between 20 and 25 psychiatrists and psychologists. That number gave them enough different points of view so that the writers could find someone on the panel who could approve a method of treatment they wanted to use in the show, since, as Rolfe says, "There was a great deal of argument and division as to what a psychiatrist or a psychologist could do at that time." Rolfe continues:

We started with the story. Every time a writer would come in with a story we liked, we would take that writer and assign him with a psychiatrist or a psychologist who did some work in that field. He would be able to call that guy with questions to help direct him along the lines that we went. And we would work it in as accurate as we could make it. We always managed to get the [character of the] psychiatrist or psychologist more involved than they normally would, probably. Some of it we just said was experimental, which turned out to be true in later life.

If the writers found the medical people were helpful, the medical people found the series helpful to them as well. Rolfe once asked the psychiatrist who was the head of the panel why they helped with the show, and the psychiatrist told him:

> You have to realize something. We send people now to lecture around the country, to explain psychiatry. How it works, how it doesn't work. We played to empty houses. We send people out now to do the same thing, and they say, "So-and-so, on the panel of *The Eleventh Hour*." We can fill the house. These people now come and listen to what we have to say.
> At least you are opening the doors to people who would never even think there's a place to go [for their] problems, to say, "There's a doctor here to help you." That's the up side of this. The bad side is they expect him to do miracles.

The Eleventh Hour only lasted two years because of an odd twist of casting fate. The psychiatrist in the series was played in the first year by Wendell Corey, who was battling alcoholism at the time. He had difficulty completing his lines, and by the end of the first year he was replaced by Ralph Bellamy, who was a better and more reliable actor than Corey. The problem was, he was not as sympathetic as Corey had been. Rolfe says, "Wendell Corey, with those clear blue eyes looking into the camera, worked for the series. Ralph didn't. I guess it was the reaction in those eyes. Never mind they were swimming in alcohol. Everybody thought they were swimming in tears."

E. Jack Neuman followed up *Dr. Kildare* with a series about a different kind of professional, a high school teacher, but *Mr. Novak* was not a comedy like *Mr. Peepers*. Neuman thought, "Maybe I can do something without a stethoscope or a gun or a lawbook." Just as he had gone to the hospital to research *Kildare*, he went to high schools, and he encouraged the writers on the series to go as well. He told them, "I know we all went to high school. Forget where you went to high school. It's different now . . . . They'll welcome you with open arms. Just go there for a day. You'll get your story. Take a smell. Talk to the kids. Talk to the teachers. Remember, you're writing about teachers, not kids." Neuman was upset when the writers came in with stories focused on teenagers. He thinks they were just too lazy to do the research required.

Like *The Defenders* and *Dr. Kildare*, *Mr. Novak* got into contemporary social issues, notably with Neuman's script "A Single Isolated Incident," which played October 22, 1963. The episode deals with the first racial incident at the school and the reaction of the faculty and staff to it. The reaction to the program was strong, even to the point of hate mail coming in. Unlike more obviously liberal shows such as *The Defenders* and *East Side, West Side* (a show about a social worker in New York), *Mr. Novak* attracted a more conservative audience.[17] When Mr. Novak took a drink in one episode, the show got 100 letters a day protesting a teacher drinking, and a professor in Texas organized a protest campaign.[18]

The idea that the hero of a television series could be a professional even extended to a series about the military. Gene Roddenberry created a show in 1963 about the Marine Corps called *The Lieutenant*. Sy Salkowitz recalls:

> Gene Roddenberry said, "This is not a show about the Marine Corps. This is a show about a junior executive whose corporation happens to be the Marine Corps." Now, we didn't have the phrase yuppie then, but that's what he was. He lived in Oceanside with a couple of other Marine lieutenants. They used to go surfing and they had girlfriends, and all kinds of things. It was wide open.

Television in the early sixties, like American society at the time, was beginning to open up.

·8·

SMALL TOWNS, TALKING HORSES, AND RELATED GALAXIES

Realistic Comedies of the Early Sixties

Allan Manings was living and working in Canada, having escaped the blacklist in New York. He and his then-wife had a 40-acre farm where they raised horses. He was told a local mushroom farmer would pay for horse manure. Meanwhile, his occasional work for American television series made by Joe Connelly and Bob Mosher at Universal required a few trips to Los Angeles and long-distance conferences. One day Universal asked if he could move to California. On the same day the mushroom farmer came to buy the manure. He paid Manings $30 for several hundred pounds. Manings said, "This is what they pay for horse shit here. I'm going to California, where they *really* pay better."

One of the shows Connelly and Mosher created was *Leave It to Beaver*. The show was on CBS in 1957–58, then on ABC from 1958 to 1963. Manings liked the show, but since his writing tried to be realistic, he had certain difficulties with its vagueness, like the kind of work Ward Cleaver did. He asked Connelly and Mosher, "What if he comes home one day and says, 'June, sit down. We have to talk. I got fired today.' She says, 'What, the peanut stand is gone?' What does she say to him?" He never got an answer. The show was also vague about other details: the boys were not allowed to ask for a glass of milk, since it was thought the show might be sold later in syndication to a soft drink company. Likewise, the only food they were allowed to ask for was "The usual" or "Junk" or "Some of that junk."

Richard Conway found other restrictions. Child labor laws limited the use of the child actors, which led to scenes where Ward comes home and asks June what the kids have been up to. She tells him, which kept them from having to shoot scenes of the kids actually doing those things, as well as giving June and Ward more screen time.

As much as he liked the show when he was writing on it, Manings later began to believe that all shows like *Beaver* and *Father Knows Best* were "a terrible distortion" because the average kid's father was not as all-wise as the fathers on those shows, and he was afraid kids might not appreciate their real fathers. The idealized portrait did appeal to audiences, and not just in the United States. In 1969 Richard Conway and his wife were traveling in the Far East. When the Conways' Japanese guide learned he had written *Leave It to Beaver*, he then introduced Conway everywhere as the show's writer. The guide told Conway the Japanese loved *Beaver* because it was about the family.

If *Leave It to Beaver* was a slightly romanticized view of suburban life, then *The Andy Griffith Show* was a slightly romanticized view of small-town life. Allan Manings describes the writing process on *Leave It to Beaver* as, "Well, I sat in an office and wrote *Leave It to Beaver*." The writing process on *The Andy Griffith Show* was more complicated. At the end of each filming season, producer Sheldon Leonard, the former character actor who had produced *The Danny Thomas Show*, and Aaron Ruben, who also wrote many episodes, would meet in a week-long seminar with the writers they hoped to use the following season. In later seasons, Griffith joined the meetings as well. The writers and producers would toss around ideas for possible episodes, and at the end of the meetings writers would either volunteer for particular ideas or be assigned to them. (Writers Guild rules were later changed so that producers could not get this free use of writers' imaginations.) The outlines and then the scripts were developed from those ideas, then read and approved by Leonard and Ruben, then read by the regular cast and revisions made, with input from the cast.[1]

The result of this scriptwriting process was a series of subtler, more complex scripts than those written for *Beaver*. The plots were not more complex, but there was a greater willingness, as the show continued, to slow down the action for character comedy, a hallmark of the Griffith show. Actor Don Knotts has pointed out that while in the beginning of the series the emphasis in the writing was on the plot, Griffith would begin to tell everybody how the people back home talked. Knotts said, "We got a little static at first because they'd say, 'We can't stop the story,' but the more we did it, the more they liked it. Soon they began to write it into the scripts, and that turned out to be one of the things in the show that people identified with the most. . . ."[2]

One reason the show could do this kind of comedy was that it was shot like a film with only one camera and without an audience present, as opposed to the three-camera shooting of *I Love Lucy*. The tendency in writing an audience show is to go for joke comedy rather than character comedy. The actors and producers feel much more comfortable if the audience is laughing constantly, or at least regularly. The audience show develops a distinctive repeated rhythm in the writing: straight-line, straight-line, punch line. Needless to say, often the jokes are arbitrary and do not come out of the characterization.[3]

The humor in *The Andy Griffith Show* was found very much in the characters and their typical small-town attitudes, and it is not surprising that one of the writing teams on the show was Jim Fritzell and Everett Greenbaum, who after leaving *Mr. Peepers* eventually wrote for several seasons on another rural comedy, *The Real McCoys*, before coming to the Griffith show. Between 1961 and 1964, they wrote 29 scripts for Griffith, including one that introduced Gomer Pyle, who was based on a mechanic Greenbaum once had work on his car.[4] Greenbaum and Fritzell were not involved in spinning off Gomer into his own series: "It was kept a secret from us." They tried writing one episode, but thought the series made Gomer dumber than he had been on the Griffith show. (On the other hand, Rick Mittleman, who wrote for *Gomer Pyle USMC*, thought of the show as *Billy Budd* in comic terms: the innocent versus the nasty sergeant.) Greenbaum and Fritzell did not write for any of the other rural comedies that sprang up on the networks, particularly CBS, after the success of the Griffith show. Greenbaum says, "I couldn't watch them," let alone write for them, since he thought they were simple-minded.

It is possible to do character comedy in a three-camera audience show, as *The Dick Van Dyke Show*, which premiered the year following *The Andy Griffith Show*, proved. Carl Reiner, after the last of Sid Caesar's shows in the late fifties, was sent several scripts for situation comedies. He did not like them, and his wife Estelle told him, "You can write better scripts than these."[5] Reiner kept thinking, "What do I know about that's different from anything else?" The answer finally occurred to him: writing for a television show. He spent the summer of 1959 developing what he called *Head of the Family*, in which he would star as a writer named Rob Petrie who worked for a television show and had a wife and child. Unlike *Beaver* and other "family" shows of the fifties, the audience would not only know what the father did, but see him do it.[6]

Reiner filmed the pilot as a one-camera show, but it did not sell. When he was put together with Sheldon Leonard, Leonard suggested two changes: that the show be done three-camera, and that Reiner *not* play the lead, which was eventually given to Dick Van Dyke.[7] Reiner had not only written the original pilot, but scripts for thirteen episodes. They were, however, written for the one-camera technique, but Leonard went over them with Reiner. As Reiner recalled, "In two short sessions in his home, he taught me how to make my thirteen one-camera shows into three-camera shows and how to extend scenes and make them more like plays."[8]

Reiner learned fast. He later said, "I was the story editor, head writer, and producer. It was the hardest single job I ever had in my life. The first year I wrote twenty scripts, the second year, about twenty-two."[9] Like the Griffith show, the Van Dyke show was not written by someone just sitting in an office. Sheldon Leonard again sat in on the story and script discussions. Writer Bill Persky described his presence:

> Sheldon would sit behind me in a high chair as I sat at the table. As the reading progressed and the script got progressively worse, Sheldon's breathing

would become deeper and deeper. I sometimes didn't hear the readings, all I heard was Sheldon's breathing! Leonard would then declare, "This script is a disaster," opening up the rewrite session. "O.K., who wants to jump in first?" We'd start on page one and fix it—nobody left.[10]

The discussions would go on at some length and then the writers would rewrite. What was being brought together here was a combination of the scriptwriting style Leonard had developed for his other shows and the intense collaborative process that Reiner knew from *Your Show of Shows.*

Because of that collaborative process, *The Dick Van Dyke Show* helped develop almost as many major television writers as *Your Show of Shows* did. One of Reiner's first teams of writers was Garry Marshall and Jerry Belson. Marshall had written gags for comedians Phil Foster and Joey Bishop.[11] Belson, who according to one studio biography began his writing career doing captions for Porky Pig comic books,[12] remembered seeing Marshall on the Desilu lot before they were paired: "Garry was the Willy Loman of comedy. He'd walk around the Desilu lot from show to show with a big bag of scripts."[13] Marshall and Belson were paired first on *The Danny Thomas Show*, then worked on the first year of *The Dick Van Dyke Show*. Reiner described them as "wonderful,"[14] and they went on to write and/or produce, collectively or individually, *The Odd Couple, Happy Days, Laverne and Shirley*, and *The Tracey Ullman Show.*

At the beginning of the 1963–64 season, Bill Persky and Sam Denoff joined the show. They had written for radio in the late fifties, then for *The Andy Williams Show*. They subsequently became story editors on *The Dick Van Dyke Show*. Rick Mittleman, who wrote for the show when they were story editors, says it was "probably the happiest experience of my half-hour writing," because when the scripts were rewritten by them or by Reiner, they would only improve them. Persky and Denoff went on to write and/or produce, collectively or individually, *That Girl* and *Kate and Allie.*

If *Dr. Kildare* and *The Defenders* were New Frontier dramas, then *The Dick Van Dyke Show* was New Frontier comedy.[15] Not only was Rob Petrie a young professional, like the heroes of the New Frontier dramas, he, like Kennedy, had an attractive young wife who had, at least once, a semi-profession herself (Jacqueline Kennedy had worked as a newspaperwoman and Laura Petrie had been a dancer). Just as the Kennedys showed an interest in culture that helped pull America out of the cultural stagnation of the fifties, *The Dick Van Dyke Show* showed a greater openness than either *Beaver* or *Griffith.* Both of the earlier shows deal with closed-off worlds of suburbia and small towns. *Van Dyke*, like the Kennedys, was very urban and open to possibilities (however limited they might be for the women in the series: Laura was only a housewife during the series, and considerable humor was found in Rob's co-writer Sally in her efforts to find a man).

It is difficult to imagine one of the most memorable of the *Van Dyke* episodes showing up on either *Beaver* or *Griffith.* For their first script for the show, Persky and Denoff wrote "That's My Boy??" in which Rob recounts, in flashback, how he became convinced that their son had been switched with that of another couple at the hospital. Sheldon Leonard suggested that the punch line of the episode be that the other couple was black. Persky said they thought it would not be possible, but Leonard ran interference for them with the network and the sponsor's representative, agreeing to reshoot the ending with a couple of another race if it did not work with a black couple, and even agreeing to pay for the show if they decided not to run it.[16]

One reason the show was able to get away with the episode is that it was performed in front of an audience. Leonard depended on the audience reaction to convince the sponsors and the network that audiences would not be upset. He guessed right. The entrance of the black couple got what Van Dyke later said was the longest laugh in the series, and they had to cut 45 seconds of the laugh out when the show was edited.[17] The network received mail "by the satchel," as Leonard put it,[18] and none of it complained about the show.[19] Leonard used the three-camera technique to show to sponsors and networks that television could deal with the opening up of American culture of the time.

Unrealistic Comedies of the Sixties

Several writers interviewed for this book tell of the famous incident in which Ray Walston, who played the title role in *My Favorite Martian*, complained to the writer of a line in the script, "A Martian wouldn't say that." The writers usually quote this story to show how weird actors are, but writers speak of their shows in the same way. One of the ways in which American television opened up in the sixties was in the development of series that did not appear to be realistic: shows about Martians, witches, talking horses, and other such creatures. What the writers of those shows tend to remember about them, however, was how necessary it was for someone writing such a show to find, if not some connection with reality, at least some sense of the world the show was trying to create. Ray Walston was probably not wrong: *this* Martian in *this* world of *this* show would not talk like this, and twenty years later actor William Daniels would likewise persuade producer Joel Rogosin he was right when he looked over his lines as the talking car in *Knight Rider* and said, "I don't think the car would say this."

Larry Rhine spent two years in the early sixties writing for *Mr. Ed*, the series about a talking horse. George Burns was one of the owners of the show and would occasionally sit in on the writing sessions. Rhine agrees completely with Burns's comment, "If you don't believe the horse talks, you can't do this show." Rhine talks about the writers' approach to the show:

> We played the horse as a teenager. We played Wilbur as the father. And Connie Hines as the mother. So consequently, [since] this was in the sixties, we

were able to have Mr. Ed letting his mane grow long, and wanting a pad of his own, meeting a filly who was taller than he and getting buildups, playing the guitar, running away from home, doing all the things that teenagers would do.
  Once again you go into realism. . . . We have all these wonderful get-togethers on Thanksgiving and Christmas. Animals don't have that, thanks to us, because we've separated them [from their families]. So we got premises out of that, [one] where Ed wanted to meet his father. We found the father working in the circus. And we had the two of them singing "My Papa."

  Richard Powell wrote a rewrite of the pilot, five of the first six episodes, and five episodes a season of *Hogan's Heroes*, a mid-sixties series set in a slapstick version of a World War II German prisoner-of-war camp. There were some concerns at the network as the show was being prepared that it might "trivialize" the war, but as Powell notes, "Once the first ratings came in, then all pressure ceased from the network about that or anything else."
  Powell himself tried to ground his episodes in reality by getting "a dramatic plot and then changing it to comedy." He avoided trivializing by not doing "the usual sitcom things, like Colonel Klink's surprise birthday party. I tried to show the German system worked by fear. Everybody was afraid of the upper echelon, so Hogan manipulated Klink's fear of the Gestapo, and the Gestapo's fear of Berlin." Once Powell wrote in a British colonel who was about to screw up one of Hogan's schemes, and Powell had Hogan say, "I think we have to kill him," which got a gasp from the cast as they read the script for the first time. Powell says, "They were shocked because they were discussing a real killing. But that was the sort of thing that was lurking in the background, and if you could fuse some of that reality into there, I always felt you had a better show." It helped that two of the cast members, Robert Clary and John Banner, had been in German camps. On the other hand, Bob Crane was, in Powell's words, "a square Republican" who was often confused by the fairly straightforward storylines: "He liked them, and he did them very well, but quite often he wouldn't understand them."
  If *The Dick Van Dyke Show* was at least a partially realistic portrait of an American family, *The Addams Family* came so close to being an idealized portrait of family life that, much to the amusement of its producer, Nat Perrin, a psychologist wrote an article about how it was the best family on television because there was no fighting among the family members. Perrin says that while that might have been wonderful from a psychologist's point of view, it made it very difficult to write the show, because after the first few weeks there was nobody in the family to bounce the comedy off of, since there was no conflict, the way there was later in *All in the Family*. On the other hand, the writers of *The Addams Family* had a distinct advantage in that they could show a very strong sexual relationship between Gomez and Morticia because the show was not taken seriously enough by the censors to bother with it.[20]

...ce, *The Munsters* appeared to be a show similar to *The Ad-* but the writers of each created their own world. In *The Addams* family knew it was weird. In the pilot for *The Munsters* the ...d wild things, but for the series the creators Bob Mosher and Joe Con..., ...ided to have the family think it was normal and play the comedy off their trying to behave normally and other people's reactions to it. Richard Conway says that he and his partner Rowland MacLane welcomed writing on the show, especially as a break from writing Mosher and Connelly's *Beaver*: "We were going from a mild family show to a wild comedy, where you could always have Grandpa blow up the lab or the dog or something." Conway later wrote for the animated version of *The Addams Family*, where they did not have to worry about the expense of sets and props and the humor got more physical.

The 1966 ABC series *Batman* also established its own camp reality. Robert Dozier was asked by his father, William Dozier, the producer of the series, to do an early episode that introduced The Joker. Robert Dozier recalls:

> *Batman* was fun because it kind of released you from the disciplines of ordinary drama, and so you kind of just let it hang out and went with it. Bunny [Lorenzo] Semple [Jr.], who was the story editor, had written the pilot, and was with the show, and later on became a fairly well known screenwriter. He was just outraged at some of the stuff I'd done. It was just too much even for Bunny. He rewrote a lot of it, but he was angry with me. I had Batman trying to prevent a robbery and he and Robin came zooming up in the car in front of a museum and racing out of the car to prevent some horrible thing from happening. A policeman goes, "Excuse me, Batman, but this is a 'no parking' zone."
>
> He said, "You're quite right, officer," and he moved his car. Well, Bunny Semple just went crazy. "That's not Gotham reality."
>
> "O.K., O.K., Bunny. It's not Gotham reality. You know more about Gotham reality than I do."

Once a show was established, its limits were set. When Rick Mittleman wrote for *Bewitched*, the writers were expected to stay with the fixed techniques and special effects for Samantha's witchcraft. In the late sixties Mittleman worked on *My World . . . And Welcome to It*, a show inspired by the writings and drawings of James Thurber. The show was mostly live action, but with some animation in the style of Thurber's work. There was no preconceived amount of time to be animated in an episode. Mittleman says, "When you are working on the story, scenes came out as being right for animation."

Unrealistic Drama Series of the Sixties

The opening up of American television also led to an increase in dramatic series that were more imaginative, although the most famous fantasy series of that period, *The Twilight Zone*, began its run in 1959. By the late fifties the live dramas Rod Serling wrote for were dying out. He had long had an idea for a radio anthology series, and the time was ripe for its development as a television series.[21] Serling looked favorably on the idea of a show he owned, which he thought would free him from sponsor influence,[22] especially at a time when the networks were moving from sponsor-ownership to network-ownership of other shows. It was also just possible in 1959 to get another anthology show on the air, although anthology shows were in theory dying as well, which is why the network insisted on a half-hour rather than an hour series.[23] Serling was enough of a "star writer" at CBS to carry an anthology show. The show could not have been done until the late fifties because it had to be done on film and needed a home at a major studio, where the backlot sets could be used. In addition to that, the growing appreciation of the weird in the semi-mass media of the fifties (science fiction B-pictures, *Mad* magazine) provided soil (and perhaps the fertilizer) *The Twilight Zone* could grow in.

Serling himself wrote, or rather dictated (he learned early he thought faster than he could type), 28 of the first season's 35 shows, writing each one in 30 to 40 hours. Because he had been thinking about a show like this for some time, he had a backlog of story ideas. The half-hour format restricted the ways stories could be done, so he spent more time writing the story than developing it.[24]

To get scripts for the episodes Serling did not write, Serling let the world know he and his staff would read submissions from anybody. They were inundated with 14,000 manuscripts in five days, nearly all of them unreadable, and none of which were used. Serling eventually settled on two professional writers, Richard Matheson and Charles Beaumont.[25] Matheson was noted as a writer of short stories in the science fiction and horror line, as well as the screenwriter of such films as *The Incredible Shrinking Man*. Only Serling wrote more *Twilight Zone* scripts than Beaumont, and writer William Nolan says, "Chuck was the perfect *Twilight Zone* writer, more than Matheson or Rod Serling, even. Matheson is very much of a realist who can mentally lose himself in those worlds. He doesn't live in them the way Chuck lived in them."[26]

Other writers were called on as well. E. Jack Neuman was working under contract to MGM at the time, so could only do one *Zone* episode, and that on the sly: "[Director] Buzz Kulik and Buck Houghton [who] was a wonderful producer friend of mine came to me . . . Sunday morning and they didn't have anything to start for Monday. I wrote it that Sunday."

When *The Twilight Zone* was renewed by CBS as mid-season replacement to start again in January 1963, the network insisted on hour shows. Matheson later noted the problem with that: "The ideal *Twilight Zone* started with a really smashing idea that hit you right in the first few seconds, then you played that out, and you had a little flip at the end; that was the structure."[27]

It was a structure that depended not on characters, or even situations, but on a particular kind of limited inventiveness on the part of the writers. The writers had to set up as unusual a situation as possible, but did not have to find a dramatic solution for it. Once writer-producer Aaron Spelling asked Serling how he could turn out so many *Zone* scripts, and Serling replied, "Easy. I don't have to write a third act. The third act is, 'That's the way it is in *The Twilight Zone.*'"[28]

Other producers on fantasy series were not as careful about storytelling and budget limitations. Don Brinkley wrote for producer Irwin Allen's *Voyage to the Bottom of the Sea*, and discovered "the greatest limitation was Irwin Allen. He had the most grandiose ideas. He encouraged you to think big, then got upset when he read the script, 'This'll cost too much.'" Brinkley also got rush calls from Allen at three or four A.M. with ideas for changes he'd heard from the elevator man, and Brinkley either tried to talk him out of them, or else just put them in the script.

In 1962 producer Norman Felton approached Sam Rolfe to help him work out the details of a proposed new series. Felton wanted to do something with spies, and had in fact met with Ian Fleming, the author of the James Bond novels, who suggested a series with a Bondlike hero called Napoleon Solo.[29] Felton could not get Fleming to write any more because Fleming feared fouling up his sale of the film rights to the Bond books to Harry Saltzman, who had just produced the first Bond movie, *Dr. No*. Rolfe, trying to help out a friend, took Felton's notes on Fleming's notes and sat down to write:

> Before I knew it I had created an outfit called U.N.C.L.E. . . . The first thing I knew, I had a headquarters and I was describing the headquarters. It was just so easy. It was just flowing together for me. I gave him about thirty-some pages. He was very excited. "Gee, that's great. What about some more?" He didn't quite say it [like] that. Norman has a way of pushing you along without pushing you. He sort of draws you along. Before I knew it, I had written something like eighty pages of this thing. I had story springboards. I had written scenes that take place to show how various things occurred.

Rolfe discovered twenty years later that Felton had put Ian Fleming's name on the proposal when he took it to NBC.

Broadcast historian Erik Barnouw has suggested that the series of spy shows which began with *The Man from U.N.C.L.E.* in 1964 grew out of the cold war,[30] but Rolfe says he "wanted to get away from the cold war. [It] isn't that I thought the Russians were right or we were wrong," but that he saw his audience watching entertainment shows to get away from things like the cold war. Besides, Rolfe says he did not have anything to contribute to it: "What am I going to say, send more spies in?" His message was slightly different: "I figured it's much nicer to do something where they work together. It's one of the few times where, underneath it all, we can make a statement here," which is why the U.N.C.L.E. organization has a variety of nationalities working for it, and why it tends to work against individual criminals and criminal organizations rather than countries.

Rolfe, in the two years he was on the show, tried to set the right tone for the series:

> The show started out and it wasn't that serious. It had a beat of reality and a beat of absurdity. It's a thing you sense. I don't know how you instill it. You either have it or you don't. And I had it. While I was with the show, I think I for the most part managed to keep one foot in a certain amount of reality.

One trick Rolfe used was to try to get an ordinary human being swept up in the adventures, which provided a realistic counterpoint to the action. Rolfe was discouraged to see after he left that the show tilted more to the absurd side, especially with the gadgets. Near the end of the series, he was living in London with his wife and they saw an episode in which Illya Kuryakin was riding a bomb down to earth. Rolfe turned to his wife and said, "We're spending the last of the royalties, I think. This is not going to go much farther." The show ended shortly thereafter. Rolfe says, "It became a parody of a parody of itself. They were trying to outsmart *Get Smart*, which came on after us."

In 1977 Rolfe prepared a screenplay for a slightly updated version of the show, but MGM decided that since it had sold off its backlot, it would have been too expensive to revive the show. He was not involved in the 1983 television movie *The Return of the Man from U.N.C.L.E.*, saying, "I was so furious with it. It is like somebody set out to figure out what it was that killed *The Man from U.N.C.L.E.* in the end, and do that."

One of the spy series that followed in the wake of *U.N.C.L.E.* was *I Spy*. On the surface it was more realistic than *U.N.C.L.E.*, especially in its use of real locations around the world, but it was still a very glamorous look at two American agents, picking up the exotic locations from the James Bond films rather than the gimmicky hardware. The producer was the ubiquitous Sheldon Leonard, of whom Eric Bercovici, one of the writers on the first season, says, "From a story point of view, I thought Sheldon was a wonderfully creative producer," adding that writing a script

> is like building a brick wall. The dramatic structure has to be there. And there was this mysterious, secret course that producers take where they learn to identify the keystone immediately. And they go for it and they pull it out. And the whole wall comes down. But Sheldon was very good about that. He wouldn't pull out a brick unless he knew there was another brick to go in.

Leonard, perhaps as a result of the success of the "That's My Boy??" episode of *The Dick Van Dyke Show*, cast a young black nightclub comedian, Bill Cosby, in one of the starring roles in the series.[31] Originally Robert Culp was to be the lead and Cosby was to be his sidekick. Bercovici suggested doing an episode in which Cosby "had the good thing to do and Culp plays the second banana." He was told it would never happen, so he wrote "Turkish Delight" with Culp having a romance in the main storyline. Shortly thereafter, Bercovici was told, "Listen, we've had an idea. We're going to have Cosby play the lead, so you're going to have to rewrite the whole show for that."

Bercovici said, "Fine," and simply changed the names over the dialogue. "I didn't do anything else." The romantic interest, who had been written as white, was cast with a black actress, Diana Sands.

Bercovici describes the show in its first season as "a very freewheeling show. You could have scenes where they would talk to each other and not make a whole lot of plot sense." This led to some scenes being ad-libbed, which was encouraged by Leonard, who told the directors to keep the camera on Culp and Cosby whatever they did or said.[32] By its third and last season, the writing was almost nonexistent as the stars ad-libbed, driving the other actors crazy because they were given no cues for their own lines.[33]

While *I Spy* depended on the chemistry and the dialogue of its two stars, *Mission: Impossible* depended on very complicated plotting, squeezing two hours of story into one hour. When Sy Salkowitz went on the show, his experience at writing for *Perry Mason* was useful:

> What you needed to do on *Mission: Impossible* was to figure out what everybody had to do at every particular moment in time. Now we had a technique we used on *Perry Mason* just to keep our ducks in a row, which was a chronological sequence of events, whether you played them or not. You had to know at 10:02 the defendant walked into the room, saw nothing, turned around and walked out and two minutes later the killer came in and killed the guy and four minutes later the defendant walked back in. So, using that chronological sequence of events, you had to lay out what everybody was doing, because your goal [was] to make the solution a little more complicated than it already was.
>
> *Mission: Impossible* was in miniature what *Topkapi* [a 1964 jewel robbery picture] was. You had to figure an absolutely ingenious way of upsetting the impossible. It was mission impossible: you couldn't do this thing. Now, you started out by selecting a mission that was impossible. And if it was too easy to beat, you had to make it more impossible. If it was impossible to beat, then loosen up on it, or put a flaw in it someplace. Because all it needed was one chink. That could be the personality of the villain, it could be something in a house that nobody knew was there, it could be anything. But then you build backwards from it, and you say, "O.K., this is how we'll approach this."
>
> You had to be a master schemer. Now, some guys have minds like that. I happen to have one. Other guys have minds that go in other directions. I wish mine did. But I'm a great schemer.

The original *Star Trek* series, which premiered in 1966, had been in development by Gene Roddenberry for several years. His assistant, D. C. Fontana, thinks that job was a benefit in writing the shows:

If anybody knew *Star Trek* as well as he did, it was me, because I had been with him from the point in 1963[34] when *Star Trek* was little more than half a dozen pieces of paper with some character ideas, the Enterprise, the main concept of the show. As it grew and developed, I was there. I was the person who was taking the dictation and transcribing the dictation tapes into the finalized versions of the format and the scripts. In that time I had sold [scripts to] *Ben Casey* and *Slattery's People*. When it came time to assign writers to the first *Star Trek* scripts, I approached Gene and said I would like to try one. He said, "O.K., fine, because I know you've written. And you know the series better than anybody but me, and what one would you like to write?"

Fontana wrote two *Trek* scripts before deciding to free-lance. The first free-lance job then became a rewrite of another *Trek* script, which led to Fontana being offered the story editorship of the series. Fontana discovered that other writers had problems coming up with stories for the series. They would come in and say, "I see this civilization," but whole civilizations can be difficult to build, especially on a television series budget.[35] And Roddenberry was not concerned with civilizations, perhaps because he had already created his own. According to Fontana, Roddenberry would say to the writers:

> Never mind about that [civilization]. Who are the people? What is the story about? Who is the story about? And how does that affect our people? Is it about our ship, our people? Is it a problem that is brought aboard the ship and creates a problem? Is it one they go to and become involved in? What is the story about in terms of people?

Fontana adds, "If you didn't tell the stories in terms of people, they just never seemed to work." In addition to creating civilizations, some writers, according to Fontana, "got overly involved in the technology and they wound up telling stories about the technology rather than about the people, and that would almost never work."

Even though Roddenberry had originally pitched *Star Trek* as "Wagon Train to the Stars," the story structure was rather different. Fontana describes the format:

> We found that we had a major story running and a minor story running. What usually happened was Kirk, Spock, and McCoy would be very intimately involved with the major story. Then supporting characters, Scott and Sulu, Uhura, maybe Nurse Chapel, Chekov, would be involved in the minor story. Or sometimes one of them would move up to the major story and the others would carry on the minor story themselves, so that we were able to give specific scene time to everybody, but they were carrying on a story. It wasn't just the gratuitous, "Oh, we've got to have a scene with Sulu in it, so let's put him in here." They always had a story they were involved in, or they were involved in the major story. I don't know if you can do that on other shows, or anybody else was doing it. But it worked well for *Star Trek*.

Fontana left the series at the end of the second season, but hardly ended all connections with the show. Fontana was involved with the animated series of the same name in 1973–75, and recalls that they were able to be more creative with both environments and creatures, since, "We [did] not have to worry about the costuming or the prostheses, or any of the things you normally have to worry about. You just draw them." Writing the animation version

> was a little harder to do [with] just 21 minutes of story [for a half-hour show] because of so many commercials in the children's animation. The one thing we did not do was make it a kiddie show. We did *Star Trek*. I thought most of the stories worked well. In only 21 minutes of storytelling we packed a lot of story in. There was very little in the way of subplot, but we did get some very complex stories in.

Fontana also returned to work briefly on *Star Trek: The Next Generation* in the late eighties, but thinks the show lacks the relationships between the main characters the original had:

> There's a coldness, I think, in the characters. Sometimes you get a little bit from Geordi and Worf, and Data is very popular, although he can't be warm. He can be funny, but he can't be warm.
> I think, too, that there are too many characters. I think there are a lot of characters that are each striving for equal time. Marina [Sirtis, who plays Deanna] gets a story, Worf gets a story, Riker gets a story, whereas the way we did it with the subplot, major plot in the original *Trek* I think worked a lot better.

The original *Star Trek* had 54 minutes of story. Most prime-time network shows by the late eighties had 48 minutes of storytelling time. A syndicated show has only 41 minutes of storytelling time. Fontana sees storytelling problems from those syndication limits:

> You have a lot less time to tell a good, full story that has relationships and action. You've got to have one or the other in 41 minutes. It's very difficult to have both. You don't have the plot, subplot as strongly as you did before. Also, instead of a teaser and four acts, it's chopped into a teaser and five acts. I say chopped advisedly, because that's what happens. You get an extremely choppy rhythm to the story, because you are telling the story in approximately eight- or nine-minute bits, with maybe a three-minute teaser, and that's about it. And I think that makes it hard to write the scripts well, because [with] that extreme choppiness, you're always having to break it off [into] extremely short scenes.

Other writers on the new series have problems with Roddenberry's view of humanity in the future. Roddenberry, speaking about the characters of the crew of the new *Enterprise*, said, "Our people do not lie, cheat or steal. They are the best of the best. When you watch the show, you say to yourself, at least once, 'My God, that's the way life should be.' "[36] Tracy Torme, one of the first-season writers, said, "All of these [regular] characters like each other all the time, and for me that was a real big disadvantage."[37] Kasey Arnold-Ince, who wrote "The Final Mission" in the 1990–91 season, agrees, saying that while both she and Roddenberry would like to have a world without conflicts, it does make it difficult to write drama.

Arnold-Ince was asked to put "more character" into her script, which surprised her agent, who thought it was all character. What they came to realize the show wanted was to make the character points and the emotions obvious. Arnold-Ince had originally written a scene between Wesley and Picard in which Wesley's feelings about Picard as a father-figure were mostly subtext. By the time the show was on the air, with a rewrite by staff writer Jeri Taylor, Wesley was talking openly about his feelings, which made for a more conventional scene, the kind of "on-the-nose" writing that television too often falls into.

·9·

COMEDY/VARIETY

Milton Berle and Sid Caesar were not the only stars heading variety shows in the early fifties. A star was a requirement if only to give such shows some identity. Stars could be difficult to come by, as Nat Perrin learned when he tried to produce a series in 1954 called *Shower of Stars*. In addition to the major studios' not wanting their stars to appear on television, stars wanted to see the script first, but how could writers write for a star without knowing *which* star, since both joke and sketch writing is very much writing-to-order? Perrin ended up with one star, but as he sagely observes, "One star is not a shower. One star is a drizzle."

Stars could be not only difficult to come by, but difficult to deal with, as many writers found out. Nat Perrin worked with Red Skelton on some of Skelton's films at MGM, so when approached to produce Skelton's TV show, he opted for the title of Executive Producer so that someone else "more fluent in Red Skelton's language than I was" had to deal directly with Skelton. Perrin just supervised the writers. Larry Rhine wrote for Skelton later and found that although Skelton took a writing credit on the show, he was never in the same room with the writers. He did not know his writers and did not want to know them. Rhine recalls that once Skelton said, "Who needs writers?" The next time he called up the writers' room for a new line, the writers said, "Let him ad-lib it." The writers were particularly bothered by Skelton's habit of gesturing to his head whenever a line got a good response, indicating he just thought it up himself. Rick Mittleman, who wrote for Skelton in 1962–63, thought Skelton feared people would learn he did not make it up, and he kept the writers out of the studio while the show was being taped. Mittleman was paired with writer Bruce Howard, and together they specialized in pantomimes. Mittleman says writers had to "think physical rather than verbal . . . rather than static." Even the pantomime writers had to bring in ten topical jokes each week, out of which jokes for the opening monologues were assembled.

Red Skelton lasted in a variety show from 1951 to 1971; Red Buttons only lasted from 1952 to 1955, and it was only a variety show the first season, then a situation comedy in 1953–54, then back to a variety show. Buttons went through staffs of writers, but he insisted to *TV Guide* in October 1954 that he was not hard on his writers, because he knew "their job is the toughest." He said he was happy with the current writers on the show, but a P.S. to the article notes that four of the five writers at the time of the writing of the article had left the show.[1] One of the tales that writers still tell is the perhaps apocryphal story that Buttons came in one day, picked up a new script, held it in his hand, then announced, "This doesn't feel funny."

Between *Mr. Peepers* and *The Andy Griffith Show*, Everett Greenbaum went to work on *The George Gobel Show* with some reluctance. He thought of himself as a storyteller and

> at first I thought I couldn't construct such deliberate jokes. And the first two weeks I couldn't, but then suddenly in the third week I became very brilliant and wrote jokes that are still being used in one form or another. Every time I run into George [Gobel] at Gelson's [Market], he tells me those jokes. He says, "Remember these jokes? And you said you couldn't write jokes."[2]

Once he got the hang of writing jokes, Greenbaum got back to storytelling by writing sketches for the guest stars. What made this "absolute hell" was that they did not know until two days before the Gobel show aired who the guest star was going to be. Once they wrote sketches for a comic who was replaced at the last minute by dramatic actor George Brent. Greenbaum recalls:

> The worst faux pas we made with a guest was Herbert Marshall. We didn't know that Herbert Marshall had a wooden leg. We wrote a sketch where he's in a submarine and they tilt the whole submarine up and down, right on the stage. We didn't know what to do. So, what we did, every time the submarine would dive, we had Herbert Marshall hang on to a pole that looked like a pole on the subway, and he would turn to the camera and say, "I hate this part of it." It was the funniest thing in the sketch.

The head writer of the Gobel show the first two years was Hal Kanter, who Greenbaum says, "rewrote everything, or put it all together. Sometimes added. Mostly subtracted. He's quite brilliant." When Kanter left, "his strong arm was gone. Everybody connected with the show was suggesting jokes and rewriting, [including] George's relatives." When a man from the advertising agency suggested changing the straight line to a joke to (a) make the joke senseless and (b) include the name of the sponsor's product, Greenbaum lost his temper, "and by the time I got home to dinner, I'd been fired."

In 1955 both Goodman Ace and Jay Burton left Milton Berle's show and helped create an hour variety show for Perry Como. With Ace in charge of the writing, the writers met from ten A.M. to one P.M. every day,[3] then had the rest of the day off. Burton says Ace did not like to write for more than three hours at a time, and "he just liked to play gin afterwards." Burton found this an immediate advantage for his social life. With Berle's demand that Burton be constantly available to write new jokes, "I didn't have a date for five years. I didn't know when to make it. On *Perry Como* I could date."

Ace supervised the writing the same way Kanter did on the Gobel show. He let everybody throw in ideas without his criticizing, but he would write down what he wanted to use. Burton says, "You didn't know until the end of the week whether your material was in the script." As befitting the more relaxed style of its star, *The Perry Como Show* had a slower pace. There was generally only one sketch, often fairly long but not physically elaborate. Some of the more domestic sketches could have come out of Ace's earlier radio show, *Easy Aces*.

The writers also had to come up with material for the crosstalk between Como and his guests, and it had to be so casual that the show, in Ace's words, "doesn't seem as if there is any writing in it."[4] This leads to the inevitable scenes in which the performers seem to throw out the script and ad-libbed. On the May 16, 1956, show,[5] the guest is Ronald Reagan, who comes out while Como is apparently having trouble with the cue card boy. Como explains the business of cue cards to Reagan, since Reagan's show, *The General Electric Theatre*, is on film. The boy drops the cards, and Como offers to let Reagan come back next week. Reagan replies in the script, "Let's go on this way. This may be funnier than the stuff we had prepared." We all know where that sort of thing led.

Mel Tolkin wrote full-time for Bob Hope for five years in the late sixties and early seventies. Tolkin and Larry Rhine, who also wrote for Hope, both think Hope was one of the nicest comedians to work with and one who fully appreciated writers. With Hope, however, writers wrote for everything. As Tolkin says,

> You work not only for his specials, you work for his gigs, his trips to Vietnam and Korea. You work on dinners, gigs in honor of somebody, charity gigs. Wherever he is, we get a poop sheet that we write jokes [from]: who's on the dais, something about the man being honored, the occasion, areas for comedy . . . and of course the poop about the places, Vietnam and Korea: the temperature, the animals around, what the soldiers eat, where they hang out.

Tolkin did not go on trips, although there were writers who did, for "the immediate, necessary jokes," on changes in base commanders, changes in routes, etc. Tolkin says of himself and the other writers who stayed home, "We wrote long distance."

For the sketches on the Hope shows, producer Mort Lachman would give the writers the subject of the sketch and the names of the guest stars, if known. Each team of writers would then sit down and write a separate sketch based on the idea. The different sketches would be turned in to the producer, who would put the sketch together using the best material from each sketch. This is why the Hope sketches have always been more a collection of gags than a developed sketch, without the consistency, the narrative build, and the characterization of the best of the sketches on *Your Show of Shows* or later on *The Carol Burnett Show*.[6]

Along with Bob Hope, one of the few comedians working in the fifties who continued to do variety and sketch comedy into the nineties was Johnny Carson. Carson first broke into nighttime television in 1955 as a summer replacement for Red Skelton. The *TV Guide* review of his show could serve as a review for his work since: "Not all his opening monologs come off and his sketches are sometimes unamusingly familiar."[7] The sketches during his thirty years on *The Tonight Show* often seem the kinds of material he was doing on his daytime show in the early fifties, e.g., his parody of a daytime television movie host that he continued doing long after local stations had given up having movie hosts. The nostalgic element of the sketch material may have been comforting to the *Tonight Show* audience as an antidote to the immediacy of the jokes in the monologue. What made Carson a success was his ability to *react* in a variety of interesting ways to material, both in the monologues and sketches, which was not working. Often Carson is funnier reacting to a joke that does not work than he is in telling a joke that does.[8]

In the seventies, Thad Mumford learned what killed the traditional variety show. He wrote for a series of variety specials, and heard Jackie Gleason, then guesting on one, say that the problem with variety television was that the singers got all the jokes. Mumford wrote for the Captain and Tennille, and he agrees with Gleason, saying, "Toni Tennille thought of herself as a sketch actress and she wasn't. We wrote some very funny things. I don't remember any of them at all, because I was too busy trying to get on a show called *Maude*."

Ernie Kovacs

Ernie Kovacs was to variety television what *The Twilight Zone* was to dramatic television: bizarre, surreal, not of the traditional American middle-class TV, and understandably the begetter of a cult.

Kovacs worked in radio before moving to local television in the early fifties.[9] His first show was *3 to Get Ready* for WPTZ in Philadelphia, beginning in the fall of 1950, and running from 7:30 to 9:00 A.M. *daily*. Kovacs's experience with live radio helped him, but quickly he began to add visual material, such as "twitching his features in synch with the records (or, sometimes, out of synch with them), then by ad-libbing to goofy props that crew members tossed to him from offstage."[10] When he did write things down, they were very brief descriptions of the actions, or gags, with only a hint of the dialogue, if any.[11] They were more lists than scripts, and his improvisations from them took him behind the scenes, showing off the mechanics of television.

His shows attracted network attention and he eventually moved to New York, doing the same kind of humor. He created recurring characters, such as Percy Dovetonsils (originally called Percy Moosetonsils), a lisping poet who read sentimental nonsense, and the Nairobi Trio, a collection of three people in gorilla masks playing a piano, a xylophone, and a conductor's baton. These characters were not created—like those of Skelton, Gleason, and others—to be loved, or to be a showcase for Kovacs's performing talents. The humor was in the concept, rather than in the performance, and it was this conceptual humor that made Kovacs a cult figure. It also most likely kept him from being a star of the magnitude of Skelton, Gleason, et al. Kovacs's biographer, Diana Rico, suggests that it was the failure of the network, NBC, to give Kovacs an adequate budget for his shows that kept him from becoming a bigger star, but Kovacs's humor was probably too intellectual to support a large audience, especially in the fifties.[12]

Kovacs is best remembered for a series of eight half-hour specials he did for ABC in 1961–62, the last one airing in January 1962 shortly after Kovacs's untimely death in an automobile accident. The emphasis in the shows is not on the performers, from whom very little is required, and what little is required is not done that well. Kovacs was more interested in the concept of the joke rather than the execution, although here again he was limited by the budgets the network provided. The money went to staging such complicated technical sequences as a symphony of kitchen appliances dancing to music or a poker game set to Beethoven. There are gags running through the show, such as a motorcycle so small it cannot be seen. It gets away from its inventor and we hear its buzz and see its path (through a cake) during the rest of the show.

In Special 7[13] there are several parodies of the typical Western cliché of a gunfight. Unlike *Your Show of Shows*, which parodied the substance of films and plays, Kovacs is more concerned with the technique and the style. An art film version is all odd angles, ending with the cowboy on a psychiatrist's couch. A Rod Serling version takes place in a misty swamp. A German version is *The Lone Ranger* in German, but the humor is not from any German doubletalk, as it would have been with Caesar, but simply the *idea* of a Western with a German accent.

Diana Rico accurately suggests that Kovacs's influence can be seen in the self-reflexive interest in technique and television itself in such shows as *Laugh-In*, *Saturday Night Live*, *SCTV*, and *The David Letterman Show*. It is not surprising that she also points out his influence on a generation of video artists, well outside the mass media mainstream.[14]

Laugh-In

The winners of the Emmy for Outstanding Writing Achievement in Variety for the 1966–67 season were the five writers for *The Sid Caesar, Imogene*

Coca, Carl Reiner, Howard Morris Special. The following year the winner was *Laugh-In*, and *ten* writers swarmed onto the stage to accept the award. One of them, Allan Manings, said, "I'm sorry we couldn't all be here tonight."

Manings had been approached by the show's producer, George Schlatter, to write the pilot episode of *Laugh-In* but had other commitments. When he and his then-partner Hugh Wedlock joined the staff of the series, he found there were so many writers that only the head writers were at the studio. The others were in a motel. Manings says:

> It was kind of jolly. It was like being a stoker on an ocean liner. Some son of a bitch is yelling down, "More coal, Scottie," and you know upstairs they are dancing and laughing and having a hell of a good time. It was that. George had a philosophy that more is more, rather than less is more. . . .
>
> [The head writers] were all in the "better" office, three blocks away, right across from the Smoke House in Burbank. We were in a couple of rooms in a motel that had probably never seen better days, and they would come down. George did have a slaveowner's attitude, a benevolent slaveowner. He would come down and throw coldcuts at the beasts, and ask for more coal. We weren't locked in to the extent that if you left, the guard shot you, but we never went to the studios to see what was going on and only were there in contact with the cast, I believe, in the beginning, at that first read-through (Thursday afternoon). All the writers would be there, seated not at the main table, but well below the salt.

Schlatter or Digby Wolfe, one of the head writers, would come down to the motel and say, "We need runners [running gags]. We need 25 Vikings. We need 16 Martians. We need six quarts of milk." Manings describes it as "Bulk orders were left." He says a first read-through script for a show would run two to three hundred pages, with a single joke on each page. Since there was no narrative structure and only occasional thematic structures, they could shoot much more material than could be used on one show, and the unused material would be kept and eventually used on other shows if, or rather when, needed. For the writers, Manings says, "it really was sitting there and grinding out an enormous amount of material to come up with the stuff." Because so much was written and then not used, Manings says the writers began to feel as if, "You write a ton, and an ounce gets on the air. . . . Not that we are as a breed necessarily competitive. Not that we are not uncompetitive. You said, 'Hey, I did four things funnier than that.' "

Manings did become the head writer/script supervisor and found he was

> up at the big house all the time. Had an office there. Had it paneled for me and everything. Got my own secretary, rather than one that was, quote, the writers' secretary. The main thing was that it was continual involvement. Rather than supplying the fodder, it was demanding the fodder. And writing, always writing, always writing.

Because Manings liked to do political material, Digby Wolfe once described him as "the conscience of *Laugh-In*," but Manings says now, "Retrospectively, it's looked upon as a show that was so biting. It was about 85 percent *kinderspiel*, and about 15 percent about something—which is, I suppose a hell of a lot." The network was against having any anti-Vietnam War material, but Manings thinks it was more the show's sponsor, Ford, which objected, since it was building equipment for the war effort. Manings also wrote a sketch in which a man comes into a drugstore in a hurry to get his medicine. The man gets the medicine and leaves a five-dollar bill. The druggist says the cost is twenty dollars, but the man has already left. The druggist picks up the five-dollar bill and says, "What the hell, four dollars profit isn't bad either." The drug industry was upset, but Manings found a newspaper clipping on congressional investigations of the drug industry that showed its markup was twelve to fifteen times the cost of the medicine. He enclosed the clipping in his reply letters and heard not another word from the industry.

In the beginning Paul Keyes, who had worked with Rowan and Martin before, wrote their *Laugh-In* monologues, and David Panich wrote most of the openings announcer Garry Owens did. The performers also contributed material. The writers generally knew who the guest stars were going to be and wrote material to fit them, or more accurately to fit how Schlatter wanted to use them. Manings wrote a bit for the ladylike actress Deborah Kerr in which she simply spoke the (clean) punch lines to the world's best-known dirty jokes. The censor objected, but it was pointed out that without the rest of the joke, the lines were not dirty. When Jack Benny was the guest star, the writers wrote what Manings calls "almost . . . a book show." On the show Benny says to Rowan and Martin that he is afraid his slower pace would not fit into the show, and they say it would be great with the girl and the waterfall. The waterfall keeps being mentioned, and at the end of the show, it is announced that the show is five minutes short, and Benny is asked to tell the waterfall story. The obvious punch line to the running gag is Benny getting doused with water, but while the show was being written, Manings told Schlatter he could not ask Benny to do that. Schlatter told him not to put it in the script. When Benny read the script, he himself suggested the dousing. Schlatter replied innocently, "Gee, would you do that?"

Manings says George Schlatter "overflowed with his love and joy of what he was doing. He's a 240-pound pixie. He loved tweaking noses. And he loved silly." Working with Schlatter was

a lot like being in the eye of a hurricane. George and I have had a wonderful relationship over the years, very good and very funny. [On the show] he was voracious. He was the quintessential cheerleader. He was wrapped totally in the show. He was wrapped up totally in the need for more and more material. Probably no one that I know of could have run the show better.

The pixie had other skills that helped the show:

He was a wizard at dealing with censorship. He was the man who put in the four [other things] so we would get the "damn." I watched him throw tantrums over things he did not care whether or not they got on. He literally once threw a chair across a studio because of something. I said, "Jesus Christ, George, let them have it." But he was protecting something else that he felt he wanted.

Manings found the network censors to be "very decent, but they were gun-shy" because the show became not only a hit but an institution noted for trying to break the boundaries. When Manings did a bit about ballistic missiles and had an Eskimo say, "I am sick and tired of these ICBMs," NBC's censor Herminio Traviesas said, "I've had it with your defecation jokes." When David Panich created the Farkle Family, the censors picked up on the similarity of "Farkle" to "fart," but let it and the suggestions of inbreeding, adultery, and incest slip by.

As the show became a hit, Manings says the dealings with the censor

became a game. The last two years—I did four years of the show—it was a wonderful relationship, and I think part of it was a game. They would see how much they would force us to give up. We would see how far we could push. To the best of my knowledge, it was never a grinding relationship. It was never, "You guys are in major trouble from here on in, forever."

Saturday Night Live

One of the junior writers on *Laugh-In* was Lorne Michaels, who found the material he and his partner Hart Pomerantz submitted to Paul Keyes, the head writer, was rewritten so much that he could scarcely recognize something of his when it got on the air. He vowed if he ever became a producer, he would run a show differently.[15]

In 1975 he got his chance with *Saturday Night Live*, and he deliberately picked writers who had not worked in television before, selecting what he liked to call "enlightened amateurs," claiming that comedy was too important to be left to the professionals. He was also limited by budgetary reasons in his hiring, since the top writer's fee the first season was $650 per week, going up to $700 in March.[16]

At the first staff meeting for the new show, on July 7, 1975, Michaels was vague in talking to the writers about what he wanted. He was not so vague about what he did *not* want. As the show's biographers note of the meeting,

Lorne made it clear that [Carol] Burnett's style encompassed everything *Saturday Night* should avoid. It lacked subtlety and nuance; it was too broad, too bourgeois, and too smug. . . . There will be more integrity and respect for the writing here, he said. From then on many an idea would be derisively dismissed on the 17th floor with the words, "That's Carol Burnett."[17]

The irony of Michaels's comments is that, with the exception of being too bourgeois, his writers fell even more deeply than Burnett's writers did into those other traps. Burnett's show was one of the best written on television, and while sketches could be broad, they are also beautifully constructed and written. The Burnett sketches are often more sharply observed than those on *Saturday Night Live*, and the "Mama's Family" sketches present in their own way as dark a view of bourgeois family life as anything on Michaels's show. There is nothing particularly subtle or nuanced about John Belushi's samurai sketches, and Chevy Chase's "Weekend Update" puts anything Burnett's show did to shame in the smug category.

The writing on *Saturday Night Live*, in trying to be as hip as possible, generally only attains smugness. The sketches run too long, even in the first few seasons, and often avoid coming to any point, which is perhaps supposed to be the point, but it makes them agony to watch. Michaels may not have interfered as much with his writers as Schlatter did, but that did not necessarily help the show.

What the writing did successfully do was provide star vehicles for the cast. Harry Shearer, who joined the show as a writer and performer in the fifth season, thought the entire show was unprofessional, and he particularly objected to Michaels's suggestion he use his own name on camera (as Chevy Chase had done). This led Shearer to suspect that Michaels "wasn't in the business of producing shows but in the business of making stars."[18] *That* Michaels and the show did, with sketches and bits that let the performers demonstrate their talents: Belushi as the samurai everything, Dan Ackroyd as Leonard Pinth-Garnell, Bill Murray as the lounge singer, and Gilda Radner as Emily Litella. The stars, and the aura of a live show that pressed the boundaries of television, became the appeal of the show: people watched to see what those people would get away with this week. Sometimes it was funny, sometimes it was just sophomoric, and often it was both. Not surprisingly, it became a cult hit, and while it has had little success in syndicated reruns, it has done reasonably well in cable reruns.

In the show's fifth season the critics and others were complaining the show had burned itself out, and Michaels told one reporter that was the plan: "*Saturday Night* is going to get worse and worse and eventually will never be funny again."[19] He was more right than he knew.

SCTV

The makers of SCTV knew from the beginning that they were not going to be *Saturday Night Live*, which was just as well. *Saturday Night Live* had started the year before Andrew Alexander, one of the producers of the theatrical comedy troupe known as The Second City, made arrangements with Canada's Global TV to do a television program. Harold Ramis, one of the original writers of *SCTV*, has said that everybody knew that some of the new forms of comedy would get to television, but as soon as they saw *Saturday Night Live*, they knew that Second City would not do it first. So they began to figure out how to do a show different from *Saturday Night Live* and still do Second City's kind of humor. At a series of brainstorming sessions the makers of the show came up with the idea that since it was being made at a local television station on a low budget, the format should be the daily programming of a local, low-rent television station. The original idea was that a storyline would connect the parodies of television, but after the first show, they all agreed the storyline kept the individual bits from working as well as they could. The station format was enough of a structure, although in later seasons a single storyline might thread through one or more shows, as in the two-part, one-hour parody in 1984 of *The Godfather*.[20]

Because the show was only shown in Canada the first year (1976–77) and then in American syndication the next four years, the budgets for the shows were very limited. Patrick Whitely, Global TV's overseer of the show's budget, said that "because we were on such a tight budget . . . the material really had to hold up. The writing had to be really good."[21]

Fortunately, the writing was of a much higher quality than on *Saturday Night Live*. The station format concentrated the writing so that *SCTV* put its satire in specific television forms, such as talk shows *(The Sammy Maudlin Show)*, educational shows *(Sunrise Semester)*, films *(Ben-Hur, The Grapes of Wrath)*, and commercials. Within those formats, they could strike at many aspects of media culture. Bringing sleazy nightclub comic Bobby Bittman (Eugene Levy) onto *The Sammy Maudlin Show* to plug the film he directed, called *Chariots of Eggs*, zings not only sleazy comics and talk shows, but arty films, directors of arty films, aerobicize tapes, and closeted homosexuals in the entertainment business. *SCTV* concentrated its fire, making its sketches much richer and more complex than the one-note sketches on *Saturday Night Live* or the one-joke bits on *Laugh-In*.

Part of the advantage *SCTV* had was that the show was on tape, not live. Martin Short, who worked on both *SCTV* and *Saturday Night Live* at different times, thought *SCTV* was a more creative experience than *Saturday Night Live*: "On *SCTV* we would have six weeks to write and six weeks to shoot six 90-minute shows. You could be dry for two weeks and make it up in the third. For *Saturday Night Live* you had Monday and Tuesday (to write). If you didn't have an idea, tough."[22]

Because of the shooting schedules, material could be shot and stockpiled, as it had been on *Laugh-In*. The McKenzie Brothers segments began after the series was sold to American television and the Canadian Broadcasting Corporation wanted to fill the extra two minutes in the Canadian version with "Canadian content." They were done in bulk. After the rest of the cast and crew had left, Dave Thomas and Rick Moranis would put on their tuques and parkas, sit down on the set and improvise a run of twenty to thirty two-minute bits, of which Thomas estimates only five or six would be used. The rest were thrown out.[23]

The other material was written, and the actors were very much involved in both the pitching and the writing sessions. The work would begin with group discussions, which were often like the improvisation sessions most of the cast had done as part of one or more of the Second City troupes. Once the material was worked out, it was written down. The process saved rehearsal time, as Harold Ramis recalled:

> There was very little read-through. When things are written by the company, the writing is the rehearsal. You don't write it down until you know you can perform it. The things you write down are the things you worked out. So rehearsal was not necessary. Camera blocking is really what the rehearsal was.[24]

Another advantage SCTV had over Saturday Night Live is that the actors on SCTV were more character actors than stars.[25] While the performers on Saturday Night Live could do three or four characters, and repeated them relentlessly, the range of the SCTV people was phenomenal. To take only one example, Eugene Levy did, among other characterizations, Hollywood agent/producer Sid Dithers, Stan Schmenge, Lorne Greene, Howard McNear as Floyd the barber from The Andy Griffith Show, Bobby Bittman, George Lucas, Ricardo Montalban, and Woody Tobias, Jr., who in turn played Bruno in the Dr. Tongue sketches. Not only did SCTV's cast have the range, they had the precision. Catherine O'Hara's devastatingly accurate Meryl Streep and Martin Short's dead-on David Steinberg made the originals virtually unwatchable for years.

In 1981 NBC picked up SCTV for its stations as a Friday-night late-night show. Since the show was being made in Canada, the network made very few attempts at interfering with its content.[26] Two years later the network dropped it (whereupon it was picked up by the Cinemax cable system), claiming that at $360,000 per show, it could not make a profit. Saturday Night Live at this point cost more than that to produce, and was considered by most to be in one of its many "brain dead" periods. The obvious solution, from the viewers' point of view, would have been to give Saturday Night Live a merciful death and replace it with SCTV. The problem was that NBC owned Saturday Night Live and therefore figured it could eventually make money on reruns of it. SCTV was not owned by the network and rerun money would not have gone to NBC.

·10·

MOVIES AND MINISERIES: THE EARLY YEARS

T Movies

*T*elevision showed movies from its infancy on, but in the fifties the networks did not show them in prime time. Partly the studios were trying to avoid television, and partly the sales of post-1948 films would require additional residual payments under guild contracts. The networks also wanted to establish their own identities with their own programming. In 1961 NBC began a series of post-1948 films in prime time on Saturday nights. By 1964 NBC, now with two movie nights per week, could not get enough theatrical films. Jennings Lang, the head of Universal television, persuaded NBC executives Mort Werner and Grant Tinker that the studio could produce feature films for television.[1] Universal did not make more than a few movies per year for television until 1967–68.

The writers were ready. In the mid-sixties E. Jack Neuman was at MGM and suggested in a memo that the studio should get into making films for television since it had the story properties (having purchased a large amount of story material over the years) and the people under contract. His suggestion fell on deaf ears, and Universal took the lead in making television movies—not surprising, since the studio had taken the lead with 90-minute series. A 1966 Universal movie, *Fame Is the Name of the Game*, became the pilot for another 90-minute series, *The Name of the Game*, which premiered in 1968. This set the pattern for the use of television movies as pilots for series.

Most of the early television movies were in the light-entertainment category. Rod Serling's 1966 film *The Doomsday Flight* was an elementary thriller about a madman who places a bomb on an airliner, and showed little of Serling's talent. Serling's former *Twilight Zone* writer Richard Matheson wrote the highest rated of the early movies, *The Night Stalker* (1972), an inventive idea (a vampire stalks women in Las Vegas) neatly worked out, although it is less inventive once they get to the vampire's traditional scary house. In 1976 Roy Huggins did the story and produced *The Invasion of Johnson County* based on the same historical incident that Michael Cimino later turned into *Heaven's Gate*. Huggins's version, with a screenplay by Nicholas Baehr, makes the lead a Maverick-type character, which makes the whole tone a lot lighter than Cimino's. Huggins rightly figured it would be easier to sell to the studio if it was lighter.

Metro-Goldwyn-Mayer did eventually get into making films for television, and like other studios, used them as pilots for potential series. In 1972 Eric Bercovici and Jerry Ludwig wrote and produced *Assignment: Munich*, starring Roy Scheider as Jake Webster, an agent for the Internal Central Bureau who operates under the cover of owning a bar. It is, as Bercovici describes it, a cross between "*Casablanca, I Spy*, and *Charade*. That was sort of our fantasy life: owning a bar, having this mysterious background. Our character was obliged to work for American Intelligence, although he didn't like to." When the show became a series, it turned into *Assignment: Vienna*, starring Robert Conrad. The series was made for ABC, which had just covered the Munich Olympics and wanted it set in another city. MGM had neglected to sign Roy Scheider to a contract for a series, and *The French Connection* made him hot in films. The series lasted six episodes.

Not every writer liked the lightweight television movies. Producer Stan Hough asked Christopher Knopf to write a television movie called *Mrs. Sundance*, about the further adventures of Etta Place, the lover of the Sundance Kid. The idea of writing it "just offended my sensibilities," says Knopf, who went to his father for his advice. Edwin Knopf said, "Have you got anything else to do?"

"No."

"Are you a professional writer?"

"Yeah."

"Do it. It's your job."

Knopf wrote it and says, "It turned out to be gold. It was a good script. It was an interesting show to write. No majesty whatsoever, but it was a lovely show." Knopf does not take all the credit for its high ratings: it starred Elizabeth Montgomery, then at the height of her television stardom.

Television movies turned serious early in their history and in effect took up the work of the old dramatic anthology shows. Richard Levinson and William Link had written for series television since the late fifties and by the late sixties were at Universal. They noticed that television series then, such as Universal's *The Bold Ones*, were dealing with contemporary political and social issues. In 1969 they began looking for a television movie project that was more than light entertainment. They found the Broadway play *My Sweet Charlie*, which dealt with the relationship between a black man and a white woman.

NBC turned down the project on the usual grounds that it had very little action and that it did not appear to be a pilot for a future series. Levinson and Link were also told off the record that "We can't have a black man and white girl living under the same roof at nine o'clock at night" (the time the movies ran) and "We are not in the business of offending our southern affiliates."[2] NBC, after three pitches, let them write the script. Levinson and Link wrote later, "After reading the script, NBC no longer seemed to think that a television version of *My Sweet Charlie* would mean the end of the free enterprise system."[3] The film was broadcast on January 20, 1970, to very high ratings and great reviews, and later in the year won three Emmies.[4]

Levinson and Link continued to do television movies of substance. In 1977, for example, they made *The Storyteller* about the writer of a television movie on arson seen by showing a young boy who then sets his school on fire. The film is a thoughtful, if dramatically flat, examination of the influence of television violence. The character of the television writer is a little too saintly, without the juice most TV writers have. The film does show an accurate view of the people and pressures a television writer deals with.[5]

In 1971 William Blinn wrote *Brian's Song*, a television movie that started two separate genres. The first genre was the docudrama, in which a real-life incident was the basis for the film. In this case it was the story of professional football players Brian Piccolo and Gayle Sayers and their professional and personal relationship. The makers of the film insist that it is only 5 percent fiction, the rest fact.[6] The second genre was what became known as the "disease of the week" story. In this case it was Brian Piccolo's death at the age of 26 from cancer. Because the film was made for ABC's new 90-minute *Movie of the Week*,[7] it runs a rushed 73 minutes, and the rushed quality also comes from the budget limitations, since it was shot in fourteen days.[8] Several of the supporting characters, particularly the wives of the two players, are not as well developed as they would have been in a longer film. The film holds up surprisingly well, however, in spite of all the other television movies that have followed in those two genres.

Brian's Song was given a theatrical release, and from time to time other films made for television have also been released theatrically. A movie about Scott Joplin was made in 1978 for television. When it was decided to release it first theatrically, the writer, Christopher Knopf, objected, saying he would have written it differently as a theatrical film, but had written it for the limits of television of the time. He did not get as deeply as he would have in a theatrical film into the life in the bordellos Joplin lived and played in, nor did he deal with Joplin's syphilis. The film was not a theatrical success.

There was the same kind of pushing and pulling with the networks on the content of television movies that there was on series. In the mid-seventies, E. Arthur Kean wrote what was supposed to be a three-hour movie pilot about Detective Headquarters called *DHQ*. NBC passed on it, but CBS decided to do it, with some changes. It was reduced to two hours, the title eventually changed to *A Killing Affair* and one of the subplots—about an adulterous affair between two cops—became the main plot. Kean was told of this by an executive, who said, "Hey, we're going to save your picture."

"What picture?"

"*DHQ*. We're going to make it. We're going to do it with O. J. Simpson."
Kean had two reactions. The first was, "This guy can't act." The second
was, "You're going to make it a black and white thing [which it was not
originally]." Kean told another executive, Paul Monash, "If you're going to
do this 'on the nose': 'Oh, God, we've got a white woman and a black man
in bed together,' I don't want any part of this." In the seven years since *My
Sweet Charlie*, the networks had discovered that television movies needed
some kind of hook to grab an audience's attention.

Monash asked Kean how he thought it should be handled, and Kean replied, "Let's take this story pretty much the way it is, and in terms of the
racial stuff, I just want to throw a few little darts. You'll be seeing it on the
screen. You don't need to lay it on." Monash and the others agreed, and
Kean remembers there being only about five lines that mentioned the racial
material at all.

In the case of Kean's rewritten script, the network censors still had their
say. Kean recalls:

> There was the word "slut." There was also a vital story point. When the man
> and the woman have just made love, there is real tension in the room. She says,
> "I don't like it rough like that."
>
> He says, "I thought we were really getting it on."
>
> She says, "No. You were really rough." They wanted to cut that scene. That
> was one of the turning points in it emotionally. It had to be there. So [producer
> David] Gerber went to bat with me. We had the actual censor sitting in the
> board room. And it was a woman. She was about 55, and she walked in. Now
> this is the censor, so you figure like a New England schoolmarm sort of thing.
> The conversation was as follows. She walks in the door. She says, "Gerber, you
> old motherfucker, how are you?" I was totally unprepared for that. You could
> have put anything in her mouth but that. I said, "I think we've got a chance
> here." I knew I was dealing with a human being who understood what it was all
> about anyway. It was not that she'd never heard the words. She was hardnosed
> about it. She's brought two of her lackies there, and they were sitting prim, Jerry
> Fallwell-faced, saying, "Well, we can't have this violent sex."
>
> I said, "This is not violent sex. It's rough sex." And I explained what was
> going on. If you look at the story, you see what this man is going through
> manifests itself to the point where he doesn't even know it. She points it out,
> and he finally gets to see it. They're saying, "Well, gee, I don't know. We can't
> have violent sex on the air."
>
> I said, "Well, then don't do the show."
>
> She said, "Twice in the story you use the word 'slut.' Now we can't have that
> either."
>
> I said, "What's wrong with 'slut'?"
>
> They said, "It means a whore."
>
> I said, "No, it doesn't." Gerber has a big dictionary this fat on his desk, one
> of his pretenses. I said, "You look over there. A slut is an unkempt woman. Yes,
> go look it up if you don't believe me."

Well, they didn't even look it up. I was telling the truth. So they said, "All right. We'll trade you one 'slut' and you get the violent sex scene. You take out one of the 'sluts' and we'll give you the violence." And that's the way it went on the air.

Because the pattern of using television movies as pilots was set early, occasionally an unneeded movie was made. In 1974 Paramount decided to make a series from the 1970 film *The Lawyer.* Rather than use the theatrical film as the pilot, they ordered another pilot. Why do another? The writer of the pilot, E. Jack Neuman, says, "Who knows? There was no reason to make that pilot at all. They had it. They had it all right there, but no, they had to have a pilot."

Not only were there light-entertainment star vehicles such as *Mrs. Sundance,* but star vehicles of a bit more substance, such as *More Than Friends,* a 1978 film starring Rob Reiner and his wife Penny Marshall, the stars of *All in the Family* and *Laverne and Shirley.* ABC was looking for a film for them, and Reiner had a production deal at Columbia with his writing partner, Phil Mishkin.

Mishkin and Reiner met at UCLA in the mid-sixties when Reiner tried out for a play Mishkin had written. Mishkin told the director that under no circumstances should Reiner be given the part. They later became friends and ran acting workshops at the Evergreen Stage, which Penny Marshall attended. She once did a scene from a Mishkin play, *Whatever Happened to Patience and Prudence?* Marshall suggested to ABC and Columbia a film of Mishkin's play.

The play deals with a young woman's relationships with several men while searching for her Prince Charming. Mishkin and Reiner did the screenplay, combining some of the men into one character, Allan (Reiner), and making him a friend of Mattie (Marshall), to whom she returns between other relationships. The film's dramatic question is whether these two are going to be friends, lovers, or both. There are similarities to both Allen's *Annie Hall,* which came out the year before, and Reiner's later *When Harry Met Sally. . . ,* especially the latter.

More Than Friends shows its genesis as a stage play, and also the sitcom-writing experience of its writers. The film begins in 1958 as Allan is trying to make out with Mattie at a party. Their long bedroom scene plays like Act I of a sitcom: funny, but funny because of the gags, some of which are related to the characters, some of which are not. In the scene Allan says he knows he's going to be bald. At the end of the scene they agree to be just friends, and he says, "You'll be my girl . . . friend," and Mattie replies, "And you'll be my bald friend." The early scenes of the film are also hurt by Reiner's not being a particularly convincing teenager; his Allan seems stupid, not just adolescent.

The film improves as it goes along, and deals better with the issue of relationships. When a stage director turns down Mattie as a girlfriend because she is a virgin, she gets Allan to take her to a motel to solve the problem. The motel scene has its quota of gags, but they are more in character. The final scene, in which Mattie, now a television sitcom star, listens to Allan read part of his novel about their relationship, is genuinely touching and within hailing distance of *Annie Hall*. The promotional material for *More Than Friends* suggested it was a thinly disguised autobiography of Reiner and Marshall, but it was based on Mishkin's play and there are considerable differences from their real lives. On the other hand, the feeling for the difficulties of man-woman relationships, although occasionally expressed in obvious gags, comes from observed reality.[9]

Given the nature of the television business, it is not always possible for a writer to get his vision on the screen as literally as he would like. Joel Rogosin produced the 1979 television movie *The Gift*, which was from an autobiographical novel by Pete Hamill. Hamill wrote the script, and the network wanted changes to make the material more dramatic. Hamill made some changes, and then additional ones were made by Rogosin and others. Hamill took his name off the script and used a pseudonym. Rogosin says:

> It was very much Pete's, but it wasn't verbatim Pete's, and Pete felt that while we may have lived up to the spirit, we did not live up to the literal words.
>
> Writers like Pete, who have that kind of passion, not that the rest of us don't have [it], but that kind of very personal intense commitment to their work, which reflects them, it's hard for them to deal with the realities [of the business]. It's a business of compromise. The question is, how much do you compromise and in what areas? Because if you are not willing to compromise to some degree or other, you are not going to be working in the business effectively.

Miniseries

Leonard Goldenson, the head of ABC, says in his memoirs that the idea of the American miniseries came about because Marty Starger, the head of network programming, was in London in the early seventies and happened to see some British Broadcasting Corporation (BBC) series that told a complete story in a limited number of episodes. Starger suggested ABC might get involved in this kind of programming, which, as Goldenson says, "was a form then unknown in America."[10] It is not clear why ABC had to waste money sending Starger to London to discover the series, since the American commercial networks had already been offered the British miniseries and had turned them down because they were made in black-and-white and the networks insisted on color. The recently reconstituted National Educational Television network, which was now called the Public Broadcasting System (PBS), decided to take a chance on a British miniseries. *The Forsyte Saga*, broadcast by PBS in the fall of 1969, established both PBS and the miniseries and was the inspiration for American miniseries that followed.

In the early seventies, producer Douglas Cramer and ABC executive Barry Diller approached screenwriter Edward Anhalt to do a long adaptation of Leon Uris's novel *QB VII*. The book tells the stories of Dr. Adam Kelno and Ben Cady, the former a doctor accused by the latter of doing illegal operations in a Nazi concentration camp. The first idea was to show it one hour each night, five nights in a row. As Anhalt said, as he was working on the script, "It's done in the manner of *Forsyte Saga*, the way the BBC did it, but all in one week."[11] Then, as Anhalt worked on the screenplay, Cramer and Diller decided they wanted to do it in eight hours rather then five, but ABC decided nobody would watch all eight hours, so it was run at six and one-quarter hours in two parts on successive nights.[12]

Anhalt wrote it differently than the British miniseries. The British series are shown one night a week, one hour at a time, and each hour is written as a complete one-hour piece. Because the American miniseries from *QB VII* on were both subjected to changing lengths and, more importantly, run on succeeding nights, there was no need to write each hour as a single unit.

Anhalt's experience in theatrical films[13] led him to write the script without worrying about act breaks.[14] He figured there were enough natural breaks in the story where commercials could be inserted. His original approach was to tell the stories of Cady and Kelno by intercutting them, unlike Uris in the novel, who told the story of Kelno first, then Cady, and then the trial. The network executives at first told Anhalt that viewers would not sit through the Kelno material first because they did not know what was coming up.[15] The intercutting did not work at the greater length of the series, and the script returned to Uris's original structure, but with a teaser added at the beginning of each segment that laid out the basic conflict between the two men.

Although *QB VII* was the first planned miniseries of the seventies, *The Blue Knight* was shown first, in November 1973. (*QB VII* was shown in April 1974.) E. Jack Neuman learned he was going on the project in a very Hollywood way. He was walking the picket lines during the Writers Guild strike in the spring of 1973, having a marvelous time listening to Carl Reiner and Hal Kanter make up limericks, when suddenly an unmarked police car drove up and two men "sailed out" of the car. They threw Neuman up against a wall and handcuffed him. One of the men took out a gun, put it to Neuman's head and said, "You're going to write the fucking *Blue Knight*, aren't you, Jack?" It was Neuman's friend and the novel's author, Los Angeles policeman Joseph Wambaugh.

The Blue Knight was produced by Lorimar, which had already signed an agreement with the Guild, so Neuman was able to go to work. Lorimar previously had Rod Serling doing a script of the novel for a four-hour miniseries, but after nine months Serling had not come up with one. Neuman did not then look at Serling's script, but read it only after he had completed his own. Neuman says, "Rod made every mistake I think I would have made if I'd been in the position he was in. . . . He was trying to think of it one hour at a time." Neuman worked as Anhalt did:

> All I wrote was "Fade In" and then four hours later I wrote "Fade Out," and they can split it up any way they want. This is the halfway mark. O.K., and this is the half of the half. I figure if I'm writing it right, at the end of any scene they can make the end of any episode they want. . . . That means that something's happened, something's going to happen, or you're scared to death, or you're interested, you're laughing, or something, but above all you're watching. I never pay any attention to act breaks.

Writing *The Blue Knight* had to be rushed. The first meeting with Lorimar took place in May, and Lorimar had a pay-or-play contract with William Holden for his first television movie. If the film did not start production by the first week of July, they *still* had to pay Holden. Neuman, who had not read the book, got Wambaugh's manuscript and found it a series of vignettes, which Neuman tied together structurally with a single crime and with the love story between Bumper Morgan (Holden) and a college teacher (Lee Remick). He began to write the script, working in a small, windowless office, as the film prepared production. The producer and the director visited Neuman in the mornings and he would describe the settings he would be writing, which meant they were location-scouting without a script, but only from what Neuman told them. He said to them, for example, "We're going to need a hotel. Not second or third class. Let us call it a fifth-class riding academy. Let us call it La Cucaracha. It's got to have some kind of atrium lobby."

Since Holden had been a movie star for over thirty years, Neuman expected problems with him, but Holden's only concern about the script was to make sure the love story was kept from the novel. Neuman says of Holden, "He was the first one on the set and the last one to leave every day."

Miniseries meant that books could be done at greater lengths than they could as feature films, and it even meant that more material than was in the book could be used. *The Company* was a novel by John Ehrlichman, one of Nixon's staff, and was originally bought by Paramount for a theatrical feature. David Rintels wrote the script, but Paramount decided (probably because the success of *All the President's Men* seemed to exhaust the feature possibilities of the story) not to do it as a film but as a television miniseries. Eric Bercovici was brought onto the project by producer Stan Kallis. Bercovici rewrote the Rintels script into the first segment of a miniseries, and notes that the novel contributed "about ninety minutes" of the miniseries. Rintels then worked out the storyline for a miniseries, but the problem as Bercovici remembers it was that "No one quite knew for a long time whether it was going to be three hours or five hours. Then it was going to be ten hours. When they decided it was going to be twelve hours, they were already shooting when I was writing the last two hours." Rintels and Bercovici shared the miniseries story credit and the teleplay credit for the first and the last two hours, and Bercovici wrote the scripts in between for *Washington: Behind Closed Doors.*

The reason the film kept growing in length is that Bercovici and Rintels arrived in Washington to do their research at just the right time. Bercovici explains, "Everyone felt the need to expiate. They wanted to unburden themselves." The writers brought this back to the meetings with the networks, whose attitude was summed up by executive Brandon Stoddard, who kept saying, "The politics are boring. Let's get into the bedrooms." (Bercovici says that later Stoddard admitted he was wrong and that the politics were "terrific." Now he tells them.) There were constant trade-offs: "O.K., you can have this political scene but we want this bedroom scene."

There were also problems with the legal side of the network, which kept thinking the film was a docudrama and, Bercovici says, "kept asking us to verify scenes we had fabricated." Bercovici and Rintels finally won when the network agreed to have the show billed as "Inspired by" but not "Based upon" the "whole political history of the period." As the Nixon White House tapes have become available, Rintels and Bercovici's tone of paranoid black comedy seems increasingly accurate.

Bercovici not only liked having the length to get deeper into the story and characters, but he loved having Jason Robards as the Nixon equivalent. One day Bercovici was on the set and heard Robards deliver a speech. Bercovici's response was "Who rewrote the speech? He made it a lot better, but who did it?" He went to the script supervisor and read the speech. He realized it was exactly as he had written it. "Jason had said it word for word. But it sure sounded a lot better when he said it than when I wrote it."

Anhalt, Neuman, Bercovici, and Rintels had the advantage of doing the scripts for their miniseries either alone or with a partner. As the miniseries proliferated, different patterns of writing developed. Roy Huggins produced several miniseries for Universal and worked the way he had in series, developing and outlining the story in detail and then letting the writers write it. On *Wheels,* Huggins developed a treatment, then drew lines across the manuscript to show where each of the five two-hour segments were. He then assigned each segment to a different writer, and did a rewrite on the drafts himself to give it a consistent tone. Like the other writers, Huggins did not worry about act breaks and told the writers not to put them in. He says, "If it's good, the act breaks are there. It will break wherever you want it to break. And if it's no good, it doesn't matter."

Huggins felt that Universal was attracted to material that was not especially exciting. He thinks most novels are "loose. They are heavy, cumbersome, cover many years. They are not very good. Some of them are, of course. We have *War and Peace*, don't we?" He found he had to tighten up the stories, even in the miniseries. He also made changes, although with best-sellers such as *Captains and the Kings*, the changes were limited.

On the 1978–79 miniseries based on James Michener's *Centennial*, the 26 hours were organized and divided up by the producer and writer John Wilder. Wilder wrote several of the episodes himself, and farmed the rest out to Jerry Zeigman and Charles Larson. Wilder told Larson there was no holding back. "If you want to write in snow, write in snow." Helpful advice, since one of Larson's chapters was "The Storm."

Eric Bercovici had a better experience with Pete Hamill than Joel Rogosin had. Bercovici read Hamill's book *Flesh and Blood*, which CBS purchased for a four-hour miniseries. Bercovici thought the book only had enough material for three hours, but knew CBS was committed to four. He talked to Hamill and suggested an additional story line, which Hamill agreed to. Bercovici started writing and ended up with a six-hour script:

> Scripts tend to do that. They never get shorter. They always get longer. And I wound up with a six-hour script, which I thought was terrific. I had a meeting at CBS about it where I was defending the six-hour script. I said, "Well, it's six hours. I can't cut it."
>
> They finally said, "Eric, Eric, it's four hours or nothing."
>
> "Oh. Well, if you put it that way . . ." Having spent a few weeks saying I couldn't cut a page out of the script, I then that afternoon cut the script down to four hours.

The trickiest element in *Flesh and Blood* was the incestuous relationship between the boxer and his mother, which everyone was nervous about dealing with. The discussions were very heated. At one meeting at the home of the producer, Gerald Abrams, on "the incest problem," Bercovici opened his briefcase to get a cigar. Everybody in the room froze. When the cigar came out, Abrams said, "Oh, my God, I thought you had a gun."

Flesh and Blood was shot and as it moved toward its 1979 airdate, Donald Wildmon, a minister from Mississippi who in 1977 had formed the National Federation for Decency, orchestrated a protest against the film.[16] The most explicit scene was edited down to a point where Bercovici felt it was simply confusing.[17] Bercovici had already won one round with the network censors, and done it in the usual way. When the character of the boxer first meets his father, Bercovici wanted him to say, "You son-of-a-bitch," but the writer knew "if I just put that one in I'd never get it, so I put four others throughout the script, and I negotiated down and managed to keep the one that was dramatically justifiable."

After wrestling with the networks, Bercovici found it a bit of a relief when in the late seventies he wrote the miniseries *Top of the Hill* about Olympic bobsledders for syndication. Because it was intended to go on at the time of the 1980 Winter Olympics, there was very little delay, which Bercovici also attributes to the syndication process:

> Very unlike a network . . . they decide to make a show. They don't stockpile scripts the way the network does and then decide what to do. They decided to make this show. My recollection is that it was simply a "go" project from the first day. "Hurry up and get it done, fellas." . . . Particularly from a writer's point of view, it's always nice to know that what you are writing is going to be made. I think if you look through the network warehouses you'll find God knows how many unproduced movie-for-television scripts. You go into any executive's office and you're always rather intimidated by the corpses piled up in the corner.

One evening in the early seventies, actors Ossie Davis and Ruby Dee were having dinner with producer David Wolper and told him about a book a friend of theirs was writing. Wolper thought the book might make a good television movie, but discovered the rights had been optioned by Columbia for a theatrical film. A few weeks later he learned the option had ended. He bought the rights and brought the project to Brandon Stoddard at ABC, who in turn recommended it to Barry Diller and Marty Starger. Starger took the idea to Elton Rule and Leonard Goldenson, who thought it sounded like a good idea. At lunch with Wolper and the author, Stoddard discovered one small problem: Alex Haley had not actually written *Roots* yet.

The project had gotten this far along because Haley was a terrific storyteller with a great story to tell: seven generations of his family, from the time they were brought from Africa to America as slaves. Stoddard admits he "was intrigued with the idea of American slavery from a black's point of view."[18] Fred Silverman, who moved from CBS to ABC after the series was in production, saw the potential problem with it: "Here's twelve hours of a story where the whites are the villains and the blacks are the heroes in a country that is 85 percent white. It doesn't sound like a good idea at first blush."[19] The story and the characters were, however, so compelling that the miniseries overcame the problem.

It did not start out to be twelve hours. The original conception was between five and six hours, but Stoddard kept telling Silverman, "It is so rich. Can we expand it?"[20] The writers, primarily William Blinn, who wrote the first three-hour episode, and Ernest Kinoy, were writing behind Haley and even occasionally ahead of him, which made the network executives nervous. When the film was completed at the twelve-hour length, the question was how to run it. Even *QB VII* could fit into two nights. *Rich Man, Poor Man*, which ran twelve hours and was broadcast in 1976, the year before *Roots*, was broadcast on successive weeks over a two-month period. It was Silverman who decided to run *Roots* over eight successive days, and its success established the broadcast pattern for later miniseries. This in turn helped confirm the narrative pattern of not breaking up the miniseries into hour segments as the British had done.

There were some complaints that, except for Haley, none of the writers on *Roots* had been black, so on the sequel, *Roots: The Next Generations* (1979), the producers made an effort to hire black television writers. There were not a lot working steadily in the business to choose from. One of them was Thad Mumford, whose credits included PBS's *Electric Company*, Flip Wilson specials, and sitcoms such as *Good Times* and *All in the Family*.

While Mumford was on *Maude*, his agent got a call from producer Stan Margulies, who wanted Mumford for a segment of *Roots: The Next Generations*. Mumford recalls:

> I was terrified of the idea. Flattered, but terrified because *Roots* was more serious, and I in no way felt capable of handling this. And I did everything in the world I could to not do it. I said to Stan, "I have a[nother] job,"
>
> "Well, we'll wait for you."
>
> "I don't feel I can."
>
> "Well, we'll give you all the help we can get." If I had said, "I have cancer," they'd say, "We'll give you an iron lung." They really wanted me to do this thing. That's where I partnered up with Dan [Wilcox], because I was not going to do this by myself. So we wrote an episode [episode five, about Alex Haley's father getting out of Cornell and returning to Palmerstown]. We both had other things, so we would write this at night, and we ended up getting a Writers Guild [Award] nomination for our script, which was more important than an Emmy nomination because it's your peers.

The head writer of the miniseries was a veteran of the original *Roots*, Ernest Kinoy, and he laid out the stories for each episode in what Mumford says was "a very detailed and wonderful way." Their episode was based on only seven pages of the book and Kinoy worked from Haley's notes as well as the book. Mumford and Wilcox got notes from Kinoy on their script, but Mumford knows that Haley read the scripts and thinks some of the notes may have come from Haley via Kinoy. Haley also told them stories, of course. Mumford agrees with everybody else that Haley is "a great storyteller."

The 1980 miniseries *Beulah Land* is not great storytelling, nor did anyone connected with it ever think it might be considered such. Producer David Gerber saw the success of *Roots* and thought *Beulah Land*, based on two novels by Lonnie Coleman, might be "the flip side of *Roots*,"[21] a romantic Civil War saga of a plantation told from the view of the white people involved. The difficulty of doing such a piece was suggested by the comments of Arthur Unger in the *Christian Science Monitor*: "The trouble with *Beulah Land* is that [it] doesn't know its place. Perhaps it was barely passable as a good old-fashioned summer print 'read' about 10 years ago. But as an electronic mass entertainment . . . liable to insult or mislead Americans of all colors, it quite simply has no place in the television of the 1980's."[22]

The writer Gerber hired to write the script was JP Miller, and Unger's comments suggest the problem of trying to get a script from the material. The novels are basically traditional Civil War romance, and *Roots* had all too recently vividly exposed the inaccuracies of that traditional genre. Miller tried to overcome those problems by working with an historian of the period, Tilden Edelstein. The scenes with the slaves can be defended on grounds of historical accuracy, but they were still deeply offensive to the black actors who read the script and were cast in the film.

Part of the problem was a question of timing. *Roots* had raised the hope of both black actors and their fans, black and white, that as a result of the success of the two miniseries, more, bigger, and better roles would open up on American television. By the time the script of *Beulah Land* was being circulated for casting, the promise of *Roots* was already not being fulfilled. While the script of *Beulah Land* seems merely insensitive and not racist to a white film historian reading it in 1990,[23] black actors in 1979 felt differently. The black actors and others agitated for changes in the script and enough were made that Miller took his name off the credits.

An example of the changes occurs early in the film. In Miller's script, Roscoe, the white overseer of the plantation, comes to whip the young black boy Floyd, who has gotten the young white master into trouble. Floyd's father, Ezra, stands by and watches, afraid of Roscoe. The scene is obviously intended to establish that Roscoe is evil, and it does so very effectively. The scene offended James McEachin, the actor playing Ezra, on the grounds that it made Ezra seem a coward.[24] As the scene finally appears in the film, Ezra holds off Roscoe with a hot poker, telling him he will punish Floyd himself by making him sharpen all the knives on the plantation. At the end of the scene, Roscoe just cracks his whip and stalks off. Historically it is unlikely that a slave like Ezra could have gotten away with such behavior without severe punishment, but the appeal of the scene as it stands to contemporary black audiences is understandable.

Whatever historical accuracy there may have been was outside the tone of the kind of story *Beulah Land* was and is. Among its many considerable achievements, *Roots* had made it impossible for the *Beulah Land* lightweight approach to that material to work artistically on film or television ever again.[25]

·11·

POLICE STORY

*JP*Miller, who has written several scripts for producer David Gerber, thinks that although Gerber is no Fred Coe or Herbert Brodkin, he is "a brilliant producer" with a "mind full of firecrackers, all ready to go off." Like many producers, "He doesn't use three words. He uses three million." Miller once taped a three-hour conference with Gerber and "couldn't understand a word of it," but realized Gerber had still gotten his point across.

Gerber. Gerb. The Gerb. Writers love him. And they hate him. They think he's full of shit. And they like him because of it. And anybody with those qualities, they can't *not* talk about, as E. Arthur Kean does in the following aria:

> David Gerber is Harry Cohn. There's more Harry than there is Jerry Wald.[1]
>
> When you are in his presence the Gerb is, number one, a brilliant entertainer. He says, "Listen, kid, I'm going to fuck you over, but it's going to be so good you're going to thank me for it." Now that's his attitude and a lot of the time he pulls it off. He has a very black side. I've never really seen it, but a lot of people have told me about it.
>
> The best thing you can do with David is say, "David, fuck you." And if you do that, whether it's in those words or in your attitude, he will respect you and you'll get along. If you're a doormat, you're dead with Gerber.
>
> By God, where Gerber's around, things happen. This is not Aaron Spelling, who sucks his thumb. I don't mean to knock Aaron. I terribly disagree with his taste. He really is gracious and stylish, whereas Gerber is the Brooklyn street bum that he was. One reason I will always tend to like him is every day you see him beat up [director] Marvin Chomsky. Anybody who can do that isn't all bad. Marvin should be beat up every day.
>
> He's got a college degree. I think he's trying to create his own legend, and he has a lot of fun doing that. I think it's part of his real enjoyment in the business.

And the writers who really like him and really hate him like him and hate him because he produced *Police Story*, the series that permanently changed how police were portrayed on television.

By 1972 Gerber had spent ten years in television and was now an independent producer at Columbia. He found in the Columbia story files a proposal for a show about a special investigation squad called *Police Story*. What impressed Gerber was that it was not idealizing cops as Jack Webb had done on *Dragnet*. One cop on the squad was just as bad as the killer they were chasing, which was why the proposal had been turned down by all three networks. He met with the author of the proposal, Joseph Wambaugh, whose realistic novels about cops had been best-sellers. The two men got along—a condition that would not last—and Gerber went about trying to sell the idea.[2]

In a typical Gerber move, he called E. Jack Neuman. Neuman had written and produced an unsold pilot at Fox under Gerber and Neuman had to order him not to talk to the director and editor. Gerber now asked him, "How'd you like to do a great police series?"

Neuman replied, "I've done all the cops I want to do."

"With Joe Wambaugh. He's anxious to buy you some lunch." You can understand why Gerber is considered the greatest salesman in Hollywood. Neuman and Wambaugh met and Neuman says Wambaugh "had an idea I'd had for a long time. I want to tell the story of the cop, not the crime. That was the whole trick." Wambaugh and Neuman went to see Larry White, the appropriate executive at NBC, and pitched the idea for the series. White's reaction was, "I'll take it. Now, who do you see in the lead?" Neuman and Wambaugh insisted it was an anthology.[3] White resisted at first, then agreed to buy it as an anthology.

Neuman's idea was that he would write and produce a two-hour movie, and they would do nine two-hour movies each year. He would produce all of them and write one or two of them. Neuman even considered setting several of the films not in Los Angeles but in other cities around the world, although he says now that Gerber never understood that part of the concept.[4] Gerber, thinking like a producer, realized the show would be easier to produce and sell if it was set in Los Angeles (although the studio, much to Wambaugh's irritation, kept deleting references to real L.A. police divisions, apparently for legal reasons). This also would give the show a crucial edge in its access to stories of Los Angeles policemen.

Neuman wrote the screenplay for the two-hour movie pilot and went skiing in Switzerland. He soon got a desperation call in Gstaad from Gerber, who said, "You've got to come home. The actors won't come out and do [the script]." Neuman flew home to learn that Gerber, thinking the speeches in the script were too long, had cut them, but in the process cut everything the actors needed to create their characters. Neuman simply gave the actors the original screenplay and told Gerber to stay off the set and away from the actors. After that, Neuman says, "It went fine." Neuman did not want to produce an hour series, so he did not stay with the show when it went to series.

The two-hour movie was made in January 1973 and the Writers Guild strike lasted from March to June, during which time no scripts could be prepared, or writers even assigned. The day the strike ended, writers began to get calls from Stan Kallis, co-executive producer with Gerber. Kallis set up a meeting of writers to see the pilot and listen to Gerber, Wambaugh, and Liam "Bill" O'Brien, whom Kallis had picked at Gerber's request as story editor. Art Kean remembers walking into the room and realizing that in addition to the production staff there were "ten of the best writers I know. I was really flattered to be in that company. Sy Salkowitz was there. Bill O'Brien. Jerry Ludwig. Eric Bercovici. Bob Collins." Gerber told them, "We haven't got a word on paper and we're on the air in six weeks."

Salkowitz remembers Wambaugh at that meeting saying, "Play the emotional jeopardy, not the physical jeopardy." Salkowitz says that "crystallized that show for me . . . . There were three or four of us who kind of looked at each other, because up to that time nobody could do that. [That's the difference between that] and any other cop show." Ed Waters, a writer and later executive story consultant on the third and fourth seasons of the show, says the idea was later expressed as "the cop works on the case, and the case works on the cop."

Unlike many creators of shows, Wambaugh stayed connected with the show for the full four-year run, although not without fireworks. As early as July 1973, when he read the first set of scripts, he criticized the writing. He often threatened to walk off the show, and both NBC and Columbia wanted him off, but Gerber insisted they keep him,[5] even though Wambaugh's most ferocious attacks were directed at Gerber. Wambaugh today takes a more benign view of Gerber, saying that "David Gerber deserves a lot of credit for the series, as does Stanley Kallis." As JP Miller says of Gerber, "When he sells a thing, he also knows how to put on the show."

A major Wambaugh contribution to the series was bringing cops in to tell their stories. Wambaugh listened to the stories first. Liam O'Brien, who coordinated the interview process, says that if Wambaugh then

> liked the story, he would call me up, and give me a briefing over the phone. I'd say, "O.K., send the guy up," or, "No, that's no good." Either one. If he sent the guy up to the studio, he'd come up about 6:30 or 7 o'clock at night and sit down and tell you the whole story. I would say, "Go home and put that down on paper the best you can. Don't worry about the words, anything. Just put it down so I don't forget it."
>
> Then I had a group of writers, whom I'd worked with on other shows. They came, eagerly, to *Police Story*, and I would sit down with them and give whatever this cop had given us. [Sometimes we'd] have the cop there, so the two of us would cross-examine the cop again. We paid the cop, and paid him well, you know. And we went from there.

The cops were paid $50 for the story, and every effort was made to hire the cop whose story it was to serve as the technical advisor on that particular episode. As tech advisor the cop was paid between $900 and $1,350 per episode.[6] E. Arthur Kean says of the cops, "They had their own language. They had their own attitudes. [It gave us] insight. Good writers love it when they find that kind of truth. We jumped all over it, [and] we got it on the air."

The interviews led to the creation of two recurring characters by Sy Salkowitz, Tony Calabrese (played by Tony LoBianco) and Bert Jameson (played by Don Meredith). Salkowitz had lunch with two detectives who handled robbery cases and one of the stories they told that day dealt with their relationship with a junkie who was their informant. Salkowitz put that at the center of his episode "Requiem for an Informant," but he based the bank robbery on several other cases they told him about. The two detectives became the models for Tony and Bert, although he found he could not use the cop's black humor, since it "took away from the importance of the moment." That kind of humor would only come to television later on *Hill Street Blues*. Salkowitz, following the two original cops, made one of them Anglo and one ethnic. The casting department proceeded to cast Don Meredith in the part Salkowitz had written as ethnic, and Tony LoBianco as the Anglo. Salkowitz "put it through my typewriter and switched the dialogue. There are the same lines, but I put it in ethnic." The characters were so popular they were brought back in other episodes.

After the interviews with the cops, the writer would then work out the story, usually in collaboration with Liam O'Brien, whom the writers on *Police Story* describe as close to a saint. Art Kean feels O'Brien respected not only the writer's work, but the writer himself, although Kean admits he could be hard on it too, since, "When you're doing that staff stuff, you just run out of patience. You run out of decency. You just run out of everything. It just grinds you down, so it can happen to anybody. But Bill was great, and I only worked with Bill."

As the stories were developed, the treatments and then the scripts were sent to Wambaugh for comment. As expected, Wambaugh could be hard on the technical accuracy, or lack of it, in the scripts. On the script for "Vice, 24 Hours," Wambaugh wrote to Stan Kallis that vice officers do not carry guns as they did in the script, and he also noted, "He pulls a search warrant out of his hat like a rabbit. . . . You cannot get a warrant for suspicion of being an asshole." Wambaugh summed it up by saying, "I don't want these cops on my police department nor on my television show."[7] Wambaugh objected not only to technical flaws, but procedural flaws. On "Contract on a Cop" he wrote "DELETE this fucking REPORT TO THE COMMISSIONER [a recent film]-style Mexican standoff where two guys point guns at each other like little kids. In real life, you start jerking the trigger the moment you THINK a guy has a gun."[8]

Wambaugh also complained when he thought writers were getting preachy. On one script he wrote, "More paternalistic, cop propaganda . . . Leave off the Jack Webb stuff about taking care of THEM. You know, *them*, the dumb civilians? Sounds pretty corny."[9] Wambaugh wrote up a list of "cop clichés" that he gave to O'Brien to pass on to the writers. He also kept making suggestions to make the scenes truer to his police experience. On one script he noted, "Do you REALLY think a cop would imply to another cop's wife that something might be dangerous? He'd lie even if it were, and tell her it's a piece of cake."[10] On the other hand, he recognized that sometimes the truth seemed too much. On "Monster Manor" he objected to a grandmother shooting an eleven-year-old full of dope: "I don't think this works. It's just too macabre. Once again, never mind that it's true, it doesn't *seem* true."[11]

For all his critical comments on their scripts, Wambaugh appreciated the writers. Of Robert Collins he wrote, "He just can't miss. Every Collins script is off-beat, right-on, and sparkling."[12] He felt the same way about Jerry Ludwig: "What can I say but that it's another Jerry Ludwig jewel. Jerry and Bob Collins could put me right out of business. With these guys writing all of them, you wouldn't really need me." (In that memo he then proceeded to criticize their scripts.)[13] He was also aware his comments could wound the writers. In notes on a script based on an experience of Wambaugh's, he told Liam O'Brien and Ed Waters of the writer, "He's a fine writer and might be tight-jawed about being totally rewritten. Just tell him I'm nuts, ego mad, see myself as Sundance Kid, etc. Tell him *anything* you can think of to keep *his* ego intact."[14]

Wambaugh was very aware that the show critiqued traditional macho attitudes of both cops and other cop shows. Three years after the pilot movie, he recalled discussions about how the film showed "another potentially frightening side to this macho kid stuff wherein you could kill another human being (not in war but on the streets of your city, your neighborhood perhaps), and drink beer, notch your gun, etc."[15] During the series he objected to Gerber's calls for more action, as in this comment: "Goddamnit, there's ENOUGH fucking macho fistfights, etc., in this piece. And this one (Douglas Fairbanks and Cary Grant) is right out of *Gunga Din* but not out of *Police Story*."[16]

He also objected to casting macho types rather than good actors. In one of his more vitriolic notes, he wrote "Is somebody over there fruit for these macho personalities to the extent that they be cast in important roles? . . . I wish the guy(s) responsible for casting he-men instead of qualified actors would hurry up and come out of the goddamn closet instead of acting out his (their) fantasies at the expense of what used to be the best dramatic show on television."[17] (Wambaugh, looking at these notes fifteen years later, wrote "These letters are proof (80 proof) that booze and correspondence don't mix.")

Wambaugh was also aware of the larger social implications of the show. He objected on one script: "Don't like the inferences that a 'well-connected' guy doesn't do time. Implies a corrupt system and that's not true. It's a liberal, easy system, not corrupt."[18] In an earlier note he wrote: "ONE OF THE BIGGEST PROBLEMS I HAVE IN INTERVIEWS WITH OUT-OF-STATE JOURNALISTS IS CONVINCING THEM THAT COPS DO NOT STEAL OR TAKE GRAFT IN LOS ANGELES AND MOST

OF WESTERN AMERICA. IT'S A BITCH CONVINCING EASTERNERS AND SOUTHERN-ERS." [19]

While on the L.A. police force, Wambaugh had worked in the predominantly Latino East Los Angeles area, so he wrote some of his most detailed notes on Mark Rodgers's script "Spanish Class." He admitted it was "one of the best things he's done," but "Having said that, I also believe we should perhaps seriously consider not shooting it." He thought that when the script went out for casting there would be complaints from Mexican-American groups. He lists six pages of things he thinks might be considered insulting to them. He writes:

> I liked the good fun of the story. I don't believe the barrio is half so wild and wooly, but I could suspend my disbelief for a good rowdy story. My real problem is that I see a charge of malice being leveled at us for the way EVERYONE turns so readily on the Establishment symbols in the story. . . . Am I biased because of my love for the Eastside and the culture? Perhaps. I know I would feel the same way if we made this a ghetto story.

If it were made into a ghetto story, he was sure blacks would object. If it were Irish dockworkers, he would not mind, but "I don't think the blacks and Mexicans can take it yet. Not when it goes this far. They haven't got enough of a middle-class, respectable image as yet to withstand this kind of raucous portrayal of an 'Eastside Saturday Night.' "[20]

Most of the excesses in the script were smoothed out and the episode was shot and shown without complaint. The problem with it, as with another Rodgers script two years previously, "The Violent Homecoming," which also deals with the Mexican-American community, is that both scripts have the feeling of having been researched rather than felt. The community is seen from the outside, even though the technical advisor on "Spanish Class" was a Latino. "Spanish Class" is the better of the two, because it does have some of the rowdy quality Wambaugh liked and the acting is much better than in the earlier show.

If *Police Story* was limited in dealing with the multi-cultural elements of Los Angeles, it was also limited in its portrayal of its women characters. The women were seen very much from the male cop's perspective, either as criminals (a hooker in Salkowitz's "Informant" script) or as wives or lovers. The wives on *Police Story*, unlike Rocky King's Mabel twenty years before, at least actually appear, but they are inevitably leaving or threatening to leave. At the end of the classic "The Wyatt Earp Syndrome," which was more accurately entitled "The John Wayne Syndrome," until Wayne threatened to sue,[21] the cop's macho behavior has become too much for his wife, and he comes home to find her gone. There are occasional policewomen, such as Barbara Altoon in "Monster Manor," but Altoon is less developed a character than the men, and more of a story function: she gets inadvertently arrested when the "manor" is being used by Vice as a sting operation for hookers just as she visits one of the cops who lives there. *Police Story* is very much an "old boys' network" show and that element hurts the show in its portrayal of women.

The "old boy" quality of the show helps it in other ways. At its best, *Police Story* gets inside not only the emotions of the men doing the job, but also the male political structure of the police system, something that no police show had done before, and few have done since. Inevitably in the stories there is some kind of political pressure on the police we are following from other branches of the department. In Ed Waters's 1975 "Officer Needs Help," Billy's captain indicates after Billy's fourth shooting in recent months he may be doing his job "too good," and later the department insists Billy see a psychiatrist, which results in his slowing his reaction time in another shooting.

One of the best of the "office politics" *Police Story* episodes is E. Arthur Kean's 1974 "Incident in a Kill Zone." Kean kept seeing tapes marked SWAT in Liam O'Brien's office and asking about them, since SWAT (Special Weapons and Tactics) teams were not well known at the time. O'Brien kept telling him, "Ah, there's nothing in that." Kean finally listened to one of the tapes, a story told by Richard Kelbaugh, who later became a television writer himself. Kean said to O'Brien, "Bill, you're out of your mind. This stuff is visual, it's cinematic." The approach Kean took was: "What would happen if Richard Nixon was running a SWAT outfit?" Kean saw his main character, Sgt. Sherman, as "a [movie] director, a director running a SWAT team. 'All for me. What do I get out of this?' " Sherman constantly makes questionable calls in the field and his second in command, Yates, usually has to save the situation. Yates's supervisors support his actions, but Sherman is not only not disciplined, but promoted to lieutenant and given a desk job. Yates comments, "We're all the time saying the department doesn't have a sense of humor."

The writers admired Wambaugh, the authenticity of his work, and the opportunity to work in that vein. The writers generally did not see Wambaugh's notes, which were passed back to them by O'Brien, who managed to persuade them to change without making it a heavy-handed "Wambaugh wants the following." Sy Salkowitz did hear directly from Wambaugh once. Salkowitz had written a 90-minute *Police Story* based on the Metro Squad, but the information he had received from the cops he talked to was wrong, and he got a note from Wambaugh saying, "That's not how the Metro Squad works and they wouldn't function that way." Salkowitz remembers, "I had to redo quite a bit because they were so used to me being right all the time they had got complacent and had not sent Joe the first draft." Because it was supposed to be the final draft they had sent him, Salkowitz had to be paid additional money for another rewrite.

Art Kean's experiences with Wambaugh were more direct more often. He would often get calls from Wambaugh complaining that "No cop in the world would do what this guy's doing."

Kean would say, "Joe, that's exactly the way the guy who lived through it told it to me."

"Ah, shit."

Writers liked *Police Story* because, as an anthology, it was of necessity, in Eric Bercovici's phrase, "a writer-oriented show." This meant, for example, the writers could take an interesting character or situation and follow it out without having to worry about continuing characters or plotlines. Sy Salkowitz came across a fingerprint expert, who told Salkowitz about a murderer who left a palm print the expert was able to lift. At that time the police did not automatically take palm prints, but the expert asked them to start on everyone arrested. One day he found a match, got to the jail just before the man was let go, and arrested him for murder.

In Salkowitz's script "Fingerprint," the expert is named Charlie, he has been with Latent Prints for eight years, and is thinking about a transfer. He arrives at the jail just *after* the man has been released, so he has to chase him down on foot. Charlie is a little too old and out of shape for this, and the problem is compounded by not having a cop car to bring the man in. He tries to get a cab to take them back to the jail, but the cabbie refuses. Charlie decides he's better off staying in Latent Prints.

Art Kean explains one of the most important reasons why writers liked writing for *Police Story*, or any other anthology:

> You didn't have any asshole [star] actor to put up with, none of the Jack Lords or the Joe Pennys, impossible people, because they don't last [on *Police Story*]. They do one show and they behave like an ass, they're never asked back. And they were banging down the doors to get on *Police Story*.
>
> In my first show, I killed off a leading man at the end of the third act. That's unheard of. But we could do things like that, which meant we could create genuine suspense. We could tell stories.

One of Kean's best episodes, the 1974 "A Dangerous Age," demonstrates his point. It was unusual for a *Police Story* in that it was not based on any particular story from a policeman. The main character, Arch Tatum, an aging cop with suicidal thoughts, is based partially on the character of Kilninsky in Wambaugh's novel *The New Centurions*, and partly on Wambaugh himself, who struck Kean as self-destructive. After hearing Arch and Vinnie, the ex-cop who runs a bar frequented by cops, talk about a cop who committed suicide, we see Arch investigate a case of a family suffocated from the fumes of a hibachi in a closed space. Later we see Arch shopping and without any expression on his face, he puts a hibachi and charcoal briquets into the shopping basket. Vinnie later saves Arch when he tries to commit suicide. Because this is an anthology show, we do not know, when Arch buys the hibachi, whether he's actually going to commit suicide or not. And while he survives this attempt, the ending leaves us with the feeling that Vinnie may not save him the next time—which might not be that far in the future.

David Gerber could also be a problem for writers during the editing. Kean wrote an episode called "The Six Foot Stretch" that was shot, but then did not show up on the air. Kean asked O'Brien what the problem was and was told that Gerber was mad because the episode was eight minutes short. Kean said, "It can't be."

O'Brien replied, "Well, by the time Gerber got done with it, it was eight minutes short." Kean had written the script so the film would cut between two teams of detectives, but the show was cut so that each team's story was told separately. Kean and the episode's director, Michael O'Herlihy, screened the cut. Kean said, "I wrote this and I don't understand it."

O'Herlihy replied, "I shot it and I don't understand it. Where is all this stuff I did?"

Kean now says, "We did some fighting and we all got together and kind of ganged up on them and they rather reluctantly said, 'Well, we'll see what we can do.' The next thing I knew it was on the air. So some of it got back in, but some of it didn't."

Kean says of Gerber's interest in editing:

> Bill [O'Brien] kept saying, "We've got to protect this show from Gerber because he fucks everything up." David does belong to what I call the "butcher block" school of film editing. I shot [directed] a show for David and [producer] Chris Morgan called me and said, "You want to see Gerber's cut?"
>
> I said, "Dare I?"
>
> He said, "Well, when you see the cafe scene, you're going to get whiplash."
>
> He [Gerber] says, "It's gotta have topspin, where's the topspin, get it over there, get it going, Jesus Christ, where are we?" He gets nervous if you have a scene where two people are saying something that's important.
>
> And yet, he's in love with film, and he was passionate about it. I watched [*One Flew Over the*] *Cuckoo's Nest* with him one evening. Now this is not a Gerber picture; there are no tire squeals or gunshots or any of this stuff. He was saying, "Jesus, this is so well edited."
>
> I thought, "How does this man know?" He doesn't know anything about editing, but he did recognize good stuff. I saw then how much he loved film. He loved the making of pictures.

According to Liam O'Brien, one of Gerber's ideas that irritated Wambaugh the most was Gerber's insistence on doing potential pilots for other series on *Police Story*. Both *Joe Forrester* and *Police Woman* began as spin-offs from *Police Story*. According to O'Brien, Gerber thought that if you could do *Police Story*, you could do *Police Woman*, which was exactly the kind of show that *Police Story* was trying *not* to be: a traditional star-driven, glamorized view of crimefighting. E. Arthur Kean came up with a Christmas story that fit the show. He says, "It [the series] was a fairy tale, so I wrote a fairy tale," which Angie Dickinson, the star of the series, told Kean was the best episode they had ever done.

Wambaugh went on to become involved with the series of *The Blue Knight*. Joel Rogosin was the producer of the series the first year and recalls that Wambaugh and the network "wanted two different things." Wambaugh's vision was what one network executive describes as "ashcan drama," meaning that it was sordid by network standards. Rogosin says that it would be "possible to do it today, but not then," and that the network said, in effect, "Clean it up or we ain't going to do it."

Gerber continued to produce other shows, including several crime shows, for which he used several *Police Story* writers. In the early eighties Gerber pitched the idea of a new series on the FBI to ABC, and the network put it on as *Today's FBI*, at least partially because of what was perceived as the more conservative trend of the times.[22] One of Gerber's producers was Sy Salkowitz, who says the Bureau was "oftentimes was a pain in the ass because they didn't want to see any warts on their officers." Coming after the accounts of the FBI's misdeeds in the Hoover years, such a clean-cut approach was simply not believable. Salkowitz says that he did try to get "more into the nitty-gritty. A little of my experience with *Police Story* rubbed off. I tried to play some of the emotional jeopardy."

He still had to deal with Gerber and his calls for action. Salkowitz says, "We had a phrase called 'Gerber's trashcans.' He owned a bunch of tin trashcans which he would set up on the curb and then have cars doing chases bump into them and knock them all over hell and make all kinds of noise. Very effective."

When Salkowitz left *Today's FBI*, Gerber hired Liam O'Brien and Ed Waters to come in during the last ten weeks to try to save it, but Waters says it was "unsavable." The problem he found was that there was no characterization and that the dialogue between the main characters was "interchangable. It was just a bad concept." When Salkowitz was developing the show, the Bureau wanted it to have a woman agent, since the Bureau was under orders to hire more women. In his research visits to Bureau offices he met "a very good-looking blond young girl who was a full agent. I said to them, 'Hey, this is terrific, and they said, 'Yeah. Use these agents.' " The problem was that no specific character was created for the woman. The actress cast in the role, Carol Potter, has not (until her recent work in Fox's *Beverly Hills 90210*) had the success she deserves because of her resemblance to Jane Fonda, but nobody connected with *Today's FBI* ever thought out what could be done with an FBI agent who looked like Fonda, then still the *bête noire* of the American right.

Liam O'Brien found on *Police Story* that as soon as he developed writers, their reputations (like those who wrote on *The Naked City*) were such that they went, in O'Brien's phrase, "up the hill" to other series. He then used his talent-spotting abilities to find and develop new writers, such as Michael Mann, who became so good at doing research that even Wambaugh was hesitant to criticize the accuracy of his pieces.[23] Mann went on later to develop *Miami Vice*. John Sacret Young came onto the show as a researcher. He started doing research on one episode and ended up writing it. He was on *Police Story* for a year, then was pulled away by another show. He later co-created *China Beach*.

One show that *Police Story* writers worked on both before and after *Police Story* was its antithesis, *Hawaii 5-0*, which was created by Leonard Freeman, who thought of the show as a "documentary," according to Eric Bercovici. Art Kean tells of the sort of thing Freeman would like:

> You're on the 25th floor of a highrise. There's a woman there with a baby in her arms. This ugly looking guy boots the door. He comes in. He slaps the woman around, picks the baby up, throws it off the lanai and says to the woman, "Now, you bitch, you're going to die." That is a 5-0. That's when Lennie would say, "Wow, we're going to go with this."

As an earlier quote in this chapter from Kean suggested, writers for *Hawaii 5-0* were not particularly fond of its star, Jack Lord. One day Eric Bercovici was rewriting an episode and ended the big fight scene with the villain knocking McGarrett off the cliff, then looking down and saying, "McGarrett is dead." He turned in the script: "They got hysterical. Lennie was having a big contractual problem with Jack Lord at the time, and kept threatening him with Steve Forrest. Lennie said, 'By God, we'll shoot it the way it is.' However, the next day they said, 'Could you give us the real page?' which I'd already rewritten." The legendary status of that original last page among television writers explains why writers preferred working on *Police Story*.

·12·

LEAR AND MARSHALL

"*Talent*, like gout, sometimes skips two generations."

That is not the message you want to get in a fortune cookie when you are the son of Carl Reiner, are in your early twenties, and have had only minor success so far as an actor. It was, however, the second time in a year Rob Reiner got that fortune, and he would get it again two years later. No wonder he was wandering down Sunset Boulevard in a daze when he ran into his once and future partner, Phil Mishkin.

Mishkin and Reiner proceeded to put on a stage production called *An Evening of Dirty Plays.* This naturally attracted the attention of television producers, and in 1970 they were brought onto a new show for Andy Griffith called *Headmaster*, about a progressive school in Los Angeles. The producers wanted young writers to deal with what Mishkin calls "real now, happening problems." Their episode on kids and drugs was creamed by the critics, especially for not being particularly relevant. Mishkin agreed and thought his and Reiner's episode was "embarrassingly unreal" and that other episodes by older writers were better.

In the summer of 1971, Reiner and Mishkin were brought onto a series starring Shirley MacLaine. Mishkin says he and Reiner, whom "they'd brought in to do all the young, happening, with-it stuff came up with this wonderful story about this old, curmudgeon sidewalk chalk artist and it had not one young person in it—which disappointed everybody."

Reiner and Mishkin did pick up some worthwhile advice from the avuncular producer of the series, Sheldon Leonard, who told them, "Now a TV show, young men, is like a trip on the freeway from San Diego to Los Angeles. You can get off at a few exits, but you remember your final destination is Los Angeles." Leonard compared the theater and television audiences: "That [TV] viewing audience is very fickle and they have *schpilkes*[1] in their pants and they can get up and turn off the set. In theater you have a captive audience. In television you've got to keep them sitting in that seat."

At the end of their summer vacation on *Shirley's World,* Reiner and Mishkin returned to their regular job: working on Norman Lear's *All in the Family.*

Norman Lear

Norman Lear broke into television in the early fifties, and with his partner Ed Simmons wrote for Martin and Lewis on *The Colgate Comedy Hour.* In the late sixties Lear read in *Variety* about a new British television show, *Till Death Do Us Part,* which featured a Cockney named Alf Garnett arguing politics with his son-in-law. Lear remembered growing up on just such battles with his father and considered the possibility of an American version of the show.[2]

Lear did two pilots for the series in 1969, both of which were turned down by ABC. In 1970 he did a third pilot, and having seen some *Headmaster* episodes Reiner and Mishkin had written, asked them to write an episode for the new series. One *Headmaster* episode featured Reiner in an acting role and Lear cast him as the son-in-law.

The premise of the series and the character of Mike allowed Reiner and Mishkin to bring some "kids of the sixties" qualities to the series. The seventh episode, "Now That You Know the Way, Let's Be Strangers," was based on an incident that happened to Mishkin and his wife, Julie, when they were not yet married but were, in his words, "significant othering." They visited Mishkin's sister, who was married and had children, and did not want the unmarried couple sleeping together in the same bedroom. Mishkin thought it hypocritical not to. Reiner and Mishkin pitched the idea to Lear of Mike and Gloria's two unmarried hippie friends spending the night and Archie's reactions. During the first seasons, Reiner and Mishkin would pitch their story ideas only to Lear and did not even have to deal with the show's story editor.

Over the summer of 1971 *All in the Family,* a slow starter in the ratings in the spring, became an enormous hit. Reiner and Mishkin wrote additional episodes. As Mishkin remembers, they did not look at episodes of the British show. "We had a whole bunch of the short precis of [them], but nobody ever used them. They didn't seem to translate in terms of what we eventually wound up doing." The third episode of the second season was their first flashback episode, titled "Flashback—Mike Meets Archie." Mishkin thinks it was director John Rich who suggested doing a flashback of the first meeting, which was the only information they were given.

The first-act "curtain" was a duet/duel of Archie and Mike talking out "God Bless America." As originally written, there was dialogue after they sang, but at the Friday run-through (the show was then a "Wednesday–Tuesday" show, with the first reading Wednesday, Thursday and Friday run-throughs, Monday on-camera rehearsal, and Tuesday dress rehearsal and taping, so Friday was the first run-through without scripts), Norman Lear fell off his chair laughing and told them the end of the song was the end of the scene. Lear at the time had a medical problem with his lip that made it hurt when he laughed, and Mishkin says, "This is a strange thing for a man dealing with comedy. He'd say, 'Don't make me laugh.' "

From the beginning, *All in the Family* was dealing with subject matter not previously dealt with in American television, at least certainly not in the explicit way this show was doing it. In the second season Mishkin alone wrote an episode about Mike becoming impotent. Just six years before, *Ben Casey* did a show on male impotency in which the subject was never named; as historians Horace Newcomb and Robert S. Alley put it, "Euphemisms alone counted for ten minutes of dialogue."[3] The *All in the Family* episode had its share of euphemisms, but they did not count for ten minutes of the dialogue. In trying to explain the problem, Archie says, "Let me put it this way, he's stuck in neutral." The line got a laugh that went on so long it had to be "desweetened" (reduced in length in the editing process). Mishkin would love to take credit for the line, but admits when people compliment him on it that it was in fact ad-libbed by Carroll O'Connor during rehearsals.

Mishkin doesn't think "you were trying to get away with as much as you could" with controversial material, but "you were trying to push the envelope." He adds, "You didn't pre-censor yourself. You'd say, 'Yeah, let's try it. What's the worst thing that can happen?' Norman was the arbiter. If it made him hurt [his lip], you knew you did something good." Lear, like Schlatter on *Laugh-In*, had material put into the scripts for trading purposes with the network censor. Mishkin describes the meetings between Lear and the censors as "almost eyeball to eyeball, Khrushchev and Kennedy."

The British series included a liberal cousin, Maude, whom Lear was dying to get into his show, and he already wanted Beatrice Arthur for the part. For a December 1971 show, Mishkin pitched an idea to Lear of having everybody in the family get sick, which had happened in his family. It was not at first a story, just scenes of people complaining. Mishkin then suggested adding a visiting professor of Mike's to whom Archie could react. A few days later, Mishkin recalls, Lear said to him, "I know what it is. It's Cousin Maude."

Mishkin had already written one draft, and story editors Bernie West, Don Nicholl, and Mickey Ross were all put on the script. Mishkin was not involved in the March 1972 episode that laid out the structure of the series *Maude*. Mishkin says:

> I thought I deserved some of that "*Maude* loot" and Norman convinced me that I was young and had a great future and I didn't need to be in the arbitration. He said, "You're not getting anything. The character was already created."
>
> I said, "Yeah, but it was in my show and I did write some of it." He talked me out of it. Oh, sure, I've been eternally grateful to Norman.

Mishkin was by then on staff as a writer, which involved rewriting other scripts as well as developing his own. One such show was "The Blockbuster," in which Archie decides to sell his house, only to discover the realtor is trying to integrate the neighborhood. It was Lear's idea originally and, as Mishkin says, Lear wanted to

> do it and wanted to get it right. He was constantly having Mickey [Ross] and Bernie [West] and Don [Nicholl] and I rewrite it. It was mainly Mickey and Bernie. There were two lines that Mickey or Bernie said. The night that it was finally shot, Norman waved to us. We were sitting on the side of the stands [where the audience sat] and Mickey or Bernie said, "I think he wants us up in his office to rewrite it again." And then one of them says, "You know what my idea of hell is? It's rewriting 'Blockbuster' for eternity."

Reiner and Mishkin's first flashback episode worked so well that in the third season Lear and/or John Rich suggested they do a two-part episode on Mike and Gloria's wedding. Reiner and Mishkin got into developing the story of the wedding being on, then off, then on, and discovered that it did not really hold up for a full hour, but by then everybody was committed to a two-parter. Mishkin feels that "Storywise it falls apart, but [has] several of the nicest scenes and the most touching little scene." The latter was based on an experience of Mishkin's as a child. He had gone to Boy Scout Camp, gotten homesick, and called his father, who drove up and brought him home. In the episode, Archie reminds Gloria of a similar incident, then says, "I want you to know, if you feel the same way [on the honeymoon], you don't have to feel ashamed."

Since Reiner was acting in the series, his writing method with Mishkin changed. Mishkin recalls:

> It got to a point where I would do one act, he would do another one. Where I would do the whole rough first draft. He would take it [and work on it]. We would very rarely be in the same room during those days. Whereas the first few things we wrote together, we were always in the same room and I was at the typewriter and he'd be pacing, or if he was writing in longhand, I'd be pacing. But then it got to the point where we'd only do that after we had a draft to work off of.

Phil Mishkin was writing for other shows when Larry Rhine and Mel Tolkin came on *All in the Family* in its sixth season. The writing process on the show had become much more complex. Partly this was because the show had become an institution and, like most institutions had developed its own staff and its own methods. Partly the writing changed because of the difficulty of keeping a continuing series fresh. Tolkin notes, "The show was set, but it was still difficult, because, after five years, most shows start getting tired. Ideas run thin. Repetition." To keep it good and fresh, Tolkin found he and the other writers "just worked [our] butt[s] off."

Ideas still came from Lear and the other staff writers, but the show also depended on ideas and scripts from other writers, although outside scripts, as well as ones developed in-house, were thoroughly rewritten.[4] The idea was first seen by the producer, Mort Lachman, and then sent up to Lear. If the idea was from someone or some team on the staff, then they were generally given the assignment to do it, although the whole staff may have helped with the development of the idea. The writers then wrote a four- to five-page outline. After the outline was accepted by Lear, the script was written, with "jokes added by other teams," as Tolkin puts it. There was a final conference with Lear and the writers of the script. Lear improvised at the conference and transcripts of the conference were later provided to the writers, who found that Lear often contradicted himself several times. The writers were encouraged not to follow Lear's suggestions completely literally, but to use them to provoke their own imaginations.

The show was by this time a "Monday–Saturday" show, with the first readings on Monday morning. The script being done the following week was read, and after lunch there was what Tolkin calls "an immense ripping of the script" by the actors. He remembers, "I never heard such brilliant, intellectual reasoning for changing" material as came from the entire cast. Larry Rhine remembers that after the reading he would watch Carroll O'Connor walking up and down outside eating an apple, and then come back with detailed comments on the script. Rhine says he has not come across any other actor who was as good at making suggestions for changes as O'Connor was. After the script was "ripped to pieces," in Tolkin's phrase, the writers of that script were sent off to rewrite it.

Also Monday morning the script being produced that week was read, and in the afternoon it was "put on its feet" in rehearsal. If it was felt the script needed a few more jokes, or if the writers had written in the script "JTC," meaning "joke to come," the current script was sent back to its writers. On Tuesday, the script was played before a small group of writers, producers, and agents, and more rewrites came out of that; and on Wednesday there was another run-through for an inside audience, with more rewrites afterwards. On Thursday the show was acted out for the writers, and Thursday night the writing staff stayed late doing revisions as necessary. This included suggestions from the actors and the director. On Friday the show was done on stage with props, and the rewriting was minimal.

By this point in the run of *All in the Family*, the show had gone to two tapings on Saturday before two separate audiences, one taping at about five, another about eight. There was dinner between tapings at what Tolkin remembers as a "long, long table" at which Norman Lear presided. Occasionally lines were changed, but often an actor such as O'Connor would insist the line was good but his own reading was off and rather than change the line, he would try to improve his reading. Tolkin says of these Saturday sessions, "I don't recall any panicky changes, just a line did get a laugh or didn't get a laugh. If a scene doesn't work, that's a problem, but by Saturday we'd tried it on audiences so that we were certain the scenes were already working very well." After the second taping, pickup shots (brief shots of reactions or line readings that were not caught in the first tapings) were done. With all the rewriting, writers hardly recognized some of the scripts, even though their names were on them—not an unusual occurrence in television.

Other Lear Shows

The enormous success of *All in the Family* lead to other Lear-produced shows that dealt with social issues in the same kind of high-intensity way. *Maude* was a direct spin-off in 1972 of *All in the Family*, and dealt with Maude involving herself in politics, having an abortion,[5] and going through menopause. These subjects created difficulties for some of the "with it, happening, now" younger writers, such as Thad Mumford, who was 24 when he started on the show. An older writer asked him, "Why do you want to write this show *[Maude]*? You're too young. You don't know how to do this. You have to live a little bit." Mumford was at the time "really offended" but thinks now the writer was right. Even though Mumford was on the show for parts of two seasons and wrote "some funny things, I was still never a part of the show because there were things to write about that I just really didn't know how to relate to. Again, I was really getting by on glibness, and that's not enough when you really want to write with substance."

Just as Lear spun off *Maude* from *All in the Family*, he spun off *Good Times* from *Maude* in 1974. He tried for some time to develop a series about Maude's maid, Florida, and her husband and their children. Lear asked Michael Evans, who played Lionel on *All in the Family*, if he had any ideas. Evans and his playwright friend Eric Monte came up with a couple of scripts, then Monte did some scripts himself. Lear asked Allan Manings to read the scripts to see if anything could be done with them. Manings liked the basic idea and wrote a new script based on the characters in the previous scripts. Lear called Manings at 1 A.M. after reading the script and said, "I just have to thank you. This is a wonderful piece of work and we can go right to the floor with this." Manings says now, "You don't get that often. Now, fourteen rewrites later, I said to him, 'Whatever happened to "I love this"?' He said, 'Oh, no, no, you must understand. I loved it for what it was going to become.'"

Manings stayed on as producer, with Monte as staff writer. Manings's idea for the show was "To present an entire black family" (the original title had been *The Black Family*), a family with both a mother and father present. Manings thinks the show was misunderstood, and that may reflect the way people watch television. People believed that family was on welfare. Maybe it was a white American view of black people, [but] even black people wrote in, "Why must we always see black people who are unemployed?" The reality was, the father was never out of work. He had shitty jobs, as befitted a man with a Mississippi grade school education, but he was continually trying to move forward. I saw the show, and I think Norman agreed, as a show about immigrants. It was my family, coming to America, and a family striving to make life better so the children will not have to go through it.

Manings thinks the show was misunderstood and/or neglected by audiences and critics "because people saw Jimmie [Walker] and not the show." Walker's stardom surprised people connected with the show as much as Edd Byrnes's stardom had to those working on *77 Sunset Strip*. Manings structured the show in the expectation that the younger son, Michael, played by Ralph Carter, would become the spokesman. Manings says,

He is the kid who has grown up out of the Civil Rights Movement, has the courage to say these things. I also said, "America will not accept any militantism coming out of John Amos's mouth. It'll be too threatening." It was really a belief. Not that he hasn't the right to say it. Of course he does, but they ain't going to watch this. That's a threatening black man.

Manings tells what happened:

In looking for the part of J.J., we had great difficulty finding [an actor]. I had seen a comic in New York, Jimmie Walker, and my wife Whitney had said, "That's your boy, young man."
I said, "No, he's a standup comic. He's not an actor." I prefer to work with actors whom I would bend. And she kept saying, "He's your man." Finally I showed Norman a piece of tape of Jimmie on *The Tonight Show* or something, and that was that. Now I was right. He was a comic. We did the first show. He heard the first laugh. He played the audience from there on in. Now when the show was over, I said, "O.K., hell of a nice show, friends. Now we're going to stay and do it without the audience."
They said, "Why?"
I said, "Because I can't edit anything because you're always looking out there." So I said, "I'm going to sit here and when you say the joke looking at the actor, I'm going to go, 'Ha, ha, ha, ha, ha."
He said, "Oh, I didn't know you wanted singles. I'm sorry I hit homers."
But he took off. I thought the young kid would take off. And he took off.

Manings's idea that the show should be about a complete black family did not survive Jimmie Walker's stardom. John Amos, who played the father, wanted a greater salary increase than the producers and the network were willing to pay, and he was written out of the show in 1976 by having his character killed off.[6] Esther Rolle, who played Florida, was unhappy with the idea of J.J. as a role model, and was temporarily written out of the show in 1977.[7] The net effect was to throw the storylines even more to Walker's J.J.

Manings was also responsible for the most non-Lear of the Lear shows, *One Day at a Time*. Manings's contract with Lear called for him to do a pilot, so Manings wrote up an idea he had been pitching for years: the life of a recently divorced woman. Manings and Lear wrote the first pilot, which was not aired. In it Ann Romano has only one daughter (Mackenzie Phillips), has a woman friend she confides in, is just moving in, and is already a nurse. Neither Lear or Manings wanted the woman to have a profession, but wanted her to try several jobs. There was also a moving man in the pilot who pinches Ann's ass. She tells him, "Do that one more time and you'll be singing soprano."

The man tells his partner, "She loves me."

The partner says, "She just threatened you."

The man replies, "Yeah, but where did she chose?" Lear thought he was too rich a character to lose, and he became Schneider, the building superintendent. Actor Pat Harrington took one look at the detailed description of him in the script and said, "I know this man."

Like *Good Times*, *One Day at a Time* went through changes, with the daughter Julie getting married in 1979 and leaving the series in 1980, Barbara getting married in 1982, and Ann remarrying the following year. Manings thinks "Well-written shows survive these things very easily." He says that in "those first hopeful days" when the show is being developed, he tries to work out where the stories and the characters will be in five years. Sometimes the show does not work out as planned, as happened on this one:

> One of the things got lost early on, and [it was] my fault as much as anyone else's. In the pilot the Barbara character, Valerie Bertinelli, has made the boy's basketball team and I wanted to carry that through, as this little, trailblazing girl, but it fell out immediately because she was so adorable that everyone kept saying, "[She's] the prettiest thing that ever happened." She became less of that and more of a pretty girl who is trying to get along, and the [character of the] sister became the more whiny problem.

Not every Lear show was a hit. In 1977, Lear produced a series for syndication called *All That Glitters*, which proposed a role-reversed world in which women were in charge. The show was an "idea comedy," but unlike the best of Lear's shows it found its comedy only in ideas, without the characterization of *All in the Family* and *One Day at a Time*. Richard Powell wrote for the show and says that Lear was not originally supposed to have any input, but "when we started, his input was considerable." Powell thinks that for a variety of reasons Lear was not at his creative best on this show. Mel Tolkin describes Lear at his best:

Demanding, but not difficult. It's difficult when you write your guts out and he writes on top of the script that it's not good. But then he says on another script, "It's wonderful." There are notes on the side of the script in pencil, in his writing, what he needs, what's necessary, where it goes wrong. And his opinions were damned good.

His opinions on *All That Glitters* were not.

Lear's Influence

Norman Lear's shows in the early to mid-seventies accelerated the opening up of American television. There were other contributing factors as well. In 1973 Rick Mittleman wrote for an aborted series based on the 1969 film *Bob & Carol & Ted & Alice*. The film deals in brilliant comic terms with the changes in sexuality among the upper middle classes. It was quite legitimately rated "R." Mittleman thinks one reason the possibility of a series based on the movie was even considered was because of a change of executives in the television industry. Mittleman found the executives younger, a reason they might have been drawn to such material. The newer executives also tended to make decisions by committee. One way of finding a consensus was to pick already-popular material such as a hit film. The executives tended to be in Programming, however, and the writers and producers still had to deal with Standards and Practices. This conflict between the two branches would only increase over the next decades. The television version of *Bob & Carol & Ted & Alice* got caught in the squeeze and died after three episodes.

Lear's success with "ethnic" shows led to similar shows. In 1976 Phil Mishkin worked on a show called *Viva Valdez*, about a Latino family in East Los Angeles trying to hold on to its traditional values in a changing world. Mishkin describes the complexities of doing the show:

> One of the trickiest problems was to keep the show on the air, to make it homogeneous and yet true to the subject that we were talking about, and those were the problems that for the first time faced me directly. I had nobody else that was telling me [how to do it]. There was no Norman Lear there. I was the main guy there. There were executive producers whom I was trying to tell how to do stuff. And I had a nice group of writers named Sol Weinstein, Harold Albrecht, Bernie Kahn, Earl Barrett.
>
> We wrote some wonderful scripts, and Marcy Carsey, who was an ABC executive at the time [and who later produced *The Cosby Show*], made a comment, "I wonder how scripts that make me laugh out loud when they cross my desk turn into such shit when I see them on the screen?"
>
> One of the problems was that we used a cast of Latino actors who were constantly at odds with us over authenticity. It was one of the great us-against-them fights that I was ever involved in. No matter what show I've ever been involved in, there's always an us-against-them. It's always, "Those writers are giving us

bullshit that we can't say." "Those damned actors can't say our bullshit." But in that case it was also ethnic mix. It seemed to give them the right to say, "You Jewish writers don't know what the hell you're talking about." I think we weren't all Jewish, but I remember somebody said to me, "Write it Jewish and their Latino accents will make it funny and Latin." That was a certain kind of ethnic divisiveness that I didn't hold with.

We also had a problem with Justicia and Nosotros [Latino advocacy groups] constantly saying, "We have to have more Latinos working on the show. We have to be able to see the scripts." And I can understand that. Boy, can I understand that. On the other hand, it made it awful hard to be funny.

We tried to [get some Latino writers for the show]. We tried to break some in. We had some apprentices, but they never worked out. They hadn't come up from the start. Still and all, we were trying to do a comedy. And they were not the people [to write comedy]. It's a profession writing comedy. It's a tough one. Just because a guy is a good writer or a good Latino writer didn't mean that he could do a good Latino comedy.

The audience just didn't buy into that confusion. Maybe they never would have. Maybe it could have been the funniest show in the world and we still never would have gone with an audience because people are just downright unwilling to accept an ethnic mix like that. It's a problem that's not going to be solved until we solve it outside of this.

Mishkin knew the importance of a strong producer like Lear in handling that kind of material. He once worked on *Chico and the Man*, which was produced by James Komack. Mishkin came up with an idea for a show in which Chico finds a statue that he brings back to the garage. The statue starts to bleed and garage business picks up. Komack loved the idea, according to Mishkin, and said, "I will fight tooth and nail for this show." Mishkin says Komack backed down "as soon as he got the first message of any kind that he had a fight on his hands."

The network thought the idea was sacrilegious and made fun of Catholics, but liked the basic idea, which Mishkin compares to "throwing away the baby and keeping the bathwater." Mishkin continues:

You know something? I'm such a whore. I'll do it because I still think there's something in this story. So I researched some Aztec, Mayan imagery and there's one earth mother, who is the equivalent of the Virgin Mary.

I wrote the script, and naturally it did not have the same kind of [impact], tell[ing] the guy to believe in an Incan statue. It took the guts out of it, and they never shot it anyway, because it was a dishonest little story. There are no miracles in that [religion]. I tried to save it. I tried to give it resuscitation, but it's just not the same thing. It's brain dead. And maybe that's my final comment on television: it's brain dead.

Garry Marshall

By 1970 Garry Marshall and his partner Jerry Belson had written hundreds of episodes of television shows. When Paramount decided to make a television series out of Neil Simon's *The Odd Couple*, the studio asked them to do it, and they became producers as well.[8] Phil Mishkin wrote for Marshall as well as Lear:

> It's as different as Garry Marshall and Norman Lear. It was much more table to *[The Odd Couple]*. The rewriting was done at the table as opposed to notes and then take it upstairs and do [the rewrite]. [For] *All in the Family* I found there was an awful lot of rewrites [from] notes given at the table, but the actual lines pitched out [Mishkin is here using the term "pitched" to mean a line suggested rather than in the more traditional sense of telling a proposed story to a producer or story editor] were not taken down by the secretary, [who] then goes and types it up. With *The Odd Couple* it was definitely done at the table and Alice James, Garry's script assistant [would take down the lines].
>
> I thought that was the best way to do television. You sit around the table with funny people and that includes the stars, in that case, Tony [Randall] and Jack [Klugman]. [Writer] Harvey Miller was there, Garry was there, Jerry Belson was there. Jerry would just come in one day a week, but he's one of the funniest people extant. And Harvey was incredible. So sitting at the table trying to pitch with these people, [you have to be] terrific. Some guys are just not good at that [who] are much more funny, but they just can't get it in there.
>
> Harvey Miller was one of the great pitching guys. That would fool you, make you think that it was funnier than it was because he was so funny. He also had this confidence: "I'm saying it's great." Then the guys would go, "I got it, I got it, I got it." [The actors would] say the line, it stinks. "It's funny, huh?"
>
> That's the way a show gets pitched, and then there's one entity at the table [who] is the man who nods, it's in or out. In that season I worked on *Odd Couple*, it was Harvey. If Garry was ever at the table, Harvey would defer to Garry. Everybody would defer to Garry Marshall. Garry wasn't a great pitcher, but if anybody understands comedy, I think Garry is probably the top. Maybe Robbie [Reiner], Robbie or Garry.
>
> Garry's contribution was knowing the two people out in the audience who were watching the show. He called them Mae and Vern. They lived in Oklahoma. What he would say is, "Mae, come in here. You the writers?" He'd do this thing in a sort of half-Bronx, half-Oklahoma accent. (Garry has this way of talking. I think [comedian] Phil Foster taught them all how to speak. Everybody winds up sitting at the table and talking exactly alike.) He says, "Oscar just said [something]." Garry said, "It's not funny. Mae doesn't think it's funny." And he knew, he knew. Sometimes you'd be surprised. You'd go, "Garry, that's cheap. It's not funny." And all of a sudden, you'd go to show night, and the audience they'd bus in from Farmer's Market [a gathering place for tourists in L.A.] was hysterical at the line, because that was Mae and Vern. So he saw Mae and Vern in these [people], he knew what was right and what wasn't.

Rick Mittleman had similar experiences with Marshall and Belson on the show:

> They were very, very creative in the meetings. You'd come in with two-line ideas and they'd go with it. Garry Marshall drove the meetings. Jerry Belson was

more of a kind of sniper. He'd be lounging around, usually in a reclining position. Then when you got into a problem, he'd come up with a solution to the stalemate. He was also strong on the floor in rehearsals, coming up with funny stuff for the actors to do.

Mishkin defines Belson's contribution:

> He was the chief cynic. And Jerry made Tony Randall laugh . . . . And when I was there, Jerry would come in and his deal was, after he saw the script, if he was bored or tired, [he would say], "It looks good. It looks nice. I'm going. I consulted." Jerry must have come up with some funny lines, but I don't remember him ever struggling.

Unlike the Norman Lear shows, *The Odd Couple* did not deal with controversial material. In "The Hideaway" Oscar finds an Eskimo quarterback, but Felix wants the man to accept a music scholarship, which turns out to be offered to him because the Conservatory needs a token Eskimo. Jerry Belson told how the story changed: "When we started rehearsing the show, it was supposed to be a black kid, but it got so preachy and so un-Odd Coupley, that we changed it to an Eskimo. We thought it couldn't possibly get preachy, trying to compare whites to the Eskimo . . . while we didn't strike a blow for civil rights, we did strike a blow for comedy."[9]

The Odd Couple was a one-camera show during its first season, but in the second season switched to three-camera. Marshall had wanted three-camera from the beginning, but it was only the clout of Randall and Klugman that allowed the change.[10] Belson was reluctant to make the change because he thought it was a more serious show about divorce and thought the one-camera technique caught more of the New York atmosphere. He changed his mind after seeing the show shot three-camera, deciding that the crucial element was the characters and the actors' ability to play those characters directly to the audience.[11] Belson recalled later, "Oddly enough, whereas the first dozen shows or so seemed funny on paper, when they aired they didn't seem as funny. When we did some of the later ones in front of a live audience, it started changing things. You begin to write a little broader and get bigger laughs."[12]

A potential problem with the Garry Marshall method of rewriting at the table was the tendency to keep changing the material. Harvey Miller thought there were some scripts that were better in their first draft forms than in their "improved" forms.[13] Mark Rothman had a chance to prove this when he produced *The New Odd Couple* in 1982, with the roles taken over by an all-black cast. He went back to the original drafts of several of the scripts from the first series and used material from those drafts. He said later, "[The material] worked. The studio audience tells you if it works, and it did."[14] The revised scripts, however, did not reflect a particular black point of view. There was also a problem because the original scripts were written specifically for Randall and Klugman, and while the new cast was good, they simply brought different qualities to the roles that the old scripts did not take into account.[15]

Marshall's biggest hit, *Happy Days*, began as a 1972 episode of *Love American Style* he was not involved with, called "Love and the Happy Days," which starred Ron Howard.[16] As a result of his role, Howard was cast in the film *American Graffiti*, which along with the Broadway success of *Grease*, persuaded ABC that the nostalgia boom for the fifties had begun.[17] Marshall produced a second pilot in which a minor character called The Fonz was pushed more into the story to contrast to Howard's Richie Cunningham, and the show got on the air in 1974.[18] Phil Mishkin wrote an episode for the show called "She Goes All the Way," about a girl with a "reputation" that Richie had helped her get by lying about her. Mishkin says it turned out to be a "fairly explicit subject for television circa 1974" and it was "kind of daring for that show. Not that anybody said that show was going to be relevant. It was going to be a comedy about the fifties." It was a show not about the real fifties, but about the nostalgia industry's vision of the fifties, in which a nice, middle-class family like the Cunninghams would actually *like* a motorcycle rider in a black leather jacket.

In the third season, the writers, according to Marshall

whipped up one [script] about a couple of bimbos from the wrong side of the tracks who the boys date. We were late and I didn't want to take a chance, so I asked Penny [Marshall, his sister, whom he had hired for a recurring role in *The Odd Couple*] and Cindy [Williams], who I knew very well, to play the characters. The first time they were on the show, the camera operator, Sam Rosen, said, "Come here." He showed me a two-shot through the camera of Penny and Cindy standing in their costumes and said, "That's a series."

I always was looking around and saying, "What's not out there?" There were no blue-collar women at all. I said I thought it's time for blue collar and took a shot at it.[19]

Marshall had already begun, as Carl Reiner and Sheldon Leonard had before him, to develop writers, and writers into producers. He said later:

I realized that, as "the boss of a sitcom," it was just too hard to turn out one show every week, and that to turn out another sitcom was just suicide. So I started developing writers. . . .

I always took a couple of solid writers who were ready to run a show, and a couple of beginners. And then on every show I always had an older writer, somebody from the old days, who had written for Jack Benny and Bob Hope. The kids would say, "Here's a new idea," and the old-timers would say, "We did that. On Eddie Cantor, we did that."

I took writers who had no phones, they lived in vans. I said, "Who cares how they live, as long as they can write." I had a lot of writers who went through that period with me. They became very powerful, you had to give them producer work, then you had to give them shows, they were too good to all be on the same show. They had trained well enough to go out on their own. So we started making up shows.[20]

After *Laverne and Shirley* had been on for two years, Marshall brought in Phil Mishkin to supervise it. The emphasis on the show by this time was not so much on the blue-collar element as on the physical slapstick, and the storylines were created the way Davis and Carroll had created stories for *I Love Lucy*: look for some physical action that can involve the characters, and then build a story from it. One week Mishkin's wife, Julie, came in and pitched an idea about industrial spies. Chris Thompson, one of the producers, said, "Oh, we can do them falling into the beer vat." Mishkin says, "That's how you said yes to a story." He adds, "Then in my season we copped out by having [them] just do a talent show. When in doubt, you did the talent show."

Marshall, because he had so many shows on the air, was not around as much as he had been on *The Odd Couple*. Mishkin remembers one of the few times Marshall came in:

We had our run-through and then our table and the rewrite, sitting around this table in the Paramount conference room. We ordered from Nickodell's or Oblath's, and everybody would be eating. Oh, we ate well. Then, after you finish eating, or while you're eating, you're starting to do your rewrite and your pitching. Garry is the one who started using apprentice writers. Young writers, before they get paid, but they're writers. They're in there pitching. Now I'm the supervising producer of his show, which he doesn't have much to do with anymore, but he comes by the conference room once, and he says, "Phil, I want to talk to you."

"What's the matter?"

He says, "I notice the apprentices are sitting at the table eating with the regular writers. Make them stand up and eat. If they eat standing up, they'll work much harder to become real writers. Marty Nadler didn't have a meal sitting down for a year. Now he's producing." The logic of it was so true.

Now, how do you do that? So I started saying, "Everybody, listen up. It's getting a little crowded around [the table], so we're going to have to start like not having everybody sit here, so who's [it] not going to be? Well, the girls and the script supervisor, they've got to sit there. The writers. They're writing. I guess, boom, boom, boom." One, Jeff Franklin, who was an apprentice during my reign at *Laverne and Shirley*, is now one of the richest men in show business. I can't believe it. I just cannot believe it. On that day I got him up out of his seat so he couldn't finish his meal from Oblath's.

By the time Thad Mumford worked on the Garry Marshall show *Angie* in 1979, Marshall was even less in evidence. Mumford thinks Marshall saw the scripts, but "He was never there. He might have been there [after] we left. 'All those guys gone? O.K., I'm coming over now.' But I met him once."

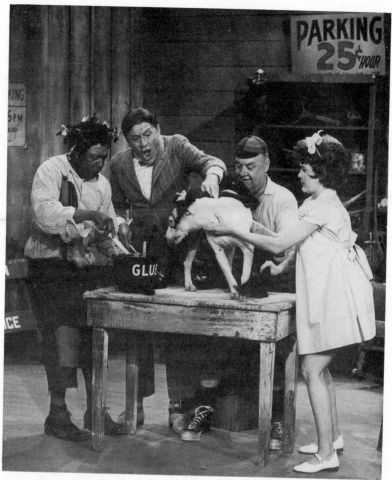

Jack Benny and his gang could do visual humor, although this take-off on "Our Gang" is not exactly vintage Benny.

It probably did not take *all* of Milton Berle's six writers to come up with the lines on the blackboard.

Lucille Ball doing one of her greatest routines; somewhere off-camera a young Madelyn Davis is upset that Ball is not getting the words *exactly* as they were written.

Your Show of Shows doing what it did best: parodying great movies, in this case *Shane*.

Two Sixties doctors: LEFT: A smiling Dr. Kildare and. . .
RIGHT: . . . a hulking Ben Casey. You do not write the same for both.

Lawyers, part 1: *The Defenders* had intelligent writing, simple sets, and a picture of Lincoln on the wall.

"Gotham reality": where do you park the Batmobile?

George Burns was right: to do *Mr. Ed* you really have to believe the horse talks.

Actress Theresa Graves, some time between *Laugh-In* (note the chains) and *Get Christie Love!* (note the long-sleeved dress).

Laugh-In kinderspiel:
Bulk orders were left.

The SCTV crowd: How many characters can these people play?

The *M*A*S*H:* crowd: Caught for once with their scripts.

M*A*S*H: "The Interview," written by Larry Gelbart and others.

Jack Klugman as Quincy, lecturing somebody as usual; offscreen it was the writers.

Lawyers, part 2: *L.A. Law* had intelligent writing, slightly more elaborate sets, and the USC Trojan Marching Band instead of a picture of Lincoln.

All right, one picture of a writer: What better than Eric Bercovici practicing what E. Arthur Kean calls Bercovici's "You say that again and you die" look, which he uses on network executives.

Dr. Kildare not smiling: Richard Chamberlain in *Shogun*.

Hill Street Blues: A world in which Nydorf (Pat Corley, right) could be a coroner.

The reason Sam Whipple (right) is smiling is that he knows what Whoopi Goldberg (left) does not yet: That the network is calling to thank her for saying "bitch" instead of "ho" at the second taping of *Bagdad Cafe*.

Michael and Elliot are paying particular attention to what Miles Drentell is saying because Ken Olin and Timothy Busfield know that David Clennon can "cut two diametrically opposed thoughts completely clean" in a single speech.

Dana Delany and the "moral weight" she brought to *China Beach*: Playing for keeps.

·13·

MTM AND M*A*S*H

MTM

*A*lthough it was the best thing he ever did for America, with the possible exception of resigning as vice-president, Spiro T. Agnew's contribution to the development of *The Mary Tyler Moore Show* was minuscule. There were others who did more. Much more.

First, of course, there was Mary Tyler Moore. In April 1969, after some time away from television, she co-starred in the special *Dick Van Dyke and the Other Woman*, which reminded both viewers and executives how good she was. CBS wanted her to appear in a series. Moore's husband, Grant Tinker, got a firm commitment from CBS to thirteen episodes without a pilot, to be developed by Tinker and Moore's production company. The company was called MTM and it was one of a group of independent television production companies (such as Norman Lear's Tandem/TAT) that started and flourished in the seventies. The Federal Communications Commission in 1970 changed the Financial Interest Rule and Syndication Rule so that independent producers would retain the syndication rights and not have to repay the networks profits the producers made on the syndication of their programs.[1] Because the independent companies were smaller and more intimate, they could and did create a more cordial atmosphere for individual artists to work in, ushering in a second Golden Age of television writing.

It is not surprising that Grant Tinker would work out such an effective business and artistic organization. His TV experience included work at advertising agencies, a network, and two major studios.[2] While at 20th Century–Fox he supervised a show called *Room 222*, a gentle, one-camera comedy about high school. The show, like *Mr. Novak* a few years before, dealt with issues such as prejudice and drugs, but in a less shrill manner than Lear's comedies. The show was created by James L. Brooks, whose previous credits were primarily David L. Wolper documentaries, and it was written and produced by Allan Burns, whose writing credits included *The Munsters, He &*

She, and *Love American Style.*[3] They had not worked together as a team when Tinker asked them to come up with a show for Moore. All he told them was that she was to be a single woman living in Minneapolis, since he knew that if she were married, the show would invariably be compared to *The Dick Van Dyke Show.*

Brooks and Burns's original idea was that she would be divorced and working as a researcher for a newspaper gossip columnist. Burns later recalled the divorce angle "as being something that was interesting." It was just at the beginning of the women's movement, and, Burns said, "We might not feel it necessary today to explain why a woman at age thirty-one is not married but at that time—curious isn't it how that would change now?—we thought it was necessary to explain."[4] Burns also realized that most writers in the industry had divorce stories that might be usable for the show.[5]

CBS had other ideas, since this was six years before Lear's *One Day at a Time* on the same network. When Brooks and Burns pitched the idea, the executives were horrified. As Burns was fond of recalling, they were told certain subjects were "forbidden" on the network, among them divorce, Jewish people, people from New York, and mustaches.[6]

This of course is where Spiro Agnew comes in. The focus of the show shifted from the single woman's social to working life, and Burns and Brooks felt that the researcher job could not carry the show, so they looked for other work. In 1969 Agnew's informal function as vice-president was castigating the news media. Brooks had worked at CBS News in New York as his first job in television, and Mary Tyler Moore thinks that Agnew's speeches and discussions of them may have helped Burns and Brooks decide to set *The Mary Tyler Moore Show* in the newsroom of a local television station.[7]

The newsroom setting makes the show more similar to *The Dick Van Dyke Show* than originally intended by picking up the earlier show's connections between the home and the workplace, but like *Room 222* the workplace is more of a family surrogate than on the Van Dyke show. Brooks and Burns also created a backstage family by hiring writers they either knew or had worked with before.[8] The writers on the Moore show became a series of what Burns calls "interlocking friendships over many years."[9] Just as Lear and Marshall's organizations expanded to create spin-off shows from *All in the Family,* so did MTM.

The writing process on *The Mary Tyler Moore Show* and the other MTM comedies was, in Phil Mishkin's word, more "communal" than on the other comedy shows. Whereas on the other shows the writer would discuss the idea in brief terms and then go off and write either the story or even a script, on the Moore show, Mishkin remembers, "The scripts were much more written in the room, even before you sat down to write your story." He met with James L. Brooks and Ed. Weinberger, one of the producers, and worked out the story in detail, then brought back the script.

Mishkin was used to working on the rewriting during the week the show was done, but on the Moore show, "I remember the first time they read the draft they said it was terrific. They loved it, and then [said], 'Look, the way we work, we won't even need a rewrite [from you]. We take it [and do the rewrite] ourselves from here. See you around.' " Mishkin attended the filming, and he says, "They shot a show that barely resembled the script that I gave them. There was a lot of stuff that they kept because a lot of lines that were in my script were lines that we got from the pitching session. It's nothing that I've ever been surprised by, [but] I know a lot of people who work television are continually shocked that their child is molested so radically."

The Mary Tyler Moore Show was what Grant Tinker called "character comedy,"[10] which is one of the reasons for the changes in the rewriting. Allan Burns thought that the creators of the series knew the characters better and the thrust of the show, and even scripts written by staff writers were heavily rewritten during the rehearsal period.[11] Steve Pritzker, one of the early staff writers on the Moore show, felt that having the staff writers involved as they constantly were on the rewrites, the rehearsals, and even the shooting "made a big difference in the nuances" of the characterizations,[12] which was a change from the tradition of the three-camera audience show's being less subtle than a one-camera show, where, as Pritzker points out, "You just write it and ship it" and the director is more in control.[13] And in spite of having his "child" molested, Mishkin thinks the Moore show and that kind of writing holds up better than the work on *All in the Family*. He says, "I watch those old *All in the Families* and they were so topical that they don't seem to have the lasting, universal appeal, except for the ones where he [Archie] is doing his stock figure stuff. But the characters in *Mary Tyler Moore* . . . hold up better."

Mishkin's experience writing another MTM show, *Paul Sand in Friends and Lovers* captures how the emphasis was put on character. Mishkin pitched an idea about two guys, one of them the character played by Paul Sand, having a fight over something. What struck Brooks about the idea was how adult men do not back down. As they discussed the scene in which Sand is using his wit to quiet a man talking in a theater, Brooks said, "The more he feels this power of his intellect, the worse it gets for him, because people are laughing. You get the feeling that you could say nothing that's not funny. And then all of a sudden the reality hits him"—that there is going to be a fight.

For all the concern about character, there was still the desire to be funny. Mishkin recalls the pitch meeting on the same episode:

> They were struggling with the ending. Everybody was trying to make the thing be true-to-life. When you're doing TV, the dirty word is "That's too sketchy," meaning it's not real. (I remember somebody else I was working with said, "You know what sketch is? Sketch is anything that the producer didn't suggest.") At one point, struggling to get Paul Sand a way out of this situation, somebody says, "He brings a vicious dog along."

"Nah, that's sketchy."

He says, "But we all were laughing."

Jim [Brooks] was one of the first ones that said, "Nah, it's sketchy." I remember he just all of a sudden stopped and he goes, "But it's funny. Guys, we're doing a comedy. This made us laugh." We went for the dog.

The writers on the MTM shows were aware of the differences between their shows and Lear's shows. This was especially true of the writers of *The Mary Tyler Moore Show.* Treva Silverman recalled the episode where Mary's parents have come to visit and Mary's mother says to her husband, "Be sure to take your pill," and both Mary and her father reply in unison, "I will." Silverman said:

> That almost gets by and then people say, "Did I just hear what I thought I heard?" And very casually we hear that Mary takes the pill. We've exonerated all the women who ask, "Oh, suppose my mother finds out?" A show on CBS about people she loves and respects, here's a woman taking the pill. And that was influential in a very private way, I think.[14]

In spite of the efforts of Agnew and his acquaintances to reverse the opening up of American public life, especially as seen on television, the writers of even "softer" shows than Lear's were able to handle subjects American television had not touched before. The emphasis on character made those issues pleasantly acceptable to American audiences. Pleasantly, because the shows were always funny, and filled with the family business atmosphere that mirrored the activities of their creators. Allan Burns attributed at least part of this to working in the three-camera technique, saying,

> Doing hour-long one-camera shows and half-hour three-camera shows is an entirely different way of working. One is conducive to the interplay of a family of players and producers and the writers' concept and the other is the reverse . . . . So it's not conducive to the same spirit. Enforced sociability went with the three-camera shows.[15]

Not entirely. In the late seventies MTM moved into hour shows, and at least in some of them in the eighties, the same kind of "enforced sociability" seemed to exist among the writers, and that, particularly on *Hill Street Blues,* changed American television as much as the MTM shows had in the seventies.

*M*A*S*H*

Battle Circus, a bland 1953 theatrical film about a Mobile Army Surgical Hospital, or MASH, unit in the Korean War, was not an artistic success, and it should be noted (you *will* learn why later) that theater plumbing was not strained by the meager crowds that saw the film.

In the late sixties, Dr. H. Richard Hornberger, a doctor who had served in a MASH unit in Korea, and a co-writer, W. C. Heinz, wrote a novel based on the doctor's experiences. It was called *M*A*S*H* and, after being turned down by seventeen publishers,[16] was published in 1968 under the pseudonym Richard Hooker. Producer Ingo Preminger bought the film rights before publication,[17] and signed former blacklisted screenwriter Ring Lardner, Jr., to adapt the book.

The book is not an easy one to adapt.[18] It is very episodic, with each story self-contained in a single chapter, and with only the surgeons continuing throughout the book. The writing is repetitive, the dialogue bland, and there is very little characterization. The first part of the novel is almost a conventional service comedy, the gore of the operating room coming in only halfway through.

Lardner's screenplay[19] improves on the novel considerably. Lardner takes several incidents from the novel and runs them throughout the script, such as the story of the doctors' Korean houseboy, Ho-Jon. He establishes the operating room gore early in the script and intensifies it as the story continues. Lardner also adds characterization, as with Corporal "Radar" O'Reilly, who is a trick (sensitive hearing) in the novel rather than a character. The script is more intellectually complex than the novel, although it does expand on the novel's tendency to humiliate the characters, specifically in creating the scene not in the novel in which head nurse Major Houlihan is exposed in the shower.

The director Preminger hired was Robert Altman, whose direction of *M*A*S*H* is seriously flawed. One story element demonstrates the problem. In chapter seven, Hooker tells the story of Ho-Jon, the houseboy drafted into the Korean army, who comes back to the unit as a patient. Hawkeye gets the recovered Ho-Jon into his old college. Lardner runs Ho-Jon's story throughout the film, with Ho-Jon returning as a patient in the third quarter of the script. The climactic football game, which in the novel has no motivation, is played to raise money to send Ho-Jon to college. After the game, the doctors learn that Ho-Jon has died while the game was on, and we see his body being taken away as the doctors play cards in the foreground.

Under Altman's direction, only a bit of Ho-Jon as a patient appears in the film, and then much earlier and with no information that Ho-Jon is the patient on the table when the electrical energy fails. Altman's letting the actors play the patient scene so casually meant the scene could not be used in its proper place, because the doctors would seem even more heartless than he has already let them be. The football game then becomes unmotivated in the film, and the impact of Ho-Jon's body being taken away is lost because we cannot identify it. The sloppiness of Altman's direction has left the film much less intense than it should have been with Lardner's script and more the conventional service comedy it was not supposed to be. The film is one (of unfortunately many, particularly American, films[20]) that succeeds in spite of its director rather than because of him.

The film of *M*A*S*H* did succeed, grossing a total of $36,720,000 (on a budget of $3 million[21]) in film rentals by 1990.[22] It is not surprising that it occurred to somebody at 20th Century-Fox that there might be a television series in the material. The studio asked Gene Reynolds, who had produced *Room 222*, to put together a pilot, and he remembered talking the year before with Larry Gelbart about working on something together.

Gelbart wrote for several comedians and eventually for Bob Hope both on radio and then on television.[23] By the time Reynolds talked to him, Gelbart, who by now was writing for stage and screen, was working in London. Reynolds and Gelbart met in London and laid out the story for the pilot, deciding what to keep from the film and what to cut (primarily the third doctor, Duke, on grounds that two, Hawkeye and Trapper John, were enough for a series). Then, Gelbart said, "Gene went back to America and I scribbled it out and sent it to him."[24]

Gelbart is being modest. What he did was return to the Ho-Jon story from the book and make that a self-contained episode, but with changes. Ho-Jon going into the Korean army was dropped, as was Ho-Jon returning as a patient. In the pilot script Hawkeye and Trapper are trying to raise money so Ho-Jon can go to Hawkeye's college. In Gelbart's script, Hawkeye and Trapper auction off a weekend in Tokyo with Lt. Dish, a beautiful nurse. The party raises $1,800 for Ho-Jon (who presumably goes off to America, although he appears as a recurring character in the first year of the series). Gelbart said of the pilot, "No one was thinking in terms of a series. We were just thinking of a successful half-hour that we could film and that the network would find attractive enough to schedule."[25]

The tone of the pilot film is more conventional comedy than the theatrical film, especially in some of the gag lines. On the other hand, Gelbart liked working with the characters, particularly Hawkeye. He said later, "It was special for me because it was the first time that I ever tried writing a character, Hawkeye, who would speak as I do, act as I do—or at least as the idealized *I* do. After years of writing material that would conform with a performer's image, I was able to try molding one of my own."[26]

Once the series was picked up, Gelbart turned to his collaborators and said, "Now what do we do?"[27] Most television series take several episodes to define themselves (and some get canceled before, or more painfully, just as they find their groove), and this happened with *M*A*S*H*. While the show was set in the Korean War of the fifties, Gelbart said, "We all felt very keenly that inasmuch as an actual war was going on, we owed it to the sensibilities and the sensitivities of an audience to take cognizance of the fact that Americans were really being killed every week."[28]

They did not want to make a traditional service comedy. The first episode shot after the pilot, "Henry—Please Come Home," was much closer than the pilot to conventional sitcom, but it was not shown until the tenth week. Burt Metcalfe, the associate producer, said, "We kind of kept hiding that one, pushing it back because we weren't terribly happy with it." [29] The third and fourth episodes come closer to hitting the mix of comedy and war than the second. The third episode, "To Market, to Market," has the doctors selling Henry Blake's desk to buy drugs for the patients, but the mix of comedy and war is not yet handled with the subtlety of later episodes. In the fourth episode, Alan Alda develops a serious edge in his performance as Hawkeye that is not there in previous episodes and this gives the series a moral weight for the rest of its run.

As the first season progressed, changes were made in the recurring characters. Lt. Dish and Spearchucker, a surgeon from the movie, were eventually dropped. Corporal Klinger, who dresses as a WAC to try to get out of the Army, and who was originally written for only a single episode, became a regular to provide what Gelbart called "a color to the show that nothing else was doing—just an absolute piece of madness every week." [30] Gelbart and the other writers were also adjusting the characters to the actors. Gelbart said that for the first seasons he was "constantly, literally, on a bicycle back and forth between my office and the sound stage, orchestrating the script for them." [31]

From the beginning, the writers experimented with both form and content. *M*A*S*H* was shot as a one-camera show without an audience and took advantage of the fact. In the pilot, there is a quick montage of shots of Hawkeye in various locations trying to persuade Lt. Dish to go along with the raffle. The pilot episode also includes a voiceover narration by Hawkeye in the form of a letter to his father. Gelbart later used this form in two first season episodes entitled "Dear Dad" and "Dear Dad . . . Again," in which several brief storylines were used in one show, a device used by the writers throughout the series. In an episode called "Sometimes You Hear the Bullet," a friend of Hawkeye's is introduced and later in the episode is killed, which upset the network on the grounds that a show should not kill off characters the audience likes. [32]

In the third season of *M*A*S*H*, Jim Fritzell and Everett Greenbaum joined the writing staff. Greenbaum had been put off by the movie's graphic operating-room sequences, but the chance to work with Gelbart was irresistible. He describes Gelbart as having "a mind like quicksilver. Larry is like a supernatural being. His mind is so brilliant, and he raises you up to his level." He also appreciated Gelbart's dealing with the network, recalling the season they started with a script about bedpans. The network censor called and said he did not want to see or hear about bedpans. "Larry's reply was to call up and have him fired, and get a different censor. Instead of getting a different script, he got a different censor. . . . You have clout when you're in the top ten."

At the end of the third season McLean Stevenson, who played Col. Blake, was written out of the show. As Greenbaum remembers, "McLean made a lot of difficulty for everybody. He kept saying he doesn't want to be one of six, he wants to be one of one, meaning stardom. And we would constantly be writing him out of [an episode of] the show because he had an engagement to perform at Las Vegas where he could cash in." Greenbaum and Fritzell wrote the script for "Abyssinia, Henry," in which Blake is discharged and sent back to the States. They did not write his death in the original script, but Gelbart asked them to do a page with the scene in which Radar O'Reilly reads the notice that Blake's plane has gone down. Gelbart, who directed the episode, kept the final scene from the cast and crew, then gave them a talk before shooting the scene about how in war people are there and then gone. The reading of the message was a surprise to the actors, and their reactions were strong. Greenbaum recalls,

> If you remember when they were reading that, one of the people in the room dropped an instrument on the floor and they left that in. I always remember that . . . and Alan [Alda] is such a wonderful actor that you could see the tears coming over his mask. And the nurses too. And the biggest tears of all were McLean Stevenson's from his dressing room. . . .[33]

It was simply unheard of to kill off a major character in a comedy. Writer Sy Salkowitz was in one of his occasional administrative jobs at the time as Vice President, Prime Time Television, for 20th Century–Fox—which made *M*A*S*H*—and he told the show's producers he did not think they should do it. He suggested they talk to the network, which they did. Salkowitz suggested to the CBS representative in Los Angeles that "This time, why don't you be the villain and not me?" The CBS man simply passed the buck to New York, which made no decision, and the ending stayed. The response was enormous. Greenbaum estimates that he got 5,000 letters from people, most of whom hated the episode. Greenbaum says that "some [people] like it." For the first daytime syndication runs, Fox cut the scene of the reading of the message, but the episode became so famous that for later syndication runs the ending was restored.[34] (Stevenson apparently did not hold Blake's death against Greenbaum and Fritzell. In 1975 he asked them to write a special for him, although when he met them, he said, "I heard one of you died.")

A problem in writing Henry Blake was that he was basically a shallow character, wavering between slightly competent and slightly not. The decision was made to replace him with a stronger counterforce to Hawkeye, a regular army Colonel. In the third season Greenbaum and Fritzell wrote an episode about a crazy general whom Henry Morgan played beautifully. Morgan was now cast as Colonel Sherman Potter. Gelbart had Greenbaum and Fritzell go to lunch with Morgan and "find out everything you can about him." The writers discovered Morgan loved horses, so this was written into Potter's character in an early episode, "Dear Mildred." The episode used the letter form again, this time to explore Potter and his attitudes. Greenbaum says of the letter form,

> The advantage is that you don't have to tell a story. The hardest part of a script is working out the story. It's sometimes easier to tell six little tiny stories, or four little stories, than to tell a whole beginning, middle, and an end for a whole script . . . . A lot of ideas can't work into a story, and this is a way to use them.

Blake was not the only character missing at the beginning of the fourth season. Wayne Rogers, who played Trapper John, left the show as well, and Gelbart and his staff were just as creative in replacing him. Trapper and Hawkeye were similar, so Trapper's replacement was B. J. Hunnicut, who unlike Hawkeye, was married, and not only married but happily so. Greenbaum and Fritzell had never seen the actor Mike Farrell before. Gelbart told them, "This actor is an open-faced American sandwich. . . . Just write him as open, honest, Midwestern."

Larry Gelbart's final episode came from a suggestion by Gene Reynolds, who was inspired by an Edward R. Murrow Korean War documentary in which Murrow asked soldiers what they thought of the war. Gelbart "wrote" the show by writing questions newsman Clete Roberts asked the cast. The cast replied in character, and the show was cut together from their responses. Gelbart said of the episode,

> To me it said, in a way I had never been able to express, that I had finished my work on the show because I couldn't improve on that . . . The irony of the show is that it says, "Written by Larry Gelbart," whereas, in fact, truthfully it was written by everyone, Roberts and whoever else was there. There are many shows that do not say "Written by Larry Gelbart," that are totally written by me, so maybe there is a little TV god who sits somewhere and figures out those credits. [35]

Sy Salkowitz recalls Gelbart's departure:

> Gelbart came into my office and said, "I can't stay."
> I went and shut my door and said, "You're not getting of here until you re-sign [a contract]."
> Larry said to me, "You're a writer. I'm going to tell you I can't write one more episode of *M*A*S*H*."
> I said, "I understand." So Larry left.

In addition to adding new characters of more depth, the writers also explored the regular characters in greater depth. Margaret Houlihan developed away from the caricature she had been in the movie and the first season of the series into a much more complicated character. Gelbart, when asked about writing "Hot Lips," said, "The trick in portraying women is to write them blindfolded, to forget they're women. In short, write them as people."[36] Nevertheless, Gelbart specifically asked Linda Bloodworth and Mary Kay Place to be the first women writers on the show.[37] In the second season, actress Loretta Swit sat down with Bloodworth and Place and discussed Houlihan's entire life for six hours.[38] The script that developed out of the meeting, "Hot Lips and Empty Arms," was the first to show Houlihan's unhappiness with her relationship with Frank Burns.[39] In the fifth season, Bloodworth (who later would create *Designing Women*) wrote "The Nurses," which is primarily about Houlihan's relationship with the nurses who work for her. By the last seasons, writer Dennis Koenig would admit that writing Houlihan was tricky for him because, not being a woman, "certain things may escape my consciousness."[40]

In the sixth season Major Frank Burns was replaced as well. Neither the writers nor Larry Linville, who played Burns, were happy with him as a continuing character, since he was difficult both to write and to play. Like Blake he was a shallow character and a very obvious target. Greenbaum and Fritzell went to lunch again, this time with David Ogden Stiers, who had been hired as the replacement. They liked the Boston accent he did and they created Charles Emerson Winchester, a much more formidable counterpoint to Hawkeye and B. J. Out of the lunch meeting came Winchester's love of classical music, which provided material for several episodes. Winchester's upper-class status gave Greenbaum and Fritzell a new variation on the mail shows: Winchester does not write letters home, he dictates them into his tape recorder.

The mail, or in Winchester's case the tape, shows performed another service. From the third season on, apprentice writers were hired to come up with story material. The younger writers, whom the older writers referred to as "The Bar Mitzvah Boys," would turn the story material over to the older writers, or in some cases write the scripts themselves. Story bits that did not make an entire show were saved and used in the mail shows. Several of the younger writers went on to write full-time for the show and later have their own series.[41]

One writing team that came on in the eighth season did not go through the "Bar Mitzvah Boys" experience. Thad Mumford and Dan Wilcox wrote the episode "Are You Now, Margaret?" as what Mumford calls "a job audition." They were also trying for a staff job on another show, so they ended up having to do "about two-thirds of the *[M*A*S*H]* script overnight." The script was turned in on Wednesday and the next Monday they got the job. The script won a Writers Guild Award, but as Mumford points out, "The bad thing about doing something like that very well overnight is that this keeps alive the myth that you can do that, and that you come to expect that, 'Oh, the boys will take care of it.' Even though there are women now, they still call us boys."

Mumford and Wilcox often worked from the research that had been developed over the life of the series. "Depressing News," in which Hawkeye receives 500,000 tongue depressors instead of 5,000, came out of research, as did "A War for All Seasons," which showed a whole year of the war in a curious way. Mumford recalls

> There were certain things that we got in research about how important the Sears Roebuck catalogue was. It seems strange that you could, in the middle of a war, order things from a catalog and actually get them there. So that was one of the themes, about how the catalogue became very helpful, even medically. There were certain utensils necessary to build a kidney dialysis machine that had come from the catalogue.

Mumford and Wilcox also did an episode featuring the recurring character of Sidney Freedman, an Army psychiatrist. The work on the character "had been done . . . before," by Gelbart, Burt Prelutsky (who wrote the first two Freedman shows), and Alan Alda (who wrote two others). Mumford describes the character as "a very odd person in the mix of larger-than-life characters whose essences were based on the tensions which were produced by war. It was a wonderful idea to have a man sit back and just look at them and," Mumford says, stroke his chin.

In the tenth season Mumford and Wilcox got promoted to producer status, which Mumford casually describes as "just a raise. It's for your next job," i.e., enables you to go into your next job at a higher level than you came into this one. Several of the writers were also producers, and Mumford says, "By that point we had worked together so long and so well that people's opinions sort of had the same weight."

As it must to all television series, the end came to *M*A*S*H*. Because of the popularity of the show, a final episode was written that eventually grew to a two-and-a-half-hour running time. Thad Mumford tells how it developed:

> First it was to be written by two writers, Elias Davis and David Pollock, who were very much the story editors on the show. Then we all got pissed off because we thought this was going to be very historic. What ended up, I think, hurting the piece [was that] they bowed to our requests and our concerns and made us all part of it. Alan [Alda, who was one of the writers and the director] was the person who was the constant, and we all spent time with Alan.
>
> The division of labor was not, "You write one scene here." We would write a certain number of pages. It was like a relay. You pick up from page 22 and you go to page 35, and I know that in the end, even though there are moments in the script that are very good and scenes that I think we're all proud of, it could have been better if one person or two people had written it. It would have hurt egos, but I think it suffered from the attempt to acknowledge all of our egos.

There are excellent elements in the show. Hawkeye's breakdown and the eventual revelation of the causes of it are well developed, as is the storyline of Winchester teaching a group of Chinese musicians Mozart. The show is too long, and it may be the writers had been too used to working in the half hour format. Several of the storylines, while they might have fit into a half-hour episode, seem extended at two-and-a-half hours. A bigger problem is that the mixture of the comedy and the drama—one of the strengths of the series—is overbalanced to the dramatic and the sentimental.

Twentieth Century–Fox was making too much money off of *M*A*S*H* to let it die a natural death.[42] After Trapper John was written out of the series, the studio and CBS developed a series about the character. At the suggestion of its writer-producer Don Brinkley, the show dealt with Trapper thirty years later, since Brinkley felt the immediate post-Korean War time was "a very dull era. It was civilian medicine. We are losing the color of the war, the excitement of the war." When *M*A*S*H* ended its run, Larry Gelbart came back and developed *AfterMash*, a 1983–84 series about Col. Potter, Klinger and Father Mulcahy at a veteran's hospital. Everett Greenbaum wrote for the series and discovered Brinkley was right: "You lost the straight line. You lost the war. The urgency was gone." The show lasted 28 episodes.

Fox tried again in 1984 with *W*A*L*T*E*R*, a spinoff featuring Radar O'Reilly as a cop. The studio at first thought of making Radar a teacher and the show a cross between *M*A*S*H* and *Mr. Peepers*. Greenbaum worked on that one as well: "At first they [the studio] started thinking properly of what kind of person he should be in civilian life. He could have been a wonderful teacher. Then the studio wanted him to be a policeman so they could do another cop show. Their minds are on tracks that do not change."

The spin-offs were disasters, with the exception of *Trapper John, M.D.*, which became more of a conventional contemporary medical series as it continued. None of the spin-offs managed to recreate the unique world of *M*A*S*H*. Like the best of American series television, *M*A*S*H* created a world of its own, full of compelling characters, both one-shot and recurring. The characters, as the writers developed them, grew on the audience in ways that only characters in a TV series can, segment by segment over a long period of time.

It is not surprising that the final episode of *M*A*S*H*, "Goodbye, Farewell and Amen," drew high ratings. Ratings, however, can only tell that sets were tuned in. It takes a different form of ratings to show how much the audience was concentrating on the final episode. In New York City, the show ran until 11 P.M. In the few minutes after 11, the water flow in Water Mains One and Two increased by a total of 320 million gallons, which Department of Environmental Protection engineers estimated meant that in those minutes one million people were flushing their toilets.[43]

·14·

CORONERS AND OTHER SEVENTIES AND EIGHTIES PROFESSIONALS

*I*t was not surprising that CBS came to Don Brinkley in the late seventies to create a show around the character of Trapper John. From 1969 to 1976, Brinkley wrote and produced what was until then the longest-running medical show in television history, *Medical Center*. *Medical Center* was very much in the tradition of the earlier medical shows, where everything was, in Brinkley's words, "clean and perfect" and the doctors were never wrong. Also, like the earlier shows, it treated controversial material, such as an episode about a transsexual, over which the network people were, Brinkley says, "fighting out one point here, one point there, one thing here, one thing there, one cautionary statement here, and so forth." Brinkley had the same kind of experiences on *Trapper John M.D.*

Since *Trapper John M.D.* was developed out of M*A*S*H, Brinkley assumed it would be rowdier than *Medical Center:*

> The pilot script and the pilot film actually were much wilder than the show itself became. They wanted it as close to the M*A*S*H quality as we could get in its own format. And as soon as it hit the air, they started saying, "Let's tone it down, let's tone it down. Let's make it a little more like *Medical Center*," which is what we didn't want to do. [We wanted it to be] wilder and crazier and brighter and more irreverent. We managed to maintain most of it, but some of the wildness was gone. It was just eroded away. They had a tendency to do that: Buy something, then as soon as it gets on the air, change it. They feel more comfortable with it that way.

The characters were certainly different from those on *Medical Center*. Brinkley suggested doing Trapper thirty years later: "He had been the maverick in his youth, [and] now he was the chief surgeon, representing the establishment, and along comes a kid right out of Vietnam, who's just like he was when he was in Korea, who was the Greg Harrison character [Gonzo Gates]. They [the network] loved that." But Trapper John was not a conventional establishment figure. He was, for example, divorced, and as Brinkley puts it, he could not make either his marriage or his divorce work. The network thought audiences would not believe he was a good doctor if he was divorced. Audiences loved it, and the shows with his ex-wife had some of the highest ratings of the series.

There were limitations on what could be done with Trapper's character. Partly this was the tradition that leading characters of a series do not change. Partly it was the difficulty of dealing with Pernell Roberts, who played Trapper. He complained a lot, saying, "This script is a piece of shit." Brinkley invited him to sit in on the story conferences, but he never showed up.

The writers were therefore more willing to develop the other characters. Dr. Stanley Riverside II started out as the typical hospital bureaucrat, Trapper's antagonist, but Brinkley says that actor Charles Siebert was so good at getting inside Riverside that the writers found they wanted to develop his character, and over the course of the series he fell in love, got married and had a child.

Don Brinkley wanted *Trapper John M.D.* to be darker and grittier, but both the network and his partner resisted and Brinkley did not have the kind of clout that Gelbart developed on *M*A*S*H*. He and the series were still able to do strong shows about contemporary issues. He recalls a show about Physicians for Nuclear Responsibility, a group that called for banning nuclear weapons, "a damned good script" written by Deborah Zoe Dawson and Victoria Johns. The network insisted they show the other side—to which Brinkley replied, "Pro-nuclear attack? You want to be in favor of it?" The network suggested they show the government was trying to do something, so Brinkley ended up quoting "whoever was in charge of civil defense at that time here in L.A. He was asked in one interview, 'What about the panic situation?' He said, 'Panic is an element we do not recognize.' " The network said that made them "look like horse's asses."

Brinkley replied, "Well, they are. This is a quote. I'm giving you an absolute direct quote from one of these guys." Brinkley says, "So it went around and around and around and finally we got the show through, but it was a long two weeks, I'll tell you: phone calls, bells, whistles."

Sy Salkowitz had similar experiences on a slightly earlier medical show he worked on, *The Doctors* (1969–73), in which the medical teams worked with what was called "space age medicine." The writers were using the subject to press for more adventurous material. Salkowitz says of the show, the changes in medical shows, and the changes in television in general:

> One, most importantly, was that the audience was getting more and more and more sophisticated, and more demanding. The second was, my own stature, if

you will, as a writer was ascending and therefore I could push certain stories that I could not have pushed ten years before, because I had more muscle now.

The producers knew that if the ratings didn't stay up, their shows were going to get canceled quicker than quicker, because that was starting to happen. So they were also pressing the boundary lines, if you will. The program people at the networks started pushing on the limitations that they had before, and they were always in constant battle with the censor. The censor was an anchor and they were the sail, and it was always that strain.

Salkowitz compares it to the audience for the moon landings of the period, noting that the television audience decreased with each successive landing:

And that's how our audience is. They say, "We've been there already. Now show me Mars." So you keep pushing against it. . . .

Now writers themselves don't understand that they themselves are pushing and shoving, because from the good writers there is always something that the censor or somebody says you can't do. In almost every script, somebody says, "Oh, we don't want to talk about that." But the good writers are always pushing against the walls that hem them in. The bad writers [just say] "Where do you want the comma?"

Producers don't like writers like that. I was privy to a conversation between a couple of producers about another writer. One of them said, "There's no excitement working with him. He asks you where you want the comma." That's the phrase. And I've never forgotten that. They self-censor as they go through that script. They hand you a script, totally undramatic, but absolutely nothing wrong with it. The censor loves it.

Quincy, M.E.

When Lou Shaw was freelancing, he would spend several hours every day coming up with ideas for series. He would write them up and, no matter how "half-assed" Shaw thought his own ideas, he would register them with the Writers Guild of America, west (the guild keeps a record of when and by whom material was created). One of them, in the mid-seventies, was about a coroner he called Quince. Shaw remembers, "The whole idea struck because at that time medical shows were very popular. Murder shows were very popular. I said, 'What if you had a medical detective?' " He decided on the name Quince because "K's were very much in fashion at the time: *Kolchak, Kojak.* I said, 'I don't want to use another K.' "

And nothing happened. Then Shaw went to work at Universal, writing for such shows as *McCloud* and *Columbo.* One day he was talking to Glen Larson, the producer of several shows at Universal. Larson told him, "Boy, they are looking for another detective show on the wheel [NBC *Mystery Movie,* which included *McCloud* and *Columbo*]."

Shaw said, "I've got a great one. It's about a coroner called Quince." He told the idea to Larson, who said he could sell it to Universal in five minutes. Shaw, who wanted his own show, says, "He put out his hand. 'Fifty-fifty partner all the way.' I said, 'You got a deal.' He got all the way to the door and he stopped like Columbo and turned around and he said, 'Quince? Sounds like jam. What would you think if we called it *Quincy?*' I said, 'Glen, I knew you'd make a contribution.'" Larson came back about an hour later and said the studio had agreed to make a two-hour pilot. The executives felt there was no way to persuade the network (Universal's shows were done almost exclusively on NBC at the time) without a pilot, so the studio would finance the pilot as "inventory," i.e., without any network financing.

The script was written but then got hung up on casting. As written, Quincy was a young, fairly hip coroner, and the original choices were actors like Anthony Franciosa or Robert Wagner, but nothing happened. Then Shaw heard that the black actor James Earl Jones was interested. He spent a day with Jones and by the end of the day he was wildly excited about the possibility of Jones doing the part. Shaw went into the office of an executive at the studio and told him Jones was interested. The executive said, "Let me ask you something, Lou. This beautiful blonde is dead. And James Earl Jones puts on the gloves and goes in alone to do an autopsy on the blond body. I don't think that would work, do you?"

Shaw, who has dealt with other industry executives whom he thinks were bigots, says of this executive, "He's not a bigot. He's so far from being that. He was being a hardnose" about what an American TV audience in 1976, the year before *Roots*, would accept. Shaw and the executive were probably right, but wouldn't Jones have been wonderful as Quincy? (As an indication of the changes in American life, consider that when Jones starred in the 1990 series *Gabriel's Fire*, the series was at first shot in half-shadows, but research showed that audiences disliked the style and wanted to *see* the characters.[1])

Jack Klugman had just finished *The Odd Couple* and every studio and network was trying to get him for another show. He read the *Quincy* script and met with Shaw and Larson. According to Shaw, Klugman thought the script was "fabulous," but wondered "if those girls would go for a balding, fat, middle-aged Jew like me." Shaw realized they had given him the "hip" *Quincy* script. Klugman told them he did not think the script was for him. Shaw persuaded Larson that Klugman would be "spectacular" in the part and they rewrote the script. With Klugman attached, Universal got a commitment from NBC for a firm six episodes to air.

Shaw had his own show, but he also had Klugman. At the first meeting on the first show, Klugman praised Shaw, hugged him, and gave him "wet kisses." Shaw told Universal executive Frank Price about this, and Price said, "Lou, wait 'til the second show." Shaw says, "Second show, Klugman started throwing out scripts and firing people." It was up to Shaw to deal with Klugman, because Klugman disliked Larson from the beginning. Klugman respected Shaw, but they still had what Shaw calls "creative fights." Shaw just

did not want to stay and face it. It was too hard, too bitter, too angry. . . .
There was no way of dealing with it because he'd scream and I'd scream. He'd
say, "I could go up there to the Tower and have you fired right now."
   I said,"Well, until you do, I'm the producer. Why don't you try acting instead
of producing. You're not doing too well in the [producing] department." We'd
have conversations like that. He was just out to get rid of anybody who would
get credit.

Shaw's Quincy was intended to be

a humanitarian who solved murders medically by the sheer brilliance of his
medical skills. That to me was the unique franchise of *Quincy*, and I think it
went away from that. It got a little preachy, it got a lot of other things, that I
didn't like particularly, but Jack had this wonderful charismatic ability to carry
the show. But I felt it went away from that kind of medical detective that I first
created.

Shaw says that the show "would have failed without him. I think Klugman was the show. I feel I made my contributions. Obviously, we all did, Glen and everybody, but Klugman in his own way was fighting for an integrity that he felt the show didn't have. I disagree with that." Shaw and Klugman still keep in touch, but Shaw says, "I was happy not to work with him after that."
   The show still needed writers. In 1978 Aubrey Solomon and his partner Steve Greenberg did a treatment for a miniseries that impressed Klugman enough to call them to pitch some story areas for *Quincy*. One led to a teleplay, and that in turn led to a rewrite on another script. They found that Klugman was in effect the producer of the show. Solomon recalls:

No doubt about it. When we got there, he had set up a unit that was totally
without any supervision from Standards and Practices or from the studio itself.
That was a unique situation. He had fought and screamed and probably thrown
so many fits in the first year that he'd won that freedom. We were fortunate to
come in after that struggle had been waged. We were no part of it.

Because of Klugman's clout, Solomon says they never had any interference on any subject matter they wanted to do,

but it was always very funny to send scripts to Standards and Practices and get
back virtually no suggestions. And even when we did get them back, we would
toss them in the garbage. With impunity. They would send us little things. I

GOVERNORS STATE UNIVERSITY
UNIVERSITY PARK
IL 60466

remember we used an expression, "chinks in the armor," and they somehow thought that was offensive and said, "Take out 'chinks.'"

Occasionally we would throw things into the script just to give them something to complain about. We were doing a show about V.D. and Steve put something in about "The Pussy Patrol" and everybody knew that was going to get a little "x." So we would throw them a few scraps to get upset about, knowing full well they would cut them.

The writers worked out storylines with Klugman, who was, according to Solomon, "the ultimate decision maker in terms of story content." This would also lead to rewriting on the set:

Very often he would be sitting in the bungalow or his trailer between scenes and he would say, "The character says something like this," and he'd go into this tirade, and we would just take our tape recorders and fashion something out of that. On the V.D. show, on location, we were chauffeured around in a limousine trying to find a [copy] machine to [copy] our handwritten scene.

Solomon adds,

The downside of it was there was no one who could say to him, "This is a little over the top." Generally, he improved everything we did. Sometimes he went a little too far. But largely the success of the show was due to his input, and his ability to know within himself what was right for the show and the character. And if he came off as foaming at the mouth too often, that was his choice.

Generally he tightened the stories. He had a terrific story sense, and a good sense of mystery. A good feeling for what is an interesting crime, and the motives behind the crimes. All this input helped us.

I think his strengths largely outweighed his weaknesses. He was open. He would listen to suggestions. But my recollection is that sometimes he would overdo things.

Because Klugman was impressed with their work, Solomon and Greenberg were asked to become story editors for the show, which meant dealing with other writers. Klugman criticized established television writers in interviews, and this made it difficult for Solomon and Greenberg to get "quality writers," who simply did not want to put up with the actor's behavior. Most of the writers Solomon and Greenberg dealt with were younger, more inexperienced writers, and most of the shows were written by the staff writers. Solomon estimates that he and Greenberg wrote about nine shows a year, and the other story editor, Robert Crais, did four or five, and only a few outside assignments were needed to make up the 22 shows. Solomon says they "found that the material we were getting was not sufficient to develop the stories the way Jack wanted them. Because it was the type of show that, unless you were on the inside, you really didn't have a good feeling for what Jack wanted." He further notes that this has become the pattern, since most series in the eighties and later "discovered that unless you have in-house writers, you are going to do a lot of rewriting. And as result, most shows now have six producers, who are all former writers, and they write all the shows."

Lou Shaw felt that the concept for the series was virtually unlimited and could have continued for twenty years because there was "an endless source of material" in the medical detective work a coroner does. Aubrey Solomon, who wrote off and on for the show for three seasons, is not so sure it could have lasted. When he and his partner came on the show in its second season of one-hour episodes [its first season had been 90- and 120-minute episodes to fit the "wheel" concept], the development of ideas was relatively easy. The story ideas came from research in articles in newspapers and magazines. Their first episode, which hooked Klugman, was based on a piece Greenberg had read about a man who developed a "Death System" for the CIA using snake venom, and it became the kind of medical detective story that Shaw envisioned for the show.

One difficulty in coming up with ideas was that Klugman began to want to deal with issues, not just cases. The writers tried for years to come up with an abortion story, but without success. Klugman finally decided that the issue was so divisive that no matter how it was done, it would alienate half the audience. On the other hand, the show did an episode on the unfairness of kidney transplants being given only to those who could afford them. Solomon learned several years later that the episode was shown in Washington and helped lead to Medicare paying for kidney transplants. (He heard this from the director of the show, Ray Danton, who later had a kidney transplant himself and was told by the people at the hospital of the connection.)

By the end of the run of the show, in its fourth and fifth seasons, it was becoming more and more difficult to find story ideas. The last script that Solomon and Greenberg wrote for the show was developed from an investigative reporter's story on possible death from breathing problems caused by hairspray. The writers could not track down the original reporter, and the technical advisor on the show felt the issue was not really proved without further research. The episode was not filmed.

Other Universal Series

Before, during, and after his involvement on *Quincy*, Lou Shaw wrote for most of the Universal dramatic series of the seventies, and he wrote mostly for producer Glen Larson, his co-creator on *Quincy*. He met Larson when he came to pitch a story for *McCloud*. The producer of the show, Michael Gleason, warned him that when he pitched to Larson, Larson would end up with a totally different story. At the meeting, Shaw warmed up by telling Larson about meeting a waif-like girl hitchhiker on the way to the studio that day. When he started to pitch the story, Larson told him they were going to do a story about the girl instead. Gleason later reminded Shaw he had been warned.

Larson wanted Shaw to work full-time on *McCloud*, but Shaw had many other commitments as a free-lancer on such shows as *Columbo, Kolchak, Ironside, Chase,* and *Barnaby Jones.* Larson said, "What the hell are you talking? Are you doing all those shows?"

"Yeah."

"Where are you on them?"

"Well, I just got a story O.K. on *Columbo. Kolchak* is in good shape because I'm doing a rewrite. I don't remember. I'll have to look at my calendar."

Larson told him he was only to work on *McCloud*, but Shaw said, "Nah, I couldn't let them down. I like them all." He would agree to come on *McCloud* if he could produce as well, and Larson agreed.

Shaw liked *McCloud* because it was an open mystery and the length, 90 to 120 minutes, let him write a movie each episode. He saw that other writers used to the one-hour format had trouble adapting to the greater length. Shaw also liked the humor of the character, since he had worked in comedy as well as drama. He learned not to write jokes for Dennis Weaver as McCloud, since Weaver and the character were not joke-tellers. The comedy had to come out of the character and the confrontation with other characters.

Shaw also wrote for another spoke in the mystery wheel, *Columbo*. He compares writing for the two shows:

> *Columbo* was harder to develop plots [for] than *McCloud*. [For] *Columbo* you needed four or five major clues that turned out awry, [a place where] he said, "I gotcha," and the guy said, "No, because da-da-da-da," and suddenly, oh, it makes sense. And then you nail him on the big one. Peter Fischer was the story editor, I remember, on *Columbo* at the time. Very excellent story editor. He's the boss on *Murder, She Wrote*. He did the same kind of format really on *Murder, She Wrote*. That was his favorite kind of format, the old *Perry Mason* type: four, five suspects, and the one you suspect least is usually the obvious one.
>
> The Columbo character, like the McCloud character, was so etched. If you really understood it, it was pretty hard not to write a great line of dialogue for him. It would just pour out. Now McCloud was taciturn. Columbo was verbose. You could write him a page, page-and-a-half scene. He'd stop, "Aw, sorry. I'm sorry, sir. One last question."

Shaw discovered what he considered the "secret" of writing *Columbo* and Peter Fischer confirmed it. Shaw says:

> The secret was: you don't tell the audience, but at a certain point you as the writer know there's a magic moment when in his heart Columbo knows who did it. And nothing changes. But it does. As a writer, there's a whole attitudinal thing that occurs, and if you didn't find that spot, I don't think the scripts worked.

It was always mystical. From that point on, the whole thing solidly moves into the new gear, and that becomes like the second act, or whatever you want to call it. That's the major turning point in *Columbo:* when he knows.

It's interesting, watching so many *Columbo*s later, they never had that point. The shows would be flat when they didn't have that point. I think Peter understood that and his shows were better because of it. When he was off the show I didn't think it was as good.

Since not every show at Universal was as classy as *Columbo, McCloud,* or *Quincy,* Lou Shaw kept trying to get off the lot, but Larson or Frank Price kept pulling him back in. In 1977 he wanted to go, and Price told him that if he would do a two-hour episode of *The Six Million Dollar Man,* he'd let him out of the rest of his contract. Shaw had never seen the show, but whipped up the script and did two more, without, apparently, the problem Sy Salkowitz had two years before on the show: how bionic to make him. The bionic man got less and less bionic as the series progressed because the more invulnerable he was, the less interesting the stories were. The producers told Salkowitz to think of him as having the strength of five men rather than a thousand, which he had in the pilot.

Lou Shaw did not get off the lot after *The Six Million Dollar Man.* Price then told him that if he would do three *Nancy Drew Mysteries,* he would let him go. The show had been canceled, but still had the three episodes to complete, but no scripts. Price made the offer on Thursday with no scripts ready to shoot the following Monday. He did a script over the weekend, then two more. A few weeks later he got a call to come up to Frank Price's office, where an NBC executive told him, "They liked the way you've taken *Nancy Drew* and changed the attitudes of everyone. They're picking up the series and they want you to go along as executive producer."

Shaw said, "Are you crazy? What are you talking about? I didn't make any change. It's a young girl and a detective." He admitted that not only had he never read the books, but he had never seen the show nor read any of the other scripts. The show stayed canceled.

Glen Larson created a show called *Switch* about an ex-cop played by Eddie Albert and an ex-con played by Robert Wagner, who create a detective agency. Larson used Shaw to run interference with Albert during a dispute. All Shaw did was listen to Albert's complaints, which satisfied the actor. Larson later asked him what he'd said, and Shaw replied that he had not said anything, but "I give great nod."

Shaw tells how Larson got him to write on *Switch:*

> I got into this very weirdly. I was producing *McCloud* and producing and writing *Quincy* at the same time. So I was a little busy. I get a call from Las Vegas and Glen said, "Look, I got the ticket. You've got to catch the plane in three hours and come to Las Vegas."
>
> "Glen, I can't."

He said, "You gotta. I don't want to lose the show. They don't like the stories, and I'm in real big trouble. We're shooting this show right here now. You've got to come." Now as I get to the airport I get a call paging me. It's Glen, "I forgot to tell you one little thing."

I said, "What?"

He said, "They're expecting you to come in with a perfect story."

They're calling "Last Call." "Glen," I said, "It's a half-hour ride." And he's off the phone. Now I come up to the [Las Vegas hotel] room. I meet Glen. He says, "Have you got a good story?"

"Glen, this is crazy." We go into the room. I knew them to say hello, but I didn't know them well. And they're standing there, "Make us laugh" kind of thing.

I'm sitting next to Glen on this little couch. "Tell them the great story you told me." Now, I was so angry on the plane I wasn't thinking. He didn't have the script on time. Somehow or other in that relationship with Glen, it was always my fault, whatever happened. Anyway, I must say in that framework, it was a lot of fun, this you might guess. But anyway, I start saying, "I have this idea that a woman shows up late with a little boy and leaves him with the Eddie Albert character and just runs away. And the Eddie Albert character takes it for granted that it is the R.J. [Robert Wagner] character's illegitimate son."

Eddie says, "What a great idea."

R.J. says, "I love it. We could raise it."

"And—" and Glen gave me a hit, and you hear it on the tape [Shaw recorded the story meeting], pow, basically [Glen was telling Shaw,] "They were hooked, you understand?" and he didn't want me to say another word, because they were starting to build the story, and he knew I didn't know where I was going. So I'm sitting there and I went, [coughs]. Now they're building the story.

Glen said, "Great. Great." Hugs and kisses, we leave.

I said, "O.K., you're out of that one."

He said, "Oh no, you've got to stay here and write it."

"What do you mean? I've got to stay here in Las Vegas and write it? What about the *Quincy* I'm writing and the *McCloud* I'm writing?" Klugman, I think, had just thrown out Glen's script, or something like that. So I said, "I can't. I can't. Glen, I can't."

He said, "You gotta. The whole show. They want you to write it."

So, anyway, that's how I ended up writing [for *Switch*]. And by the way, I'd never read a *Switch* script, and I wrote two *Switches* back to back. And to this day I've never seen a *Switch* show.

Shaw got away from Universal and Larson and was in San Francisco producing and directing a stage show of Tom Lehrer songs. He got a call from Larson, who said he desperately needed help on *The Fall Guy*,[2] a show about a movie stunt man/bounty hunter. Shaw insisted he had not seen the show, but Larson said, "Oh, you can always write them. Just write one." The network liked the one so much they asked him to do a second. Larson then got him to write and produce seven of the next season's 22. At one point while doing those, he got into a fight with Larson while the network people were there, and when Larson fired him, one of the network executives said, "If it gets to that, I think you'll be the one to go, Glen. I'd be very cautious." Larson talked Shaw into staying and Shaw brought in for some episodes writers he'd worked with before, such as Aubrey Solomon and Steve Greenberg. Solomon describes working with Shaw as a producer:

> We got along very well with Lou. He's a good friend and he's a great storyteller, and he loves just to have someone he can talk to and just enjoy their company. And we enjoyed working with him.
> Lou is a funny kind of producer, because he'll spend three weeks trying to get act one right, and then you'll have two days to figure out the other three acts, so a large part of our time is spent working on that first act.

Glen Larson also created *Knight Rider*, but by the time Joel Rogosin came on the show as a producer in later seasons he was no longer actively involved. Rogosin says, "We used to send Glen *Knight Rider* scripts. I think his contract demanded that. And I never heard from him. Never. Nobody ever called up and said, 'We got the script. We didn't get the script. We like it. We don't like it.' And frankly, I'm sure he didn't care. He's very, very comfortable, Glen, with his residuals and royalties."

Producer Cy Chermak once told Sy Salkowitz that to be a successful producer, "You always had to have a writer in your pocket that could be thrown in at the last minute to fix something, or give you something in a hurry." Lou Shaw was Glen Larson's "pocket writer," as Shaw admits:

> Glen, as a high-flying producer, never wanted me to leave because he had in me someone who could do whatever is necessary. And to me it was very good, because it becomes a little gold mine. In my heart I know if I have to write a two-hour script based on no plot, whatever it needs, I can do it . . . . Glen could always talk me into anything, I must say.

The Rockford Files

There are at least two versions of how *The Rockford Files* was created. In the first version[3] producer Roy Huggins and writer Stephen J. Cannell were on the spot with a cop series called *Toma*. In the spring of 1973 the fourth show of the series would not make its airdate and ABC needed something to fill in. Cannell had an idea that Toma could hand off a case to a private investigator. Toma would appear at the beginning and end, but the rest of the show could be shot while another *Toma* episode was being filmed. Cannell and Huggins decided to throw in anything that would undo the private-eye clichés: private eyes did not have relatives, so Rockford had a father; they had sexy secretaries, so Rockford had an answering machine; they had seedy offices, so Rockford worked out of a trailer at the beach. Cannell only had five days to do the screenplay and found himself writing fifteen to twenty pages a day. He had "so much fun breaking all the rules" that the screenplay ended up 90 pages long, half again the length for an hour show. ABC wanted to cut it to an hour and take out the humor. Cannell and Huggins refused, and Universal, the producer of *Toma*, decided to do *The Rockford Files* as a 90-minute TV movie and pilot.

Roy Huggins remembers the development a little differently. The star of *Toma* was Tony Musante, an intense New York actor, and Huggins ran the stories he came up with for the show by Musante and Musante's wife before he had them written. When Musante's wife said she thought one was not a particularly *Toma* story, Huggins filed it away. A week later he got a call from his old *Maverick* star, James Garner, who told him, "Roy, I've decided I'm going to go back into television."

Huggins replied, "Yeah, but you don't like Universal."

Garner said, "I've decided I'll even work at Universal if you can come up with something."

Huggins, remembering his *Toma* story, said, "Hold your horses, James, I may have something." He reworked the story, making the character *Maverick* as a private eye. He gave the story to Cannell, who wrote the script. (The credits for the movie read "Teleplay by Stephen J. Cannell. From a story by John Thomas James," which was Huggins's pseudonym.) ABC passed on the movie and Universal took it to NBC, which bought it and the series.

As Huggins points out, what he brought to the show was the combination of action and humor that was a hallmark of his work on *Maverick*:

> The character [of Rockford] was the guarantee that it would be funny. Any guy who is the reluctant hero, who can argue with the girl over who's going to pick up the check, who turns all the cliches upside down is going to be funny. And the guy was sneaky. A guy who's waiting for the heavy to come in and puts soap all over the bathroom floor so that he will have an easier time winning is funny. So it's going to be funny whether it is action or not action. Because it isn't verbal wit. It's character wit.

The *Rockford Files* series goes beyond the character wit Huggins refers to. Particularly in the writing of Cannell, David Chase, and especially Juanita Bartlett, Rockford's attitudes toward the police, the FBI, the CIA, the Mafia, or any other American authority figures present a consistently anti-authoritarian viewpoint. This was usually present in traditional private-eye shows, but *Rockford* takes it a step further. It also goes further than Huggins did in *Maverick*. In the Western, the authority figures were those of the past, while on *Rockford* they are contemporary. In other series, representatives of the Federal Government and the Mafia are both treated seriously. In *Rockford*, they are not. They are smart, because, as Bartlett says, "There's no triumph in overcoming a stupid person. So we tried to make them human." They have human failings, especially the bureaucrats, whether legal or illegal. Bartlett's insights "just come from dealing with them, the idiocies of bureaucracies. It's from life. And it doesn't get any better. It seems to be getting worse."

Juanita Bartlett had written for Garner before. After trying unsuccessfully for years to sell scripts, she finally broke in on Garner's show *Nichols*. She remembers sitting watching the first dailies of Garner saying her lines, and, recalling that she had been rejected by *Lassie*, she turned to the producer, Frank Pierson, and said, "Do you realize what it means to sit here in the projection room and hear my words coming out of Jim Garner's mouth? My first dailies could have been 'Arf.' " Bartlett says now of writing for Garner:

> Instead [of Lassie] I have this marvelous actor. As Steve [Cannell] said, when you're in the series business, you never have enough time, and invariably there would be a line that you'd think, "There's a better line. There's a better line in there. I just don't have time to find it." And you go to dailies and it would come back at you as the wittiest, most wonderful line anybody could ever have written. Because Jim knew how to deliver it. He's such a joy.

Bartlett says of working with Garner on *Rockford*, "We were as enthusiastic in the sixth year as we were in the first . . . . There wasn't anybody on that show who would not have been ready to do murder for Jim Garner." As opposed to Jack Klugman on *Quincy*.

Juanita Bartlett describes the writing process on *The Rockford Files*:

> We would sit down and we would have story meetings and if I had a story to do, we would work on mine. For the first two years Steve and I pretty well [did most of the scripts]. Steve's faster than I am, so he wrote more. "You're up . . . I'm up . . . You're up . . . I'm up." We did have some outside writers. Most of those we rewrote, which is not a reflection on the writer necessarily. It's just a fact that if you are working on a show, you know those characters so well that it's just easier. You give the outside writer an opportunity to do the second draft and the polish, and if it's not there, then you go in and do the fine tuning and make sure that it's *Rockford*.
>
> Then David Chase joined us, and there were three of us who put the stories together. And usually we would start either with a character that we liked, [or] sometimes it would be a situation.
>
> An episode that I wrote called "Trouble in Chapter 13" was the result of a cover story in *Time* about Marabel Morgan, the woman who told you to wrap yourself in cellophane and greet your husband that way. What you looked for were characters that would generate some kind of heat with Rockford. Rockford was a character who was totally without bullshit in him, and didn't appreciate it in others. And if you put him with somebody who was 99 and 44/100th percent bullshit, you knew you were going to get something, so that's pretty much the way we did it.

Bartlett tells of the genesis of one of the show's most memorable characters:

On one occasion we were sitting there and I had to do it. I was up at bat and he [Stephen Cannell] said, "Well, do you have any ideas?"

I said, "No."

"Any characters you are dying to write?"

"No."

It was just nothing. So he said, "Why don't we go for something really unique, really unusual. The hooker with the heart of gold." And that's how the Rita Capkovic [character was created, which won Rita Moreno an Emmy in 1978]. It started out as a gag.

I said, "Oh, that's wonderful, Stephen. The hooker with the heart of gold?" As a matter of fact, the *Nichols* that I wrote was about a saloon keeper who was a little more than a saloon keeper. My first *Toma* for Roy was about a madame, a kind of Xaviera Hollander character. *The Cowboys* that I wrote was about a lady with a shady reputation. I thought, "What is it? Why do I keep writing about these people?"

I have some story [meeting] tapes that are so funny and so dirty because when we were putting together the Rita show, Steve and Dave [Chase] would do everything in their power to get to me. They are so filthy with what they are saying, and you can hear me on the tape saying, "All right. Are you guys finished? Fine. Now can we continue? Can we get this out of the locker room?" They were trying to make me laugh. And I was not going to laugh at their filthy jokes.

An example of how the staff on *The Rockford Files* collaborated can be seen in the development of "So Help Me God," which deals with the abuses of the Federal Grand Jury system. Bartlett had been developing another script and was stuck for a "B" story (the "A" story is the main story of the episode, the "B" story is a subplot). One morning David Chase came down the hall with a copy of *The New Yorker* and he showed Bartlett a story on the grand jury system, suggesting it might make the "B" story. Bartlett read it and said to him, "This isn't the subplot. This is one on its own. I love this." Bartlett says today, "Of course I know as much about law as I do about hooking, so when I finished the script, I sent a copy to the ACLU and the ABA and asked if they would read the material and tell me if I had made any horrendous gaffes." There was one step in the procedure she had missed, and that change was made. The show received numerous awards from lawyers' groups.

The Rockford Files, with its own lighter touch, managed to deal with issues as well as attitudes, blending them together so that the episodes never appeared to be preaching, unlike many of the *Quincy* episodes. *Rockford* was moving away from dealing with issues as issues and toward integrating them into the storylines and conventions of the show. In addition to being highly entertaining, the show was part of a transition from earlier shows like *The Defenders* and *Dr. Kildare*, which dealt with an issue a week, to the more integrated later shows like *Hill Street Blues* and *China Beach*.

·15·

MOVIES AND MINISERIES:
THE LATER YEARS

Given the success Paramount had with Eric Bercovici's work on the miniseries *Washington: Behind Closed Doors*, it is not surprising they thought of him when they purchased the rights to James Clavell's novel of feudal Japan, *Shogun*. Bercovici was sent a copy of the massive novel with instructions "Read this tonight." He got through the first three hundred pages, and then was told at the studio the next day not to bother. Paramount assigned the project to others.

A year later, Bercovici was called by the president of Paramount and told to meet with Clavell. Bercovici had begun to develop an idea of how to do the film version of *Shogun* the year before:

> So I went over and met with James for the first time and I told him my idea of how to do *Shogun*, which was to change the whole view of the book. The book is written from God's point of view: you know what everybody is thinking, characters are speaking Japanese, Portuguese, Latin, English, Dutch, everything. Obviously, you can't do that. However, I wanted to shift the emphasis and tell the movie from Blackthorne's point of view and have him understand, and have the others understand, only what he understands by having the Japanese speak only Japanese. But James was [saying], "But what about all the scenes where Toranaga and all the Japanese are sitting around talking all that wonderful political stuff?"
>
> I said, "It's got to go. You can't do it." He looked rather grumpy at that, and I said, "I didn't get this job."
>
> He said, "Meet me at the house tomorrow at ten o'clock." So I go up to his house, and I knew that I had displeased him. I rang the doorbell and he opened it and he was a totally different James Clavell. He was a smiling man. He had torn up a copy of the book and torn out everything I said I was going to leave out of the script. He handed me this. He said, "By God, it works."
>
> At that point I entered into this mystical relationship with James Clavell that continues to this day. Mystical in that he started to place all his faith in me, without question. And when you are working for someone who likes what you are doing, you do better work with encouragement. He encouraged me mightily.

Bercovici did no research on his own while writing the script, relying on the novel. When he went to Japan as producer of the miniseries he spent a week with a Japanese historian who corrected what Bercovici calls "the misinterpretations of Japanese history." In spite of that, there were battles over the history during the production, sometimes over very trivial matters. When the crew was getting ready to shoot a scene with swans in the background, some of the Japanese assistants were taking away the swans, saying at this period in history they did not know how to clip swans' wings. Bercovici, who took the attitude that it was drama, not history, had them replace the swans.

Since Bercovici wanted to tell the story from the point of view of Blackthorne, the English navigator, he wanted to keep the Japanese speaking Japanese. He wrote the entire script in English, then had his assistant, Chiho Adachi, translate the Japanese characters' dialogue into Japanese. Bercovici himself translated Blackthorne's Japanese speeches so they would be in awkward Japanese. He turned the script in to Deanne Barkley, the head of miniseries for NBC, who read it and said, "It's terrific. Go." Bercovici points out that among executives "there is a reluctance to read in Hollywood [and New York], especially something like [the size] of the New York phone book." He thinks no other executive, either at NBC or Paramount did read it. The network's censors read it and there was what Bercovici felt were relatively minor negotiations about content, specifically the pissing scene, the decapitation, and a few uses of the word "bastard."

The shooting schedule ended up helping keep the Japanese language in the miniseries. The original schedule was upset when the actress first hired for Mariko wanted to add "another zero" to her contract. While they searched for another actress, they shot the shipwreck scenes first, using as many as eight cameras, and scenes with the English crew of the ship. This resulted in "endless, endless footage," which was processed in Japan and sent back to Paramount and NBC. Bercovici is convinced that after the first month of this, nobody at Paramount or NBC was watching any of the dailies. The first time anybody at the studio or the network realized that much of the film was in Japanese was when they saw the first cut, and Bercovici began to get calls from the executives asking him if *any* of the rest of the show was in English. There were constant debates with the network executives, who wanted to subtitle the Japanese scenes, but Bercovici eventually prevailed, pointing out that it would make Mariko's translations redundant. Bercovici adds,

They also kept changing the format. Originally it was three hours, two hours, two hours, two hours, and three hours. Then it became three hours, one hour, two hours, three hours, one hour. [It ended up three, two, two, two, and three.] We kept changing the format, changing the focus, and saying, "What are we going to do about the Japanese?" The whole end of that show was done with an endless stomach cramp.

In addition to writing the script, Bercovici also ended up having to write a sea shanty. In the script he had just written that Blackthorne sings a shanty. When they got to Japan they realized they did not have one, and the tapes Paramount had UCLA send of historical shanties did not work. Bercovici told director Jerry London he would write one.

> I wrote it in a car. It was inspiration out of desperation. Richard [Chamberlain] had to learn it, and it was fairly Keystone Comedy, because I had this shanty in my head. I said, "Get me a piano." [If] I can pick it on the piano, I can write it down. First we had to find a piano. Not that easy to do. They finally found a piano and I wrote the music and the lyrics down. Since I was too shy to sing it myself, I gathered a few people and taught them the song. So we all sang it together so we could make a tape to give to Richard, because they were certainly more on key than I was.

As the writer and producer, Bercovici was involved in the post-production phase and beyond. For the first run of the miniseries in 1980, he wrote the "legends" setting the scene, as well as the narration for Orson Welles to deliver. For the second run, NBC wanted more legends and subtitling and Bercovici supervised those, as well as writing more narration for Welles. Bercovici was also involved in writing and cutting different versions of the film. While they were in production he was told they would have to prepare a two-hour version, so he cut the script down to a two-hour version that was filled with "telephone booth scenes" (although there were no telephone booths in feudal Japan) in which characters describe what happened in the scenes that had been cut: "Oh my God, you should have seen what just happened. It's incredible." Bercovici kept insisting that this version made no sense. Gary Nardino, an executive at Paramount agreed, but insisted there be a two-hour version. Bercovici still thinks the two-hour version is "dreadful."

> Then, there are three other versions. We then made a two-and-a-half-hour version that at least filled in some of the holes. Not all of them, but some of them, which NBC played as three hours. That was a little bit better. Then there was a Japanese version, 2 hours and 47 minutes. In the two-hour version and also the two-and-a-half-hour version we took out most of the Japanese-language scenes. In the Japanese version we took out most of the English-language scenes. None of them is any good, I don't think. The twelve hours are the twelve hours. That I am happy to have my name on. The rest of it is nothing terribly valuable.

At least Eric Bercovici had the advantage of having all the historical characters in *Shogun* safely dead when he wrote that miniseries, and the only people who complained were Japanese historians and Jesuits who did not like the way the missionaries were portrayed. E. Jack Neuman did not have it so easy on his 1982 miniseries based on Albert Speer's autobiography, *Inside the*

Third Reich. Speer was still alive and Neuman spent a year with Speer in Germany, asking questions.

> Speer was totally frank with me about everything. He never evaded a question, never eluded anything. And I began to understand a very, very complex man, and in spite of myself, after a couple of years I began to grow fond of him. But I did not make him a great sympathetic man on the screen at all. I told the story of the worst Nazi of them all, because he knew better. And I think the audience understood that.

Neuman had first developed an interest in doing a miniseries of *Inside the Third Reich* when he read in a literary trade journal that the book had sold 19 million copies. He then learned that the book had been optioned at different times by several different companies for a total of $300,000 in options, but had never been filmed (Neuman also learned by accident that Speer had not kept the money from the book but turned it over to the United Jewish Relief). The book was by then un-optioned and he went to the head of NBC, John McMahon, who told him to do it, even though Neuman wanted to do it as a ten-hour miniseries. A deal was made to do it at Paramount, and then both McMahon and the head of Paramount were fired. The new head of NBC, Fred Silverman, wanted to do it, but as Neuman found out, "Some guy in New York had decided to de-fang Freddie and also decided they didn't want *Inside the Third Reich* at their network." The problem, Neuman discovered, was that the senior executive at NBC did not believe Speer.

Neuman managed a meeting with him and asked him if he believed Erich Fromm, Telford Taylor, Simon Weisenthal, and William Shirer—all of whom Neuman had also talked to. The executive said he did, but still did not believe Speer. Neuman's agent, Frank Cooper, knew how much work Neuman had already put in on the project, and he managed to get it away from NBC and Paramount and took it to Brandon Stoddard at ABC, who said, "Let's go, baby." Stoddard did insist on cutting Neuman's script from ten hours to five hours, which is all he felt he could give the film.

Neuman did not get much help from either the author or the main character in his next miniseries, the 1985 *A Death in California*. The four-hour film was based on Joan Barthel's book about a true-life crime, in which Hope Masters, a Beverly Hills socialite, has a love/hate relationship with the man who killed her fiancé and raped her. Neuman called Barthel, "who didn't want to have anything to do with me." He hired a researcher to pull together all the coverage of the case, and he talked to nearly everybody connected with the case. "I stayed away from Hope herself, because I figured she was a flake anyway. I finally met her after the picture was made. Absolutely fucking gorgeous. She made Cheryl Ladd [who played the part] look like a tramp. But a flake, a real flake. She was still going to visit the guy." According to Neuman, the murderer still has a suit against him and ABC for defamation of character, and Neuman says, "I'm sure he's going to knock on the door one day when he gets out of the slam."

Neuman's next movie was also based on a true story, told in an article by Michael Daly in *New York* magazine, about a Queens mother who becomes an undercover agent for the DEA when she discovers her son is hooked on drugs. The network, CBS, only wanted a two-hour movie, but Neuman persuaded them it had enough material for three hours. He thinks it could have even gone longer, since Daly had done enough research for more, and Neuman had difficulty getting *Courage* down to three hours.

For his four-hour 1990 movie *Voices Within*, about a woman with multiple personalities, Neuman looked at the two famous films on the subject, the 1957 theatrical film *The Three Faces of Eve* and the 1976 television miniseries *Sybil*, but felt they were both "pretty dull pictures," done with the same formula, starting with a troubled person coming to the psychiatrist and then flashing back to when the person was sane. His version started out with the young woman "young, vibrant, pretty, and successful, with all the confidence in the world about life. Slowly but surely you find out that there's more than one of them." Neuman had some reservations about the final results, since he did not think Shelley Long, who played the lead was "quite up to it," but he thought Lamont Johnson directed it "very well." Neuman produced it and thinks "the trick is to ride it through and make them keep their nose on the script. You know, even Monty [Johnson] has a tendency to [do] a little creating or something. 'No, I'll do the creating Monty, thank you. Just do what it says.' They don't like that but I'm not bashful a bit. A blithe personality I'm not."

Not every television movie of the eighties had a serious subject. *Midnight Offerings*, a 1981 two-hour movie written by Juanita Bartlett and Stephen J. Cannell, puts a witch in conflict with a college girl with supernatural powers. Bartlett and Cannell, who had worked together on *The Rockford Files*, sat down on a Sunday to work out the story. Bartlett is fascinated by the occult and has an extensive library on the subject. Cannell admitted he knew very little about it, so Bartlett explained such things as what witches do, and Cannell, like a kid with a new toy, wanted to include everything. Bartlett told him it would be too gimmicky. Bartlett, talking of this and *Rockford*, says what she misses most no longer working with him is "the laughing. I have laughed my way through so many story meetings with Steve."

In the eighties, as in the seventies, there were also star-vehicle television movies, and two that E. Arthur Kean wrote were star biographies as well. He was somewhat reluctantly drawn into doing the 1982 two-hour film *Mae West* because he hoped to be able to direct it as well. At the first meeting with executives at ABC, he told them, "I am not going to tell lies about this woman. Now, that's the deal breaker." They assured him they did not want him to do that, and he went to work on the script. Ironically, because of the network's insisting that the material be as raunchy as possible, Kean had no problems with the network censors. "They didn't dare censor this, because it was about censorship." Kean found himself fighting with "the ABC guy," Stu Samuels, who

> wanted to do all the stuff I said up front I'm not going to do, so we continually went around about this. He just wanted to make it more crass, more commercially viable. I said, "No. We're lying about her. We can't do that. She's recently dead. Too many people know her and love her and we can't offend these people. It's not right."
>
> He said, "Aw, fuck this. Come on, we're making pictures, guy." That was essentially the attitude.

Kean thinks the arguments with Samuels led to his not directing the film. Kean was sent a copy of the shooting script, and he did not recognize a third of the pages.

There were also changes in the characterization. Kean had written West's mother as a duchess who falls in love with an Irish stable boy, which shows West what can happen when a woman is overcome by love, thus motivating West's determination not to be at the mercy of men. Piper Laurie was cast in the role, and she, in Kean's words, "decided she knew more about writing than I did." She changed the duchess into what Kean calls "a nasty little guttersnipe . . . a nice, feisty woman [who] had nothing to do" with the original characterization and therefore changed the dynamics of the story.

Kean did not have much better luck the next year with *Rita Hayworth: The Love Goddess*. Kean's old producer from *Police Story*, Stan Kallis, asked him to work on the project, which already had a script by a woman writer. Kean read it and thought it was "stillborn. It was essentially two hours of the same scene [of] Harry Cohn [dumping] on Rita Hayworth." Kean read the biography the script was based on, then called Kallis and said, "Stan, I don't know who this lady is, but somehow, she has studiously gone through this biography and removed all the good stuff." Kallis agreed and Kean worked out a storyline.

The production of *Rita Hayworth* came about in the first place because of Lynda Carter's big success with the *Wonder Woman* series, which started on ABC but moved to CBS. Carter's CBS deal included television movies, but by the early eighties the network, Kean says, was "stuck with this commitment with her and they wanted to dump it. They just wanted it over with." David Susskind said he could produce the film for a million dollars, and the network agreed. There was a rush to get the film done and Kean went into the first production meeting with only an outline, from which he explained the story and the characters. Kean recalls that the unit production manager, who handles the minute details of the production ("and these people are not known for their generosity, or their humanity, and their effulgence," Kean notes) said, "Now we've got a story to tell." Kean felt "very good that this guy is so moved," and while they were casting and scouting locations, he whipped up a script in about a week. Susskind called up him and said, "Art, you dazzle me," which was followed by a similar call from Stan Kallis.

Three or four days later Kean learned the company had not acquired the rights to use any of Hayworth's movies, and furthermore they did not think they could get them, with the possible exception of the "Put the Blame on Mame" song from *Gilda*, and while Kean would be allowed to use the number, he could not use the scene. And they needed the revised script the next day. Kean recalls:

> I remember in the middle of this saying, "This is a catastrophe. Why am I having so much fun?" I was having a wonderful time with no known reason. So I remember saying, "O.K., I can solve this," and I left. I came back in two or three days, and I'd solved it all. And Susskind called and said, "Art, you did it again. You dazzle me. It's absolutely wonderful. How do you do these things?"
>
> I said, "I don't know, but I did it. And I'm very glad."
>
> When they read the "Put the Blame on Mame" scene they called me and said, "We can't do this! We can't do this! You're showing the scene."
>
> I said, "Have you finished reading the scene?"
>
> They said, "No."
>
> I said, "Well, you call me later." She's in the gown and she does the whole number, and when it's over, you expect maybe somebody to say, "Cut," or whatever, but it's the wrap party [at the close of shooting] and she was performing it for everybody, and that got into the key confrontation with Harry Cohn. And that worked very well.

The director hired, James Goldstone, was not enthusiastic about Lynda Carter. He told Kean, "She can't act. She can't sing. She can't dance. This picture's going to be a disaster." Kean thinks that Carter is "a nice lady," but at the first cast reading of the script, she was mumbling. He thought she was just nervous, but "little did I know that was the top of her form." At the reading, Kean thought the show might work, but he went back after seven days of rehearsal for the final read-through, and felt it was like a funeral: "Goldstone had in seven days destroyed everybody's spirit." Kean describes David Susskind at this point as "suicidal. Everyone was way down, and I knew we were on our way to a catastrophe." Kean later said on a radio interview that he felt that Goldstone had ruined the film without changing a word. What he meant was that, for example, the big final confrontation scene, which was supposed to be a big screaming match, was played quietly. At the industry screening of the film Goldstone introduced Kean by saying, "His dialogue is so easy to cut." Kean had to be restrained by his wife.

The original screenwriter asked for a Guild arbitration on the writing credit, and Kean was "in the odd position of arguing to protect my screen credit, which I am considering removing." Kean's sole credit stood, and in spite of his opinion of the film he has received heavy residuals from both the domestic cable sales and overseas sales.

In the early eighties, Christopher Knopf wrote two biographical films rather different from Kean's. For the first one, Procter and Gamble approached Knopf and his partner, Stan Hough, about sponsoring a four-hour miniseries based on the lives of the apostles Peter and Paul. Basing the script of *Peter and Paul* on the Acts of the Apostles from the Bible, Knopf was getting "constant, constant feedback" from a variety of religious advisors. The Catholic advisors took exception to his reference, straight from the Bible, that Joseph, Jesus's brother, took over running the church after Jesus's death. The Catholics contended that Mary remained a virgin all her life and had no other children. The Catholics also insisted that the film had to show Peter in Rome, although the Bible never says he went to Rome, only to Babylon, which the Catholics insisted was a code word for Rome. Knopf felt that the constraints on him and his collaborators made the film "stodgy. I think it was written a little stodgily. Everybody else added their stodginess to it. I think the problem was that we were totally inhibited from breaking away from the Bible and adding any theatricality to it. We just stayed with what the Bible had." On the other hand, Knopf says that "extremely religious people" liked the film very much because it was so literally the Acts of the Apostles.

Knopf had almost no problems with the Catholic Church on his next film, three years later, the 1984 *Pope John Paul II*, which dealt with the early life of Karol Wojtyla. Knopf worked primarily through the archdiocese of New York. He had problems instead with CBS, which thought the film was too slow. They also may have thought they were going to get a different kind of film. One CBS executive knew that Wojtyla had been anti-Nazi during the war and expected this to provide some action scenes. Knopf explained to him that Wojtyla's activities were confined to an underground theater group and told the executive, "I can't put a gun in the Pope's hands."

The executive replied with the classic show-business phrase, "Isn't that negotiable?"

Knopf told him, "I don't think so."

Ed Waters ran into network problems as well on his first television movie, the 1981 thriller *The Intruder Within*. He says that compared to writing for episodic series, television movies are "an easier form, but it's a much dicier game. If you are doing episodes, if you are any good, you know they are going to be on. When you're doing movies for television, maybe one in three gets on, or that was the average in those days. And you're dealing much more closely with the network. They're really controlling it." With this film, the production company came to him and wanted to do what was essentially a remake of *Boom Town*, the 1940 Clark Gable–Spencer Tracy movie about oil wildcatters. Waters looked at the film and did not think there was much story there, but decided an interesting story could be done on an offshore oil rig. ABC then generated an internal memo describing the film as a horror movie. The producer, John Furia, Jr., gave Waters a chance to back out, since it was not the film he had intended to write. Waters decided to do it since he had never done a horror story before, but the script was changed after he left to make it more of a rip-off of the current theatrical hit *Alien*.

As the eighties progressed, there were more and more co-production deals, which involved more than just network influence. In the early eighties David Simons talked to Christopher Knopf about the possibility of a TV movie about a real Cambodian teenaged girl who came to America in 1970 speaking no English and who went on to win a spelling bee four years later. The show, which was finally called *The Girl Who Spelled Freedom*, was written for the British production company Marble Arch for broadcast on CBS, but the network decided it was "too soft" and did not run it. Disney was starting a two-hour anthology show and got hold of the script and made a co-production deal with Marble Arch's successor, ITC. The ITC executive put in charge of the project hated the script. Knopf prevailed, and the show went on to win a number of awards, several of which the executive happily accepted. Knopf notes, "He loves those plaques."

In the mid-eighties, Sam Rolfe moved from television movies into miniseries. He had not done miniseries before that because "Nobody ever asked me." In the case of the 1985 miniseries *The Key to Rebecca*, Taft Entertainment had Rolfe under contract and asked him if he could do a script from the book. Rolfe believes the book's author Ken Follett is "a marvelous book writer, and I don't think he'll ever want me to write anything else of his, and I don't think I ever want to touch anything of his." The main character in the book, a German agent in World War II, is told to go to Cairo and just generally help win the war. Rolfe told the executives at Taft, "You can get away with writing this because, somehow or other, in a book you're just looking at the words and a good wordsmith can just carry you along." On the screen, he said, "You're going to be watching this, and the [dramatic] flaws are going to jump out at you." The company agreed and Rolfe went to work.

> So I really had to lay in a lot of stuff to make that work. It was a bitch. Ken Follett hated me for that. First of all, I had to give the guy a mission. Do something, and not just steal things until you get the right one. I had to find a way to get him directed to what he wanted.
>
> I also had to work up the relationship between the man and the woman, which I think I did rather well. Some of the best dialogue I've written. I stuck in a couple of those scenes between the protagonist and the woman he uses in this. I had to cut down on the sexual stuff, not because I wanted to, but because that's what you had to do in television. I just had to reshape an awful lot of things. People who are in the know congratulated me on making that story work. Never mind it was a best-seller. Making it into a screenplay is a whole different ballgame.

The Key to Rebecca ran 200 minutes, and the following year Rolfe wrote what became a five-hour miniseries, *On Wings of Eagles*. Based on Follett's nonfiction account of H. Ross Perot's attempt to rescue two of his employees held hostage in Iran, the project was originally to be a theatrical film, but Taft at some point decided to do it as a miniseries. Rolfe did not know it was to be five hours when he began writing. He wrote "my normal long first draft, and then when they said, 'Let's find some more,' I just wrote another exceptionally longer [draft, with] incidents, people, and things. [I] just took it and made it longer than it had to be, and just cut it back down."

The material was not very dramatic: the team arrived in Iran with a plan, the plan was clearly not going to work, and through events they had not planned, they were able to rescue the hostages. The material could well have been written as a black-comedy adventure, but Perot was insistent that his men appear to be "heroes." Rolfe did not object to this: "My whole story depends on them being heroes. And secondly, I think they were very brave to do it. Even if it didn't work out [as planned], it's a gutsy thing to try to do." Perot showed up in the middle of the mission, which could have been a stupid thing to do, but it was easy enough to make it look heroic as well. Rolfe invented several incidents to make it more dramatic, doing "a lot of creative work in there. But the thing that made it tough was that it was based on a story that's supposed to be true, and the characters really did live. But everybody sort of approved of it and it turned out very well, I think."

When Rolfe was interviewed for this book, he had just finished a script for a television movie on redwoods. His script was two hours and the company wanted to stretch it to three, but he told them it would just be speeches and no drama at three hours, but better and more dramatic at two. He accepted the assignment reluctantly, telling the company, "Don't give me a subject like that. Give me an ax murderer, give me a war, give me something I can sink my teeth into. You give me redwoods and it's tough." He describes it as "one of the toughest things I've ever written."

Eric Bercovici had more lively subject matter when he wrote the 1986 three-hour movie *The Fifth Missile*, based on the book *The Gold Crew* which shows what happens when war games on a Trident submarine get out of hand and two officers try to avert a nuclear war. When the script was completed, it was sent to the Navy with a request for cooperation. The Navy told Bercovici they knew of the book, did not approve of it, and would not cooperate. When Bercovici drove up the submarine base at Bremerton, Washington, to look around, the sentry told him, "We've been expecting you. Get out of here." MGM had developed the project but turned it down, and they told Bercovici that if he set up a co-production that included MGM, they would be willing to be part of it. He set up a co-production in four days with European financing—which meant the film was shot on sound stages in Rome and at the Italian naval base at Taranto.

After moving out of television and into theatrical films in the sixties, Reginald Rose returned in the seventies to work in the longer forms. In 1979 he did *Studs Lonigan*, a six-hour (originally planned for eight) adaptation of

James T. Farrell's trilogy, and in 1982 he did an original miniseries, *The Rules of Marriage*, about a marriage that breaks up. He said in an interview at the time that he was shifting from writing about issues, as he had in the early days of live television, to writing about relationships. He noted that Paddy Chayefsky had gone the other way, from relationship television plays like "Marty" to theatrical films about issues like *Network*. [1]

Rose returned to issues with the three-hour 1987 television movie *Escape from Sobibor* about the biggest and most successful escape from a concentration camp. The final film was a bit unbalanced, spending all but the last ten minutes on the preparations for the escape. The film was originally to have a second part, which was to run two hours, dealing with the escape. The script was written, but Rose says, "The CBS executives did their biennial dance," and a new set of executives came in who did not want to do it, since it was not their project and they did not want to see a project from the old regime turn into a hit. The first part became the complete film.

In 1988 the creators of *Shogun* collaborated again, this time on the eight-hour miniseries called officially *James Clavell's Noble House*. The material does not lend itself to a miniseries as well as *Shogun* does (but not many novels do). The plot deals with attempts to take over or ruin the Hong Kong banking house of Struan's, so there is a lot of exposition in dialogue about banking in general and "Hong Kong rules" in particular. The story also does not lend itself to Bercovici's approach to *Shogun*. The major character of *Noble House* is Ian Dunross, the *tai-pan*, or boss, of Struan's. He is already on the inside of the world of the story, and is protecting his world rather than exploring another one.

There is also a certain amount of back-story about the bank to get it, since its history was told by Clavell in his earlier novel *Tai-pan*, which was made into a dreadful theatrical film in 1986. *Noble House* does work better as a miniseries, and *Tai-pan* probably would have as well. The characters in *Noble House* are interesting, and the Hong Kong scenery is, as usual, spectacular, as are the sequences of the fire on the floating restaurant and the collapse of an apartment building (although the major characters seem to remain superhumanly cool through both disasters).

Shogun, in 1980, had been a co-production involving Paramount, Toho, the Ashai National Broadcasting Company of Japan, and the Jardine Matheson Company. The trend in movies and especially in the more expensive miniseries throughout the eighties was toward that same kind of co-production, as in the cases of *Peter and Paul*, *Pope John Paul II*, *The Girl Who Spelled Freedom*, and *The Fifth Missile*. This meant an increase in the kind and variety of executives involved in the production of the films. The impact of the American networks did not necessarily abate.

When *Noble House* was first published, there was a slight interest from NBC, but they turned it down since they were not sure the business storyline was that interesting. Clavell then worked out a deal with the Beta Taurus company of Munich to develop the project. Bercovici's first script was for twelve hours, but there were no takers for three years. Then CAA, the agency handling the material, sold the project to Dino De Laurentiis and his De Laurentiis Entertainment Group. But there were still no network takers. Finally, Bercovici went to a meeting with Brandon Tartikoff and Susan Baerwald of NBC for what he thought was to be a discussion of cutting the series down to eight hours. There was very little discussion. Baerwald said, "Yeah, Eric can cut it down to eight hours."

Tartikoff replied, "Can I have it on the air in February?" It was agreed it could be done, and Bercovici walked out of the room with an agreement to do the show. As did other writers in their dealings with the networks, Bercovici suspected that, as usual, there were things going on behind the scenes that he simply did not know about.

·16·

PROFESSIONAL STATUS

The Guild

Since television evolved out of both radio and the movies, unions connected with both showed interest in organizing the writers of the new medium. As early as February 1949, some writers in the Authors' League of America (ALA), but without the backing of the ALA itself, were trying to organize a Television Writers Guild.[1] The Radio Writers Guild (RWG), a branch of the ALA, later in 1949 called for a joint effort with the Screen Writers Guild (SWG) to work out representation for TV writers,[2] but many radio writers felt the SWG did not understand the problems of television writers, particularly the question of residual payments. Radio had for years paid writers additional payments when shows were rebroadcast, but there was nothing equivalent in the motion picture business. In June 1949 the SWG stated it would seek residual payments for writers when theatrical films were shown on television.[3]

By 1954 television writers were covered by the Writers Guild of America, a merger of the SWG and RWG that broke away from the ALA. Richard Powell says that at the time of the merger the film writers treated the television writers as "stepchildren." The conflict between the television and screen writers was not smoothed over by the reorganization and continues in some degree to this day.

The guild got agreements in principle on residuals in the early negotiations, but it took the six-month strike in 1959–60 to get the money as well as the principle. By the middle of 1991, the guild had collected over $700 million in residuals for its members, the largest source of which was television reruns.[4] One writer interviewed for this book noted that he gets about $20,000 in residuals and royalties per year, and judging by some of the houses I interviewed people in, other writers make a lot more than that. Because the television business can be so cyclical, residuals are necessary to keep writers in the business during the slow times.

Throughout the fifties and early sixties, the screenwriters' branch of the guild was the most powerful branch. In 1965 Christopher Knopf was the first television writer elected president of the WGAW (Writers Guild of America, west). The vote was on branch (screen vs. television) lines, and he beat screenwriter Michael Blankfort by seven votes. Knopf does not think his guild involvement has created any negative network or studio reaction to him as a writer.

Knopf, who has been through several guild strikes, thinks, "You have to strike for everything. Nobody hands you anything, unfortunately." He sees the changes in the industry now, as the conglomerates take over the networks and the studios, and he wonders "whether the strikes are going to work anymore. You're striking Coca-Cola [the one-time owner of Columbia], Cap Cities [the owner of ABC]. You're not striking Louis B. Mayer or Lew Wasserman."

Many younger writers entering the industry in the seventies and eighties did not come in with high opinions of the guild. Because the guild services those writers already working, it does not particularly help those trying to break into the business. Writers who struggle for years to make a sale suddenly find the guild representative there insisting they have to join. Younger writers are often ignorant of the history of writers in Hollywood and the guild's efforts on their behalf, and do not appreciate those efforts.

Joseph Dougherty, a writer on *thirtysomething*, felt that way when he was asked to join. The first season of the show was shortened by the 1988 WGAW strike, the longest strike in the history of the guild (154 days), in which the studios tried to reduce residual payments for one-hour dramas on the grounds that one-hours were not selling well in syndication. (The issue was finally settled with a change in the formula for computing residuals, a slight win for the guild, or at least not a loss.)

Dougherty became "weirdly radicalized" when the strike was in its fourth month and a tentative contract was put to the vote. Dougherty was attending a Writers Guild of America, east meeting in New York and astonished himself by going up to the microphone to speak. He called for the members to vote the contract down, and was booed by the East Coast writers, who thought the issues were not of importance to them. Dougherty returned to his seat and looked up to see that the next speaker, supporting his position, was Budd Schulberg. Dougherty said to himself, "I think I've just done something cool," and says now, "Budd Schulberg and I are up there with these union guys. It was great." He adds:

> Schulberg was astonishing. He just simply stood there and in five sentences reminded people of what it was like before, when you didn't tell people you were going to a meeting. When you couldn't park in front of a house, because this was when the Disney people were going around taking pictures of license plates of people who were picketing. He said, "There was a time when you couldn't even get together in a house."

The 1988 strike continued until August, and as typical of guild strikes, it produced both hardship and fun. Lydia Woodward recalls how she spent the 1988 strike:

> After *St. Elsewhere* ended, we had a wonderful . . . writers' strike, which was a great reprieve from working, [from] having to feel guilty about not working. We got to go to the Dodger day games, which was fun. I joined up with a bunch of writers that we all kind of met in the strike line and other places and we played softball every week. It was a wonderful five months, what can I tell you? I was so depressed when it was over and we had to go back to work.

The 1988 strike was perceived by many writers as an attempt to destroy the guild, as President Reagan had destroyed the air traffic controllers' union earlier in the decade. George Kirgo, the guild president, did not go that far, pointing out that the guild was valuable for bookkeeping of residual payments and for arbitration of writers' credits.[5] Even so, the studios' behavior, in Joseph Dougherty's words "radicalized a lot of writers who had not been radical before. . . . I think the studios burned a lot of bridges with a lot of good writers, who now simply do not trust them and just will not go there."

Speed

In 1954, when the dispute over which guild would represent television writers was in full bloom, Cy Howard noted that one reason why radio writers would be better for television is that the new medium needed writers who could write fast, adding, "Screen writers simply cannot write that fast."[6] In early television, Richard Conway notes, the saying was, "Get the script in by Wednesday, or we'll have half an hour of organ music on Friday." On some shows, Conway remembers, "We were so busy putting out scripts, we hardly got out of the room. We had one script in a drawer in case of a tie. . . . We'd have to do a script overnight. Somebody's sick and they're featured in this week's script, so you have to rewrite for the sets and the outside people [actors] you have."

Allan Manings is blunt about what the time pressures can do to a writer: "If I'd never written series television, I'd be a much better writer. The time constraints are so pressurized to get that damn show on, that when you come to a situation where you have essentially the same situation, you tend to solve it the same way." Manings also quotes writer Hugh Wedlock on the perils of late-night rewriting sessions, particularly on comedies: "At three o'clock in the morning either nothing is funny or everything is funny."

On the other hand, many TV writers feel they need a deadline and even thrive on the pressures of television. Mental speed and agility, and not just speed at writing, is essential for television writers to maintain their position in the industry. When writers freelance, they often keep several scripts in mind

at the same time, as Lou Shaw did. Robert Ward was a novelist before he
got into writing TV, and he was astonished to discover he could keep in mind
several different scripts for different episodes for a series he was writing and
producing. He allows as how some of them had what one of the show's producers called "The cringe factor"—you cringe when you see the results. Ward
adds,

> It's obvious the pressure is bad. What's not so obvious is that having a long
> time can be bad. Sometimes under pressure you come up with stuff that would
> never come up if you didn't have the pressure, which I think is why people force
> themselves to work at the end of deadlines. "O.K., I got six weeks. That means
> I can do nothing for five-and-a-half weeks. O.K., now I've got three days, now
> I can be creative."

Ed Waters made his major contribution to the *Kung Fu* series at deadline
time. Waters "basically got them [the wise little sayings of Master Po] from
deadlines. People thought I was deeply versed in Eastern philosophies and so
forth. I had a few things [books] around, but basically it was 'My God, we
have to do something here,' and you came up with it."

Juanita Bartlett also has to have deadlines, but notes that you can concentrate so much on the script "you can't see problems. If you can put it away
for a week or so and then get it out and read it again, it'll pop right out at
you and you'll find it, but you never have that two-week grace period."

Joseph Dougherty was a playwright before he started working for television,
and has become a faster writer because of his television work. He would write
the first draft of a *thirtysomething* episode in two to three weeks, and found
non-television writers "just slackjawed" at his pace. Dougherty feels

> You have no time to second-guess yourself on a first draft. You have to just try
> it. If you do the first draft [like that], you write some horribly clunky stuff, but if
> you get a good riff going, you're doing it . . .
>
> I think if you've been doing it for a while and you're comfortable with the
> scenes and the characters and the physical limitations of the production, you can
> fall into the *thirtysomething* trance, which you do. If you kill yourself and it
> takes you months, you're not doing it right. It really should come easily.

As Dougherty discovered, television writers learn to let the time pressures
of television work for them. One of the fastest writers in television—Lou
Shaw—says,

> I didn't get agonized or eaten up. I've seen a lot of writers eaten up alive by
> that kind of pressure. It wasn't even that kind of pressure on me. The only
> pressure on me was: How do I do all three shows simultaneously? Because I do
> get very concentrated when I'm writing. I get very monomaniacal on that one
> show. But if I've got to do three at the same time, it gets a little tough.

Dealing with the Bosses

Because of the institutional as well as time pressures, writers' dealings with their bosses, whom Phil Mishkin calls sarcastically "the brain trust of television," are often not smooth. Not even close to smooth.

When Richard Powell worked with the networks developing pilots for series, he began to think it was like being surrounded by Pygmies in Africa who want to look at your Jeep, and "while they have no idea at all what makes it work, they will infallibly reach in there and extract the part [whose absence] makes the whole thing not work. It's amazing how they manage to hit on that." Allan Manings quotes the head of the BBC as once saying, "In America you have the writers, you have the directors, you have the producers, you have the actors—every bit as good as ours. What you don't have is the people who will let you do it."

When E. Jack Neuman was writing and producing at MGM in the early sixties, he followed Reginald Rose's approach and insisted the network and studio people write everything down in a memo, since he felt that as soon as they started to write down their complaints, they would realize how stupid they are. E. Arthur Kean says, "When you're dealing with episodic television, you're just getting the notes," which is why he prefers doing television movies, where he can talk to people directly. Kean quotes a lawyer as saying, "You can't cross-examine a note." He adds:

> A writer has to learn to cultivate every possible power of intimidation. The master of that in my view was Eric Bercovici, who has grown this fierce countenance. He looks like he can murder you at any moment. It's wonderful in a network meeting to have that kind of presence. And he uses it brilliantly. And it's all a fake. And I love it. It's marvelous the way he does that. "You say that again and you'll die."

You can see why producer Gerald Abrams might have thought Bercovici had a gun in his briefcase.

Both Joel Rogosin and Sam Rolfe have noted similar changes in network involvement since the early sixties. Then, the networks were relatively passively involved in the creation of the shows, but in the following years there were increasing layers of executives, with, as Rogosin says, more and more people being copied on the memos and more and more people in the story conferences. Rogosin and Rolfe agree that often the executives are very bright, but Rogosin notes that the network representatives to a show are usually middle-management types whom the network is developing for advancement—which means they are less concerned about the quality of the show and more about their own careers. Both Rogosin and Rolfe agree the executives are bright and can be creative and make contributions, but, like Powell's Pygmies, they suggest changes that will hurt the script. Rolfe notes that most of them studied film in college and tend to think in visual rather than narrative terms. He sits in story conferences with them and is "reminded of a bunch of kittens batting at bright-colored moths flying by," who say things like "Hey, that's a gas. Let's stick this in," without any sense of how it will connect to the story. Rolfe adds, "It's so much fun they want to play with it."

Although there was less involvement from Standards and Practices in the eighties as the networks cut back network staffing and at the same time were in competition with the more open cable channels, writers still had to deal with some censorship from the networks. As Phil Mishkin says, "They had practices, but they sure didn't have standards." Robert Ward recalls that on *Miami Vice*, NBC "would get bent out of shape if a character took drugs or if a character was drinking too much." He says the network was so puritanical they would not even allow jokes on the subject, as if to joke about it meant one was not serious about the war on drugs.

On *thirtysomething*, Joseph Dougherty says,

> They leave us almost completely alone. The fights we've had have been kind of pathetic. We get Standards and Practices notes and we fight about them and we trade-off and some things we get and some things we don't and some things we put in there just to get. Usually, you put in at least one "Jesus" and a "God damn," so it comes back in the notes and you change it to "Jeeze," and you answer the note.
>
> We went to the mat with "God damn" in the episode [broadcast] February 5th, [1991,] because it's actually about blasphemy. They said, "You can't say, 'God damn.' "
>
> We said, "We have to. We have to say it this time." I wrote it in the script twice, so the first thing we said was, "Well, we'll only say it once."
>
> They came back and said, "Well, we can't."
>
> We said, "Will you look at the scene? It's Elliot and his mother. It's about God. It's about religion. It's about blasphemy. Look at the scene."
>
> They came back and said, "O.K. You can say, 'God damn' once if, immediately after that, another character says, 'It's blasphemy and against one of the Ten Commandments.' " Scott Winant [a producer] told me this on the phone.
>
> I said, "O.K. Call the network and tell them I will definitely write a line of dialogue where [she] says, 'It's against the Ten Commandments,' if the next time somebody is killed on an ABC detective series, somebody standing over the body says, 'It's a shame she's dead. It's against one of the Ten Commandments, too, did you know that?' " So we got it. . . . They backed down on the Ten Commandments part of it. [In the episode as broadcast, Elliot's "God damn" is part of the conversation and Mom replies, "Please don't curse at the table. Don't take the Lord's name in vain."]

Dougherty thinks the worst part of dealing with the networks was that they were worried about the characters being wrong, whether it was a political opinion, or an opinion about a product or a procedure. The *thirtysomething* writers assumed their characters could be wrong, but the network got very nervous. Dougherty wrote a scene where Nancy said something that was wrong, as a later scene made clear, but a network representative called after reading only the first scene and Dougherty had to tell him, "Read on."

Dougherty says that, as expected, "They're bad on sex too. There was a terrible fight about the concept of orgasms, which was I think the biggest fight we ever had here." The network's first reaction was that an orgasm could not be shown, but the show negotiated with the network to find a way to do it. After the show was shot and delivered to the network, they cut the end of the scene off. Unfortunately that was a setup for another joke, the punchline of which they left, but which made no sense at all on the air.

Writing for cable channels is not necessarily easier than writing for the networks. Aubrey Solomon wrote a special on Howard Hughes for cable and found that the dramatic structure was the same, down to the act breaks. "They don't break for commercials, but ultimately that show is going to be syndicated somewhere, so you are going to need the commercial breaks." He feels that as at the networks, cable executives do not "know what they want until they see it. You can give them any number of variations that they can say yes to, but somehow there is something nagging at the back of their mind that says, 'This isn't quite it.' " Solomon says it can then be "hell" trying to figure out what the "it" is.

Solomon also worked in his native Canada, and the first thing a producer there told him was that it was "a kinder, gentler nation," which he says it was in terms of having fewer hassles with the Canadian network, since the network had fewer executives involved. This also meant less input and critical evaluation of the scripts, and Solomon thinks this was both a blessing and problem in that sometimes he missed not having somebody pushing him to make it a little better.

In 1986 Phil Mishkin worked on a half-hour show for HBO called *First and Ten*. A major difference he saw was that all the scripts for the order of twelve episodes were written, and then shot together like a movie. Because of the way the material was cut together, scenes a particular writer wrote ended up in different episodes. While the writers were being well paid, Mishkin says often "you wind up seeing a scene that was taken out of your episode and put into somebody else's episode, or stretched to a point that you didn't feel like you were getting fair recompense."

Mishkin stayed with the show through 1988, and sometimes he stayed with scripts through the preparation stages, which called for rewriting for production changes: not getting the set or location they originally wanted, or changes in actors. One character was written as white, but when the producers found they could get O. J. Simpson, the scripts were rewritten to make him black. There was also a lot of what Mishkin calls "ancillary writing to be done, mainly what they called 'TV versions.' I would have to take a script and take out the 'fuck yous' and put in 'Get out of here' or 'Lay off' for subsequent usage in commercial television. For syndication some scenes would have to be redone. I guess it's like dubbing a foreign film."

Writer–Producers

One way writers could get a little leverage in their dealings with the bosses was to become bosses themselves. By the time television production moved to Hollywood, the tradition of writers becoming producers was well established in the motion picture industry.[7] The tradition became even more established in television, especially series television. Because of budget limitations in series TV, the major characters, sets, and locations were generally the same each week, and the function of the producer was to develop scripts. Nat Perrin, who started in the thirties as a screenwriter with the Marx Brothers and then moved into producing films, got into TV in the early days more as a producer than as a writer, but this often involved rewriting other writers' scripts, which he did not particularly enjoy, but felt he had to do as part of his responsibility as a producer in order to improve the show. Perrin's description of his "producing" Red Skelton's show makes it sound easier than it was: "I would look at the material [the writers brought in], and say, 'Keep going, boys.' Or, 'It needs a little work.' Tough job. The higher up you go, the more money and the less work."

Some writers either could not do that, or else did not want to. Many preferred to spend their time writing. Everett Greenbaum compared writing and producing to his days as an officer in naval aviation during World War II: "I loved the flying. I was not a leader of men."

Most writers became producers to maintain control of their material as best they could, although most writer–producers realize they do not have as much control as they would like, but as Don Brinkley says, "You at least get your licks in." Christopher Knopf, however, says that "sometimes protecting your own material is not necessarily a good thing. Sometimes material should not be protected. Sometimes you should listen to somebody else [if] they've got a pretty good idea." That collaborative process is why writers often become producers. Sam Rolfe was drawn to both writing and producing and would alternate years at each:

> One year I would be nothing but a writer, the next year I would be nothing but a producer. I still think it's a great way to live, if you can do it. Now as a writer, it's a nice, lonely, sole life. You sit by yourself and you work and you write and you think and you wander, and it's almost bucolic in the way you live. It's relaxing and it's good. When you're a producer, you're never alone. You're tummuling, you're mixing, you're always dealing with people. You're in a roomful of people and people are waiting for you to talk, and people are looking for you to say something, and so your mind starts racing and it pushes you, because you have to come up with things.

Every writer–producer can list the disadvantages of doing both. Eric Bercovici starts off with: "Grief. Lack of sleep. Phone calls that wake you up at three o'clock in the morning saying, 'We're pulling the plug.' " Thad Mumford continues with: "Alcoholism. Gray hair. Ulcers. Kidney problems. Failed marriages. It's a lot of work." It is even a lot of work, maybe even more, on shows that are not that good. Lou Shaw worked fifteen- and sixteen-hour days on *The Fall Guy* to "do it properly . . . for it to be accepted by *its* public."

Phil Mishkin learned that producing could make for tension around the home *and* the office when his wife came in to pitch a script for one of his shows. He was afraid he would be accused by his staff of nepotism, and was relieved when the first draft his wife turned in pleased the story editors. Then on revisions it became, "Will you understand this, *dear*? That it's nothing personal? That if you were Jane Austin you would be getting this?"

The collaborative process that the writer–producer is part of involves the writers working on the series. As Robert Ward puts it, "It's better not to be rewritten. It's better to be able to be the guy who can rewrite somebody else." Robert Dozier became a producer on writer–producer Jerry Thorpe's series *Harry O*, and he discovered producing was not as simple as he thought it would be. When he was asked later at a college seminar what quality, as a producer, he valued most in a writer,

out of my mouth came, "Obedience." I said, "I said that? I actually said that. Stet. Let it stand. That's exactly what I mean. God, I really said that?" You get that way when you're there, and things aren't coming in right, and if they're not right, you fall into the trap: you're the only one who can do it right. It's the trap that everybody falls into: you end up rewriting 50 percent of everything. It should all sound alike. And if it doesn't sound like you, it doesn't sound alike. So I went into it, because I thought, "I won't have to write for a while." I did more writing in those two years than I've ever done in my life.

In addition to dealing with other writers, the writer–producer has to deal with the director. Roy Huggins is of the opinion that one reason to become a producer is to protect your material from the director. Some writers want to become directors, but most television writers prefer producing rather than directing, since control in television is held more by the producer. Given the time and money pressures of TV, the director has little opportunity to "be creative" in the ways that can disfigure theatrical films. He simply has to shoot he material as best he can, which may well be why the best American television in the eighties and nineties was often better than American films.

Sam Rolfe has had several opportunities to direct, but turned them down, not only because he does not want to get up at four in the morning, but because he values having another mind to challenge his. If a director tells him the scene cannot be done the way Rolfe wrote it, and Rolfe cannot persuade him otherwise, Rolfe will make the changes since "if he says he can't, it's not going to come out the way I want it. I've got to listen to him. He's the guy that's got to do it."

Writer–producers also have a collaborative relationship with the actors, unless they can avoid it. Roy Huggins did exactly that on *The Lawyers*. The first pilot starred Guy Stockwell, who came into Huggins's office when it looked as though the show was going on the air. In Huggins's words, Stockwell "did something that I really, really appreciated, because most actors won't do this." According to Huggins, Stockwell said, "Roy, I'm not a piece of meat hanging on a hook. I'm an actor and I just came in to tell you I expect to be part of the decision-making on this show."

Huggins replied, "Jesus! Boy, am I glad you told me this. Because I don't want you to be part [of the show]. I don't want actors to tell me how to do this, because it's very difficult *without* the actors telling me what to do. But they often do, and very few of them are honest enough to come and tell me beforehand. So don't worry about it. You're off the show." Huggins says now, "I must confess that I was not very kind about it, because he was not kind in his approach to me." Huggins says Stockwell started to back-pedal, but Huggins replaced him with James Farentino.

On *The Line-up* in the late fifties, E. Jack Neuman had to take over producing from Jaime del Valle, and he learned how to handle actors from the experience:

> They couldn't go to Jaime because he was either unavailable or smashed or gone or something, so they would come to me. There were two grown men (Warner Anderson, Tom Tully) playing leads in the series, and one would come to me and say, "You know he's got 185 lines and I've got 162, and I'm supposed to be the senior officer." Or vice versa.
>
> I'd say, "Get the fuck out of here." That's the way I learned how to say that to actors.
>
> "I'm going to call my agent."
>
> "Get on somebody else's phone, not mine. I don't give a shit who you call. Get out of here." This is the way I found out how to handle that pouty, little-child bullshit that actors are inclined to do. And of course both of them were making a pisspot full of money [on the series, as opposed to their earlier work on Broadway or as character actors in movies].

When Phil Mishkin took over as producer on *Laverne and Shirley*, he had known Penny Marshall earlier, which did not make things easier:

> It's just that it's hard to work with somebody who was once an equal and is now one of the two major [stars] in the number-one show in America.
>
> One time, my first or second week there, she and Cindy had me called down from the office to the set, and gave me what-for about some scene that had come down to them. "What's going on? What are you guys doing? Who cooks up this stuff? I mean, Phil, aren't you on top of these things? I mean, that's why we

hired you." Then one of them held out a cigarette. I don't know if it was Penny. I smoked at the time, and I was expected to light it, after being bawled out. I lit Penny's cigarette, or Cindy's, and then they gave me another, "Get with it, will you?" and I turned around [and] left. It came back to me, from Alice James [Garry Marshall's script supervisor] that the girls skittered away laughing that they had Phil lighting their cigarette and shaking. Those mean, whatever you call those kinds of people. It was a very nasty little thing. So I had to deal with that.

When Ed Waters was hired as producer of the Robert Blake show *Baretta*, his friends gave him an escape ladder he could roll out the window if necessary. Waters learned there was no controlling what happened to the script after it left the office, because Blake would change everything on a whim, sometimes to a point where it was impossible to cut the footage together. Blake was notoriously difficult with people he thought were "the suits" (executives), but Waters says Blake did him "a great favor. He used to chew tobacco, and he used to spit it on the carpet when he came in to talk to people. When he came to talk to me, he'd spit it out the window."

Roy Huggins

Beginning with his work at Warner Brothers in the fifties, Roy Huggins created his own method of developing stories for the series he ran as producer or executive producer. He would spend hours driving in his car, thinking up stories, recording them on tape. Back at the office, he would then dictate the stories to a story assistant, who would type them up in a narrative form that included only suggestions of dialogue.

> I then bring in a writer. I don't hand him this transcript. I now tell him the story, and it's once more put on tape, and it is once more transcribed, so that the writer gets a transcription of the second draft. Because I've thought it out and I've refined it.
>
> I found many writers who would change my story. Not many, but a few, and they would always change it for the worse, and it wouldn't work any more. In other words, they were doing what producers do, and I would say, "Hey, don't do that. Here's why that doesn't work. So go back to the original." And if you look at my record, you will find the names of writers that I never used again. Those are guys I had to rewrite completely. I mean, they just didn't do it. They got the story all worked out. They gave me back junk. Or something I didn't want to use. When I say junk, I'm talking like a producer. They gave me back things that, who knows, maybe what they did was one way of doing it, but it wasn't my way of doing it. And then I would rewrite them, never with credit. I wouldn't even ask for credit, unless the rewrite was so complete that it went back to my story and their version wasn't my story. Then I would ask for credit and I would usually get it. I'd use a pseudonym [John Thomas James].

Joel Rogosin went to work as a producer at Universal in the early sixties to "mind the creative store" on Huggins's shows when Huggins wanted time to work on his Ph.D. Rogosin considers Huggins a "very talented, bright creative man" whose "filing cabinet is filled with versions of stories which he had originated and told and retold until they were at a stage when he was comfortable enough to pitch them to a writer." Rogosin remembers that there were writers who resented Huggins's method of working, since Huggins took credit—which he was certainly entitled to—on the stories. Rogosin says,

> They resented it because there are a lot of people like me around who gave stories away. A writer would come in with something that didn't work and I would tell him something else, and I frankly, and this is no reflection on Roy, never took credit. It was my sense, and wrongly I think, in retrospect, that it was part of the producing function. As a result, Roy has a lot more writing residuals than I do.

Huggins thinks only one writer ever improved on his stories: Juanita Bartlett, with whom he worked on several series before *The Rockford Files*. He says, "She was absolutely wonderful. But she changed the stories! And made them better! So I discovered something important: I didn't really object to having my stories changed; I only objected to having them fucked up." She says it was "a little intimidating" the first time she worked by Huggins's method, because she was putting into script form his vision, not hers, and she felt an obligation to protect that vision.

Not every writer was impressed with Huggins and his method. Don Brinkley had difficulties cutting through Huggins's associates and getting direct answers from him. Sy Salkowitz is even more vehement about his two experiences with Huggins. The first one occurred in the sixties at Fox. Salkowitz had written a story for story editor Marion Hargrove and they were now going to meet Huggins. Salkowitz recalls:

> It was so hot we were baked, and we were kept waiting about 25 minutes in the outer office. When we were finally allowed in, Mr. Huggins was stretched out on his couch, wearing a pair of tennis shorts and some kind of light pullover. I'm wearing a shirt and jacket because that's the first time I'm meeting with the producer. When we walked in, Mr. Huggins was being handed, on a tray, a glass of ice water, which he takes and he drinks and he hands [it] back to the secretary. She leaves. [Huggins] never says, "Would you like some water? Would you like a cold drink? Would you like anything? Kiss my foot?" Nothing. Then [Huggins] proceeds to tell me how he really doesn't like my story at all, doesn't think they should go ahead with it. My thought was, a simple phone call in the coolness of the beach would have taken care of that.

In the early seventies Salkowitz was working at Universal. Glen Larson asked Salkowitz to look at the pilot he had done for a rip-off of *Butch Cassidy and the Sundance Kid* called *Alias Smith and Jones*, with the idea of Salkowitz writing some episodes. Salkowitz liked it and went to talk to Larson, only to discover that Huggins was now the executive producer, which Larson himself had only found out the night before. Salkowitz continues the story:

> Understand what my frame of mind is: I do not care to work with [him]. Had I known up front I was going to work with him, I would have said no, but I've at least verbally agreed with Universal to do it. At the moment, there are three secretaries hovering around him. One is holding a microphone to his mouth so that every word he says is recorded. Another one is pouring him a cup of coffee, and another one is handing him a note on some outside business. The secretary disappears with the outside business. The other one, with the microphone never left his mouth as Roy Huggins said to me, "I'm going to do the story, you're going to do the screenplay."
>
> Now I expected this, because Roy Huggins's pseudonym is John Charles Thomas [sic. The actual pseudonym is John Thomas James], which you will find on practically every damn episode he ever did, because he gets a lot of residuals. Now he lays out a story and I'm listening to it and taking notes. One would think, by the way, that the recording is being done to hand me a cassette to take home so I don't forget anything. Wrong. The recording is being done so he has a record of the fact that he created the story and nobody can ever contest that. I have to go home with my own memory.
>
> Now at some point during that meeting, he gives a story point and I interrupt him. I say, "Roy, that won't work."
>
> He's incensed. "Of course it will." This was called "The Macready Bust" and I say, "Roy, it won't work. It's going to come out [of the script]. So let's not even bother with it, since it's going to be something else. I don't even think you should have it in." He insists it's going to work. So I say O.K.
>
> So I go home and I write the first draft, and the thing that didn't work still doesn't work and I leave it out. I send in the first draft and I get a call from Glen saying, "We think you did a terrific job. Roy says, 'Thank you very much,' and he feels that he can do the final work on it quicker than he can tell you and then you can go home, etc." Now I want you to understand that I have been known to write a 60-minute script from scratch in 24 consecutive hours. So he thinks he can do it quicker than telling me. But O.K.

Salkowitz was given the succeeding drafts of the script and noticed that the story point he left out was now in, then out, as well as other changes. He also noticed

> a very interesting thing on the front page. It says, "Story by John Thomas Charles [sic. see above], Screenplay by Sy Salkowitz and John Thomas Charles," then it says "John Thomas Charles and Sy Salkowitz," and the last draft I did says "Written by John Thomas Charles."
>
> I'm off it. I asked for arbitration and I knew how it was going to come out: "Story by John Thomas Charles, Screenplay by Sy Salkowitz." Period. Mr. Huggins was incensed. He wrote that entire thing from word one. How could the Guild possibly ever have given me credit?

Glen once called and said, "You want to do another one?"
I said, "Not on your life."

Mr. Huggins's credits include *Maverick, The Fugitive, Run for Your Life,*
and *The Rockford Files.* Mr. Salkowitz's credits include *The Naked City, The
Untouchables, Mission Impossible,* and *Police Story.* Mr. Huggins and Mr.
Salkowitz did not, I believe, socialize.

Aaron Spelling

When Aaron Spelling acted in *Dragnet,* Jack Webb let him visit the set to
learn about production, since Spelling wanted to write for television. Spelling
soon connected with Dick Powell, who was being talked into hosting *The
Zane Grey Theatre.* Spelling suggested that Powell do humorous and historically informative introductions to each week's show. Powell liked the idea,
and Spelling, who knew very little about the history of the West in spite of
coming from Texas (he later told interviewers that being "from a Jewish family in Dallas you don't ride a lot of horses"), went to the library and researched the introductions. Spelling ended up producing six series at Four
Star.[8]

Christopher Knopf wrote for Spelling's shows at Four Star and thinks Spelling was "incredibly bright. He could keep four things going at once. . . . He
always had an idea. His ideas were superficial, but he would allow you to dig
deep if you wanted to, but he always had an idea that would get you going
in some sort of direction if you were stuck. He was fun. He was pleasant to
be around."

The only time Knopf did not find Spelling "fun" led him to learn why
Powell valued him so much. Knopf had mentioned an idea for a *Zane Grey
Theatre* episode, and Spelling pitched it to Powell. When Powell asked whose
idea it was, Spelling claimed it as his. Knopf heard of this and complained to
Powell that Spelling was a thief and asked him why he kept him around.
Powell replied, "I'll tell you why. I got you and Dick [Richard Alan] Sim-
mons and Bruce Geller and the rest of you, and you're all trying to win
Emmies. He's keeping me on the air. He's doing twenty hours while you're
doing two." Knopf had to admit that was true. He now adds:

> I've always felt Aaron was superficial. I'll tell you something. If you put a gun
> to Aaron's head and said, "You will write an opera that the New York Opera
> will accept, in three months," he'll do it. He'll do whatever he has to do. He
> had to be what he's been [in order] to do what he's done. I think if Aaron ever
> said, "O.K., I'm going to concentrate on something and dig in deep," I think
> he'd do it. He just hasn't had to. He's had great success with trivia. It's very
> entertaining and I've enjoyed it.

The term Spelling himself has used for the kinds of shows he does, and which writers love to quote against him, is "mind candy."

Ed Waters had "spent my whole career never writing anything for Aaron Spelling," when he was "gulled" into writing for *T. J. Hooker* after they told him they wanted it to be more like *Police Story*. He went on the show and "quickly found out they had no intention of doing that." He tried to use some stories of patrol cops that had not been done on *Police Story*, but the mind-candy tone of the show worked against them. E. Arthur Kean was approached to write for another Spelling cop show, *Macgruder and Loud*. He was told it was going to be "gritty street action," but Kean told them he knew it was going to be "gritty Rodeo Drive street action" and wrote them "a fairy tale."

Both Rick Mittleman and Everett Greenbaum wrote for Spelling's hit *The Love Boat*. Mittleman calls it "pleasant, lightweight writing," and Greenbaum says, "If I had known what the residuals were like on that show, I would have written as many as I could have, under a different name." Greenbaum describes writing for the show:

> It's very complicated. You had to write all the stories, and they all had to allow for the boat to leave and to stop in Acapulco, or wherever it was going, and all the stories had to fit the stop and the layover. And you couldn't interfere with the characters. You couldn't interfere with one another's stories. It helped if you helped one another's stories. It was quite complicated. Everything has to come out at the end.

E. Arthur Kean wrote an episode for a Spelling show called *The New People*, in which a group of young people are stranded on an island. The main titles for the show establish the premise of the series each week. When Kean went in to look at the rough cut of his episode, he thought the first and second reels had been reversed, since the second act of the show played first. He was told by the producer that Spelling felt there was more "island" material in the second act and he was afraid that with the first act the audience would not know they were on the island. Kean pointed out that the titles establish that, but Spelling's cut went on the air.

Ed Waters thinks that kind of writing, which Spelling demands for his shows, is too obvious, so that "first you tell the audience what you are going to do, then you do it, then you tell the audience what's been done." Spelling's insistence on this kind of storytelling may be a major reason for the success of many of his shows, since there has always been a segment, of varying size, in the American television audience that wants "mind candy."

The Longer View

Television writers not only move "up" into the role of producer, but some of them move even further "up" to work as executives for studios or networks.

Sy Salkowitz has served in several executive capacities, and when he went to Fox as a vice-president for development, he listened to pitches from writers. He felt many of them had not bothered to work out the story, and when he asked them to do it he never heard from them again. He also saw situations that confirmed what Allan Manings heard from the head of the BBC. Salkowitz had to remove producers from shows because they were not letting the writers be as good as they could be.

Being in the business for a long time can also change a writer's perspective. Sam Rolfe looks at the changes in forty years of television:

> We started out in television and we were doing what was essentially crap. Now I see we were doing art. Yesterday's crap is today's art. *Have Gun—Will Travel* and *Man from U.N.C.L.E.* are considered very classy shows. Well, they were just ordinary, everyday [shows]. I think today's art is tomorrow's crap because people are taking this whole thing so much more seriously than it really deserves to be taken. It is essentially the ordinary man's escape from the vicissitudes of life.
>
> Everybody expects it now to educate people and to raise their consciousness and do all sorts of things which it is not equipped to do. What it is is a mild diversion. Now you can say things and you may be able to instill messages into it, but they have to be under the entertainment you are getting to people, or they're not going to tune you in, so your message is useless. It does me no good to come out with a marvelous, important thing if we only want to get remarked on by the critics.
>
> I really felt like the Marx Brothers at the beginning, the Keystone Kops running up and down on the street banging into each other as we developed this thing. Now it's being taught scientifically in schools. They are turning out hordes of people to do this thing. You know something? In the end I don't think they are turning out any more product than we did with a small group at the beginning. We did 39 episodes a season. Now you're doing 19. That's a season. I think they are still turning out essentially about the same amount of material. The only thing is, they're using ten times as many people to do it.

Rolfe has read analyses of his stuff that "staggers" him as to what the analyst thinks was in his mind. He sees himself as "an old-fashioned yarn spinner. I tell the tale. That's all I do. I didn't know I was trying to change the world until I read the interpretations of some of the things I've done." He continues, "The big summation for me is that the fun has gone out of the game. It's become too serious."

·17·

UNSOLD PILOTS AND FLOPS

Unsold Pilots

*P*robably thousands of the ideas for television series are pitched in any given year, for one simple reason: a successful television series can make a fortune, at least some of which gets back to its creators and writers. Writers, of course, pitch ideas to producers, studios, and the networks, but networks, studios, and producers also pitch ideas to writers. Most ideas pitched die early.

As many as a few hundred survive to a stage where enough money changes hands for a writer to write a script for a pilot film, which is supposed to demonstrate what the show is going to be like. It is relatively easy to tell by reading a script if it is not going to work, but it is not so easy to tell if it will work on film. Many scripts for pilots die relatively early, but many are made. In the 1991–92 "selling season," the four networks (including Fox) commissioned a total of 120 pilots.[1]

Writers who have been in the pilot-making business for some time have noticed that networks have increased their involvement in the process over the years. In the early days, Roy Huggins says, there was "a kind of unstated agreement" between him and the networks that he would be left alone on the pilots, but with each new incoming group of executives "the arrogance of power grew" and there was less and less respect for the producer. Phil Mishkin swears that on every project pitched to the networks, the executives will protect themselves by writing what he calls "the yes–no memos," one memo saying the network should pick up the show, another explaining why it should not.

Some writers love writing pilots. E. Jack Neuman developed a taste for it early on, not only because of the royalties a creator of a show got, but because of the challenge of figuring out what the format of the show is going to be and what its hundredth episode is going to be like. His formula for grabbing the audience's attention was to "let the audience know, in the most dramatic way, as quickly as you can, and in the briefest way you can, how your protagonist, how your series' lead feels about God, marriage, politics, money, all of the important things."

The odds of success for a pilot are not large—which is not necessarily a terrible thing for a writer. When Don Brinkley was between *Medical Center* and *Trapper John M.D.*, he and his partner spent three years writing pilots that did not sell. Brinkley describes it, only half-facetiously, as "the best period of my life. I would write these pilots, we would produce them, we'd make lots of money, they wouldn't sell, and we'd have no responsibility after that. We'd go on to the next one."

As noted, most pilots die, some thankfully, some not so thankfully. What follows are some stories about unsold pilots, which provide another perspective on the history of writing for American television.

In 1959 E. Jack Neuman wrote and produced a pilot for a private-eye show called *Carter's Eye*, and Neuman is very explicit on why it did not sell: "Tom McDermott didn't have any brains." McDermott was what Neuman calls the "boy wonder" of the advertising agency Benton and Boles, and in those days the advertisers and their agencies decided which shows got on and which did not. McDermott instead went for a Western with a man with a withered arm.

In 1961 Sam Rolfe did a pilot called *Hurricane Island*. CBS executives had seen a movie about dinosaurs and liked the idea of a series about travelers shipwrecked on an island with prehistoric terrors. Rolfe was "amazed at how many kinds of stories I could come up with in that situation," the special effects were workable on a series budget, but the project suddenly died. Rolfe was told that William S. Paley's children were afraid of dinosaurs.

In 1960 Lou Shaw heard there was one more script needed for the series *The Rebel*, so he called the producer, Andrew Fenady, who said he had all the scripts he needed. Shaw said, "Geez, I hope they don't work, because I've got a great pilot idea that would be the greatest spin-off on *The Rebel*."

Fenady had Shaw, who actually had no idea at all, drive over to his office. During the 45-minute drive, Shaw came with an idea about the first real detective in the West, "a Sherlock Holmes out West." Shaw pitched it, and the series story editor David Victor started to say, "This will be a great dram—" and Fenady said, "This is funny." As Shaw remembers it, Victor shifted in mid-sentence: "This will be a great dram—comedy."

Shaw looked at Victor and said, "Comedy?"

Victor said to Fenady, "Oh, I was talking to Lou just a minute ago what a comedy this will be."

Fenady said, "All right! This is going to be terrific. And I got a better idea."

Shaw said, "It's going to be hard to beat this one." Shaw had no idea where he was at this point. The script was written, the pilot made, and the pilot sank without a trace.[2]

Sam Rolfe was upset that he let his agency, Ashley Famous, talk him into accepting a "developed by" instead of a "created by" credit on *The Man from U.N.C.L.E.*, because it meant he lost creator royalties not only on *Man*, but on its spin-off, *The Girl from U.N.C.L.E.* While still a client of the agency, Rolfe wrote a pilot called *The Long Hunt of April Savage*, but by the time ABC wanted to do it as a series, Rolfe had left the agency and refused to do the series on the grounds that it would make money for his former agency. ABC passed on the series without him.

Richard Powell originally wanted a black woman to play the lead in his 1967 pilot *Mrs. Thursday*. The network, ABC, said there would be no creative interference, but insisted on a white woman being cast in the lead. On the other hand, the 1971 E. Jack Neuman pilot *Crosscurrent* starred black actor Robert Hooks as a police lieutenant. Hooks was hot at the time, but the executive at Warner Brothers forgot to hire Hooks for a series when he signed him for the pilot.

Two years later Neuman wrote a pilot called *Stat!* about a hospital emergency room. When asked why it did not sell, Neuman says, "Damned if I know. They were wild about it. Christ Almighty, it was exactly what they wanted."

In 1973 Eric Bercovici and Jerry Ludwig wrote and produced *Wheeler and Murdock*, and the director was Joseph Sargent. Everyone, including Sargent, whom Bercovici describes as "terrific," liked the script, and as Bercovici and Ludwig kept rewriting the script, it kept getting longer. Sargent insisted they not cut it, and that to fit it into the 47 minutes required, he would have the actors "talk fast." The first cut ran 75 minutes, and when it was cut to 47 minutes it made no sense. The longer version was finally released in syndication as a television movie.

For a 1973 special, Rob Reiner and Phil Mishkin wrote an episode called "Sonny Boy," about a middle-aged son trying to get out from the control of his mother. (Carroll O'Connor originally wanted to do a piece by Chekhov, but Mishkin was glad their script was chosen: "So I've always been able to say we beat out Chekhov for one job. I used to say [mimicking network executives], 'Chekhov and who? Who's he writing with?' ") The special's producer, Bob Precht, felt the idea might work as a pilot, so Reiner and Mishkin rewrote it. The part played by O'Connor went to Allen Garfield, whom Mishkin thinks was "not quite right. He was a little heavy for the part." They went with Garfield because he was a better actor than the others tested, but he was simply not funny in that part. The other casting was wrong, as well. Mishkin says, "It was the worst case of casting I was involved in. It was [the] decisions that we made, and yet we made the wrong decision on every single one of them."

Allan Manings also feels there were casting problems, although of an opposite kind, with the 1976 pilot *Roxy Page*. The half-hour comedy dealt with an ambitious young singer trying to make it on Broadway, and NBC insisted on casting Janice Lynde, whom Manings felt was too good-looking and too good a singer for the audience to believe she would have any difficulty at all becoming a Broadway star.

The 1979 pilot *Pleasure Cove* came from a suggestion by NBC executive Paul Klein, who wanted a show about a resort where your dreams could come true. Lou Shaw was called in to write the two-hour movie pilot. Shaw's agent paired him with David Gerber as producer on the show, telling Shaw, "You want to get on the air? That's the best route." Shaw says now, "So the whole show was a present to Gerber. He came within an inch of selling it, I must say. Just didn't go. Go fight City Hall."

For the 1981 pilot *Quarrel*, Sam Rolfe returned to the spy business, but is not sure why he wanted to make this one more realistic and darker than the *U.N.C.L.E.* shows. "It may have been a different stage in my life. It was just, I think, mostly at that point I felt that there was nothing on the air that dealt in that area. I think I was also a lot more disillusioned about the possibility of [the United States and Russia] working together."

In 1982 Robert Dozier wrote a pilot script called *Streets of Beverly Hills* that had not yet been made when he was interviewed in October 1990. It had, however, just been optioned yet again. In the course of the recent negotiations, MGM discovered its options had lapsed and that it did not actually own the property:

> You cannot imagine the bullshit we went through with their Business Affairs [people]. The lady from MGM called my agent, "Well, we have this old piece of shit here from Robert. Maybe there's some life in it. Maybe we could—"
>
> My agent called and I said, "Jeff, nobody goes through old scripts. Number one, they're dead. So something's up, so just say, 'Yeah, we'll talk.' And find out what's going on." Well, we found out they'd sold it to ABC and they're negotiating with Walter Matthau to do it.
>
> I said, "Jeff, we have a cannon at their head. Let's not fire it. Let's just make a very good deal." So we did. Then Walter Matthau backed out and it didn't work. But in the meantime we'd made this terrific deal if it did go on the air. Then they renewed the option the following year, and they just renewed it again. Now they are developing it as a half-hour sitcom. I'm not sure it will bear any resemblance to what it was I did, but I don't really give a shit because the beauty part is that I'll have a great deal of money, and the real beauty part is I won't have to have anything to do with it. I wish them well.

Dozier also had casting problems on his 1983 pilot *Inspector Perez*. He was trying to get something racially different on the air, but was disappointed with José Perez's performance in the pilot. He thinks that Perez suddenly wanted to be a real cop, even though the show was "make-believe." Dozier says, "I had the feeling he didn't want to embarrass himself in front of his cop friends in Spanish Harlem. The charm he had in *Steambath* [Perez played the bath attendant, who is more or less God] just wasn't there. I don't know where it went. It was written for that. It needed the charm."

Technically, Lou Shaw's 1986 television movie *Dalton: Code of Vengeance II* is not an unsold pilot, since the show was eventually picked up by NBC, which ran two of the four pilots and two episodes, but the episodes were probably all or part of some of the pilots, if Shaw's experience is any indication. He was working at Universal for what he now calls the last time, and the studio had made five hour shows, he recalls, that were "so bad that Universal called NBC and asked that the show get canceled" even before it was on. The five shows were not even completely edited and most of them were too short for the hour format. NBC did not want to throw away the money it had spent, so it asked Universal to see what it could do, which is what Universal turned around and asked Shaw.

Shaw resisted, but Universal assured him that whatever he did would be buried where nobody could see it. Shaw looked at the five episodes: "One was worse than the other." Shaw took the two worst hours, which had no storylines in common, and changed the story by adding voice-over narration. He was given no money for reshooting, but could recut. The editors found what Shaw describes as "garbage" footage of the hero, an ex-Special Forces veteran of Viet Nam, doing martial arts. Shaw used that as the frame for the two hours, putting the narration over it. Shaw says the work was "really hard . . . and it took every skill I had." The network finally ran it in sweeps months [the months the most extensive ratings are taken for the networks] opposite the miniseries *North and South Book II*, and as Shaw says, "It nearly beat it." Shaw later learned Universal had received "huge compliments" on how well it turned out.

Sometimes it is difficult to save even a better pilot. Joel Rogosin got called in late in the process on a 1986 pilot *Lily*, which Shelly Duvall, whom Rogosin liked very much, both produced and starred in. Rogosin says of his experience,

> I don't know that it worked as well as it ought to have worked as a concept. I don't know that the material, which was written by a very talented, bright young writer, Andy Borowitz, was as strong as it should have been. I don't know that the show was as good as it should have been. I don't know that the story they elected to tell for the pilot was the most appropriate choice.

Rogosin notes that, in situations such as this, he is often brought in after the pilot is written and the commitment made, so his input is limited to what the creators are willing to discuss. In the case of *Lily*,

> They were very, very responsive to discussions of the material. However, by the time I got to it, it had already gone through a lot of discussions, so there's a limit . . . People worked very hard, and when the network looked at it, they obviously didn't feel it was something they wanted to make a further commitment to, with all the best intentions all around.

Flops

Not all series that get beyond pilots stay on the air. In the 1986 "selling season," for example, 103 pilots were made but only 36 became series, and only 13 of those lasted more than a season.[3] But then, most television shows are flops, either creatively or commercially, and are canceled sooner or later. What follows are some stories about flops that writers have been involved in, which provide yet another perspective on the history of writing for American television.

Roy Huggins has probably had as many hit shows on television as anyone, but *Cool Million*, in the 1972–73 season, was not one of them. Herb Schlosser, an executive at NBC, brought to him an idea about a private eye who does not take cases on for less than a million dollars. Huggins believed "that was rather romantic and unrealistic, but I thought, 'What the hell, maybe I can do something with it,' so I took it on. But I took it on without conviction, and it did not succeed."

Phil Mishkin had the experience of both writing and acting in the thirteen-episode flop *The Super* in 1972. Mishkin and Rob Reiner took an idea by producer Gerald Isenberg about the tenants of an apartment building and focused it on the building superintendent. What Mishkin calls their "really wonderful pilot script" interested Richard Castellano. Castellano had just made a big impact in the theatrical film *Lovers and Other Strangers* and was about to appear in *The Godfather* as well. Mishkin thought Castellano "was the part," but was appalled when Castellano insisted that his girlfriend play his wife. Reiner said to Mishkin of her, "She can't act. She's not good looking. She's not very smart. She's nothing like the part. Aside from that she's perfect." She was too young to be the mother of the super's sons as written, so one of them was turned into the super's brother, and Mishkin took the part: "I didn't mind the fact of becoming a TV star."

As the rehearsals progressed, there was "such tension on the set, trying to make the part work for her. It was a process of cutting out the part, cutting the part down, cutting it down until it was down to nothing." Castellano saw this happening and was not happy. The director arranged to show the dress rehearsal of the first show on closed-circuit cameras to the executives at ABC. The executives told the producers to get rid of her. The word got back to Castellano, who threw a desk through a wall, aiming at director Hal Cooper, and then threatened another executive as well. Both Castellano and his girlfriend stayed on the show, but it was shot one-camera without an audience.

Mishkin liked working with Castellano as an actor, which made things difficult for him as a writer:

> Working with Castellano as an actor was strange because I knew that the man was bringing in other people [which] was ruining my scripts, but, on the other

hand, he was wonderful in the show, and he was wonderful to work with [as an actor]. I was working with a real professional actor in the sense of a man who was available, who gave you something. He let you take a scene, which was really interesting. I felt good about that part of it. So I was schized out.

Mishkin was the co-creator of *Free Country*, another short-lived series he is much prouder of. In 1978, since he and Rob Reiner already had a contract at Columbia to develop shows, they pitched an idea for an unconventional sitcom about Mishkin's grandparents, who came to this country in the early years of the twentieth century. Mishkin calls it a "saga, the first continuing sitcom." The first five episodes ran in the summer of 1978, but it was not picked up. Mishkin thinks it may have been too ethnic, along with the problem that it was

not fish or fowl. There was something basically wrong with doing a zany sitcom [about this kind of subject]. We were trying to do bringing the bed up the steps. In a certain way I can understand how our Chicano friends were feeling about *Viva Valdez*. They were saying, "Hey, to us it was not a laughing matter," but unless it is, it isn't going to be a matter at all. . . . It wasn't a bad show. Some people that have seen them, still talk.

Sam Rolfe still thinks the 1978 series *Kaz*, about an ex-cop/ex-con turned lawyer, is one of the best series he was ever connected with. Some time after it was canceled, he was told by a network executive that they should not have killed it because it might have caught on. Rolfe thinks the reason it was canceled was that in interviews the star, Ron Liebman, was, "being very smart-mouthed about the network, and everybody got very sore at this and said, 'Who needs this?' "

The following year Rolfe worked on *Big Shamus, Little Shamus*, about a hotel detective and his thirteen-year-old son. The star here was Brian Dennehy, whom Rolfe admires because "He's professional. He shows up ready to work, doesn't bitch, takes it and tries to make it work. It's always a good experience to work with a guy like that. You try your best for him." Rolfe pointed out to Lee Rich, the head of the production company, that the problem was that the audience was not even sampling the show. He said, "This is humiliating. If they're not even going to look at you and say, 'You're bad,' or, 'You're good.' " The production company asked the network to pull the show.

In 1979 Robert Dozier was the executive producer on a series produced at Paramount called *Sweepstakes*. Dozier did not think much of the people at Paramount, although he did like executive Gary Nardino, of whom he says, "He was kind of an animal like Gerber. I got along with him." The other executives kept trying to change what had started out as a comedy-drama into what Dozier calls "a little kind of slapstick piece of shit." It ran for ten episodes.

Dozier left Paramount ("If my children ask, 'What do you do for a living, Daddy?' I don't want to have to say, 'I deal with people who have no concept of right or wrong' ") and went to work at Universal—"Another great mistake I made in my life, although compared to Paramount, working for Universal was like working for the Medicis," i.e., they are ruthless, but occasionally they will support an artist. Dozier and Herman Groves developed a thirteen-episode miniseries about a prizefighter, but it ran afoul of a network executive whom Dozier describes in his most printable language as "this little pig-faced swine, with a bouffant hairpiece . . . he was known in New York as Bill Paley's pet rock . . . he was an accountant, an actuary, who acceded to high places by kissing ass and trying not to do the wrong thing, I suppose, but he angered up the blood just to have to sit with him." The executive had the scripts rewritten and virtually nothing of Dozier's appeared on the series as he wrote it. The series, *The Contender*, ran five episodes. Dozier shortly got out of the business and moved to Bear Valley, California. He gets more satisfaction now out of making furniture in his basement than he did writing for television: "Besides, nobody tells you when you're done, 'Take three inches off this, and I want three more knotholes in it here.' "

In 1980 NBC bought the rights, and the scripts, of a raunchy Australian show about the sexual activities of the residents of an apartment building. Allan Manings was under contract to Paramount at the time, and tells what happened:

> They got some of the best writers in town, David Lloyd particularly, who I think is really one of the finest, if not currently the finest, half-hour comedy writer. David said, "I will not write this shit, but I will do a show based on it." It was a highrise with a lot of people and their relationships.
>
> David got Bob Ellison and Barry Kemp involved, and Bob Ellison, who had worked with me on the [David] Frost show [in 1971], said, "Can you come in and help us with this and produce a few of these?"
>
> I said, "Sure. I'll work with you guys again." The network wanted to make it sleazier. They wanted to call it 69. It was only a compromise to get it called *Number 96*, believe me. They wanted to have 69 with the two letters whirling, whirling, whirling in space so that they got mixed together.
>
> Conceptually what I wanted to do with the show was to make it as upscale as possible. It should be about wealthy, sophisticated people, because to do a show that was essentially to deal with the sexual peccadillos, my belief was that you can have powerful people doing these things. America watching television accepts it because they are looking at people they are not in contact with. It's a little further away. Much as *Dallas* works because very few of us hang out with oil millionaires daily. . . . They wanted it to be as blue collar as possible.
>
> I must tell you, the show is seen as a cult show by people. Twelve episodes were written, six aired. Of the six episodes that aired, no two went on at the same time or the same day. It was such a running hassle, I can't tell you. One time NBC said, "We're going to write a promo for the show for just the stations that'll buy the show. It'll never air."

So I said to Bob Ellison, "Let us do it." Bob and I wrote a piece where we had everyone in the cast in a hot tub, to send up the whole ugly thing. They ran pieces of it on the air, and the only joy I had was that they had not contracted with the actors and had to pay them a tremendous amount of money.

I remember taping the first show, where the earthquake hits, and there's a couple in bed, and the woman is running wrapped in a sheet. The Paramount executives said, "Pull the sheet down more. Let us see."

As can be imagined from that last story, the writers and producers found themselves

too uptight for the network. . . . . Programming wants it to be as sleazy as possible, but they haven't got the agreement of Standards and Practices. Then you say [to Programming], "Go to bat with us."

I don't believe in sleaze. I don't believe television moves forward by being raunchy as much as it would by dealing with ideas.

In 1981 Joel Rogosin was brought onto the series *Foul Play* after significant changes had been made from the pilot in the relationships and histories of the main characters. He says now, "I'm not sure that those changes were for the good. I think there were some things in the pilot that I think they probably should have kept." According to Rogosin, the two stars, Barry Bostwick and Deborah Raffin, were not "as harmoniously matched was they might have been. [They were both] well intentioned and caring and talented and energetic, and each felt they had a certain . . . vested interest to protect, and those vested interests might not have been compatible."

Sometimes the actors in a series could get along too well. In 1981 Eric Bercovici was asked to create a show for James Arness. In *McClain's Law* Arness plays an older cop paired with a younger cop. As Bercovici sees it, that conflict between the cops "somehow just melted away, because aside from everything else Jim and Marshall Colt [the young cop] really liked each other and you could see it on film. Nobody wanted to pursue the mild animosity between the characters. That's what softened it up. And I can hardly blame anybody but myself for that."

The writers on the 1984 series *The Mississippi* had to deal with a star in charge, in this case Ralph Waite. The show was shot along the river, but the scripts were written in Los Angeles. Waite was changing the scripts as they came out, although Aubrey Solomon contends his scripts were not changed as much as ones he had written for other shows. Solomon thinks the story editors were feeling that they were not trusted by Waite, and Solomon says that if that was the case, "then they had to doubt why they were there creatively." Waite had other writers and story editors brought in in an attempt to control the show, but Ed Waters, who came in for the last nine episodes, thinks the problem was in Waite's concept of the show:

Ralph Waite contributed to the demise of his own show, I think, by trying to make himself a leading man. That's a personal opinion. I think Ralph was a good actor, but I don't think he's the man to carry a show. I think that show had the potential, when it worked right, to build up the guest characters into important roles, with Ralph filling in the framework. But when he took control, I think he became more central to the stories, and I think that failed to hold the audience.

By 1984 *M*A*S*H* was over and Thad Mumford had gone to work at MTM. One of the shows he worked on was *The Duck Factory*, a half-hour situation comedy about an animation studio. He tells why he thinks the show did not go more than thirteen episodes:

> Grant Tinker [the former head of MTM] didn't like the show. He had just gone to NBC. I don't think we did the best to make him like it. This show was shot like *M*A*S*H*, with one camera, without an audience, and it took place inside. Now, ordinarily when you shoot a show with one camera, it's because you need to go outside and take advantage of life and not the studio walls.
>
> People are trained to look at certain kinds of things. He would get a print from *Night Court* and it would have lots of audience laughs and cheers, and then he would get our print that had no laughs on it, and I think it very much didn't work [for him], and [he had] all the other executives to look at it and see why it might be funny. I don't have any proof, [but] I just know from what was told us, Grant soured on the show early, and I don't think he was ever able to dissuade it [his sourness toward the show].
>
> I think if it had been given some time it could have become a pretty good show. I think that, not just in terms of people catching it, but the things that we realized didn't work about it, [such as] the actors had less rehearsal. I think we would have changed the format and shot the show with an audience, but we just didn't have the time.

In 1985 Glen Larson asked Lou Shaw to lunch, telling him, "We've got a series." Shaw went reluctantly to lunch, where Larson said that Brandon Tartikoff, the head of NBC, had come up with an idea.

Shaw said, "Give it to me."

Larson said, "It's about a short detective."

"Yeah?"

"That's it."

"No wonder he's the head of the network. A short detective. That's exciting."

Shaw and Larson wrote a pilot script. Shaw liked the actor cast, Joe Pesci, but Shaw came to realize he was wrong for the part. "He was not in our mind when we wrote it. We were thinking of a Dudley Moore . . . Pesci's different. He's ethnic, he's a lot of things. But he's not what you'd call a charming guy who's going to knock women over, and that was the character of the guy." Shaw had been through this before with Quincy, and in that case had time to rewrite it for Klugman. With *Half Nelson*, the first scripts were written before Pesci was cast, and the Writers Guild strike of 1985 made it impossible to rewrite them for the actor.

One of the most difficult types of series to bring off is the science-fiction series. In addition to the regular series difficulties, there are usually budgetary restraints as well. There is also the problem of creating and presenting a believable world to the series audience. D. C. Fontana, who has written for several science-fiction series, suggests some of the problems the writers face:

> You have to introduce people suddenly to [the world]. Here's the ship, or here's the technology you have to deal with, and here are the people, and they do this, letting the technology take care of itself. Which is what *Star Trek* basically did. We didn't stop and say, "This is the transporter. This is how it works." They got in, they beamed down. O.K., you got the idea of how it worked when you saw it work, so you didn't have somebody standing there explaining that.

Fantastic Journey, a 1977 series about a scientific party marooned on an uncharted island where a man from the twenty-third century has the key to time travel, was put together in a hurry. Fontana came on as story editor in December 1976, with the first show going on the air in February 1977, and had to deal with the changes that had been ordered, which included changes in the cast. In the first hour episode, two supposedly regulars had to be "sent back in time," off the show, and a new alien character was added. In the second episode, the villain that Roddy McDowall played in the pilot and first episode had to be transformed into a "nice" guy so he could continue on the series. Fortunately Fontana was working with several free-lance writers who could all work on their episodes at once. Fontana thinks the series was finding its way by the sixth episode, but by then the ratings were so bad it was dropped.

The 1980 science fiction debacle *Beyond Westworld* started as a Lou Shaw pitch to MGM (where the *Westworld* films had been made) in which Westworld had been destroyed and the robots were on the loose. It was pitched to CBS, where the then-head of development liked the script written for the pilot. But a new head of development was appointed, and he did not like it. Shaw agreed with his comments and rewrote the script. The people at the network loved it and said, "Do the pilot." The problems now came from the studio, since its owner, Kirk Kerkorian, was, as usual, trying to sell the studio and did not want to spend any money on anything. Shaw hustled some extra money from the head of MGM-TV, six episode scripts were prepared, and the pilot was shot. It was shown to William Paley, who reportedly loved it, but the head of programming was now the first head of development whom Shaw had dealt with, and he wanted to go back to the original idea, which by this time only he liked. Shaw went quickly from having a pilot everybody loved, and six scripts, to having nothing, "With two weeks to get it all set up."

Two writers he brought in were old Quincy hands, Steve Greenberg and Aubrey Solomon, who says of *Beyond Westworld* that it "was changing every five minutes. . . . And the high cost of production meant that MGM was constantly involved with the scripts for financial reasons. I don't think any of our stories were excessive for budgetary areas, but because of the special effects and the action, there were constant changes and requests for cuts and slim-downs in terms of action." Solomon, who lives in the San Fernando Valley near Universal, compares the experience of working at MGM and Universal: "It's a much longer drive to [MGM]. You think I'm kidding. It was the rainy season. It took me an hour and a half to get to work." Seriously, he adds, "We had been in a very organized situation at Universal, where the producers really knew what was happening. . . . Universal is more an example of controlled chaos. This was uncontrolled chaos."

One of the legendary flops in the history of television was the 1984 series *Jessie*, which starred Lindsay Wagner as a police psychiatrist and ran for seven episodes. Appropriately, the story of this series begins with Aaron Spelling's dog. In 1967 Eric Bercovici was writing a World War II story for the anthology show Spelling produced. One day Spelling asked Bercovici to write in a part for his big white dog, Adam, which Spelling used to bring to work. Bercovici says, "I didn't quite know how to take that," but he wrote in a scene when the main characters come across a dog in the woods and kill it and go on. Bercovici turned in the script and the dog was never mentioned again. As for Bercovici's relationship with Spelling, Bercovici says, "After I killed his dog, [it] went downhill," and he did not work again with Spelling until *Jessie*.

In 1984 Bercovici got a call from his agents, who told him that Spelling wanted to talk to him. With some trepidation, Bercovici went to Spelling's office and was "treated like the old friend I wasn't." Spelling insisted that only Bercovici could do the series he had in mind, which would star Lindsay Wagner. Bercovici had no idea who Wagner was and a meeting was arranged at CAA. Bercovici met Wagner, looked into her eyes and did not like what he saw. He told his partner about the meeting and his partner told him not to be ridiculous.

Spelling's original idea was that Wagner would be a psychologist, but she wanted to be a psychiatrist, so, as Bercovici says, "We gave her an M.D." Bercovici began to write the pilot script. He had about 90 pages done, which he found agonizing to do. He gave them to writer Jerry Ludwig and said, "Tell me they're as bad as I think they are."

Ludwig read them and said, "Finish the script. It's on the air."

"It can't be."

"It's on the air." Everybody congratulated him on the pilot script and the shooting of the pilot went reasonably well. There was was one small problem, however. Bercovici explains:

Lindsay had wanted to do the show about holistic medicine, which ABC had instructed me to totally ignore. Lou Erlicht, the head of ABC, was saying [to me], "You, listen, you chicken shit, you tell that Lindsay Wagner. You tell her that show is not about holistic medicine."

I kept saying, "Lou, but—"

He says, "I'll tell her. I'll look her right in the eye and I'll tell her." We go to New York. We got to ABC for a meeting, Lindsay and her mother, to meet Lou Erlicht and he's going to tell her off. Hooray. We get into the office and he says, "Lindsay, I'm going to look you right in the eye and I'm going to tell you that you're a beautiful woman."

I said, "The war is over." It's finished. Sure enough, they bought the series. And it was a nightmare. The very first day of production, she was talking to me about holistic medicine. We called it the "h" word. You couldn't say the "h" word in the office. She hated the scripts, hated them.

Bercovici preferred not to do an show about holistic medicine for two reasons. The first is, he knew very little about it and from what he did know he did not think it was very dramatic. The second reason was that ABC kept telling him it was an action show. Did Wagner know what ABC wanted? Bercovici says, "I was at the meeting with her [when they told her]. But she decided to do her own show." According to another account, ABC executive Ann Davis told Wagner, "You realize this is an action show," to which Wagner replied, "You realize I don't do action."[4] Bercovici continues:

What happened at the end, it quickly reached the point where it was impossible. It was impossible to get on with writing the scripts. She was trying to get everybody fired. [Ed Waters, one of the writers Bercovici brought on the show, says that Wagner was hiring her own writer and "doing the scripts the way she wanted them."] She tried to get all the writers fired.

It reached the point where my lawyer was saying, "Don't quit. Don't quit. Make them fire you." MGM was willing to fire me, but they can't find anyone willing to take the show. I finally said, "Give it to Gerber. He'll do anything." So they gave the show to Gerber and I was then removed from the show, and a lot of people called me names.

At least some ABC executives felt badly about how Bercovici was treated. Bercovici says today, "Gus [Lucas] told me a year ago he goes to church every weekend and Peter [Roth] goes to temple every weekend to beg forgiveness for what they did to me on *Jessie*."

Gerber only had a few weeks to get the show on, so he called on his old professionals to help bail him out. One was Sy Salkowitz, who did two scripts for the series, one produced and one not produced. As usual, Salkowitz pondered the concept of the show: how do you get the psychiatrist involved in the cases? He made the villain in one a corrupt cop, a rip-off of a *Police Story* episode he had done, but the character was too dark for Gerber, and *Jessie* was dropped before Salkowitz could do a rewrite. Salkowitz says now that Gerber "must have thought I'd lost my touch. And maybe I had." Which did not stop Gerber from calling Salkowitz after the latter's surgery several years later and saying, "What do you mean you had surgery? Suppose I need you to come up here and do a rewrite for me?"

Gerber was not upset Salkowitz had ripped off a *Police Story* episode. Gerber told Morgan Gendel for an article about *Jessie* that, in view of the short time he had, he gave *Police Story* scripts and cassettes to writers to show them "the kind of quality we did on *Police Story* and say, 'This is the kind of thing we want.' "[5] When the article appeared, Gerber wrote to the *Los Angeles Times*, "When asked, I told him clearly the story in question was being taken from an original file case, the same file upon which the *Police Story* script was drawn, and the script written [sic], as well as the real-life participants."[6]

One writer who recognized the scripts of *Jessie* as *Police Story* rip-offs was the author of one of the *Police Story* scripts, E. Arthur Kean. He had been aware that something was going on when Stan Kallis, who was now working on *Jessie*, asked Kean the name of his technical advisor on a *Police Story* episode called "Wolf." The author of the *Jessie* episode was Sy Salkowitz, who now says, "I didn't take that episode, I took the source material and ran it in a different direction." The direction was not different enough on that and other episodes based on Kean's scripts for Kean not to be "even more offended that they ripped them off so badly. The shows were embarrassing." Kean called the guild to complain of plagiarism, and eventually Kean received credit on the *Jessie* episodes.

Gerber was upset that Kean took the matter to the guild. He later told a writer, "Art Kean murdered me. He went to the guild and says I'm ripping him off."

The writer asked, "Well, aren't you?"

"Well, yeah."

"Well?"

Gerber said, "Well, he murdered me. I'll never work again."[7]

Gerber, as of this writing, heads the television division of MGM. Several years after *Jessie*, Gerber and Kean were at a party together. Kean, who by then had forgotten the arbitration, went up to Gerber and they exchanged hugs and, in Kean's words, had "lots of laughs." Ten minutes later, Gerber's wife, the beautiful and talented actress Laraine Stephens, came over to Kean and said, "David never holds a grudge, you know."

·18·

HILL STREET BLUES

The Eighties

*T*raditional kinds of series continued to be produced in the eighties, with the traditional kinds of problems associated with them. Ed Waters was approached to write for the second season of *Jake and the Fatman*, which was being relocated from Southern California to Hawaii. The show was made a little more hard-edged, but Waters says the stars made it difficult for the writers:

> [Joe] Penny and [William] Conrad hate each other, to put it mildly, and Joe Penny is a nervous guy who sweats every moment in the script. Conrad is a man I don't think you can please unless you make him center stage. But with his physical liabilities he can't move around very much. And the story doesn't move if it's centered on Bill. You get much more activity if you escalate Joe Penny's part, which I think was what I was trying to do, but I rubbed Bill Conrad the wrong way. And I think that's why I left.

In the third season of *Magnum P.I.*, Joel Rogosin came on as supervising producer. He had no problems with the star, but in finding writers who could capture the tone of the show. The original pilot script by Glen Larson was a conventional detective show until Don Bellisario, in Rogosin's words, "infused it with the *Magnum* personality. It was all sort of tongue-in-cheek. It was a very difficult style to write in. Nobody but Don Bellisario could ever really write it very well. There were a couple of people who came marginally close, but not like him."

Traditionally in TV, drama writers write drama, comedy writers write comedy, and they very seldom switch over. For all the lightness Roy Huggins brought to *Maverick* and *The Rockford Files*, his one attempt at a situation comedy, the 1963 pilot for *The Ginger Rogers Show*, did not sell. Huggins says, "That's not my field." Two writers who have made the transition are Rick Mittleman and Phil Mishkin.

Mittleman in the eighties moved into hour dramas with comedy overtones such as *Remington Steele* and *Simon and Simon*. The big difference for him is that "In comedy you have to hone every line, because every line is either a punchline or leading to a punchline. That's very hard. Sometimes you sit all day working on one line. When you don't have to go for the joke, the down-and-dirty writing is easier in drama than in a comedy. A story editor's job [on a comedy] sometimes is to take out funny lines" that do not fit the story. One story editor told Mittleman he kept a large manila envelope to save all the funny lines he had to cut out. Phil Mishkin moved to hour dramas and says, "I still have a hard time having a character in *Matlock* leave a scene without a blow-off line, that line that says, 'I'm gone,' big laugh, boom. [In] an hour [drama], a guy can actually say, 'Goodbye,' and leave a room."

As in any decade, there were writers who were trying to expand the boundaries of series television. One was Eric Bercovici. Fred Silverman, then head of NBC, asked Bercovici to "Go to Chicago and do a 90-minute show, doctors, lawyers, policemen, a wheel [of different shows that could be programmed in one time slot under a generic name]." Bercovici was not comfortable with the wheel idea and wanted to put them all into the same show. Silverman agreed and the series *Chicago Story* premiered in March 1982.

The pilot had six continuing characters but the series had more. Bercovici felt that "because of all the intertwined stories, it had a lot more juice to it than the usual one-hour episodic." The stories were structured so each episode involved all the characters, "but not equally. Some shows the lawyers would be number one, the police would be number two, the doctors would be number three. On other shows it would be the reverse of that." By organizing the stories this way, Bercovici was able to have two units shooting two separate episodes at the same time, a help when shooting in Chicago in the winter.

The story complexities made it a hard show to write for. Unlike Bercovici, E. Arthur Kean recalls that Bercovici wanted to use all of the main characters equally, but for the episode he wrote and directed, Kean reduced the number of characters he followed. He had no problem with Bercovici. After Kean took the script through the first set of revisions, he did not hear further from Bercovici. Kean finally called him to tell him he was leaving for Chicago the next day. Bercovici replied, "Yeah, I know. Good luck."

"Well, what about revisions?"

"Good luck." Bercovici says now he stopped giving notes "when you get it right. Nowhere is it written that you have to have eight drafts." On the other hand, when Kean got to Chicago and started auditioning actors with scenes from the script, he decided it did need more revisions, so he spent the weekend in his hotel room doing a rewrite. Kean thinks Bercovici gave him "the best treatment I ever got" on a show on *Chicago Story*.

The treatment the show got from NBC was not quite as good. By the time it was ready to go on the air, Silverman had left, taking any enthusiasm for the show with him. The show was pulled after thirteen episodes, but Bercovici says that when he does press tours for other shows now, *Chicago Story* is still the one he gets asked about most.

Perhaps one reason NBC was not so interested in *Chicago Story* was that it already had another show on the air doing what *Chicago Story* did, but doing it better. The show was *Hill Street Blues*.

Hill Street Blues

Fred Silverman had another idea for an NBC series. Silverman was thinking about a cop show like *Barney Miller*, with an ethnically mixed cast, done not as a half-hour comedy but as an hour drama, set in a bad neighborhood like the upcoming feature film *Fort Apache, The Bronx* (the same area where the Raymonds's documentary *The Police Tapes* was shot), with the absurdist humor of Chayefsky's feature film *The Hospital*, and dealing with the private lives of the police as *Police Story* did. The thinking was, as social historian Todd Gitlin puts it, "recombinant."[1]

One of Silverman's executives was Michael Zinberg, who had previously produced and directed at MTM, and it was Zinberg who suggested the network's pitching the project to MTM. MTM had by this time gotten into making hour dramas, by the unprecedented device of spinning off a character from a sitcom, Lou Grant, into his own hour dramatic series. The specific writer–producers Zinberg suggested Silverman talk to were Michael Kozoll and Steven Bochco.

Kozoll had published in literary journals as a college student, then later taught English at community colleges. He then decided he could write for television, and spec scripts got him work at Universal on such shows as *Quincy*, *McCloud*, and *Delvecchio*, a cop show where he met Bochco.[2] Bochco had started working for Universal while still in college, and had written scenes to fill out one-hour *Chrysler Theater* episodes to feature length for European release. He later wrote for *The Name of the Game, Columbo,* and *McMillan and Wife.*[3] According to one producer there, his plotting was often not clear.[4] When Bochco got tired of the big-studio atmosphere at Universal, he went to work at MTM. In January 1980 Kozoll, whom Bochco had brought to MTM, was about to leave, and the company asked him to work with Bochco on the NBC project.[5]

Neither writer was happy about the idea of doing a cop show, since both had done them before. They proposed to the network a show based on Arthur Hailey's novel *Hotel*, which would allow them to intertwine several storylines, much as Aaron Spelling was doing on *The Love Boat.* The network was insistent on a cop show (Spelling himself later did *Hotel* as a series), and let Bochco and Kozoll use the multiple-storyline idea in the cop format with an ensemble cast. While the network was focusing on what was "recombinant," Bochco and Kozoll were looking for something different. Bochco also insisted on a meeting with Broadcast Standards to set the limits for the show before they even wrote the pilot.[6]

More than most pilots, the one for *Hill Street Blues* demonstrates the tone and feel of the series. It also shows the distinctive narrative patterns Bochco and Kozoll intended to use. As do most of the series episodes, the pilot begins with the roll call Kozoll brought over from *The Police Tapes,* including the final "Let's be careful out there."[7] The first "item" Sgt. Esterhaus reads deals with a purse snatcher who dresses in drag; the second item is about gang homicides. The juxtaposition of humor (primarily humor of character rather than gag humor) and seriousness, which is an element of both *The Police Tapes* and *Law and Order,* is made immediately.

The first act, after the credits, establishes Furillo as the captain of the division, then brings on public defender Joyce Davenport breathing fire about one of her clients being "lost" in the system. Detective LaRue continues an earlier effort to charm Davenport, and in the final scene of the act officers Hill and Renko chase two crooks who turn a liquor store into a hostage situation that will be settled by the end of the episode.

As much as the *Hill Street* pilot (and the series) borrow visually from the direct cinema films like *The Police Tapes* and *Law and Order,* it does not borrow from their narrative structure. In both the Raymonds and Wiseman films, the pattern consists of long sequences complete in themselves, such as the door-battering sequence in *Police Tapes,* rather than *Hill Street's* interweaving storylines, which borrow more from the narrative pattern of *The Love Boat.* The difference is that while Spelling's show would have three stories combined, the *Hill Street* pilot has at least seven, not counting different elements of the hostage situation.

Hill Street also establishes much more vivid characters more quickly than any previous show on television, yet conversely, unlike Spelling's shows, it does not tell the audience everything as soon as possible. In the pilot we are led to believe that Hill and Renko are going to be major figures in the series (the first scene after the roll call is between them), but they are shot at the end of the third act (and in the original pilot were killed, but kept alive in the pilot as broadcast, and the series, because test audiences liked them the best). LaRue's seduction efforts with Davenport lead us to expect a romantic relationship, but in the final scene we learn that Davenport and Furillo are lovers. The series does the same thing with Furillo, not telling us until the last episode of the first season that he is a recovering alcoholic. This withholding of information about the characters and sometimes the story action is also perhaps borrowed from Wiseman's documentaries which, without narration, plunge us into the action and let us figure it out for ourselves.

The visual look of *Hill Street Blues* borrowed from the hand-held camera approach of the direct cinema documentaries, and some critics began to complain the series was using it less than the pilot did, and returning to a more conventional television look of an establishing shot of characters followed by exchanges of close-ups. One reason for this change was the strength of the writing of the show, which emphasized character over action. Curiously, this follows an element in direct cinema as well, which is to focus on the characters; and some of the later series episodes seem more like direct cinema in content than in style. A late first-season episode called "Fecund Hand Rose" has the fiftyish Sgt. Esterhaus preparing to marry a high school cheerleader. The pacing is slower than the pilot because there are longer character scenes, particularly between Esterhaus and Grace Gardner, the policeman's widow he has had a steamy affair with.

Gardner had been created by Bochco for actress Barbara Babcock and was intended to appear in only two episodes, but was so good a character she was written into enough other episodes that Babcock won an Emmy in 1981 for Outstanding Lead Actress in a Series. Babcock later put together a film of all her *Hill Street* scenes from the entire 146 hour episodes of the show, and the film only ran a hour and twenty minutes, which gives some idea of how quickly and vividly the writers created characters.[8]

The first half-season of *Hill Street*, from January to May 1981, did not get good ratings. NBC, which had low ratings as a network, renewed the show, but with the insistence that there be at least one storyline completed per episode, since the network felt audiences had trouble following storylines wandering through many episodes. Bochco agreed, and said at the time ("putting on a brave face," as Todd Gitlin wrote), "I see the validity of that. . . . I hate having to do it, in a sense, because I loved the freedom we had last season with our stories."[9] A few years later he told Levinson and Link about the change, "The network had a valid complaint, and we responded with great pleasure. We were creating our form as we went along, and that [difficulty in following all the storylines] was something we hadn't anticipated."[10] In the second season, the show also made some continuing stories more distinct, as in a four-episode set centered on Captain Freedom, a man dressed in tights and a cape who tries to help the cops.

Bochco and Kozoll wrote most of the first season's episodes themselves, with single episodes by other individual writers. By the second season Kozoll was not writing scripts, although he was still involved in the creation of the stories, and other writers were coming to the fore, including Anthony Yerkovich, who had written during the first season, and Jeffrey Lewis. Lewis was a Yale alumnus who graduated from Harvard Law School. He worked as an Assistant District Attorney in New York County while writing unpublished novels. He wrote to Bochco telling him he had a lot of cop stories from his legal days—which was true—and enclosing a spec script he had written for *Lou Grant*. His first script for *Hill Street*, "Fruits of the Poisonous Tree," deals with the legal question of the admissibility of evidence obtained in a deceptive way. He wrote other scripts and quickly became part of the staff.[11]

Lewis subsequently brought his college roommate, David Milch, onto the show. Milch had written a novel in college, lived through a coup d'état in Greece, and got himself expelled from Yale Law School for shooting the lights of a police car with a shotgun.[12] His first script, "Trial by Fury," opened the 1982–83 season and went on to win an Emmy and a Humanitas Award, which is given to writers for scripts that promote "values which most fully enrich the human person." The episode was one of the occasional "stand alone" episodes the series did that focused on a single storyline complete in one episode. (This is one of the reasons it appealed to award givers: a panelist on the awards committee could make sense of the show without knowing the series.)

Based on a news story Milch read in the *New York Post*, the episode centers on the rape and murder of a nun. The two men responsible are caught but because he does not have enough evidence Furillo gets the prosecutor to indict them on lesser charges, which would let them go free on minimum bail. But it is made clear to the suspects that the public is in a lynching mood over the case. The pressure makes one suspect, Gerald, confess and agree to testify against the other, Celestine. Davenport is furious and later in Furillo's office he defends his action to her, saying he trusts his instincts. She says she trusts *his* instincts, but prefers the rule of law since there are others whose instincts she does not trust. In the last scene, we see Furillo go into a confessional and say, "Bless me father, for I have sinned."

The episode is very much in the tradition of *The Defenders* and even *Police Story*, the former in its dealing with an "issue" in intelligent if somewhat didactic terms, the latter in showing the moral complexities of police work. While "Trial by Fury" would have been a great *Defenders* or a great *Police Story*, it is only a reasonably good *Hill Street Blues*, simply because *Hill Street* had by then upped the stakes for this kind of show. The Davenport–Furillo scene is preachy in a politically correct way (perhaps the main reason the episode won awards), and the subplots, particularly a second murder that does not get solved because it does not get the public attention the nun's murder did, are very obvious counterpoints to the main story. The lack of continuing stories keeps the show from having the loose texture of the best of the *Hill Streets* and there are, probably inevitably given the basic storyline, not the sudden comic counterpoints that keep the series surprising.

Milch and Lewis became the mainstays of the writing staff, and Bochco told Levinson and Link how the writing process worked during the years he and they were in charge:

Basically, Jeffrey Lewis, David Milch, and I collect all kinds of material, things that we know will function well as purely modular stories within an hour. Each segment has one story that has a beginning, a middle, and an end, along with other storylines that we may weave through three, four, six, or ten hours. We come up with single stories as well as the ones that will carry us through a number of episodes.

The way it generally works is that David and Jeffrey and I will sit down and structure an hour show, scene by scene. We'll talk it through, and I'm usually sitting at the desk with a pad and pencil. I'll take all of the stories within an episode and weave them into a four-act structure. Or Jeffrey will do it. We eventually come up with a four- or five-page step outline for internal purposes. Then we decide who's going to write the teleplay. Usually it's divided among three or four writers. Sometimes it's divided into acts, or even scenes. Then one of the writers has to assume primary responsibility for the sections where we bring stories from the outside into the squad room. That's where all kinds of things overlap, and someone has to take all of those elements and weave them so that things crisscross in the appropriate fashion.[13]

"Mayo, Hold the Pickle," which opened the 1984–85 season, is an example of what *Hill Street* does best. The previous season Michael Conrad, who played the avuncular Sgt. Esterhaus, died and the episode plunges right into roll call with new sergeant Stan Jablonski's first lines: "And what is Stan Jablonski, 22 years at Polk Avenue, doing at Hill Street, day one? Three or four of you may have heard rumors. Let me tell you one thing: Stan Jablonski never coldcocked no woman. O.K.? That's it." Then he gets into the items for the day, which include the news that Celestine Gray, who murdered the nun two years before in "Trial by Fury," is sentenced to die the next day.

The main storylines of the episode cover the typical *Hill Street* interconnection of emotional, legal, political, and social issues: tension between Davenport and Furillo, who have separated, at least partially as a result of the Celestine Gray case; a burglary-assault case that is intertwined with a fencing sting that LaRue and Washington are running; Belker working undercover as a clerk at the hotel where LaRue and Washington are set up as fences; what looks like a comic subplot about a man stealing bags of ice and then an ice cream truck, but which turns out to be a murder case when Bates and Coffey discover the body of the man's mother in the back of the ice cream truck; and the beginning of a storyline about a married couple from out of town whose car is stolen and who are put up at Belker's hotel by Furillo's ex-wife, now a victim's aid helper. At the end of the episode Furillo is almost seduced by new detective Patsy Mayo, but returns to Davenport. As Bochco said, "We were putting more information on, frame by frame, than any other show in prime time. If I'm proud of anything about *Hill Street*, it's that we redefined for the audience the terms of the agreement under which they turned on the set."[14]

In 1985 Bochco left the show fulltime to develop *L.A. Law,* and Milch and Lewis took over the daily running of it, which meant they were in the market for new writers. One was Walon Green, who had written National Geographic specials for television and theatrical films, most notably *The Hellstrom Chronicle* and *The Wild Bunch.* Green had learned that while the filmscripts he wrote became big-budget films, not a lot of the budget went to the script. He could make a lot more as a weekly staff writer, plus, unlike the development hell of motion pictures, a writer could see what he wrote on the screen within weeks of writing it.[15]

Another writer whom Milch and Lewis brought on the show was Robert Ward. He had graduated from the University of Arkansas in creative writing, then after being on the road ("All the good things happened to Jack Kerouac, all the bad things happened to me"), he taught at various colleges and wrote novels. He got into magazine writing and wrote two more novels, but they were not making him much money. He told his agent he had to find "a real paying gig." The agent asked if he would consider television, but Ward had never worked in TV and *Hill Street Blues* was the only show he watched. The agent suggested she could get him a job on that, and he assumed she was just talking agent-talk. The next day she called to say Milch and Lewis had read his novel about steel workers and wanted him to come out and pitch ideas.

Ward had picked up enough police stories in his free-lancing days that he could work into material for the show, so he met with the producers. His best idea was about a cop who falls in love with a woman with a child, then feels the relationship is going too far, and when the cop and the woman fight, the child gets the cop's gun and shoots him. They asked him whom he saw the story for, and he said Neal Washington. Ward recalls, "Jeff and David both smiled. They knew I understood the show. They said, 'He's right. He's the perfect guy for it.' "

Ward describes the writing process when he was on the show:

> In general we worked every way you can imagine a group of guys could work. That is, we tried every combination. Here's one way to work, the way my first script turned out: they [Milch and Lewis] came up with one idea for one story in that, but the rest of them were mine; I went off and wrote the whole script; it came out great; we shot it. That's one way to work. Every guy on the staff did at least one of those that way that year. Some came out better than others, but everybody had at least one episode.
>
> The other way you can work is this: three guys sit around and kick around a story. They go, "O.K., we're going to get Belker married [an episode Ward helped develop the story for]. Let's see what happens. O.K., O.K., he needs this, he does this. No wait, let's try this." You go back and forth, all right? Eventually you work out the beats to that story. That means you've done the story with these other guys. However, maybe because you're working on two different scripts, or three different scripts simultaneously, maybe I don't end up writing those stories.

Maybe some other guy ends up writing it with somebody else. We give that to him while I work on another story that I have an interest in. So that's another way to work.

Another way to work is to assign two guys [to a script]. We assign Jacob Epstein and Bob Ward to write a script. They work out a story together and they take different acts. Jacob Epstein writes Act I, Bob Ward Act II, Jacob takes III, I take IV. We then meet, meld our stuff together until it's seamless, or tries to be seamless. That's another way to work. So there's any number of ways you can work, and we tried them all on *Hill Street* that year.

In addition there are scripts that come in from outside writers, which the staff writers have to fit into the patterns of the show.

Ward says that with the story "arcs" that cover several episodes, "The guy who's hot on the story, you might give him the story . . . all the way through. Somebody wrote a story that was an arc, but they didn't do a good job, you take them off it and get somebody else on it, or if it's just too much for them, keep two groups of guys, or two guys might work on it." The staff writers would meld together the storylines as best they could, and the material was then worked over by Lewis and Milch. Ward and the other writers found themselves exhausted by having done eleven shows by Christmas, only to realize they had to do eleven more. They were writing weekends as well. Ward says, "TV shows tend to be [a] fairly all-inclusive lifestyle. When you're writing the shows, that's pretty much all you're doing."

Ward often saw the story being changed by Milch after it had supposedly been approved, which would require wholesale rewrites. Ward found it tough at first.

But this is how one learns. I was beat up. In TV [and] movies, you have to be able to talk a story. I was used to being a novelist, sitting in a room, working on characters for years at a time. These guys would come in and go, "Beat one: Belker does this. Beat two: he does that. Beat three: no, no, we switch this around. Beat four: now this guy comes in here."

"What guy? What guy are we talking about?" They've invented him on the spot. I remember the first time I saw these guys doing this, I thought, "Either these guys are geniuses or they have some magic I don't know about," because I couldn't do that. I can now, because it's a habit of thinking about story that literary intellectuals never do, because first of all, growing up in the fifties and sixties, we were [not] taught [that] in English classes, in graduate classes. All of us [on the show then] have [college] English backgrounds.

Walon Green was a wonderful writer there. I learned a lot from him. This was great education to be taught by these guys because they were the best writers in town. When it came to dialogue, nobody could write dialogue any better than me, but I didn't know how to do stories. That was the difference. Those guys could write the dialogue and do the story. I couldn't do that. And that was the thing that was really tough to learn. But you learn it, because if you don't, you're out. They used to say to me, "Go to your room and write a five-beat story on

Furillo and Davenport." I'd go in the room and sweat would just come down my face. I'd think, "Five scenes?" That was like asking me to move a mountain. I just didn't know how to do it. Finally, though, [it was] like on a bicycle. You know how you try to ride a bicycle, you fall down, and one day suddenly you're up there and you're going, "What's so hard about this?" That's how it literally was, psychologically. One day I was going, "O.K., Belker does this, Belker does this, ping, ping, ping." I suddenly realized, "Hey, I can do story." It was like osmosis. I'd heard it so many times that finally I could do it.

It's a question of seeing, inherently. First of all, you know certain things about story. You know that [Belker's] a cop. You know that he's got to go out on a case. You know that he's probably going to go undercover, because that's what Belker did best. Now it's a question of what does he go undercover on. What haven't we seen before? What would be fun for Belker? Now the big mistake that a lot of novice writers make is that they like to make up wonderful guest stars. They go, "O.K., he meets this guy, the guy's dressed like Dracula, blah, blah, he's really funny, the guy does this, the guy does that." He's always telling, "The guy does [something]." The question will always be then, what does Belker have to do with any of this shit? The story is about Belker and his relationship to the guy and everything has to go back onto Belker. The audience doesn't care about this guy that much. They want him to be colorful, but they want to see Belker's involvement with him. And that's where we used to have trouble, because the writers were going, "What's Belker doing? He's just a cop?" But no, we had to find a way to make Belker emotionally involved with this person.

Once you started realizing that was the center of a story, not the surrealistic goings-on and shenanigans of the guest star, which was what a lot of people thought *Hill Street* was about when they saw it on the surface, then O.K., you start to see the beats then. Beat one is: he's undercover; beat two: he meets the guy; beat three: there's some kind of twist or turn of the plot which endangers their relationship. Maybe Belker likes the kid or something, and the kid is going to get killed because of his own foolhardiness, or tries to be too much like Belker, which makes feel him guilty for somehow involving him. In other words, the whole-out point is to try to find stories that have Belker's involvement.

That's true of all the other characters as well. And once you learned those secrets, then writing scripts became a whole lot easier. You started to realize, "Oh, this isn't just some magical thing guys do." It's that they understand the mechanics of storytelling.

In the third season of *Hill Street*, actor Dennis Franz created a memorably corrupt cop, Sal Benedetto. Benedetto died, but Milch and Lewis wanted to bring back Franz in a similar role, which they did in the sixth season, creating the role of Detective Norman Buntz. Several writers wrote Buntz stories, establishing him in Robert Ward's words as "a tough, no-nonsense guy who was willing to take the law in his own hands, which put him in direct conflict with Furillo." Ward says Buntz is "such a great guy to write for," whereas Furillo was the hardest character to write for because "It's no fun to write for a guy with no flaw. He's always fair. He's always stern, true, good. It's a drag to write for somebody like that. It's much more fun to write for a guy that might take the law into his own hands and may go off the deep end."

Walon Green's fans among writers, and there are many of them, generally think his script for *The Wild Bunch* is the best work he ever did, but a good case could also be made for the February 13, 1986, episode of *Hill Street*, "Remembrance of Hits Past." It is in some ways atypical for the show in that it is a "stand alone," although appreciation of its richness does depend on a knowledge of the series. It also focuses more on Davenport than episodes normally do, which helps give it a different perspective on the characters and the show. The episode opens with a pre–roll call scene of Davenport and Furillo getting dressed at home, and then at roll call we learn Furillo is testifying at Viamonte's retrial today. At the courthouse Furillo is shot by a gun with a silencer.

In Act I, Chief of Police Daniels and Henry Goldblume are at the hospital, leaving a phone message for Davenport. When we see her at the hospital, she has already heard on the radio on the way over. Green (and Lewis and Milch, who worked on the story with him) avoid the obvious scene of her hearing to move the story forward.

By this point other cops on the hill have heard of the shooting, and we expect a scene in which one of them shows up at the hospital to comfort Davenport. Rather than an obvious choice, Lewis, Milch, and Green bring Buntz into the intensive care unit. Davenport says he probably should not be here, and Buntz replies, "Yeah, I had to tell the doctors I was from the Medical Examiner's office"—an oblique reference to a third-season character, a sloppy, alcoholic coroner named Nydorf. In a world in which Nydorf is a coroner, doctors would believe Buntz works for the Medical Examiner. Buntz tells Davenport that if everybody's positive, it will help Furillo, and she replies with a slight smile, "It helped me." Buntz, who is always chewing gum, offers the elegant Davenport a stick of gum, which she takes. It is a lovely scene, played beautifully by Veronica Hamel with stoic coolness and by Franz with surprising delicacy.

In Act II Davenport hears Viamonte on television insisting he did not order the shooting and that his prayers go out to Furillo and his family. Then there are the first of a continuing series of flashbacks to the first meeting of Furillo and Davenport, after Viamonte's aborted first trial, intercut with the efforts of the cops either to find out about Furillo (Belker is undercover at a meat packing plant—a nice visual juxtaposition with the operating room se-quences—and has trouble getting a break to make a phone call) or to track the shooter.

In Act III the flashbacks continue, with Furillo and Davenport's first date, reluctant on her part because she wants her independence. This flashback is followed by a scene in the hospital between Davenport and Chief Daniels. Green here gives us a new slant on the normally pompous Daniels, showing us his affection, usually hidden, for Furillo.

In Act IV the cops discover that the shooter was not hired by Viamonte, but is a former mental patient who had attempted to shoot other public figures. Intercut with flashbacks of Furillo and Davenport starting their romantic relationship, the cops track the shooter to the hospital. Buntz chases him into a stairway, takes careful aim and shoots him, even though he is several floors below. Other cops express amazement at the shot. Buntz chuckles and says, "Wasn't that one hell of a shot, huh?" In Furillo's room Davenport learns his vital signs have begun to stabilize.

There were some pressures on the show to go out with a two-hour finale, in the manner of M*A*S*H, but according to Ward, the writers on *Hill Street* thought the finale of M*A*S*H was overdone and they wanted to avoid that. Ward says, "We decided basically to make it like any other episode and that'd be the end of it. So that's what we did. Understatement. The show's strength was understatement. That's the way we wanted to go out." The last episode, "It Ain't Over Till It's Over," telecast on May 12, 1987, was so understated that it did not have as much of an impact as it might have.

Todd Gitlin reports that midway through the second season of the show its co-creator, Michael Kozoll, told him that he had finally found a metaphor for series television. Doing series television, Kozoll thought, was like rearing a retarded child. There were only so many things it could do, no matter how much effort you put in.[16]

Kozoll left *Hill Street Blues* to write theatrical films. His first-produced script after the series was *First Blood*, the initial Rambo movie. If pressed to select whether *Hill Street Blues* or *First Blood* is most like a retarded child. . . .

·19·

THE CHILDREN
OF HILL STREET

*E*ven the vicar of American television production, Grant Tinker, once referred to the project that became *St. Elsewhere* as "*Hill Street* in the Hospital."[1] *St. Elsewhere* was the first of several post-*Hill Street* hour dramas to use the pattern the police show had established: a large ensemble cast, set in an institution, several intersecting storylines per episode, story arcs covering several episodes, and literate, witty writing.

When *St. Elsewhere* premiered the year after *Hill Street*, it seemed very much like a rip-off. The setting was the Boston hospital St. Eligius, nicknamed St. Elsewhere because, like the Hill Street area in the earlier show, it was very much in a lower-class, ethnically mixed neighborhood. *St. Elsewhere*'s Furillo was Dr. Donald Westphall, the chief of staff; the cops were the assorted doctors, nurses, and interns; and the crooks and their victims were the patients. As the first and succeeding seasons continued (the show was renewed after its first season in spite of low ratings, at least in part because its ratings pattern followed that of *Hill Street* the previous year[2]), the show began to develop its own tone. There was more out-and-out surrealism on *St. Elsewhere*, including dream sequences, and there were not only running jokes, but series of in-jokes complete in individual sequences. *Hill Street* would not have even attempted something like the *St. Elsewhere* episode in which the doctors go to the bar from *Cheers*. The episode did not work, simply because the rhythms of the writing of the two shows is so dissimilar the two styles could not mesh. It was also one of the few dramatic shows on television that could end with a suggestion the entire series was a figment of the imagination of an autistic child (perhaps its makers' reply to Michael Kozoll's observation).

The *St. Elsewhere* style was firmly in place when Lydia Woodward was hired as a writer and story editor on the show in its last season. Woodward had produced a film at the American Film Institute, then been both an agent (a bad one, she admits, because she could not sell scripts she did not believe in: "I could not do the old CAA attitude, 'Don't smell it, sell it'") and a development executive before turning to writing. A script for the sitcom *Slap*

Maxwell got her the *St. Elsewhere* position. The show was run by its creators, Joshua Brand and John Falsey. Woodward says that all the stories were generated by the producers and then handed to the writers. Woodward did two scripts on her own and was teamed on a third one with Grace McKeaney, although "teamed" is perhaps the wrong term, since they did not work directly together. They were given storylines, some as short as a line or two, and developed some others themselves.

Each storyline was written as a separate script, and then the producers integrated them into a whole script. So Grace probably had two storylines and I had two storylines, which I wrote from beginning to end, and which she wrote from beginning to end. And then, after the script was integrated, it was given back to us to do rewrites on, and that's when I was writing on the first act and the third and she was writing on the second act and the fourth. Grace wandered into my office and said, "How are you doing on your half?"

"I don't know. How are you doing on your half?" And we didn't have any idea. She'd be finishing storylines that I was starting, but she didn't know what I was doing with it.

St. Elsewhere always had these little funny insider themes in their shows. In this one, the name of it was "Fairy Tale Theatre," so all the storylines reflected fairy tales in certain ways. What was funny was that because Grace and I really weren't working together on it, we kept using the same fairy-tale references, because you go to your most basic ones. So there are all these Jack and the Beanstalk references in her stuff and then in my stuff, so we had to go back and clean that out. Our instincts were all the same everywhere.

So it was not exactly a collaborative process. It was great. At points it was a little crazy, but it was fun.

Woodward describes writing for *St. Elsewhere* as being "like writers' boot camp. You shoved the pages out under the door and they would shove in the food. It was a lot of fun and a lot of writing, because you did so much rewriting on free-lancer scripts." Woodward started her work as a story editor, "which is only another word for writer," rewriting scripts that had been farmed out to free-lancers. Woodward or another story editor would do two drafts of the script, then turn it over to the producers, who did their drafts. Woodward says, "I think I was pretty lucky. I actually saw a lot of my stuff kind of get through. Not always in the same form or in the same place."

The story editors on *St. Elsewhere* were often asked to come up with a scene quickly to fit a script about to shoot. Woodward remembers when

they came to Doug [Steinberg, also a story editor] and me once and said, "We don't have an ending for the show. We need a final scene for the show, Ehrlich and his wife, about the baby." And we did it in half an hour. We knew roughly what the show was about. We'd seen it through its various stages, so it wasn't like they just handcuffed and blindfolded us. We just shut the door of one of our offices and panicked and came up with a final scene for the show, which they did not rewrite. They put it in. It was shot.

As with *Hill Street*, one of the great strengths of *St. Elsewhere* was the characters, but in the final season the characters seemed less consistent than in previous seasons. Woodward replies, "Are you asking if logic played a role in any of this? In a television show? Certainly not," adding seriously, "I don't really remember being aware of that [unevenness], quite honestly." She relates:

> I think the thing that I loved about the *St. Elsewhere* characters and [why] I loved writing about them, is that every character there had the ability to accidently spit on himself. Drool, that's the word I want to use. Every character had the ability to drool on himself, which you don't often see in television characters. They're usually straighter, stronger, more confident, not as much vulnerability as I think the *St. Elsewhere* characters [had]. I think that's why the success of that show really came out of the writing of those characters. They had more dimension, and that's why they were more interesting to write and more fun to write.

Steven Bochco's second attempt at an ensemble cast show was not as successful as his first and his third. In 1983 he and Jeffrey Lewis created *Bay City Blues* about a minor league baseball team. Thad Mumford, who had been a batboy for the New York Yankees ("and it's been downhill since then"), and his partner, Dan Wilcox, were brought to MTM to write for the series, but the series was delayed by a financial dispute between MTM and NBC. The delay did not help the writing. Mumford admits, "I think there was about a month or five weeks where we couldn't do anything. We would sit down and we would talk about ideas, but it was like waiting in a hospital room to find out if somebody was going to die or not. 'Do we make plans to go shopping or do we make plans to get the crypt?' "

Mumford and Wilcox had been given the impression when they were hired that they would be running the show, but as it developed, Bochco made it clear Lewis and David Milch were in charge. Mumford says he and Wilcox "felt like hired hands or story editors." They did one episode and left the show. Only four episodes were run on primetime, and the remaining four ran on NBC-owned stations late at night later in the season. Mumford thinks the problem with the concept was that

> Steven tried to compare the lives of athletes to policemen. I think he was looking for the same kind of pathos and drama [as in *Hill Street*] and it wasn't that kind . . . in minor league baseball. People who are in minor league baseball are happy, even the ones who don't get a lot of money, because they have a chance at the big leagues. Not to say there is no unhappiness, but it's not the same complexity.

The problem for viewers was simply telling the various players apart, since there were several in their early twenties on their way up, and several older and on their way down.

Bochco's third ensemble series turned out better. In 1984 he read in a newspaper column that the head of NBC, Grant Tinker, had asked him to do a series on the law. Tinker called him that day, having seen the item, to ask Bochco to refresh his memory about the conversation. Bochco could not, since they had never talked about such a series. Both agreed, however, that it was a good idea. Bochco thought about the idea and later pitched it to Brandon Tartikoff at NBC. Tartikoff bought it, and Bochco looked for an attorney to collaborate with him, since he did not feel he knew enough about the law. His co-creator was Terry Louise Fisher, a former deputy district attorney and producer–writer of *Cagney and Lacy*.

Bochco and Fisher wrote a two-hour television movie pilot for what became *L.A. Law*. It opens with the husband of an ex-client coming into a divorce lawyer's office with a gun, and then a senior partner is found dead in his office, his face in a plate of beans. When the firm's divorce attorney learns of the death, he calls dibs on the late partner's office. Bochco said,

> The pilot opening is designed, very consciously, for effect, to very quickly loosen up your expectations about a show about the law. *Perry Mason, The Defenders*—they're earnest shows. There's nothing wrong with them. But there was precious little humor in them. The cases were all resolved, usually heroically, by the end of each episode. I don't want that kind of show . . . and I want the audience to know that right away.[3]

Bochco saw early on that the writing of *L.A. Law* had to be even better than the writing of *Hill Street Blues*, since the newer show had no action scenes to cut to. Fisher said, "This show is talking heads. The talk better be good. . . . We've learned already [in the first few scripts] that when the words aren't good, the show is awful, the scenes endlessly boring."[4]

It took the show from its opening in October 1986 to its episodes in January 1987 to find the right balance. Scripts that other writers did were rewritten by Fisher and/or Bochco.[5] Several of the writers were lawyers themselves. One of them was David E. Kelley, who had decided in the mid-eighties to write a screenplay for a feature film about his legal experiences. (The script became the 1987 film *From the Hip*, which is not quite the retarded child film legend has it; Judd Nelson is just not Corbin Bernsen.) The script got to Bochco when he was looking for writers for the series. Bochco later said,

> I only read about the first thirty pages of his script, and you could see in the courtroom stuff—he wrote it with such real feeling and it was very funny. And that's exactly the voice you want to locate for *LA Law*. You want to take the viewer into the courtroom and make it come very much alive and also find the

humor inherent in the environment. Most TV writers fall into the trap of writing courtroom stuff very ponderously; it's so overwritten. It's like bad French cooking where everything is bathed in too much cream sauce.[6]

At the beginning of the 1989–90 season Bochco left the show and Kelley took over the running of it. In March 1991, Executive Producer Rick Wallace noted the difference in the emphasis: "The first three years under Steven's tutelage and guidance was 65 percent relationship and 35 percent legal. What's happened since David has taken over is that it went the other way and it become [sic] more like 65 percent legal and 35 percent relationship."[7]

In February 1991 it looked as though Kelley might be pushing the show back into relationships. New characters had been added, including an English woman lawyer, C. J. Lamb. After Lamb and Abby Perkins, another woman attorney, have dinner together to celebrate a deal they have made on a case, Lamb kisses Perkins, who is startled. The next day Perkins tells Lamb that she likes men, and Lamb says she does too, admitting to being "flexible." After further discussion, the relationship is left up in the air for several episodes, as if the writer [Kelley wrote the episode] and the network were awaiting the public response. The Los Angeles NBC affiliate reported the next night that they had received only 85 calls about the scene, only a little more than half negative. Wallace said later that very few viewers had objected to the scene,[8] but Kelley said later there was pressure from NBC not to continue the storyline.[9] The more freewheeling days of the earlier Bochco shows were, perhaps, coming to a close.

On its pastel surface, *Miami Vice* would not seem to be an obvious child of *Hill Street*, but in typical network recombinant thinking, it evolved out of the earlier show. The network wanted a combination of *Hill Street Blues* and *Starsky and Hutch*, a traditional buddy cop show, and they decided to approach *Hill Street* writer Anthony Yerkovich, who had a reputation for writing the Hill and Renko characters. The network shorthand was "MTV Cops," since they wanted to play the show against contemporary music and envisioned cutting the scenes like the music videos on MTV. Yerkovich was tired of shooting in Los Angeles and suggested making the show in Florida.[10]

The style of the show made an immediate impact, as the style of *Hill Street* had done, but the earlier series had also developed its characters and its content; the characters on *Miami Vice* were never particularly interesting and did not develop over the course of the series in interesting ways. *Miami Vice's* main stories, because of the locale, inevitably had to be about drugs, and they became repetitive. The flashy visual style got tiresome very quickly without the substance to back it up. Getting the visual style was often at the expense of the story. Ed Waters, who worked on the show its second season, recalls:

In an effort to keep that visual look that they did so successfully on that show, they would go to a location that would take them three to four hours to get to, and they would shoot a page and a half that day, so something had to give. You have a 55-page script and seven days to shoot it in, you have to shoot seven and a half pages, or whatever, and if you shoot one and half pages one day, you're in trouble. So a lot of things were sacrificed to preserve that style. Many of the stories suffered. When you're scrambling to meet the schedule, story values and plot points are going to fall by the wayside. They did.

The producer in Florida was more concerned about the look of the show, and Waters kept seeing dailies that were "oftentimes not reflective of what was in the script." (Communication and understanding between the writers and production staff is often a problem on shows shot some distance away from Los Angeles. Waters noticed similar problems on *The Equalizer*, and Joel Rogosin also saw it happen on *Magnum P.I.*)

Robert Ward came on *Miami Vice* as producer in its fifth year and tried to develop tighter stories about a greater variety of subjects, but by then the show had run its course. It was one of many shows in the history of television, like Milton Berle's first show, *The Man from U.N.C.L.E.*, and *Mork and Mindy*, that made a strong immediate impact but burned out quickly.

Having done a show with great visual style, Anthony Yerkovich turned in 1987 to one with great verbal style, *Private Eye*, set in Los Angeles in the mid-fifties. Joseph Dougherty, a big Raymond Chandler fan, did two scripts for the show, and comments, "The problem is, you've kinda, gotta have Bogart to hang a show like that on. I don't think anybody realized how tough it is to do Chandleresque material." Not so much for Dougherty, who claims he "could write this stuff by the long yard." He got the assignment to work on the show by showing up one day when they had an episode that needed some extra narration for it to make sense. Dougherty says, "I just sat down in the office and I wrote four and a half minutes of narration. I'm sorry, but it's the best thing in the episode. It's great. It's these big, sweeping Chandleresque metaphors. It's fun to do." The series never quite worked and was pulled after twelve episodes.

For his 1986 police series *Heart of the City*, E. Arthur Kean focused on the relationship of the cop and his two teenaged kids. The relationship struck a nerve in viewers and Kean began to get what he describes as "love letters" from parents telling him how it helped them talk to their teenagers. Kean describes what he learned from the show and its audiences:

> Now I know there are about 12 million people out there that are interested in that kind of thing. It's putrid [numbers] by television standards. Well, we opened in 63rd place, and I said, "I'm going to be diligent. I'm going to hang in there." And I persisted. And I managed with great force of will on my own personal behalf to keep it at 63rd place. Which was the bottom. But I managed to keep it there. It's to my credit that it never rose a single point.

The show was scheduled at nine on Saturday night on ABC against *The Golden Girls*. ABC never found another time period for it and it was canceled after thirteen episodes.

Call to Glory, a 1984–85 series, also tried to interweave the personal and professional lives of its characters. The problem was that the profession was Air Force officers in the early sixties, and unlike most previous one-hour series, the personal lives were serialized, with continuing developments each week. Joel Rogosin, a producer on the series, says,

> So you not only dealt with the personal lives against the professional lives against the [production] logistics [of shooting] at Edwards [Air Force Base] with the cooperation of the Air Force, and the integration of stock footage and second-unit stuff which we shot, but you dealt with the continuity of the storylines that were going on. In 48 minutes that's a lot to juggle and have it coherent. Very difficult.

Even writers who wrote for years before *Hill Street* began to adapt to the style. Christopher Knopf, whose credits go back to the late fifties, co-wrote a pilot in 1988 called *Mad Avenue*, which would have been an ensemble show set in an advertising agency. Knopf says, "There's no question that Steve Bochco set the tone for it, for that kind of show." The problem with the idea for the series was similar to the problem with *Bay City Blues*, or, as Knopf puts it, "How concerned can you get about a twenty-million-dollar [advertising] account?"

Later, he was working with his partner, David Simons, on a show about the criminal justice system, and ABC put them together with Thomas Carter, one of the most successful directors of pilots in television, who was also thinking about a law show. Their collaboration became the 1990 series *Equal Justice*, which focuses primarily on the prosecutor's office and the people working in it. Robert Ward's description of everybody doing everything on *Hill Street* also applies to *Equal Justice*. Talking in November 1990, Christopher Knopf describes the then-current process: "We're starting a brand-new story right now. [The staff writers] go into the office of Deborah Joy LaVine, a very good writer. She has a big white board up there you can write with ink crayons on that you can erase right off. [She] draws four lines down. Act I, Act II, Act III, Act IV, and we'll start talking." They will need to develop three stories. One will be a case story, but they found that case stories can only take eleven pages, which still requires two days of shooting, because of the necessity of covering all the participants in a trial. They will need a legal story outside the courtroom, and a personal story for one or more of their characters.

Not all of the five writers can spend too much time on the story, since they are busy planning their own new stories, writing their own scripts, and doing rewrites. Thomas Carter, the co-creator of the show, can help some, but he is involved with shooting and cutting. Knopf says, "When you first begin the year, you're all sitting around, 'Isn't it wonderful? We're all here to help everybody.' But right now [November] it's you catch what you can catch. You go knocking on somebody's door and say, 'You got five minutes for me? I got a problem with this scene.' So it gets a little hectic."

Knopf has found that several older writers resent being asked to show they can adapt to the newer style, but he recommends the older writers write a spec *L.A. Law* script to show they can handle it. He knows writers who have, and have gotten work from it.

The spring of 1990 saw the beginning of several months of premieres of series following the *Hill Street* pattern. The most heavily promoted—to the point of creating a frenzied cult about it—was *Twin Peaks*. The co-creators were film director David Lynch and Mark Frost. While most of the talk about the series centered on Lynch because the series was seen as being very much in his portentous and surrealist style, the *Hill Street* connection was through Frost, who had written for that show. In one interview with Frost (as opposed to the many with Lynch), he was quoted as saying, "*Hill Street* was very good, but it was very impersonal work for me. I wrote about that place as if I was a visitor. It wasn't what my life was like. It was a great place to learn the craft of how to shape a scene, but I wanted a chance to write about more personal themes and obsessions. My point of view has always been more offbeat."

The two-hour pilot of *Twin Peaks*, written by Lynch and Frost, shows the connections with *Hill Street*, most notably in not revealing until the end of the pilot that Sheriff Truman and Josie Packard are involved in a romantic relationship. The biggest delay in revealing story details to the audience came in the structure of the series, which begins in the pilot with the investigation of the murder of Laura Palmer. The killer is not revealed in the pilot, or even the first series of episodes, run in the spring of 1990, but only in a new series of episodes in the fall of that year. The problem Lynch and Frost set for themselves with the delayed payoff of the murder story is that while the investigation is continuing, they were not creating other stories, and more importantly, not developing compelling characters to hold the audience's attention past the revelation of Laura Palmer's killing. Like *Miami Vice*, *Twin Peaks* tried to get by on style without substance. Unlike *Miami Vice*, it could not do it for more than a season.

Twin Peaks was followed in the summer by *Northern Exposure*, created by Joshua Brand and John Falsey, the creators of *St. Elsewhere*. Like Lynch and Frost's show, Brand and Falsey's is set in an odd small town in the northwest, in this case Alaska. Unlike *Twin Peaks*, *Northern Exposure* began early in its run to develop a set of offbeat and interesting characters. While it was often hard to tell the two or three young dark-haired women or the two or three young dark-haired men on *Twin Peaks* apart, each character on *Northern Exposure* is precisely defined and well rounded, often in surprising ways. Returning in the spring of 1991, *Northern Exposure* began to catch on with audiences and was renewed after *Twin Peaks* was canceled.

The fall of 1990 saw three children of *Hill Street* start the season, with all three to be canceled before the season was over. David Milch, one of the stalwarts of the *Hill Street* writing staff, was the principal creator of *Capital News*, an ensemble show about a Washington newspaper, and John Eisendrath and Kathryn Pratt created *WIOU*, a show about local television news. The most heavily promoted of the three was Bochco's *Cop Rock*, in which he tried to integrate musical numbers into a realistic cop show. *Cop Rock's* characters and location were too similar to *Hill Street*, so the show produced a sense of déjà vu. The musical numbers did not fit into the show's realism and felt like commercials instead of the show.[11] It was not only a question of realism. Bochco's skill, as seen in his successful shows, is to create compelling characters in strong storylines. The musical numbers in *Cop Rock* were so aggravating precisely because they took audiences away from the characters and the storylines.

By the end of the 1990–91 season ABC cancelled *Equal Justice* and *Cop Rock* as well as *China Beach* and *thirtysomething*. The other networks were dropping hour dramas, particularly with ensemble casts, although *L.A. Law* and *Northern Exposure* held on, and there were continuing hour dramas with one or two stars, such as *Matlock*, *In the Heat of the Night* and even *Jake and the Fatman*. But the heyday of the children of *Hill Street* was clearly over, even as critics were willing to admit that it had been another Golden Age of television.[12] The large ensemble shows were dying out for several reasons. One may have been that audiences found it too hard to keep *that* many characters in *that* many shows in mind. The style may have worn out its welcome.

There were other considerations as well. The networks were losing viewers, which in turn caused a loss of advertising revenue. So-called "reality shows" were much cheaper to make and got as good or better ratings. (An interesting irony: the direct cinema documentary techniques first led documentary into examining character, which is an element the ensemble shows picked up from documentary. The "reality" shows tended to use the same techniques in a shallower way, avoiding character and turning the documentary into the sensationalized mind candy that the best fictional shows were more and more avoiding.) The ensemble shows were expensive to make, not only in costs of the actors, but also in terms of writers, because of the large number of staff writers, usually with salary-increasing titles like Story Consultant, Executive Story Consultant, and Producer, which were necessary to keep these shows running. Such expenses could possibly have been covered by the production companies, to be made up for when the series were sold in syndication, but the market for hour dramas—particularly serialized shows like *Hill Street Blues*, *St. Elsewhere*, and even *Dallas* and *Dynasty*, had collapsed (although several such shows did well in cable showings, cable reruns are much less lucrative than traditional syndication to local stations). Half-hour comedies did much better on the networks and in syndication. The hour ensemble dramas were simply too good, and too demanding, for the conventional audience for syndicated re-runs.

·20·

YET ANOTHER PERSPECTIVE

Like most American institutions, network television has been very much an old boys' club. In discussing their careers, writers talk about how they got jobs through friends and contacts made on other shows. Most of the writers for American television have been men, but from the beginning there have been women writers as well as women stars, and even women producers and directors, and they too got jobs through contacts. Network television has in some ways been less sexist than many American institutions, and the changes in women's roles in TV both on-screen and off-screen mirror the changes in women's roles in American society. Looking at the history of television writing by observing women writers and women characters provides yet another perspective on that history.

One reason Catherine Turney was able to find work in the early days of television was her previous experience writing women's pictures in Hollywood. She worked on *Mildred Pierce* as well as several Bette Davis films, but as stars like Davis left the studios for independent production, writers like Turney were let out of their contracts. Among her early television work, Turney did an adaptation for the *Lux Video Theatre* of the old Bette Davis film (not one she had written) *Jezebel.*

Madelyn Davis got into radio because the newspaper she wanted to work for "didn't want Journalism Graduate ladies on their paper." She was willing to start as a secretary in radio, but landed a job writing commercials first. In radio and then TV situation comedy, it was helpful for her to have a male partner to deal with people who might be uncomfortable with a woman writer. Being a woman writer helped her get work on shows with major women characters. Many of the women she wrote in the fifties and sixties were scatterbrained, and she says, "It would probably bother me today, but we hadn't had our consciousnesses raised yet. And that was sort of a style: Gracie Allen, Marie Wilson, Mary Livingstone, Blondie, Joan Davis." (Nat Perrin worked within that style as well, first on *My Friend Irma,* and later in the fifties when he decided that the focus of the series version of *How to Marry a Millionaire* should be on the "funny" girl, since the show was supposed to be a comedy.) Davis looks now with what she admits is hindsight at what she wrote and says of the changes that have taken place:

> There were a couple of things in that pilot that didn't get aired [the original unaired pilot of *I Love Lucy* was shown on CBS in April 1990] that I thought, "Oh, my," [such as] Ricky saying, "I want you to stay home and cook my meals and have my children." I would never write that today. It was a long time ago.
>
> People say, "Has comedy changed?" Well, life has changed. So if you're going to be funny, you write about the funny problems today, which are a little different from the funny problems then. When we did *Alice* [1977–85], I noticed we got into more of today's themes, were more aware of the times . . .

Davis had more difficulties as a woman producer than as a writer:

> I found I had to be rather careful, because men didn't particularly want to be working for a woman producer. It wasn't very overt, but I learned to handle it. Whereas a man would never have to do that. I just learned to say, "What do you think?" a lot. "I need some help on this." A lot of times they'd have good ideas. It wasn't that it was a big chore or anything, but you just learned to be rather . . . careful.[1]

Being a woman could be difficult in the early days of TV, for a variety of reasons. Lucille Kallen, one of Mel Tolkin's "outsiders" on *Your Show of Shows*, later remembered the problem of office space: "We were in a rather seedy part of the city, and there was very little space. So Mel [Tolkin] and I got the boys' dressing room, the dancers' dressing room. So we sat there surrounded by jockstraps, if you please."[2] According to Allan Manings, when Kallen worked on *The Imogene Coca Show*, she had just had her first child and "was having difficulty being a mother because she was devoting so much time to the show. I remember she came in and she said, 'I dropped him. Well, of course, what else would I do? I mean, I don't know what to do with a child. A sketch I'll fix, a child is different.' " Kallen eventually got out of television and into writing mystery novels.

From the beginning of filmed television, it has not been uncommon for women to move from being secretaries to being writers. Dorothy Fontana's first job after she graduated from college in 1959 was as a secretary at Revue. Assigned to the show *Overland Stage* as a secretary, she later pitched a story to the same producers for another of their shows, *The Tall Man*, and they bought it. She continued working as a secretary for several years because, until *Star Trek*, she was not making enough writing to support herself. Fontana wrote for several Western series using her full first name, then she

> was trying to write a *Combat* or whatever, and I found I was running into, "Oh, well, a woman can't write *our* series."

I said, "Well that's silly." But I decided to start putting the initials [D. C.] down because then if they were reading a submitted script, as a sample script, they wouldn't have any built-in prejudices as to whether it was a man or a woman.

That was how I sold the *Ben Casey* [script]. They didn't know who had written it. They didn't care. They just liked the story and bought it. I found that was lucky, so I kept on with it.

As D. C. Fontana she continued to write Westerns. On *The Big Valley* she wrote for the matriarch of the ranch, Barbara Stanwyck. Stanwyck read the first draft and told Fontana, "Look, I'm just Ruby Stevens [Stanwyck's real name] from Brooklyn. I don't talk like this. Make it simpler"—which Fontana did.

In the seventies Fontana was called in to write a *Streets of San Francisco* because the show wanted to do a woman's story. Fontana talked to police-women and relates, "Some of the things they said, which were true at that time, are in the script, about the fact that a woman has to work harder to gain rank, that mostly they wound up being desksitters at that point because then you didn't have what you have now, with the women actively in patrol cars or on the beat doing more dangerous things." Fontana was told she was the first woman writer hired by that production company, Quinn Martin Productions, and they wanted her to use her full name. She agreed to let them use "Dorothy C. Fontana" on that one script, provided they went back to "D. C." on any others. They agreed, and wanted her to do another woman's story, but to avoid being typecast she wrote an episode that was "all male." She later wrote for the show a recurring woman police-lieutenant character who had a romance with the Karl Malden character.

Another secretary who moved into writing was Juanita Bartlett. Bartlett tried to write scripts for years, but without making any sales. Once a friend working on a medical show suggested she submit a script. The producer refused to read Bartlett's material, telling the friend, "You know we've never had success from women writers." Bartlett went to work as a secretary to Meta Rosenberg, who was executive producer of the James Garner series *Nichols*. One day Bartlett asked the producer of the series, Frank Pierson, "Have you assigned any Bertha stories yet?" He asked, "Who's Bertha?"

Bartlett had noticed on the Western street standing set where the show was filmed that there was a saloon called Bertha's. Pierson said he had not thought of any character to go with it, and Bartlett asked if she could submit a story. Pierson asked Rosenberg if she had any objections, and when she did not, Pierson agreed to read the story. After several days of waiting nervously, Bartlett got a call from Pierson saying, "Congratulations, Juanita. You're no longer a secretary, you're a writer." Bartlett was afraid she would not be able to sell another script, so Rosenberg agreed to hire only a temporary replacement, and if at the end of three months Bartlett wanted her old job back, she could have it. Bartlett plunged into writing scripts for *Nichols*, including a rewrite of another script. She says, "It was sort of a baptism of fire. Somebody was standing below the window practically, and as I would finish pages, I'd throw them out. So I really didn't have any opportunity to get too nervous, because there wasn't any time." This did not stop Bartlett from continuing for some time to come by Rosenberg's office and make coffee. The new secretary finally had to say to her, "Juanita, I know how to make coffee."

Like Davis, Bartlett found more problems as a woman producer than as a writer, but she remembers a conversation she had with Rosenberg on the subject:

> When I had just started to work for Meta Rosenberg years ago, I was in her office one day and she said, "Let me ask you something, Juanita. Just out of curiosity. How do you feel about working for a woman?"
>
> I said, "I don't think about it one way or the other. The one thing that I care about is that I have respect for the person that I'm working for. And if they're a man, fine; if they're a woman, fine. But it doesn't bother me to work for a woman."
>
> She said, "Well, there are some women who don't want to work for another woman."
>
> I said, "There is a disadvantage, and that is you can't throw your apron over your face, or tear up, or bat your eyes, and say, 'Oh, silly me. What a terrible mistake to have made. Can you ever forgive me?' You're on your own."

Some producers, especially writer–producers, agree with E. Jack Neuman, who says, "I don't care what they are as long as they can write. Color, sex means nothing to me. Just gimme a writer." Ironically, he makes this comment in discussing the 1975 series he created about a woman lawyer, and Neuman can no longer remember whether he had any women writers on the staff of *Kate McShane* or not. What he does remember is that in the original script the lawyer was a man, the son of a cop who raised five children alone. Neuman felt that for it to work the lawyer had to be a son, but Fred Silverman, then the head of CBS programming, insisted it be cast with a woman, Anne Meara. Neuman thinks she is "a nice lady," but simply wrong for how he had conceived the series.

One reason it may have occurred to Silverman to make the lawyer a woman was not only the women's movement in this country, but the way the sensibilities of the movement showed up in weekly series. Some of those sensibilities came from the women writing the shows, such as Treva Silverman on *Mary Tyler Moore*; Charlotte Brown on *Rhoda*, Linda Bloodworth, Mary Kay Place, and Karen Hall on *M*A*S*H*; and Irma Kalish, who co-wrote the episode of *All in the Family* in which Edith thinks she might have a breast tumor. The women (and some men) writers may have been running slightly ahead of the public on the issues. *TV Guide* noted in a 1977 article that a poll in December 1976 showed that 46 percent of all viewers, and 47 percent of all women viewers, thought that women on TV were *more* liberated than women really are, while only 3 percent thought they were *less* liberated.[3]

There were male writers and writer–producers who wanted to explore a more liberated view of women. Allan Manings is married to actress Whitney Blake, who played the mother in the series *Hazel*. Blake had in real life raised three children alone, and she and Manings thought there was a show in that. Manings tried unsuccessfully for eight years to sell the idea. He started out by pitching the idea as "What happens to Nora after she leaves the doll's house?" Manings recalls the reactions of most executives: "I would get the blankest looks you have ever seen in your life. I'd say, 'Ibsen. Play?' [The executives would grumble.] And finally I'd say, 'This is the story of a woman who jumps up and down on the diving board and as she launches herself, on the way down she notices there's no water in the pool.' And that's essentially it."

In 1975 Manings pitched the idea to Norman Lear, who had always wanted to do something about the emerging woman. The show was *One Day at a Time*, and even though Whitney Blake was the co-creator she had reservations about Schneider, the building superintendent who constantly came into the apartment of the mother and two teenage girls. Manings recalls, "Whitney always used to say, 'That man should not be allowed to walk into that apartment.' And she's right. She says, 'A mother would not allow this. Don't these people ever lock their door?' I said, 'No one in television locks their doors, because you always have that funny neighbor next door who's got to walk in with the joke.' "

Lou Shaw also saw an opportunity in the 1974–75 season to help the television presence of both women and blacks. As usual, it began with a phone call from Glen Larson, who had taken over a series that had debuted that September, *Get Christie Love!* The show starred Teresa Graves, a black singer and dancer, as a police officer. Shaw says, "I was very excited about the whole idea. . . . I thought it would be a very exciting thing to have a black woman as a lead. And it could work. . . . That could have been a massive hit." Shaw's motives for agreeing to be a story editor on the show were not entirely altruistic. He did not know what a story editor was at the time, but thought it would help him "get his hooks" into Universal and become a producer.

Shaw wrote a script for the show and then had his first meeting with Graves, who brought along a man Shaw "guess[es] you'd best call her manager/preacher." Graves had recently converted to a fundamentalist religion, and told Shaw the manager/preacher would discuss the script with him. Thus began what Shaw remembers as a seven-to-eight-hour meeting: The script opened with Christie Love coming into the police station dressed from having played tennis; the police raise a glass of champagne and wish her a happy birthday. The manager spent an hour and a half explaining all that would have to go: birthdays are heathen since "Only Jesus has a birthday"; drinking is "barbaric and heathen"; making toasts is all right as long as no person is praised, since only the Lord can be praised; and in athletics a woman does not show her legs.

Shaw began to wonder if he was being put on. He reminded them that on *Laugh-In* Graves danced in a bikini, but the manager said, "That was a former life." Now she would be fully covered at all times and would never show her body or her legs. Shaw made what he now calls a "feeble joke" about hiding one of the assets of the show, and the man replied, "That kind of joke could never happen on *Christie Love.*" As the meeting finally ended, the manager added, "By the way, it would be a good idea maybe if I was hired to be an actor on the show so that I could keep close track of what is going on every minute, you know."

The whole thrust of the show was that Christie Love was anti-establishment and, in the cop show tradition, disagreed with her superior, who was a man. The manager told Shaw, "A woman does not disagree with her boss . . . a woman's position is secondary to a man." All the scripts had to be rewritten, with the manager constantly saying, "Oh, no, Teresa doesn't say this. Teresa doesn't say that." Shaw thought the scripts "reduced" in the rewriting. He also thought the manager ruined Graves's performances. Shaw says, "She was an absolutely charming woman, and she had charisma on the screen. Except, this guy just was with her and flattened it out."

Get Christie Love! would never have become great drama. It was always intended as light entertainment, but within its formula it could have broken new ground if Graves had used her position wisely in dealing with the politics of the studio and the network. She did not, and while it may have been a religious victory, it was at least as much of a loss for women and blacks on American television. The same thing can be said about Lindsay Wagner's later experience with *Jessie.* Wagner was trying to use her power as a star to shape the show to her viewpoint, but did not handle her dealings with the writers and the network well. Just as Bercovici should probably have pulled out of the show at the first meeting, so perhaps should have Wagner (*her* autobiography will undoubtedly tell us what *she* saw in *his* eyes) when it was clear she, Bercovici, and the network were not in agreement on what the show was to be. The uses of power, particularly in a collaborative medium such as television, need to be handled skillfully and often are not, particularly by actors and actresses.

Writers who are sympathetic to women and women's stories often are confounded by actresses as Bercovici and Shaw were by Wagner and Graves. Phil Mishkin had such an experience on a 1982 television movie finally titled *Not Just Another Affair.* The original script, by Rick Podell and Michael S. Preminger, called *The Last American Virgin,* was about a woman marine biologist saving herself for marriage. Mishkin was called in to do a rewrite and the CBS executive in charge told Mishkin that Victoria Principal wanted to play the lead. Mishkin said that he thought she was a little too old to play a virgin.

The executive said she could not be a virgin. Mishkin replied, "But Norman, that's what the movie is about. It's about a virgin. You're saying, 'Let's do *Sands of Iwo Jima* but it's not going to be about a war.' " The network decided to make the character celibate, so Mishkin reconceived the character as someone who does not want to give in until she is swept away by romantic love, as in the old movies. The old movie connection was a running theme in the script, and according to Mishkin, Principal simply did not understand that and asked why she had to wear the "old-fashioned clothes" the script called for in a scene that paid homage to the old films. The movie tries to capture the spirit of the screwball comedies, but the dialogue sounds rather flat, and it is not helped by both lethargic direction and the lack of light-comedy skills of Principal and her leading man, Gil Girard.

Just as there are actors writers like, there are also actresses with whom writers have good professional relationships. In 1984 Juanita Bartlett wrote a two-hour movie pilot about a woman sheriff in the West that starred Stella Stevens, and Bartlett says, "She's a joy to work with." Rick Mittleman sold free-lance scripts to *Remington Steele* for a year, and then was executive story consultant for another year, and he admired Stephanie Zimbalist's professionalism. She and her co-star, Pierce Brosnan, did not particularly like each other, but they never let it interfere with the work. On the other hand, when it was suggested the show could continue for another year if the two characters got married, both Zimbalist and Brosnan "refused to play married," in Mittleman's phrase, and the show went off the air. Mittleman thinks Zimbalist learned her professionalism from her father Efrem Zimbalist, Jr. Mittleman says she developed the idea, "You go to work with your lunch pail."[4]

Phil Mishkin, somewhat to his surprise, enjoyed writing for Suzanne Somers on the late-eighties syndicated series, *She's the Sheriff*. Part of it was that the show itself was undemanding to write for ("No one involved in that show thought they were curing cancer, or even a headache"), but part of it was that Somers was "wonderful. I'd come to expect a person with an attitude problem [because of her publicized disputes with the management of *Three's Company*] and found just the opposite. She worked hard. She didn't have any presumptions of doing anything great. And she didn't think she was that good. She knew she had limitations."

In addition to *Kate McShane* and *Get Christie Love!*, other dramas in the late seventies focused on women leads. The series *Julie Farr M.D.* in 1978 began as a series of three movie pilots: *Having Babies, Having Babies II*, and *Having Babies III*. All three had scripts by women writers and dealt with the medical and emotional problems of birth and adoption. In the second film the character of Dr. Julie Farr first appears as an obstetrician/gynecologist, and after the third film, the series evolved. Joel Rogosin, who was brought on to produce the series, says, "We began to feel that that (specialty) was going to be very limited on a week-to-week basis, and we made her into an internist." The limitations of network television in terms of explicitness probably made a series about a gynecologist impossible, but might not women producers as well as women writers have found ways to tell stories that would have worked for a female audience? But would there have been enough of a male audience as well to satisfy the demands of a network?

Just as Madelyn Davis thought it was useful to have a male writing partner, having a male producer can be useful to women writers in promoting and protecting their ideas. In 1974, writers Barbara Corday and Barbara Avedon wrote a script for a theatrical film about two women police detectives. *Cagney and Lacey* was turned down by all the studios, but Corday's husband, producer Barney Rosenzweig, kept trying to sell it. It was also turned down as a proposed series by all three networks, and turned down as a television movie by two networks. In 1981, CBS agreed to do it as a television movie starring Tyne Daly as Mary Beth Lacey and Loretta Swit as Chris Cagney. The movie got high ratings and the network wanted a series.[5] Swit was still tied up with *M*A*S*H*, so the part was recast with classy and attractive Meg Foster. The immediate ratings of the series were low, and a definitely unclassy CBS executive was quoted in *TV Guide* as saying Cagney and Lacey were seen as "too harshly women's lib," and that "We perceived them as dykes."[6] Foster was replaced at the network's insistence by the equally classy and attractive Sharon Gless.[7]

The show was canceled twice, but brought back by complaints from the audience, encouraged by Rosenzweig, who kept a careful watch on the production of the show and the network's treatment of it. Rosenzweig kept in contact with women's groups over the status of the show,[8] which eventually ran for six years. The series focused on both the professional and personal lives of the two detectives and provides an interesting counterpoint to its contemporary, *Hill Street Blues*.

Hill Street takes a wider and denser view of the lives and work of the police, while *Cagney and Lacey* focuses specifically on the women. A recurring criticism of *Hill Street*[9] is that it shortchanged its women characters. Davenport is presented as an intelligent, professional woman, and the makers of the show resisted the network's pressure to hire a more conventional bombshell type for the show,[10] but much is also made of her sex appeal. It is a definite step forward from both *Rocky King, Detective* and *Police Story* that Davenport is seen at the end of the episodes with Furillo and is both supportive and critical of him, but she is usually seen in bed or in the bath with him. The "Remembrance" episode is the only one primarily focused on Davenport, but even there most of what we see of her is her reaction to what the men are doing. In the series we see Furillo's family but never hers, and we do not get inside her in the way *Cagney and Lacey* gets inside its heroines.

The family lives of Cagney and Lacey are a source for both subplots and occasionally major plots. We learn more about how Cagney and Lacey think and feel about everything than we learn about Davenport (or any of the women) in *Hill Street*. Partly this is because Daly and Gless both have greater emotional palettes as actresses to work with than Hamel does, and the writers for *Cagney and Lacey* use their actresses' resources extraordinarily well. (Walon Green, in the "Remembrance" episode of *Hill Street*, does an excellent job of using Hamel's strengths and avoiding her limitations.) By being a star vehicle for the two actresses, *Cagney and Lacey* avoids a problem that many ensemble shows like *Hill Street* fall into. The ensemble shows were generally run by male writer–producers, and while they include women characters, there is a tendency to deal with characters they feel closest to.

This was true of *St. Elsewhere*. In the pilot script, Dr. Wendy Armstrong was described as a "pert redhead," but the producers decided to cast Asian-American actress Kim Miyori. The role was never fully developed, and at the end of the second season, Miyori was called into producers Tom Fontana and John Masius's office and told that the character would be committing suicide. Miyori at first thought they were joking, then realized they were not and asked Fontana why. Miyori said, "He told me that they couldn't write as well for my character. . . . He said that my character hadn't developed like the others, wasn't as interesting. . . . How *could* it be? You never saw Wendy Armstrong out of St. Eligius Hospital, not with her family or friends. And you don't see any Asian writers involved, obviously."[11] Viewers, and not only Asian-American ones, never entirely forgave the show for killing off one of its most potentially interesting characters.

In a February 1990 article,[12] Lydia Woodward was quoted as saying she had been hired on the last season of *St. Elsewhere* because of network pressure on the show to hire women writers. In the interview for this book a year later, Woodward says,

> I never said that in the interview. It wasn't the network. I think there was pressure on MTM at the time because they had a lousy hiring record in terms of women. To tell you the truth, I don't think that particularly mattered. They were surely not people who were going to hire you because you were a woman. They hired you because they liked your work and they liked you. At that point, it probably was like, "Oh good, she's a woman, too. You can kill off a couple of birds here."
>
> I don't think it was by any means the deciding factor why I was hired at *St. Elsewhere*. One of the guys from *St. Elsewhere* called me after that article and said, "We didn't hire you because you're a woman."
> I said, "I know that, John."

Woodward says she has "never been terribly interested in all the women's issues stuff, quite honestly," and her view of *St. Elsewhere* from that perspective is that she does not

> think their show was primarily about women. I think they cared about their women characters, but I don't think they really wrote for women characters, particularly. And I don't think I was even remotely hired to write for the women

characters. I was hired to write the show. I was hired to sit in the office and turn out stuff. I don't say any of that as a criticism of them particularly. I just think it was not what the focus of their show was.

I guess the one example that I could use would be the Nurse Rosenthal character played very nicely by Christina Pickles. I think that they, without realizing it, had created a rather strong character. I think there were probably times when they would have liked to have killed her off. She was strong. She kept fighting back.

They certainly took some of the women through some very, very interesting story arcs on that show, so it's not like they ignored the women characters. I mean, Dr. Craig's wife and that divorce in that last year, Nurse Rosenthal becoming a drug addict, all sorts of stuff. They took the women characters through interesting arcs, but I just don't think that was the primary focus of the show.

Hiring a woman writer does not necessarily overcome pressures from the networks. In the mid-eighties a producer came to Reginald Rose with the idea of doing a TV film about a woman discovering her bisexuality. Rose describes the result, *My Two Loves*, as "TV gone Hollywood," and his script for it as "not much like you saw" in the film. He learned later that the producer hired novelist Rita Mae Brown, who has been open about her own bisexuality, to provide what Rose calls "*that* point of view." Rose did not like the final results, which he thought was filled with "terrible, terrible clichés." Brown was also not happy with the results. She has written that in "theme" shows such as this,

> a therapist appears in the fourth act, if not before. That's right, folks. Rub a little therapy on it and that nasty rash of incest just disappears. Do I like it? No. Do the producers like it? No. (Don't underestimate network executives. They have tremendous intelligence but so few of them have any real power—or guts.) Do the sponsors like it? I expect they do. It's a little "safer." Do the censors like it? You bet. Do therapists like it? Hell, yes. It's got to be bringing them business.

Brown adds that if called upon to write "one of those shows . . . you smack that therapist in there. It's a formula and once you know when and where to look for it, an unintentionally funny one."[13]

One of the basest canards of the seventies was that the feminists had no sense of humor, which was ironic in that there were several successful professional women television comedy writers at the time (not all of whom would necessarily wish to be considered feminists, but still . . .). One was Susan Harris, who went on to create *Soap*, *The Golden Girls*, and *Empty Nest*. Another was Linda Bloodworth-Thomason, who in the mid-eighties had an idea for a series about a group of women running a decorating business. She called CBS to pitch the show and sold it within twenty minutes, and "about thirty seconds after I sold it"[14] she decided to set *Designing Women* in the South. She felt the South had been maligned, and said, "What I originally intended was to entertain, but I also wanted to influence the media about women and the region. We're definitely doing something subversive." Once the show got on and was renewed, there was no trouble with the network: "They have other holes in their ship, so they just let our dinghy set sail."

One "subversive" element of *Designing Women* is the rhythm of its dialogue, particularly in the episodes Bloodworth-Thomason wrote herself. It is not the traditional sitcom structure of repeated setup, setup, punchline. The speeches in the show tend to be longer, and the sentences within the speeches longer, than in traditional television writing. The rhythm of the speeches is not just very Southern, but very Southern *woman*, particularly in some of the "arias" Bloodworth-Thomason has written for Julia Sugarbaker (Dixie Carter). *Designing Women* has the most distinctive regional writing to appear on television since the heyday of Chayefsky and Foote (and perhaps *The Andy Griffith Show*).

In the early seasons, the scripts were written by either Bloodworth-Thomason or Pam Norris, who also writes effectively in the Southern rhythm. Bloodworth-Thomason said in 1990 that the show was never a script ahead, except "Once we got a script ahead, put it in a room and called it a stockpile." The show rehearsed and filmed Monday through Thursday, and Bloodworth-Thomason and Norris wrote the first drafts Friday through Sunday. The ideas came from anywhere. Bloodworth-Thomason, like Roy Huggins, gets ideas while driving, and sometimes the cast suggested ideas. Delta Burke went in to talk to Bloodworth-Thomason one Friday about the possibility of doing a show on people's obsession with weight, and by Monday the script for "They Shoot Fat Women, Don't They?" was done.[15] The scripts then went through rewriting in rehearsal, with changes continuing up to the day of shooting, with sometimes as much as 90 percent changed.[16]

In 1990 Bloodworth-Thomason left writing the show to develop another Southern show, *Evening Shade*, and it took the new writers on *Designing Women* several episodes to find the distinctive tone. *Evening Shade* had some trouble in its first season finding an equally distinctive tone, but CBS was happy enough with the work of Bloodworth-Thomason and her producer–husband Harry Thomason in December 1990 to sign them to an eight-year deal to create five new series. The deal is expected to be worth between $45 and $50 million to the Thomasons.[17]

Diane English, the creator of *Murphy Brown*, also works on ideas while she drives. Her husband, producer Joel Shukovsky, said, "Diane tends to do her thinking in a car on the freeway. She puts on her music and she'll just kind of think and meander. It's not good to drive with her when she's in this state. She won't say anything to you for thirty-five miles."[18] (A word here about producer-husbands like Thomason and Shukovsky. Writers have always depended on the kindness of strange producers, so it is probably better for them to have producers they know well and who know them well and who are of a gender to deal with the [declining] number of male [and female] executives who may have difficulty dealing directly with strong, talented women.)

English also works in the office. A lot. The writing procedure on *Murphy Brown* in its first seasons was more complicated than on *Designing Women*. English recalled:

> A half a dozen times each season we lock ourselves in a room for a whole hiatus week [a week when the show is not shooting], and we just pitch story ideas. We pinpoint the ones that we like, and then we spend a full day or more together [the show had several staff writers], working the story out, scene by scene, beat by beat, until we've got something we feel has a beginning, a middle, and an end, a good arc.[19]

The writer assigned the script will first do a detailed outline that includes not only plot, but character attitudes as well. The outline is reviewed by the entire staff, and then the writer takes notes from that review and writes a first draft script. That draft is read by English and writer Korby Siamis, the show's supervising producer. From their notes, the writer does a second draft, which is reviewed by the staff; then English and/or Siamis will do the "final" draft, which is finally provided to the cast on the weekend prior to the first reading Monday morning. As with other shows, there are rewrites until the shooting Friday night.[20]

Like many women television writers, English does not think of herself as a feminist,

> but if feminism means that my female characters or my friends or myself are respected, in all walks of life, then I'm a feminist. But I don't get involved in the politics of it very often. I don't waste my time pointing at men, blaming them for holding us back, because that has not been my personal experience. I don't like to refer to myself as *woman* writer. I think those kinds of labels are very limiting and I look forward to the day when no one refers to me as woman writer anymore, because I'm just a writer, as an artist is just an artist and a singer a singer.[21]

It is perhaps not surprising that one of the most "feminist" episodes of the series, in which Murphy tries to get into an all-male club, was written by two of the male writers on the show.[22]

Because *Murphy Brown* deals with a woman successfully working in a world of men, there is less of a distinctive rhythm in the dialogue than in *Designing Women*. Where *Murphy Brown* has made a change in sitcoms is in the rhythm of scene construction and storytelling. Prior to the show, half-hour sitcoms were broken up into two acts of equal lengths, with in some cases a "teaser" (short scene) before the first commercial break and/or a "tag" (short scene) after the last commercial break. In *Murphy Brown*, the scenes are of greatly different lengths, with commercial breaks likely to arrive at any time during the show. This gives the series a greater degree of flexibility in the kinds of scenes it can have, changing the rigid rhythm of traditional sitcom storytelling.[23]

Thad Mumford has also written shows not just for women, but for black women. When it was decided in 1987 to spin off Lisa Bonet from *The Cosby Show* into her own show, Mumford was brought on *A Different World*. Unfortunately, Bonet simply could not carry her own show. As Mumford says, "Lisa Bonet has gifts . . . she's very good in an ensemble, and I think she's perfect where she is, back on *The Cosby Show* as part of an ensemble."

After three years on *A Different World*, Mumford worked on *Bagdad Café*, and saw firsthand how the networks have begun to accept black women as strong characters. In one episode, the word "ho" (meaning, as Mumford explains it for those who might think it is an abbreviation for a garden utensil, "a derogatory reference to a woman") was used because Whoopi Goldberg "didn't feel the rhythm of the line was right without some third word. The network didn't want her to use the word 'ho,' so in the second [taping] she used the word 'bitch' . . . . The network called and was so grateful, 'Thank you. Thank you for saying, 'Bitch.' "

Like women writers who had male partners or producers, Mumford had a white male partner for several years, and thinks "unofficially that helped people see me differently from some of my black peers. I think people do get ghettoized and stereotyped easily." This has changed in the years he has been in the business. When he started in the seventies, he thinks there was greater concern about getting new black writers.

> But it doesn't go on much any more. I think people sort of feel that it's O.K. now. We have a lot of shows with black characters. And I think there is this feeling, maybe we have it ourselves, of complacency, because we now get to look at more than just Bill Cosby. We get to look at a lot of our people.
>
> On the other hand, I think that we are the ones probably who are better at writing about our own lives. You see, it's a real fine line, and I'm picking words carefully because I don't want to say the wrong thing. It's not to say that white people can't write about black people. Of course that's just as stupid as saying that we can't write about white people. But sometimes a black person might have a better instinct, or, because of exposure, you might just hear the language better. I am sure the same thing is true for white people too. You just don't want people to make decisions about writers based on things like that. You want people to make decisions on the basis of an instinct on whether you can write this material because of your skill, not because of your ethnicity, or your gender, or anything like that.

For women writers, Kasey Arnold-Ince sees it also as a question of attitudes. In her relatively few years in the industry she has not run into any overtly chauvinist men who would not hire women, but she sees certain problems women writers have. One is that in our society women have not been trained to promote themselves, since society does not reward women who do. In TV self-promotion is necessary for advancement, even in what is supposed to be a solitary endeavor like writing. Television writing of course is not, but as Arnold-Ince notes, women, because of their lack of self-promotion, are more likely to focus on the work of writing, "not the [seduction] of the secretarial pool," as men writers might.

A second problem for women is a question of time, particularly for those like her who are mothers, which inevitably means difficulty in keeping up with the time pressures of television writing. Because of the time demands of a staff position, Arnold-Ince has kept to free-lancing, which has its own element of seduction, as she observes: "I compare it to being single, not having a steady boyfriend, going to parties, being charming, flirting. Developing the story is like you get to dance with Fred Astaire in the moonlight, champagne, roses, and then you turn in the script and the next morning it's Andrew Dice Clay who gets out of bed and goes to the window and yells, 'I broke the bitch.' "

There are frequent studies of female employment in the television industry, most of them semi-encouraging at best. The opening of American television and American society has begun to include women, but neither are as yet as open as they might be. Consider the uni-sex restroom I used in a writer's building on one of the studio lots in 1991 while I was conducting interviews for this book. Tacked up over the back of the toilet was a poster-sized picture of a beautiful girl in a bikini. The picture had an inscription from the would-be actress who had sent it to the writer–producers in the building, and additional inscriptions had been added by other writers. As I turned to leave, I noticed by the door a picture of a shirtless hunk of a man, with inscriptions. In what appeared to be women's handwriting.

The picture was about half the size of the poster.

·21·

MATURITY

*I*n December 1978 Larry Gelbart pitched to NBC's Fred Silverman what Gelbart described as "a comedy but not a situation comedy." Gelbart wanted to "avoid writing problems and the mediocrity that a lot of television is."[1] Silverman agreed, and Gelbart intended to have a full season's worth of scripts completed before the series went into production. Gelbart said while working on the scripts, "Most people who work in television feel somewhat illegitimate, and few are writing as honestly as they'd like to. I'm lucky that I can."[2]

The series, *United States*, premiered in March 1980 and it focused on a young married couple, Richard and Libby Chapin. They seldom left their house. No funny neighbors came in through an unlocked door and made wisecracks. Libby did not try to break into show business. They did not talk in setup, setup, punchline. But did they talk. All the couple did was talk. A lot. About their problems. About their feelings. The show was very literate, mature, intelligent. And dull. The couple and their problems simply did not connect with an audience enough to compel people to watch. Nor was it compelling to at least one writer who worked on it. Gelbart asked Everett Greenbaum to do some episodes. Greenbaum did, but felt the show "Too conversational, too personal. . . . The trouble was, I just didn't like the people. I couldn't get attached to them." By the end of April the show was off the air, having telecast only eight of the completed thirteen episodes.

In 1983 *The Big Chill*, the upscale rip-off of John Sayles's 1980 *Return of the Secaucus Seven*, was a box-office hit in theaters, and in 1985 CBS presented its television rip-off of *The Big Chill*, a series called *Hometown* about a group of friends in their mid-thirties. There was, as in *United States*, a lot of talk about their feelings and attitudes, and the series died after nine episodes.

thirtysomething

Marhsall Herskovitz and Edward Zwick were in their twenties when they met in a filmmaking class at the American Film Institute. According to Richard

Kramer, what happened then was that "recognizing each other as the *other* smartest person around, they had declared a pact of mutual disarmament."[3] They worked individually after that, writing for such quiet dramas as *Family* (Zwick) and *The White Shadow* (Herskovitz). They first teamed up to write the story for the 1983 television movie *Special Bulletin*,[4] a masterful blend of a fictional story of nuclear protestors threatening the destruction of Charleston, South Carolina, told in the form of a simulated news special.

Later Zwick had a development deal at MGM/UA, which wanted to sell a series to ABC.[5] Two days before they were scheduled to meet with people from ABC, they still had no ideas. According to one source, Zwick said later the breakthrough came from his wife, Liberty Godshall, who referred to a cartoon of a blocked writer in a room full of dogs whose wife tells him to write about dogs.[6] According to another source, it was Herskovitz who suggested doing "something about our generation."[7] Eventually they worked up a memo on their idea:

> It's about a group of people, all of a certain age, who know enough about life to be totally confused by it. It's about growing up—no matter how old you are.
> Which means owning up to certain realities. Swallowing a pill or two. Not necessarily the compromise of principles, but rather the recognition that many of our notions of the future were idealizations and can't be lived in the world.[8]

That generalized description could apply to people of different ages, but Herskovitz and Zwick began to work in the memo toward more specifics:

> And since everyone knows this is the first generation ever to have children, or buy houses, or try to have careers, it naturally assumes that everyone else will be interested in its noble endeavors. The truth is we know there's nothing inherently noble or even particularly interesting about people in their thirties. It just happens to be the territory we know best. And the fact that we *aren't* the first to attempt any of the things we're stumbling through that leads us to hope that twentysomethings and fiftysomethings will identify with it as well. It's about people. Not ages. . . .[9]

Film and television are very specific, realistic media, and the more precise the story and characters were made, the more specifically "thirtysomething" they became. In the pilot episode, Hope's final speech answers Michael's question about why everything is so hard: "Because we expect too much. Because we've always gotten too much. I think that our parents got together in 1946 and said let's all have lots of kids and give them everything they want so they can grow up and be totally messed up and unable to cope with real life." What Herskovitz and Zwick beautifully articulated was the self-absorption of the specific generation they were writing about, which in turn was what made the show both more aggravating and more successful than *United States* and *Hometown*. Generally those viewers both older and younger (and even some the same age) than the characters in the series found the characters whiny and self-indulgent. The show and its creators took the angst of a generation seriously, and those of that generation returned the favor by taking the show seriously.

What brought the viewers at least partially together finally was laughter. Near the end of the first season of the show, there was a program on it as part of the Museum of Broadcasting's Festival of Television at the Los Angeles County Museum of Art. An early episode, entitled "Therapy," about Elliot and Nancy's attempt to save their marriage, was shown. It was written by Herskovitz's wife, Susan Shilliday, and she was afraid of what the audience reaction might be to such a depressing episode. She later wrote: "But a shocking thing happened. The audience got into it. They *laughed*. I had never written for the stage, never witnessed an audience responding to my writing, certainly never thought of myself as *funny*. And I had certainly never thought of 'Therapy' as funny. I became completely intoxicated."[10]

It became apparent to those creating *thirtysomething* that viewers, even loyal ones, sometimes found the agonies of Hope, Michael, Elliot, Nancy, Ellyn, and the others funny, and that was part of the reality of the generation as well. It opened up the show to a new texture.

The sale of the movie rights to Joseph Dougherty's play *Digby* brought him to Hollywood. In 1987 he was working on Anthony Yerkovich's series *Private Eye* and talked to Herskovitz and Zwick about doing some first-season *thirtysomething* episodes. He worked on both shows simultaneously—a form of culture shock. Dougherty would sit in the office with Yerkovich for five or six hours in two or three meetings and work out every story beat, ending up with a seven-page outline. It was different down the street:

> With Ed and Marshall you come in, you knock things around for an hour, an hour and a half. You figure roughly the beats in an act, then you are totally on your own. There were mornings where I would actually spend from about nine to one with Tony Yerkovich at Universal, then have to drive down here [the series was made for MGM/UA but at the MTM studios, about a mile away from Universal] to work on *thirtysomething*, and basically, somehow I had to use Ventura Boulevard to stop thinking about hookers and cops and people driving in De Sotos, and come down here and just all of a sudden start working on an atmosphere which was much closer to my play.
>
> Actually I'm very proud of the fact that in the same year I was writing for these two incredibly different shows, just because it eliminated the chance that I was being typecast. Although I am finding out now as I go out looking for something to do after this show, my agent's astonished that I am just perceived as a dramatic writer. I say, "Don't they watch the shows? They're funny."

Dougherty, a fan since age twelve of Preston Sturges's ability to shift between comedy and drama, uses comedy as an "ingratiating tool to elicit trust: 'It's going to be O.K. Come with me. I'm going to take care of you. You're going to have a good time.' And once people have committed to a piece, they will stay with you."

When *Private Eye* was canceled, Dougherty joined the staff of *thirtysomething*. The show was written then primarily by Herskovitz, Zwick, their wives, and Richard Kramer, who had known them for years. Ann Lewis Hamilton was something of an outsider on the staff, and she at first assumed Dougherty was, in Dougherty's words, "another film school dweeb." She was in his office when he was unpacking. The first picture out of the box was his wife, but the second was Sturges. She told him later that she knew then it would be O.K.

Dougherty thinks he and Hamilton, as outsiders, have brought a little "vinegar" to the show, that they avoid "the more self-congratulatory aspects" of the show, those elements that make audiences complain of the "whining" of the characters. Dougherty says, "When people tell me Michael whines, I say, 'No he doesn't.' " Dougherty explains, "I take a much more sophisticated view of Michael Steadman. He's like a doctor who just understands the symptoms of his own disease too much. He's incredibly self-reflective, but I only think about him in terms of how I write him." Dougherty says that Ken Olin (Michael) once said to him after a reading of a new Dougherty script, "God! Plot!" Dougherty gave himself the title of Executive in Charge of Plot and Plot-like Substances.

Dougherty and Hamilton's professional relationship led to a December 1990 episode he wrote that she directed, in which Ellyn meets an old flame, Billy, and starts seeing him, all the while pretending with Gary that she and Gary are sleeping together. Dougherty tells how the episode came about:

> It's the first one she directed, so the deal we had was that I directed one of her scripts and she would direct one of mine, so we'd see if either one of us was talking to the other at the end of the experience. It was me desperately wanting to write for Polly [Draper, who played Ellyn]. I thought Ellyn was underserviced as a character and I wanted her to be happy. I wanted her to be fixed up with a guy and I wanted Ann to have a good sexy script to direct.
>
> And, basically, it had to do with the fact that since Ann and I hang out so much together we became the subject of an office rumor. We found out that Ed and Marshall were wondering if we were sleeping together. That's kind of where it came from: "You and I will be Peter [Horton, who played Gary] and Polly, and Michael and Hope will be Ed and Marshall, and it's just these people thinking we're sleeping together." Now at every given opportunity we always allude to the fact that we have slept together.

Because both Dougherty and Hamilton have worked in low-budget action adventure films (Hamilton's husband produced Dougherty's script of *Steel and Lace*), Dougherty considers them "genetically close as writers." He also sees the two of them as "the bad kids. We can't believe they're letting us sit together this semester. We shouldn't be allowed to sit together at read-throughs."

As with the last two years of *Hill Street Blues*, the writing on *thirtysome-thing* was done in a variety of ways. Dougherty says this is one reason the show is "so good" and "so uneven" at the same time. Richard Kramer wrote that the show was fun to write because "Ed and Marshall had created in the pilot the chance for me and other writers to write in our own voices."[11] Dougherty expands on this:

> I think there are six people formally on staff right now, and no two of us work exactly the same way. My assessment of Richard [Kramer] is he's very detail oriented. I think he thinks he has to be perfect early in the process. This is a very comparative statement, [but] I think Richard is a slower writer than some. He takes it very seriously.
>
> Right now Ann Hamilton and I write the fastest of anyone here. Ann and I, for different reasons, the lesson we learned from television is the ability to give the certain effort. Does the language do the job or not? If it doesn't, fix it. If it isn't [right], throw it out and do it again.
>
> Ann does something that I can't do. Ann doesn't have to through-draft the first time. She can go to an outline and look at an outline and pick the place where she wants to start and just go all over the place writing scenes. I couldn't do that to save my life. I've got to get through it at least once.
>
> I'm looked on as an incredible eccentric in that I have to write my first draft longhand. Because I can't type it the first time through. Winnie Holzman and Richard sometimes work on stuff together and might collaborate. I don't quite know how the collaboration stuff works. Winnie's pretty fast. Richard's slowed down but I hate to say that as a negative.

thirtysomething began as an ensemble show, but during the first season, the writers found it increasingly difficult to use all the characters all the time. In the second season, the writers began to focus on individual characters, or couples, in each episode, such as the series of episodes dealing with the collapse of Elliot and Michael's business and their going to work for Miles Drentell. This focus on characters led the writers to write in certain areas. Dougherty did several of the business shows, and says, "Richard [Kramer] adopted Melissa. Winnie [Holzman] is adopting Melissa to a certain extent, too, and also Ellyn. Before Susan [Shilliday] left, Nancy and Elliot were basically her bailiwick. Liberty did Hope and Michael. Sometimes the lines would be crossed."

Richard Kramer, from the beginning of the show, spent time with the actors discussing their characters, and discovered they often knew what he was trying to write for them before he did.[12] Joseph Dougherty's experience is

> almost that turned on its side, in that I look at the actors now and I know what their voices are and I know what their characters are, so I know what I can do with them. This is a case with somebody like David Clennon, who is Miles

Drentell, which is a character I've written a lot. There are some times that you say to yourself, "There's something I want to write about. Who are the best characters I can run this story [through]? Who'd be the most interesting to put in this situation?"

You get to a point after three years when you're dealing with actors that the physical text of their speeches on the page is different than the text for the other characters. The two people who it leaps out to me about are Tim Busfield and Polly Draper, but it's also true with David Clennon. It's like having actors available to you in repertoire. You hear their voices. You know how they corner in a scene, so that with Tim Busfield, you can give him a speech that consists of nothing but incomplete sentences, with ellipses and run-ons, and Timmy can make sense of these things. Timmy can fill in the ellipses.

Polly is wonderful. Again, you can give Polly Draper non-sentences, but if you give Tim Busfield a non-sentence, you have to end it with an ellipse to indicate a trail-off. With Polly you can actually do two words and a full stop.

You can put two diametrically opposed thoughts next to each in a Miles Drentell speech and David will cut them completely clean. It's astonishing. I've seen him do it. And he's always done it. He does it in *Being There* [and] *Missing*. He's able to play somebody who in his mind can play three different chess games, and uses it and can corner like that.

My philosophy is that these people are instruments and they came in with very different things. It's like a choice of colors that would be like a palette for a writer to have access to on a regular basis. So it's kind of the flip of what Richard's talking about. So I think now each one of us approaches the characters differently.

In an episode in the last season of the show (1990–91), Dougherty wrote a monologue for Polly Draper that ran seven minutes in the first cut. The last two minutes had to be cut, since the entire episode ran thirteen minutes long. Dougherty says, "Just because we came in an act over, I don't see any reason we couldn't have aired it and just told Ted Koppel to stay home for an extra fifteen minutes," but television had changed since the days of Desi Arnaz and U.S. Steel.

One reason Dougherty wrote for Draper in the last season is that at the end of the previous season he had written several "business" shows and made it part of his deal to return for the fourth season that he have "access to the women [characters]." Dougherty feels that he and Hamilton were doing "damage control in a strange way" in their handling of the women characters. He says the two of them were

very pugnacious in terms of defending characters, particularly the women. In an overall sense Ann and I are eager for every opportunity to try and keep the women strong, and to try and keep them healthy, since there's a tendency to make them mentally neurotic and physically ill because of their neuroses. We are desperately trying to keep Melissa happy, but there's some kind of glacial feeling from the corner office, from Ed and Marshall, that Melissa is not permitted to be happy.

This happens a lot with Melissa and Ellyn. I sometimes don't know how Polly and Melanie [Mayron, who played Melissa] deal with [being] the most radically differently written characters over the course of the year. When Ann and I write either one of them, they usually tend to be pretty integrated people. But when Richard and Winnie write them, they tend to be very neurotic and lock themselves in bathrooms. And it's kind of like, "Weren't they O.K., last week?" I think it's there that we basically feel different ways. We want to do different things with these characters. I'd like people to look at these people and say, "It's O.K. to be single. It's O.K. to be sexually ambivalent." I'd love it if at the last show of the season Melissa would finally realize she's gay, or something. "Please, could we just let the woman be happy somewhere in her life?"

Polly Draper took the job of Ellyn based on the assumption, which was the same assumption I had, that it was not always going to be Ellyn who was always going to be jealous of Hope, but Hope was going to be jealous of Ellyn because Ellyn was single and fucking like a bunny. Unfortunately there is this kind of neo-conservative agenda, which I've run afoul of in very strange ways. It's my opinion that Ed and Marshall do not like strong women, as characters or as writers or as people. I think their problem is translated into the choices they make for the show.

For a while there, Ellyn was supposed to have an ectopic pregnancy resulting in a hysterectomy. And Ann and I have been saying, "Excuse me? You're going to take out the sex organs of two out of the four female characters?" That's fifty percent. That's a little statistically significant. That was nipped after much screaming.

There was, as befits a semi-democracy, even more yelling and screaming the year before when Herskovitz and Zwick decided to give Nancy ovarian cancer. The issue was discussed at what is now a legendary staff meeting,[13] with several of the writers objecting strongly, for a variety of reasons. Ann Hamilton felt that the show's women had suffered enough, and Susan Shilliday thought that it would be impossible to get back to dealing with daily life after introducing a problem of that size.[14] Dougherty says that Zwick's defense was "We can do it better than anybody else. We can be straighter about it. We can go someplace where no one's ever gone before."

The cancer "arc" was enormously compelling, if controversial, and the writers of the show were able to get at the range of emotions patients and their families go through.[15] The arc of stories dealt with it not just as an issue, as other shows had done, or even just in terms of the emotions of the characters, but the fact that it was a group of episodes made it clear cancer was a war with many battles. As should have been expected, women went for checkups as a result of the show, as well as writing and calling the show. The makers of the series were aware of their responsibilities. Dougherty says,

> I'm appalled at how many people in television don't accept the fact that television is the primary culturalization force in America today. They just out and out deny it. The only people I have met who have not denied that are Ed and

Marshall. They accept the fact that this particular medium actually does shape [public attitudes].

I had a theory that one of the reasons a lot of people are unhappy in this country is because they couldn't figure out why they weren't as happy as the people on television. Why couldn't they solve problems that way? Here was a show that was going to say you could be angry with somebody you love. You can go through periods where you can't stand to have them touch you. You can be dissatisfied. You can have problems that won't get solved right away.

The writers of the show were also aware that, however much a conservative agenda they might think there was on it, there are people who do not think the show was conservative enough. Because the series suggested all the complexities that Dougherty mentions above, the proponents of a narrower American society have objected to the openness of the show, especially in its positive portrayal of a brief affair between two gay men. The conservatives put pressure on the sponsors of the show and succeeded in getting ABC not to rerun one of the episodes in which the two men appear in bed together. In retaliation, Joseph Dougherty wrote into a Halloween party scene an exchange between two gay characters, one of whom identifies himself as Jesse Helms, the other as Donald Wildmon. Dougherty expected some kind of reaction, but as of the January 1991 interview for this book, there was none. Dougherty says, "We wanted them to know that we are aware that they are monitoring the show. 'We just wanted to wave to you.' " Eternal vigilance is the price of freedom of expression.

In the last season, Dougherty and Ann Hamilton's scripts were written differently from scripts in earlier seasons. He thinks they were more subtle, with more emotional subtext and less language. They decided, "Let's see what's the smallest amount of words we can use to do this." Their writing was different from that of other writers, and the show and the characters, like the last year of *St. Elsewhere*, were more uneven. Dougherty thinks the show would have been much more successful and certainly more homogeneous if it were a more conventional show with more conventional writers. He says, "We fuck up, easily, as often as we succeed. . . . We may fall flat on our face, and usually if we do it's with a rather flatulent pomposity, but you've got to give us points for trying. And sometimes we hit our goals."

Dougherty defines the mixture of attitudes necessary to write the show, and television in general:

You're doomed when you say to yourself, "I'm writing *thirtysomething*. I'm writing important television." I've always felt that Marshall should have two signs on the door to the producers' suite. On the front door going in it should say, "It's not television, it's *thirtysomething*." And on the door going out it should say, "It's a TV show." Because really, "It's a TV show" is very liberating. I feel free to try anything. It may not work, and I may have to come up with something else, but I can try it. I can sit down and I can write this heavy dramatic episode and say to myself, "I really want to do this right here," and you believe in it and you just go with it. You have to be free to kind of [do it]. You can't be afraid of the paper.

I don't think there's any excuse for bad television. There just isn't, except for a failure to take pride in what you are doing and an assumption that "Everybody else is doing shit, I might as well do it." There's no excuse. . . . I don't care what people say. "Oh, it's what the public wants." The public wants what's there. The public would not miss bad shows. The public is not going to wake up tomorrow morning and realize *Full House* is not on the air. If *Full House* had not existed, it would not have been necessary to invent it.

As uneven as the writing process on *thirtysomething* may have been during the last season, the writing staff came up with an astonishing series of shows, particularly those shown in February and May 1991. On the February 12 episode, written by Ann Lewis Hamilton, Nancy goes into the hospital for a "second look" for her cancer after her chemotherapy treatments. Hamilton holds off the results until the end of the second act, not letting us hear the doctor tell Nancy, but letting us see the scene we want to see: Nancy telling Elliot, and their reactions. In the third act, the major characters celebrate in Nancy's room, and we begin to get suspicious because Gary is late in arriving. Michael goes out to call him and learns from a cop who has left a message on Michael's machine that Gary has been killed in an accident. Hamilton handles the balance between the happiness about Nancy and the sadness about Gary beautifully.

Joseph Dougherty's script the following week gives us the reactions of the women in Gary's life to his death, showing Susannah, his wife, handling the situation better than anybody else, including Michael. Although Dougherty generally tried to avoid the flashback/surrealist shows other series writers did, here he uses both flashbacks and the ghost of Gary very effectively, in the almost-casual way they had become part of the grammar of *thirtysomething*.

Winnie Holzman's episode the following week shows the respective bachelor parties of Ellyn and Billy, the "feminists" on the staff having triumphed with Ellyn getting a husband instead of a hysterectomy.

The final episode of the series, telecast May 28, was intended only as the season finale, but the network decided not to renew the show. Herskovitz said, "If we knew the show was gonna end, we would have tried to come up with a more comprehensive final episode."[16] In some ways, the episode is more typical of the show by *not* tying up all the loose ends and leaving situations and relationships open.

thirtysomething was produced for MGM/UA, but made at the old MTM lot. While the producers undoubtedly visited the MGM administrative offices, on at least one occasion the head of MGM/UA Television visited them. He told the show's staff, "Jesus, I love coming over here. This is the way it should be in this business. This is *fun*."[17]

And if anybody would know about the fun of making television, it would be David Gerber.

China Beach

The young woman in the swimsuit sits on the beach. It could be any beach. It is a peaceful day.

The camera pans across the beach and we begin to hear a mechanical sound. The camera is on the back of the woman's head. She hears the sound, and there is tension in her neck as she turns her head to one side, then bows her head. The sound is clear: helicopters.

She starts walking into the underbrush up from the beach, soldiers running past her. She goes into a hut, puts on a surgical gown and opens the door to see the choppers with the wounded. The actress is Dana Delany; her face, her expression, and her presence carry a moral weight. The pilot for *China Beach* has begun.

The nurse, Colleen McMurphy, is scheduled to leave the China Beach hospital and recreation area in Vietnam. She is given a farewell party, and she is hustled by a visiting singing group into being a backup singer for them. The base is attacked, and McMurphy and a singer in the group help the wounded. The singer admires what McMurphy does, and McMurphy decides to stay at China Beach.

The question the pilot only begins to answer is: how do you do a series about a combat area hospital and make it different enough from one of the great series on television, *M*A*S*H*? The *China Beach* pilot seems to have more similarities than differences, but the hints of the differences are there. First of all, the focus is not on a man but on a woman, McMurphy. As created by John Sacret Young and William Broyles, Jr., she was originally much tougher, a character who had seen it all, but Young was impressed with Delany and shifted the character to suit her talents, which included an ability to be still. Delany told an interviewer in 1989, "Well, one thing I've learned from doing *China Beach* is the value of stillness, so that you let the audience come to you, and then they can project whatever they want onto you. There's great value in that. I mean, you see all the old movies, that's what they used to do." [18] It is this stillness that gives her the moral weight, that draws the audience into not only her emotions but her choices of action.

Not only is the focus on McMurphy, but the experience is seen from her point of view. In a scene later in the pilot, she and the primary doctor in the series, Dr. Richards, come into the wards, and while Richards is making Hawkeye-type jokes, the scene's focus stays on McMurphy and her reactions to what she sees.

The pilot and the first six episodes of the series ran in the spring of 1988, and it was clear from them that the series was darker than *M*A*S*H*. The storylines followed not only McMurphy, but Cherry White, a naive young

Red Cross worker who volunteered to come to Vietnam to look for her brother, who is listed as missing in action. Her search takes her into some of the more disreputable areas of Vietnam, where she finds he has become a drug addict. Within the first few episodes of the fall season, Cherry White is killed.

William Broyles, Jr., who had written a book about Vietnam[19] and wanted to do a show about war from women's point of view,[20] said in the fall of 1988, "We wanted to do a character show from the very beginning. We're not doing a documentary about the war any more than *M*A*S*H* or *Full Metal Jacket*. We want to bend realism here, something in the way *M*A*S*H* did. There's an absurdity to our show that I think is realistic. If you try to deal with [the war] like a camera, like a documentary, you miss the sort of absurd truth about it."[21] Another series about Vietnam, *Tour of Duty*, got letters from Vietnam veterans who put down *China Beach* because it was about human relationships rather than combat. Broyles replied, "I think they've managed to attract the veterans. The audience of veterans is an important audience, but we want to reach people who *weren't* there as well."[22] *China Beach* began with that broader view both of the war and what the series was about, a view that expanded as the show continued.

John Sacret Young, whose credits include *Police Story* and the television movies *A Rumor of War* and *Testament*,[23] wanted women on the show in several capacities, especially writers. Lydia Woodward, who went from *St. Elsewhere* to *China Beach*, says

> It's worked out great. We've fulfilled Warner Brothers's entire minority hiring program. Especially this year [1990–91]. We hired three staff writers this year. Two of them were women. One of those women was a vet who served in Vietnam. And the third person we hired was a black guy, so we *really* fulfilled their minority hiring this year.
>
> We got into making lots of what we called our gender gap jokes in the office. Stuff in story meetings, "You're a guy. Of course you don't get it." That kind of stuff, silly stuff. Obviously it was a very different experience for me from *St. Elsewhere*, but John was very insistent on having a lot of women involved, and had a lot of women involved in the show at every level: women editors, Mimi Leder was the producer–director.

Woodward got on *China Beach* in the fall of 1988 because its staff read her *St. Elsewhere* and *Slap Maxwell* scripts.

> They had gotten a pickup for the full season, so they were staffing up. I went over and met with them. I talked to a few other shows, but *China Beach* was very intriguing to me. I knew of John Young from other work he had done, specifically *Testament*, and thought, "This was an interesting guy." I had seen all six [episodes], and I thought they'd done a pretty interesting job with them.
>
> It seemed unrelentingly dark and depressing, and I think in part I was hired because there was a little more humor in my writing examples from *St. Else-*

where and from *Slap*. [They] were things that had a little more comedy relief, if you will, and I think at the time the network was pressuring them to lighten up a little.

From the beginning, the show had people interviewing veterans. Carol Flint, who later became one of the show's best writers, started as a researcher, and it was her research that Woodward read through when she went on the series. For the first weeks Woodward got "more and more depressed reading about Vietnam until you couldn't even take any more in. Emotionally it became too overwhelming, so at some point you just kind of stopped and started the process of doing the show."

While she may have been hired to lighten the show, Woodward "immediately became as dark and depressing as everybody else there. I've now ended up on the darkest, most depressing show on television and loving it." It was a show that did things like killing off Cherry White, but unlike the suicide of Wendy Armstrong on *St. Elsewhere*, Cherry White's character had grown and developed. As Woodward recalls,

> We had pushed the Cherry White character as far as she could go with the show in any kind of interesting way. And women did die in Vietnam, and Red Cross women, so we decided to go ahead and do it.
>
> It was slightly controversial and there were a lot of people who loved that character who said, "I never forgave you for killing Cherry White." We didn't think it was that big of a deal. I don't think the network was crazy about it, either. The network said, "You don't kill off your regulars. What are you doing?"
>
> What was kind of fun and great about working with John Young is that he didn't really care. If he thought it was a good idea and we were going to be doing something interesting with it, then he was completely supportive of that kind of thing, as opposed to just, "Oh, yeah, the rules of the game are you don't kill off a regular this early." [*M*A*S*H* had obviously defined how early you can kill a regular. His attitude was] "Forget the rules. Throw the rules out and do what you think is going to be interesting for our small but loyal audience." It wasn't that small, actually. It wasn't as small as it's rumored to be.

Woodward saw the writing process on *China Beach* as "a very different experience from *St. Elsewhere*. Very, very differently run show. *China Beach* is a democracy. *St. Elsewhere* is not." She continues, talking about establishing whatever overall story arcs *China Beach* had in the first season she was on it, "It was a collective process. We would sit around and throw out all sorts of things and then we'd kind of weed through them. We'd marry certain stories to others. The show was still very new and was experimenting with its form and its characters were changing." The democratic process of story development continued over the run of the series. In March 1990, writer Carol Flint said the process that season began with all the writers sitting in a room with a big board on the wall with open spaces for episode ideas. The writers discussed possible ideas, then each writer went off and wrote the scripts he or she wanted to do. She felt it involved the best of both kinds of writing, collaborative and solo, and described it as "Part café society, part art."[24]

John Young kept an eye on the writing. Woodward says Young "has an enormous respect for writing. . . . Not that he would let you off the hook and let you do anything with it. The expression we always used was 'Dig deeper, dig deeper.' Because that was always [Young's] comment on all the scripts." Broyles described his own function as executive consultant on the series as "They show me the scripts. I read them and send them notes. Sometimes they pay attention to what I say."[25]

It is common for television series, particularly if they get behind in production, to do a show consisting primarily of flashbacks. *China Beach* did its in 1989 the hard way. John Sacret Young said that they were suffering "midseason fatigue" and realized one Thursday night at ten they did not have a script for the following week. Writer John Wells suggested using filmed interviews with veterans intercut with material from the show. They had interviewed over five hundred vets, and they now had between 40 and 50, some of whom had been interviewed before, some of whom had not, come in and give filmed interviews. In some cases the material in the interviews had been the basis for story material in the pilot or earlier episodes, but in others it was just coincidence that the material matched. Unlike "The Interview" episode of *M*A*S*H*, the "Vets" episode used the real interviews, rather than fictionalizing them. The network objected to "Vets" on the grounds that people would tune out, thinking it was a documentary. Young thought the *China Beach* audience knew the show well enough to appreciate it, and it was shown, getting more response from veterans and children of veterans than any other episode until then. The following season the show did a similarly structured, if not quite as powerful, episode, "Souvenirs," without any objection from the network.[26]

The end of the 1988–89 season saw a two-part episode, "The World," written by John Wells, in which McMurphy returns to her home in the Midwest for the death of her father. The thinking on the staff was that they wanted to deal with two issues:[27] the treatment soldiers in Vietnam received when they got home and McMurphy's relationship to her family. Wells's script is particularly good at laying out in subtle and complex ways the tensions within the family.

The beginning of the 1989–90 season saw the introduction of new characters, particularly Holly, a Red Cross worker; Frankie Bunsen, a black woman mechanic; and Sgt. Pepper, a grizzled long-timer who runs the car pool. Unlike the traditional pattern of introduction of new characters in shows, the writers of *China Beach* wrote no great entrances for their new characters. They often hovered in the background for an episode or two, then moved into more substantial stories.

Lydia Woodward explains the purpose of the new characters and how the show itself defeated that purpose:

> The war was a very dark experience. We were always trying to find ways to kind of lighten things somewhat, and it was usually through the introduction of a new character. Invariably what would happen is that we would introduce characters and they would turn dark on us, because we turned them dark. It's because it's essentially what the show was. The show was really about the emotional costs of war. Even with these characters, we brought them on and they could sing and they could dance and they could be funny, and we would immediately put them into dark storylines. It just happened. We just couldn't help ourselves.

Holly, for example, later became the subject of the abortion episode, "Holly's Choice." When Carol Flint first thought of the story, she was afraid that it would become a traditional "issue" episode in which the issue would be debated in a balanced style. What she ended up doing was telling the story in reverse order, beginning after Holly's abortion, then having each scene go another step backward in time. She felt—and rightly so—that this would focus on the characters rather than the debate.[28] The show did not immediately get as much trouble from the network as the writers anticipated, at least partially because the leading character, McMurphy, came out against the abortion, but there was pressure on the sponsors of the show and the network pulled the show from its scheduled rerun, just as it did with the "gay" episode of *thirtysomething*.[29]

The same darkening came when the network asked the show to include a romance for McMurphy. The writers came up with an older French doctor who had been in Vietnam for years, which gave him a different perspective on the war and the American presence. The relationship contained echoes of Nellie Forbush's relationship with Émile de Becque in Rodgers and Hammerstein's *South Pacific*, and another relationship, between a Vietnamese woman and Beckett, the soldier in charge of preparing the bodies of dead soldiers for return to the States, also parallels the Liat–Lt. Cable relationship in the same musical.

One limitation of the series was that the Vietnamese characters were generally not as well conceived as the Americans, although the season opener of the 1989–90 season, in which McMurphy and K.C., the more-explicit Miss Kitty of China Beach, are caught in a Viet Cong cave provided a conscious opportunity to show the Vietnamese side. Lydia Woodward says, "Obviously the tunnels were a pretty extraordinary metaphor for how the Vietnamese survived and won the American war in Vietnam. It was their land and they dug in and it worked, and I think we wanted to show that. And that there was another life, a whole other kind of underground life that you would be exposed to." The most interestingly conceived Vietnamese character, Trieu Au, the woman who took care of K.C.'s baby, did not show up in the series until the final season.

In February 1990 *China Beach* brought one of its characters home for good in "Thanks of a Grateful Nation," and the 1990–91 season expanded on that idea. It was typical that the writers did not choose to do it in a simple way. Woodward explains in her matter-of-fact way how the season's narratively complex arc was constructed:

> We wanted to bring the characters home. We wanted to move forward in time and explore their lives on through the years. And we did not want to do it in a strict chronological, linear fashion—for a number of reasons. One, that felt a little too much like we were doing straight soap opera: and then this happened, and then this happened. So we wanted the ability to jump all the way into the future. I think the most forward we ever go is 1988. The opening of the season was 1985, and then flashbacked to 1967, which is another era we never showed. The pilot took place in '68, and the first two years of the show took place in 1968, so we'd never shown any of the kind of pre-stuff, and we'd never shown that 1969 stuff at the base, and the war was very different in 1969. But we really wanted to be able to jump around in time.
>
> We also had some just practical considerations in that one of our actresses, Marg Helgenberger [who played K.C.] was pregnant, so we knew there were X number of episodes that she was going to be out of. And, we also knew that if we did it in a strict linear fashion, we'd run out of China Beach stuff at some point and we wouldn't be able to shoot the compound. So a lot of the decision of integrating time periods within shows was basically a financial consideration to shoot on location and also still be able to use the compound that we already were paying for. But I think that foremost we were not interested in telling linear storylines.
>
> There was no bible for this. We never sat down and said, "This is where every character is going to go for the next 15 years." We knew some of what we wanted to do with characters, so it's not like it lacked any direction. It did have some direction, but we left a lot of it open to just discover as we went along.
>
> My feeling is that it's resulted in, I think, some of our best work, and I think that our successes were bigger and maybe some of our failures were bigger. It was a lot of fun to do. I think it was probably difficult for an audience. Your hardcore, loyal audience is with you. I mean, heaven forbid you should be a new viewer. You wouldn't have a clue what was going on. So, politically, maybe it wasn't a smart thing to do, but again, we didn't play by those rules particularly.

It was more than just their best work. What turned out to be the final season of *China Beach* was an astonishing attempt, that mostly succeeded, in presenting on an American television series a serious, epic, multi-level vision of the past twenty years of American emotional history. In view of the way it was put together, it is amazing it held together as well as it did, flaws and all.

In the first episode of the season, "The Big Bang," John Wells establishes the structure of intercutting between later, in this case 1985, and earlier at China Beach. Boonie, the former lifeguard at China Beach, his wife, and his children (or those we assume to be his children) visit Dr. Richards and his wife in 1985. Richards has not married McMurphy, but another woman named Colleen who reminds us very much of McMurphy. The visit provokes a series of flashbacks to Dr. Richards's first day at China Beach.

The next episode, "She Sells More Than Sea Shells," written by Carol Flint from a story by four writers, lets us know that one of Boonie's daughters is in fact K.C.'s daughter. "You Babe," by two new writers to the series, Susan Rhinehart and Cathryn Michon, shows us McMurphy in Vietnam having to deliver K.C.'s baby in the streets of Saigon—a harrowing scene that is a long way from the gentility of the birth of Ricky Jr. on *I Love Lucy*, which set the television precedent this scene builds on. Woodward's "Fever" cuts between McMurphy in Vietnam in 1967 and her adjustment, or lack of it, to returning home in 1970. The episode ends with McMurphy getting on a bus and hitting the road. Woodward says of writing for Delany:

> How do you write the quiet stuff? I don't know. She's sort of a stoic Western hero, that's really who she is. She's kind of Gary Cooper in some respects, with a little stronger emotional life. I really don't have an answer for that question. We seem to do it. The thing about *China Beach* is the whole thing is subtext, so it always kind of comes out. You're never really writing about what you're writing about, it's all about something underneath. And the actors certainly understood that and were very good at delivering that.

The director of this episode was Diane Keaton, and as well written as the episode is, Keaton's direction is a little off. The rhythm is perhaps too distinctively Keaton. She does not use Delany's stillness as well as the best of the series directors, John Sacret Young and especially Mimi Leder.[30] (Woodward, on the other hand, thinks Keaton's direction was "great" and "got it.")

Young both wrote and directed one of the best of the season's episodes, "Juice," in which we find Richards in Miami Beach in 1972 with a girl we come to realize is the Colleen he later married. They run into McMurphy, who now wears leather jackets and works at a juice plant. At the end of the episode she is leaving Miami Beach and helps a vet in a wheelchair off a curb. He tells her he is going to his first demonstration, at the Republican National Convention. She does not go with him, but rides a bit of the way on her motorcycle, stops, then looks at the demonstrators. She is lost, both emotionally and historically. The scene's imagery suggests both *Easy Rider* and *Born on the Fourth of July* without the pomposities of either. The series was looking at the past, but not as most television does in terms of nostalgia. The Cunninghams of *Happy Days* would not let this McMurphy live with them.

China Beach's time slot for the first two and a half seasons was Wednesday nights at ten P.M., where it had an average 21 percent of the audience watching television at that time. In the fall of 1990, ABC moved the show to Saturday night at nine as a lead-in to *Twin Peaks*. *Twin Peaks* died for the reasons mentioned in Chapter 19, and took *China Beach*, which was then opposite the very popular *Golden Girls* and *Empty Nest*, with it. *China Beach's* share was reduced to 12 percent.[31] In December 1990, as the deadline for Iraq to leave Kuwait drew closer, ABC put *China Beach* on hiatus. After the war started in January, the cast and crew of the show spoke out. For John Sacret Young, the war was

> a good reason to bring the show back.
> Our whole reason for doing the show has changed. We did an episode [yet to be broadcast] called "Rewind," where Karen [Christine Elise], the daughter of K.C. [Marg Helgenberger], was doing home movies and talking to our characters about the Vietnam War. When you watch what they say and suddenly think about the Middle East, there's a whole different level going on. There's a whole added sadness, a whole added complexity. It may make our show tougher to watch.[32]

It was not until June 1991, after the Gulf War was over and the interminable parades had begun, that ABC brought back the series and ran the last of its episodes. Two episodes follow K.C.'s decision to give up her child, and both cover enough of the same material that they might have been condensed into one more conventionally written show. What the two episodes do, however, is articulate what had always been a subtext in the series: that the most important relationship in the series is not the conventional McMurphy–Richards semi-romance, but the thorny, difficult relationship between McMurphy and K.C.

The focus on this relationship becomes a continuing thread in the season and series finale, the two-hour "Hello and Goodbye," which begins with a reunion of the China Beach personnel in 1988 to which K.C.'s daughter, Karen, comes, hoping finally to meet her mother. K.C. does not appear at the reunion, and the second half of the episode has some of the group, including Karen, driving to Washington to see the Vietnam Memorial. Karen finally meets her mother, who has become an international businesswoman dealing with Japanese businessmen.

Like the final episode of *M*A*S*H*, the "Hello and Goodbye" episode of *China Beach* is probably too long, and the scenes at the memorial wall are unfocused. Those between McMurphy, K.C., and Karen do not seem strong enough to end the series, or even the season, since when they were written and shot, it was not yet clear the series was being canceled. The K.C. and Karen material is better handled in "Rewind," the episode that ran two weeks before the finale.

Written by Carol Flint and John Wells, the episode begins with videotaped interviews of people talking about Vietnam. Some know about it, some (especially the younger ones) do not. (Are the interviews real, or made up for the episode? We cannot tell by looking or listening.[33]) The show is tying together reality and fiction in an even tighter knot than it has done before. The interviews are part of a school project by K.C.'s now-teenaged daughter Karen, who is living with Boonie and his family.

Boonie sees the interviews and winces when a kid says his grandfather was in Vietnam. Boonie asks Karen if she is only going to talk to kids, and she turns the camera on him and he asks her if this is about K.C. She says it is just for a communications class, but he gives her the names of people who knew her mother. In Act II she interviews some of the main characters of the show, ending with now-General Miller. In a brilliantly written, directed, and acted scene, the general slowly realizes that Karen is his daughter, but all he can remember about K.C. is that she was good in bed.

In Act III Karen talks to K.C.'s sister, the aunt whom Karen did not know she had, and Act IV begins with the awaited scene in which Karen interviews McMurphy, who claims not to remember that much, although it is clear through Delany's performance that she remembers too much. This is followed by an interview with Trieu Au, and then Sgt. Pepper, who now says that the movies and television shows about Vietnam are becoming his memories, that they are "better than my messy old memories. Vietnam is just becoming a little war in history now, a little half-page sandwiched between Kennedy's assassination and Watergate. Pretty soon all we'll have left is the clichés."

Karen is back with Boonie, showing him the tapes, ending with a montage of people asking her to turn the camera off. Boonie tells her it's great, but Karen says, "I still feel lost." After Boonie leaves, she interviews herself, talking to the K.C. who is not there. Karen wants to call it quits, but then admits it is not finished.

The series, unfortunately, was.

CONCLUSION

There is, because of the institutional structures and their pressures on it, a lot of junk on American television, just as there are bad movies shown and bad books and magazines published. American television, like American filmmaking and American publishing, is a moneymaking business, which is why the people who run the structures of American TV are willing to make and show junk: Sponsors are willing to pay for it because audiences are willing to watch it, just as viewers are willing to watch bad movies and read bad books.

But there is also as much work of quality and substance on American television, and often more, than in American films and literature. It happens when the writers (yes, and actors and directors) are given the chance to do it, and when the audiences are given the chance to appreciate it. For every nostalgic wallowing in the worst of American TV, there is at least some awareness, love, and appreciation for the best of American TV.

And the reason is because audiences know that when the best of the writers for American television are at their best, they are not playing for anything so trivial as money, power, glory, titles, or credits. They are playing for the soul of America and they are playing for keeps.

Notes

To reduce the length of these notes, material clearly from the interviews conducted for this book has not been footnoted. A complete list of those writers who were interviewed can be found in the Acknowledgments.

Introduction

1. William MacAdams, *Ben Hecht: The Man Behind the Legend* (New York: Scribners, 1990), p. xi.

2. Tom Stempel, *FrameWork: A History of Screenwriting in the American Film* (New York: Continuum, 1988, paperback, 1991).

3. Joel Engel, *Rod Serling: The Dreams and Nightmares of Life in the Twilight Zone* (Chicago: Contemporary Books, 1989).

Chapter 1

1. A more thorough history of the development of television from radio can be found in Erik Barnouw's *Tube of Plenty: The Evolution of American Television* (Oxford: Oxford University Press, 1982).

2. Burton interview, also Burton's unpublished memoirs *(Hello King)*.

3. Charles Champlin, "Reunion of Uncle Miltie's Million-Member Family," *Los Angeles Times Sunday Calendar*, March 26, 1978, p. 47.

4. Milton Berle, with Haskell Frankel, *An Autobiography* (New York: Dell, 1974), pp. 296–97.

5. Ibid., p. 298.

6. Lawrence Christon, "At 77, Uncle Miltie Still Rates as Mr. Television," *Los Angeles Times Calendar*, May 15, 1985, p. 5.

7. Jay Burton's complete collection of scripts for the Berle shows is in the Special Collections section of the Doheny Library of the University of Southern California. Notes on the scripts are from the scripts in this collection.

8. Alex McNeil, *Total Television* (New York: Penguin Books, 1984, 2nd Ed.), p. 430.

9. Bob Cunliff, "The Great Comeback, Part I," *TV Guide*, June 12, 1953, p. 12.

10. Ibid.

11. Berle, pp. 334–35.

12. David Crook, "Uncle Miltie: Out at NBC, But in, Perhaps, on Pluto," *Los Angeles Times Sunday Calendar*, September 13, 1981, p. 2.

13. Milt Josefsberg, *The Jack Benny Show* (New Rochelle: Arlington House, 1977), pp. 380–83; see also Jack Benny and His Daughter Joan, *Sunday Nights at Seven: The Jack Benny Story* (New York: Warner Books, 1990), pp. 236, 279–81.

14. Ibid., pp. 71–2.

15. Josefsberg, p. 390.

16. Quoted in Milt Josefsberg, *Comedy Writing for Television and Hollywood* (New York: Perennial Library, 1987), p. 138.

17. Cheryl Blythe and Susan Sackett, *Say Goodnight, Gracie* (New York: Dutton, 1986), p. 24.

18. Ibid., p. 21.

19. Ibid.

20. Ibid., pp. 21–22.

21. The scripts for both the radio and television shows of Burns and Allen are in the Special Collections of the Doheny Library at the University of Southern California.

22. Blythe and Sackett, p. 169.

23. Ibid., pp. 93–95.

24. A history of the radio and television life of *The Lone Ranger* can be found in David Rothel, *Who Was That Masked Man?* (San Diego: A. S. Barnes, 1981).

25. Rothel, p. 54.

26. Ibid., p. 201.

27. In the summer of 1989, the Gene Autry Western Heritage Museum ran several of the radio and television episodes of *The Lone Ranger*, including these two.

28. SuzAnne Barabas and Gabor Barabas, *Gunsmoke: A Complete History* (Jefferson, N. C.: McFarland, 1990), p. 83.

29. Ibid., p. 97.

30. Ibid., p. 104.

31. Ibid. The book has complete summaries of both the radio and television episodes, pp. 359–725.

32. Ibid., p. 105.

33. " 'Death Valley Days' Can't Be Numbered," *TV Guide*, November 12, 1960, p. 9.

34. Perrin.

35. See Chapter 21 for the *thirtysomething* equivalent of that.

36. "Armchair Spectator," *TV Guide*, October 7, 1950, pg. 22.

37. Robert Taylor, *Fred Allen: His Life and Wit* (Boston: Little, Brown, 1989), p. 290.

Chapter 2

1. "The Fifth Network," *TV Guide*, August 20, 1955, p. 16.

2. Dan Jenkins, "The Man Who Bet on Television," *TV Guide*, June 11, 1955, pp. 4–7.

3. Ibid.

4. "Fifth Network," p. 17.

5. The collection of *Racket Squad* scripts, with production notes on the scripts, is in the Special Collections section of the Doheny Library at the University of Southern California.

6. "Old Horse Operas Never Die," *TV Guide*, January 15, 1954, p. 21.

7. Ibid.

8. Rothel, p. 195.

9. Hal Erickson, *Syndicated Television: The First Forty Years, 1947–1987* (Jefferson, N. C.: McFarland, 1989), pp. 5–8.

10. "Now Hear This," *TV Guide*, March 2, 1957, pp. 14–5.

11. " 'Death Valley Days' Can't Be Numbered," pp. 8–10.

12. Madelyn Davis began her life and her career as Madelyn Pugh, and her *I Love Lucy* scripts are signed that way. She was Madelyn Martin for a while thereafter, and has been Madelyn Davis personally and professionally for several years.

13. Davis interview; also Bart Andrews, *The "I Love Lucy" Book* (New York: Doubleday, 1985), pp. 36–37.

14. Andrews, p. 1. Andrews writes that Carroll and Davis did a pilot script for a television version of *My Favorite Husband*, but Davis in the interview said they did not.

15. Davis quoting Ball in *I Love Lucy: The Unaired Pilot*, broadcast April 30, 1990.

16. Andrews, p. 15, quotes Arnaz as saying there was a pilot script written in which Ball and Arnaz played married movie stars, but Davis does not recall any such script.

17. Quoted in Andrews, p. 141.

18. Andrews, pp. 92–94.

19. Ibid., pp. 192–93.

Chapter 3

1. "Six Candles," *TV Guide*, May 1, 1953, p. 13.

2. "Final Curtain for Kraft Theatre," *TV Guide*, September 13, 1958, pp. 6–7.

3. Ibid., pp. 6–7.

4. "Six Candles," p. 14.

5. The UCLA Theatre Arts Reading Room in the Graduate Research Library has a collection of *Kraft* scripts of one of the early *Kraft* directors, Richard Dunlap, and the scripts included the blueprints for the set construction, as well as Dunlap's handwritten notes.

6. "They Never Had It So Good," *TV Guide*, August 6, 1955, p. 14.

7. Brooks Atkinson review, *New York Times*, September 22, 1933, p. 15.

8. "Six Candles," p. 14.

9. "Trends in TV Drama," *TV Guide*, January 19, 1957, pp. 26–27.

10. "104 Plays a Year," *TV Guide*, November 6, 1953, p. 9.

11. Engel, p. 120.

12. Barnouw, p. 131.

13. Roscoe Karns, "Why You Never See My TV Family," *TV Guide*, December 7, 1951, p. 24.

14. Background on Tolkin: Tolkin interview; background on Liebman: Ted Sennett, *Your Show of Shows* (New York: MacMillan, 1977), pp. 7–9.

15. Sennett, pp. 9–10.

16. Ibid., p. 10.

17. Ibid., p. 12.

18. Ibid., pp. 18–20.

19. Quoted in "Great Caesar's Ghost," *Esquire*, May 1972, p. 142.

20. *FrameWork*, p. 28.

21. Sennett, p. 26.

22. Ibid., p. 85.

23. Ibid., p. 133.

24. See *FrameWork*, Chapter 9, for a discussion of this phenomenon. Also see Ibid., p. 211 for the cure.

25. Eric Lax, *On Being Funny: Woody Allen and Comedy* (New York: Charterhouse Press, 1975) pp. 183–84.

26. Sennett, pp. 171–73.

27. "Dialogue on Film: Neil Simon," *American Film*, March 1978, p. 40. Simon is nominally describing the writing on *Your Show of Shows* but the description is more accurately the process on *Caesar's Hour*.

28. Neil Simon was the model for the writer in the 1982 film *My Favorite Year* who keeps whispering into another writer's ear. The film is a reasonably accurate demonstration of the writing process of the Caesar shows, although Joe Bologna's comedy star bears more relationship to Berle than he does to Caesar.

29. Eric Lax, *Woody Allen* (New York: Knopf, 1991), pp. 110–11.

30. Available on videocassette from Reel Images, Video Yesteryear series.

31. Tom Shales, "Caesar's Hour May Have Just Begun," *Los Angeles Times*, November 26, 1982, p. IV20.

32. David Swift, at the UCLA Archives screening of four *Mr. Peepers* episodes, July 28, 1989.

33. Greenbaum interview.

34. Ibid.

35. Quoted by Fritzell in Max Wilk, *The Golden Age of Television* (New York: Delacorte Press, 1976), p. 75.

36. Wilk, p. 82.

37. Greenbaum at UCLA screenings.

38. "The Rise and Fall of Mr. Peepers," *TV Guide*, July 30, 1955, p. 21.

39. Ibid.

40. Ibid.

41. Michael Wilmington, "Special Screenings," *Los Angeles Times*, July 24, 1989, p. VI5.

Chapter 4

1. "Produced by Fred Coe," *TV Guide*, July 9, 1954, p. 11.

2. Wilk, p. 127. The beginnings of *Philco* are from Wilk, pp. 125–27.

3. "Produced by Fred Coe," pg. 11.

4. Gore Vidal, ed., *Best Television Plays* (New York: Ballantine Books, 1956), p. 139.

5. Gore Vidal, *Visit to a Small Planet* (Boston: Little, Brown, 1957) p. xvii. This

is the published edition of the stage play. The television version appears in *Best Television Plays*, for which Vidal was the editor.

6. "They Never Had It So Good," *TV Guide*, August 6, 1955, p. 15.

7. Vidal, *Visit*, pp. xviii–xix.

8. Ibid., p. xix.

9. Arthur Knight, "Paddy Chayefsky Becomes Part of the Big Picture," *Los Angeles Times Sunday Calendar Magazine*, March 26, 1972, p. 12. Other sources for Chayefsky's background: John Brady, *The Craft of the Screenwriter* (New York: Simon and Schuster, 1981), pp. 29–30; also *Best Television Plays*, p. 249; also press release biography of Chayefsky for *The Hospital*, included in the Chayefsky clipping file at the UCLA Theatre Arts Reading Room.

10. *Hospital* biography.

11. Paddy Chayefsky, *Television Plays* (New York: Simon and Schuster, 1955), p. 37.

12. Ibid., p. 126.

13. Swift, UCLA screenings.

14. The creation of "Marty" is from Delbert Mann on two occasions. One is Cecil Smith, "Paddy Made TV's 'Small Moment' An Art Form," *Los Angeles Times*, August 5, 1981, pp. VI4–5. The other is Mann at the Museum of Broadcasting's 8th Annual Television Festival in Los Angeles, March 8, 1991.

15. Chayefsky, p. 173.

16. "Playwright Turns Self Critic," *TV Guide*, October 22, 1955, p. 15.

17. Chayefsky, pp. 259–68.

18. Brady, p. 52.

19. Ibid., pp. 38 and 66.

20. For a discussion of Chayefsky's film work, see *FrameWork*, pp. 182–83.

21. Tim Brooks and Earle Marsh, *The Complete Directory to Prime Time Network TV Shows* (New York: Ballantine Books, 1988, 4th Ed.), p. 754.

22. Reginald Rose, *Six Television Plays* (New York: Simon and Schuster, 1956), p. 303.

23. Rex Polier, "Reflections On TV's Golden Age," *Los Angeles Times*, January 1, 1982, Part VI, p. 9.

24. Rose, pg. ix.

25. Rose interview.

26. Rose, p. 53.

27. Rose, p. xi.

28. Rose, p. 105.

29. Ibid., p. 107.

30. Ibid., p. 108.

31. Ibid.

32. Ibid., pp. 155–56.

33. Ibid., pp. 156–57.

34. Ibid., p. 249.

35. Rose interview.

36. Bob Stahl, " 'Studio One' Goes West," *TV Guide*, December 28, 1957, pp. 5–6.

37. Ibid., pp. 6–7.

38. "Strictly for Adults," *TV Guide*, October 12, 1957, p. 19.

39. Engel, p. 86.

40. Ibid., p. 116.

41. Ibid., pp. 136–38; also see comments by the director Ralph Nelson on the video release, Wood Knapp Video.

42. Brooks and Marsh, pp. 628–29.

43. Wilk, pp. 260–61.

Chapter 5

1. The Subcommittee of the House of Representatives on Un-American Activities. For a brief history of the Subcommittee's investigations on Hollywood and its connections with writers, see *FrameWork*, pp. 136–152, 164–175.

2. Barnouw, p. 125.

3. I have for space reasons had to leave out some of Polonsky's stories about his adventures on the black market, but he assures me that Walter Bernstein, who wrote the script for the film about their activities *The Front*, is writing a memoir of the period that will include all his great tales.

4. In Powell's case it was Martin Berkeley's article, "The Reds in Your Living Room," *The American Mercury*, August, 1953. Berkeley was one of the most voluble witnesses before the committee. He named 161 names. He was also one of the least accurate, with at least a dozen misidentifications: Victory Navasky, *Naming Names* (New York: Penguin Books, 1981), pp. 75 and 85.

5. "Now He's a TV Hero Who Fights Communism," *TV Guide*, December 4, 1953, pp. 6–7.

6. Dick Holeson, "TV's Disastrous Brain Drain," *TV Guide*, June 15, 1968, p. 8.

7. The original owners included Joel McCrea and Rosalind Russell, but they were replaced early by Lupino and Niven.

8. Christopher Knopf, "If My Aunt in Little Rock Doesn't Like It," *Daily Variety 43rd Anniversary Issue*, October 26, 1976, p. 182. Previous background on Knopf from Knopf interview.

9. "Ceiling Unlimited," *TV Guide*, February 23, 1957, pp. 12–13.

10. Richard Schickel, *The Disney Version* (New York: Avon, 1968), p. 11.

11. Ibid., pp. 266–67; also Leonard Goldenson with Marvin J. Wolf, *Beating the Odds* (New York: Scribners, 1991), pp. 121–24.

12. Ward Kimball, talking to a class at Los Angeles City College, November 9, 1973.

13. Dan Jenkins, "Hollywood Stubs Its Toe," *TV Guide*, December 17, 1955, p. 6.

14. Quoted in Goldenson, p. 124.

15. Background on Huggins: Huggins interview, and Navasky, p. 258.

16. Goldenson, p. 129; McNeil, pp. 791, 901.

17. Lynn Woolley, Robert W. Malsbary, and Robert G. Strange, Jr., *Warner Brothers Television* (Jefferson, N. C.: McFarland, 1985), p. 143. The book also lists the Warners series by episodes, indicating which ones are rewrites of other shows.

18. Knowledge can be disillusioning: When Leith Adams was growing up in the fifties, he loved the Warner Brothers Western series such as *Cheyenne*. He has since become the archivist for the collection of Warner Brothers papers at the University of

Southern California and learned from looking at the papers that all the scenes he remembered from the shows were in fact stock material taken from theatrical films.

Chapter 6

1. Interviews with writers; biographies from Vidal, ed., *Best Television Plays*, pp. 249–50.
2. "Dragnet Catches 38 Million Viewers," *TV Guide*, April 10, 1953, p. 7.
3. "Strong Medicine," *TV Guide*, October 9, 1954, p. 17.
4. "The Sponsor Sits in the Audience," *TV Guide*, March 19, 1960, p. 19.
5. Barnouw, p. 187.
6. Stockton Helffrich, "Nobody Loves Me! (or, the Lament of a Censor)," *TV Guide*, March 3, 1956, p. 5.
7. Sorry to disappoint you, but this one was *way* off the record.
8. Holeson, p. 8.
9. "The Time of Our Lives," *TV Guide*, November 30, 1957, pp. 20–23.
10. Robert Drew, "An Independent with the Networks," reprinted in Alan Rosenthal, ed., *New Challenges for Documentary* (Berkeley: University of California Press, 1988), p. 391. The entire article is on pp. 389–401.
11. I've shown *Primary* in my History of Documentary Film class at Los Angeles City College for many years, and it varies from semester to semester whether the class thinks the film favors Kennedy or Humphrey.
12. Erik Barnouw makes the distinction between the two filmmaking styles in his *Documentary* (New York: Oxford University Press, 1983), pp. 235–55.
13. For an excellent account of making the film and the subsequent controversy, see Mary Ann Watson, *The Expanding Vista* (New York: Oxford University Press, 1990), pp. 144–51. See also Stephen Mamber, *Cinema Verite in America* (Cambridge, Mass.: MIT Press, 1974), pp. 105–14.
14. Watson, p. 150.
15. The most detailed look at Wiseman's work is Thomas W. Benson and Carolyn Anderson's appropriately titled *Reality Fictions: The Films of Frederick Wiseman* (Carbondale, Ill.: Southern Illinois University Press, 1989).
16. The Raymonds returned to Antony Bouza for their 1990 film *Police Chiefs*. Bouza was by then chief of police of Minneapolis.

Chapter 7

1. "He Sticks With Cattle," *TV Guide*, September 10, 1960, p. 23.
2. Ibid., p. 22.
3. Sally Bedell Smith, *In All His Glory* (New York: Simon and Schuster, 1990), pp. 435–36.
4. Knopf interview, although he admits, "That's the story I heard. I don't know if it's true or not, but the fact of it was, we were all fired."
5. McNeil, pp. 901 and 905.
6. Lou Shaw says it happened to him as well.
7. Kean.
8. Ibid.

9. See Goldenson, pp. 238–42, for a more detailed account from Huggins of exactly how much everybody else disliked it.

10. Edith Efron, "The Eternal Conflict Between Good and Evil," *TV Guide*, March 17, 1962, p. 8.

11. Both Stone and Vlahos quoted in Ibid.

12. Efron, p. 8.

13. Ibid., p. 9.

14. Rose.

15. A similar idea was tried in 1990 with the series *Law and Order*, but in that series the attorneys are prosecutors, so they were working with the police.

16. Watson, p. 43.

17. Ibid., pp. 61–62.

18. Edith Efron, "Can TV Drama Survive," *TV Guide*, September 25, 1965, p. 10.

Chapter 8

1. Richard Kelly, *The Andy Griffith Show* (Winston-Salem, N.C.: John Blair, Rev. Ed., 1989), pp. 25, 108–9; Greenbaum interview. Kelly's book is a model of how to write about a series. It is also very encouraging to note that in the 1989 revision of the 1981 original, Kelly added sections on two of the series writers, Harvey Bullock and Everett Greenbaum.

2. Kelly, p. 8.

3. There is an excellent discussion of the differences between one-camera and three-camera shooting in Kelly, pp. 28–35. This has been augmented here by material from the Greenbaum, Tolkin, and Mumford interviews.

4. Kelly, p. 115.

5. Ginny Weissman and Coyne Steven Sanders, *The Dick Van Dyke Show* (New York: St. Martin's Press, 1983) p. 1.

6. Ibid., pp. 1–2.

7. Ibid., pp. 3–6. David Marc, in *Comic Visions* (Boston: Unwin Hyman, 1989, pp. 97–99), raises an issue that Weissman and Sanders avoid: that one reason Reiner was replaced with Dick Van Dyke is that Reiner would have seemed too Jewish for Middle America whereas Van Dyke was from there.

8. Weissman and Sanders, p. 31.

9. Ibid., p. 67.

10. Ibid., p. 30.

11. Fred Graver and Terri Minsky, "Garry Marshall Is Asking For It," *Esquire*, March 1990, p. 167.

12. Jerry Belson Studio Biography 1981.

13. Graver and Minsky, p. 167.

14. Weissman and Sanders, p. 67.

15. See Watson, pp. 44, 59–60; also Marc, pp. 84–76.

16. Weissman and Sanders, pp. 63–65; also·John Rich, the director of the episode, at "The Expanding Vista" forum at UCLA.

17. Van Dyke: Weissman and Sanders, p. 65; cutting 45 seconds: Rich at UCLA.

18. Weissman and Sanders, p. 65.

19. Rich at UCLA.

20. Perrin.

21. For a more detailed history of the development of *The Twilight Zone*, see Marc Scott Zicree, *The Twilight Zone Companion* (New York: Bantam Books, 1982), pp. 17–29; see also Engel, pp. 151–83.

22. Engel, p. 169.

23. Ibid., p. 154.

24. Zicree, p. 36.

25. Ibid., p. 54.

26. Ibid., p. 74.

27. Ibid., p. 296.

28. Engel, p. 173.

29. For more detail about the creation and writing of the series, see John Heitland, *The Man from U.N.C.L.E. Book* (New York: St. Martin's Press, 1987).

30. Barnouw, *Tube of Plenty*, pp. 366–68.

31. Weissman and Sanders, p. 65.

32. Salkowitz.

33. Mittleman.

34. Roddenberry had actually been tinkering with the idea since as early as 1960: Stephen E. Whitfield and Gene Roddenberry, *The Making of* Star Trek (New York: Ballantine Books, 1968), p. 21.

35. Fontana remembers the budgets as $190,000 per episode the first season of shows, then dropped to $180,000 for the second. Whitfield and Roddenberry quote memos indicating the second set were to be budgeted at $185,000.

36. Daniel Cerone, "Roddenberry's Trek Record," *The Los Angeles Times TV Times*, October 28, 1990, p. 3.

37. Sheldon Teitelbaum, "Trekking to the Top," *Los Angeles Times Magazine*, May 5, 1991, p. 18.

Chapter 9

1. "Buttons at Bat Again," *TV Guide*, October 16, 1954, pp. 13–15.

2. The interview with Greenbaum was conducted before Gobel's death.

3. A *TV Guide* article (Cindy Adams, "Life Among the Gag Writers," *TV Guide*, December 3, 1960, p. 13) says the writers were on the job from 10:30 to 4:30, but Burton remembers them quitting for lunch and not coming back.

4. "What's Wrong with Television," *TV Guide*, December 7, 1957, p. 6.

5. Burton's scripts for *The Perry Como Show* are also at the Special Collections of the Doheny Library at the University of Southern California.

6. The description of the creation of the Hope sketches is from the Tolkin and Rhine interviews, but the critical judgments are mine.

7. "Reviews," *TV Guide*, August 20, 1955, p. 19.

8. For a look at the process of writing for Carson on *The Tonight Show*, see Lawrence Leamer, *King of the Night* (New York: Morrow, 1989), especially pp. 155–57, 195, and 263–67.

9. Background on Kovacs: Diana Rico's excellent *Kovacsland* (San Diego: Harcourt Brace Jovanovich, 1990).

10. Rico, p. 83.

11. Ibid., pp. 85–78. The Kovacs papers are in the UCLA Special Collections, but only beginning with material from 1951.

12. Rico, pp. 194–95.

13. Specials 4, 5, 6, and 7 were run as part of the program *Kovacs and Kaufman* at the Long Beach Museum of Art, November 1989–January 1990.

14. Rico, p. x.

15. Doug Hill and Jeff Weingrad, *Saturday Night* (New York: Beech Tree Books, 1986), p. 37.

16. Ibid., p. 50.

17. Ibid., p. 60.

18. Ibid., p. 348.

19. Ibid., p. 347.

20. Donna McCrohan, *The Second City* (New York: Perigee Books, 1987), pp. 213–14.

21. Ibid., p. 219.

22. Susan King, "Exploring Comedian Martin Short's Inner space," *Los Angeles Herald-Examiner*, June 28, 1987, p. E11.

23. McCrohan, pp. 222–3.

24. Ibid., p. 228. See also Lawrence Christon, "SCTV: Let's Create a Show," *Los Angeles Times Sunday Calendar Magazine*, December 11, 1983, pp. 1, 5–7, for a more or less transcript of a writing session on the show, and his follow-up, "How SCTV Finally Got Act Together," *Los Angeles Times Sunday Calendar Magazine*, December 18, 1983, p. 56.

25. While the performers on *Saturday Night Live* have gone on to star in films and television, the SCTV people have done primarily supporting work in films, and even those who have had starring roles, such as John Candy, have generally been better in supporting parts.

26. McCrohan, pp. 216–17.

Chapter 10

1. Steve Weinstein, "A Quarter-Century of Television Movies . . ." *Los Angeles Times Sunday Calendar Magazine*, April 23, 1989, p. 24.

2. Richard Levinson and William Link, *Stay Tuned* (New York: St. Martin's Press, 1981) pp. 29–30. While this memoir does deal with some of their series work, particularly *Columbo*, it is more detailed about their television movie work.

3. Ibid., pp. 31–32.

4. Ibid., pp. 62–63.

5. I have used the opening pitch scene in *The Storyteller* in my screenwriting class to show students how it happens in the real world.

6. Symposium on *Brian's Song*, the Museum of Broadcasting's 8th Annual Television Festival in Los Angeles, Los Angeles County Museum of Art, March 22, 1991.

7. See Goldenson, p. 330, for the development of the 90-minute movie.

8. Ibid.

9. The background on the film is from Mishkin: the observations on the completed film are mine.

10. Goldenson, p. 345.

11. William Froug, *The Screenwriter Looks at the Screenwriter* (New York: MacMillan, 1972), p. 279.

12. Edward Anhalt, "America at the Movies: The Screenwriters in the American Film Seminar," American Film Institute, October 20, 1988.

13. For a brief look at Anhalt's film career, see *FrameWork*, pp. 179–80.

14. Anhalt, AFI.

15. Froug, pp. 281–82.

16. Kathryn C. Montgomery, *Target: Prime Time* (New York: Oxford University Press, 1989), pp. 154–55.

17. Montgomery indicates the scene was cut completely, but it remained in drastically reduced form.

18. The mini-history of *Roots*, including the quote from Stoddard, is from Goldenson, pp. 363–64.

19. Ibid., p. 365.

20. Ibid.

21. Howard Rosenberg, "Protests Erupt Over *Beulah Land*," *Los Angeles Times*, March 3, 1980, quoted in Montgomery, p. 125. Montgomery's chapter on the controversy over the film, pp. 123–53, is a sharp-eyed look at the conflicting forces, their stands, and their excesses.

22. Arthur Unger, "A Bargain Basement *Gone With the Wind*," *Christian Science Monitor*, October 6, 1980, quoted in Montgomery, pp. 151–52.

23. The script is in the Louis B. Mayer Library of the AFI.

24. Montgomery, pp. 130–31.

25. In spite of the protests, *Beulah Land* did run on NBC in October 1980 and again in 1983, and is available on videocassette.

Chapter 11

1. For the distinction between Cohn and Wald, see *FrameWork*, pp. 100–1 on Cohn, p. 127 on Wald.

2. Dwight Whitney, "Cop vs Showman," *TV Guide*, August 17, 1974, p. 21.

3. Neuman recalls that it was his idea to do it as an anthology. Wambaugh recalls that it was either himself or Gerber who had the idea.

4. This idea was picked up the late-eighties documentary series *Cops*, which had groups of episodes taped in different cities, including a one-hour *Cops in Moscow*.

5. Whitney, p. 22.

6. Don Freeman, " 'We Saw It Happen. Who Could Make That Up?' " *TV Guide*, April 10, 1976, p. 33.

7. Wambaugh memo to Kallis, October 11, 1975, pp. 2 and 3. The Wambaugh memos are in the possession of Liam O'Brien.

8. Wambaugh memo to Kallis, May 29, 1975.

9. Wambaugh memo to Kallis, September 25, 1975.

10. Wambaugh memo to O'Brien, July 28, 1976.

11. Wambaugh memo to O'Brien, July 23, 1976.

12. Wambaugh memo to Kallis, June 19, 1975.

13. Wambaugh notes, November 10, 1975.

14. Wambaugh memo to O'Brien and Waters, September 1976. Wambaugh

threatened a lawsuit if the script went on as written, but later decided he liked the show and asked for a cassette of it.

15. Wambaugh memo to O'Brien and Waters, September 10, 1976.

16. Wambaugh memo to O'Brien and Waters, August 16, 1976.

17. Wambaugh memo to O'Brien and Waters, December 19, 1976.

18. Wambaugh memo to O'Brien, December 24, 1976.

19. Wambaugh memo to O'Brien and Waters, September 3, 1976.

20. Wambaugh memo to Kallis, June 2, 1975.

21. Whitney, p. 26.

22. Todd Gitlin, *Inside Prime Time* (New York: Pantheon, 1983), pp. 242–46, has a good section on *Today's FBI* as an attempt to do a "conservative" show.

23. Wambaugh memo to O'Brien, June 22, 1976.

Chapter 12

1. Literally, *schpilkes* means "something in the pants," so *"schpilkes* in the pants" is redundant, but why kvetch?

2. Donna McCrohan, *Archie & Edith, Mike & Gloria* (New York: Workman Publishing, 1987), pp. 9–11.

3. Horace Newcomb and Robert S. Alley, *The Producer's Medium* (New York: Oxford University Press, 1983), p. 176.

4. The writing process on the later *All in the Family* is from the Tolkin and Rhine interviews. There is also a less detailed description of it in McCrohan, *Archie,* pp. 114–18.

5. Montgomery, pp. 27–50, has a good section on the controversy over the abortion episodes.

6. Manings.

7. Brooks and Marsh, p. 306.

8. Edward Gross, *The 25th Anniversary Odd Couple Companion* (Las Vegas: Pioneer, 1989), p. 22.

9. Ibid., p. 32.

10. Ibid., p. 40.

11. Ibid.

12. Ibid., p. 56.

13. Ibid., pp. 45, 69.

14. Ibid., p. 100.

15. Joel Zwick, quoted in Ibid., p. 101.

16. Brooks and Marsh, p. 324.

17. David Wallace, "Blue-Collar Knight," *Los Angeles Times Sunday Calendar Magazine,* June 16, 1991, p. 38.

18. Goldenson, p. 348.

19. Wallace, p. 39.

20. Graver and Minsky, p. 171.

Chapter 13

1. The beginnings of *The Mary Tyler Moore Show* and MTM are from two major sources: Robert S. Alley and Irby B. Brown, *Love Is All Around: The Making of the*

Mary Tyler Moore Show (New York: Delta, 1989), pp. 1–2; and Paul Kerr, "The Making of (The) MTM (Show)," in Jane Feuer, Paul Kerr, and Tise Vahimagi, eds., *MTM: 'Quality Television,'* (London: British Film Institute, 1984), pp. 61–69. Kerr's article is from public sources and places the show in the cultural, business, and political trends of the period, while Alley and Brown were able to interview most of the participants in the show and have more firsthand accounts of working on the show.

2. Jane Feuer, "MTM Enterprises: An Overview," in Feuer, et al., p. 5.

3. Background on Brooks and Burns: Horace Newcomb and Robert S. Alley, *The Producer's Medium* (New York: Oxford University Press, 1983), pp. 196–97.

4. Ibid., p. 220.

5. Quoted in Kerr, p. 74, from an article in *TV Guide*, February 8, 1975, p. 32.

6. Alley and Brown, p. 4.

7. Kerr, p. 71, from Don Freeman, "Mary Tyler Moore: 'I'm Not a Comedienne; I React Funny,' " *Show*, October 1972.

8. Alley and Brown, pp. 39–40, 47, 51.

9. Newcomb and Alley, p. 211.

10. Ibid., p. 227.

11. Ibid., p. 209.

12. Alley and Brown, p. 48.

13. Ibid., p. 47.

14. Ibid., p. 46.

15. Newcomb and Alley, pp. 221–22.

16. David S. Reiss, *M*A*S*H: The Exclusive, Inside Story of T.V.'s Most Popular Show* (Indianapolis: Bobbs-Merrill, 1980, rev. ed. 1983), p. 12.

17. *Variety*, July 12, 1968.

18. "Richard Hooker," *M*A*S*H* (New York: Pocket Books, 1969).

19. Ring Lardner, Jr., *M*A*S*H*, Final Draft, February 26, 1970. The script is in the Margaret Herrick Library of the Academy of Motion Picture Arts and Sciences, Beverly Hills, California.

20. See, for example, *Thelma and Louise, The Color Purple*, and, just to show you it's not entirely an American phenomenon, *Chariots of Fire*.

21. Wayne Warga, " 'M*A*S*H' Mangles Film-making Axiom," *Los Angeles Times*, March 8, 1970, Calendar, p. 1.

22. "All-Time Film Rental Champs," weekly *Variety*, October 15, 1990, p. M170.

23. Marshall Berges, "Home Q & A: Pat and Larry Gelbart," *Los Angeles Times Home Magazine*, July 16, 1978, p. 27.

24. Jack Searles, " 'A Once-in-a-Lifetime experience,' " *Los Angeles Herald-Examiner*, February 28, 1983, p. C1.

25. Ibid.

26. Berges, p. 28.

27. Burt Metcalfe, quoted in Searles, p. C-4.

28. Searles, p. C1.

29. Ibid., p. C4.

30. Reiss, pp. 112 and 51.

31. Ibid., p. 112.

32. Metcalfe, in Searles, p. C1.

33. Greenbaum. In *Memories of M*A*S*H* (Producer: Michael Hirsh, broadcast

on CBS, November 25, 1991), Gelbart indicates he gave copies of the last page to the actors before the scene was shot and that they gasped when they read it.

34. Salkowitz.

35. Reiss, p. 112.

36. Berges, p. 28.

37. Linda Bloodworth-Thomason, in *Memories of M*A*S*H*.

38. *Making M*A*S*H* (Producer: Michael Hirsh, broadcast on PBS, 1983).

39. Reiss, p. 98.

40. *Making M*A*S*H*.

41. Greenbaum.

42. See the weekly *Variety* special section on the show, February 23, 1983, pp. 82–92, which shows how much some local stations paid for and received in advertising rates from the syndicated reruns of *M*A*S*H*.

43. "How *M*A*S*H* Reached Its Final High-Water Mark," *Los Angeles Herald-Examiner*, March 15, 1983, p. A6.

Chapter 14

1. Monica Collins, "The Collins Report," *TV Guide* (Los Angeles Metropolitan Edition), January 26, 1991, p. 36.

2. *The Fall Guy* was actually produced by Fox and not Universal, but with a lot of the Universal "regulars" connected with it—which is why it is squeezed in here.

3. Jean Vallely, "The James Garner Files," *Esquire*, July 13–19, 1979, pp. 70–80. The section on the development of the show is on pages 70 and 73, and appears to have come primarily from Stephen J. Cannell, although Vallely does not list her sources. The quotes from Cannell are from this article.

Chapter 15

1. Polier, p. 8.

Chapter 16

1. "Guilds Clash on 4 Fronts in Jostle for TV Jurisdiction," *Daily Variety*, February 16, 1949; Notes from Erik Barnouw, Former Chairman, WGA. For a brief history of the Screen Writers Guild, see *FrameWork*, pp. 136–43.

2. "Six Writers Guilds Mapping One Big Television Council," *Daily Variety*, June 16, 1949.

3. Ibid.

4. "WGA Resids Pass $700 Mil Mark," weekly *Variety*, July 22, 1991, p. 12.

5. Louis Chunovic, "Conciliatory Words Flow in Aftermath of Bitter Strike," *Los Angeles Times*, August 6, 1988, p. V1.

6. "Cy Howard Curls a Scornful Lip at 'Country Club' Writers," *Daily Variety*, March 31, 1954.

7. See *FrameWork*, pp. 123–28, for a discussion of this trend in movies.

8. Background on Spelling: Richard Levinson and William Link, *Off Camera* (New York: New American Library, 1986), pp. 229–35; also "He Scored a Bingo with 'Ringo,' " *TV Guide*, March 26, 1960, pp. 20–22.

Chapter 17

1. J. Max Robbins, "War Webs Dine on Humble Pie During Prudent Pilot Roll-outs," weekly *Variety*, March 25, 1991, p. 50.

2. There is no record of it in Lee Goldberg's book, *Unsold Television Pilots* (Jefferson, North Carolina: McFarland, 1990). Goldberg's book is a mine of information and it would not have been possible to do this section of this book without his book, since it gave me basic information to ask the writers about. Citadel Press published an abridged paperback edition entitled *Unsold TV Pilots* in 1991.

3. Goldberg, p. 1.

4. Morgan Gendel, "Lindsay Wagner and the Series of Doom," *Los Angeles Times Sunday Calendar*, November 18, 1984, p. 3.

5. Ibid., p. 5.

6. *Los Angeles Times Sunday Calendar*, Letters, November 25, 1984.

7. Kean tells this story but cannot remember precisely who the writer was.

Chapter 18

1. Gitlin, p. 279. Gitlin's chapter on the creation of *Hill Street*, pp. 273–324, is an excellent example of writing intelligently about a television show.

2. Ibid., pp. 277–78.

3. Levinson and Link, *Off Camera*, pp. 18–19.

4. Gitlin, p. 276.

5. Levinson and Link, *Off Camera*, p. 21.

6. Ibid., pp. 22–23.

7. Kozoll, quoted in Elvis Mitchell, "It Was the Old Pros Who Put 'Hill Street Blues' on Map," *Los Angeles Herald-Examiner*, February 28, 1985, p. B8.

8. Barbara Babcock, talking to a combination of Television and Theatre classes, Los Angeles City College, December 12, 1988.

9. Gitlin, p. 306.

10. Levinson and Link, *Off Camera*, p. 32.

11. Michael Austin Taylor, "Alumni: A Little Bit of Art," *Yale Alumni Magazine*, April 1985, pp. 34–36.

12. Ibid.

13. Levinson and Link, *Off Camera*, p. 31.

14. Mark Christensen and Cameron Stauth, *The Sweeps: Behind the Scenes in Network TV* (New York: William Morrow, 1984), p. 118.

15. Walon Green, at the seminar "America and the Movies: The Screenwriter in the American Film," American Film Institute, Los Angeles, November 3, 1988.

16. Gitlin, p. 324.

Chapter 19

1. Gitlin, p. 76.

2. Michael Leahy *TV Guide* article, November 12, 1983, quoted in Feuer et al, pp. 268–69.

3. Beginnings of *L.A. Law* and quote from Bochco: David Shaw, "The Partner

Lay There Dead . . . Face Down in a Dish of Beans," *TV Guide*, October 11, 1986, pp. 34–38.

4. Ibid., p. 35.

5. Ibid., p. 36.

6. Steve Weinstein, "He's the Final Authority on *L.A. Law*," *Los Angeles Times Sunday Calendar Magazine*, August 12, 1990, pp. 7 and 94.

7. Susan King, "The Wheels of Justice," *Los Angeles Times TV Times*, March 24, 1991, p. 3.

8. Ibid.

9. On *Entertainment Daily Journal*, broadcast July 19, 1991.

10. Beginnings of *Miami Vice*: Brandon Tartikoff, quoted in Levinson and Link, *Off Camera*, pp. 251–52.

11. One person I was watching an episode with got up when one number started and said, "As long as the commercial's on, I'm going to the bathroom." I think she realized she was making a joke.

12. See, for example, Rick Du Brow, "Humanity Loses to Reality," *Los Angeles Times*, March 30, 1991, pp. F1 and F12.

Chapter 20

1. All the writers I interviewed who had worked with Madelyn Davis highly praised her and her professionalism.

2. Sennett, p. 24.

3. Ellen Torgerson, "Even Edith Bunker Has a Paying Job," *TV Guide*, September 17, 1977, pp. 16–17.

4. In her father's case this was literally true: When he was at Warners in the late fifties, he brought his lunch to work with him in a workman's lunch pail: Grace Lee Whitney, quoted in Woolley et al., p. 189.

5. Beginnings of *Cagney and Lacey*: Barbara Corday, in Levinson and Link, *Off Camera*, pp. 225–26.

6. Quoted in Brooks and Marsh, p. 123, along with some comments made by other organizations and people on the controversy that followed. Gitlin, p. 9, identifies the CBS executive as its head of research, a man named Arnold Becker. Terry Louise Fisher, who wrote for *Cagney and Lacey*, co-created *L.A. Law*, whose sleazy divorce lawyer is named Arnie Becker. Do you think that is just a coincidence?

7. An indication of the class of both women: When Gless started her own series, *The Trials of Rosie O'Neill*, in 1990, Foster was hired for a recurring role as an assistant district attorney.

8. See Montgomery, pp. 201–15, for Rosenzweig's working with women's groups on an episode on abortion.

9. See Steve Jenkins, "*Hill Street Blues*," in Feuer et al., pp. 183–99.

10. Gitlin, p. 289.

11. Michael Leahy and Wallis Annenberg, "Discrimination in Hollywood: How Bad Is It?" *TV Guide*, October 13, 1984, pp. 10–11.

12. Sharon Bernstein, "The Women of TV's Vietnam," *Los Angeles Times Sunday Calendar*, February 18, 1990, pp. 9, 90, 94.

13. Rita Mae Brown, *Starting from Scratch* (New York: Bantam Books, 1988), pp. 183–84.

14. Linda Bloodworth-Thomason, Museum of Broadcasting's Festival of Television, Los Angeles County Museum of Art, March 10, 1990. Unless otherwise noted, quotes from Bloodworth-Thomason are from this source.

15. Delta Burke, Museum of Broadcasting Festival, March 10, 1990.

16. Arnold-Ince; she was a coordinator on the show for a season.

17. Rick Du Brow, "CBS Shows Faith in Its Future with 'Designing Women' Deal," *Los Angeles Times*, December 22, 1990, p. F1.

18. Robert S. Alley and Irby B. Brown, *Murphy Brown: Anatomy of a Sitcom* (New York: Delta, 1990), p. 21. This is interesting to read in juxtaposition to the same authors' *Love Is All Around*, about *The Mary Tyler Moore Show*.

19. Ibid., p. 54.

20. Ibid., pp. 54–62.

21. Ibid., p. 22.

22. Ibid., p. 61.

23. I am surprised that in their book Alley and Brown make no mention of this at all, since it is a step in the liberation of the sitcom format.

Chapter 21

1. Wayne Warga, "Gelbart, Slade: Through the Ranks to the Theatre," *Los Angeles Times Sunday Calendar*, June 10, 1979, p. 60.

2. Ibid.

3. Richard Kramer, "The *thirtysomething* Journal," *Playboy*, December 1989, p. 156.

4. Terri Minsky, "The Unbearable Heaviness of Being," *Esquire*, November 1990, p. 163.

5. The beginnings of *thirtysomething*: Kramer, pg. 156; Minsky, pp. 163–64.

6. Kramer, p. 156.

7. Minsky, p. 164.

8. Reprinted in *thirtysomething Stories* (New York: Pocket Books, 1991), p. 3.

9. Ibid., p. 4.

10. In *thirtysomething Stories*, p. 60.

11. Kramer, p. 203.

12. Ibid., p. 204.

13. See Minsky, pp. 219–20, for an account of it.

14. Ibid., p. 219.

15. I speak from experience; my wife had breast cancer two years before Nancy's cancer, and while I would like to think we handled it all better than Elliot and Nancy, the show covered familiar ground.

16. Howard Rosenberg, "Are the Nights of Yuppie *Angst* Really Over?" *Los Angeles Times*, May 28, 1991, p. F5.

17. Kramer, p. 154.

18. Tom Shales, "Critics Corner," *Los Angeles Times TV Times*, August 20, 1989, p. 6.

19. William Broyles, Jr., *Brothers In Arms: A Journey from War to Peace* (New York: Knopf, 1986).

20. William Broyles, Jr., at the Museum of Broadcasting's Festival of Television, Los Angeles County Museum of Art, March 24, 1990.

21. Diane Haithman, "TV's 60's: War and Remembrance," *Los Angeles Times*, November 30, 1988, p. VI7.

22. Ibid.

23. Yes, *Testament* was released first theatrically, but it was originally made for PBS's *American Playhouse*.

24. Carol Flint, Festival of Television.

25. Broyles, Festival of Television.

26. John Sacret Young, Festival of Television.

27. Woodward.

28. Flint, Festival of Television.

29. Woodward.

30. I have to admit a little bias here. Mimi Leder was a student of mine in the film program at Los Angeles City College in the early seventies, and I have followed her career with great interest. At LACC she was my student projectionist, and I can say without fear of contradiction she is a much better director than she ever was a projectionist.

31. Steven Herbert, "*China Beach* Winds Up Production," *Los Angeles Times*, February 15, 1991, p. F28.

32. Ibid.

33. The giveaway that they are mostly real is a credit at the end of the episode for "interview coordinator." Mimi Leder says the interviews were shot *before* the script was written. The questions were based on the treatment for the script: Phone conversation with Mimi Leder, March 5, 1992.

Index of Names and TV Shows